NAMING THE LOST:
The Fresno Poets Interviews & Essays

EDITED BY

CHRISTOPHER BUCKLEY

STEPHEN F. AUSTIN STATE UNIVERSITY PRESS

Production Manager: Kimberly Verhines
Book Design: Jerri Bourrous

IBSN: 978-1-62288-904-4

For more information:
Stephen F. Austin State University Press
P.O. Box 13007 SFA Station
Nacogdoches, Texas 75962
sfapress@sfasu.edu
www.sfasu.edu/sfapress
936-468-1078

Distributed by Texas A&M University Press Consortium
www.tamupress.com

Cover image: L to R: Philip Levine, Peter Everwine, and Larry Levis standing in the hallway of the old administrative building at Fresno State, c. mid-1960s. From the archive of Peter Everwine.

I believe the truth is we form a family with other poets, living and dead, or we risk going nowhere.
—Philip Levine, "Two Journeys"

"By the time I entered graduate school in 1974, there was a style associated with Fresno poetry, almost as if one could say there was a Fresno School, as there was a New York school, of poets. That is not the case, of course. But it is clear to me that without Philip Levine's presence, the importance of poetry coming from Fresno would have been diminished. . . . Why else did Larry Levis have his canny sense of class consciousness, mixed with surreal imagery, and a shrewd colloquial voice? Why else did Gary Soto present to the poetry world the clipped, free verse lyrics of a working class Hispanic who knew the earth and weather of the San Joaquin? Why else did David St. John weave together intricate narratives pivoting on conditional tenses of the imagination?"

—Mark Jarman, from the Introduction to HOW MUCH EARTH

CONTENTS

INTRODUCTION

NAMING THE LOST: THE FRESNO POETS—Interviews & Essays presents and preserves an amazing nexus of poetic talent and fellowship, and documents the providence that brought so many outstanding poets to Fresno—early '60s through the '80s—a confluence and coincidence of talent and personalities unlikely to be seen again.

The first question is, who would want to come to Fresno, "Dust and Wind State" as Larry Levis named Fresno State College? To start, Philip Levine—to take a job and find an environment good for a son's asthma; Peter Everwine to join Phil in developing a creative writing program, and a few years later, Chuck Hanzlicek to join a burgeoning program. Many poets to be were ready and waiting in the Valley; the earliest poets to come through were Lawson Inada and Sherley Anne Williams, locals. Followed by Larry Levis whose family had a ranch in nearby Selma. David St. John's grandfather had been Chair of the English Department at Fresno State and was the Dean of Humanities who hired Phil. Luis Omar Salinas had moved to Fresno with his family in the '60s. Gary Soto grew up in Fresno and Ernesto Trejo came to study economics and work at his aunt's restaurant. Jon Veinberg's family moved here when he was a young teenager after leaving Estonia and escaping the Russians via Germany; and Tom Emery came on a baseball scholarship. Roberta Spear grew up in Hanford nearby, David Oliveira in Armona, Greg Pape lived in Fresno from the age of six. Marty Williams grew up in Fresno, went to UC Berkeley, and came back to Fresno for poetry. There are many more such stories. Then, as the reputation of the creative program and its faculty grew, young poets began to arrive for the M.A. program as well as for the undergraduate program, joining the poets from the Valley already here.

In her essay for this book, Connie Hales speaks to a good part of the necessity and serendipity of the situation:

> At one dinner party, I asked Phil why he thought Fresno State got so many talented poets to enroll in our program. I realized as soon as I said it that, of course, the obvious answer was the three superb poets sitting here in the room with me. . . . But that wasn't where Phil went with it. He paused, leaned forward and said with all seriousness: Where else can they go? It was an acknowledgement of a simple fact. Many of our students had considerable family obligations and full time jobs—or simply could not afford financially or logistically to move away for a couple of years to study creative writing. UC Merced didn't exist then and there were only a few low-residency programs across the country. Even Bakersfield was a 2-hour drive. This is still the case for a large number of our students, and this valley is filled with people who are living profound lives, who have important stories to tell—stories that we need to hear.

In 2001 I co-edited *HOW MUCH EARTH* with Fresno poets David Oliveira and M.L. Williams. It was the third anthology of Fresno poets and poems following *Down at the Santa Fe Depot*, 1970, and *Piecework: 19 Fresno Poets*, 1987. *How Much Earth* was, as much as possible, comprehensive, covering early and recent poets—most every one that had come through Fresno to date.

With the death of Peter Everwine in October of 2018, the untimely death of Jon Veinberg in 2017, and Philip Levine's passing in 2015, the stark reality was that the Fresno Poets, the early core group, had become pretty thin on the ground. That added to the fact that too many poets were lost far too early in the proceedings: Ernesto Trejo in 1991, C.W.Moulton 1995, Larry Levis in 1996, Sherley Ann Williams and Andres Montoya in 1999, Roberta Spear 2003, Luis Omar Salinas in 2008, and several others including Bruce Boston who died in February and Dennis Saleh who passed in November 2020 as this ms. was being completed.

Philip Levine came to teach at Fresno State in 1958 and Peter Everwine followed in 1962; C.G. Hanclicek came in 1966 and the initial group of Fresno poets collected here became students and colleagues of theirs. Sadly, about one third of the poets in *NAMING THE LOST* are no longer with us. This book focuses then on the community of poets, first coming through Fresno, the formative contingent beginning in the early 1960s, starting it all off.

The interviews and essays present the poets speaking in their own voices about the ideas and processes behind their poems as well as about their comrades, the community of poets in Fresno, their interaction, mutual development, and support—what it was like working together in those early days. Out of necessity as well as respect, one Fresno poet often offers a tribute to and appreciation of another poet lost to us. Especially noteworthy are Philip Levine's essays on Larry Levis, Ernesto Trejo, and Roberta Spear, but there are many more by other poets testifying to the character, accomplishment, and original talents of their fellow poets.

The concept behind the book then is to preserve the voices of the poets talking about their work, their beginnings and development in interviews they have given over the years. The essays by the poets and about the poets—short and long—are not so much critical/ scholarly pieces as they are memoir and "ars poeticas" looking into the background of the growth of these poets' poetic talents and voices, the community and fellowship in which they grew into those voices.

As often is the case in assembling any anthology, I was not able to include all the original poets I had hoped to. Some had passed on with no contact; there were no materials available for others; some could not/did not respond. However *NAMING THE LOST* is substantially representative of that essential core, the early group who wrote and published books and made a poetic life that began in Fresno, and whose work and accomplishments contributed to the continuing zeitgeist of the Fresno community of poets. The book focuses on those poets lost to us, and those of us still standing—if a little wobbly—in our 60s and 70s. This, I believe, is a collection of historical and aesthetic value to contemporary poetry and creative writing in the 20th and 21st centuries.

There hasn't been another grouping of poets like this in the U.S. in the last 60 years. It seems unlikely there will be another.

Philip Levine 1928-2015

In 1958 Philip Levine joined the English Department at Fresno State where he taught until his retirement in 1992. In 1970 he was chosen Outstanding Professor at Fresno State, and the following year he was chosen Outstanding Professor for the California State University System. Levine also taught at many other major universities, among them New York University as Distinguished Writer-in-Residence, at Columbia, Princeton, Brown, Tufts, and the University of California at Berkeley. He was Elliston Professor of Poetry, University of Cincinnati, 1976; poet-in-residence, National University of Australia, Canberra, summer, 1978, and was visiting professor of poetry at Vassar College, University of Houston, and Vanderbilt University. He has served as Chair of the literature board, National Endowment for the Arts, was inducted into the American Academy of Arts and Letters in 1997, and in 2000, was elected a Chancellor of the Academy of American Poets. In 2011 he was appointed the 18th U.S. Poet Laureate by the Library of Congress.

Among Philip Levine's many prizes for poetry are the Ruth Lilly Poetry Prize, the Frank O'Hara Prize, the Levinson Prize from *POETRY* magazine, the Harriet Monroe Poetry Award from the University of Chicago, an award of merit from the American Academy of Arts and Letters, the Elmer Holmes Bobst Award from New York University, and the Golden Rose from the New England Poetry Society. He was elected to the American Academy of Arts and Sciences in 2002.

He received two Guggenheim Fellowships, the Lenore Marshall Poetry Prize, the National Book Critics Circle Award, twice received the National Book Award, and was awarded the Pulitzer Prize for *The Simple Truth* in 1995. Commenting on this book Harold Bloom said, "I wonder if any American poet since Walt Whitman himself has written elegies this consistently magnificent. The controlled pathos of every poem in the volume is immense. . ." Philip Levine has published two books of essays and interviews, a book of nonfiction, two books of poems translated from Spanish, and twenty books of poems. About his last book, *News of the World*, Terrence Rafferty, writing in *The New York Times*, said "What gives Levine's work its urgency is that impulse to commemorate, the need to restore to life people who were never, despite their deadening work, dead things themselves, and who deserve to be rescued from the longer death of being forgotten."

The Last Shift (poems) and *My Lost Poets* (memoir) were published posthumously.

from *How Much Earth*, 2001—Philip Levine

I first came to Fresno in the spring of '58 to interview for a teaching job. It was on a day after a week of hard rain, but the sun was bright, & the fields dotted with wildflowers & the fruit orchards looked freshly scrubbed. Even the pools of standing water reflected the light. The place looked better than it is. I got the job. The less said about the college & the city of Fresno, which at this very moment is sending its strip malls up into the foothills, the better.

Teaching literature and creative writing at Fresno State turned out to be more rewarding than I ever would have dreamed. Once Peter Everwine joined the staff I had a brother in poetry & and some years later another when Charles Hanzlicek was hired. Our poetry writing program flourished & so did my life, for among the young poets and the poets to be I found many of my best friends. Very quickly I discovered I could write poetry in Fresno, though most of it was not about Fresno or the Central Valley. Franny, my wife, claims I can write anywhere, but I don't agree. My ability to write there, my house, my friends, have kept me coming back to the place. When I'm living in Brooklyn or somewhere else there are times I miss it, & when I'm there & working there are times I almost love it.

"An Interview With Philip Levine by Rex Burwell and Gordon Preston," Fresno, California, January 29, 1977, from *Five Points,* 2015

(Over 40 years ago Rex Burwell was teaching as a grad student at UC Davis when he anchored an interview with Philip Levine for the then California Quarterly. *He knew Gordon Preston from San Diego State University where he studied creative writing with Glover Davis, one of Levine's early students, and together they drove to Fresno. The original transcript was 26 pages, and was edited down to 11. Phil then gave his approval.* California Quarterly *was back-logged, and the interview was then submitted to* Antaeus, The Iowa Review, *and* Field *who all reluctantly declined. The interview was never published. On hearing of Phil's death, Gordon Preston reviewed his personal library and found the 11 page interview, and sent a copy to Christopher Buckley for the poetry journal* MIRAMAR. *Buckley thought it worked perfectly with the essay he had just finished on Levine and that together they might find a larger audience in* FIVE POINTS *where it was first published.)*

Rex Burwell: I'm curious about the cover of your latest book, *The Names of the Lost*. Let me guess what the photograph shows. It looks to me like a column of Republican prisoners just after the Spanish Civil War. Is that right?
Philip Levine: You're close, but you're wrong. It's a column of the survivors crossing into France.

RB: And the man in the uniform?
PL: He's a French cop. And that looks like a road, but it's the beach.

RB: Are those men the ones who were never able to go back?
PL: I think they could now go back. I think that about thirty years after the end of the war, 1969, Franco finally declared an amnesty. He's a very patient man. A great many of those survivors, of course have gone to live in other Spanish-speaking countries. The present Spanish republic has a government but it doesn't have a country. The President is a plumber in Mexico City. By the way, the camp where those survivors went was where Antonio Machado died. He made that walk. His dying request was that he be buried in Spanish earth, and after he died some of his friends sneaked back to Spain and got some earth and brought it back to France and put it in his grave. I asked a Spanish friend of mine, a man whose father had been an anarchist and who had been there when Machado died, what Machado had died of, and he said that his father said that he had died of a broken heart. I guess he probably did, because he was so committed to the Republic in his last years.

RB: What do you think the relation is between a poet's attitude toward humanity as a whole and whether he made good poems or not. Does it matter?
PL: It does to me.

RB: What about somebody like Pound, say, who was a fascist?

PL: Well, I think he was an important poet in spite of that. But at every juncture where the fascism shows, he's writing shit. The same is true of Neruda on the other side where he writes like a Stalinist—crap, just junk—but a lot of his poems written out of a deep commitment to the idea of communality or communism as apart, say, from Soviet or Eastern politics, but as an ideal, a socialist ideal—I think a lot of those poems are very powerful because of the great ideals.

RB: Before we start talking about your poems, I wonder if you could talk about your background. I read an interview that Glover Davis and Dennis Saleh did with you about four years ago, a good interview except it didn't say anything about your personal history. We get a general idea of your background from your poems, but maybe you're willing to talk about your childhood and where you lived and what you did until you were twenty-five or thirty or so.

PL: Yes, it's very fresh in my mind. I've been back to Detroit several times because I've just been living in Cincinnati. I went to all the old neighborhoods. I was born in 1928. I'm an identical twin, which is the most significant fact about me. My brother still lives in Detroit, he's a painter.

RB: House painter or artist?

PL: He's an artist. He also sells bearings. But I think gradually he is going to cease selling bearings, and just be a painter. I think as he gets better at painting and more confident, that more and more time will be spent on art and less and less in business. My family was totally composed of immigrants. My mother was born in what was Russia and which later became Poland. Same for my father. My grandfather had originally come as the first member of my family to emigrate to America. He came to escape the draft for the Russo-Japanese war of 1905. He came with a brother who so hated Detroit, which is where they wound up, that he went back. He was willing to go back. By the time he had worked his way back, the First World War had started and he settled himself in France, so I have part of a family there.

RB: You have a cousin there?

PL: Yes, the son of that man. Then my father's brother was killed in Russia for political activities. So my father left Russia and went to England where he was drafted and served in the First World War. He was running a prison camp in the Near East and he deserted and came to the United states under another name and lasted till the statute of limitations ran out and then resumed his own name. And I suppose the knowledge of that was of extraordinary importance to me later on. Also the death of my father; my father died when I was five and my mother went to work. I grew up having no one to tell me yes or no. At the same time, I felt the death of my father was the most extraordinary deprivation, and in some ways I still think so. But later on, through the experience of my students, I saw how, in a way, good can come out of evil. I mean, I see my students struggling against their parents, against the father figure especially; the father tells them not to to be poets, for example. I have some very gifted students whose parents, whose fathers, were very opposed to their becoming poets.

GP: When did you first start writing?

PL: I first began writing when I was nineteen. Fiction–poetry very shortly thereafter. When I took freshman English at Wayne University in Detroit, I had a teacher who called me in–he hadn't paid any attention to me all semester. For our last paper, he'd asked us just to state our ideals and what kind of a world we would like to live in, and I wrote a very bullshit-eloquent thing, very anarchistic, about the destruction of government and the idea of some kind of unchaining of people and the destruction of all the organs of lies and imprisonment, that sort of thing. And the guy was very moved by it and he said, "You know you have a real gift for writing; you ought to try to be a writer." His name was John Sinclair, never saw him again. And I didn't take him too seriously. You know: 'Yeah, that's great.'

RB: Had you been thinking yourself about writing at that time?
PL: No, but I did write. I wasn't thinking about it too seriously though. I was eighteen then. When I was very young, thirteen or fourteen, my house tended to be a tiny bit explosive. My people would argue ferociously and I would want to get out of it. I would sense in the evening that there was going to be this big family argument, so I would get out of the house. Because of the war we had moved away from where I had grown up. There was a freeze on housing, on the building of houses, and so there were vast areas of open field, which no one would believe now. Now there's rubble, but no fields. As I walked around these fields I would sort of talk to myself about my life, what I was living, because I could give a shit about the ninth grade, you know. What are you going to say about the ninth grade? But I had several of these 'talks.' They were poems in a way, and I would polish them, and I enjoyed reciting them enormously, quietly to whomever wanted to hear. The birds didn't answer. I didn't seem to upset anything. The trees went on being trees. I often say I recited to the moon and stars, but now I remember in Detroit you never saw the moon and the stars anyway. So I guess I was reciting to what I thought the moon and stars might look like. That was probably my earliest contact with poetry. I had several teachers who told me, "Gee, you write well. You ought to think about writing." But at that time writing to me meant journalism. It wasn't until I began to go to college that I began to read good books. As a freshman I read Dostoevsky, and then *Moby Dick*, Faulkner, you know. This stuff was unbelievable! Why didn't someone tell me about it? I didn't have to flunk English in high school . . . . If only we hadn't been reading Whittier.

RB: So when you finished high school, did you start going to college at Wayne State right away?
PL: Yes, it was called Wayne University then, not Wayne State.

GP: You were working and going to school at the same time?
PL: Most of the time, yes. And then I graduated and kept working till I was twenty-five or so.

GP: How old were you when you were first married?
PL: Twenty-two, so then I just worked.

GP: You worked in factories; how did you like that?
PL: I was scared by the factories. In this plumbing place where I worked, I came in one day for work and at lunch they had a little party for me because I had worked there a year. "I quit." I said, "I quit, I quit." Right then and there I said "I quit." And they said, "What are you talking about?" And I said, "Well, I thank you for the party and all that, but I had lost touch with the fact that this was a year. And before I know it, it will be two years. I better get my ass out of here." So I always had that fear: I gotta get my ass out of here. My mother used to make a great remark: "Philip is testing American social mobility. He was born in the middle class, and he's moved to the working class. The idea is to go up, Philip, not down." I guess that was it: the idea of being one of the exploiters was just too

sickening to accept. Some of the jobs weren't all that hard either. Some of them were very brutal, but some of them weren't that hard. The plumbing thing was very uncomfortable, but not that hard. It was boring, tedious, you know. But I had my life arranged when I was working there. I worked four to midnight and I would go home, have a beer or something and go to sleep and get up in the morning and feel pretty fresh. I'd have seven or eight hours in which I could do what I wanted. I guess that's why I wasn't going to school—I really wanted to write.

GP: Then you later wanted to go to a school like Iowa.

PL: Well, I went to Iowa for want of a better thing to do, really. At that time I was free, in a sense. I wasn't married anymore. I continued to work for a while in Detroit and I lived very humbly. One of the guys that I had gone to Wayne with, a poet named Paul Petrie who now teaches at the University of Rhode Island, told me he was going to Iowa, and I asked why, and he said, "Well, they offer this degree there and Robert Lowell will be teaching there." That excited me. I mean I was excited about Lowell as a teacher, but then I don't think Lowell was too excited about me there [laughter]. I went there to study with Lowell and Berryman, although I actually didn't enroll. I didn't want to pay the tuition. I just sat in the class and heard what they had to say, and gave them my poems. And they'd say, 'Your name's not on the roster.' And I'd say, 'I dunno, why's that?' I wasn't interested in earning college credits. The poetry workshop was fourteen or fifteen people. Fiction was so much more popular then in America. People were saying, "Oh boy, novelists make a fortune." And there must have been fifty people in the fiction thing, and it was out of hand, really. There were three teachers instead of one. Although Lowell did nothing to bring us together as a group, we supported each other. And Berryman was very good at that—bringing people together. He made us into a group even though he never applied any rigid class structure. He threw a couple people out who were no good. He just made them leave: "You're no good, get out." He was very brutal. And then he said, "Okay, the rest of you can become poets. Right? Right?" He created a situation in which we became friendly toward each other, and shared our work with each other.

RB: How long were you there?

PL: I was there almost a year and then I ran out of money.

RB: That was in 1952, '53?

PL: No, '53 and '54. From the fall of '53 to some point in the spring of '54 I was there. And then I went back to Detroit and worked.

RB: You're talking about wage jobs?

PL: Yes, by this time I'd learned some skilled jobs that paid more. And I could get work more easily because I could do certain things. And I went back to Detroit and worked until July, and then I went to North Carolina and married my wife Fran. I mean I just didn't pick her off the street. I already knew her. She was working in North Carolina.

RB: Was she from Detroit too?

PL: No, from Iowa. And then she taught drama and acting and costuming in northern Florida, at Florida State University. And when our second kid came along, I decided I would try teaching. And by this time I was published in Poetry, and I wrote Iowa and they gave me a job teaching Engineering English, which was just up a poet's alley. Technical Writing, they called it. I taught there two years. I taught Technical Writing and a course in Greek and Biblical literature. I faked this guy out: 'Of course I know Greek and Biblical literature.' Which I'd forgotten completely. I had known it as a kid, but I'd completely forgotten it.

RB: And then you went to Stanford in what year?
PL: 1957.

RB: How long were you there?
PL: One year. I went there on a writing grant. But it wasn't much money. I was thinking of Iowa City and how inexpensive it was to live there at that time, and when I went to Stanford, I thought, what the hell, I can live on $3000. But I couldn't, and I ran out of money.

RB: How many children did you have then?
PL: Two. I wound up working at the post office. The people at Stanford were very angry at me for that: 'We didn't bring you out here to work at the post office.' They had a room for me in the library, and I was supposed to sit down and write poetry there, and I said, 'Well, you go work in the post office and give me the money, and I'll go sit in the room.' And the university itself paid very little salary. They kept the Jews out. They wanted gentlemen teachers, gentlemen students and all that. But there was this new breed of graduate student who was coming to college on the GI bill and this kind of thing, and it was mixing things up. And I didn't know what Stanford was till I got there.

RB: Stanford still has that kind of reputation, doesn't it?
PL: I think it probably still deserves it, although I read on campus there a couple years ago and there were Black people there and Chicanos. There weren't any when I was there; it was absolutely lily white. I was very uncomfortable. The first day I was on campus I was walking to the office to get my check, my 3,000 bucks, and I thought I looked dressed up, in my own eyes. And a guy dressed in a Railway Express uniform—I'd worked for Railway Express in Detroit for about six months—this guy comes up and says to me, "Don't ever deliver trunks to this fucking place; you carry them up to the third floor and those bitches don't even give you a quarter tip." And I'm so nonplussed by the fact that he could pick me out of all those people, he could pick out the shitkicker, you know, that I went home and said to my wife, "How could this guy spot me so easily?" She said, "Gee, I don't know; you look fine." I said, "Yeah, but this guy just came right to *me*."

GP: You're a poet of the proletariat in a certain way, would you agree?
PL: Well, it's a very curious thing; it will sound kind of bullshitty, but when I was very young and working in a factory and trying to write poetry, I made a vow to myself. There was no poetry of this experience. I never heard it, and if there was, I didn't know it. And I made a vow I was going to write it. Then later a very strange thing happened to me. When I was about thirty-four, I had a dream which really changed my poetry. I dreamt that a guy I worked with in Detroit called me from Bakersfield, California–a Black man–and I said, 'Hi, Eugene, how are you? Blah, blah, blah.' And it was clear that he was calling me so that I would invite him here to Fresno, and in the dream I didn't do it. I told him I hoped he had a good time in L.A, because he mentioned that he had to go to L.A, but it was clear that he called me so that I would invite him, and I didn't. And then when I woke up from the dream I said to myself, "What a prick you are. You're a teacher now and you live in a white neighborhood, and you didn't invite your old buddy back." And I was very depressed by this, and I remembered this old vow. And then it occurred to me that it was

a dream; I didn't do it. It was a warning. Then I did a strange thing: I told my wife to call the school and tell them that I'm sick. And I got in bed for about ten days. I wrote and wrote and wrote. I wrote about Detroit for the first time. I wrote a good portion of *Not This Pig* in bed—all the poems in there, like "Heaven," which are about people in Detroit. And a poem about that very guy, one of the first poems in the book, called "In a Grove." So suddenly I discovered that subject was enormously alive in me, and I remembered it with great clarity.

GP: With his realization, how do you view race relations in the South, having lived there, as opposed to those in northern cities, like Detroit?
PL: I was just in Cincinnati, right near Kentucky, and it seemed to me that in terms of the race situation in America, Kentucky was somewhat better than Cleveland, Chicago, Detroit, New York, Boston. . . .

RB: It was that much better?
PL: Oh, much better.

RB: Is it because of the unemployment problem in the big cities?
PL: A lot of things. Yeah, in the South there isn't the unemployment. After all, what you have in Detroit are the people who were driven off the land of South so they could work in the factories. Now automation has made them unemployable. They're sitting there getting more and more pissed off. There's no money for urban renewal, although they've torn down vast stretches of these cities, and the ghetto becomes more and more of a prison. You don't have this in the South. I think too that in the South Black people and white people have lived together for a longer time. If you leave Detroit and drive for an hour straight north, you ain't going to see any Black people and you can keep driving for hundreds of miles and you ain't going to see any!

RB: There's even some sort of belt, some street or road in the northern part of Detroit, that's the dividing line between ghettoized Detroit and the suburban white part of it.
PL: Yeah, that's right. Dearborn and Michigan, which is where the world's biggest factory is located—the Ford River Rouge factory. When I lived there, there were probably twenty thousand, thirty, forty thousand Black people working in the factory, and there wasn't a single Black citizen of Dearborn. There are now about eight or ten—all doctors, lawyers they've allowed in. Eight or ten! And there are a hundred eighty or two hundred thousand people living there. Yes, it's much worse. You go to northern Michigan and you encounter racial attitudes that Jefferson Davis would have endorsed. It's more the conflict between rural and urban sometimes than it is between the North and the South. But I think the fact that Black people and white people have been living close to each other for a long time in the South makes it impossible to maintain such an incredible racial mythology there, such as one could encounter in a small Michigan town, and makes it impossible to meet people there who really believe such shit.

GP: Can we get back out west? You are there at Stanford studying with Mr. Winters, Yvor Winters.
PL: Arthur. His real name was Arthur. Yvor was his middle name. When he first began writing, there was another guy in the United States, a fiction writer, with the name Arthur Winters, so Winters used his middle name.

RB: I can imagine that anybody could be a student of anybody else, but somehow I can't imagine . . .

PL: That he chose me?

RB: Yes.

PL: It's hard to figure out. I never did figure it out either. I got along with him very well on a personal level. We rarely talked about my poetry because at that juncture, friendliness ended. He was a terrible teacher. He was a hopeless teacher, a frightened man—very irrational, very paranoid. He was a very sad man, one of the saddest men I've ever known, but he was a very gifted man, a sensitive man. He had a great feeling for poetry but not for people. He was kind to me and my family, but he was not a good teacher.

GP: There has become not only a larger audience for poetry, but more people are now participating. And now with all these poets, especially poets of my generation now in the mid-twenties, all off on these "careers in poetry" [laughter]—what's it going to be like, say in twenty years?

PL: I don't know. It's very strange. I'm amazed at what's happened. When I went to Wayne University in Detroit, a university of about twenty thousand students when I went there, there were about five of us writing poetry. As far as I knew there were two more in the whole city. And there were two million people in Detroit. Even here in Fresno I've seen it happen. I came here and taught poetry writing courses and at first had one class of five or six students. And today we might be offering six sections with fifteen or twenty students in each. I caught in the way you asked the question a kind of terror: "It's bad enough in your generation, what's going to come in the next?" There are obviously more poets in San Diego, say or Santa Cruz today than there were in all of California twenty-five years ago. And the number of magazines that exist and the number of books that come out! I don't know what it's going to mean. There is a certain scary quality to it: maybe there's too much poetry, maybe the best poems will be lost in this extraordinary volume of stuff, maybe it will be hard to find the really good poets. And maybe they will tend to write too much alike because they will all be going to the same sources to get their material. On the other hand, if you don't write your poetry nobody is going to write it for you. If you want to write your poetry, you are going to write it. And I think it's a good thing that more and more people learn that poetry might be an alternative in their lives. They might write their poetry; they might not necessarily sell somebody else's Buick, and in that sense it's a tremendous thing that more and more people would take that up as a thing to do with their lives, knowing how difficult it is, because it's hard now, as hard as it was when I started. There was a certain period when one was able to get a teaching job. Now that's stopped. And yet young people go on writing. The say "fuck you" to all the difficulties, and they live on welfare, they live badly, and the most exciting moments of their lives are when they write the poems they wanted to write. I guess that outweighs everything else. It does to me. I think it's a valuable thing to write your own poetry, and to speak for yourself, and do it well because you recognize certain things about yourself. You are a very rare creature, you are the one of you, you are unique, and that your experience is perfectly valid, totally valid. That everything you've lived is important enough to make poetry of. I meet people who say, "How can I write, nothing has happened to me?" I say, "What do you mean, nothing has happened? You got born." Look how much Roethke made of that! It's not a question of vanity. It's that I'm a worthy human being and what happened to me ought to be told, ought to be sung. The people who nourished me and fostered me were valuable and I want to immortalize that, memorialize that. In that way, I think poetry writing is good.

RB: Do you think writing programs can delude students into thinking that they are writers? I've known of programs in which teachers have coddled their students along, I suppose to keep the program growing. It seemed some programs could do disservice to writers because the writers weren't getting a lot of criticism, and nobody was really telling them what they needed to know. They were just being told, "Yeah, keep turning in poems, this could be fixed up, this is okay. . ."

PL: Well, given the wrong teachers, it's hard to think of the damage. Any writing program could screw people up. I have seen teachers use students in a very ugly way: exploiting them, manipulating them and using them for their own advantage. I have seen teachers put such an extraordinary emphasis, not upon the quality of the writing, but on the length of the bibliography and the "success" of the poet, so as to impart a shitty set of values to young people. Yes, writing programs can be just terrible. I suppose that's why I never have gone to a big one. I've had lots of offers to join big poetry writing programs and I've never gone to one because I think a lot of them are just bureaucracies, as you've described. I like to teach young kids how to write and let them take it from there.

GP: Do you like teaching? Do you like what it has developed into for you? How do you see yourself now that you have a generation of students who are out writing creatively or out teaching? Do you ever sit back and say, 'Look what I have done?'

PL: Yes, I did do that once. An awful thing: 'Look what I've done, look what I've created, this monster factory of poets.' I'm not ashamed of my accomplishments. I shouldn't laugh at them. I've had a lot of good students and I didn't stop them from writing. I kept on encouraging, they kept on writing. Obviously most of them did the work on their own; I mean, you just don't make poets. Most of them trusted me and some of them have become by best friends. I like teaching, I like it a great deal. Teaching is very exciting for me. I still get a kick out of it. I like to teach the very young people, young in the sense that poetry is new to them.

GP: Are you a father figure to them?

PL: Oh, sure.

GP: Do you take it on?

PL: No, I don't take it on. It's forced on me. I mean, I have three kids of my own and I don't need any more. There are so many students that really don't get along with their parents. But I try to avoid being a surrogate father. I think relationships that are healthy are going to be based on equality, and I don't think parental relationships are equal. I think the student ought to have the right to hate his teacher at times. Your function as a teacher isn't to be liked by the students, but to teach them something, to help them learn to become a better poet. And if you have to tell them at times, "Hey, this is shit, cut it out. James Wright already wrote this poem"—if you have to tell them that, you better tell them. As I get older I don't get as close to as many students as I did when I was in my thirties because there is a kind of natural barrier. It isn't that I don't like making new friends; I did in Cincinnati and enjoyed it enormously. I like to think that I teach poetry well, that I'm entertaining in class. I'm very funny. Galway Kinnell, who taught with me a couple of times, said, 'I can't say the things to the students you say.' In class with him, I'd say, "Galway, what do you think of this poem?" And he'd say, "Oh, about what you think." One day I said, "Galway, goddammit, I'm not going to do all the work," and he said, "But when I say the poem is bad everybody cries, and when you say it's bad they laugh. I can't make them laugh, I don't have the gift to make them laugh. So it gets very hard to criticize." Galway has a serious way of saying things, he is a serious man, he's serious all the way through. I'm serious in the center, and a buffoon on the outside, and I enjoy that. It's the way I've been all my life.

RB: How important is it as a poet to "succeed," to be accepted by critics, to win prizes? Can a poet really be a poet if no one recognizes his talent?

PL: I think if you keep your head on straight you realize that all the prizes and all the publications and all that can go to people with extraordinarily little talent for writing but terrific talent for promotion. And remember that you can revere a handwritten poem as much as one that appears in *The New Yorker*. We don't yet know, for example, the strengths or weaknesses of the poetry written in my generation. You realize that a poet like Williams had almost no influence on his own generation. His contemporaries couldn't see him for what he was. They missed him altogether, yet he revolutionized my generation. It took so long because he was so obviously poor at self-promotion. Besides, he was a doctor, and he was busy, and Ezra Pound kept telling him he was a dummy. Although he didn't believe it. He knew how good he was and he persisted. I remember going to the YMHA to hear Dylan Thomas read, and somebody had given me a letter to give to Oscar Williams, so that Oscar Williams could introduce me to Dylan Thomas. I went up to the guy who was running the thing, John Malcolm Brinnin, and I said, "Is Mr. Williams here. I have a letter . . ." And he said, "Do you mean Oscar, or the Great One?" Well, I didn't know William Carlos Williams was a great poet. I didn't know what he was talking about. "What do you mean, the Great One?" He said, "William Carlos Williams." I said, "No, no, I mean Oscar." I was a little puzzled—I was only about twenty—a little dazzled by his response. Later I realized Brinnin was a pretty hip character.

GP: Who else gave you that sense of belonging? Who else did you think was exciting then?

PL: Some of my teachers helped me to get that sense—Berryman certainly. His knowledge of poetry was extraordinary. And Winters too, though probably the only good thing he gave me was a sense of an ongoing tradition of what he called "the plain style." And whatever else you'd say about my poetry, it wasn't the plain style he was describing, although it was, is kind of a plain style.

RB: Speaking of style, how has the change in your style been accepted, the change, say from that of *Not This Pig* to that of *They Feed They Lion*?

PL: *They Feed They Lion* was rejected by about a dozen publishers. It was rejected twice by Wesleyan, for example. They had done *Not This Pig* and they wanted another book just like it: *Not This Wolf*, or something. They especially disliked the title poem. It was violent. They had thought of me in one way and here I was writing in another way. They weren't prepared for it. And I think this is probably the story with a lot of writers who, as they change, lose a certain portion of their audience. If you're twenty-some years old and writing a certain kind of poem, there's no guarantee you'll always write that way. As you grow older, you feel differently about a lot of things, and so the way you write changes, your attitudes change, your subjects change. . . .

GP: Early success can influence writers sometimes a wrong way, a very sad way, do you agree?

PL: Yes, I agree. I can see this as damaging to writers. They put themselves under terrible pressure. They get treated as stars before they are ready. I think one of the luckiest things that happened to me was not publishing a book in a sizeable edition, one which anybody saw, until I was forty. It was almost too late then to ruin me. I think I had a perspective that a lot of other guys didn't because I was aware of the fact that those poems that were being praised had been rejected by nearly everybody who was now praising them. I would always have to say to myself, "Don't listen to these guys—you know how good you are, you know how good you aren't, you know how far you're come. You haven't come far enough, and let's stick at it."

"Keeping Faith: An Interview with Philip Levine"—Richard Jackson, *Poetry Miscellany*, Summer 1986

Poetry Miscellany: I would like to begin by referring to the following long quote from Milan Kundera: "I invent stories, confront one with another, and by this means I ask questions. The stupidity of people comes from having an answer for everything. The wisdom of the novel comes from having a question for everything. When Don Quixote went out into the world, that world turned into mystery before his eyes. . . . The novelist teaches the reader to comprehend the world as a question. There is a wisdom and tolerance in that attitude. In a world built on sacrosanct certainties the novel is dead. The totalitarian world, whether founded on Marx, Islam, or anything else, is a world of answers rather than questions. There, the novel has no place. In any case, it seems to me that all over the world people nowadays prefer to judge rather than to understand, to answer rather than ask, so that the voice of the novel can hardly be heard over the noisy foolishness of human certainties."

That's a helpful thing to keep in mind at the beginning: we're not looking for answers. We only want to extend the questions. I think of the closing lines from "The Conductor of Nothing"—

> I come back to life each day
> miraculously among the dead,
> a sort of living monument
> to what a man can never be—
> someone who can say "yes" or "no"
> kindly and with a real meaning,
> and bending to hear you out, place
> a hand upon your shoulder, open
> my eyes fully to your eyes, lift
> your burden down, and point the way.

Philip Levine: I basically agree with what he says. I'm reading a book right now, H. G. Wells' *THE RESEARCH MAGNIFICENT*. It's the old kind of novel, with answers, published in 1914. It's about a man who's making a great research to find out how to live. Though I'm not done with the book, and although clearly he's found a lot of ways not to live, he hasn't found a way to live. I suppose that in 1914 people picked up books in hopes there would be perhaps a design for how to shape your life. I mean, my life has been shaped to an enormous degree by what I've read.

The other day I was answering a question for the Gallup Poll. George Gallup picked at random some names from Who's Who—which means I guess that you're successful—and he asked how you'd become successful. What were the models for living. Well, the answer was there weren't any, but there were a lot of people in the books I was reading. And I realized that my role models were in Tolstoy, Dostoyevsky, Twain, and were more alive to me than anyone in my neighborhood. Kundera lives with real totalitarianism, not our watered down version of it. And I'm very much in agreement with his notion that it's in the novel we have to look. Trust the novel, not the novelist; trust the poem, not the poet. The minute I start generalizing outside the poem, I start sounding ridiculous. I mean, I might as well run for office. I think we all recognize when we pick up a novel and it starts urging us, as say this Wells book does, towards a certain way of living. It stops telling us about how people actually live and we yawn, put it down. I've already turned away from the people who would tell me how to live. I can turn the T.V. on any Sunday morning and find some idiot telling me that. The minute the poet gets into those large generalities I start to distrust the voice.

Although, I'm reading some Rexroth at M.I.T tonight. In a lot of his poems he tells you how you ought to cut the mustard, and he ruins a lot them that way, but not all. But in his translations he shows his own enormous gift for language, and an erudition comes to play without the opinionated Kenneth who knew everything. He was the best educated man I've ever come across. He was enormously articulate and his memory was incredible. So he could tell you everything. Poetry was difficult for him because once he got going he wanted to tell you everything again.

PM: He's had an enormous influence. Snyder, for instance, is another poet who knows a lot, but it's a different kind of knowledge.
PL: When he starts lecturing he's so abysmally boring. I think that outside of his poems he's dull. Rexroth invented Ginsberg and he invented Snyder, and he never got credit for it. Both became far more famous, but the models are there. Look at Rexroth's poems on the death of Dylan Thomas and you'll see it's a real model for *HOWL*. And in the Sierra Nevada the way the language moves, the way the nature images are used; those high mountain images, you could be reading Snyder at his best. The poems are that good.

PM: There's a Soviet writer, Mikhail Bakhtin, who describes the best writing as a mix of language groups, cultures, classes—something he hopes guarantees a perpetual revolution in language, values, that prevents any official language of truth. To write is to change, he'd say, yourself and others. But you have to contradict, challenge yourself. Or it's Satchel Page: "Don't look back. Something might be gaining on you."
PL: Well, ten years ago I'd have said so. Now I find that while my work has been constantly changing, and while I'm still aware of an overriding truth, I don't make many choices in my writing—about what I write, I mean. I get something, and I go with it. I go wherever it seems to be going. I'm not the commander. I don't say, well, today we'll have anti-Reagan poems, tomorrow we'll write about childhood, Thursday's good for eggs. In the last 3 or 4 years it isn't changing as radically as I'd like it to change. It doesn't do me any good to dislike that. I'm aware I can take a poem in a direction I've already gone, and so day by day I have to struggle not to do this. And the struggle gets harder to win. I mean, I've gotten 40 lines into a poem, maybe I should start over. And there was a time I'd start over. Now a little voice says—20 more lines, you're there!

I've been a guy who's written—I've had no dry spells in my whole life, at least not more than 3 months. I don't know what writer's block is. I think that if I had skipped years and years the way some people I know have, that I would never have changed as much as a writer as I have because I've been there waiting for poems when remarkable changes occurred. I was once a person who wrote a poem line by line I got a sense of structure, stanza, line lengths, rhyme—all that stuff. I was 30 say, writing that kind of poem. Somewhere before I became 40 that notion changed and I began writing a poem in which I would not know what the structure would look like for a long time. Then maybe it would begin to tell me what it looked like. Later on in my mid forties I would sit down and write for 3 or 4 hours, 200 or 300 lines. It just poured out. I would eventually shape it, but I trusted myself in the meantime.

A friend of mine was using my study once and found a big pile of papers. He liked lots of it, but thought it was a mess. He said: "It's like you're throwing it away." I said: "No, it's just a first draft." "When did you write it," he said. "Yesterday morning." Then he said: "You wrote it all yesterday morning? How did you do it?" I said: "Well, you know, you get up, you drink a cup of tea, you sit down, and you get thunderstruck." He was totally puzzled. And I realized he might have had opportunities like that, but he spent years not writing. When the thing came to him, he probably didn't write anything. He probably thought he had a fever. Maybe there was this huge urge to language and he didn't know how to cope with it. Now his poems are right back where he started from. He writes tiny little rhymed poems, crystal clear, boring little poems. He went back to the past. I think I'm lucky that I've been so determined. My friend believes in his talent far more than I believe in my own. I believe in myself far more than he believes in himself. I think my experiences are universal. When somebody gets hit by a car I think my responses are human. He thinks: "Maybe I'm jaded." But he believes in his verbal talent. I've always doubted my verbal talent, and so worked harder at it.

PM: He's trying to shape experiences, validate them from the beginning, by language.
PL: He's trying to have it easy. He thought he wouldn't have to work so hard.

PM: So many of the more recent poems are subjunctive in the way they work. "I could believe," goes one poem. Or a title like "Let Me Be."
PL: I suppose. It's like Willy Loman in *Death of a Salesman*. There's no sense trying to tamper with the future because it isn't there. So you have to go back and change the past – "I could have done this." I never thought about it, but I guess it's that sort of thing. If you see most of your life behind you, you're going to stick with it. I have to go back to 1936 to change the world.

PM: Well there's a whole revisionary stance that comes from the desire just to talk. "What shall I say because talk I must, "Williams opens "The Yellow Flower." The need to talk can lead to revaluating what you say.
PL: I'm distrustful of that, but only because I have felt that way, and have written those poems. They're there. I wrote a lot of poems because I just felt I had to write poems. Now I've come to another point of view which is—I don't have to write any more poems. It's no big tragedy. I would rather not write again the poems I have already written. I have a new book coming out and enough work for another after that. I'm 57, and I'm not going to rescue everything at the 11th hour. So rather than rewrite what I have already written I will forgo that poem. I will wait. I could reduce the pressure by diddling around, and that way I could say, "that's wonderful, I'm writing a lot." Maybe the need to write worked for Williams, but not for me anymore. You can look through Williams and throw half of it away. But that's not a bad average. It's better than Ty Cobb. You'd be a .500 hitter.

PM: There's a sense of joy in your poems that counter balances the sadness. It's like the way Byron makes Don Juan progressively sadder and happier as the poem goes on. I think it's related to a sense of presencing things. What I mean is, say in "On the Murder of Lieutenant Jose Del Castillo..." where the focus on the first 2/3 is on the murder and the context around it, the way things are and aren't noticed, are both present and absent in a sense. In the last 9 lines, you say that the more to be said can only be said by someone who has suffered essentially. Yet the poem does go on, and makes him present by noticing what he might notice. There's a triumph there.

PL: Yeah, you know, a lot of people don't see that in my poems. They think I'm a depressing poet. I'm trying to redeem a lot. I am a person who enjoys life enormously, at the same time I'm aware of the infinite rage of people who don't. I think that up until 40 this other aspect you mention doesn't really emerge. But now I'm happy with it. My favorite book of my own is *One for the Rose* where that redeeming attitude is dominant.

PM: You write yourself into impossible situations to see if you can write out of them.

PL: That is something I like to do. That's a good description of it. It's like channeling a poem down a road so that I either get out of it, out of the trap, or I fuck it up. I have a manuscript of things that didn't work out. I like to find out where the poem's going right near the end. I have a kind of faith that that happens, a faith in the imagination. It's working all the time.

PM: There's a stance in your poems that is very important. It comes perhaps through Hardy and Whitman—a witnessing. There's an odd religious connotation to that word, where I'm now living, and I don't mean that. I think of Roethke's "I'm Here" where the woman just wants you to notice—here I am, I'm alive, I'm flesh, I'm like you. I think of the end of "7 Years from Somewhere" which goes "that/ means you are, you/are, and you are home." There's a desire to embrace: "Why give up anything?" you say in another poem.

PL: I was reading in Tuscaloosa recently and Dara Wier told me that when I announced I was going to read a poem about being reborn several students just perked right up. Then the air went out when they found out it was about being literally reborn. They think they own the term, and if you use it in a way they don't, that you're the one that misused it. So I understand what you mean about the word "witnessing."

It seems to me that witnessing is such a central urge in the poetry of this century. It may be THE central urge. Not just to pain and terrible events, and how they work, and effect you. There's a whole world here, and somehow seeing it and being touched by it for a day or an hour is a way of celebrating it, of seeing how valuable it is. It's a faith in the kind of world we live. Catalogue becomes important, enumerating things. You have to combat a cast of mind like Reagan's that says": "once you've seen one redwood tree you've seen them all." That's obviously idiotic. It is the predator's remark—"I'm not killing your pet lamb, I'm killing 14 pounds of chop." "The poet's witnessing may inhibit the predatory thing in himself, and hopefully the poems will do the same for others. I think the most fundamental function of poetry is there.

PM: Your poems find the beautiful. So many poets today try to get the ugly in, to say, look, you want ugly and tough, I'll show you ugly and tough. Your poems transform those things. The poem "Sources" does that triumphantly. The end of "One For The Rose" turns all that you discovered in the bleakness earlier in the poem into a love of "every turn" of your life: "and each one smells like an overblown rose,/yellow,

American, beautiful, and true." I think of the way Blake does something like that: "You become what you behold," he says.

PL: Blake has those incredible portraits of the ghastly industrial age, yet the poems are so beautiful. They have a mystery and a magic. There's not much point in adding a piece of grime to a grimey poem. *1933* was reviewed by Richard Howard who said how much I had to face the ugliness in my life so that I could go on living. I read that and thought—he's talking about my family! my uncle! my father! What I think is unbelievably touched with glory and dignity, he thinks is ugly. I wouldn't put Richard in the category of those poets you were talking about, though. His is just a different sensibility. My poems are a discovery, and a kind of history of what I believe in, and found beautiful.

Joyce Jenkins—"Putting the People In: An Interview with Philip Levine," *Poetry Flash,* Number 196, July 1989

Philip Levine is the distinguished author of seventeen books of poetry and has been a Professor of English at California State University in Fresno since 1958. He has been the recipient of many awards, including the Ruth Lilly Poetry Prize, the National Book Critics Award, and the American Book Award. It has been written of his work, "Of all contemporary poets, he has probably remained most faithful to the world of the American underclass and working class, who know as he does what it is to endure 'a succession of stupid jobs.'" In March, he received the Bay Area Book Reviewers 1988 Award for Poetry for A Walk with Tom Jefferson, *his most recent book of poems. This interview took place at his Fresno home soon after the BABRA Awards Ceremony in San Francisco, and is of special interest because of how graphically it illustrates the differences of print and radio: the full taped interview from which this piece was taken will be aired on KPFA A-FM, 94.1, Berkeley, on Sunday, July 16 at 5:30 p.m.*

Joyce Jenkins: I wanted to talk to you about the innately political nature of your poems. In a lot of your poems you have been described as an "urban poet," a "poet of the underclass." It seems to be a kind of political poem that doesn't really talk about politics. You talk about the politics of everyday life.

Philip Levine: Well, I think we live in the world that Orwell was describing and dreading, in which everything is political. And I don't, myself, have a kind of political platform. I have in the past at times felt that I knew the proper politics that the world ought to assume. But, as I get older, I get less and less sure that, with me at the helm… well, the nation would be in a hell of a lot better shape than it is now—but that's not saying much. What I'm most interested in is the politics of everyday life. It seems to me that I grew up in a world in which most of the people I knew and cared about did not exist in the literature I was reading and the movies I was seeing and the radio programs I heard. And, as I began to write poetry, like many beginners, I was attracted to the subjects of other poets. I was reading people like Keats and Yeats and T.S. Elliot, etc. I was reading everything. But, by the time I was 22, it dawned on me that I wasn't in any poetry. And my mother wasn't in any poetry. And my uncle wasn't in any poetry. And all these people that I worked with weren't in any poetry, and, if I didn't put 'em in poetry, they weren't gonna *be* in any poetry. And so, as young people often do, I made a sort of foolish pact with myself, that this was gonna be my career. I was gonna put 'em in poetry. And lo and behold, that's what I've gone and done.

JJ: I want to talk to you more about this autobiographical angle. I heard you say, once, at a reading, that your poems are talking from the 'I', but the 'I' isn't always you. And

you started talking a little bit about the imagination of your poems. They often seem to be life stories, but would you say they're stories about your family?

PL: I think in the beginning the 'I' was largely a device for talking about myself. But I think in the poetry I've written in the last 25 years there's very little that's autobiographical. I mean, there are all sorts of autobiographical elements that inform the poems. But I feel totally free to invent for the purpose of heightening. And also, because my life is not nearly as interesting as the things I can imagine. I never met, for example, the character in the poem, "A Walk with Tom Jefferson." He is an amalgamation of various people I've known and other people I've wanted to know. I know that neighborhood; I've worked there. I know it well. I knew it very well as a young guy. And I've gone back; every couple of years I go back home to Detroit and look at the spoliation of the place. And I went back there, oh, I guess it was two years ago, for the retirement party of an old teacher of mine. I went back as a surprise to him. I had a long day to spend in Detroit, and I just wound up in this neighborhood. I met a guy there who recognized me. He came up to me and said, "You're Philip Levine, the poet, aren't you?" And I said, "Yeah." And he said, "Oh, I read your work," and blah-blah-blah. And he took me around the neighborhood and showed me some of these things that wound up in the poem. But the whole story of this man's life, Tom Jefferson's life, is really an invention. I have a poem where I'm a fox in the poem. I have a poem in which the 'I' is a magical child. I remember one time I got a review in the *Village Voice*, and this woman writing the review began by saying I was an autobiographical poet and then she said, "It's really strange that, having been born in 1928, he was able to fight in the Spanish Civil War, which ended when he was 11." But she did not draw the obvious conclusion: that the speaker in the poem was not me; it was clearly somebody else. Somebody I invented.

JJ: In the autobiographical information in your books you always say, "after a succession of stupid jobs," you finally left the city of Detroit. And you've kept that in there, book to book. I always thought that was interesting and fun, that the publisher let you get away with that.

PL: Everytime it happens, we argue. He says, Will you please take this out?" and I say, "No." A couple of people have gotten angry at me because, they say, the jobs aren't stupid. And I say, "You didn't do 'em. I did 'em."

JJ: I wanted to talk a little bit about how your work changes. I've heard people say many times that you're a poet who's found a strong voice, that you absolutely have your voice. And they say that your voice doesn't change that much, that if you've read a Levine poem, if you've read a Levine book, you know Levine's work, now and into the future. I disagree with that, because in closely studying your work, I find a difference, a real change from book to book. More poems about transcendence and 'soul' topics, and more ambiguity, and cosmic, if you will, topics, than some in the previous books — like *Ashes*. And then, in *One for the Rose*, I notice that your work seemed to be incorporating more of the story, more of the narrative line, with that same sense of transcendence. And I think you've completed that synthesis in *Tom Jefferson*. Would you like to say anything about that?

PL: I see my work as having changed enormously. If you looked at my first book, if was almost entirely in traditional meters, for example. All the poems were formal, in one-way or another, either accentuals or syllabics, or traditional meters. The attitudes in the book were very different. I got even angrier in my second book. I think my anger climaxed at my fourth book. My third book, *Red Dust*, much of which is in *Ashes*, was my most obscure, difficult, and surreal book. Much was written during the Vietnam War; maybe I was at my most disturbed. Somewhere around my early forties, perhaps through the writing of this poetry, itself, or maybe it's 'cause my life got better, I think *I* began to change. Strong changes took place in *me*. I've been writing poetry now for over forty years, so naturally I think the poetry does reflect not only changes in craft and changes in technique and changes in attitude, but changes even, you might say, in the mission of the poem. The early mission was to enunciate my rage against America, for what it was doing to the people I loved. But, as I lived longer and got older, I realized that even though we were cheated and lied to and deprived of a great deal, we gave each other a great deal, and our lives were rich. Maybe it was because I had a good family life, too—that was within the family my wife and I created—there were rewards that I didn't anticipate. When my children were young and I was poor, until my children were six, they had asthma. That's why I came to California, to get out of the Midwest and out of asthma country. I was in a rage with being unable to provide medical care for my kids and having to sit in public hospitals for hours and hours, knowing that many of my friends, people that I worked with, had the same kinds of... burdens. But life changed. I became this teacher. I loved teaching; I'm a natural ham. Here in Fresno I got *wonderful* students; my students are just *fabulous*!—some of whom have become, I think, terrific poets, very well-known poets. So naturally my attitudes changes over the years, and I confess I see each book as being quite different. Joyce Carol Oates once said to me—I was sitting in a lecture she was giving, and she was talking about voice—"Well, like Phil here, he's got a voice. His voice is always identifiable and always recognizable, and" (she said) "I always find it interesting, and so I'll read anything he writes." You can see a common thread in terms of the voice, in terms of the kind of diction that I gravitate to, and certain attitudes, etc., but I think the poems change radically: I think they've gotten freer; they've gotten funnier. I remember at the age of 38 or so a friend of mine said, "Ya' know? You're the funniest guy I know, and your poems are never funny; they're just incredibly serious. How come you're never funny in your poems?" I started thinking about it, and I thought, "Well, ya' know, I'm really writing about what's troubling me, and my sense of humor doesn't trouble me at all!" The fact that I can laugh about almost everything—that doesn't trouble me, so I never write about it. But I took it as a valid criticism. I'm one of these people who believes you should get criticism wherever you can. I thought, yes, you can't have too many really funny poems. I mean, I *love* funny poems! So, for example, in *One for the Rose*, there are quite a few funny poems. And in my next book, which is untitled, but which I'm working on, there'll also be a lot of them.

JJ: It's interesting to hear you talk about you feeling that the poems in *A Walk with Tom Jefferson* are freer, because I experienced that freeness, and I experienced the poems as more prosey; not any less poems, not any less poetically important, but with a kind of prosey swing to them, much more of a story, which is interesting. I just want to tell you that people I know that aren't usually acquainted with poetry, literary people, literate people, have loved this book, buy copies of it for their friends, that sort of thing. I think that something about that style is very accessible.

PL: My friend, Thom Gunn, who I don't see a lot of, alas, wrote me a wonderful letter about the book; and he used the phrase that it always sounded spontaneous, as though it were just being invented. The *Tom Jefferson* poem, which was his favorite, and the poem called "Twenty-Eight," seemed so spontaneous; and yet, when he looked carefully, they were very conscious and crafted. Thom is a guy whose poetry I love, so I took it as the highest praise. I'm pleased with the book. The *Jefferson* poem was a very hard poem for me to write.

It took three years. I say it took three years, but it took two weeks; that is, it was written in two sections, each about a week long, but separated by all these years. So the poem sat there half-done for a couple of years. There was a time in my early writing life when I couldn't have tolerated that. If I couldn't finish a poem I just went into a *frenzy*. I gotta' finish it! I gotta' finish it! But, as I've gotten older, I've gotten much more patient. I have two virtues: my sense of humor and my patience. I have a third one, my stubbornness, and I know when to get up and walk away from a poem. And so I just put the poem down. I had some confidence that I'd get this right. It's crazy, because I had met a guy that day, a cab driver, and he had made a remark to me that lingered in my head. I told him I was going back to this reunion, and he said, "This is your old teacher," and I said, "Yeah," and he said, "An' you've come all the way from where? You're from California, aren't ya', but you're born in Detroit?" I said, "How'd you know?", and he said, "Well, you know the city, so you obviously grew up here, but you look too happy and healthy to live here. Yeah, all the smart ones went to California. So, you're going back for your old teacher now?" I said, "Yeah." And then he said, "That's Biblical!" That phrase hadn't gotten into the poem yet, and as I began thinking about that guy I thought, "Oh, he's a Born-Again, and that's what he means," but no, then he described what he meant by its being Biblical. He said, "For example, if you got out of the cab on the wrong side and got hit by a truck and got killed. I like you. Every year I would pull up right here. See that bar over there? I'd go over there, and I'd order two drinks, and I'd drink one for me, and then I would drink one for you and say your name. I don't know your name, but I'd find out, and I'd say your name, and then I'd read a poem, one of your poems. That would be Biblical." That stuck in my head, and [I thought], "How am I going to get that in the poem?" Well, I got it in the poem, but it took me years!

JJ: That's wonderful! It's a refrain in the poem, actually. It appears again and again. Could you read us one poem from this book? The first poem is also wonderful, I think.
PL: "Buying and Selling"? Which one would you prefer? That, or "Making Light," or…?

JJ: Either one. "Buying and Selling" has more of a storyline; "Making Light of It" is more of the transcendence that we were talking about.
PL: Yeah. Let me read the transcendent poem. So that people can believe that I deal with such things. "Making Light of It."

Making Light of It

I call out a secret name, the name
of the angel who guards my sleep,
and light grows in the east, a new light
like no other, as soft as the petals
of the blown rose of late summer.
Yes, it is late summer in the West.
Even the grasses climbing the Sierras
reach for the next outcropping of rock
with tough, burned fingers. The thistle
sheds its royal robes and quivers
awake in the hot winds off the sun.

A cloudless sky fills my room, the room
I was born in and where my father sleeps
his long dark sleep guarding the name
he shared with me. I can follow the day
to the black rags and corners it will
scatter to because someone always
goes ahead burning the little candle
of his breath, making light of it all.

From *A Walk With Tom Jefferson*,
Alfred A. Knopf, New York, 1988

JJ: That was lovely. You don't have to convince me that you can write transcendent poems. As a matter of fact, it's what strikes me again and again in your work, and is one of the things I love so much in it.

PL: You know, in the poem "Twenty-Eight," I talk about being faithless at 28. And, in a way, I was faithless. That's one of the changes that's come over me. But I've seen a lot of miracles. You know, as you get older, you see a lot of miracles, I've seen my children transform into men. My wife and I have been together for thirty-something years, and we still love each other. That's kind of a miracle. I see the annual miracle of her garden. I've gone crazy and recovered; that was a miracle. And I've been miserable, and then I've been happy. I see my mother aging. My mother is 85, she's blind now. In spite of that, she's a woman of great dignity, strength and intelligence. And, as she gets older, she gets wittier and more accepting. I've seen so many amazing and transcendent things.

JJ: At the risk of repeating something, I want to mention how non-sentimental your work is. I know we've been talking about family and things like that, but, for me, there's not a sentimental bone in any of your poems. You use really simple words for titles. "Clouds," for example. That's it. Just a single word. And you just break everything down into these basic units of meaning, without losing any power.

PL: I try to use an available and simple vocabulary, too. Talking about sentimentality— many years ago I sent Thom Gunn all my books, and he wrote back a wonderful letter about that book. I don't remember which book it was. But he said, "You know, Phil, if you just romanticize that child you're writing about," who was the child I was, "a little bit more, you're gonna kill him with sentimentality. I mean, you've gone right to the edge." And I looked back at the poems, and I thought, "He's absolutely right. I've gotta draw back. Enough halos around children!" As I say, I get my criticism where I can.

JJ: You selected a collection of John Keats for the Ecco Press, *The Essential Keats*, and you wrote a little bit in the preface to that book about romanticism, his romanticism, from the early 1800s, as it relates to your own. And then you mention him again in several poems. You mention him in the first poem of *A Walk with Tom Jefferson* and in a couple of the other poems in other books.

PL: He was the first great poet I fell in love with. And it wasn't just his poetry that thrilled and awed me. It was also his letters, which to me are even more impressive than his poetry, and his life. Lionel Trilling, in a wonderful essay on Keats, says in some ways he was larger than life — he was a hero. And he was kind of a hero to me. He was a guy out of the working class who suffered great misfortunes and had to do his best to support a family even as an adolescent. And yet made this covenant with himself, with the world itself, that he would write poetry. And he did. At the age of 26 I had already outlived him and written nothing that anyone would want to read. But I wasn't discouraged. I took heart from… you know, I just had this belief, we develop at different stages. It has always been my belief, something I try to inform my students with: don't be impatient. Some people grow fast; some people don't. Of course, his talent was an extraordinary, remarkable talent—way beyond anything I was gifted with. He's just someone who's always been there for me. And I think his letters are the greatest book I've ever read about what it's like to be a poet.

JJ: I found, in a book of poets' biographies, this title quote from you, where they asked you what your major obsessions were. And you wrote, "Detroit. The dying of America. Search for communion. Admiration for cactus, pigs, thistles. Thorny people who refuse to die." I love that quote!
PL: Well, I wouldn't change much there. Except I would add foxes to that now. Yes, "thorny people who refuse to die." That's right. The country asks a lot of us: won't we please just go and drown in the pacific. And a lot of us say, "No, we won't. No, we're gonna hang around." I feel this is my America too. I left the United States, during the Vietnam War, for two years; and I came back because I got this sense that if everybody who hated the war went off and left the place, it would be left to the warmongers. And that the rest of us had to come back and make a lot of noise, do what we could. I feel like a patriot, really. I was the head of the resistance here in Fresno, then, when I came back. And people called me all kinds of names and cursed me and bugged me on the telephone. But I'd say to them, "Look, I'm really the patriot, not you, you jerk. Because I'm trying to make this country what it promised it would be. Not America's version of Nazi Germany."

JJ: Some of your poems about the Spanish Civil War maybe reflect that same feeling, only about a different era.
PL: For several years, I considered myself an anarchist and tried to live by anarchist principles. And, as such, I really was fascinated by the whole anarchist movement, that took place in Catalonia, especially before the Civil War, and during the Civil War. I went over there and met people, talked to them, and got some real sense of what there lives had been like. Anarchism is probably like Catholicism, with the faith. I'm not going to communion very often, these days. I bought a house. Property is theft, and I bought a house. So I'm not living by my anarchist principles anymore, and I don't honor myself with that title anymore. But I still have great admiration. And, again, one of the things I did in those poems was to try to call attention to the heroism of those men and women and what they had done. History had bypassed them. I thought, well, they're just like the people I grew up with in Detroit; somebody's gotta pay attention to them. Put them in poems. They weren't in poems in English, so I *put* 'em in poems in English.

JJ: I want to ask one more question about influences on your writing. I have another quote from you. This was from the early seventies, and I'm sure this has changed quite a bit, which is one reason why I want to ask you about it. You said that the critical writings of Kenneth Rexroth and Robert Bly helped you to open up. And then you talked about Spanish poets—Hernandez, Alberti, Neruda, and Vallejo—and said that they "exploded" you. And you talked about modern Polish poets. I wondered if you've had any recent experiences with other poets and other poetries that seemed to be important or maybe poetries that you would like your students to become more acquainted with.

PL: Well, I'm sorry I said some of what I said there. Rexroth, yes. Rexroth was a powerful influence on me. But I think as the years went on I got more and more bored with Bly. But he became more boring; you know, as a young guy he was a really very fascinating, interesting man. He was not nearly as wise and all knowing as he's become. He was just one of us, a person, and I think his early magazine, *The Fifties,* later re-titled *The Sixties* and *The Seventies,* was interesting, and he was interesting. And it was through those early magazines in the fifties that I started turning to Spanish poetry, and then, when I lived in Spain, I learned Spanish and translated a lot of them, or just read them in Spanish. They were doing things that excited me, and I was at this time also abandoning traditional form in English and looking for another way to write. I was a little bored with what I had been doing, and the surrealism of northern Spain—it's kind of surrealist atmosphere—[interested me]. There's something so ancient about it, and something so modern about it, and they're both going on at the same time. There's something crazy about the life there that really appealed to me yet at the same time frightened me. And I think it got reflected in the poetry that I wrote in those years. But I think that as I grow older what happens is I return more and more to English poetry, or poetry in English — to my great earlier loves: Chaucer, Milton, Shakespeare, Keats, Witman, William Carlos Williams — and find in our language this extraordinary body of poetry. I love Robert Frost, Hardy, Yeats, Dylan Thomas. I seem to be turning back more to Sir Thomas Wyatt, who I just love and reread. For example, right now I'm reading Wyatt; I'm rereading all of Williams, and I'm reading Hardy. I seem to be returning to those old guys for sustenance; and Emily Dickinson; I'm completing my voyage out. For awhile, an East German poet had an influence on me; there was a delicacy in him that's in Machado and Jiménez that I just couldn't find in myself, or translate into English poetry. But I don't want to disparage what we did, what we've done, with our language. I feel very lucky to be someone who writes in English. I remember once I was helping a woman, a Flemish woman, translate her poetry into English. And she said to me, "You don't know what it's like to write in Flemish. There are only two million people who can read you." And I said, "Oh, God, I never thought of that!" She said, "You're so lucky; you write in English. Everybody in the world can read you." There's a truth to that; it's such a vital language. Constantly borrowing from other languages. It's just a great language.

from "A Conversation with Philip Levine"—Christopher Buckley, *Quarterly West* #43 Autumn/Winter 1996/97

Philip Levine, one of our most acclaimed and prominent poets, has published sixteen books of poetry. The Simple Truth *received the Pulitzer Prize for 1994 and* What Work Is *was awarded the National Book Award in Poetry for 1991. This interview was conducted August 17th, 1996 at the poet's home in Fresno, CA. Buckley visited with Levine as he paused between a full schedule of travel for readings and conferences. He was working on the ms. for his seventeenth book of poetry,* Unselected Poems, *Greenhouse Review Press, Santa Cruz, CA, 1997, and preparing to leave California at the end of the month to teach at NYU for the fall semester.*

Christopher Buckley: You retired from teaching at Fresno State in 1992 where you had taught since 1958. You had also been teaching at Tufts and other places such as Princeton and Columbia. Was the idea to save time and energy for your own writing? You're still traveling a good deal giving readings and almost every fall now you're teaching at NYU. Are you still managing to write about as much now as you have in the past and in recent years?

Philip Levine: Yes. I think I'm doing about as much. When I teach at NYU I teach one night a week. I think the class is two and half hours. I get as much out of teaching the class as the students do. I probably steal their energy. They steal my something. We fire each other up, we excite each other. I find that much teaching, one class, one semester, is an asset. The summer writing conferences I do less and less of because I think they're a drag, a drain, although last year I did one in Santa Monica and the students were quite terrific, as serious as hell. I like the students at NYU and the spirit of the place—I don't know that there's another place in the country that I would go to every fall the way I go there. I think Sharon Olds and Galway Kinnell have created a wonderful atmosphere, one that I can fit into and feel a part of with great satisfaction.

CB: I'm not by any means alone in thinking that over the last 30 years or more you have been one of the most active, helpful and influential teachers of poetry writing in America. While there are no formulas or shortcuts or prescriptions, is there a particular advice have you found yourself giving most often to young writers and those in your classes? Has it changed over the years?
PL: It probably has; but I don't know what the changes are. At NYU last fall, two students came by who had been my students the first time I taught at NYU which was perhaps ten years before. And afterwards they both said to me, The students aren't nearly as good, and you're so gentle now, and on and on about how there was this terrible change in me, I wasn't the ogre that they'd come to love. Of course, the two were wrong. As far as I was concerned, I was still the ogre and the students were no worse than when they were there. They were romanticizing their own past. I'm sure there are changes, I just don't know what they are.

CB: Tragically, Fresno has lost a number of poets over the recent years. As part of the Fresno Poets Assoc. that published Chuck Moulton's posthumous book, you wrote the introduction. In it you mentioned early days of teaching and traditional assignments in workshops and it seems somehow Moulton's presence in an early class came at a time you were thinking about moving away from assignments in prosody. How do you feel today about the viability of such assignments in workshops?
PL: Well, the first thing you have to recognize is that in writing the introduction to the book of Moulton's poetry, I made it as dramatic as I could—shall we leave it there? Moulton didn't change the way I taught; I tired of it. It took too much energy. It takes a lot of energy to force a beginning class of twenty-five students to write iambic pentameter, then syllabics, tetrameter, accentuals and so on. After a while I said, This is too much work, let them write their own quacky poems. Also the late '60s came along and two things were happening. One, I was myself reaching into more open forms while still writing syllabics—I'm still writing syllabics and metrical poems at times too—but I thought, I'm tired of teaching this way.

CB: You've not spoken much in interviews or in your prose about your own process of writing poems. Has your writing process changed over the years and/ or does writing come any easier after all the years and successes?
PL: It's changed over the years. But then I think I'm a very fortunate poet; I've never really had what you could call a writer's block. I've been lucky. Or maybe Dashiell Hammet's right that there is no such thing, as he says to Lillian Hellman: Lillian, just put your ass on the chair and you'll start writing again. I have been there when poems have come in different ways.

When I was a youngster, let's say from the age of 18 into my late 20s, poems came line by line. When I began to write in syllabics—I was 29—poems began coming to me you could almost say in paragraphs. That kept going I would say into my 40s when poems started coming to me in great rushes of language. I remember one morning—this has happened more than once—writing several hundred lines in a morning, just huge rushes where I just sat there and wrote what kept coming to me. Then the art became one of editing and shaping.

The poem "A Walk With Tom Jefferson" really is a poem born on two separate days, separated by over a year and a half. The first half of the poem which is about 320 lines came along with another 600 lines in a day and a half, which I then boiled down to the first half of the poem which sat unfinished for close to a year and half. When I got an idea for completing it, I did it in a morning—got the idea that morning and finished it that morning—another 300 lines—whoosh, off I went. So I've become much more patient. Something that I've discovered in the recent past, something I never would have done which I've only been doing about a year, is, I often read poetry before I write. And I use the poetry I read to stimulate me, and the things that stimulate me are very odd. It might be a single reference in a poem—recently, the last one I can remember was a poem by Pavese; there was a reference to a sea breeze—that's all I used, *sea breeze*. It was about 112 degrees here in Fresno; I wrote a poem from the point of view of someone who would never get across those hills to that sea. All he would see to let him know that it was there would be a seagull. In this poem a seagull comes down into a field in the western part of the valley, and just gives up suddenly and says, Oi, This is Fresno,—how the fuck did I get here, and the seagull dies and a guy gets out of a pick-up truck and buries him. All I got from Pavese was *sea breeze*, and I took it and ran with it. Often I get poems in this curious way. I'm accomplishing two things—I'm reacquainting myself with my beloved Pavese, and if it works it works, if it doesn't it doesn't, and I enjoy myself. I've used a number of poets. Pessoa was another. I read two books of Pessoa, I guess it was this winter, and a little phrase in Pessoa which triggered a poem had to do with a shop . . . Meanwhile, if I don't get any writing done, I do spend a lot of time with Pessoa and Pavese or Machado or whoever it happens to be that week.

CB: Your friend and former student, Larry Levis—whom poetry and the world lost last May—was the main person who responded to your work, critiqued the poems. How far back does your working and poetic relationship with Larry go?

PL: Well, actually Larry began reading my poems twenty-five years ago as a critic—that long ago. I realized even when he was my student what an extraordinary touch he had. I saw him in class helping his classmates rewrite their poems. I thought, This guy is just terrific, and then I inherited some of his students, so I knew how savvy he was. When I was putting together *The Names of The Lost* in 1975, he helped me a lot, and since then he became my main critic, and I think I was probably his. We just traded poems constantly. When I put my papers in the Berg room in the New York Public Library, I was amazed at how much help he had given me. There were a couple hundred letters. Then he put his letters from me into the Berg room. I think he had something like 250 in which I had tried to help him with his poetry. So it was a wonderful reciprocal relationship. Just after he died I was reading at Ohio University in Athens, Ohio, and I happened to read a poem and realized I owed the ending of the poem to Larry; he had said to me, You know, the timing is all wrong in this ending. So I had rewritten it, and then it struck me as I was reading that nobody else in the audience knew it; nobody in the audience knew. And then the next poem—same thing. There was a point in the poem where I realized I'd sent Larry an early draft of it and he has said, Rewrite this passage, and he gave me a suggestion how I might do it, and I had done it. So I told the audience how these poems would not be without his help. He was extraordinarily important to me; I've mentioned all this in a piece I wrote for the Academy of American Poets.

CB: You're now editing Larry's last book. What is your sense of his last book and his poetic achievement?

PL: He had a huge voice. I think there's so much invention, vitality and imagination in his work. There are so many different landscapes in the work, there's such intensity—emotional intensity—so many surprises, such daring. I have found his mature work so inspiring; it's shown me the value of not finding your niche and getting cozy in it. In these new poems once again Larry was journeying out, trying to create a kind of poem that didn't exist until that moment. The daring, the sheer inventiveness, the power of these poems is going to shock a great many people. There was no one quite like Larry as a poet or as a person. I think he was easily the best poet of his generation, at times I truly believe he was writing the best poems in the country. Many of the poets I've talked to since his death feel the same way. But even greater than the loss of the poems he would have gone on to write is the loss of Larry. Being with him was a feast, he was so honest and brilliant and funny. He was special.

CB: In _The Simple Truth_ there are poems about your "sister." In recent books there are poems such as "I Was Born In Lucerne" and "M. Degas Teaches Art & Science at Durfee Intermediate School, Detroit 1942," In the new book, _Unselected Poems,_ there is a poem "Those Were The Days" and the speaker is someone very wealthy, growing up with great privilege. And in _One For The Rose_ you have the poem "The Fox" which Helen Vendler must have missed in her reading, claiming in her review that the book was "all too real." Can you discuss the working of the imagination in those and other poems not literally grounded in experience and say something about Poetic Truth as you see it?

PL: I write as everyone else does, I write what comes to me. I have always admired foxes. I like the way they live. I like the way they kill chickens, the way they attack the hen house. I used to make a remark in class which I meant very seriously. I would say to my students after a month or two of poems about why the world didn't love them quite enough, I would say—I would lean forward and in some sort of pontifical way say, "Why be yourself when you can be somebody interesting?" And that's what all that's about. Why shouldn't I be a little child and on my own? Why shouldn't I be someone quite different from who I am. I mean my imagination can haunt and invade and exist in the minds and hearts of others. Let it go. Let it lead me where it goes, and let me follow.

CB: What about metaphysics, a notion of some spirituality. I'm thinking about later poems whose themes seem openly metaphysical, poems like "Belief," "Let Me Begin Again," "Let Me Be," "The Whole Soul," and "The Voice." There's a very compelling vision in back of the humanity and sense of mortality in these poems, albeit a very secular, elemental or pantheistic one. How important are such ideas to the poetry now?

PL: Well, there was no program to do this. I don't think the world is crying for another poem about mortality—we could pile them up until they reach the ceiling. But now and then there's something in me that's crying to talk about it or deal with it, deal with it in a poem. And I'm constantly being reminded of it, especially as I get older and more weary, and my friends die. So, I turn to these subjects. But I don't have a program to turn to them, only of course when the mood seizes me. And sometimes you look at it with "calm belief" in a way, the unreality of death, the way everything keeps recreating itself. In some ways, I am a recreation of what has died, we all are. I mean that's a vision born of extraordinary optimism, which happened to be what I was living with at the time. In those periods of my life when I am not living with that kind of optimism, when I am in mourning or in grief, grieving at the loss of someone, that poem about death is quite different. I might make the same statements, but with undercurrents of irony or disbelief

A good deal of what happens in these poems has everything to do with how I was when I wrote the poems. I don't use, as you notice, a metaphysical vocabulary. I really do still believe in drama, in narrative drama, characters, visual detail. I don't want to give my poems up to some sort of high abstract diction.

CB: You've been working on new poems this summer. Dou you see any shifts in subjects or concern, in style? And which aspects of your work do you see unchanged over the years?
PL: The only thing that I see unchanged are the subjects, and when I say the subjects I really mean the material itself you might say, not even the language. I have a poem in Ashes in which I describe working on a road gang—we're building US 24. There are two main characters in the poem, me and a guy named Cal. Cal was gay and he talks about being discovered by his father with his boyfriend. I recently wrote about two other characters from that same job, so, the same material, the same road gang, the same guys, the same boss, the same foreman, the same long hot days on US 24. They are in the poems but the attitudes arid the details are very different.

The landscape of this valley remains in my poems. The attitude towards it changes. I read "Magpiety" (from *The Simple Truth*) the other day and I read this other poem about the valley and I realized there's such a different attitude towards the same landscape. "Magpiety" is a poem about discovering wonderment in this hideous landscape, discovering beauty too, the magpie itself, the rather exotic trees that grow here. But the new poem looks at the great harshness and the punishing nature of this landscape. I think that the things that really remain are this sort of cast of characters which I add to constantly. For example there is a poem in *Unselected Poems* called "You Can Cry." A guy by the name of Cherry Dorn is on that same road gang, but there is a guy who was on that road gang I never wrote about; he was a bank robber, Little Jerome. How come I never wrote about that little weasel? He was such a little liar, a marvelous liar. He was paroled to the guy who ran the work gang and he entertained us every lunch by telling us stories. He never did any work. He was too weak to do any work, or too lazy. Wouldn't even pick up his shovel. We had to do his work for him, but he was a wonderful entertainer. And there was a moral to his stories: Don't fall in love with romance, or you'll wind up in Jackson prison.

CB: About *Unselected Poems*. Your selection is pretty spare, especially with regard to uncollected poems. How do you feel overall about this grouping of poems. And secondly, does your evaluation of your poems change over time or do you find your judgments of poems early and recent to be pretty consistent?
PL: My friend Peter Everwine was invaluable in helping me choose and place those poems which would make this collection of poems written over forty years seem like a unified book. Right off he convinced me to avoid the poems in my first book, *On the Edge*, because they just don't suggest what is to come. I also used his structure of the final section, those poems which had been rejected for my most recent three books. He

had a marvelous sense of such things, much better than my own. Of course the book is rather small, less than 100 pages, mainly because I'm the person responsible for all the final choices, and so I was able to make that book I always wanted, a selected poems you could stick in your pocket when you took the bus to Toledo or Bakersfield. Of course these were unselected selected poems.

To answer your other question, Yes my attitudes toward my own poems have changed quite a lot. My attitudes towards the poems of others have changed, my attitudes toward damn near everything. I'm twice as old as the person who wrote some of the poems; I no longer possess that blind love born of the fever of creation. But the poems I truly disliked because they seemed windy or obvious or simply didn't age well I left out, or at least I believe I did. What surprised me was how much affection I had for some of these poems; I couldn't for the life of me understand why I'd left them out of my *Selected* or left them out of any book, and I'm delighted they are no longer languishing in the dark. I believe they will go out into the world with their heads high, with pride and dignity, and work like hell.

"The Unwritten Biography: Philip Levine and Edward Hirsch in Conversation," from the Academy of American Poets POETS.ORG 2001

Edward Hirsch: What are the reverberations of the word mercy in the title of your new book?
Philip Levine: First, *The Mercy* is the name of the ship that brings my mother from Europe to the U. S. when she's a girl. As I say in the poem, mercy is something she can never get enough of. I think that reflects my sense of the world, though I'm not sure why. I have received mercy from those I love and about none from those I mistakenly thought loved me. In my Hart Crane-García Lorca poem in *The Simple Truth* I speak of a merciless God who pushed these hideous images at the speaker, who is clearly me, images of my young son falling from the roof he works on, of my father dead. I'm afraid we live at the mercy of a power, maybe a God, without mercy. And yet we find it, as I have, from others.

EH: The word tenderness comes up in the first poem, "Smoke." How did a feeling of tenderness come into your poems?
PL: In that poem I list the names of the guys coming out into the morning air after a night of work, Bernie, Stash, Williams, and I. One of us uses the word tenderness, and I know it wasn't me. I know who it was, I remember the moment forty-seven years ago in a bar in downriver Detroit. Bernie Strempek and I were watching this beautiful second-rate jazz singer, and Bernie—divining my state of mind—began to speak of tenderness and how above all else it was what he desired. I'm going to sound like a moron, but I had no idea what he was talking about. My thoughts were large and elsewhere. Bernie was a guy of amazing smarts who seemed almost too gentle and delicate for this world, the world in which he did not long remain. His mother was and still is one of my heroes. The father had abandoned the family of four, and she supported them by working at Ford Rouge on nights; furthermore she totally supported Bernie's wish to become a poet. She appears in two poems in the new book. Years later I heard Galway Kinnell remark how much he valued a poetry of tenderness, and I thought, Wow, I could use some in mine, which at the time was dominated by rage toward American racism and imperialism. In the book *1933* you can see my first efforts in that direction.

EH: I wonder if you would say something about the final three lines of "Reinventing America," which seem to be a description of the Detroit of your boyhood.

> It was merely village life,
> exactly what our parents left in Europe
> brought to America with pure fidelity.

PL: I'm talking about the racial and ethnic hatreds that seemed asleep until they exploded in violence. I have a hunch this was inspired by Williams's *In the American Grain*. Detroit may have been something Europe never knew—though it must know it now—but it did not submit to the new world in the manner that Williams hoped. We lived with the old poisons still intact. An act, or more likely a rumored act, sets the place on fire. If you were Phil Levine aged fourteen, five-feet-two, 125 pounds, it was a nightmare. Detroit was the most anti-Semitic city west of Munich, and all these Jew haters—in my imagination—were coming after me, and in fact a lot of them were. But in spite of that the kid in the poem is learning to accommodate all the madness and to live in the eye of the hurricane and survive. In that way the title is not ironic.

EH: Would it be fair to say there's a sense of orphanhood running through this book?
PL: In an odd way, yes. I don't mean I personally felt I was an orphan. My father died when I was five, but I grew up in a strong family. My mother worked full-time so I was largely ungoverned, free to roam the streets of Detroit from an early age and research the poems to come, a tiny Walt Whitman going among powerful, uneducated people. I have a sense that many Americans, especially those like me with European or foreign parents, feel they have to invent their families just as they have to invent themselves.

EH: American poets have sometimes been criticized for writing about their families. Is there any validity in this critique?
PL: American poets have been criticized for anything you can think of. For being too English, recently for not being English enough. For free verse, for formal verse. For being obscure. For assuming words have meaning. For using their imaginations to invent an America more interesting than the ones they got. For writing about their love lives, for not writing about their love lives. Each of us has a family or doesn't have a family. Those who do might naturally turn to that experience and try to transform it into poetry. Look what Williams did with the elderly women in his family starting with Emily Dickinson Wellcome. Would we not want to have those poems? The test is the quality of the work. Period.

EH: The poets Vallejo and Lorca come into your new book. What have they meant to you?
PL: More than I can find words for. In *The Bread of Time* I described how *Poet in New York* directed me toward my first decent poems of rage against Detroit and General Motors for whom I worked. I soon learned not to imitate Lorca. For one thing it's too easy, for another it always shows. Back in '94 I reread a lot of Lorca to write that essay, and the day I reread *Poet in New York* I put the book down and couldn't stop talking like Lorca. "Hunger is a boy in a dark room with brown shoes that pinch," and so on. I was seeing the world through his images. Something like that happened when I first visited the Prado back in '66. I spent more than an hour with Goya's black paintings, and when I left the museum I entered the Madrid of Goya. Wherever I looked I saw the punished bodies, the torn mouths, the eyes bursting with fear or rage.

Vallejo I came to much later, in my early thirties, in the translations of Jim Wright, Thomas Merton, Lillian Lowenfels, Nan Braymer, Charles Guenther, which are still the best translations we have. I later learned Spanish and struggled with the originals which are very difficult, and then many friends, the scholar José Elgorriaga and the Mexican poet Ernesto Trejo, led me patiently through them, and I got an idea of their majesty. If his collected works were available in great translations he'd be as famous here in the States as Neruda.

No one can write like Vallejo and not sound like a fraud. He's just too much himself and not you. I did swipe one thing from him. In his great poem to Pedro Rojas he gives this railroad worker a little silver spoon with which to eat his lunch on the job. It's just a perfect tiny insight into the man. In my poem to P. L., the soldier who died in Spain, I give P. L. a little knife he wears at all times. Maybe someday someone will find the person who gets the fork.

EH: How much do you think of yourself as poet of work? I think there's a deeper commitment to saving from oblivion what is thought of as ordinary life.
PL: In my twenties, before I learned how to write poems of work, I thought of myself as the person who would capture this world. There'll always be working people in my poems because I grew up with them, and I am a poet of memory. There was always music in the poetry of Jimmy Merrill and Bill Matthews; music was just part of who they were and in their poems still are. For sure I once thought of myself as the poet who would save the ordinary from oblivion. Now I think poetry will save nothing from oblivion, but I keep writing about the ordinary because for me it's the home of the extraordinary, the only home.

EH: Your early years of working in Detroit seem inexhaustible. Do you ever feel you're overdrawing the account?
PL: Probably not nearly as often as others do, especially those who have no idea how poetry comes to be. I write what's given me to write. I don't sit down with the notion, I will celebrate those who work or even those I worked with. I sit down with a pad of paper and a pen. On good days I'm ready to celebrate, as García Lorca would put it, "the constant baptism of newly created things." I see nothing wrong with poems about work or people who work. If half the most celebrated poets want to pay homage to Wittgenstein, I won't complain. Whatever the drive is, we follow it: if the poem is about killing and devouring a rabbit or seducing a statue or singing in an empty warehouse to make my peace with the demons of filth, so be it. All of this may produce garbage, but we do our best.

EH: I love the poem "The Unknowable." Would you say something about its genesis? It seems as if jazz has had a great influence on you as a poet.
PL: The Sonny Rollins poem. I love his sound. I can hear it right now on "Lover Man" with Brownie and Max Roach; it's such a full and unapologetically sensual blooming. In the late sixties before his second "retirement" he recorded "East Broadway Rundown." I listened to that over and over, couldn't get enough of his sound. What made him my hero was his ability to remove himself from the music scene just at that point in his career when he was becoming the dominant saxophonist, to stop playing publicly and retire into himself and his instrument. For close to two years he lived like a monk alone in Brooklyn, lifting weights, practicing his music on the Williamsburg Bridge when the weather permitted, just living with both of his instruments. That dedication amazed me; he withdrew from the whole commercial thing into the monastery of his art.

I don't know how much the music has influenced my writing; I know it's inspired me, and the young jazz musicians I went to school with in Detroit—Kenny Burrell, Pepper Adams,

Bess Bonier, Tommy Flanagan, Barry Harris—were the first people I knew who were living the creative lives of artists. In age they were kids like me, and I thought, if they can do it then I can do it. There were many others who did their best and wound up as footnotes, like my friend Marion in the poem "Flowering Midnight," but they too were part of the enterprise. It's just like poetry: you can give it your all and find out later it wasn't enough.

EH: At times you seem to be mythologizing the world of your parents before you were born. Why is that so important to you?

PL: What I inherited were myths and maybe even a few facts. My father's life seemed and still seems utterly mysterious to me. He came alone to the States from Russia at age eleven. He settled in New York City with two sisters and their families. A few years ago I learned there were three sisters. He enlisted in the English army at age nineteen. He was stationed in Palestine. He deserted. He found a new identity and a passport in Cairo. Or maybe none of this happened. I recall a tall, loving, dark, very handsome man, one who spoke perfect English, Yiddish, Russian, Arabic, who read Latin poetry and Russian and French fiction, who voted for Hoover and not F. D. R. A Jew voting for Hoover? He was thirty-five when he died. My mother carried on and supported us; her ambition had been to write poetry and songs. I never heard or saw one. They and my grandfather seemed mythic: people who crossed a continent, an ocean, landed in a strange country, learned "our ways, our language," and lived with gusto and style. They mythologized themselves.

EH: There's a revealing moment in "Salt and Oil" in which you say,

> [This] . . . is a moment
> in the daily life of the world,
> a moment that will pass into
> the unwritten biography
> of your city or my city
> unless it is frozen into the fine print
> of our eyes. . . .

Do you see this recent work as saving that moment and writing that unwritten biography?

PL: I want a record, a visual one will do. I'm saying look, here they come, pay attention. Let your eyes transform what appears ordinary, commonplace, into what it is, a moment in time, an observed fragment of eternity. Millions of us are walking the streets, and at any moment literally dozens of us are seeing. I'm saying if you're awake, if I'm awake, this is what we could see. Any one of us can transform the moment into what it is. Salt and Oil are based on two poets I knew and loved who passed from breath before they did the work they were meant to do. The hero of one, Salt, the name I give Bernie Strempek, was Hart Crane. Oil had two heroes, Homer and Rilke. I can't write like either Rilke or Homer, so I fed at the trough of Hart Crane for this poem. Of course there is a third person in the drama, but I never name or describe him. I invite the reader to mortalize him.

EH: I wonder if you'd say something about the structure of *The Mercy*.

PL: Originally I saw the book very differently, but my editor, Harry Ford, asked me to write a description of the book even before I began to put it together. I wrote one description and my wife disliked it, so I wrote a second in which I called it a book of journeys, from youth to age, from innocence to experience, from sanity to madness and back again. When I then looked at the poetry I'd assembled I saw about fifty pages of it didn't belong; then I had to put the rest together. I quickly saw three sections and a building toward intimacy, intensity. That final section is mainly family poems and includes actual as well as spiritual brothers and sisters and parents. You and Larry Levis helped me with my previous book and together you gave me the notion of building the sections to a sort of climax and keeping that high into the next section, then gradually coming down to rebuild again to another climax. I tried it again. My friend Peter Everwine gave me the notion of the coda at the end, the little elegy for my mother who died while I was putting the book together. If this is a successful structure I owe it to you, Eddie, and Larry, and Peter. If it's not I still owe it to you, not that I had to take your advice.

EH: Do you know where you're going next?

PL: Brooklyn in April. Not really. I never do. I'm seventy-one now, so it's hard to imagine a dramatic change. I don't expect to embark on anything like The Cantos or The Dream Songs. Or even a Brooklyn poem based on Paterson. It would be nice to stumble onto one of those great projects so I could stay busy right through my dotage, but I'm not counting on it. Work might keep me from turning into an ash tree or a cabbage tune on the wind I should be hearing. I've never known where I'm going until I've gone and come back, and then it takes me ages to see what the trip was about. I've never truly planned a book ahead of time. I know that works for others, and to paraphrase Frost, "It might work for me, but it hasn't yet."

EH: Have I forgotten someone or something?

PL: Cesare Pavese. I first read him thirty years ago in a Penguin translation I found in London. I fell in love with his way of making a poem. Then later *Hard Labor* translated by William Arrowsmith, and I must have read it fifteen times before I found it could help me. He's in this book, he and—as usual—Williams. And for a change Hart Crane and Antonio Machado. But Pavese is the inspiration or maybe the trickster to whom I owe much of this work or whatever is worthy in the book. He blamed himself enough; he doesn't need my fuck-ups on his shoulders.

EH: *The Mercy* is dedicated to your mother. Does she cast a retrospective light over the book?

PL: I was very lucky to have a mother who encouraged me to become a poet. As a fourteen-year-old I fell in love with horse racing, and she hated that. I think she was so glad I quit the track and went to college when I turned eighteen that I could have studied lion taming, and she would have said, "That's an old and honorable profession." But she loved poetry, fiction, music; that a son of hers would devote himself to this art thrilled her. Only the final poem in the book was written after her death, which was in the spring of last year just after she turned ninety-four. I did not see her death coming. The last time I spoke with her she sounded very snappy and was looking forward to my new book. I hope the book contains some of her zest for life, some of her belief in the power of beauty, some of her great humor. As a teacher you too must have known many young people who wanted to pursue poetry but were discouraged by their families. I'm one lucky guy to have had Esther Levine for my mother.

"The Magic of Failure"—from *FIRST LIGHT: A Festschrift for Philip Levine on his 85th Birthday*—Jon Vienberg

If I would've known what I was doing, I never would have discovered poetry. It was 1972 and I had accumulated enough credits to graduate from Fresno State College twice except I didn't know it until the registrar's office notified me that it was about time to declare a major. The good part was that I loved learning and the design of classes I orchestrated for myself ranged from Accounting to Meteorology to Western Civilization. The bad parts were that I had a cavalier attitude toward anything that smacked of authority and I dreaded a commitment that might lead to a job that I would hold on to until I died, even though at the time I was working at a hospital cleaning out infected wounds and emptying bedpans. In the maze of cubicles at Fresno State's Administration Building the woman who scrutinized my file proudly proclaimed me a rare graduate by accident in the field of Psychology, and all I had to do was pay my fees at an adjacent window, which took me another three years to do. Instead I picked up a schedule of courses to choose two classes that I felt I had overlooked or had been deficient in selecting during my accidental and failed scholarly pursuits. One was Genetics taught by Woodwick, and the other was Poetry by a guy named Levine.

I liked Philip Levine before he ever said a word. He wore white Addidas, denim jeans, and a horizontal, wide striped, black and white tee shirt. Later in the semester, when it got cold, he wore a dark, Eisenhower jacket with the word " Messenger " sewn above the pocket, which I coveted. The class was a night class held in the upstairs of the Ed Psych building that he hurriedly bounded up as if floodwaters were storming his heels, then with the patience of Job, he listened to five chattering conversations directed at him at once, never flinching toward brusqueness. He turned on the glaring lights and gave a twenty minute comedy shtick on the mundane status of Fresno State architecture, what he ate for dinner and nobody better ruin it through bad poetry, his sore shoulder, his first piece of advice being not to get old, Bobby Riggs, the enormous bulk of the cows being nurtured in the Ag Dept., and how he once met Lenny Bruce in a restroom in New York. Then he asked for poems written by us. That's when I asked the guy sitting next to me what that was supposed to mean. I thought I had signed up for an academic class in Poetry. This was a writing class and he's a published poet, a big deal, I was told. But it didn't matter. I couldn't get out. I was drugged or hypnotized, enthralled by his plain and common speech, his stiletto wit and humor. I was addicted without ever having written a poem.

In a class where imagination was King and originality its slowly ascending daughter I wrote my first poem. " Green Eyed Ants " was a recklessly surreal account of two opposing groups of ants battling over a stale, leftover piece of wedding cake, which I handwrote on a piece of yellow, legal pad paper. Philip Levine's comments were acerbic and to the point, encouraged by his forgiving comments, " this line was a nice athletic try by a poet who lost focus and the game," I nearly pissed my pants that he called me a poet. On the legal pad of my poem he wrote, in part, " now you're rolling, remember to keep it tight, uptight and out of sight like Stevie Wonder says". My next poem ruined his dinner and he told me so. Mostly he was expansive in his generosity, a quality that to this day I admire as one might a religion, and I still remember many of his aphorisms: " why write about yourself when you can write about something interesting " or " you have more poems in your pocket than in your head " or one he told me privately, " lose a lot of what you might know of poetry, but try not to lose that bluesy voice." What I thought of poetry, pre-Levine, was scant and that it had to be safe, self absorbed and reflective. With his electric enthusiasm he burned those notions away in the first few meetings. Poetry could be fiery and perilous, risky and dangerous, and if it wasn't you weren't trying hard enough and as a consequence were betraying poetry and the many selves that inhabited you, namely your experience/history. And it was not without what I came to refer to as the 4C's or pitfalls of poetry: the Cartoon image, the Clever line, an attitude of Conceit, and the forever-dreaded Cliché and all its remnants. It was an ominous amount to consider, turning failures into magic and that's why I came, stayed for the humor and ended up getting serious.

Even after a friendship that has lasted over thirty-five years, I don't know if Philip Levine believes in magic, not the rabbit-in-the-hat, dime behind the ear lobe, sleight of hand card trick, no illusory lost wallets in this class, not even one weeping Ouija board or sleepy séance or the collecting of off-campus bat wings. And even though it was still a study of wonders and surprises, it was the opposite of disappearing acts and deceptions. It was the finding of what had vanished from our lives and brought back through the music of words, a personal world trying to find its seam. It was the magic that took a Beginning Poetry Writing class, five of whom became published poets, and taught them more than how to soothe the unsettling image, or how to put a choke hold on the mixed metaphor or level a humpy rhythm. It was a group who at one time or another gazed at the August stars, heard car crashes from their apartment patios and in winter, immersed themselves beneath the fleece of tule fog, and in summer were scoured by heat in their backyards and corrupted by the swirling dust spores of Valley Fever. Philip Levine taught us how to laugh at ourselves, how to respect poetry by carving out time to " let the silence enter us " and just maybe we might hear the furious beating heart of childhood, or get a glimpse of the thread of light wiggling beneath the moth's wing, watch it as it ignites into a wheel of fire so bright and beautiful and bold that it so deeply touches the human spirit that I am inadequate to call it anything but magic.

from "Philip Levine"—*Pacific Review* 1990; & *On the Poetry of Philip Levine: Stranger to Nothing,*1991; & *A Condition of the Spirit,* 2004—Larry Levis

To attempt to be at all objective about my friend and my first teacher Philip Levine is impossible for me. For to have been a student in Levine's classes from the mid to late 1960s was to have a life, or what has turned out to be my life, given to me by another. And certainly then, at the age of seventeen, I had no life, or no passionate life animated by a purpose, and I was unaware that one might be possible. . . .

It isn't enough to say that Levine was a brilliant young poet and teacher. Levine was amazing. His classes during those four years at Fresno State College were wonders, and they still suggest how much good someone might do in the world, even a world limited by the penitentiary-like architecture and stultifying sameness of a state college. For in any of those fifty-minute periods, there was more passion, sense, hilarity and feeling filling that classroom than one could have found anywhere in 1964. If the class was difficult, if Levine refused to coddle students or protect the vanities of the lazy and mediocre from the truth about their work, if his criticism was harsh at times, all of this was justified and beautiful: justified because some students thought that an A could be had for repeating the clichés on greeting cards or that everything they did would be judged as mildly as finger-painting in grade school; and it was beautiful because there poetry was given the respect it deserves and was never compromised to appease the culture surrounding it in the vast sleep of its suburbs, highways, and miles of dark packing sheds (all of which, I might add, if left without the intelligence and beauty of art, is in its mute entirety absolutely worthless).

But beneath the difficulty of the class, of studying and writing in traditional prosody, beneath the harshness of the criticism Levine gave to us, impartially and democratically, there was in the way he taught a humor and a talent for making the most self-conscious young students laugh at themselves and at their mistakes; by doing so, they could suddenly go beyond the uselessly narrow, brittle egos they had carried with them since junior high like a life savings in the wrong currency; that laughter woke them from the sleep of adolescence into something far larger; what was larger was the world of poetry, not only the study of it (passionate rather than impartial in Levine's readings of it), but also the possibility of writing it. If you could forget awhile your whining, hungry, sulking selves, Levine seemed to say to us, you could enter this larger world where the only president was Imagination. Levine made this the necessary world. And doing this made him unforgettable. It was a class like no other if only because it dared all of us in it to be considerably more alive than we wanted to be. . . .

Levine was the funniest and most unflinchingly honest man I have ever known. In those years, class after class would literally shake with laughter. A kind of rare, almost giddy intelligence constantly surfaced in Levine in comments that were so right and so outrageous that they kept us all howling, for he kept brimming over with the kind of insouciant truths most people suppress in themselves, and none of us in the class were spared from those truths about our work, and, by extension, about ourselves. "Amazing! You write like the Duke of Windsor on acid!" he said to one passively stoned, yet remarkably pompous student. Or, to another, "For a moment there your imagination made an appearance in this poem and its loveliness astonished us all, but then. . .right. . .here—where you say, 'Love is golden, Daddy, and forever,' the grim voice of Puritan duty comes back in and overwhelms you with a sense of obligation even you couldn't possibly believe in. Remember, in poetry you don't owe anyone a thing." Or: "Look at this absolutely gorgeous line crying out to escape from all its dumb brothers snoring beside it there!" Or, to a young woman who had written a wonderfully sophisticated poem about a detested ski instructor: " 'With practiced stance which he has made his own'—notice all of you please, in the deafness of this age, this line. It's amazingly perfect for what it's doing here, lean, scrupulous, and innocent in tone at the outset. And, just now, it's a pentameter that seems to be light-years beyond anything the rest of you can do. Oh, I know you have ears, I mean, I can see them right there on the sides of your heads, and yet on some days they strike me as vestigial, like the appendix, and as the age evolves I can see them creeping toward extinction; soon, all that will be left of ears will be their occasional appearance on postage stamps, along with the passenger pigeon, the Great Auk, Adlai Stevenson." Or, to a student full of pretentiously profound yet completely trite statements concerning God, Love, Death, and Time—a two-page endeavor with all the lines italicized in the typescript: "Writing like this suggests that you might need to find something to do with your hands. Tennis is an excellent sport!"

Something animated him. He is the only person I have ever known who seemed to be fully awake to this life, his own and the lives of others. An amazing talker, it surprised me when I noticed how deeply and closely he listened to students. And when someone was really troubled, a special kind of listening seemed to go on, and there was often a generous if sometimes unsettling frankness in his response.

Why in the world did he care so much about what we did? Because we mattered so much to him, we began to matter to ourselves. And to matter in this way, to feel that what one did and how one wrote actually might make a difference, was a crucial gift Levine gave to each of us. All you had to do was open it, and it became quite clear, after awhile, that only cowardice or self-deceit could keep you from doing that.

His care for us seems all the more amazing when I recall that these years were crucially difficult and ultimately triumphant years for him as a poet. For in 1965 he went to Spain for the first time, and what changed him deeply there is apparent everywhere in the poems of *Not This Pig*. Shortly after this, he would begin to write the poems that constitute the vision of *They Feed They Lion*. What still strikes me as amazing, and right, and sane, was his capacity to share all that energy, that fire, with those around him: students and poets and friends. The only discernible principle I gathered from this kind of generosity seems to be this: to try to conserve one's energy for some later use, to try to teach as if one isn't quite there and has more important things to do, is a way to lose that energy completely, a way, quite simply, of betraying oneself. Levine was always totally there, in the poems and right there in front of me before the green sea of the blackboard. . . .

Could I have written poems in isolation? I doubt it. I grew up in a town where, in the high school library, Yeats's Collected Poems was removed, censored in fact, because two students had been found laughing out loud at "Leda and the Swan." That left Eliot. For two years, largely in secret, I read and reread Eliot, and I told no one of this. But finally one afternoon in journalism class, while the teacher was out of the room, Zamora stretched out, lying over three desk tops, and began yelling at the little, evenly spaced holes in the plyboard ceiling: "O Stars, Oh Stars!" The others around us talked on in a mild roar. Then Zamora turned to me and said: "I saw that book you always got with you. Once again, guy, I see through you like a just wiped windshield." There was this little pause, and then he said, "What is it, you wanna be a poet?" I said, "Yeah. You think that's really stupid?" His smile had disappeared by the time he answered, "No, it isn't stupid. It isn't stupid at all, but I'd get out of town if I were you."

It was true. A town like that could fill a young man with such rage and boredom that the bars of Saigon might twinkle like a brief paradise. You could die in a town like that without lifting a finger.

Whenever I try to imagine the life I might have had if I hadn't met Levine, if he had never been my teacher, if we had not become friends and exchanged poems and hundreds of letters over the past twenty-five years, I can't imagine it. That is, nothing at all appears when I try to do this. No other life of any kind appears. I cannot see myself walking down one of those streets as a lawyer, or the boss of a packing shed, or even as the farmer my father wished I would become. When I try to do this, no one's there; it seems instead that I simply had never been at all. All there is on that street, the leaves on the shade trees that line it curled and black and closeted against noon heat, is a space where I am not.

"Philip Levine," from *First Light: A Festschrift for Philip Levine on his 85th Birthday*, 2013—C.G. Hanzlicek

When Phil called to tell us that he was going to be named the Poet Laureate of the United States, my wife and I did a little victory dance around the house. Well, metaphorically at least. What a perfect match: a poet who writes almost exclusively about people was to become the people's poet. I don't know a single writer who has worked harder at his art than Phil, so it follows that I don't know anyone more deserving of the accolades he has received. Let me talk a bit about Phil as a poet and also as a teacher, since he has filled both shoes so admirably. Phil's 1981 collection, *One for the Rose*, contains a poem—"To Cipriano, in the Wind"—that has always seemed to me to be at the center of what he has been up to. Cipriano, a Spanish immigrant, is a pants presser at the Peerless Cleaners, and as he bends, shirtless, over the steaming mangle, there are scars gleaming across his shoulders: "a gift/of my country" he explains. As the speaker of the poem recollects this scene from his boyhood, he remembers Cipriano's credo that has stayed with him ever since it was spoken to him in 1941: "Dignidad . . .without is no riches." These days, when we listen to Newton Gingrich excoriate the disadvantaged, it is sometimes difficult to remember that the human animal is capable of behaving with dignity. But the search for and the revelation of human dignity are at the heart of a large part of Phil's work. The heroic anarchist fighters in the Spanish Civil War are obvious examples of humanity at its best, but Phil also finds dignity in the struggle of his two brothers and his mother and himself trying to work their way through the early and sudden death of the father and husband, in his aunts and uncles and grandparents and even great aunt Tsipie communing with a trinity of crows, in Michelangelo (not the artist but the tree remover on a highway construction crew), in even minor characters like Mrs. Strempell planting her tulip bulbs, but perhaps most of all, in the men and women who work long, punishing shifts with their hands, doing what one of them calls "serf work." Phil's loyalty to the workers among whom he spent his early years has been unwavering, and they roam through book after book throughout his career. I'll never forget the day when he told me that his publisher had informed him that a trade union had bought several hundred copies of *What Work Is* to distribute to its members. There was no mistaking the quiet pride Phil took in this.

As an undergraduate, I was fortunate enough to have a professor, the poet James Wright, who picked me up and set me back down in an entirely different place. It was a change of worlds that I never could have anticipated. Countless students have had their lives changed in the same way by Phil. Phil was an expert winnower in his classes. I don't know if he maintained the practice throughout his career, but I know that early on he used to make students memorize a poem and recite it to the class. This had the brilliant effect of eliminating students who had no idea where poems could be found. They sensed very quickly that his class was going to involve real work and concentration, never a delicious prospect to some. So after that initial week or two of winnowing, what was left was a group of young men and women who were prepared for some earnest labor. Many of them were ill read or ill educated or both, but that was going to begin to come to an end right there. After all is said and done, I think Phil's great gift as a teacher is that almost every single person who studied with him ended up writing a little or a lot better than they ever dreamed they could. Many of them went on to become major lights in the literary firmament, and some did not, but all of them, in the face of their craft, were given both the necessary modesty and the necessary pride to pursue their poetry. He gave them—dare I say it?—a little dignity.

"Remarks on Philip Levine: On the Occasion of the Ceremony in His Honor as Poet Laureate," Fresno State University, January 28, 2012—Peter Everwine

I met Phil Levine in Iowa City in the mid-1950s. We were classmates in the Poetry Workshop and shared a rental house that sat a few yards from the railroad tracks—Phil and his family upstairs, my family and I downstairs. Since then, over the course of more than fifty years, Phil has reminded me—with some frequency—that during the long months of the Iowa winter the thermostat was located in my warm half of the house while he bravely endured living in his sub-zero half. You may understand, then, why his most recent honor comes as no surprise to me. Anyone who can bear a grudge over such a long period of time has the kind of superlative dedication and willpower that one needs to achieve such a long and distinguished career. Had I known then I would be standing here this evening listening to people refer to him as a national treasure, I would have been kinder to him. Actually, what I have to say this evening has very much to do with dedication and steadfastness. Phil published his first book, *On the Edge*, not long after he began teaching at Fresno State. I want to read a passage from one of the poems:

> Today on the
> eve of Thanksgiving, I said
> I will close my eyes, girl-like,
> and when I open them there
> will be something here to love
> and to celebrate.

As the title suggests, *On the Edge* is an angry book. The anger has mellowed over the years, the idealism grown more shadowed and complex, but what has been constant is his undistracted search for what there is to love and to celebrate in a world that so often is indifferent and unjust. And surely one hears, from his very first book, what continues to be Phil's singular voice: his insistence on memory, personal and historical, as a way of keeping a perspective on the rush of the immediate and the fashionable; his dedication to clear speech in opposition to the constant hum of political, social, and cultural cant; his joy in freedom and eccentricity, his aspirations for what is most decent in us, his sense of narrative which binds us to our common humanity. There's much to celebrate this evening—a distinguished career of writing and by word and example, of teaching those who would write. If I were wearing a hat, I'd tip it to my old friend and laureate.

Philip and Frances Levine, c. late 1970s.

Peter Everwine — 1930 - 2018

Peter Everwine was born in Detroit in and grew up in western Pennsylvania. He attended Northwestern University and the University of Iowa. In 1962 he began teaching at Fresno State and retired from CSU Fresno in 1992. He is the author of eight collections of poetry including *Collecting the Animals* (Atheneum) which won the Lamont Poetry Prize, *Keeping the Night*, (Atheneum), and *From the Meadow: New & Selected Poems* (2004) from the Univ. of Pittsburgh Press. Everwine's recent collections of poetry are *The Countries We Live In: Selected Poems of Natan Zach 1955-1979* (Tavern Books, 2011), and *Listening Long and Late* (University of Pittsburgh Press, 2013), and the limited edition poetry chapbook *A Small Clearing* (Aureole Press, 2016). *Pulling the Heavy but Invisible Cart*, his posthumous book, was published by Stephen F. Austin State University Press in 2019.

At California State University Fresno, with Philip Levine, and later C.G. Hanzlicek, Everwine was responsible for one of the most renowned creative writing programs in America—often referred to as "the Fresno School," though in fact there was no "school" aspect to it, given the wide range of talents and voices among the poets. Many nationally recognized poets today owe their careers and writing lives in large part to their time in Fresno working with Everwine, Levine, and Hanzlicek. The poets Larry Levis, David St. John, Roberta Spear, Gary Soto, Dixie Salazar, Ernesto Trejo, Kathy Fagan, Greg Pape, Jon Veinberg, and Luis Omar Salinas are but a few whose skills and poetic sensibilities were influenced and shaped at Fresno State.

Along with his poetry workshops, Everwine taught Eastern European poetry, Aztec, Swedish, Chinese, and Israeli poetry. He published translations of the Nauhuatl/Aztec, in a volume, *In the House of Light*, with Stone Wall Press 1970, published *The Static Element: Selected Poems of Natan Zach*, the Israeli poet, with Atheneum, in 1983, and then more translations from the Aztecs in *Working the Song Fields*, with Eastern Washington University Press, 2009. These voices and strategies had a deep effect on the poetry Everwine began to write in the 1960s and afterwards.

Everwine's long and estimable career included the Lamont Poetry Prize, a senior Lecturer Fulbright award for the University of Haifa, Israel, fellowships from the National Endowment for the Arts and Guggenheim Foundation, and an American Academy of Arts and Letters Award in Literature. His poems were published in *The Paris Review*, *POETRY*, *Western Review*, *The New Yorker*, *Antaeus*, *Field*, *The Iowa Review*, *The Ohio Review*, *Crazyhorse*, *Kayak*, and *Kenyon Review* among many other prominent literary journals, and his work has been widely anthologized for the last fifty years.

from *Pulling the Invisible but Heavy Cart*, 2019—Philip Levine

Everwine's poems are like no other in our language: they possess the simplicity and clarity I find in the great Spanish poems of Antonio Machado and his contemporary Juan Ramon Jiminez but in contemporary American English and in the rhythms of our speech that rhythm glorified. He presents us with Poetry in which each moment is recorded, laid bare, and sanctified, which is to say the poems possess a quality one finds only in the greatest poetry.

"Feeling Back To That Voice: An Interview with Peter Everwine," 1979—with Jon Veinberg & Christopher Buckley, from *Snake Nation Review,* 1983

Peter Everwine is one of the most accomplished and valued poets and translators writing in the United States today. His long and estimable career includes the Lamont Poetry Prize, a senior Lecturer Fulbright award for the University of Haifa, Israel, fellowships from the National Endowment for the Arts and Guggenheim Foundation, and an American Academy of Arts and Letters Award in Literature. "There is something shining and pure—a radiant clarity," poet Edward Hirsch writes, "a luminous stillness at the heart of Peter Everwine's beautiful, mysterious, and necessary work."

This interview was conducted in Fresno, CA, before Peter left to spend a sabbatical year (1982-'83) in Israel and Italy. My memory says it was done in 1979 when I was living in Fresno and teaching at Fresno State. Peter did not like the interview when it was done (Jon and I no doubt doing too much cheerleading) and it sat in a folder for a couple years until I re-edited it. He approved of the newer tighter version and it was published in *Snake Nation Review.* (CB)

Snake Nation Review: Do you remember anything from childhood or your early years that may have had some effect on your work?
Peter Everwine: One of the things I supposed that happened was that my first language was Italian, not English. I was raised with my grandmother who spoke only Italian then, so until I was six or seven and going to school, there were still occasions where I had difficulty remembering the English word and I would substitute the Italian word, especially if I got excited, so even as a kid I didn't come to know English at first . . . and I have a feeling that's an influence. I don't quite know how, but I feel it has to do with the sound of language, the rhythm of language, and I can remember that.

SNR: Do you have any sense of why you started writing?
PE: I came out of the army and I guess just about the time I was coming out I was interested in writing—not poetry so much, fiction. And at the end of my army business I wrote some poems and sent them to Cid Corman, who at the time was editing *Origin* magazine, and they were really awful poems, but as it happens you write an editor you've never heard of and Corman at that time was publishing Creely and Snyder, Levertov, the whole Williams factor that came out of the Black Mountains, and so I sent him some poems and they were very rhetorical and odd poems, very amateurish. And he was extraordinarily kind. I've never met him. I've never had any correspondence with him except those first letters when I was young. And he was an extraordinarily kind man. He kept telling me that these were awful poems and who to read and to send more stuff and I would send more stuff and he'd tell me these were awful poems, read this . . . . And he had an amazing capacity, just energy of responding to bad poetry, and that was exactly what I needed at that point; I was in the army, I was isolated, I didn't know what in the hell was going on. And he was extraordinarily helpful, not because he published me, not because he told me what in the hell was going on, but because he was extraordinarily kind. And that was my first real contact with "a poet"—and so I'm remarkably fond of him in a very oblique way, because we've never met.

SNR: When do you think you realized the concept of poetry that you now have? When did you start mining that background of yours?

PE: Sort of late . . . I think after I got to Iowa, which is really where I began to take poetry seriously. Yeah, if I guess I had to isolate an influence that grew in Iowa, it would be Yvor Winters, in an odd way. And I don't think that the early stuff was sort of in the Wintersian direction. It was very rhetorical, very, almost archaic in diction, and I guess I didn't get back to what you're talking about until I picked up writing again which must have been about 1969 or '70 in Mexico.

SNR: When did you stop writing? You went through Iowa and wrote there?

PE: I wrote in Iowa, went to Stanford on a fellowship with Winters, and gave up poetry . . . about 1960, and didn't write again until about 1970, so there was a period of about 10 years when I didn't really write at all.

SNR: Why do you think you stopped?

PE: I don't know. I think I looked at the poems and didn't like what I was doing very much.

SNR: Do you feel part of it was the influence of the poetry around you, the notion then that all good writing sounded a certain way, a similar way?

PE: I don't think it was that theoretical; I don't think it was sort of an intellectual decision, deciding what's being written and what's not being written. I think I just looked at what I was writing and didn't think I was a poet—simple as that. You look at it and say, "that doesn't really seem very interesting or very good compared to what everyone else is doing," and so I think I just decided at that point that I really wasn't much of a writer.

SNR: Well then, what got you started writing again? It wasn't really so many shots of tequila and the portrait of Poncho Villa, was it?

PE: No, but it's as good a reason as any. I went to Mexico for a year; I didn't know what to do with that year. I had gone through sort of traumatic experiences, just personal experiences, and through, I guess, those experiences, it struck me that what I'd better do was to put my life in some kind of order, do something with it, so I was just sitting in Mexico in a kind of isolation, having gone through that stuff, just that need to start putting something down on paper, which I guess was an old need that I had just pushed aside.

SNR: Did you discover the Nahuatl poems there?

PE: Yes. That helped me too. I got hold of some books, and was struck by how extraordinarily simple and beautiful and clear and resonant those poems were and I guess I started to work with those and feed back and forth my own work into that. They were influential, I think, somehow they fit, if not my style or my voice or whatever it is one talks about in poetry, they filled some sense of need you have to be in touch with what you think of as legitimate poetry, and that was an important source I think; it fed something, if not by direct imitation, it feeds your sense of what is important in language, what is important to do with words.

SNR: In the beginning of *Collecting The Animals* you mention that the Nahuatl word for poet means, "one who knows something." In "putting your life back together" and beginning to write again, was that done in order to "know something," to discover something?

PE: I felt too that I was a, well it must be a common enough experience, that when things start falling apart very badly, you sort of weather yourself through that; you always feel as though you've sort of shed some skins—as if you're somehow, well totally new, you don't feel "reborn," but like with a different perspective for material, and I think I felt that sense in Mexico and that's what pushed me to writing again. And at that time I didn't think about whether it was good, bad, indifferent, career, or anything of this sort. It was just something that seemed to work out and it was good . . .

SNR: When you were at Iowa, in addition to Winters, were there any other influences or models? Was Justice a help? Did others say, read this or that?
PE: Yes there were. Justice was there, Snodgrass was there, later on Phil, Mezey . . . I met a guy by the name of Don Peterson who was sort of the Dr. Johnson of Iowa City; he would feed me poems over and over again—not just contemporary poems but a whole range of stuff and that was enormously helpful and enriching—just people who were there constantly pointing out poems, talking about poems. It's easy to sort of down play Iowa; now everybody who's been to Iowa says, "oh yea, that awful place" . . . and there were a lot of things that were awful, cliques, politics, but I bless that place. I learned more about poetry than I ever learned . . . it was tremendously influential.

SNR: There's hardly anyone in poetry now who is not aware of all the poets who have come from or through Fresno and benefited enormously from the "Fresno experience." How do you feel about the teaching and all the people who have come through here?
PE: The notion of having people come through who have been as talented as they've been . . . most of the time when you teach standard writing courses, students go out somewhere, they have a degree and they do something. People who have come through here and who have gone on to become exceptional poets—I don't know that you can take too much pride in that, in the sense of saying, "Jesus, I did that." It doesn't work that way. But to have that contact, that talent, seems to me a rich experience.

There are three of us here . . . I think probably Phil, I don't know exactly how Phil teaches, it's been a long time since I sat in on any of his classes, or how Chuck teaches . . . but I have a feeling that there are differences, because we do have differences in taste, different ideas about how we work, what constitutes a good poem, a bad poem, and this and so on, and I have a feeling that that exposure is probably good too—a sense of multiple things happening instead of one single voice or teacher.

SNR: What are some of the models you're using now with writing students?
PE: Many of the models that I start with are not even, I suppose, in that range called "literary poetry" . . . sometimes I do folk poems, tribal poems, sometimes oriental poems, sometimes I have different traditions—oriental poems especially, poems that just seem to be looking at something clearly, to get that sense of how language can deal with something very simple, very direct. So you start feeding models that way, hoping that they will catch something that's . . . it's not even literature anymore, it's a, maybe what you're teaching at that point is really the mechanization of imagination, so you're not calling it a particular kind of poem you're saying, look in all of these situations, how similar at times the imaginative process works. You can read an 8th century Chinese poet and he sounds a little bit like an African poet in the 12th century and he sounds a little bit like this poet over here writing in Greek, and what kind of pulls it all together? You say it's somehow similar to what people do with the imagination when it fits in terms of language, image, music, etc. . . .

SNR: Perhaps then we're asking about ways of knowing, of finding things anchored in an identifiable human emotion. What about a poem we both like very much, "How It Is," would you say it is about as close to a poetic statement as there is as far as your writing is concerned?

PE: That's a pretty fair statement I think.

How It Is

This is how it is—

One turns away
and walks out into the evening.
There is a white horse on the prairie, or a river
that slips away among dark rocks

One speaks, or is about to speak,
not that it matters.

What matters is this—

It is evening.
I have been away a long time.
Something is singing in the grass.

SNR: This poem, by way of symbol, at one in the same time grabs what is most universal in the past and ties it emotionally together to what is most immediate in the present. Can you talk about the sources of that poem?

PE: A little bit. . . . One of the responses to the poem that I like best, not necessarily my own poem, is that I like the poem that stays very close to the impulse, and I find that there is at least in me a peculiar sense of impulse to a poem. I'm aware of those poems that come from an occasion and you have to give information about the occasion but there's a way in which when you write that kind of poem you spend part of the time writing the occasion—I did this, I was doing that, this happened and it all leads to this. . . . . And, I guess I get more and more interested in the kind of poem that doesn't need all the information coming into it, is very close to that sense of—it's almost a physical sense, a kind of suspended sense where everything is just about ready to break into meaning. I'm not sure where all those images come from, but it's part of that almost standing in the doorway of something, trying to catch that sense of the past, and a present, and a kind of presence, and I guess I want language to begin to intimate that sense of presence and stay a little mysterious.

I mean there are people you know—my sense of poets who have done this kind of thing—I think of the poems of Ungaretti which I love dearly, some of the smaller poems of Jimenez, even Machado. . . . And, especially Bobrowski; he has that sense of, it's a lyrical voice, but in touch always with that kind of imminence, and he's the poet among all those others I've mentioned who I really feel most is the spirit of poetry, or what is the spirit of poetry for me. I'm not trying now to talk about direct imitation of a technique or a voice, just that sense of where does the poem sit, for your spirit.

SNR: Can you say something about the politics and the position and the ambition that you've sort of stayed away from?

PE: My basic assumption really is that if you get too tangled up in the career of being a poet, you may not be a worse poet, but your character suffers. It's like any field where you get wrapped up in too much careerism; you may be very good at it but your character suffers after all. That doesn't say that to not get wrapped up in it makes you a sterling character, but the predictability is that your character suffers—it's an ignoble ambition to want to be a poet. Auden says somewhere in his notebooks, I forget the exact quote, talking about the character of the great poet, and he sort of makes the observation, (it must really be a cliché), that most really great poets, as characters, are assholes. There may be a real germ of truth as far as I can tell. I read the biography of Neruda and I much prefer the poems of Neruda to the biography.

SNR: In the reviews of your work and in other places, do you think that the notion of Solitude and Silence is made too much of? We find more of a meditative progression of symbols and images, precise concentrations and not personal complaints—the poems take on the larger stance, the spiritual stance. Aren't you tired of hearing "Everwine and his silence, Everwine and his solitude," as if the poems were wholly about that—as if the white space on the page were really that important? Isn't it rather what you say?

PE: I think I'm enormously aware of those qualities that surround the poem and I think that's more a matter of aesthetic choice, a matter of temperament. You sit down and you want to write a poem and there are a lot of other people who have talked about this, you hear a voice that you think is your own, and if you hear a voice other than that, it's not your poem; it's somebody else's poem which you can admire, but it doesn't sound like where your poems come from. And I suppose that sense of sitting down and listening to a voice probably comes close to a sense of a kind of meditative voice—that is what I begin to associate with my poems, that sounds to me the most authentic I can get. And I guess it also proceeds from that assumption I talked of earlier that I am less and less interested in writing the poem that is deeply occasional or anecdotal, or informational, and I want to stay very close to that impulse that feeds the poem, and that impulse for me comes very close to a sense of silence which surrounds the act of the poem, rather than one that is the center of the poem.

When I respond most to a poem in a way that's what I'm responding to; it sounds right to me, and it comes out and it doesn't sound quite biographical, it doesn't quite sound personally historical; what I want it to sound like is a hell of a lot better than what I am, or a hell of a lot wiser than what I am, or more knowledgeable, maybe that's all it is. It's a pitch you hear in the back of your head, a pitch, a voice and it hits, it's not like a note or anything, and that's the voice when you try to write the poem. You feel your way back until you can hear that voice, and if you hear that voice, you say, "Ah ha, there it is, let it talk," it's going to know what to say—and I think that's always the process. Maybe that's meditation, maybe it isn't, but it's feeling back to that voice until you hear and say, let it talk because that's the voice. And if it falters or goes into some other kind of voice, the poem breaks apart, the poem changes; it's not your poem, it's somebody else's poem.

SNR: What about the term "witnessing" as something poets do? Isn't the strategy of the witnessing poem different than other occasional poems? The Italian poems in *Keeping The Night* seem to be very clear and beautiful poems of witnessing in which it's not this or that happened, but rather the right incidents or particulars have a cumulative emotional effect which do not resolve, 1, 2, 3, but altogether show us

the right things or resolve emotionally that way. How do they work and why are they important?

PE: Well in a way some of those poems, like the one for example about my grandmother coming on the train and so on, in a sense that poem was almost directly given to me by my mother who said, "This is the way it happened . . ." So in a way, in writing that kind of poem, it's a family poem, it's not in a sense just a family poem; I try to deal with a whole range that was personal and at the same time dealt with immigrant families and Italians at home, I suppose what you try to do in that poem is to locate the incident or the image, or the symbol if you will, that most releases the quality of that life. I've written a couple of poems about my grandmother—she was a wonderful woman, and I thought if I could release one of the real qualities of her life without being too wordy about it, just holding it to its own being, then it would work. I would say something about her and I would say something about my relationship to her and so the idea was not to comment too much or to give too much about her life, but to choose the moment that in a way most revealed her life, and that story I thought was the most revealing of the woman. So in a way that kind of witnessing, I meant it to go in a couple of directions, I wanted it to be a personal witnessing, of my own roots, my own family, and at the same time I didn't want it to get locked into a sort of biographical, anecdotal, informational poem—I wanted that sequence to play off the whole of one part to the other part, the man something different than the woman, a man and woman in relationship to myself, the village in relationship to what I return to, what I try to find, etc. So I think witnessing there is a . . . usually when you think of the witnessing poet you think of it in a kind of political context, witnessing some sort of political degradation, corruption, witnessing values in the midst of corruption, and that tends to put a political cast on the poet. Those poems weren't political witnessing, but I think they're trying to witness what is valuable in lives, what holds it to be valuable, my grandmother in a sense was nobody, a small Italian woman, she had enormous value for me, because in a way whenever I go back to her or think of her I know exactly what virtues, what responses are there, and I think that's a way of witnessing too; say this is what is valuable, this is what was there, this is what creates my own sense of work, my own sense of love. It's not political at all, but it's a way of reaffirming some kind of real continuity, and a kind of life that really doesn't have much continuity—I don't have much continuity, my children don't have much continuity. In a way, she gave me continuity, and I wanted to reaffirm that I suppose.

SNR: The poem that witnesses, then, is a lot larger than those poems in which the poet simply recounts events, personally, saying, I didn't get this or that out of the experience, as opposed to making a larger statement about values?

PE: I suppose the other quality attached to that isn't political. In many ways I guess, many of those poems from the book, certainly that sequence in the Italian poems, are elegiac; if they're witnessing, they're witnessing in the sense of mourning what's past, to a degree. So maybe for me that act of witnessing is often that relationship, maybe it always has that melancholy cast, I don't know . . . and that may be my temperament too.

SNR: Your first book is almost like a celebrating of the past, rejoicing of the past, and you're becoming a part of the past. The second book seems to be more brooding, to have a lot more anger in it, more of a mourning of the past, and, comparing the first book with the second, what is the general turn of attitude?

PE: I think the first book, for example, is more scattered than the second—it's less cohesive to my taste. The second book was very cohesive, and I think perhaps to a number of reviewers, almost overly cohesive; that is to say narrowed in range—some complaint that the voice seemed too similar, that the poems seemed narrowed down in range, so that I tend to discount that. I like the second book better than the first book; it's a darker book, I agree with that . . . and that may be a number of things, that may be a matter of aging which is not to be discounted, it may be a matter of shifting of time where I'm starting to write again, to settling into writing, being truer to the elements that move that book. It may have been because I spent a long time alone doing that book. One of the elements I liked in that second book was its consistency, its voice. I have to agree it's a darker book in a sense that it is both narrower and much less openly celebratory or joyous if you want to call it that. That seems to me one of the givens that you have to accept, that if a book is of that nature, that is what's happening in the life, in the thinking, and you sort of accept it in its framework, and so I'm willing to say I understand the criticism of the book because it has darkened and narrowed in its kind of concerns, and then I have to really step back and say, but that's what I wanted.

SNR: Despite the difference between the two books, despite the more celebrating and brooding side of each we read them as equally mature and spiritually realized. Would you agree with that?

PE: It would sound arrogant if I did . . . . when you talk about childhood, for example, even if you exclude it from the normal terms of spirituality, it seems to me you can go several directions-you can write about childhood in the sense of what I did when I was in my past: I was a kid, this happened, and I had this relationship with my father . . . and sometimes you can write the poem in which childhood is continuous, present, that is to say it is not something that you achieve simply through recollection or nostalgia, or put in the framework of the poem as being time past, but in the framework of the poem it can also be time immediately present, continuous. And, I think one of the senses I have sort of using the childhood detail, the childhood image, whatever it is, is that it is absolutely continuous, it's present, and that's close again to my sense of getting at the impulse of the poem; when you don't feel your childhood as something sort of past, you feel it as an absolute, immediate, locatable present; it's there, and the ability to move in and out, in and out, and to hold it all at the moment, seems to me the most interesting possibility . . . not to just talk about it as I did that, or I was that, I am this! It's happening now! The moments where I'm most pleased at times in the *Keeping The Night* poems, is when that can occur, when the whole thing is flooded by that sense of absolute immediacy, but tempered.

SNR: What role do objects play in the life of your poems; your use of objects is comparatively spare. Do you see objects symbolically?

PE: In a way, I have a limited range of objects. I'm not terribly . . . when you really talk about a poet who brings a lot of objects into a poem you're talking about a catologist, I mean that's really the art of bringing objects to a poem. I guess for me objects in poems have almost very little literal life. I bring objects into poems maybe because they have a start in a literal life, but for me, objects always take on the resonance of metaphor, or symbol, or whatever, and that's a fairly limited range. I think in most ways the vocabulary I use, the objects I use, are probably very simple, very commonplace. I don't think they're eccentric or unique or even very inventive. They always manifest themselves to me in some sort of special meaning, and I think that when you stay with relatively simple objects, they tend to take on more meaning than elaborate and eccentric objects simply because they've been around so long, or maybe because they've been in so many frameworks of literature or meaning or proverbs or whatever you say . . . or maybe because they are so familiar with our lives and those seem to me the most luminous for poetry.

SNR: How do you see yourself standing in the world as a poetic voice—that is, your poems and voice are unique and totally distinct from any other poet or group?

PE: I don't think I ever measure that. I'm not sure I ever clearly distinguish my voice, other voices, other styles. I think that calls for almost stepping outside your own boundaries for examining where you are inside that boundary.

SNR: How do you see man standing in the rush of existence, the spiritual and human structures of existence? Would it be correct to say your views are not so much concerned with the immediate manifestations of our society, that your views could even be called primordial, elemental? Does this present problems for you?

PE: My notion is that human beings sort of sit at the center of an immense desire. They desire things; it's simple, like other people or women, but a kind of immense longing that goes on in the world. I don't think I'm normally religious, dogmatically religious, but that sense of a . . . maybe it's a matter of perspective, maybe I tend to take a stand that's way out somewhere. I mean people talk about the lack of, to use a reviewer's phrase, "author commitment," if that means what I think it means . . . I guess I always stand way back from things and look at it in maybe a larger scope—I'm not that socially minded; I'm not that interested in the structures that we usually call social. I don't think I write many social poems. It's a hard question for me to answer because you have to be awfully self-aware of where the voice comes from, what your philosophy about life is, and I'm not so sure I've ever been self-aware of that.

SNR: To go back a bit to what you said about the more simple objects of the earth being used in poems—wouldn't you say that they are more reasonably cherished than more eccentric or private objects or events?

PE: I like a certain weight in language, and a certain weight in poetry, and I think, God help me, that was one of the things that attracted me way back then to Yvor Winters. It's very simple these days, and even then, to make great sport of Winters, his pronouncements, his judgments, his this, his that. In many ways he was a very silly and crotchety man, but I think what I most responded to in Winters as a critic and even more as a poet, was the immense authoritative weight that he had to his poetry, which I thought was synonymous with poetry at the time.

SNR: Like his poem "To The Holy Spirit"?

PE: Exactly. That great heady voice, that a . . . he was almost baffled by experience, baffled by death, baffled by all the boundaries one walked into. And yet, there was that deep, grave sensibility, and that heaviness, and orderliness of language, and I thought, that's what poetry really ought to be. And I think I maybe haven't lost that, and I've abandoned the notion of rhetorical poetry, formal poetry; I think I've abandoned a lot of what Winters had, ideas of what poetry should be, but I think that kind of gravity of voice is for me always something I've found in poetry that I've loved. And it needn't be archaic, and it needn't be high-falutin—just a heavy seriousness, and I must say I've never been able to write comic poems.

SNR: Can you tell us a little about folklore, myth, fable, and your own work?

PE: I love fable. Fables are as close as I can get to being able to write in a different voice. I just finished talking about this great voice . . . the fable allows you to, in many ways, really release from that. It also does a lot of things; for one thing it tells a very nice simple story and yet keeps to a serious point, a point that isn't just locatable in an odd historical moment. It allows you to have more a sense of play than I might have in a poem; it allows me to have a little more whimsy than I might have in a poem. It's just that it opens another kind of small door or window and says, "Hell, you can do that and still stay within the strictures of what you think an art form ought to do," and still at the same time be fun to do. In a way, fables are more fun to write—sometimes poetry is lovely to write, but it may not be fun—fables are fun.

SNR: Can you say something about "The Fish / Lago Chapala" from *Keeping The Night*—how do you see the primary rituals of people, say not even so much rituals, just things they do to survive which carry over to us?

PE: You're referring to that little myth at the last section that talks about the tear pots—that's sort of adapted from a real myth. It's adapted from really the function of those tear pots; there was a real function, I mean they did collect blood. I think its value there is the same value as art, what it is is sort of a nonverbal dramatic enactment of their whole life meaning, I mean the whole life cycle. It's a prayer, it's a benediction, it's an acknowledgment of their lives, an acknowledgment of what's outside their lives. It takes no verbal form but in a way, like a ritual, it seizes upon the dramatic components of what their life means—you give something to the water, the water gives something back to you. I think it was my temperament that saw that act as blood and somehow pain. I'm not sure they did at all, maybe they did, but they must have, they knew better than that. I worked on it for a long time. I had the first section as an incident—the burial—and the section about the fish, everything turning into fish, but I couldn't find the link between them. I knew there had to be a link, and I think it was the myth that gave me the link—that is what myth always does, myth is that thing that creates connections, and it seems to me that the poem is that thing which creates connections. The two functions are very close together; if you can bring the myth and make it the same as the poem, then you've fulfilled something, you've made the connection, the significance of the discrete elements of our life—a burial, fish drying on the landscape of the road; the myth holds it all together, the poem holds it all together—you bring it into the poem.

SNR: You have a marvelous poem of curses. Is that close to the fable concept, but say, a bit on the lighter side?

PE: That's an old format, that notion of . . . in Italy I came across this; it's an old tradition that each village has its form of sort of making fun of other villages, and at every sort of yearly celebration of the village, they used to enact this, that is, it was a sort of literal litany of insults, and that's a very old folkloric element. It's one of those things that you can take right into your own literary tradition and make it work, but once again it's something that's been part of a literary tradition—it's something that's been valuable, it's something that's been persistent; it's useable as any literary tradition of Keats or Shelly or anyone else and it's also marvelous fun. It's the old premise, one of the old definitions of the poem, or the old definition of language—you reach out and you name something, you name it and you got it. This is a way of naming, the folk tradition names, the poem names; if you name it you can identify what you love in the world, you can identify what you hate in the world, and to do that is to recognize it. Or to put it another way to come back to an earlier question, it's a kind of witnessing, you name it and say, "There it is," and that just to witness in a way—so that's the old tradition.

SNR: About translations—you've just published a collection of poems by Natan Zach. What moved you to do him? What's special or unique about him, and then again, how do you choose who you translate, and what if any effect does translating have on your own work?

PE: Well I think in the case of Zach, I got exposed to a few of his poems. Shula read me a few of his poems and I liked what I heard, and so I began doing some for the sake of doing some, without any sense that I would go much further than that. And then it seemed to me that I got interested in him and you get interested in people for the strangest coincidences—he's my age, what is an Israeli poet my age doing at this point? He also doesn't write very much like me—in part yes, in part no—he's different. I feel a closer affinity to say the Aztec stuff if I were talking about relationships of technique and so on, than I do to Zach, because Zach is in many ways a very intellectual poet, that is to say he really does know how to think inside a poem. And, I think very few, this will sound very prejudiced, but I think in general there are probably in American poetry very few who really think in poems—there is thought, there is logic, there is metaphor, but there's not really any intellectual structure, and Zach is often a man who works in intellectual structures and ironic structures, and I found that immensely attractive, partly because I didn't know how to do it, because to a degree it's almost foreign to my own sense of writing and I thought maybe I could learn something. Because he really does sort of move through, and you can see it in a poem, you can hear it, this is a man not looking at self drama, but outside at a kind of problem, and thinking about it in terms of not logic but the movement of the poem and that's immensely attractive to get into that kind of poem and work inside of it without ever claiming it as your own. You say, "I wonder if I can manage this by somehow approximating his voice," and obviously approximating my voice because that's obviously the only thing you can do with it, taking it into your own language anyway. It turns out that to be neither Zach nor quite myself, but an amalgamation maybe, closer to Zach obviously than to me I hope, if I'm accurate in my translation, but he's a very attractive poet and he's a great ironist; he's really an ironist of allusion, experience, he's a wonderful poet. He hadn't been done, no one had touched him in the sense that there are very few English translations, and those available, with one or two exceptions, are just not adequate, that is to say they don't really capture what he's doing in a poem; they're not accurate, and he's damn good.

SNR: Do you see Zach as sitting in the same areas of the theater as you are when we're looking at the big poetry screen as far as witnessing and staying outside of the idiosyncratic kind of writing?
PE: He can be very idiosyncratic insofar as he opens himself to the possibility of, well for example the use of the pun—because he is using Hebrew the possibilities of the pun are enormous, sometimes almost untranslatable. But to sit inside the ironic usage of language as well by way of the pun and so on, to me is a relatively unfamiliar technique. I don't really see myself as an employer of the pun; he does it fairly consistently, so in many ways he is remarkably foreign from what I know as my own voice, what I'm interested in as a poet. He also seems one of these relatively isolated, to the side of things, poets—maybe that's why I like him.

SNR: How is your Hebrew?
PE: Poor. Shula is indispensable; I couldn't even come close to him without her notes, without her gloss. In some sense, she is really the co-translator of this work; I couldn't even get through him because his use of language is very complicated and dependent on a whole network of playing-off these Biblical allusions, and unless you have that awareness of how a language can play off and create ironies off the Bible, you're lost in Zach; you can't follow him.

SNR: Do you wear, so to speak, two hats? Do you translate and then give yourself time for your own poems? Are they totally different; does one affect the other?

PE: I don't really see them so much as two hats, to me they're involved with poetry, which is one of the reasons I suppose I include translations in my own collections. I don't see a hell of a lot of difference in writing a book that has your work and including translations of some body else's poetry—in a way that's your work too, and I sort of like the idea that you create a book that is not just your work in terms of your own original poems. You sort of touch base with things that are around you and outside of you, and sort of feed the book; that's why I put the Nahuatl stuff in the first book and why I put the Zach in the second book. I was writing a sequence of stuff that had to do with Israel and it seemed to me that after a while you are a literary person-you don't make those neat distinctions between literature and experience, I mean literature and experience go together for me, one feeds the other, vice versa, etc., very little distinction. So, if you're writing a section about Israel which concerns somehow the experience of that, well, the literary experience is part of that experience too. So Zach, the translations, tend to feed and vice versa; it's part of the same, to me, cohesive world, and why compartmentalize it and say, "Here, this is my work, this is somebody else's work—this is A; this is B.

SNR: Who are some of the European and foreign poets you read? Also what subjects outside of poetry interest you, what books and writers do you think are neglected or overlooked?
PE: I think I read most of the European people I can get a hold of. That's that strange balance I guess since Williams, since Whitman there's that notion that there is a distinct American poetry, a distinct European poetry. You create the American poetry and you abandon the European poetry, and I don't know, but maybe it's just fashionable these days. It seems I read an enormous amount of European poetry in translation, sometimes by way of almost a kind of preference.

One of the things the Europeans have provided is subject matter, I mean it really comes back to an almost archaic term, the very fact that they've been exposed to most of the important currents of history, that they've been witness to an appalling kind of history. In an odd way, American poets have almost been luxuriating in a sense of what could poetry deal with? What is the subject matter? What could it do? How can it deal with the real stuff of our lives? And I think European poets in part have answered that out of hand "It can do this!" Which is an odd way to restore—I don't mean to denigrate American poetry at all—but that sense of what really is the importance of poetry, what it can do, what is its value, and I think the European poets have an enormous sense of what it can do—that it's not just poetry that deals with self-examination, self-therapy, or this or that; it really has a legitimate way of dealing with the major blocks of experience: war, death, poverty—all these things. And I think that's been enormously influential, if only a kind of oddly therapeutic way—by God, poetry does mean something after all—here are these guys to witness that sort of meaning, that sort of coming to grips with experience. And also, because they're not locked into certain kinds of techniques that have become almost synonymous with us, and that's tremendously valuable as a way of sort of restoring one's optimism in poetry, if only that. . . .

SNR: What fears do you have about writing poetry, about inspiration? Do you ever feel you're losing it or repeating yourself, writing the same poem? What about the element of time, etc.?
PE: I think it's difficult to pinpoint what feeds your poetry, for any given person what feeds it, what creates not just a need to do it or to write it, but what actually creates the substance of it, and I think because it is to a degree somewhat mysterious and you're not totally familiar

with it always, you're afraid it's going to go away. I've always lived with that because I go through long periods of time when I don't write, when I don't feel like writing, when I don't feel like I've ever written before, and those days are always scary. It's as if what ever came to you unknown has also left unknown; you are no more aware of its coming than you are aware of its going and so I think there's that immense feeling that at any given moment whatever gift you had has become a failure and that you end up almost literally speechless. And I think that's frightening not because it has anything to do with money or fame or anything else, but because it is one of the ways that you value yourself and if you value yourself in that way and you find the way you value yourself is to a degree mysterious, then it's frightening, because you don't know that you can summon it back and say, "Don't go away."

SNR: What do you look for in your work now? Are you working toward a third collection?
PE: It's a mishmash at the moment. I never quite know what directions I've been going in. I sort of sit down and say, I'm pretty close to a book. I think the last book surprised me because it was so consistent; I didn't realize how consistent it was until I sat down and said, "Okay, it's about time to put it together. So at the moment, I don't really know where I'm going; it's not that close to being finished, about half a book. . . . The Zach's has taken up a lot of time—a lot of stuff I've not been very happy with also, I've put it aside or thrown away or said, "These are not quite the directions I'm going in." In a way, the next book is still very ambiguous. I sort of know what I don't want to do but I'm not sure of what I want to do.

SNR: What is it that you don't want to do?
PE: Repeat the second book. Not that I need to come out with something wholly new, I think that's sort of foolish—that sort of constant seeking for something novel. But I don't want to write the same poem over and over again. And I guess I don't know what to do with some of the darknesses in that last book. I want it to either get a hell of a lot darker or change some aspect of whatever it is, and that's been the problem so far—knowing what to pursue in that, how to step off from that book.

SNR: Although *Keeping The Night* is darker than *Collecting The Animals*, what you have to say overall comes to some larger spiritual resolution and so doesn't that maybe take some of the burden off worrying about whether one is darker or lighter?
PE: Yeah, I don't worry about whether it's darker or lighter, frankly. I'm not really terribly interested in whether it is or not, as long as it seems to be authentic, then I don't care really what it says at that point.

SNR: What hope do you have for your poetry and poetry in general?
PE: Let me answer the second one first as it seems to be easiest. I don't think you have to have hope for poetry, I mean I think it's independent of anyone's hope for it. I think that it is so anchored to somebody's need, I'm not talking about audience, but just somebody's need, that you don't even have to hope for it, it's like a given—and if it's not poetry, it's something very close to it, and there's no way to hope for its being as if it's in some danger of survival; I don't think it is. For my own poetry, what the hell can you hope for? You want to write another good poem, and after that, maybe you want to write another good poem . . . and that's all you can say. You hope for the next thing to come, that it will be right, that it will be good

"In the Moment: An Interview with Peter Everwine," by Jon Veinberg & Christopher Buckley, *New Letters*, Vol. 83, No. 1, 2016

Everwine's recent collections of poetry include *The Countries We Live In: Selected Poems Natan Zach 1955-1979* (Tavern Books, 2011), *Listening Long and Late* (University of Pittsburgh Press, 2013), and the limited edition poetry chapbook *A Small Clearing* (Aureole Press, 2016), which is discussed here, along with recent and new poems, their sources, the lyric crucible and his recent achievements.

New Letters: I'd like to begin with a poem on the Poetry Foundation's website, "Designs on a Point of View," originally published in *Poetry* magazine (1958), which resonates still with the singular quality of your voice and vision. It is from your first book, *The Broken Frieze,* and it's a mix of Petrarchan and Shakespearian strategies, right? Despite the formal mode—compulsory in those days—can you hear any threads connecting this poem's voice to the newest poems?

Designs On A Point of View

Thus, on a summer evening, how the light
Will never startle birds or quite define
That tree, that port in air, unleaved to night
And thickening to an atmosphere no line
Will measure. Yet the swallow at his trade
Revels upon this density—the lift
To the stunting wing, the thrust and accolade
Of air that vectors to the fruitful drift.
Design means supper to the birds, not flight,
Not simply the release, although that, too
Is part of it. And the tree that shapes the night
Will also aim the bird, give contour to
A local habitation where the eye
Is rooted, where the bird defines the sky.

Peter Everwine: Lord, this is more an archaeological site than a poem. This was among the first poems I published. You have to dig down through the layers of allusions, derivations, get past that pompous drumroll of "Thus" and maybe you'd find something—a kind of phrasing, a way of teasing out or playing off meaning from a couple of simple images, a voice that a reviewer of later work called "disembodied"? What I like in the poem is the word "supper," especially placed against so many of the other words in the poem. And maybe "vectors." For an early, formal sonnet, it has its moments, though overly infatuated with literature.

NL: I think "The Train Station of Milan" from *Listening Long and Late* (2013) is genius, the true and objective pathos of one moment—expanding to indict all our lives—that one hopeful gesture in a train station all that time ago. This is the second half of the poem:

. . .

The old man surely is dead now,

and I am of the age he was
when I first saw him—as I see
him now—that winter afternoon
in Milan, his hand extended, palm up,

his fingers opening and closing,
as if he were setting free something
he held, if only for a moment,
then beckoning it to come back.

How does the first impulse for the poem develop for you, and how does the sensibility of a "moment" become a discipline in your poetry? How does the implication follow, no matter how subtle, about the notion of time, our common mortality?

PE: I was raised in an Italian family; gestures are language. I remembered the scene in the station years later, and "saw" the scene again, but slowed it down, found myself in the old man. So now the gesture was not only an illustration of the arc of memory but also an enactment of farewell, loss, and at the same time a yearning for the moment to return and stay, to welcome back—an impossible gesture to our passing moments. The poem depends on time and our common mortality, although I was hardly thinking of abstractions at the time of writing. The old man's gesture was also mine—so much slipping away, so much reluctance and yearning for its return, by any means. The train station was the perfect setting for departure and arrival; without it, the poem would not have come to mind. The man's small gesture suggested an entire history.

NL: One of the qualities of your poetry that I find astonishing is how you have maintained a lyrical integrity and intactness of vision throughout your career, a great deal of which relies on memory and loss. "Drinking Cold Water," an early poem like the more recent "Rain," infuses memory and loss through the detail of water. How fundamental has the theme of memory been in transforming the thought and vision of your poetry over 60 years of writing?

PE: It's always been important to me, though in earlier poems it may have been more veiled. As I've aged, especially in more recent work, memory has grown more central because so much of my life exists in remembering and because I believe I've dropped so many veils, become more intimate and transparent. In a curious way, growing old has taken away some of the luxuries of poetry but also has given me a certain freedom to speak more openly and plainly. I've never worried too much about being fashionable, at least in my later years, but it feels terrific not to give a damn except to write with integrity to the moment.

NL: Recently, in 2016, you published *A Small Clearing*. One of the most memorable poems in that collection is "We Were Running."

We Were Running
in memory of Annie

We were running up the slope of a hill,
that dog and I, an early winter rain

beginning to fall, wind-driven and sharp,
the clouds so black the edges of the hills
were etched and incandescent. That dog
and I were running, the two of us
apart and yet together, and even now,
in the solitude of a quiet hour—the days
and that dog long gone—I can follow
those far-blown traces of unexpected joy
and find my way back again: heart wild,
lungs filling with the breath of winter,
and that dog beside me running headlong
into the world without end.

Can you speak to that instant you capture here? It is near impossible, as we know, to write an effective, unsentimental poem on the subject of a pet. The dog is a coefficient for that distilled point of life that comes back in a much larger way. It is just amazing. How did the gathering of specifics establish the moment in the poem and then lead to the suggestion of the larger themes?
PE: The opening is fairly exact. I really did feel in touch with that dog, the wildness of the day, that incredible joy and intimacy I shared with that lovely dog. The poem tries to return to that experience, a tracing of images back through time. Also, a key for me was the sense of "apart and yet together," which leads into the last lines and their implications.

NL: To us, few contemporary poets give more music and elegance to grief with such startling, vivid imagery. In recent years, your poems have softened in tone but heightened in brevity and the weight of specific experience. "Elegy For the Poet Charles Moulton," from _Listening Long and Late,_ and the recent "We Were Running" include joy, loss, humor, and mystery all bundled together by metaphysical string. Is this a conscious act on your part or has experience led you there?
PE: It's a hard question, because it suggests an either/or choice. I like when an ordinary word or small phrase suddenly expands into more than one meaning, even expresses contradictions. That always seems possible in the act of writing. There's always the experience pushing at you to get it right; at the same time there's the possibility, the expectation or alertness of the poet who is looking for the word or words that will tear themselves open to you. I think this happens in both poems that you mention. How many of us have listened to beautiful music and felt so much joy that we weep? I don't think that our emotional lives are easily simplified.

NL: To continue along this line, "At the Hermitage" mentions St. Benedict as advising you, "stay in your cell ... and your cell will teach you."

At the Hermitage

This morning, before light, the voices
of the monks at matins lifted the sun
into one more day of the Creation.
Now, the headlands lean
into haze, the sea milk-blue and motionless.
In silence the hours drowse.

Only a small dun-colored bird
rummages in the underbrush, hunting
for something I can't see.
I have been reading Po Chu-i. Unencumbered,
but for the years he carried, he chose the path
of solitude into mountains much like these.
The clear sound of a bell from the mist,
a heron lifting from a pool of water—solace enough
for him and, sometimes, for me as well,
but when I turn away from my book
the old disquiet tugs and frets at my sleeve,
and I can find no peace.
Sit in your cell, St. Benedict said,
and your cell will teach you.
The hours drowse, the dun-colored bird
with his fierce appetite for the present
is hard at work, the gentle Po Chu-i is gone,
and under words, under everything is silence.
O Lord of Silence, I can no longer tell apart
what was abandoned, what gained or lost—
so much, so many lives tangled into years,
and how would I not carry them with me
even to the border of your Kingdom
and beyond it, if I could?

What has your cell taught you? What regrets might you have in writing poetry? Or to take it a few steps beyond: Is it possible through the art of poetry to grow into your own poems?

PE: I'm not sure if the poem is much about writing or the regrets of pursuing poetry. Poetry has been a good life. Silence and solitude are the conditions of the hermitage, just as they often are those of writing. The bird lives in the immediate; to go back to the beginning of this interview, "design means supper to the bird." Perhaps to live in the present—the bell, the heron—is enough. What the cell teaches me isn't the peace found in solitude, isn't the detachment one requires. What I find is what lies beneath the Word: silence. I bring to it my life, my memories, my history, and I don't wish to give them up, or can't give them up without becoming something other than who I am.

NL: A new poem, "Lines Written for Elmo Castelnuovo" [first published elsewhere in this issue] includes personal and family recollections, as we see in Keeping the Night, the small particulars from childhood that become emblematic for longings and insights we come to, usually later in life. I don't think I know a more powerful elegy. This poem in particular seems to have started with recalling that pat on the head—would that be right? Who are you recalling from your childhood in Pennsylvania? The specifics remind me a little of the Spiritual Exercises of St. Ignatius of Loyola. Is that fair?

PE: Elmo was my uncle, and I've written about him in more oblique ways. I grew up with him and my mother in my grandmother's house, a truly essential part of my life. I had a difficult time writing this poem. I had the first section but wasn't sure how to go on. I thought then to move the poem forward in time, then to return to him in the classic sense of emerging from the underworld to a vanished world that existed within me. In a sense, the poem built somewhat, unconsciously, on the gesture of the man in the station of Milan. The emotional center of the poem was the pale crescent of his skin that appears in the first section.

NL: Now, more than ever, the poems pursuing love of silence and solitude are wiser and much more haunting. How have these two elements affected your work and understanding of the world of which you write, and have they centered on your growth and learning through time, age, and absences, including your self-imposed gaps of not writing?

PE: I think "At the Hermitage" is perhaps the only poem in which silence and solitude are the major subjects. I'm really not sure why I've earned this reputation. I do write rather spare poems, and I often speak from a position of solitude. Also I often invite the speechless absent into a poem. I live a rather private life, though I'm far from reclusive. As for those periods during which I've not written, they may be a curse or a blessing, but certainly not a moral choice. I've not thought of myself as a career poet; I'm not claiming this as a virtue.

NL: At the memorial last February on campus at California State University, Fresno, close to 20 of us testified to the generosity and importance of Philip Levine as mentor and friend—many had been students. Your talk was easily the most moving, and you read a new poem you wrote for Phil, an elegy, titled "Nellie" [published in this issue]. You were Phil's closest friend in poetry and in the world for something like 60 years, and I know he depended on you for help and feedback on his poems. While most all the speakers that day were appropriately thanking and praising Phil, your poem spoke to the man, to a brotherhood, to a personal tenderness and common humanity you shared. Can you say a little about that poem and that relationship of so many years?

PE: I could never figure out why Phil signed his letters—and sometimes his books to me—Nellie, the name of an odd cat; Phil wasn't a man to have pets. He wrote a fine poem about a fox, and he had that painting of a fox that he dearly loved. On a pure hunch, and it is a hunch, I put Nellie and Fox together, which made "Phil-sense" to me. We both enjoyed, in a friendly way, sticking it to each other. Phil's fox poem suggests a world of anti-fops. I wanted also to suggest one of anti-fads. And I wanted Phil's spirit to have the last laugh, one true to the friend I knew.

NL: It's no secret that you have been a much revered and endearing teacher. If you had yourself as a student in this day and age, what suggestions would you have for him?

PE: Being a student in my day was pretty simple. Now you've got a zillion conferences, summer camps, lectures, poetry cruises, discussions, forums, advice, how to use flowers as inspiration, how to emulate suffering by wearing your shoes on the wrong feet, etc. Give it up. Find some poems or poets who move you; take them to heart. Feel like it's an honor to be in their company. I had, as a student, a small anthology by Oscar Williams. It was like a door into the Muse's bedroom. You didn't even have to knock, just open it.

NL: I want to go back to voice, and a new poem "The Day" [published in this issue]. It has always seemed to us that the great achievement of our greatest poets is to speak directly, to make the artifice of the poem disappear. I think of Levine, Kunitz, William Stafford, and Gerald Stern, and also of Milosz, Szymborska, Herbert,

Jaroslav Siefert, and, of course, Antonio Machado. To present the specifics that lead to the universal in lines that are direct, clear, and yet luminous and exact seems to be the great task, and the true achievement of your poems, especially the new ones. You manage to have an idea as common as "happiness" grounded in this poem and then have it resonate to suggest a complex understanding of that in time. Can you talk about the voice and strategies of this poem, and, forgive us, the vision?

PE: Wow! What answer could follow that question? Vision seems so large a word. I don't want to over-explain what the poem comes to. I wanted to speak of a particular day, as sparely as possible. A day of happiness, a day without regret. Then, as it often happens in my poems, to move the experience in time, roughly parallel, and return to it in the light of a different or larger view, one altered by what had been encountered in time. I don't know if I'm approaching anything one might call "vision." It might be nothing other than reaching a certain age and trying to write as truthfully as I can at this stage of my life. Everything lies open to question. I have no answers.

"A KR Conversation/short interview" (August 2018) in *Kenyon Review*—Claire Oleson

Claire Oleson: There's a song mentioned in your poem of which the words, singer, and sound are never quite revealed. What do you think or hope this occlusion does to your readers' understanding or perception of the song? Is it meant to have a sound somewhere in thought or does the silence of the page do something to signal your persona's incomplete memory of the melody?

Peter Everwine: The first poem in my first book (*Collecting the Animals*) was "How It Is," a short and rather elliptical lyric based on a couple of images. The poem contained more silence than speech, and its last line became the beginning line of "How It Is (Later)": *Something is singing in the grass.* After almost five decades, I wanted to return to that poem, thus the present tense. The first poem was youthful, a poem stunned by the wonder and mystery of a natural world beyond a need for speech or explanation, a poem of renewal. The "singing" never had a particular melody; it was more metaphor than something that reached the Billboard charts. Since then, that world has become not less of a mystery, but one subjected to time and experience. An aging face often begins to reveal character, even its beauty. Both poems, especially "How It Is (Later)," are concerned with how limited words are in pinning things down, and what an extended "ambiguous chorus of songs" we hear in a world we love—one that now includes so many memories—knowing it will vanish with our passing. In that sense, the celebration and joy has acquired for me also a sense of loss and sorrow, which seems more complex and truthful.

CO: The beginning of your poem quotes another, said to have been written before, does this poem exist anywhere? Does it matter, to you, whether or not this poem's quotation of another comes across as authentic or humorous, real or in existence only in the reality and authority of "How It Is (Later)" alone?

PE: I couldn't expect a reader to know the earlier poem. I believe one enters a poem on its own terms and, in good faith, goes from there; the poem stands or fails on its own, as does the first line. Whether real or imagined it finally doesn't matter, although it is an actual line I wrote. The movement and development of the poem is what matters.

CO: How has your writing or writing process changed since you started out?
PE: It seems difficult and unimportant to me to stand back and view a career of writing poems, even if I don't have a large body of work. My apprentice poems were formal; later ones more image-based, loosened and associative. I think of Zbigniew Herbert's depiction of poets who have "gardens in their hair." I'm not much good at gardening, and I now have less hair. I like rather spare poetry and try to avoid the overly narrative. I hope I've grown more open as I age, more interested in clarity than in drama or complex poetics.

CO: Which non-writing-related aspect of your life most influences your writing?
PE: In a curious way, my best answer to your question concerns the experience of growing up among the woods and streams of Pennsylvania. I learned to hunt and fish, both of which forced me to acquire a keen eye and ear, a sense of direction, humility and wonder before the power of the mysterious, the value of silence, a deep reverence for life and death, and the discipline of patience, all of which have been enormously useful to me in writing poems.

CO: What is either the best or the worst piece of writing advice you've received or given?
PE: In 1954 I got serious about writing poetry. I was near my date of discharge from the army and had landed in Baltimore. I read *Origin*, edited by Cid Corman, who published many of the Black Mountain poets. Foolishly, I sent Corman some of the first poems I was writing. They were terrible, of course, and yet Corman sent me a letter telling me, in a polite way, how terrible they were, but suggesting I should read W. C. Williams, among other poets, telling me to compare what I'd sent him to specific poems other poets had written. It was not simply a rejection but an entire lesson in how one might go about writing a poem rather then writing "poetically." And so we corresponded a few times after that, and Corman's generosity and patience were simply astonishing. Needless to say, he never published anything I sent him and I soon left Baltimore for Iowa City, against his advice, yet I am forever indebted to that man. He became even more helpful, *in absentia*, years later. So I thank you, Cid.

from *How Much Earth*, 2001—Peter Everwine

Zbgniew Herbert once said that you didn't need much to make a place livable: a church, a market, a saloon or two, a brothel. Fortunately I found much more when I arrived in Fresno in 1962: Phil and Franny Levine were here, I had the promise of a teaching job at Fresno Sate, mountains and clear streams were close at hand. One day Phil observed—with more truth than he probably knew—that I met my classes looking as if I'd just come in from a duck blind. It dawned on me then that I'd never make it to Harvard, and I was relieved to be free of such ambition. Then Chuck Hanzlicek came from Iowa and settled in. Fresno, with its rough edges—perhaps even because of its rough edges—felt more and more like home.

I've been asked how it is that this hot, nowhere farm town has witnessed such a bumper crop of poets and writers—as if the imagination could be found only at a certain street address in London or New York City. I'd like to say it's because I was a hair-raising genius of a teacher, but not even my mirror, who is quite gullible, would buy that. Does it really matter? Early on, I knew I was lucky to be living and working in a community based on mutual respect, genuine friendship, and abiding faith in the power of art to give solace when everything else fails us.

"Concerning 'In the Last Days'" from *Poetry East,* 2005—Peter Everwine

In the late 1950s I wrote a poem about the death of my father; I called it "The Glass Tent" and the title alluded to a hospital oxygen tent transformed by metaphor into a deep sea diving bell. Separated from him by that transparent wall, I had watched as he drifted in and out of his final delirium. In the process of writing, I tried to use images that suggested what he might have seen—an old aunt, a tintype parlor, etc.—particulars of possible memories, all of them undergoing sea-changes in the metaphor of descent. The poem ended, as one might expect, when the glass cracked and the sea rushed in.

I thought I had made a marvelous poem, one in which I had found a language and a line free from the formal constraints I had been using. It was only much later that I realized how flawed it was. I had managed to load it down with fanciful images and turn it into a cartoon. I have never reprinted it.

I write of this early poem because "In the Last Days," almost fifty years later, grew out of its failure and a unremitting memory. And so I began again with separateness and the act of watching, remembering one of my father's gestures at the time, which became central to the poem. This time I wanted to stay close to the event, to speak of it directly and without unnecessary detail (stanzas one and two). More important, I now saw my father's death in a different and far larger world of time and memory, one that included my own aging and sense of uncertainty (stanza three). The shifting ambiguities of time and the acts of "seeing" or watching were charged with something more elusive and mysterious, and I felt a kinship with my father that I had not known in that early poem. Back then, I had been preoccupied with the process—and, yes, the delight--of image making. But I've come to believe that simple words and details grow powerful and haunting as they move back into the shadows. Moreover, a structure that is mechanical and one-dimensional is not equal to a form rising from resonant, complex rhythms of recurrence and surprise. Clarity doesn't have to mean shallowness, image isn't the whole of poetry, and form isn't a sack stuffed with particulars.

from *Bear Flag Republic: Prose Poems & Poetics from California,* 2008—Peter Everwine

I rarely write a prose poem, and I have little more than a passing acquaintance with the form and its history. To use the form one must abandon any notion of poetic line, and I have difficulty doing this. Early in my writing career I wrote in traditional meters, so that even now, having long abandoned them, I still hear "metrical ghosts" informing the way words and syntax move from silence into speech. The few prose poems I've tried to write came from the dilemma of having a potential subject matter but no sense of line with which to develop it. In short: my prose poem begins in failure.

Having said this, I should also add that abandoning the line for the paragraph is like having a large but definite space in which to roam about. I have a sense of freedom, though I still look for compression. Recurrence, expectation, surprise: these are as important to the prose poem as they are to the lyrical poem. So is silence and pacing, as ways of impeding the rush of sentences And there's another bonus for me: I get to try out another side of my temperament, something looser, more playful or ironic, than when I'm writing what I call "my poem." That I can count my prose poems on the fingers of one hand may suggest, alas, a different sort of failure.

"On Kees" from *Aspects of Robinson: Homage to Weldon Kees,* 2011—Peter Everwine

I first read Kees in Iowa City near the end of the 1950s. Don Justice and Kim Merker were preparing the splendid Stone Wall Press edition of his *Collected Poems* and Kees' work was getting a lot of attention from the workshop poets, especially the "Robinson" poems and those written in complicated French forms.

Kees' reputation, since then, has diminished, but he remains a significant poet for me. To explain why, I'd like to talk about a poem that's been close to me over the years: "Homage to Arthur Waley." The poem is set in a room overlooking the Seattle train yard. Kees describes weeks of gray rainy days in a few simple images, all of them suggestive of that sense of displacement, tedium, and loneliness that often affects the solitary traveler. He has been reading Waley's Chinese translations (it's clear he's read them often, the pages are "worn") and wonders if Waley is still alive, then concludes his poem by quoting a line from one of the translations: "By misty waters and rainy sands, while the yellow dusk thickens."

The line is from Po Chu-I, the 9th century poet, and is the conclusion of a poem in which he describes traveling alone in his boat as a rainy evening settles in on the river. With this line, Kees brings everything into fusion, inviting into his own poem, across the abyss of death, years, absence, loneliness, and distance, the immediacy of what is shared and timeless among the three poets.

There is nothing in this quiet poem that strikes one as especially brilliant of flashy—the language is spare, there is no ornamentation or stylistic elegance, no drawing of attention to anything other than the few particulars. And yet the understated simplicity here—especially the abrupt shift of time and place—has everything to do with the complex depth of the emotions evoked. Kees' poem has the same classical movement and undiminished freshness of Waley's Po Chu-i, whereas the "Robinson" poems already seem rather dated to me.

"Homage to Arthur Waley" is an early poem and somewhat atypical. Kees is usually thought of as an ironic and satiric poet and here he exposes more personal vulnerability than he normally allows. No matter. My comments are appropriate to many of his other poems. Kees may easily be overlooked these days but what he can teach us remains valid. "Homage to Arthur Waley" and my own poem, "Rain," are examples not of imitation or conscious "borrowing," but an acknowledgment that the work of the poet is a long conversation in which one is not always certain who listens who speaks.

"HOW IT WAS: An Afterword" from *Pulling the Invisible but Heavy Cart,* 2019—David St. John

I first saw Peter Everwine in 1965 or 1966 when I was a junior at McLane high school in Fresno and was attending every folk music performance that I could find. One night, some lucky friends and I found The Sweets Mill Mountain Boys with Kenny Hall, Frank Hicks, Ron Hughey and, of course, Peter Everwine. In the more than fifty years since that time, I've thought of that first sighting with more awe than nostalgia, as I remember Pete said almost nothing that whole evening, instead smiling, laughing his rich, infectious laugh at something Kenny or Ron or Frank had said, playing effortlessly his style of old-timey three-fingered banjo, and between songs smoking his unfiltered Camels.

It wouldn't be until 1967 that I would actually meet Pete, when Larry Levis introduced me to him outside the old Fresno State English department building. During those next few years, I was able to watch as Pete moved back to poetry, his own poetry, finding also while translating Aztec poetry the exquisite lyric simplicity and luminous beauty that would become the hallmark of his poems. In Pete's poems, I am always struck by the way the natural world awakens beneath his human gaze, at how the silence of that world holds for him an urgent intensity; and I am also astonished by the many ways even Pete's most narrative poems are, in truth, actual songs.

From Peter Everwine, I learned that there is no greater grace that can be experienced than discovering a poetry of unsurpassed integrity, dignity, simplicity and transcendent joy. Those of us who knew him think how very fortunate we are; and to those who are just discovering Peter Everwine's poetry, I'd say how very fortunate you are as well. Now, as we did, you are able to bring his poems into your lives.

from *Pulling the Invisible but Heavy Cart,* 2019—C.G. Hanzlicek

Peter Everwine and I were friends for 52 years. He called me his poetry brother, but truth be told, that was pure flattery. Our relationship was more like mentor and mentee, but to me he was even more than a mentor: he was a lodestar, my guide to navigating the currents of both life and poetry.

Peter was, above all, a man of enormous kindness. He radiated a warmth that everyone around him felt. After people, his great love was poetry, and he cherished every poet from the Aztecs to Christopher Smart to the great moderns of Middle Europe and Israel. After poetry came music, especially 50's and 60's jazz; his favorite jazz musician was the tenor saxophone player, Ben Webster. And then there was string band music. In his day, he was quite adept at the banjo and sat in with many musicians in the rural beer joints of Fresno County. Late career, he played with a group called the String Bandits, and he was fond of saying that the group got its name because when anyone paid them to play, it was highway robbery. To the list of his loves has to be added art, both primitive and modern, which he collected avidly.

Reading through his last poems, I am struck again by their beauty. They speak in a singular voice, one of clarity and simple diction, and always the voice responds to passion, not poetic fashion. It seems a little quaint to speak of beauty in poetry, but in these poems, forged in a lovely quietude, there is no roaring, no clamor, just words that arise from the surrounding silence, words that strike one as infallibly well-spoken. His poems have an inner glow, like moonlight on dew. They speak to us of the things that matter: family, love, the grace of the physical world, and our sorrow that we must someday part from these things. I love the poems because they belong utterly to him. I love them because they embrace the world. I love them because they elevate my species.

Many of the old Navajo songs have the refrain, "I walk in beauty." In the very words you can see the singer walking atop the mesas or through the canyons of their homeland, feeling the power of the landscape flood the body.

Peter, old friend, you walk in beauty.

C. G. Hanzlicek

C. G. Hanzlicek was born in Owatonna, Minnesota, in 1942. He received a B.A. from the University of Minnesota in 1964 and an M.F.A. from the Writers' Workshop at the University of Iowa in 1966. He is the author of nine books of poetry: *Living in It, Stars* (winner of the 1977 Devins Award for Poetry), *Calling the Dead, A Dozen for Leah, When There Are No Secrets, Mahler: Poems and Etchings, Against Dreaming, The Cave: Selected and New Poems,* and, most recently, *The Lives of Birds,* which appeared in 2013. He has translated Native American Songs, *A Bird's Companion,* and poems from the Czech, *Mirroring: Selected Poems of Vladimir Holan,* which won the Robert Payne Award from the Columbia University Translation Center in 1985. In the summer of 2001, he retired from California State University, Fresno, where he taught for 35 years and was for most of those years the Director of the Creative Writing Program.

from *How Much Earth,* 2001

When I first arrived in Fresno to begin my teaching career in 1966, Philip Levine and Peter Everwine had already been here for several years. I can't begin to tell you how important it has been to me to be able to spend most of my adult life working with and becoming the friend of these poets whose work I so deeply admire.

Because of the powerful teaching of these two men, there had also grown up around them a community of writers, and that community has increased steadily throughout my years here. What is astonishing about this community is how little envy there is in it, and how much pleasure is taken by its individuals when another member of the community has a success of one sort or another. Most writers don't have the good fortune to live among such support.

The Sierra Nevada foothills and mountains around Fresno have become central to my life and work, but no mountain could loom large enough to overshadow the importance in my life of my fellow local writers, many of whom grace these pages.

from *Bear Flag Republic: Prose Poems & Poetics from California,* 2008—C.G. Hanzlicek

I've always been a fan of the prose form called the feuilleton, which comes from feuille, meaning "leaf," as in a sheet of paper. The implication is that the feuilleton should be brief enough to fit on a single sheet. These brief essays or chronicles became very popular in Middle Europe in the nineteenth century, where they often appeared in newspapers, sometimes serialized, when newspapers still had literary aspirations. Jan Neruda (yes, Pablo Neruda took his name from a Czech romantic poet) was a master of the form, and in the early twentieth century, the novelist and playwright Karel Čapek wrote hundreds of charming pieces, and toward the end of the century, the form was again revived by Ludvik Vaculík. The pieces are most often very intimate in tone, and they sometimes have an ironic or humorous turn at the end. My prose pieces are even shorter than the norm; I guess they could be called mini-feuilletons. I hope they carry a feeling of intimacy, and I suppose half a leaf is better than none.

"Interview: Chuck Hanzlicek," by Sallie Perez Saiz, June 14, 2006

In an e-mail interview, MFA student Sallie Perez Saiz asked Hanzlicek—pictured fourth from right in the photo above—about his role in linking the community to the creative writing program at Fresno State, his poetic inspiration, and the inspiration he brings to Fresno audiences through the FPA reading series.

After twelve years of directing the Fresno Poets' Association, longtime Fresno State poetry professor Chuck Hanzlicek received the special Horizon Award at the annual Fresno Arts Council award ceremony this past May. The award was given in acknowledgment of his contribution to Fresno's arts community, recognizing his writing, his work as an educator, and his stewardship of the annual FPA reading series, which takes place at the Fresno Art Museum the first Thursday of each month from October through April. Hanzlicek's diligence to poetry and the role he plays in bringing acclaimed poets and writers to Fresno has made him a central figure in the arts community. The Fresno Arts Council says of Hanzlicek, "His outstanding work as an arts organizer and volunteer, as an arts educator, and as a marvelous poet have dramatically improved the community's access to and appreciation of the literary arts."

Sallie Perez Saiz: You received seven or eight nominations for the Horizon Award. This is the highest number of nominations the Fresno Arts Council has received for a single prizewinner for many years. What did receiving the award mean for you as a poet, as an educator, and as an administrator?
Chuck Hanzlicek: The nominations were largely the result of a nefarious campaign by [MFA alumnus] Stephen Barile. I was pleased to accept the award because I think Fresno poets have been insufficiently recognized by the council. Prior to this year, only three poets had received awards, and two were in the Special category and the third in the Educator rather than the Artist category. Mine was also a Special category award, but [local poet and essayist] David Mas Masumoto won an Artist award this year, so at long last a writer has been recognized as an Artist.

I would hope that one of these years we will see a poet become an Artist winner. It seems odd that Philip Levine has won a Pulitzer Prize and just about every other literary award known to man, but he has never won a Horizon Award. But enough of that screed.

I was also happy to accept the award because it gave me a chance to thank Fresno for what it has given me: a community of writers, many of whom have been my friends for more than three decades; a terrific audience for poetry; generations of students who are for the most part unafraid of work; kufta, that most sublime version of a meatball; and, saving the best for last, Dianne, my wife of 38 years. I believe that living in Fresno has helped me to become a better writer and maybe even a better human being.

SPS: You have directed the Fresno Poets' Association since 1994. Who or what has been your inspiration?
CH: The audience is the major reason I stick with running the series. I can't tell you how many writers have left here saying that this was the best audience they'd ever read to. The Fresno audience has no trouble following a poem, and you can feel their concentration in the room. No joke in a poem goes unlaughed at, and no emotional subtlety escapes notice.

One reader this past year, Judith Vollmer, referred to the FPA series as a national treasure. I think maybe it is.

What is uninspiring about running the series is when the MFA students don't attend readings. The last two seasons have seen a real decline in student support, and I don't get it. Why would a student poet not attend every reading that comes their way? In the past there was a student or two who couldn't afford the $4 admission, but when that came to my attention, I printed scholarship tickets for them. Sheesh, another screed.

The second reason I continue to direct the reading series is that I get to meet new writers and reconnect with old writer-friends. Almost every single writer I've invited here for a dozen years has been great to be around. Of course, when I'm considering a writer for the series, I read their work very carefully looking for a hidden jackass factor, and so far there has been only one jackass. I completely misread her poems. Most of the others have been a fine group of writers almost all of whom have become my friends.

SPS: Do you see your role as director of the FPA as an extension of your work as the first coordinator of the MFA program at Fresno State?
CH: One of the things about the FPA that makes me proud is that it is a community-based series rather than a university-based series. Most universities have a reading series, no matter how shabbily funded, but how many cities support a reading series?

We do cross paths with the university in that every writer I bring to Fresno also visits an MFA workshop. The university pays an honorarium for the class visit, but the funding for the reading itself comes from small grants, from member donations, and from the admission charged at readings. Several readers have said, "You mean people in Fresno actually pay to go to a reading!"

When I first started directing the FPA there was almost no university funding for on-campus readings, so if we wanted readings, it had to be on a do-it-yourself basis. I like the fact that more than half, sometimes way more than half, of the FPA audience is from the community. I once read for the series years before I became its director, and after the reading a guy came up to me in the lobby and told me how moved he was by my poems. The exposed skin of this man was so touched by the sun that I knew he had to have been outside every day, driving a tractor, or shingling roofs, or pounding grape stakes into rows. That's an "only in Fresno" moment.

I've also been very grateful for the financial support from FPA members. Several of our members donate $100 every year, and they really keep the wheels turning.

SPS: The FPA has a history of bringing accomplished poets and authors into the classroom at Fresno State. In your experience as a poet and an educator, how important is this for an MFA student?
CH: It's important for a lot of reasons. The atmosphere in the workshops is always very relaxed, and it's nice for students to meet a writer face to face before they see them behind a podium. The students get to hear their poems workshopped in a different voice by someone who has no history with them.

I've also tried to bring in writers who have doubled as editors. I brought Dave Smith, who was then the editor of *The Southern Review*, and Peter Cooley, who was at the time the poetry editor of the *North American Review*. This gave students the chance to look at journal publishing from the other side of the fence. Cooley talked about the thousands of poems he received every year, out of which he could only publish around forty. This kind of talk can be both dispiriting and encouraging. It's dispiriting to learn that acceptance rates at literary magazines are always a fraction of one percent. It's encouraging because you find out that thousands of people are staring at rejection slips at the same moment you are, and it also tells you that when you do get something accepted for publication, it means something, at least to everyone who knows the score. I've also brought Ed Ochester here twice, first and foremost because I'm a fan of his poetry, but also because he is a book editor. He edits the Pitt Poetry Series, a university press poetry series that actually earns a profit.

SPS: How does the role of the visiting poet or author affect the community?
CH: The community is instantly seized by a spirit of idealism. People insist on donating their own money to enhance funding of social services. They no longer tolerate political hacks and will support only candidates of real substance. They live their lives in the sweetness of the moment. They laugh more. They name their children after authors. They become better cooks and parents and lovers.

SPS: Is there a Fresno school of poets?
CH: Not in the sense of the Black Mountain School or the New York School or the Language Poets. Those groups have readily identifiable styles. Some might argue that the essence of Fresno poetry is narrative, but there are many exceptions to that rule.

Peter Everwine, especially in his work after *Collecting the Animals*, is driven by lyricism rather than narration. I find myself writing fewer and fewer narrative poems. And there's the crazy gypsy, Luis Omar Salinas, who writes only like himself. Whenever I look for a common thread among the Fresno poets, I find diversity. Levine and Jean Janzen. Roberta Spear and Jon Veinberg. Connie Hales and Suzanne Lummis. And Larry Levis, out there in a classroom by himself. These potatoes just won't mash.

What we do have in Fresno is a community of poets, almost all of whom are close friends. What always astonishes and pleases me is how supportive the Fresno poets are of each other's work; this has to be the most non-competitive group of poets on earth. Okay, let's call it the Enviable School.

SPS: What's new on the horizon that furthers the work you've begun?
CH: The older I've gotten, the less I've written. I think my poems have gotten better, but they sure do seem to require a lot of breathing room between them. After a long dry spell, I've just finished a ninety-line poem. I'm hoping it's a prelude rather than a coda.

from "An Interview with Maria Bosch," MFA student at CSU Fresno for the MFA program's Facebook page, Nov. 16, 2018

Maria Bosch: How would you categorize or describe your larger body of work? Most recently, you've written *The Lives of Birds,* a book preoccupied with mortality and family life—how has that book in particular come out of your recent life/concerns?
Chuck Hanzlicek: The aforementioned Irish poet, W. B. Yeats once said: "The only two things worthy of occupying the serious mind are sex and death." He meant that in the broadest sense, of course, and those themes have indeed occupied my mind. I have been in love with the same woman for fifty years, so I've written countless love poems in that span. My father died of a heart attack when he was only 58 years old, so death came early to me as subject matter, and I have perhaps been too occupied with it, but it is the blunt fact of our lives. The natural world is the most common setting for my poems. My childhood home was on the edge of town, and I spent my growing years exploring the woods and fields of Minnesota. My mother had one of the first bird feeders in town, so birds also came early into my life.

MB: As a follow up, how do you put together collections of poetry? Do you have an idea for what a book will be before you begin to work on it, or do you write poems first and go from there?

CH: The individual poems always come first, and then I try to figure out a logical order for them. I sometimes go for a long spell without writing, so there's never a plan for a book that seems like a project for me. Would that it were not true.

MB: Are you working on anything new? I've also heard about an upcoming chapbook—could you talk about that?

CH: My last stretch of not writing was the longest I've endured, and it went on for years. I thought I was done writing and had pretty much reconciled myself to that fact. I have a friend, Chris Buckley, who lives in Santa Barbara, so we usually see each other only once or twice a year, but every time we do meet he asks, "Are you writing?" It always pained me to answer him, so I finally decided that I had to write something just to quiet him down. Before I'd stopped writing, my poems were mostly a single long stanza, and my approach was narrative. I thought that if I was going to kick-start myself, I needed to try something completely different, so I began writing in two line stanzas with an approach that was more lyrical than narrative. The form seemed to click for me, and I was comfortable in it. And now Chris Buckley has published ten of those poems in a letterpress chapbook from his Miramar Editions imprint.

MB: As a writer trying to figure out my own style and voice, I think I've focused a lot on what my process is and how that's working (or sometimes not working) for me. Describe your writing process – has it changed from book to book or with your interests? What kind of environment do you need/want to be in & do you have any specific "tools"? (i.e. a computer, a legal pad, napkins) Do you find yourself stuck on a particular form or style, almost going through phases?

CH: I keep notebooks in which I jot down images that seem urgent at the time, but which can sometimes look feeble when pondered later, but if I don't write them down, I won't remember them. Sometimes one image leads to another in the notebooks, and when that happens I move to the computer and try knocking them into some kind of shape. With luck, a poem appears.

MB: From your perspective, how has the MFA program changed and/or grown after Phil Levine? Do you feel any kinds of shifts in Fresno poetics?

CH: Back in the day, Phil Levine and Peter Everwine and I had only an MA option in creative writing. We had a good number of undergraduate students but only a handful of graduate students at any given time. We also had no budget to work with; we'd have been happy with a shoestring. Now, I'm pleased to say, the MFA has drawn critical support from the administration, and the program has grown to a size we never would have imagined.

MB: What role do you think poetry has at this particular moment in time? What role does it play for you?

CH: Well, when you live with a government run by The Liars' Club, it can be a comfort to turn to poetry, since poets are only part time liars. Poetry in America will never have the political force that it has had in Latin America and Europe and especially Middle Europe, but at least there is a scrap of dignity and nobility in pursuing a craft where one can unearth a truth, even if it's only a small truth.

"Constellation of Memory: An Interview with C.G. Hanzlicek," 2019—Christopher Buckley from *The Normal School,* 2020

Christopher Buckley: You grew up in Minnesota and your parents were not professors, or artists, but your father was a craftsman, a tool maker and wood worker; did that have some influence on how you saw experience and work, and ultimately on how you wrote when you later came to writing poems?
C.G. Hanzlicek: My mother came from a family of nine children, and they were, you can imagine, quite poor. My mother's childhood was difficult and abbreviated. Her parents took her out of school after the eighth grade and put her to work as a housemaid. She worked for a doctor for several years, and he was kinder to her than her parents. I was named after him.

My father grew up in a very affectionate family of Czech extraction. He had three older sisters who doted on him. When he graduated high school, his oldest sister, who was teaching deaf children in New York City, offered to pay his way through college if he moved to New York, but he was already courting my mother, so he declined that future and went to work in the tool factory where my grandfather worked. Being a tool and die man in those days was a very skilled profession, and he mastered the skills quite quickly. During WWII, the tool company had many defense contracts, so my father's skills also kept him out of the war.

Much of my childhood was spent in the wood shop my father had in our basement. He spent the days hunched over milling machines, and when he came home, his idea of relaxation was, as I once said in a poem, to "get lost in the softness of wood." He was always making something, often from black walnut, and through him I learned the satisfaction that comes with making something, be it a table leg finely turned on lathe or a humble poem.

CB: How did you come to poetry; weren't you initially interested in being a painter?
CH: Maybe the initial question should be how I came to education. I had no idea what I was going to do after high school, but the most logical answer would probably have been to go to work in the factory alongside my father.

Back in 1960, the University of Minnesota was actually sending recruiters to the high schools in search of students. One of them came to my study hall and asked us to write an essay. Clear writing had always come quite naturally to me, and lo and behold, a few weeks later I got a letter from the university inviting me to apply. A few weeks after that, I was accepted, opening a future I hadn't even dreamed about.

I immediately loved the freedom of campus life and threw myself into it "whole hog," as they said in the Midwest. Because I was attracted to making things, I was also attracted to the idea of drawing and painting. One painting class was enough to disabuse me of that notion; I knew that I just didn't have a skilled enough hand to please myself. I switched to an art history major, thinking that I might want to go into museum curating, but I hated the way art history was taught then. We looked at slide after slide of works of art without really ever talking about art. The exams for the courses were slide tests: name the artist, the date, the country of origin. I used to have a memory in those days, so I could do well on the tests, but I couldn't imagine pursuing undergraduate and graduate degrees doing nothing but testing my powers of memory.

Since I'd done well in English classes in high school, I switched to an English major and began to dabble in poetry. I had the good fortune of socially encountering a professor, Sarah Youngblood, who taught Shakespeare and W. B. Yeats and had an abiding interest in poetry. She invited me to stop by her office at any time and show her my poetry. I had been reading Gerard Manley Hopkins, never a good idea for a beginning poet, and the first poems I showed to Sarah were full of alliteration and pompous gas. That lovely woman had the patience of Job, and she couldn't have been more generous with her time. I worked hard and eventually began to publish poems in the student literary magazine. Every time I saw Sarah, she would recommend someone for me to read, and it was she who told me that I should read James Wright and take courses from him.

CB: You attended the Univ. of Minnesota from 1960-64 and studied with James Wright. Did he actually teach poetry workshops there? What classes did you take with Wright?

CH: The only creative writing course at the University of Minnesota at the time was a seminar restricted to graduate students and taught by Allen Tate, so my first workshop was in Sarah Youngblood's office, and my second workshop was being around James Wright. I wouldn't have traded either of these experiences for, as Shylock says, "a wilderness of monkeys."

Wright primarily taught courses in the English novel (his PhD dissertation was on humor in the late Dickens). I took the three courses in that sequence from him.

Fortunately, the university also had a very strong Humanities department. There were only a couple of permanent faculty in that department, and they drew people from other disciplines to teach the courses. I had more units of Humanities courses from Wright than I had units in my English major. They were 5 unit courses, meaning they met every day of the week. We read the Russians, Kierkegaard, Nietzsche, Marx, Flaubert, you name it. It was fantastic. It made my brain buzz.

Wright was gifted with eidetic memory and remembered damned near every poem he'd ever read, and he would constantly recite poems to us, no matter what the subject matter of the course was. He once recited to me his favorite three pages of Flaubert's prose as we were walking across campus together. When he met a poet for the first time, he would recite one of their poems to them. Believe me when I say this was not rehearsed, because I saw it happen spontaneously on several occasions.

CB: What specifically did you learn from Wright, other than the lessons one can pick up from reading his great work?

CH: I only showed him one of my poems, to which he responded, "Write shorter sentences!" It was clear that he didn't enjoy critiquing poems, so I left him alone on that score, but he was a model of a teacher and poet for me, and because of him I decided that I wanted to be a poet/professor. What could be better than spending one's life in a classroom talking about necessary things?

CB: Describe the years, your writing life, before you went to Iowa, and how was it you ended up there? What poets were your early models? How many poems did you have in hand that you felt were "finished" when you landed at the Writers Workshop?

CH: I didn't know the Writers Workshop existed when I went to Iowa. I went there to get a PhD, and I chose Iowa because graduate students paid resident tuition ($150 per semester at that time), which meant I could make it through on part time jobs.

I hit a rough patch in my second semester when I took a course in Pope, Dryden, and Swift. Since Swift was always pulling a fast one, he was okay, but I sincerely believed that Dryden was going to be the death of me. That same semester I was taking a seminar in James Joyce from Robert Scholes, who later became famous as a semiotic critic at Brown. Scholes and I lived in the same neighborhood, so we often walked home together after the Joyce seminar, and usually stopped for a beer on the way. One day I was weeping into my beer about Dryden and lamenting that I'd probably be a failure at getting a PhD. Scholes said, "You don't belong in the PhD program, you belong in the Writers Workshop." God bless that man. He told me where the Workshop office was, and armed with about ten poems, I sat down with Mark Strand. He made fun of one of my poems but accepted me into the program.

People I was reading in those days: Wright, of course, and Bly, Kinnell, Merwin, Justice, and one of my poetry gods, Theodore Roethke. Confessional poetry was becoming the rage then, so I read Lowell's *Life Studies* and Sylvia Plath and Anne Sexton. Sexton seemed less jittery than Plath, so I preferred her. I once wrote Sexton a fan letter, which she very sweetly answered. I was also reading a lot of poetry in translation— Wright had turned me on to Juan Ramon Jimenez—and Penguin was publishing that terrific series of Penguin European Poets.

CB: Who did you work with at Iowa—main influences? Was it mainly Marvin Bell? Were there any other poets in the workshop whose work or critiques you found helpful?
CH: My first workshop was with George Starbuck, and thereafter I worked with Marvin Bell. I missed Donald Justice until my last summer semester since he was away on a two year Ford Grant. The workshops were huge back in the day, Paul Engle wanted to grow the program as much as possible, so workshops had 30-40 people, which meant getting only one or two poems workshopped per semester. Marvin, however, held a lot of one on one conferences over coffee in the student union, and he was a meticulous close critic, which was exactly what I needed at the time.

Jon Anderson and James Tate were both in my workshops, and I was good friends with Steve Orlen—we had rooms next door to each other. There was a very flamboyant and eccentric guy named Bob White who really enlivened workshops. Someone had a poem called "Sparrow," and Bob did an entire critique filled with bird puns and ending with, "I like the way the poem dovetails at the end." As if he, himself, wasn't a bird pun.

CB: Having read your work for 40 some years now, I am impressed with its consistency, how it is absolutely your voice, your way of translating the world. Would you say the "Pure Clear Word" of James Wright, (as Dave Smith coined it) was the main influence in your direction? And when do you think you developed or decided on your Voice, the style of poem you would write?
CH: When people start writing, they imitate the voices of what they have been reading, what they love. I think one finds ones voice when the other voices eventually fade and you're left standing naked in the voice that was actually yours all along. Certain things can help shed those other voices. For me it was reading the poets in Czeslaw Milosz's anthology of postwar Polish poets, and also the Czech poets Miroslav Holub, Vladimir Holan, Josef Hanzlik, and Jaroslav Seifert. These Middle Europeans all worked in very direct voices, with minimal showiness. Milosz, in introducing the poems of Tadeusz Rozewicz, said that Rozewicz emerged from WWII with the feeling that art was an offense to human suffering, so his poems were both stripped down and terribly urgent. That notion has stuck with me all of my life, and I do my best not to be an offense to human suffering.

CB: Can you follow up with some thoughts on the value of clarity and accessibility as an aesthetic. Little, of course, goes much of anywhere without image and invention, and a turn on predictable outcomes. But the precision clarity requires, on top of imagination, has always made your poetry stand out from most of what is presented.

CH: A quote from the poem "Route" by George Oppen comes to mind: "Clarity, clarity, surely clarity is the most beautiful / thing in the world, / A limited, limiting clarity // I have not and never did have any motive of poetry / But to achieve clarity." Clarity can look easy on the page, but we all know how much easier it is to be vague and sloppy. A lack of clarity, for me, is an intellectual and artistic collapse.

CB: You came to teach at Fresno State in 1966. How did you obtain the position? Had you ever heard of Fresno at that time? Did you interview with Phil and Peter? What was the process like then?

CH: I spent a lot of time in the placement office at the University of Iowa, checking out the job listings. It was urgent that I get a job immediately after graduating so that I would qualify for a teaching deferment to keep me out of the war in Vietnam. Most of the listings were strictly for composition, but then I noticed a listing from Fresno State that said they were looking for a poet. As I later learned, they were looking for a poet because Philip Levine and Peter Everwine were among the most popular teachers in the department; if it had worked twice, it might work again. I applied in a heartbeat. I had never heard of Fresno, so I looked it up in an encyclopedia, and it said that Fresno's average temperature was 70 degrees. It did not specify that this number was arrived at by averaging temperatures from lows in the 30's and 40's and highs in the 100's. But I really didn't give a damn; I was tired of Minnesota and Iowa winters. There was no budget for flying me out for an interview. I had a phone interview with the department chair, Russ Leavenworth. Russ was an architecture buff, and he knew that my home town, Owatonna, had a Louis Sullivan designed bank. I think he hired me just so we could talk about Sullivan.

CB: Did you have any initial reservations about moving to a town inland in the middle of California? What was Fresno like in those early days? Wasn't it mostly Orchards with a railroad running through it? A much smaller population?

CH: Short answer to the first question: Midwest winters, snow, below zero. And yes, there were a lot of orchards, both to the north and east of the city, figs and citrus mostly. I was from a small town, 12,000, and Fresno was around 130,000 then, so it seemed like a big small town. We're at 500,000 now, so I spend more time in my car.

CB: And how old were you then? Didn't some of the poets there become friends and poetry colleagues? Were you teaching classes with Larry Levis and Bruce Boston in them or were they gone on to MFA programs by that time? Did they and other Fresno poets become colleagues? Was there already a community of poets in place in Fresno?

CH: I was 23 when I was hired, and had just turned 24 at the end of August before I started teaching in September. Phil Levine had just returned from a full year sabbatical in Spain, and he was so high on Spain that he was wearing espadrilles on the day I met him. He knew as much as anybody about the Spanish Civil War, and he had visited all of the hallowed places of his war heroes. I read Hugh Thomas's *The Spanish Civil War* just so I could carry on a decent conversation with Phil.

Phil and his wife, Franny, were the hub around which the Fresno poetry wheel turned. When poets came here to read, they were the ones who hosted dinner parties. Phil was one of the funniest people on earth; he definitely could have done stand-up. He could also be a physical comedian: he once drop-kicked a book of poems—I won't say whose book—directly into the fireplace flames. If laughter is the best medicine, then we always left an evening at the Levines healed. Comedy was also a teaching tool for Phil. He could dismantle a poem line by line, but he did it in such a funny way that the poet laughed all the way through revisions.

Another tool of Phil's was to have students memorize a poem to recite to the class. Just reading a poem enough times to have it in memory teaches many things, not the least of which is rhythm. (Aside: I learned more about rhythm from reading Samuel Beckett's novels than from any other source).

Phil was also a model for how the work of poetry gets done. He went into his study every morning, six days a week, and didn't come out until lunch. He said that some days he just straightened paper clips and sharpened pencils, but if he wasn't present when the muse dropped in, poems would be lost. The quantity and quality of his life's work is a testament to his availability, his sweet surrender, to his art.

CB: You've told a story about a cheese omelet and Larry coming over for breakfast? Did you remain close to Larry, did you see any connection between his work and James Wright's as you both were admirers of Wright's poems?
CH: Larry was in the first class I taught at Fresno State. I mean this literally: 8:00 on a Monday morning. I think Larry was in his junior year then. He must have sensed that I was lonely in my new situation, and early on he introduced himself after class and invited me to have coffee. We began hanging out after most classes, and he introduced me to Bruce Boston. Bruce and his wife, Marsha, had a lot of parties to which I was invited, and all of a sudden I had a social life.

Larry lived in my neighborhood, so early on I invited him to have breakfast with me. When he arrived, I had Schubert's "Trout Quintet" playing on the stereo, and Larry seemed impressed. I don't think he had much interest in the music—he was rock and roll to the bone—but it seemed to interest him that someone of my age was listening to classical music. He asked what we were having for breakfast, and I told him cheese omelets, which he said was great. When we sat down to eat, he opened his omelet with a fork and scraped all of the cheese out of it.

It was Larry who introduced me to Dianne, who later, lucky me, became my wife. We've been married for 51 years now.

Larry shared my enthusiasm for James Wright, and you could see traces of Wright in his early poems, some of them lingering into *Wrecking Crew*, his first book.

Larry and I stayed fairly close over the years. I have a pool table in my garage/study, and whenever Larry was in town, he'd come for dinner and a few games of pool.

CB: I remember Omar Salinas and others talking about the Café Midi in the early days; it seemed like a great place to gather and talk. Did most of the poets congregate there? Was it on Olive Street in the Tower District? What was it like back then?
CH: Cafe Midi was one block north of Olive in the Tower District. It also greatly expanded my social life. Mort, the owner, was a piss-poor capitalist because he didn't mind if you nursed a single cup of coffee for several hours. The chess players also hung out there, and there were usually two or three matches going at all times. On Friday nights, Mort sometimes showed films, whatever he could find to rent for his 16mm projector. On Saturday nights there was usually folk or blues by local musicians, and on Sunday afternoons there was live jazz. One Saturday night, Lightning Hopkins showed up and played an hour and half set. I don't have any idea how that happened. Since many of the writers occupied the place, there were also poetry readings. Mort grilled a really good hamburger, so he could feed body as well as soul.

CB: The first anthology of Fresno Poets was *Down at the Santa Fe Depot*. Can you talk a bit about how that came about, some of the poets in that volume—that iconic photo on the cover.

CH: I really didn't have much to do with *Down at the Santa Fe Depot* other than being represented in it. The idea for it came from the editors, Jimmy Beloian and David Kherdian. I assumed it wouldn't really go anywhere, but David Kherdian knew how to flog books, and it ended up selling several thousand copies. The cover photo was taken on a cold and foggy Saturday morning, which explains why all of us look overdressed for California. A handful of people who no longer lived in Fresno weren't there for the picture.

CB: *Living In It,* 1971, your first book, is a handsome hand made letterpress book from Kim Merker's Stone Wall Press. It's 5 ½ x 9 ½ and the shape of the book fits the shape of the poems—a beautiful book on hand-made English Paper. Merker also printed Phil's first book, *On the Edge*. Did you meet Kim at Iowa, take his printing class? How did the book come about?

CH: I only met Merker once in Iowa City. It was at an afternoon lawn party thrown by the aforementioned Robert Scholes, and Merker made a fabulous entrance as he and his wife drove up in an amazing rarity of a car—the body style was called a landaulet—from the 1930's.

The book happened a few years later, due to Robert Scholes—what a friend—telling Kim that I had a book. Dianne and I made a stop in Iowa City on our way to visit my parents. We went to Kim's print shop, and by grand coincidence he was setting type for my book, so we got to watch his hands at work. The book Kim did just before mine had been printed on machine-made paper, and Kim didn't like the look of it, so he went back to hand-made paper for mine.

CB: *Living In It* seems to carry a little of the Iowa imagistic influence. The title poem, however, was one of only two you chose to reprint in the landmark *Down at the Santa Fe Depot*. This poem seems more direct and risks more personal emotion and narrative gravitas. Did this poem point the way for following poems and books?

CH: Yeah, "Living in It" was one of the poems that revealed my own voice to me. It allowed me an openness that I truly wanted.

CB: *STARS* was the 1977-78 Devins Award winning book from the Univ. of Missouri Press, an important poetry prize they offered for several years. The poems are, to me, in your mature voice and vision. They risk an honest lyric voice, a keen and deep appreciation of nature and the environment, and close attention is paid to relatives and others you know closely. And off the top of my head, I can't think of any other poets whose books have a blurb from James Wright—who said in part: "Hanzlicek prunes and thereby truly liberates his gift for beautiful sounds by taking great care to use precise diction. The poems are full of clear and unmistakably genuine emotion, and they are thoroughly lucid and coherent from beginning to end." Can you speak to the journey from your first book to *STARS?*

CH: When I look back at it, *Living in It* was a very dark book. It was written during the Vietnam war. There were frequent rumors that the government was going to stop granting teaching deferments, so Dianne and I were constantly trying to figure out what we'd do if I got drafted. Move to Canada? Go to jail? It was oppressive, and it shows in the poems.

CB: "Eclipse," the long poem that ends *STARS*, seems to me the "star" of the book. How did this one evolve? The personal narrative is compelling as it selects the emblematic events of the past, and then section 7 takes us to more of a time present and focuses on the simple details of nature, the irony of belief in nothing but the present. How representative then is this poem of your work in general, the work that comes after this poem?

CH: Old W. B. Yeats once said that the only two things worthy of occupying the serious mind are sex and death. He meant sex in the broadest sense, of course. Both are the core explorations of "Eclipse," and you could easily say that they are still occupying me. I've written a lot of love poems over the years, because Dianne's love is what has gotten me through those years. My beloved paternal grandfather died when I was a senior in high school, so that set me to early brooding on inevitability.

CB: Your next book, *Calling the Dead,* is anchored by a 14-part elegy for your father. In the middle of the book, it is an amazing constellation of memory, imagination, and thinking that pulls in much of the struggle in life, leading to death—the implicit fact that we must face in our lives—as well as the loss, the absence, that calls so much into question. You balance the dark weight of such loss with a poetic inquiry and resolution, that is philosophical in its view, but not in the phrasing. Rather, the syntax and diction here are clear and exact, and risk a great deal in their directness without the voice ever becoming self-conscious or reflexive. How did this poem develop, how do you see the parts working symphonically?

CH: My father was only 58 when he died of a heart attack, so it came as a real shock. I remember that on the drive to the airport after the funeral, I was telling myself that if I couldn't write my way out of what I was feeling, I would be as good as dead. I began working on those poems just a few days after getting back home. No emotion recollected in tranquility; it was all heat of the moment. I've written quite a few sequences over the years, and I never begin thinking that I'm writing a sequence. One poem comes, and then another, and if I'm lucky, some more, and it's only at the end that I start thinking about the order of the poems. In that sequence, I wanted to bring some kind of nobility to a man who was unfailingly kind to me, who worked his ass off all of his life, and who died an agonizing death.

CB: "Room for Doubt," as I remember, was a poem you often read around the time of the publication of *Calling the Dead.* A number of your poems refuse to suffer fools, and this one especially is fierce with its appreciation of life, the implicit and explicit morality in that. Talk a bit about its intention.

CH: Those boys were unthinkingly cruel. They were torturing a creature, in this case an angel shark, almost out of habit. I probably inflicted some cruelties myself as a boy. Let's face it, boys are neanderthals. But these boys were old enough to know better. I could have given them a lecture on karma, but it would have been like whistling into an empty beer bottle. So I got even with them in a poem, which has been read by tens of people.

CB: "Portrait of Peter Everwine" had to be written around 1980 or so. Peter was a close friend of yours for over 50 years, and this kind of a poem is difficult to write, to find a credible strategy for. And now Peter is gone almost a year; you have a poem, and elegy for him in the latest issue of *MIRAMAR.* Tell us a little about Peter and your friendship, the writing of these poems? Here's the most recent one:

Elegy for Peter Everwine

I'm hoping that in your last moment
You were lifted out of time

And let gently down onto a train in Italy,
Chuffing through a star-driven night.

Two men across from you played scopa,
But your mind was far from cards.

At the depot in Piemonte,
You were met by the village elders

Who took you to a candlelit house.
Around the table, family stories unfolded,

And you had a last glass of Barolo,
Never so sweet to the tongue,

And then you threw back your head
And released your final, glorious guffaw.

CH: As you say, Peter and I were friends for over 50 years, and it was a friendship that grew closer with each passing year. We shared tastes in art, music, poetry, everything that matters. In the last twenty years or so, I became increasingly dependent on him as a critic for my work. He knew me so well that he also knew my limits, so his critiques took that into account. If he made a suggestion that I might at first think required too big a stretch on my part, I would think my way into accomplishing it, because, after all, Peter *thinks* I can do it. I never considered a poem finished until I had at least a provisional imprimatur from Peter. I emailed him every poem I wrote. We were in touch several times a week, and we went to lunch together every Thursday afternoon. In the poem quoted above, I end with his laughter because everyone who knew Peter loved to hear him laugh. I often turned into a comedian in his presence, just to provoke that laugh. The hardest part about getting older is not what happens to you, it's what happens to those around you.

On the Thursday before he died, Peter said he didn't feel up to going to lunch, so I said I would come to see him, and we talked at his dining room table. He handed me his two volume set of Audubon bird watercolors, saying, "You should have these."

I didn't see this as something as portentous as it was, because I, too, am beginning to think about shedding things. He also said, at one point, that he thought he was writing better than he ever had, to which I added my most profound agreement.

On the following Sunday morning, his companion, Connie, who lives sixty miles south of here, called me to say that Peter was not answering his phone. I went to check on him, but I had grabbed the wrong key and couldn't get into his house. After going to every window and shouting his name, I called 911. I don't want to talk about what happened after that except to say that I'm glad I had the wrong key, or I would have been the one to find him, my brother, my father, whatever masculine words would describe our relationship, *mon semblable, mon frère.*

It seems to me that Fresno poets have come into an unfair amount of losses. It started years ago with Robert L. Jones, and then it was Larry, and Ernesto Trejo, and Roberta Spear, all of whom died young, and the list goes on and on.

CB: *Secrets* has poems in which the poet takes a look inward, but with a wry objective angle, with some wit, and almost affection for an "other." I am thinking here of three especially that occur in a row, "In the Dark Again," "A Short Ode to My Shoes," and "C.G. Hanzlicek." I admire how the persona of each poem becomes an everyman almost. Did turning 40 have a lot to do with this stance? Tell us about these poems in relation to where you saw yourself in your poetic career and about the idea of staying "grounded" as a writer/poet?

CH: I guess you could read all three of those poems as being against the notion of self improvement. The psyche or soul or whatever you want to call it, isn't something that can be remodeled like bathroom. After a certain point, you're pretty much stuck with the brain-plumbing that got you that far. Since it's all you've got, you might as well enjoy it. Or at least accept it.

CB: In addition to the sequence of twelve poems for your daughter, *Secrets* has another longer poem that concludes the book, "The Long Arc." What drove the narrative here, the emotional center?

CH: It's just a stream of memories from childhood, mostly pleasant, but some are more ominous. Most of the memories involve my feeling of comfort in the natural world. I was an only child, so much of my play was solitary, but in the woods or next to the river, I never felt lonely.

CB: "Flycasting at Sunset," a short poem, is one of my favorites of yours and I think could be a hallmark of your voice and vision; with great concision it manages to preserve the landscape of the past (I'm guessing this is Minnesota?) and move far into the future:

Flycasting At Sunset

Ripe wheat runs down the hillside
To where the lily pads begin.
I launch the canoe
And paddle through waveless water
The color of whiskey.
Purple martins
Clear the insects from my course.
I have no anchor;
I ship the oar and drift.
With a pliers
I straighten and bend the hook
On my fly until it snaps,
Then cast out as far as I can
And wait for stars.

When we were talking about this poem you said you had forgotten it somewhat, the kind of joke of bending the hook. I think though that you were being way too modest. To me, this is a very serious poem, though sonorous and highly lyric. The precision of detail here, the calm and specific order of observation leads emblematically, absolutely to a conclusion which is both resonant and unexpected and which, I have always felt, moves outward with both a suggestion of mortality and of a larger, almost universal, vision of life. Isn't that what the poem achieves, what most of your work aims for?

CH: Again, it's a scene of comfort in the natural world. My parents had a cabin on a lake in Minnesota. I liked to go out in the canoe at sunset, after the water-skiers had gone home and I had the lake pretty much to myself. My flyfishing was just a ruse. I broke the hook off the fly so that no fish would disturb my meditation.

CB: "Men at Forty-Five" opens your 1994 book, *Against Dreaming.* The wit counterpointed with the gravitas of mortality makes for a powerful opening poem. How does that poem set up the book? And how was it that you went back to the University of Missouri Press after two books with Carnegie Mellon?

CH: Donald Justice had a poem called "Men at Forty," and I was riffing on that. His men at forty are bleak, and I was thinking, "C'mon, Don, give us at least another five years before we're good as dead." The poem is a little bit tongue-in-cheek, but its serious side is to face the futility of trying to weigh whether your life has amounted to what you might have wanted. If the only thing you see in the mirror every day is the face of failure, you might as well curl up and die.

University of Missouri Press for years only published first books, for the Devins Award, and then suddenly they started a poetry series. I'd had a very pleasant experience with them when *Stars* was published, so I submitted *Against Dreaming*, and that led to another pleasant experience. Then they asked me to be an outside reader for the series. I picked a book, they published it, and shortly after they stopped publishing poetry altogether. I hope I didn't kill the series.

CB: The majority of this book is divided between poems about your Czech heritage and visits to Prague and the Mahler Sequence that ends the book. First, talk a bit about the inspiration for the Czech poems. You made a visit to Prague when it was still under the boot heel of Russia. What did you discover there other than that there were no crowds of tourists on the Charles Bridge? You were looking up family, right?

CH: We were in Prague for three weeks with our daughter, who was five at the time. All three of us had a glorious time. I had just published a book of translations of Vladimir Holan, with enormous help from Dana Habova, who was a simultaneous translator of English to Czech in Prague. She often worked for the government, translating at conferences and that sort of thing, and she also worked in the film industry when they were dubbing movies from English to Czech. She could feed the dubbing actors their dialog in an instant. Holan was a sort of national hero. He had been banned from publishing from 1948 until the Prague Spring of 1968, which ushered in a brief period of liberalization. Through all those years of being banned, Holan still wrote every day. His collected poems are published in ten volumes of perhaps an average of 250 pages each. Having published my English versions of Holan opened all sorts of doors for us in Prague. We also got to spend a good deal of time with Miroslav Holub, who had read twice in Fresno and stayed with us for several days on both occasions.

Dana Habova and her husband drove us to my grandfather's village in northern Bohemia. He had left for America when he was in his teens, but I still felt that he was present there. I climbed a hill on the edge of the village, and below me was a man hand-cutting hay with a scythe. At that point, I felt like I was standing inside my grandfather's boyhood body; he must have witnessed exactly the same scene. There were almost no tourists then in Prague: a few Germans, a few Brits, and we only ran into one couple from America.

CB: The Mahler sequence is a great symphonic—pun intended—movement. How did this develop for you, how did the music inspire the poems as the poems do not really take up the music per se, but rather range through a lyric landscape and use the symphonies as a jumping off point for a larger imagination and personal engagement with the world?

CH: Well, I've been a Mahlerian since my undergraduate days. I still listen to him all of the time. To me, he is the most expansive soul in music. Our daughter recently took us to see Gustavo Dudamel conduct Mahler's Ninth Symphony at Disney Hall in Los Angeles. Fantastic Frank Gehry building, and an overwhelming performance of my favorite Mahler. I started with just one poem, a sort of thank-you to Mahler for having given me music of such dimension. I speak directly to Mahler in all of the poems. I got a second poem, and then a third, and after some months I was up to seven poems, at which point I told myself I had to come up with two more, since Mahler had nine symphonies in all. As it turned out, the ninth poem was my favorite. Although the poems aren't direct responses to the music, in the course of my conversations with him—he's a strangely quiet guy—images that have their background in the music do occasionally come up. Mahler was born and raised in Bohemia, so some Czech themes also arise. The main framework, though, is a humble man trying to converse with a giant.

CB: The University of Pittsburgh Press published *The Cave: Selected and New Poems* in 2001. Peter Everwine commented that "Hanzlicek has the power to surprise in us a conviction that "in the end, beyond the metaphors,/We can't help loving life."

There is a lovely and moving elegy for Larry Levis among the new poems, "Sierra Noon" and this is a profound poem of place, a poem that shows how place marks our lives. When did this poem come to you?

CH: I don't remember. I don't even remember when I had good memory, but I'm guessing that I just started off writing about that landscape, and then at some point Larry entered my mind and therefore the poem. This arrival at an unexpected point happens often for me, and when it happens, it always delights me. Larry was definitely a man of place. As I point out in the poem, the landscape of his youth never left him, and it kept appearing in poems throughout his life. I also consider myself a man of place, but at some point in my life, I ceased being a Midwesterner and became a man of the West, the landscape that I now feel most at home in.

CB: You do not write many prose poems, nor much about politics. "DeStalinization in Prague" does both, and with sly insight and wit. Talk about this one.

CH: The Czechs have faced many calamities in their history, and often their defensive weapon of choice has been humor, most often tinged with irony. Jaroslav Hasek's *The Good Soldier Svejk* is a prime literary example of deflation by irony. The monument mentioned in my poem—Stalin leading a group of workers and peasants into the future—was a gigantic eyesore perched on a hill above the Vlatava river. The Czechs called the monument "The Bread Queue," and said that Stalin was smiling so broadly because he was first in line. They had to wait until the era of deStalinization to dynamite the statue, but they had long ago blown it to pieces with irony.

I don't write much about politics, yet I'm a deeply political person, and with Trump around, it has become a full time job. It's hard to write about politics and make it interesting, much less beautiful. I have a recent little poem about an avocet, a beautiful bird of the marshes. Originally, Trump was in it: "Waddling the walls of the White House / Tweeting twaddle at 4:00 AM." I loved the sound of those lines, but Trump is too grotesque to share the avocet's world, so I yanked him out by the neck. There are vaguely political lines remaining in my description of the avocet: "She does not care / About the powers that be" and "She moves in a world / That seeks its own level, / A world of quietude. // She lives outside of history." So in a way, I describe politics by its absence.

CB: The title poem "The Cave" is a hard and experiential look into factory work mid-century in America, which moves seamlessly into a memory from childhood visiting a tourist cave, and finally ends in a larger appreciation of the seen world. The ending is classic Hanzlicek, resolving in a realization that is surprising but which is earned from the sum of all the specifics. How did this poem come together.
CH: Well, again, there was accidental arrival taking place in that poem. I began with the image of workers in the pre-OSHA era gradually going deaf from the thunderous noises in the forge shop. Pondering deafness led me to thinking that the sense I would least like to lose is sight, since I live and work in a world of imagery. That led to the childhood memory of visiting a cave and being plunged into total darkness by the tour guide. That led to my embrace of the seen rather than the unseen world at the end of the poem. Pascal's wager lurks behind this. My theory is that if there is a God, He is by nature a skeptic, so if I manufacture faith just to possibly come out on the positive side of a wager, God will see through my choice and take all of my chips anyway. Ergo, I might as well go with my gut and embrace *this* world as the only paradise we are likely to witness.

CB: In 2013 *The Lives of Birds* was published by Tebot Bach in the Ash Tree Poetry series which David St. John got going to publish Fresno poets. Again, I defer to Peter Everwine—how could one not—in his evaluation of the project and accomplishment of this book. In part he says, "Hanzlicek is drawn to those occasions when the common and familiar give way to what is transcendent or redemptive, which is to say that he is essentially a poet of celebrations." I think that is a perfect evaluation of these poems. I love how these poems celebrate, often, as advertised, in the life of birds, the small but luminous detail, and how we all reach for some transcendence as lives on this planet. I feel that poem after poem, this is one of your best books, if not your best. Authenticity of voice, real subject and the ability to sing it directly, are the hallmarks of great poetry. The title poem is the last in the book and offers us that great earned affection for life that close attention and appreciation rewards. Your eye and imagination cherish the tenuous connection of all of our lives. Can you say something about the composition of the title poem then, its wit as well as its gravity, and how the two almost always come together in your poems?

CH: I always think of a poem as a balancing act. I like to find a balance between thought and feeling, the tragic and the comic, etc. I think I achieved a pretty good balance in this poem. The main mission of the poem is to be a love poem to my wife, and also a love poem to the world of birds. The poem begins with a crow murdering a young jay, but then the poem balances that with delights that have come to me from both crows and jays. And there's humor in the poem, too, the balancing act.

CB: Translations. I recall that back in the '70s you published *A Bird's Companion*, translations of Native American poems and songs. Were you working from a prose gloss, did you have some knowledge of the languages?

CH: I taught a course in Native American literature several times, and I was always unhappy with the translations of tribal poetry. The language of the translations was always the language of the translator at that moment, which was often at a distance from us, so the poems were too flowery, too ornamental to be believed. I just didn't think that Sitting Bull could have spoken in Longfellow's diction. My sources, with one exception, were from Frances Densmore. Densmore was an anthropologist and musicologist who traveled to many tribes and recorded their songs. As a byproduct, she also wrote down, very literally, the words to the songs, all of which were printed in various issues of the Bureau of Ethnology Bulletins. In these, I felt I was as close as I could get to originals, and I worked from them, and used the translations in my classes.

CB: Later, you published *Mirroring: Selected Poems of Vladimir Holan* which won the Robert Payne Award from the Columbia University Translation Center. Did you meet him in Prague? How did that project come about? And also I seem to remember Miroslav Holub reading at Fresno State in the late '70s, in a science classroom? Did you know him, invite him to campus?

CH: As mentioned earlier, Holub read at Fresno State twice and stayed with us both times. On his second visit, we were standing at the center and on top of the Millerton Dam, watching the hawks below us hunting along the San Joaquin River. Holub told me that Vladimir Holan had recently died, and I said, "God, I'd give my left leg to translate Holan." Holub thought for a moment, and then said, "This could be done!" He talked to Holan's editor in Prague, and put me in touch with Dana Habova, who had co-translated some of Miroslav's books in the *Field* translation series. We were off and running. Holan's editor selected the poems and gave them to Dana, and she sent me very literal translations. It took a year, and this was before email, so if I had a question about something, it took ten days for the airmail exchange to answer my question. I didn't write a single poem of my own during that period, since anything I would have said would have been tinged with Holan's voice. Prior to that, the only Holan in English was a slim Penguin edition that was not distributed in America. Wesleyan University Press took the book quite quickly. They called me on a Saturday afternoon and told me they needed an introduction that had to be mailed on Monday for a board meeting the next week, so I hammered out a six-page introduction in one day.

CB: Now for an important subject: Poetry, and pool. I remember when you converted your garage into a poolroom, re-stuccoed the walls, installed a fine table with leather pockets. I remember shooting 14.1 with you and Jon Veinberg there a few times, but by then I had lost the stroke I had mastered at 16 and 17 when I used to hustle games in the three bowling alleys in Santa Barbara. For a number

of years each time I called Jon he had recently been over to your place to shoot a few games. Jon was a great poet and great soul; was he any good at pool? And in one of the poems published in your chapbook, *A Dozen for Leah*, 1982, there was a poem about several special cues made of exotic woods? Did you actually have many of those? It was finally a kind of metaphysical poem, right? And I think that whenever Larry was in town he came over to shoot pool. As I recall, the talk was usually more about pool than poetry, but certainly the table was a source of some community?

CH: Jon Veinberg was an above average pool player and consummate poor loser, but amid the tensions of competition, we shared many stories and much laughter. Jon was of Estonian heritage, and we both had a deep respect for the poetry of oppressed societies, and we both liked to crack wise, so there was a lot of back and forth between the sacred and the profane. Those were my fondest days at the pool table.

I did have one custom cue made by a man named Paul Huebler from Kansas City. I couldn't afford one of his cues made from exotic woods, mine was his base level cue, but it was perfectly balanced and a pleasure to hold. I said earlier that Larry and I shot pool whenever he came on a visit to Fresno, but he wasn't a fan of 14.1 continuous, also called straight pool, which is played to 125 points. When there's only one ball left on the table, you rack the other fourteen balls and try to break the rack with the ball left on the table, which goes on until one player has scored 125. Willie Mosconi, the greatest pool player ever to live, once sank over 400 balls in a row in an exhibition. That was too much of a grind for Larry, who liked to live fast, so we usually played one game of 14.1 continuous and then switched to 8-ball.

Yes, the pool poem in the sequence of poems to Leah is kind of metaphysical in that I'm in heaven, which is a pool parlor where I play with six of the old greats of the game. Minnesota Fats is not among them. He was a fraud, and Mosconi could wipe the floor with him even after he'd suffered two strokes.

CB: I want to touch on poetry citizenship. You worked with Phil and Peter for close to 40 years, and Directed the creative writing and MFA programs toward the end of your time at CSU Fresno. You must have helped many young writers?

CH: The program was small for most of my time here because we only had an MA option in creative writing. We were dealing almost exclusively with local students, but that was fine, because we liked them. A lot of our students had grown up in poverty of one degree or another, and that meant that they were not afraid of work. And poetry is work of the loneliest sort. Many of those students went on to lives of real accomplishment. When Bill Matthews came here to read, I asked him why he came here from New York to read for so little money. He said, "Fresno is on the poetry map, and I had to see it." Students as much as the faculty put us on the map.

CB: And you headed the Fresno Poets Association and ran the reading series for 15 years. What was the scene like in Fresno, on campus and in the various venues for the Poets' Association. What are some of the memories of the poets who came to Fresno to read. Did Local poets draw as well as poets from across the country?

CH: The FPA series was held at the Fresno Art Museum, which had a very nice auditorium that they rented to us for $100 a night. We charged admission so that I could cover airfare for several readings a year, and we also had many annual donors. I did a mailing for each reading and included a poem or two so people had an inkling of what they were going to hear. I don't want to test my memory by trying to rattle off a list of who came to read over the fifteen years, but Belle Waring, Nancy Willard, Bill Matthews, Robert Wrigley, B. H. Fairchild, Milena Morling, Dorianne Laux, Beverly Lowry (a prose writer), Brian Turner, and Joseph Stroud, a princely poet in my book, were among them.

CB: Lastly, a question about the amazing community of poets from Fresno, and "The Fresno School". Looking back to the early days when you first arrived through more recent times, what strikes you, what do you cherish?

CH: The first anthology of Fresno poets, *Down at the Santa Fe Depot,* appeared in 1970. That was followed by *Piecework* in 1987 and *How Much Earth* in 2001. As new voices emerged, each anthology grew a little longer to accommodate them. The Fresno Poets became something spoken about. Some called it the Fresno school, but I never liked that designation. What I cherish is that in Fresno, poetry is not a competitive sport. We all support each other, and everyone is happy when one of us publishes a new book. "Are you writing" is as familiar a form of greeting as "hello" here. There is no school of similar aims and styles but there is a vibrant community of vastly different aims and styles. I don't want to disparage any city, so I'll just randomly say that no one speaks of the Tampa poets, or the Kansas City poets or the Phoenix poets. But the Fresno poets is a thing, a beautiful, unlikely, but real thing. It has been an inspiring place to spend a career and has given me many rich friendships.

Lawson Fusao Inada

Lawson Fusao Inada was born in 1938 and raised in Fresno, except for three years in American concentration camps. His books are *Before the War: Poems as They Happened*, New York: Morrow, 1971; *The Buddha Bandits Down Highway 99*, Mountain View: Buddhahead Press, 1978 (With Garrett Kaoru Hongo and Alan Chong Lau); *Legends from Camp* Coffee House Press, 1993, winner, American Book Award, finalist, Los Angeles Times Book Award for Poetry; and *Drawing the Line* Coffee House Press, 1997, winner, Oregon Book Award for Poetry. He also edited *Only What We Could Carry: The*
Japanese American Interment Experience, Heyday Books, 2000. In 1994, *Legends from Camp* won an American Book Award. Inada has received several poetry fellowships from the National Endowment for the Arts, and he also won the 1997 Stafford/ Hall Award for Poetry. In 2006 Inada was named Oregon's fifth poet laureate, the first person to fill the position since William Stafford in 1990. Until his retirement, he was Professor of English at Southern Oregon University.

from *Down at the Santa Fe Depot,* 1970—Lawson Fusao Inada

I'm a Sansei, and was born in Fresno in 1938. Father's people were sharecroppers but he became a dentist. Mother's father started the Fresno Fish Store. During the War we live in "camps" in Fresno, Arkansas, and Colorado.

After the War, I went to Lincoln, then Edison High School. A non-Buddhist, I joined the Black and Chicano set. The main thing then was music: Johnny Ace, the Clovers, Little Walter, etc., and on into Pres and Bird. They made me want to "say" something.

After a year at Fresno State, I went to Cal (The Black Hawk, actually) and saw The Lady, Bud, Miles, and Coltrane, so when I got back to State I was studying the bass. Then Phil Levine got me interested in writing.

The bass became lost during subsequent stays in New York, New England, and the Midwest, but there are three Inadas with me now: Janet and the boys—Miles and Lowell.

We're living in Oregon, listening to the Great Ones and singing. I've completed one book, *The Great Bassist.* "West Side Songs" are from a work in progress. *The Death of Coltrane.*

from *How Much Earth,* 2001—Lawson Fusao Inada

In this collection, were I to be included in a section of "West Fresno" poetry (along with Sherley Anne Williams), that would feel fitting to me for West Fresno (or the West Side) is a distinct and historic community, as old as Fresno itself.(My place in the history: Grandfather Saito founded Fresno's first fish store in 1912.) And in its heyday before the Highway 99 freeway gouged through residential neighborhoods, and "Urban Renewal" demolished much of the commercial district— West Fresno was not only the major multicultural mecca of the Valley, but one of the most globally rich places on earth.

The above-mentioned "forty-eight,"(different nationalities) for instance, might well have been found in one grade school, and the impressive number does not do justice to the actual diversity. For example, the Chinese community consisted of several languages and religions, likewise the composite Filipino community, and the Japanese society was not without complexity and variety, as expected of people form islands that span a territory equivalent to the distance from, say, Kiev to Cairo, or Boston to Havana. West Fresno was considerable.

And if it had a flag, it would look like this: railroad tracks across the top, cotton plants and grape vines around the other borders surrounding a swirling expanse of colors—black, brown, and yellow—with splashes of "ethnic" white intermingled (Armenians, Basques, Germans, Greeks, Irish, Italians, Portuguese, Scandinavians, Slavs, etc.), and at the center would be the Tiger of Edison High, which before the advent of desegregation busing, was the shining centerpiece of the community—the University of West Fresno.

So West Fresno it was and is, and Edison is where I had my first success as a writer. It was the spring of 1955 and as the class recited Shakespeare, I simply began scribbling in a tablet, starting with the word "Macbop" a the top. Words kept coming, and after class I showed Sam Jones and Frank Flores what I had done. They cracked up, contributed licks, and by next day I had a bunch of scribbled pages incorporating the vernacular and nuances of our community. While it was the natural, down home thing to do, it was also unavoidable hip, sophisticated, and downright funny. For instance, when Sam (Macbeth) exhorted "Ease up off me, ese" Frank (McDuff) retorted with a cool reference to Mexican golf—chopping cotton.

Our teacher, Miss Bennett, was duly impressed (my first good review) and asked us to produce it. Casting was easy from our class, for our "class," our "caste," was full of skilled and experienced performers at adaptation, with talents for survival. (Two colleagues watched appreciatively, for they hardly spoke English: a deeply scarred young man from war-torn China, and a Jewish refugee from Latvia, with a far-away look in her eyes. They made our class international, and fit right in, for many of us were recent arrivals also: Sam from segregated Georgia, Frank from a Southwest Indian reservation—where he was to die—and I had the concentration camps behind me. And this was just one *ordinary* class at Edison.)

In short order, with the scribbled script, we had our act together, performed it for an uproarious Edison audience, and were then selected to take part in a cultural-exchange program with Fresno High. They brought us classical renditions, Broadway medleys, and we transported them to the heart of West Fresno, the street corner where Sam's father preached, jukeboxes jubilated in tongues, and the labor buses lined up at dawn. . . .

I long ago lost the script, but I've been scribbling in a tablet since.

"The Surprising Chill" from *Coming Close*, 2013—Lawson Fusao Inada

The entire line was, is—"The surprising chill of a September morn"—by poet Carol Howard, but it was recited by the teacher, several times—with the grace and gestures of a conductor—before he wrote it on the board in his elegant script. Ah, yes—the flow . . .

And there we were in a clunky Cold War complex on the steppes—but in a classroom with the air of a conservatory, where the teacher regarded us with warmth, respect. As poets.

Thus, even the conventional textbook took on a transformative aura, and even though an Emily Dickinson, for instance, could be dispensed with in short order, as an "assignment," she was a tall order for her fellow poets who hunched over her in library recesses, cloistered, mouths moving to her music. And mystery. How did she do it?

Evenings, while I tended to a plot of words, my father, a former fieldworker, would intone passages of poetry, over and over, varying pauses, being trained in shigin-traditional, songlike recitation—which, upon approval of the teacher, could lead to being called upon to preside at ceremonial occasions. It was a calling; still, poetry was poetry, and it all fit.

Our teacher, our sensei, was also a master of recitation, and with an uncanny immediacy, urgency, could project, transport us to a "contagious hospital" in New Jersey, and then we'd be in a "flee from me" location in olde England. Poetry is poetry . . .

Meanwhile, we huddled masses had miles to go, since so much depends on a jar in Tennessee, and my initial attempt at "verse"—unlike my scribblings, sprawlings in a tablet—was laboriously typed, clunked out on my mother's college machine. The "verse" began—"What sort of man was Charlie Parker, who"—and thus began a further relationship with the teacher, who had "heard the Bird" in Detroit. The Bard! Wonder of wonders—in the English Department—which coincided with the fact that, several months earlier, on a meandering sojourn at Cal, I had managed to matriculate under the tutelage of, not only "The Pres," but the Muse herself—"Lady Day"! In order to "woodshed," I returned home.

We took it from there, listening sessions private "bom-Bard-ments"in our respective homes; but as for his own "blowing," all I knew was that he was "writing poetry," so I assumed he was "woodshedding" also. Then, too, as a new teacher, and young at that, his only distinction was that he taught "elective" classes.

However, when asked, he did mention some recent appearances in publications not available in the campus library—the "periodicals" alcove akin to a walk-in closet. This was, after all, a former normal school where parking was a priority. Ah, but the teacher, always generous, loaned me his personal copies. What a revelation! A "surprising chill"! Formidable verse! The teacher could really "blow"! His poetry could have readily graced, enhanced, expanded the textbook—and here he was in a cubicle!

Poet Philip Levine!

Sherley Anne Williams—1944-1999

Sherley Anne Williams was born and grew up in Fresno, graduating from Edison High School and receiving her B.A. in English from Fresno State in 1966 and her master's degree at Brown University in 1972. Sherley published two books of poetry: *The Peacock Poems*, Weslyean, 1975 which was nominated for the National Book Award, and *Some One Sweet Angel Chile*, William Morrow, 1986, was adapted into an Emmy Award winning television performance. Also in 1986, William Morrow published her first novel, *Dessa Rose*. Williams' one-woman play, *Letters from a New England Negro* (1992) was performed at the National Black Theater Festival in 1991 and at the Chicago International Theater Festival in 1992. She also published two picture books, *Working Cotton* (1992), which won the Caldecott Award of the American Library Association and a Coretta Scott King book award, and *Girls Together* (1997). For television, Williams wrote the programs, *Ours to Make* (1973), and *The Sherley Williams Special* (1977). Williams published the groundbreaking critical study of African American writing *Give Birth to Brightness: A Thematic Study of Neo-Black Literature* in 1972. She was also selected to write the introduction for Zora Neale Hurston's 1991 edition of *Their Eyes Were Watching God*.

In 1973 Williams joined the University of California, San Diego as a professor of literature. She would later serve as the chair of the department from 1977 to 1980. In addition to her 26-year teaching career at UC San Diego, Williams traveled to Ghana as a Senior Fulbright Lecturer in 1984 and had visiting professorships at the University of Southern California, Cornell University, Stanford University and Sweet Briar College. In 1987 she was named the Distinguished Professor of the Year by the UC San Diego Alumni Association. She died in July of 1999.

from *The Geography of Home: California's Poetry of Place,* 1999—Sherley Anne Williams

I was born in California near the end of World War II at a time when most black people were still in the South. As a child I was impressed with California's size, the economic richness I learned about in school, with the fact that California was not the Old South country my parents had escaped from, and also, I was totally alienated by the reality of California as I knew it: poverty and back-breaking labor.

I moved to Southern California in the early seventies at a time when one could still see, even in its sprawling urbanopolises, vestiges of what its primal landscape might have looked like. This was very liberating for me: I had been so focused on cities—San Francisco, L.A.—and on the land as agri-business made it in the Valley that I hadn't seen the landscapes around me. I imagined the world as anthropomorphic with personalities pretty much like some black people I know and created "Myths for the 21st Century" (unpublished). I'm also working on a novel set in 1969 in the Valley. The state today is run by people who want to turn circumstances back to a time when white people didn't think there were consequences—or thought somebody else would pay them. In my mind the state is still the land of giants and elemental forces where black people roam and make songs and are free.

from *PIECEWORK: 19 Fresno Poets,* 1987—Sherley Anne Williams

Though there are many she credits as having heartened and nurtured her many talents as a poet, storyteller, essayist, playwright, and novelist, it was Philip Levine at Fresno State whom she emphasizes as "the first to encourage, affirm and insist in finding a voice."

the wishon line

i

The end of the line
is movement the
process of getting
on, getting off, of
moving right along

The dank corridors
of the hospital
swallowed him up
(moving right along
now—from distant
sanatorium
to local health care
unit—the end of
that line is song:
T. B. *is killing*
me We traveled some
to see Daddy on
that old Wishon route
but the dusty grave
swallowed him up.

ii

These
are the buses of
the century running
through the old wealth of
the town, Huntington
Park, Van Ness Extension
the way stops of
servants; rest after
miles of walking and
working: cotton, working
grapes, working hay. The
end of this line is
the County: County
Hospital, County

Welfare. County Home—
(moving right on—No
one died of T.B.
in the 50's; no one
rides that line for free.

from "Sherley Williams–From Fresno to La Jolla: Raised Not to Hope Too Hard"—*Jangchup Phelgyal San Diego Reader*, April 13, 2000

(This is roughly one-third of the entire article; in this portion Phelgyal interviews Philip and Franny Levine about Sherley Anne Williams.)

Frances and Philip Levine on Williams: "She wrote about her life in West Fresno, and she made her world come alive for the reader."

Frequent-flyer miles on Southwest Airlines got me to New York City; the number 2 subway of the Manhattan Transit Authority got me the rest of the way to Brooklyn Heights. There was no nearby six-lane freeway, no blue California sky; here the houses crowded in close, making the streets seem narrower and the curbs taller. The urban colors were deeply saturated. It was October 12, and the autumn air had the fruity taste of Comice pears. Gray pigeons pecked at the pavement where eleven o'clock sunlight fell through a lacy scrim of ginkgo leaves in a drizzle of gold. Manhattan, that massive crunch of concrete and steel, was just across the Brooklyn Bridge, five minutes from here. But the metropolis with its hordes and mayhem seemed to belong to another distant world. When I rang the doorbell of the multiple-unit brownstone, the sound tore through the stillness and sent the pigeons scrambling into the air.

On the other side of the clear-glass panel of the front door, Philip Levine descended to the foyer. "Hello," he said, unlocking the door and opening it. I stepped into a thick, sweet smell of warm chocolate. "Someone's baking," he explained, leading the way upstairs to the third floor, where the chocolate smell had faded into the mixed stale odors of an old building. His wife met me at the door.

Frances Levine was around the same age as her husband, who is 71. She wore no makeup, and her hair, thick and gray and falling below her shoulders, set off the bony intelligence of her face. She was cleaning the house, dressed in a loose shirt and jeans that had been bleached of much of their original denim color. Levine wore an olive green cashmere sweater, sweat pants, and a black baseball cap pulled down low. Husband and wife were both slim and looked fit, and between them was held an intimacy at once easy and unspoken. She was at the moment stripping the bed to wash the sheets.

The large living room led to a roomy kitchen and both had a woodsy Scandinavian sparseness. The furniture was of undistinguished design and vintage, the second-house stuff found in beach cottages and summer homes. The Levines live in Brooklyn half the year with their children and grandchildren nearby; they return to Fresno for the winter and spring. I took a seat on the couch.

"So you wanted to talk about Sherley…"

Philip Levine won the Pulitzer Prize for his poems in 1995, the first American Book Award for poetry in 1980, the National Book Award in 1991, and twice received the National Book Critics Circle Award. After 30 years at the California State University,

Fresno, he retired and now teaches one course at New York University in the fall term. He spends most of his days writing but agreed to give me a few minutes to talk about Sherley because she had been his colleague and friend. Their relationship began in his classroom when she was a freshman. My search for Sherley Anne thus formally starts in 1963 when she is 18. Her life was already a third over.

"I was a young professor, and she was clearly a very bright, very talented student. In over 30 years of teaching poetry, I have found that it is the rarest of events to come across a supremely gifted student. I was lucky." Levine counted back, reflecting that Sherley was enrolled in his Introduction to Literature course that was offered in the second semester of her first year. He remembered that she liked to sit in the front of the class, near the door, that she favored brightly colored clothes, and that in those first years she wore her hair short. "She dominated the class, there is no doubt about it. The other students listened to what she said and praised what she wrote. There was no question in anyone's mind that she was bright."

Levine paused and sat back, looking at the ceiling. In the background, the washing machine churned through its wash cycle. "You know," I said, choosing this moment to come clean, "she certainly can write — you can tell that right away — but I'm having trouble with the novel." "Why is that?" I explained that I'd grown to care so much for the characters, I could not bear to learn something bad happens to them. I'd had this deep identification with a book's characters only twice before, when reading Pearl Buck's *Good Earth* about starving Chinese peasants, and a suspense novel, *The Collector* by John Fowles, in which a young woman is held captive by a psychopath. "No, finish it. It's worth it," he assured me.

I asked Levine what Sherley looked like. Slender, he answered, and very attractive. "She had beautiful, expressive eyes. She was physically very energetic," he clenched his fists to illustrate, "and very articulate. Sherley liked to talk and was highly opinionated about what she read. She took a strong position, and we argued." I wondered how difficult that was, coming from a student. He looked over at me. "Once I understood how serious she was, how she was absorbing the material, I went with her. She was eager, eating everything up, and what teacher doesn't thrill to have a student like that?" He said that he assigned the class to read Ralph Ellison's *Invisible Man*. "It was a savage and amusing book," Levine recalled, "and discussion was heated." At the end of the class period, Sherley and he were still in disagreement on some point. He waved his hand in the air, as if to grasp that point now so many decades old. But in the end, his palm open and his fingers spread wide, he admitted that while they'd gone back to his office and continued to debate, he could no longer remember what it was they had argued about. "I do know that at the next class I stood up and said that I had been forced to reconsider my position and that Sherley's point was better taken." It must have been a pretty heady moment for a freshman.

"The next semester she took a poetry course from me, and her poems were often masterful. She wrote about her life in West Fresno, and she made her world come alive for the reader." He recalled her poem "the wishon line" that was collected in her second volume of verse, *Some One Sweet Angel Chile*. "From the first, she had three great strengths. Sherley always had a strong story line, a narrative. She always had characters. And because she was reading a lot, she was developing her sense of pacing, her ear. She had an excellent ear."

He pointed a finger at me. "But her strength was also her greatest weakness. She had a lot of pride. God knows she needed it, but sometimes that pride got in her way."

Levine recounted how one afternoon she brought in work that was not up to her standard. "The fact was, it was not a very good poem, but the other students were afraid to say so. Some of them had tried to write like her, but they did not have her talent. And when this poem came along, they did not know how to respond. I explained why it wasn't very good. Sherley was not happy, but I did it because I knew what she was capable of. I owed it to the poet I knew she could become." During the course of the criticism, he said, Sherley remained quiet, sitting absolutely still. It was only when he was through that she raised her hand. Levine interrupted himself to say that all his students called him Phil. "Sherley too," he went on. "But this time she said, 'Professor, may I say something?' She was staring and had not taken her eyes off me. I was standing in the front of the class, and I said, 'Of course, Sherley. What would you like to say?' 'GO FUCK YOURSELF, LEVINE!'" With this, the poet whipped off his cap and laughed. "Then she gathered her things and stormed out of the classroom." What did you do? I asked. "What did I do? At the next class meeting, she appeared and nothing was said of the incident."

I was not sure what surprised me more, an angry outburst from a teenage undergraduate or an instructor's decision to let the incident pass. With his cap off, I had my first full look at Levine's eyes. They were a clear child's blue. And at the moment they were twinkling. "You had to know Sherley," he explained. "At the next class, we just looked at each other and that was it, the incident was finished. We understood each other. She participated in class and we never had another problem."

In her second year, she told Levine she wanted to go to a black college and wondered what he thought about her transferring to Fisk. He urged her to apply.

"She got in and studied under Sterling Brown, I think. He is a superb poet. He writes exquisitely in the tongue of black Americans, and I think you see his influence in her work."

But she was not happy at Fisk and returned to Fresno, where she graduated. She went on to Brown University for graduate work, but she dropped out in 1972 after earning her master's degree. She returned to California, with a baby. "She came back to Fresno State and sat in on a poetry course of mine. But she did not need me. She was writing poetry and fiction and needed a community of writers. And she found one."

I described the challenge I'd found in assembling copies of everything she had published. "There is one book you will not be able to find," he said. "It was her first novel."

Her story, he said, was an account of a poor young black woman living in West Fresno, "more or less like Sherley." The woman supports her child and a brother by working as a domestic for a white jeweler and his wife. The jeweler is a louse who hopes to sleep with the girl. At the same time, a black street hood is trying to charm her while organizing a hustle that would draw the young woman's brother into trouble. "Sherley had submitted the manuscript, still incomplete, to a publishing house for consideration. This was why she asked me to read it. She told me that in her ending, as she conceived it, the sister and brother would affirm their affection for each other and work together to pull themselves out of the situation. I said it sounded wonderful and that she should get it published. And that was her dilemma. The publishers apparently had agreed to print the book but said it lacked violence. They suggested that the brother kill the hustler. And they wanted more sex in it too, something about the woman being a prostitute. And poor Sherley, this was her first novel and she really wanted to see it published."

I thought about Sherley Anne Williams before the honors, before the tenured spot at UCSD She was ambitious and talented, and, like her heroine, she was a single mother with a child to raise. "I told her, 'Sherley, you made those characters, and the most beautiful thing in it is the relationship between the brother and sister. I think you should finish the book on your own terms.' " Levine's eyes conveyed a weary sadness. "And that's what she did. She finished the book as she had planned it, with the love between the siblings defining the book and giving the characters the strength to survive. She finished the book her way, and she never sold it." There's a voice at the window that calls me by a name only the brotha should know. I'd have to leave my house to answer yet one night I was tempted to go.

How did she do at a reading, I asked. "She had a remarkable voice and could use it to great effect. She may have been professionally trained. She would go back and forth, breaking into the black voices of her characters, and then returning to the neutral voice of the narrator." She worked hard to get her material across, he said, and referred to a reading they did together in 1981 in Birmingham, Alabama. The theater had a raked auditorium and good acoustics. It was a perfect setting for Sherley, Levine said, and she brought a real class act to the community of black people who had come to hear her. Suddenly Levine called out to his wife in the kitchen. What, he asked, did Sherley wear that night in Birmingham? Frances stepped into the living room. "She wore a two-piece turquoise outfit with large gold earrings." Later, in San Diego, Sherley's sister Birdson would describe how, after their father's death, the family went on welfare and the four girls wore Goodwill "hand-me-downs" and charity offerings. The hardest part about wearing other people's clothes, according to Birdson, "was fixing yourself so that the clothes didn't stand out, so you looked like everybody else." That night in Birmingham, Williams stepped onstage so well put together that years later a friend could instantly recall the blue shade of her dress, the size of her earrings. But few in the audience knew how hard she had worked to earn that turquoise blue outfit and those big gold earrings.

By the time of the Birmingham reading, Philip Levine and Sherley Anne Williams were colleagues, established faculty members with acclaimed books to their credit. But there was that interim period, after Sherley returned from Brown University, no longer a student but still not established in her own right. She was writing the ending of a book that would never be published. Levine remembers that time for its racial climate. "This was the late '60s and early '70s, and there was a lot of racial stuff going on. Somebody called Sherley a 'nigger.' " I asked if she had a problem with whites. "Sherley?" said Frances, who had remained in the living room. "No. She had a problem with phonies and hypocrites, and in the end it didn't matter what color they were." At that reading in Birmingham, Alabama, she stood before the audience of 300 people and thanked Philip Levine for encouraging her to become herself. "She was generous to me," he recalled.

I collected my things. By the way, I asked, why was the movie of *Dessa Rose* never made? Levine remembered that the cast was assembled and on location when word came that filming was not going to happen. Cicely Tyson, Donald Sutherland, and Natasha Richardson, a British actress just beginning her career, were reportedly signed for parts. Later I would read that the studio had been sold and in the shuffle of properties, *Dessa Rose* got lost. "We were sitting in the kitchen in our place in Fresno when she told us," Levine said. It had been early morning and their small wooden house, surrounded and made private by tall trees, had been quiet. Williams talked of how she had been with the film crew in South Carolina, ready to film, when the phone call came. "Oh, Phil, I wanted that money," she told him. "But that was it. We packed our bags and came back home." Levine could see that she was disappointed. "But when she told me that they'd killed the project — 'They just killed the whole thing' — she laughed. That was Sherley. She just laughed."

On the train ride back to Manhattan, I jotted down what the couple had said of their last meeting with Sherley Anne. It was in the summer of 1996 and Williams had traveled to Fresno for a reading. She brought her grandson, Malcolm (named after his father, Sherley's son). Levine recalled that the child, who must have been eight or nine, was disruptive during the reading. Later, he asked Sherley what was going to happen to the boy. "I'm going to raise him," she said. She had raised her son alone, and now she was going to raise her grandson. At the time she was over 50. The next day, before returning to California, I ducked into the Museum of Modern Art. The museum is just a few blocks from the Donnell Library on 53rd Street where, in the spring of 1978, at an evening sponsored by the Academy of American Poets, Sherley read her poems. It was among her finest hours.

I thought of that on the second floor of the museum when I came upon a sculpture by Aristide Maillol of an immense young woman lying on her side. Small-breasted and naked, she was falling off what looked like a plank or a mattress or the edge of the world.

The day before, Phil Levine had described for me how at the Academy of American Poets reading the library had been packed with people, including Amiri Baraka, the celebrated playwright and activist. "It was that kind of evening, and Sherley shined."

She was staying in Brooklyn with the Levines, and the next morning she and Phil were in the kitchen going over the highlights of the evening before when Frances walked in. She had taken a shower and was wrapped in a white floor-length terry-cloth robe.

"Goddamn!" exclaimed Sherley, when she saw her. "I wish I looked that good."

Now, at the museum, studying the Maillol, I imagined Sherley in the Brooklyn Heights kitchen the morning when Frances entered the room dressed in the robe. Here was a woman with an adoring husband, children who were prospering in the world, two homes. At her public triumph the night before, Sherley had had no partner to share that experience, no one to lighten the immense burden of responsibility she felt for her nine-year-old son. Was she not the woman represented by that Maillol sculpture — small-breasted and ripe, and dangerously balanced on what might be a mattress, or a plank, or the edge of the world?

"I would trip through / neon-lit city nights tryin / to make it fast through all my / young woman years till I could / be old and not be called on / to love no man, but just to / have what I have suffice and / all this wantin be covered by / a spreadin body, buried / in a old woman heart."

She did achieve the "old woman heart," but she never got to be old.

C.W. Moulton—1936-1995

For over thirty years, until his accidental death in 1995, C.W. "Chuck" Moulton was one of the most colorful figures in the Fresno area poetry scene. He was born and raised in the San Joaquin Valley, spending much of his youth in Visalia. In recent years he was the unofficial poet-in-residence in the cafés and coffee shops of Fresno's Tower District. He was not only a poet, but a poetry writing teacher, an artist (sculptor and painter), astrologer, firefighter, and teacher's aide for severely handicapped children. As the founder

and director of the Fresno Poets Association, he organized readings by some of the country's best poets and encouraged Valley poets of all ages. He gave frequent readings himself, and his work appeared in many publications including the anthologies *Piecework: 19 Fresno Poets* and *California Heartland* as well as journals such as *Transpacific* and *Common Wages*. Moulton was also the host of the radio program "Poetry in Fresno." The Fresno Area Council of Teachers of English honored him with the Contemporary Lifetime Achievement Award in Literature for his efforts to promote poetry in the schools.

from *PIECEWORK: 19 Fresno Poets,* 1987—C.W. Moulton

I was born May 19, 1936 in Modesto, California. My first recollections are of running away, mostly out of curiosity, looking into puddles—some muddy, some receptive to their shining bottoms (they were scuffling footprints of a sad meteorological pig going around and around the world.) Santa Claus interested me. I had an appreciation for his work and proper joy. I loved merry-go-rounds, playmates, and rumbling traffic. Police brought me back many times and I was locked in the house. When the windows were nailed shut I learned to sing all 27 verses of "O My Darlin' Clementine" and got kisses at my mother's parties and began to dance. A 12-foot fence was ordered and built through which I vanished into the future. A howling revival schooled the faculty of my assbones. Before my decision-making faculties were further altered I threw all the Christmas tree ornaments against the basement wall, stole a kitchen knife and towel and flew off the garage but not far enough. My therapy consisted of digging holes. I threw dirt in the air. Forts. Barricades. Then thinking I could get somewhere—gold, buried treasures—I honeycombed the lot next door. All I found were tears and a mosaic of minds. I read the dictionary on rainy days and played my first and last game of canasta throwing the cards into the air. When my sex glands erupted I had visions of diamond rings and fierce Sears & Roebuck catalog models. . . . I kicked rubber balls into the air, gathered up worms and toads, flashed knives and tomahawks from my hands. I both attacked and made love to the sycamore, climbing to become its captain. The sky filled with bombers; WW II was in full swing and I envisioned the war and peeled off in a Grumman "Hellcat" wing-guns blazing straight into the mouth of hell with absolute and complete control of gravity. It took a long, long time but I kept the nose pointed straight down until I could see that war was a piece of maggot-sucked horseshit compared to each man, woman and child's crisis.

When I was 7 years old I discovered language, its absolute ideal, by falling into a cistern. I didn't think my breath would come back. A futureless nothing. How can people know when to give and when to take? And even if there was a rope there are some things that will not climb a rope. And how can people remain calm with this crime being committed by all?

from *Lion in the Fire,* 1996—C.W. Moulton

Try to Save the Fresno Bluffs and San Joaquin River Bottom from the Land Developers Poem

If you can't get it through the eye of a needle
don't put it there, and if you do you'll be
a lot deeper in the almighty wrath sooner
than you suckers think.
        —Amos

Man's integrity, intelligence, and performance
are based in a wilderness of unvarying natural
form.
        —Black Elk

When I was a kid
I went out to Scout Island because I wanted to
find out, and now I don't want to be guided
into difficulties by lawyers of land developers.
I want to be guided by reliable blue herons
standing in the spirit of the San Joaquin river bluffs.
I want to be guided along the bluffs by doves that coo.
I want to be able to get off a bike and sit down somewhere
leaving the highway bridge behind like a graveyard
and watch bunting and little green towhee zip freely
back and forth across the river from tree to tree,
reed to reed like skillful reconciliations.
It occurs to me that the land developers
are not as shrewd as the hawk in the sycamore.
It occurs to me that the fresh water clams
paying attention to business at the bottom of the river
have a better sense of preservation and groping
than that which has emerged wishing to tear the place
    apart and litter.
It comes to me that it took this river 2,000,000 years to
carve this composition that molds and remolds the lives
of hundreds of species of animals, and if I had a dollar
for every year and animal that lives here I could call
the bank and bulldozer and cut into its brow
and make 2 or 3 million more putting in tract houses

egotistically spaced apart. It occurs to me
that a timid, greedy child grown old could pick up a rock
and throw his conscience into the river;
and the kit fox, if the kit fox had hands,
he could go through the night and strangle
the land developers as they sleep in their beds.
A violent act committed by a kit fox in good taste.

> (January '79)

"Foreword" from *Lion in the Fire,* 1996—Philip Levine

In the spring of 1961 at the age of thirty-three I decided to take a gigantic step backwards toward adolescence, and at Wilson's Motorcycle shop in downtown Fresno for $475 I purchased a year-old but unused 250cc Zundapp, a German two-cycle bike which at that moment I thought a splendidly handsome machine with its baby-blue and chromed tank. I had no idea how to drive the thing, so the better-natured of the Wilson brothers took me out back in the cindered alley and gave me a twenty minute lesson. He made extra sure I knew where the controls for the brakes were. Somehow I got the thing home to my place on East Dayton near the airport, and all that weekend I perfected my riding style. By Monday morning I was ready to drive it to my morning class at Fresno State. By some coincidence on the way there I saw another fellow about my age driving a similar bike a few hundred yards ahead of me; when I caught up with him he gave me a snaggled grin and we tweedled along side by side and parked our machines in the space reserved for motorcycles near the business building where the English Department had its offices. It turned out that this fellow's bike was not a Zundapp but a Czech Jawa of almost identically hideous design. As we dismounted the owner said, "They're no beauties but they get the job done." These were the first words I heard out of the mouth of Charles Moulton. He spoke in such a singular and fervent style, a sort of raw western style that suggested what John Wayne might have sounded like had he not been corrupted by money and egotism, that I immediately decided to get to know this man. We introduced ourselves, and I informed him I was the poetry writing teacher on campus (at the time there was only one). "Poetry," he said, chewing his lower lip and obviously giving it serious thought, "I should get to know something about that shit." It turned out he was unsure what to major in, psychology, art, philosophy, he was attracted to them all. "Maybe I'll give poetry a shot, what you think?" I assured him that he had a flair for language. I was about to start a night class for beginning poets, and he was certainly welcome to join.

Join he did, and thus we began our thirty-five year long mutual study of poetry. The first thing I learned was that Moulton would go his own way; he knew who he was and what he wanted to use poetry for and he wasn't going to let an academic lead him by the nose. At that time I was something of a strong-willed director of fledgling poets. I required them to write in specific forms before they were released to the chaos of free verse. Chuck sat through my lectures on the charms and strengths of iambic pentameter, accentuals, and syllabics. He handed in no efforts at any of them. The first poem he presented to the class was something of a show stopper. He rose, unasked, from his seat in the back of the room and asked if he might be permitted to offer us a poem. "Sure," I said, "just bring it here." "I don't have it written down, Phil, so can I just recite it?" I was more than a little taken aback, but naively I thought no harm could come from this, so I let him go ahead. I never saw the poem on paper—it may never have been consigned to paper—and I never heard him recite it again, so I can only present a general idea of its originality. It began something like:

> If a broken-down roan in a fenced-in field had only two legs
>   would it be a man?
> If a spotted dog wearing a napkin had one leg would it be a
>   Republican?
> If a man had common sense would the governor make him pick
>   clover for the next two thousand years?
> In my last incarnation I looked for the perfect apple and so walked
>   from Albany to Sacramento
> And chain-smoked the entire way.
> My health is better for it, so don't believe anything you read.

This went on for less than ten minutes, and then Moulton thanked the class for its courtesy and attention and sat down. To say we never quite recovered from the experience is an understatement. What in fact happened was that in those minutes Chuck managed to fire the imaginations of twenty young and not so young poets who suddenly understood that it was open house: whatever the brain concocted was material for the poem. For the next several weeks surrealist poems fell from the light bulbs in that dingy room in the old Ed Psych building "like paratroopers in Kansas," to quote Chuck's friend Omar Salinas. The person who learned the most from these events was Assistant Professor Levine, for I had believed without the least doubt that THE way to release the imagination was by means of the discipline of metered forms. I believed that without something defined and solid to hold on to the beginning poet—or older one for that matter—would fall into a paralyzing freedom, but I was forced to recognize that some of us make our peace with freedom without the least difficulty. Moulton was the genuine article, a free man of the West, and the universe carried within himself was various and without limit. To shackle his gifts would have been a crime against the human imagination, and in the very heart of his being Chuck knew this and lived without the least hesitation. It was what made him a unique and priceless man and such a useful poet. Blake had already written his motto, though he may never have read it:

> If the Sun & Moon should doubt,
> They'd immediately go out.

Years later Chuck asked me to testify as a character witness on his behalf in a civil disobedience case at a courtroom in downtown Fresno. The other defendants—represented by a single lawyer—had swapped a promise to behave themselves for their release. Chuck stood fast and made no such promise, and chose to defend himself, for he believed in the dignity of the single person against the tyranny of the state and its codes. All that morning I saw in the courtroom and listened to the foolish prattle of the district attorney who was failing to convince a jury that Moulton, by placing his body between American capitalism and its need to despoil the land he loved, was a threat to every American's God-given right to make as much money as possible. All through the charade I was practicing what I might say in Moulton's defense, but within moments of being called to the stand I was rebuked by the judge—at the urging of the DA—for presenting my views of Chuck in a narrative mode. I asked the judge, "How else can I tell the story if not in a narrative mode?" the judge glared at me and stated I was there to answer questions and not to ask them. I grew more and more frustrated by my inability to depict Moulton as the person he was, and finally simply blurted out, "Charles Moulton is the free American artisan that Tom Paine and Jefferson put their faith in when they created the republic." The judge slammed his hand down and shouted, "Are you trying to show contempt for this court?" Much to my shame, I did not answer, as Chuck would have, "No, I'm trying to hide it." But in fact Chuck had no fear of showing his contempt for all that corrupted and dirtied his America, the independent people, the beasts, all the growing things, and the land itself, the America he so loved and gave his extraordinary gifts to preserve.

Michael Clifton

Michael Clifton was born in Reedley, California, in 1949 and grew up on various army bases around the world before his family settled in Fresno in 1960. He attended California State University, Fresno, where he received both a BA and an MA in English before getting a PhD in American Literature at Indiana University, Bloomington. He taught at California State University, Fresno, from 1982-2015 and has published in a variety of scholarly journals. He has poems in *Down at the Santa Fe Depot: Twenty Fresno Poets* and *How Much Earth: The Fresno Poets.* Tebot Bach published his collection *Whatever Lasts in Winter* in 2004.

from *How Much Earth,* 2001—Michael Clifton

I was born in Reedley but grew up on various Army bases until I was eleven, when my family moved to Fresno and the suburbs. Walking home from school that first day, I got so lost in all the tract homes that I couldn't find the right street until almost five o'clock. But my grandparents owned farms out in the Valley itself, first in Wasco, outside Bakersfield, and then just outside Yettem near Cutler-Orosi, and I spent every school break I had on those farms on a kind of working holiday. When I wasn't chopping cotton, irrigating cotton, spraying Johnson grass around the ditches, or harrowing the bare fields, I was wandering around, shooting birds sometimes, eating all the fruit I could find, and generally just looking. The older I got, the less important the BB gun or .22 became. I learned how private it was under a grown orange tree, and I can still imitate a dove's call with my cupped hands near enough to make them answer.

These are the scenes, the landscapes, that shaped and shape my writing. Those farms—as well as reading Keats in a high school literature anthology and discovering that I wanted very badly to know how to make music with words like that—are the really bedrock elements, I think.

Whatever skill I have, I learned first at Fresno State in some really remarkable workshops with poets like Phil Levine, Peter Everwine, and Chuck Hanzlicek and fellow students like David St. John, Roberta Spear, and Greg Pape. It was an amazing time and place to be a student writer.

Indiana University, a good writing program there, and a Ph.D. came later, but it's always the Valley and its light I come back to: the place is so flat you can see for miles; that's a lot of light, and it gets under your skin somehow.

"Right by Yettem," 2020—Michael Clifton

Because my parents moved here in 1960, Fresno was home from the fourth-grade, and when I graduated from McLane High in 1967 I was upset: my grades and test scores were good enough for UC, but I didn't have the money to go. In my mind, I was stuck with Fresno State. I was also writing bad poetry because my family's bipolar, my first major depression hit during fall of my senior year, and I discovered writing poetry gave me what felt like a little bit of a handle on it when I was recovering in the spring.

Phil wasn't on campus at first—he may have been in Spain—but my high school girlfriend was crushing hard on her English professor named Hanzlicek, so I signed up for Chuck's beginning classes in freshman composition and then literature before signing up for his poetry-writing classes as well. It was in one of those that I wrote my first good poem, "Poem for Papa Bear," later published in *Down at the Santa Fe Depot*. Chuck was great: he invited me into his home, praised the writing I was doing, and introduced me to contemporary American poetry in general, to Donald Justice, Robert Bly, and James Wright, whose poems from *The Branch Will Not Break* changed my life.

Wright's poem "The Jewel" in particular struck me: that sense of something crucial and intricately structured, both precious and threatened somehow by the outside world, made immediate sense to me. I knew that he was right and that I needed to know more about it. And it turned out I had a knack, what felt to me like a little room with a door I could open and listen into. Sometimes, there was music that was language and sound and rhythm at once. So I kept going.

David St. John was crucial. Because we went to the same high school and had mutual friends, he'd already read and praised the mishmash of Keats and Tolkien's ballads and songs from *Lord of the Rings* I was writing at the time; then he persuaded me to take Levine's upper-division poetry section despite my fear of Levine's reputation for blunt honesty and impatience with bad writing.

And the two sections of that I took were magic, filled with people who went on to publish later. We were meeting across from campus in Roberta Spears' apartment, and I had a bad habit of imitating Wright if I got stuck on ending a poem, so that sessions on my work turned more often than I liked into accusations from the other students that I'd done it again, which I always denied, even when I knew it was true.

Those workshops were intense. Whether it was Phil's absolute dedication to poetry, that particular time in our history (it was 1968 and felt a little like things were falling apart), or just the random good luck of having that mix of writers—it began to feel, at least to me, like we were part of something. There were lots of poetry readings at the time—the English Department had just begun the Fourth-Hour Programs (literary readings, lectures, and sometimes concerts) to justify bumping its literature courses to 4 units—and attendance was strongly encouraged. There were lots of opportunities for student-poets to read, and other people in the department, both students and faculty, began to notice.

Then Mike Cole, friend and student-poet, was appointed editor of *Backwash*, the literary magazine at the time, and made David and I the poetry editors. Fellow student-poets Lance Patigian and his friend Curt were part of it, too. I remember spending lots of time selecting the poems and proofing the copy later, and we basically blew the budget on the fall issue alone, so that Mike had to spend personal funds on the smaller spring issue. But we won an award for the magazine that year for being the best in the country for a school our size—from the Coordinating Council of Literary Magazines.

The *Backwash* staff is important to my story, too, because it was after a meeting selecting the magazine's final contents for one issue that four of us piled into Curt's VW bug and drove over to a poetry-reading at Gene Zumwalt's, the chair of the English Department at the time. It was dark, we were stoned, and Gene was intimidating— Greatest Generation, combat fighter pilot, etc.—so I was appointed to go to the door to see if we were in the right place because I had the shortest hair and looked straighter than anyone else in the car.

At one point during the reading I was sitting on the couch next to Chuck Moulton, who was reading a long, hilarious poem and only gradually noticed that the poem he was reciting had nothing to do with what was on the page he was holding. To this day I don't know whether he was reciting something he'd memorized or if he was inventing it on the fly. And at the end of the reading David Kherdian, an Armenian-American poet and editor from Milwaukee, introduced himself and asked if he could see some of my poems for an anthology he was thinking of editing.

That anthology soon became *Down at the Santa Fe Depot: 20 Fresno Poets*, of course, and being in it was double-edged for me. On the one hand it was wonderful: there I was with all the heavy hitters, the professionals, and I was the youngest poet in the book (Roberta Spear and I had a bet; I won by a couple of months). On the other, people began paying attention to me, and that made me uncomfortable. And in my family stress leads to mania leads to self-medication.

Which may have been the reason why, when Kherdian called one afternoon to tell me to be at the Santa Fe Depot at 8:00 in the morning I said, ok, I'd be there, walked to the bar nearest my apartment and drank 5 brandies over. So I was completely hung-over the morning of the photo-shoot and asked the photographer not to make me smile but he did anyway. I remember that the group photo on the stairs took a long time to shoot and that the reason Phil is looking off to his left is that Jock Ries, a member of the English Department at Fresno State and a colleague of Chuck, Phil, and Pete, had just pulled into the parking-lot. I guess he wanted to be able to say he was there when it happened.

I was convinced at the time that graduate work at the Iowa Writers Workshop would be really iffy for me and decided instead to get a critical degree, beginning with a Master's at Fresno State and then a PhD at Indiana University, figuring I could teach poetry and literature but not poetry writing itself and continue to write on my own. The idea was to ride the horse rather than the other way round.

So in 1980, after three years at IU, my wife and I moved back to Fresno (I promised), and I started working on my dissertation, analyzing the presence of jewel and flower imagery like that in Wright's poem. (It's visionary, typical of an altered state of consciousness.) By 1982, I was far enough along in it to begin teaching at Fresno State at the same time I was writing the dissertation. A few times during the Eighties and early Nineties, Chuck Moulton asked me to read at the Wild Blue Yonder, I think whenever he was really broke and needed money since he never paid me. I liked reading there though: you could take a beer with you up to the mic.

It was during this time that I shared an office with and got to know Pete Everwine, who had the best radio voice of any poet I've ever heard. While Chuck and Phil were both excellent readers on their own, Pete had such a set of pipes I could easily have sat and listened to him read aloud from the phone-book. Hearing him read poetry was always a treat, and he had one of the world's best laughs.

Some time at the end of the 90's or the very early 2000's, David St. John, with whom I'd kept in touch, said send me all your stuff, since he knew I'd been writing poetry steadily at Indiana and afterwards, though without much effort to publish. I'm still amazed at the coherence he found and made apparent: in his hands all those separate poems became my collection *Whatever Lasts in Winter*, the first book in the Ash Tree Series David started with Tebot Bach Press for Fresno poets. That was published in 2004.

In 2005 David and I gave a reading for the Fresno Poets Association at the Art Museum, and in 2010, there was a reading for all the poets in the Ash Tree Series on Fresno State's campus. At that one, a guy from the Bay area who said he'd been in one of my English classes back in the day came up and introduced himself, said he was a fan, and remembered the small motorcycle I rode at the time and the redhead who sometimes rode with me to the fourth-hour readings.

I was both amazed that anyone was paying attention and a little unsurprised, if that makes any sense. Because that's the kind of contradiction Fresno is: hot, flat, dusty, and uninteresting on the one hand and hours away from anyplace more comfortable like the beach, the Bay Area, or Southern California.

But it is an astonishing place to write poetry and has been since Phil first got here and started it all up. Because of that my undergraduate years became not just any ordinary four-year degree but a literary adventure—not only for me but for others as well. And for a loner Okie kid like me, who loved to read and had a decent sense of rhythm, it was perfect.

* *"Yettem" is Armenian for "Eden." My grandparents' farm was just down the road.*

James Baloian

James C. Baloian is an Armenian-American poet who has been writing, teaching, and performing his poetry for the last 40 years. Born in the San Joaquin valley in Fresno, California, He earned a B.A. degree from California State University, Fresno while studying with Philip Levine; and went on to graduate from the University of California, Irvine with a M.F.A. in Creative Writing.

He co-edited and appeared in the anthology *Down at the Santa Fe Depot: 20 Fresno Poets* (Giligia Press, 1970) and followed it with two more books of poetry, *Looking In* (UC Press) and *The Ararat Papers* (Ararat Press.) His poems have appeared nationally and internationally in journals, magazines, and several anthologies including *The Reporter, Antioch Review, Carolina Quarterly, Sow's Ear Poetry Review, Rockford Review, Ararat, Rain City Review, Sonora Review, Papyrus, Midwest Quarterly, Midwest Poetry Review, Cold Mountain Review,* and *Americas Review.* In addition, Baloian has published three chapbooks: *Poems, Winter Afternoon,* and *Eclipses,* as well as *The Ararat Papers.*

Baloian's poetry was selected for the *Anthology of Magazine Verse Yearbook of American Poetry* 1997 Edition (Monitor Book Company) as well as the anthologies *How Much Earth: The Fresno Poets* (Roundhouse Press,) and *Armenian Town* (The William Saroyan Society) both released in 2001.

Baloian farmed for 25 years in the San Joaquin Valley, and has been a guest lecturer and instructor at Fresno State university and Columbia University. Recently retiring from teaching in the San Francisco Bay Area, Baloian currently lives in El Granada, CA 20 miles south of San Francisco with his wife. Always proud and concerned with his Armenian heritage, he writes about looking back at his past, looking in on the present, and looking forward to where his life is going.

from *How Much Earth*, 2001—James Baloian

I remember the first Levine class I took with great clarity. The class at its inception had over thirty students who had enrolled for a variety of reasons. Levine quickly changed the tone of the class by asking all those who had come to take the class as an elective to find another course. His reasoning was honest and to the point: "Writing poetry is my life and I expect my students to embrace this attitude, or leave." By the third meeting, the class had reduced to ten students, part of the nucleus that would later be known as the first generation of Fresno Poets. The anthology, *Down at the Santa Fe Depot: 20 Fresno Poets* represented and celebrated the first two generations of Fresno poets and our work with Levine.

Influencing our poetry and lives was the turbulent and energetic era of the 1960s, which redefined America and its values as no previous era since the 1920s had done. Much of the writing produce by the Fresno poets reflected the tone and imagery of this metamorphosis occurring in the country. Our workshops addressed not only our poems, but events occurring both nationally and internationally. Many of us supported and participated in marches, rallies and poetry readings that challenged America to reevaluate its conscience.

Our relationship with mentors, poetry and each other did not stop when we departed in 1967 from Fresno. In fact, the bond we established in those four years grew stronger and continued to gain strength after leaving our mentors and the Fresno "scene". Many of us went on to graduate school, but always continued to keep in contact through letters and poetry readings. After our departure, the Fresno State poets, including Peter Everwine, Gene Bluestein, and others, continued to influence new generations of poets to follow. In the years since then I have continued to feel what a unique period of growth and revelation this time in Fresno was to me and to others. In addition, the voice of Levine still drives me in my writing to embrace and celebrate life and the earth.

"Looking Back at the Past," 2020—James Baloian

I hadn't planned on going to go to college after graduation from high school, due to the fact that my grades where average and my father had informed me that I would begin training in learning the business and operation of the Wholesale Produce Business. My father also informed me that if I went to Fresno State I would have to major in Business to also help me prepare for my business career with the family business. I again explained to him that I would take a full course load in Business, but that I was required to take four semesters of English to graduate. I enjoyed the subject of English especially from the study of the Novel and the writing and subject of Poetry. I had been writing poetry my last two years in High School, following in the footsteps of my grandfather Arpiar, who always seemed to be writing stories or poems of our homeland, Armenia. I would climb under his desk while he was typing and pretended I had a typewriter and type invisible stories about my life. This was my first introduction to the world and love of poetry I would treasure and work at for the rest of my life.

My mother's father, Arpiar, also a businessman, had a second love in life, poetry. He wrote extensively night and day, at home or work, in fact every moment of free time he had. One of my favorite things to do, as a child was when we would visit him at his office, where he would always be writing or typing poetry or stories from his life in Armenia and America. I don't even think I knew what a poem was then, only the fact that it was something personal, but also as Arpiar would say in Armenian his own way, "it should be universal in thought and theme."

I continued as a child and in adolescence to compose poems and stories; as I matured my world and knowledge expanded into new ideas and journeys that would contribute to my garden of new ideas to explore. Poetry was always a way to define the thoughts and activities I was introduced to as well as the keys (books, essays, and lectures, etc.) which would open the doors to expand and study these new opportunities.

So, in 1963 I began taking classes in English and literature. In the fall, 1964 I secretly changed my major at Fresno State from Business to English, and during the spring of 1964 semester I began to inquire about teachers in the English Department at Fresno State. Friends who were English majors were all talking about an instructor who they said wrote and published poetry and kept the class stimulated with his lecturers and books. His reputation was well known as a professor who demanded excellence in essays and class discussions. I was in the second semester of English 1A, which was based around discussions, and essays of World Literature. The class was after lunch and the teacher was a woman who had taught college in Russia (Soviet Union) and had come to America to teach for a year. It happened that on a Spring Day in April in mid afternoon most of the class had dozed off with open eyes or were engaged in finishing homework for the next class. The spring air had ignited my blood to write and in each of my previous classes I had began a poem that followed me from morning classes in to afternoon. I was in the middle of a poetic line, and the teacher was strolling up and down the rows of old fashioned desks when I suddenly realized she was standing behind me. "And now class, I want to show you how focused my class is! She remarked, "What do we have here, Mr. Baloian," she said in a very calm voice, "A poem, class! A poem!! She looked down at me and smiled, "At least, Mr. Baloian was writing poetry." She then read the poem to my surprise and asked me if I had ever taken a class from Philip Levine. "No I replied. I don't recognize the name."

"He's a poet who teaches here."

When I entered Philip Levine's beginning class of poetry in 1964 the class was packed. Every seat in the classroom was filled with 30+ students in ages ranging from 60+ to 18 years old. Levine entered the class after the bell and called the overzealous crowd to order. He was thin but spoke with a strong and intelligent voice that brought quiet to the once loud and over active room. He called the roll, and as he approached the last name on his roster, quietly said, "Thirty people! My, My there are too many people registered for this poetry class. Is there anyone here that will leave, now?" No one moved. He called out 5 names and politely said, "Leave." This elimination continued for three weeks, some of the students in the next 3 meetings left on their own, those who came waited for the list to name the next 5 students. After 3 more weeks 3 more left. Finally, there were only 10 poets left and then there were 9. This class held together the rest of the semester and with a few additions every year of new students, he kept the class at around 10. It was a beginning class in poetry, so at the end of that semester we all waited to see if we made the cut to move up to poetry classes from beginning poetry classes to advanced poetry classes. Members of the group were: Robert L Jones, Larry Levis, James Baloian, Dewayne Rail, Bruce Boston, Charles Moulton, Dennis Saleh, Luis Omar Salinas, Sherley Anne Williams.

Phillip Levine was a teacher who inspired his students through his own love and dedication to the subject of poetry and the women and men who gave their lives not only to creating excellent poetry, but to exploring all styles and themes of poetry to express and explore the complexities of an idea or subject. Levine possessed a powerful voice which always kept his audience fixed and engaged not only with the musical movement of the language in the poems of rhyme and meter that he read, but he also could bring a presence to the images and metaphors in poems written in free verse. He expected his students to engage their reading to all styles of poetry and the poets who wrote it. Levine's love of poetry was even more apparent in his public readings of poets and poems that had encouraged him to write as well as stimulate his students; he engaged his fellow poets, friends, and lover's of poetry, his culture and environment for the audiences that attended lectures and readings. Levine's voice echoed through each person in the auditorium, but more importantly through each listener's heart and mind.

My four years at Fresno State and poetry not only opened a new door and direction in my life, but also introduced me to a new family of men and women who practiced and devoted their lives and understanding to poetry. Poetry was not only a catalyst of images and language, but also a human reaction, a transformation. I was fortunate to participate weekly with poets who shared the same love and intensity, who were dedicated to discovering and reading poets from the Americas to Europe and Asia. Levine had us read and discuss poetry before attempting it, solo. I hung out with Larry Levis, Dennis Saleh, Dewayne Rail, Charles Moulton, Bruce Boston, Gary Johnson, Omar Salinas, and Roberta Spear. I had a close friendship with Larry Levis whose rhythms and images could bring tears to the heart and awaken one's spirit to the language of life through poetry. Larry always encouraged me to write even when I felt my poems weren't good enough.

The group would get together at a local pub and plan the event or poetry night. Fresno State offered large event rooms that we used for poetry readings, and Levine brought many well know American poets to read and conduct seminars before or after the readings that we all attended and supported. I graduated from Fresno State in the spring of 1967 with no future for developing my poetry or using it to support myself. Many poets of our small group had applied and were accepted to universities that offered an MFA in writing. Levine called me into his office a couple days before the end of the term and asked me what I was going to do. I told him I didn't think I would be accepted to a university that offered an MFA in creative writing. Phil then said to me "Baloian, I want you to go home and write a letter to the University Of California, Irvine requesting the paper work for admittance to the graduate program."

Not too long after my meeting with Levine, I returned home one afternoon and upon entering, my mother handed me a special delivery letter. Before opening the letter, I noticed the return address University of California, Irvine. I opened it slowly and read the opening news that the UCI was accepting me for its graduate program on a recommendation from their English Department. I was to find out from Charles Wright that a letter from Phillip Levine to the UCI English Department had made the recommendation to consider James Baloian for an MFA degree. I wanted to dance and scream out my thanks and jubilation all at the same time but reserved myself for a celebration at a later date.

In 1969 I began putting together an idea for a book of poetry, more an anthology of the Poetry and the poets who had the fortunate experience to work with Phil as well learn to write and understand the art of poetry. Phil had been hired by Fresno State in 1958 and I knew a few of Phil's first students interested in pursuing a life of poetry. Former students, William Childress, Lawson Inada and Glover Davis would return to Fresno from Graduate Schools they were attending and visit family and friends. It was at these functions and social events that I had a chance to speak with them. I asked each of these fellow poets their feelings about an anthology of Fresno Poets (students) who had had Phil as a mentor, and continued their careers in poetry and teaching. I asked each poet for their opinions and feelings about an anthology of Fresno poets and received a positive response. The biggest problem, however, was finding a publisher to publish it.

I met David Kherdian in the Fall/Winter of 1970 in Fresno at a party given by Gene Bluestein for faculty and graduate students. Kherdian had published a book on Beat Poets and had published articles about William Saroyan and his writings. We were introduced and sat for a couple hours talking about books of poetry and poets. During these discussions I introduced my idea and dream of an anthology of Fresno poets that Levine and Peter Everwine, also a professor of English and poetry at Fresno State, had instructed in their poetry writing classes. Kherdian liked the idea and we made arrangements to meet and discuss the idea further. A few days later we got together in Fresno and discussed our opinions and feelings about the anthology, and its chances to succeed or fail.

I then met with Levine and Everwine for their thoughts and opinions. Their response, "It's was a good idea and to make a "go of it." I also met with Larry Levis, who like myself came from a family of farmers. Larry also was respected as the "top writer" in all the poetry classes. Larry also gave his support for the project. I informed Kherdian that we had the support of Levine and Everwine and the poets, and that we could begin the project when he felt he was ready.

I was very grateful to Kherdian for accepting and promoting the idea of a Fresno Poets anthology as well as publishing it. David also made me a co-editor of the book, which was an honor. Our first task was to outline how the book would be structured and then to write a letter to the poets I selected explaining the structure and theme of the book, number of poems for each poet to send, as well as a short biography and picture of each poet.

I also ran idea for the book by another close friend and poet, Dennis Saleh. Dennis and I had known each other for many years and we reunited with each other at Fresno State in Levine's poetry classes. He also liked the idea and encouraged me to continue working on getting it published. Kherdian informed me he not only wrote poetry and prose, but also had created and developed his own press for publishing books, The Giligia Press.

David and I worked from 1969 into 1970 at his mother's house in Fresno to write letters to each of the poets about the anthology, and requesting their poems for possible inclusion in the book. All the poets chosen for the book responded back with poems and letters in support for the book. I think the most creative time we shared was selecting the poems that would represent each poet. The biggest question that needed to be answered was a title for the book. David had suggested taking a group picture for the book's cover at "Fresno's Santa Fe Train Station" to compliment the individual photos of each poet in the book, giving credit to Fresno for being the current home of the poets. I agreed and checked with Levine, who nodded his approval for the title: *DOWN AT THE SANTA FE DEPOT: 20 FRESNO POETS.*

In the spring of 1970 the book was introduced with a Poetry Reading at Fresno State College and sale of the new anthology. I organized the reading in an outdoor area of the college that would hold at least 750-1000 people for an event. Musician friends donated their time to play music, and David and I felt that after the reading would also be a good time to sell the books. The outdoor auditorium was close to being filled, and the poetry reading went smoothly. The book was a hit and a good portion of the 1st edition was sold.

David told me a year or so later that the first edition had sold out, and he had reprinted a second edition of the book to sell. The reviews were mixed, but most of the journalists had good words for the book and some of the book's poets like Phil, Bob Mezey, Larry Levis, Glover Davis, Dennis Saleh, and Peter Everwine received excellent reviews for their poetry. The book was also praised for its originality, as well as being one of the first anthologies of poets who knew each other and studied poetry under one person. After the publication of *Down At The Santa Fe Depot,* each poet continued on his or her path in writing and publishing. Many of the poets in the book went on to teach English and poetry in colleges and universities throughout America. Along the way we lost some of our brothers and sisters in poetry to life's final journey: Larry Levis, Erenesto Trejo, Roberta Spear, Robert L Jones, Khatchik Minasian, Luis Omar Salinas and alas several others. In 2015 Philip Levine our guide, friend, and teacher passed away, and in 2018 we lost Peter Everwine. It's hard to write this final part of this story, but the memory of Phillip Levine will never pass away. His words, poems, and style of teaching will always live in the hearts and minds of his students and all who heard him read, teach, or just exchange ideas and thoughts as he encouraged human interactions such as poetry as a means to open the door to oneself, the world, and each other.

Thomas Emery

Thomas Emery graduated from California State University, Fresno, in 1960, with an AB degree in journalism, received an M.A. degree in Language Arts (fiction writing) from California State University, San Francisco, in 1964 and received an M.F.A. in fiction writing from the University of Iowa Writers Workshop in 1966. He taught at DePauw University from 1967-2000 and retired as the Richard Peck Professor of Creative Writing. He has published short stories, essays, and poems. He wrote the entry on the late Welsh poet Leslie Norris in the *Dictionary of Literary Biography: Poets of Great Britain & Ireland, 1945-1960*, has a hand-made illustrated chapbook, *Baker's Dozen*, and a 44-minute video of his own poetry, *Pretty Country*. He created a video of the reading done by participants in the book launch for *How Much Earth, The Fresno Poets* in March 2001, in Fresno. He lives in Greencastle, Indiana.

"Phil Levine In Fresno," 2019, Thomas Emery

I first heard of Fresno State College from Tom Yost, the coach of our baseball team my junior year at Placer Union High School in Auburn, CA. Coach Yost worked with the system he had learned at FSC from Pete Beiden, the coach, who produced excellent teams year in and year out by focusing on basics and undergoing constant fundamental drills with his players. He emphasized discipline and conditioning. (He later once observed that most of his ball players said they would rather play baseball than eat but he hadn't noticed much abstention at the dinner table). We were our league champions and a powerful team in the Sacramento area. We were not as good my senior year after Yost left but I applied for a baseball scholarship to FSC and received one for the 1956-57 year.

I played baseball at FSC and was on the very good junior varsity team in '58 with a 10-2 pitching record. In my junior year on the varsity team, I was in a car accident on the way to spring baseball practice and injured my pitching hand covering my face from hitting the windshield. I never fully recovered but did some relief pitching and lettered on the team that finished 3rd in the nation in Division I rankings. At the same time, I was sports editor of *The Collegian* that spring and also was under contract with ROTC to go into the air force after graduation (this was preferable to being drafted). Because I had to undergo ROTC officer training that summer, I couldn't play summer semi-pro baseball in Canada. Because my friend, Herb Strentz, took a job with *The Fresno Bee* instead of becoming editor of *The Collegian*, I took his place as editor for the year in 1959-60.

The prospect of playing Division I college baseball, starting ROTC pilot training, completing my senior year classes and being editor of the college newspaper three times a week was all too much. I quit baseball and resigned from ROTC. I was lucky to survive as a full-time student and still be editor.

Philip Levine was new to FSC in 1958 having come from Stanford on a post-graduate grant where he worked with the literary critic, Yvor Winters. My friends,

Tom Peck and Mickey Hazen, reported Levine to be a bright, energetic, athletic poet with a no-nonsense, razor-edge teaching style and a lovely helpful wife, Fran, whom he featured so centrally in his first book, *On the Edge.* Early in my term as editor, I asked him to submit any poems he deemed worthy for the paper and he said he would remember it but most of his students were beginners. Later, as editor, I noted that Levine could find no campus funding for his invitation to record his poetry at the Library of Congress whereas the FSC cattle judging team was being transported all over the country at school expense. Earlier, my managing editor, Jamie Williams, had entitled my editorial about sorority rush, "Cattlemen Judge More Tactfully." We explored the conflicting values in a growing college located in the middle of a rich agricultural area. I was exploring writing as editor in the only way I knew how in a college new to the ways of creative writing brought by Levine from the Iowa Workshop and it was shocking how fast that change brought change, sped even faster when Peter Everwine joined Levine in 1962. Iowa seemed then, before easy air travel, such an exotic, foreign place deep in the green mid-west.

I graduated in 1960 and began working at the *Merced Sun-Star* covering city council, planning commission, police and fire for the city. In about six months, an opening came on *The Fresno Bee* and I took the job. It was a considerable raise. Carol Anne Gregg and I married the next summer and settled down until the Cuban Missile Crisis occurred with its threat of nuclear war and I received my draft notice. I had 10 days before I had to report. I applied to join the California Air National guard but there was no space available for California basic trainees in the Texas training center. Miraculously, a spot opened up before the 10-day deadline and I was assigned to basic training at Lackland Air Force base. Years later, I learned that George Bush the younger and Dan Quayle both endured similar dilemmas but they had no trouble finding basic training space. I had come within days of being drafted into an army that soon would be involved in developing the Vietnam war. Ten years later, as a young college professor, I became eligible for military service in Vietnam again as a reservist without a local base assignment in rural Indiana.

Carol was pursuing graduate studies at FSC that would lead to a public schools counseling certificate and later a long career in Indiana. She also was teaching full time in the Clovis School District. I returned from basic training, which was much more pleasant when I did it as an officer candidate. In time, I learned that I technically could have entered the Air National Guard without attending standard basic training because of my ROTC training. I took up my work with *The Fresno Bee* as a general assignment reporter and substitute for the beats on police, sheriff's office, and fire department and county, state and federal government, including the FBI. I learned handball playing with an FBI agent named Clarence, who taught me a spin serve by serving a ball that appeared to be heading to my right side but suddenly skipped into my chest smartly before I could touch it. At some point, I decided to try my hand at Levine's night course in poetry writing and in the next year and a half I would take two of them and one of Peter Everwine's excellent night courses in fiction writing.

Levine's course was unlike any other I had in college. In my introduction to my contributions to *How Much Earth: The Fresno Poets* in 2001, I spoke of how my keen relationships with good students at DePauw and 33 years of reading, writing and traveling for myself and my family came from the attraction of Philip Levine's evening poetry writing class while I worked for *The Fresno Bee* and I said it was the best class I ever took, opened up worlds for me, and remained my standard of teaching excellence.

I've never stopped thinking of why Levine was so appealing. He did not lecture as most FSC professors did. He used a textbook but did not rely on it heavily. He often brought mimeographed contemporary poems as examples to discuss and commented on them. He often told stories about his past, about other poets, and was a very interesting and entertaining performer with a wicked sense of humor. He mimeographed some of our poems and we discussed them. The rule was that the author could not defend or explain their poems until the end of the discussion unless asked. He was brutally honest in his criticisms and just as frank in praise, sometimes in the same poem. He discussed prosody and encouraged us to imitate poems or poets. He pointed out his frequent use of lines measured by syllables and he extolled the virtue of the disciplined line. He advocated using odd numbers of syllables—5,7, 9—rather than even numbers to avoid unintentionally falling into an iambic pattern.

Most of all, Levine was focused. He paid attention and his attention was sharp and quick. At the beginning of one session, two of the students—Ollie Simpson, who later married poet Robert Mezey, and the poet, Dennis Saleh—were goofing off, giggling over something, as Levine was trying to bring us to focus. "Knock it off," he said. They paused for a moment and then resumed their banter. "Knock it off," he said, a bit louder. Which they did but then made nervous responses to one another. "Get out!" Levine said. When they showed bewilderment, he added, "I mean it." They left the class, as embarrassed as those of us remaining, and the class began. That moment stayed with me all the while I taught and I have thought about it over the years. At times I have thought that it was an overuse of professorial prerogative, an excessive use of power. But over time, I came to see it as something essential to Levine. He truly believed in the value and sanctity of poetry as an enterprise and that extended to the class devoted to it. He demanded that the process be respected. Levine's classes always had a certain tension in them. He used that tension that worked to keep our attention and focus. They were not times to relax, nor was it his to relax as a poet and teacher. He had to "stay on duty," as he described the poet's job, "to be ready to receive the poems when they come." It was something I remembered and tried to emulate in my own way: if I had the students' attention, at least I had the chance of making education happen between us.

Levine was an unusual man with unusual energy. He found a niche in the world where his energy was able to gain an outlet as poet and teacher and we were the recipients of it in both ways. But he also was at the forefront of the creative writing phenomenon (or educational phenomenon) that coincided with his beginning teaching around 1960. It focused on education that succeeded, not on education that was presumed to be succeeding. As every writer knows, bad writing is just as common as good writing. That is why we rewrite. The poet or fiction teacher's job is to help the student succeed with his best writing, not to grade the worst and average it with the best for a grade. This sounds like a simple thing and it is; but for the most part college classes before this approach (and many long after) were designed to make distinctions between people's performances in order to rank them with grades, not to produce excellent products and rank the projects after the fact. Levine and other good creative writing teachers wanted the best they could get from their students. Levine wrote a recommendation for me to the Lilly Endowment for a grant to create poetry videos in which he pointed out I had moved from writing "scraps" of poems to a full-fledged and polished poem in the class. It was true and I think he was talking about "To the Dirt, the Grass and the People of Hanford, Washington, Who Live with a Plutonium Plant" that I did in the first class with him. It was a good poem that I wrote under the influence of an astounding article I had just read. The article was very grim about that nasty plant and its by-products that would last almost forever. I was overcome with the unified thrust of its argument and that spirit give me a voice. Its many facts gave me details. When Phil visited my senior seminar in writing at DePauw in 1994, I asked him what he wanted in a good poem. He had been asked before and he had a ready answer: 1. Vibrant physical imagery (details from life); 2. Music in the language or just chopped up prose? 3. Story. Is it good? Does it move? 4. Clarity. 5. Urgency—a need for the poem to exist ("psychic weight," Robert Bly's phrase).

Then he added this additional advice: "Don't be afraid to write badly." I think that gets to the heart of Levine's teaching and outlook. How can you get at your deepest, most honest self without confronting your fears and writing about them? Don't be afraid of yourself! Not a good prescription for performing for a teacher who wanted his or her deepest opinion repeated correctly back to them, something more in line with poet Robert Lowell's attitudes than the attitudes of Levine's poet-mentor, John Berryman. The two poets taught at the Iowa Workshop as described in "Mine Own John Berryman," the first chapter in Levine's *The Bread of Time*, 1994. In that chapter, Levine details at length lessons learned through his mentor as he heard them: don't "bootlick" or suck up to your teacher; prefer "ordinary" events in poems to the miraculous or grand; don't select untruths as subjects; "write good prose diction in a usual prose order unless you've got a damn good reason for doing otherwise;" try to write the poem you are unable to write; there is great poetry hiding where you least suspect it...; we must find our touchstones where we can...; there is no adequate book on prosody... we are all thrown on our own ... better to learn from a poet who doesn't intoxicate you; write everything that occurs to you; a teacher must stand ground as teacher apart from students; the fellowship of a class is a delicate and lovely thing; tell the truth but remember Blake, "A truth that's told with bad intent/Beats all the Lies you can invent." Like John Berryman, never fail your obligations as a teacher and bring a depth of insight and care to your students. Levine's chapter is rich and full in a strong voice that celebrates Berryman, a brilliant Shakespeare scholar and student of English and American poetry. "He (Berryman) did it for the love of poetry," Levine says.

I began casting around for comments about Phil later in his active teaching career and came across Anne Whitehouse's piece in *The Baltimore Sun* in 1994 reviewing *The Bread of Time*. She had been a student of Phil's at Columbia University in 1978. "I recognized his own teaching style in his descriptions of Berryman. I cannot imagine, however, that Berryman's gift for ribaldry surpassed Mr. Levine's. I have never had a teacher with such an inventive, wicked and explosive sense of humor. For a semester, he kept the class laughing with witty and often unprintable jokes... As with Berryman this sense of humor coexists with an essential seriousness of purpose, a suspicion and dislike of pretentiousness, and a passionate commitment to poetry. . . . Mr. Levine, like Berryman, was a force to be reckoned with. He reserved his scathing criticism for poems where he judged the expressions and feelings were inauthentic, and we sat in trepidation of his disapproval. He was a memorable teacher...."

So, to put it another way, the Philip Levine in 1978 in New York City was the same Philip Levine as in 1961 in Fresno.

After Phil's death, Fran sent me a picture from my time at the Iowa Writers Workshop ('64-'65, '65-66, '66-'67) which I had forgotten all about. The workshop at that time was still the preeminent workshop in the country (as it arguably still is) and there were five of us there, all Phil's students: Mickey Hazen, Tom Emery, Herb Scott, Glover Davis and Harold Tinkle. There were some 200 fiction writers and poets in the workshop from all over the country. We had all arrived there independently in the course of pursuing our own lives after taking Phil's classes and all went our separate ways afterwards. I got to know Herb and Glover best, Herb with his five children, and stories about working at night in a grocery store to support the family while he got his AB from FSC (his second book was *Groceries*); and Glover, with his stories of living as a child in a Catholic residential school, pulling toys out of cereal boxes before they set them on the breakfast table. Glover used to drink a beer with us at the three-story apartment building we lived in across the street from the university hospital; I served the building as a kind of superintendent for half rent. Herb eventually was deeply involved in publishing at Western Michigan University and Glover had an entire career at California State, San Diego.

One of the changes that came out of the creative writing phenomenon was the present sense of community created from its readings and publications. When I was at San Francisco and Iowa, there were few poetry or fiction readings. Especially at San Francisco, we were just taking very special classes in a suburban campus. There were not many writing centers in the whole country.

At Iowa, there were frequent parties, usually centered on the writers: Donald Justice, Marvin Bell, George Starbuck, R. V. Cassill, Richard Yates, Vance Bourjaily, Nelson Algren, Kurt Vonnegut and Jose Dinoso. Cassill and Bourjaily were permanent writer/teachers and had their own followings. We were very much aware of our special situation in the workshop and standard PhD faculty members were wary of workshop students in their classes and vice versa. I studied fiction writing in both workshops and returned to poetry almost exclusively in the 80s while teaching at DePauw.

There were athletic contests between the Fiction Workshop and the Poetry Workshop members. I remember a laughable moment in a volleyball game between the fiction writers and the poets when the fine poet, Donald Justice (one of Phil's original classmates from 1953) vehemently contested a ball called out of bounds for his side on a rough, dirt play field not even marked. Generally, we worked hard at our craft and prepared for our classes. In both places, Carol taught in the local schools, so our lives were more regular and conventional than many of the students there.

As for the rigor of the discussions of stories and poems at either San Francisco or Iowa, I felt fully prepared. Once you had been through Levine's scrutiny, you could stand up with anyone

At DePauw in 1967 when I started, one young professor was curious about the New Left and the rising anti-Vietnam War activity and wondered how prevalent they were at the famous Iowa Workshop. I replied that we largely worked hard as writers to make good sentences, not act out political philosophies. I served as an Instructor in Fiction Writing in the Undergraduate Workshop in my third year at Iowa and my office mate was novelist John Irving, who was also an instructor.

Some of my students included novelist, short story writer and essayist Barbara Kingsolver; novelist, story writer and essayist Susan Neville; journalist and non-fiction writer James B. Stewart, who won a Pulitzer prize; poet Mark Cox; journalist, Doug Frantz; novelist/naturalist Greg Schwipps, who teaches at DePauw, and John McWethy, the dynamic White House reporter and ABC correspondent who died in a skiing accident in 2008.

Call it any name you want, but Phil Levine wanted his students to write good poems and they did and they got their students to write good poems too. He wasn't the only creative writing teacher at that creative time but no one was better. "We must constantly rededicate ourselves," he once said.

I stayed in touch with Phil, including two one-week workshops he conducted in 1994 and 1995 at DePauw. Of all his memorable qualities, probably the most memorable was his steadfastness. He was always ready to help with your next step, always ready with a good word if the writing wasn't coming. Your part of the bargain was to hold your own in your writing, in your teaching, and with your students.

Kurt Vonnegut, who was an interesting and innovative teacher himself ("Write your paper like a writer. Interest me, amuse me.") when I was his student in Iowa said after spending a week at DePauw in 1968: "I continue to be gratified by how respected you old Iowa M.F.A.'s have become in the academic community. The degree was said to be a joke, but there was nothing funny about what good teachers so many of you turned out to be."

Glover Davis

Glover Davis is professor Emeritus of Creative Writing at San Diego State University. His books of poetry are *Bandaging Bread*, *August Fires*, *Legend*, *Separate Lives*, *Spring Drive*, and *My Cap of Darkness*. At Fresno State he studied with Philip Levine, and then attended the Iowa Writers Workshop where he studied with Donald Justice. Davis's work has appeared in *POETRY*, *Ploughshares*, *Shenandoah Review*, *The New England Review*, *The Southern Review*, and *Southwest Review*. He now lives in Mason, TX near San Antonio.

"Grace" from *First Light: A Festschrift for Philip Levine on his 85th Birthday*, 2013—Glover Davis

Almost by accident and luck I walked into Philip Levine's beginning poetry writing class, and this changed my life. Perhaps only former fellow students at the Iowa Writers' Workshop and Yvor Winter's graduate students at Stanford knew about Philip in those days, but the students interested in literature and writing at Fresno State College, as it was called in those days, discussed this inspiring, charismatic teacher.

I didn't particularly want to write poetry but I did want to be a writer. At first it was difficult. I didn't know very much. I hadn't read enough. I had to train my ear.

Phil was demanding. He wanted poetic excellence and as a great martial artist once said, a person would "have to eat bitterness" to achieve excellence in his art. So it was with Phil. Some of us in his classes were veterans who believed in what was difficult, yet few of us had done that well in high school. Some of our first poems were laughable and Phil was witty. He was, at times, as funny as a great stand up comedian and we suffered. But I, for one, had never progressed so quickly in anything else.

Like few, a very few great teachers, there were times in a classroom when something like a special grace seemed to infuse Phil. He would rise above any personal prejudice, if he had any, and do this under influence of an aesthetic truth or as he said "the truth as it is given to me to see the truth."

There would be waves of good poets coming out of what Larry Levis, one of the best of them, called "Wind and Dust State," as the campus was new, raw, devoid of vegetation. Lawson Inada was one of his first students but just after Lawson there were Bill Childress, Herb Scott, Ollie Simpson and myself. Every four years or so there would be a new group including people like Larry Levis, Bruce Boston, Bob Jones, Shirley Williams, Roberta Spear, Jon Veinberg, Omar Salinas and many others.

By the time we were juniors we were publishing in some of the best literary journals such as *Poetry*, *The North American Review* and *The Southern Review*. Many of us were awarded writing fellowships at the University of Iowa's Writers' Workshop or the University of California at Irvine's MFA Program. But Philip Levine's teaching and help extended beyond graduate school. He helped sustain me when I was a young teacher and poet.

"Introduction: Glover Davis and *SPRING DRIVE*," 2010—David St. John

The many admirers of Glover Davis's previous four collections of poetry—*Bandaging Bread, August Fires, Legend,* and *Separate Lives*—know well the singular achievements of his poetry. Glover Davis is a formal master whose lyricism is coupled with a natural colloquial, conversational diction and a deceptive modesty. His poems have a poise and composure, even a kind of stateliness, rare in our contemporary poetry. Yet the urgencies of memory and the immediacies of daily life resonate in all of his work.

Many of Glover Davis's poems celebrate the shifting seasons and the minute changes of the natural world even as they chart the subtle shifts in his speaker. These meditations are by turns celebratory and valedictory, as Glover Davis recalls passages and events from both personal and public pasts. He offers us portraits of family members, of himself as a boy and young man. He lets us see our world at times of war. One of the constants in his poems is a concern with the erosion of time; his speakers struggle to gather up memory as urgently as they wish to gather those elements of the natural world we also see eroding and passing as well. Davis knows that we often need to turn to the natural world in order to feel grounded again and relevant to our own lives and landscapes.

The limits of language—even while we try to honor and reflect the passages of our natural and human worlds—arise in nearly every one of Glover Davis's poems. Even as the reader is carried forward by his flawless iambic pentameter lines, across those dazzling webs of his rhymes, he acknowledges that the naming he is seeking remains, as it does for all poets, at best provisional. Calm and reflective, and sometimes humorous, these poems look squarely at the dilemma of trying to capture memory, at the frustrations of trying to name experience. These questions feel most urgent in those Davis poems in which we feel the encroachment of the "real" world—of war, family deaths—upon the elements of the natural world. Some of his most powerful poems are drawn from the 1940s and 1950s and the influence of wartime upon the speaker and his family and his friends.

Conversational eloquence is always a given in Glover Davis's poetry. Ordinary men and women are lifted by the clarity and intimacy of their observations to something resembling a state of grace. From the carnal meat—both animal and human—that he considers in his sequence of poems based on paintings by Chaim Soutine to his vision of deliverance in the collection's concluding poem, "*Burial Dream*," Glover Davis has placed the question mark of mortality, inverted like a hook, hanging before our eyes. Maturity and experience are said to breed wisdom. You are holding a book of profound wisdoms in your hands.

"from An Interview with Glover Davis," 2019—Gordon Preston and Christopher Buckley

Q: We'll start with background, going way back...you grew up in San Luis Obispo. Did you enlist in the Navy right out of high school instead of applying to college?
A: First, I did not grow up in San Luis Obispo. I was born there, but I only lived there one year in third grade with my grandmother when my chaotic family had reached a crisis point, the first of many. No surprise, as my father was an alcoholic whose instability exacerbated my mother's mental illness. So I actually grew up in a series of towns and schools: kindergarten in Berkeley Hills, Mrs. Hester's boarding school in Descanso, first grade in Point Loma, second grade in East San Diego, then St. John Bosco's in Montebello. Then Kansas, where my father got a job before he abandoned us again. My mother returned to California and put all three

of us children in Nazareth House, an orphanage in San Diego, as she suffered a mental breakdown and was hospitalized. I lived there for four years until I aged out of the system and my Aunt Kay and Uncle Glen Hooper took us all to live with them—and their four children— in Felton, a small town in the Santa Cruz mountains. A year later, my uncle Glen died, so when I graduated from high school there, obviously my Aunt had no resources to help me with college. The military seemed the logical option. I wanted to join the Marines but since I was only 17, my Aunt had to sign off and she would only do it if I joined the Navy.

Q: When and how did you decide to attend Fresno State? Had you heard of Levine then and were you interested in creative writing? If not, how did you discover Levine's workshops?

A: By the end of my three years in the Navy, I had two correspondence courses from the University of California and six hours of engineering credit for my work in the military. I always intended to go to college, but my grades in high school were too uneven to get into a top university—if I liked a class I got an A; if not, I was satisfied with a C. I could get into Fresno State, and my sister was already there, enjoying her classes. I had always wanted to be a writer, but poetry never entered my mind. In high school my journalism teacher recommended me when the Santa Cruz Sentinel came looking for someone to report on our San Lorenzo Valley football games. Which was interesting, since I was writing about games in which I was playing.

When I began taking courses in English at Fresno State, a number of student colleagues would discuss with awe and sometimes anger but always intense interest this poet and teacher, Philip Levine. I didn't especially like poetry then, but at schools like Fresno State you go where the talent is. Once I enrolled in my first poetry workshop with Phil, I knew I had found my calling.

Phil wasn't yet famous, but he was an incredible teacher—tough, demanding, absolutely honest. In those days, masculine egos would cause students to challenge him in a kind of intellectual shootout. I kept my mouth shut and watched as these guys licked their heads. One never knew where a dialogue would go, fueled as it was by inspiration. I hadn't known poetry could be this way and I began writing seriously.

Q: Did you take any classes with Peter Everwine? And who were the poets on campus and in the community there that became your friends; who was helpful in workshops? Were you there with, before, or after Larry Levis?

A: I did take one class with Peter Everwine near the end of my coursework at Fresno State, but it was a contemporary literature class, not creative writing. Pete had a period when he stopped writing poetry, and my time there coincided with this. We would later become friends and supporters of each other's work. My close classmates in Phil's workshop were Herb Scott, Bill Childress, and Ollie Simpson Mezey. Larry Levis was about six years behind me at Fresno State, but I would meet him later under other circumstances.

Q: When did you start to write poems that you thought might be keepers? Who were you reading early on as models, what books, anthologies? When and where did you publish your first poems?

A: With Phil Levine's tough encouragement, I started writing poems I thought might be publishable. If they weren't "keepers" I kept working on them until I thought they were. During this time, in workshop we were reading Robert Lowell, Elizabeth Bishop, William Carlos Williams, Frost, Stevens, James Wright, W.D. Snodgrass, Gary Snyder, Whitman— and our teachers Levine, Bob Mezey, Henry Collette. For me, inspiration and influence came also from the Elizabethans, Shakespeare, Ben Jonson, Donne, Herbert, Yeats, Ted

Hughes, Eliot, Louise Bogan, James Dickey, and some of Ginsberg. Within two years of my participation in Phil's workshops, I had poems published in some of the best literary journals, including *The Southern Review* and *Poetry*, as well as numerous other journals, some of which no longer exist.

Q: What do you remember about the anthology *Down at the Santa Fe Depot*? How did that develop, and what do you remember about that now famous photograph on the cover in which you are included?

A: Since I had been teaching at San Diego State for a while, I was involved just as a contributor with the development of the anthology. I remember that being a good weekend, as I stayed at Phil's, where we talked and drank. One of the interesting things about that photograph is that the only non-poet featured is the famous writer William Saroyan. I'm not sure why he was there, but it might well have had something to do with the fact that the editors were also Armenian Americans. In the photograph, I'm sitting squarely facing the camera on the front right at Phil's feet—somehow fitting. I look like the jock I was for much of my life. Tom Emory, another Fresno student at the Iowa Writers Workshop, said I looked like a determined coach who had to whip these guys into shape.

Q: Did you go right to the Iowa Writers Workshop from Fresno State? What year was that? How many poems did you have to submit with your application in those days? Did Phil and Peter write letters for you?

A: I went to the University of Iowa's Writers Workshop in the fall semester of 1964. I had graduated in January of 1964, and while I was waiting for the next step I took a poetry workshop with Phil in the spring and wrote when I had free time as I was working to support myself. I cannot remember how many poems I had to submit for admission. Phil recommended me, along with my other English professors—not Everwine as he was not familiar with my work at that time.

Q: Who did you study with at Iowa and what poets in the workshop were you closest with?

A: My first year at Iowa I worked with George Starbuck and occasionally Paul Engel. I was close to some other students such as Harold Tinkle, Herb Scot, Tom Emory and a guy from L.A. named Glen Miller Epstein. There were fiction writers I hung out with, sometimes Andre Dubus, Bob Lacey, and especially Jim Crumley. Then in my second year Donald Justice came back from his leave, and I focused my studies with him. I loved Don's book *Summer Anniversaries*, even memorized some of his poems. He directed my thesis.

Q: In those days Harry Duncan had his Cummington Press at Iowa and taught a printing class. How did you connect with him? You printed a chapbook of Levine's "Silent in America" in his class. Tell us that story.

A: I met Harry Duncan through Bob Mezey, who was friends with Duncan. Bob visited Iowa and introduced me to Harry. In his typography class, I learned the history of printing books, their design, and type faces. Images from that experience have appeared in my poems ever since. My project for that course was a chapbook. I chose Phil Levine's "Silent in America" because several sections had been published in *The North American Review*, but no one had published this whole long poem. I don't remember how many copies I printed, but I do remember I gave half of them to Phil and sold most of the rest at the local arts bookstore to pay for the high quality paper I had used. I kept a few copies and when I began teaching at San Diego State, I lent them to students who never returned them. My chapbook became a rare book. Booksellers would later offer Phil a fortune for a copy, but none could be found by then.

Q: Your first book *Bandaging Bread* was printed by Harry in 1970; was that after you left Iowa or did you participate in the printing and production? There were just 300 copies printed on a thick Japanese Hosho paper, the cover a pressed green kind of burlap or grass weave. A beautiful example of book art. Were you consulted on choices and design?
A: I had been away from Iowa for four years teaching at San Diego State when Harry published *Bandaging Bread*, a beautiful example of his art. My only participation in the physical production of this book was insisting on a classical type face with letters clear and straight "driven into the soft Hosho" of my oneiric poems, as Richard Howard said in his article on The Cummington Press in *The American Poetry Review*.

Q: When you finished the MFA at Iowa, did you go right into teaching at San Diego State? When was that? What was it like applying for creative writing jobs back then? I recall in your first years in San Diego you were living in a trailer and carrying water uphill to it. Were you underpaid as an assistant professor there to begin?
A: When I finished my MFA at Iowa in the spring of 1966, I went directly into teaching at San Diego State University, teaching a summer school class and then full time in the fall of 1966. It was easier for creative writers to find jobs then, but we did have to teach four classes, including two English composition courses. The pay for assistant professors wasn't that good for San Diego even then. So when I had saved enough, I bought two unimproved lots in the hills above Harbison Canyon east of El Cajon. I put a trailer up there. My stove and hot water heater ran on propane and batteries made other things work. I had to haul in five-gallon containers of water every day, but it was beautiful there. Huge boulders and you could look down through shadows green and shifting over the landscape and hear the hawk's hunting cries.

Q: Poems I especially remember from *Bandaging Bread* all that time ago are "From the Dark Room" and "America," both for their subtle hint of apocalyptic conclusion and as well for their ear and eclectic use of diction. What were your concerns for craft and voice in those early days?
A: There was a mixture of free verse and formal poetry in that first book. I was concerned with both modes. I had a lot of images and immediate experiences that led me to use free verse, but the formal poems like "From the Dark Room" are more lyrical. There's a kind of subtle music to the formal which I find very attractive. In both modes I was concerned with internal structure proceeding from some problem and internal solution. Even then, I felt you ought to be able to do both—free verse and traditional forms—if you were a poet.

Q: The other poem that has always stood out for me in that volume is "Anonymous Phonecalls"—a longer poem in three sections. The subject is fairly mysterious, almost film noir? What was the impetus for the poem? Also—it could just be me—but there seems to be a slight influence in tone from "Silent in America"? Do you think that is so?
A: Remember, I was a young man back then, and there would be flirting in the cafeteria at the university. I would imagine what might happen with some of these young women. Later, I'm not sure if it's contemporaneous with the writing of this poem, one of them actually did repeatedly call me anonymously, although I was pretty sure who it was. As far as influence from "Silent in America," I think you might be right, although I hadn't thought of this myself before.

Q: Thinking back to teaching now…I think you taught at SDSU for something like 35 years? As an early student of yours I wondered about the design of your writing workshops, was the influence from Fresno, Iowa, or of your own making?

A: Actually, I taught at SDSU for 39 years! I learned to teach writing workshops from Phil Levine; I wanted to emulate his toughness, his insistence on excellence because I felt this approach had made me into a serious poet. Phil said, "I tell the truth as it is given to me to see the truth." And this is what I tried to do with my own students. At Iowa, Donald Justice, who was a great formalist, encouraged my work. I remember once in workshop I had a blank verse poem the other students didn't like because it was "too iambic." Justice immediately defended the poem: "What about the great tradition?" he said. Because of his teaching and my own inclinations, I worked more with formal poetry with my students than Phil had. Both Fresno under Levine and Iowa under Justice provided an environment of rigor and serious regard for the work of poetry. I tried to give this to my own students at SDSU.

Q: Could you elaborate on your expectation for including the poetry anthology _Naked Poetry_ on your syllabus?

A: _Naked Poetry_ was published in 1969 with the subtitle of _Recent American Poetry in Open Forms_. I included this anthology in my syllabus because my friend Bob Mezey was one of the editors and more important because it contained a lot of poems I liked by poets like Levine, Mezey, Kinnell, Roethke, James Wright, Weldon Kees, Berryman, Robert Lowell, Gary Snyder, and some of Ginsberg. This anthology came out when the debate over what form new poetry should take was still vigorous. Donald Justice said, "It's time for poetry to put its clothes back on." I thought he should have been included in this anthology, though of course the main point was to show poets throwing off traditional poetic devices such as rhyme and meter. Although I had no intention of rejecting traditional forms, I knew it was important for my students to read this new work.

Q: In the advanced workshop in 1972 you ordered both Levine's _They Feed They Lion_ and Everwine's _Collecting the Animals_ for the class. And while they were both Fresno poets and former teachers of yours, weren't they about the best two books published that year? They became the early benchmarks for my life in poetry; did most of the students respond as positively?

A: Yes, these books were two of the very best books published that year. _They Feed They Lion_ may well have been the best book of that decade. Although Everwine didn't become famous like Phil, he was a terrific poet, and I'm glad my students were exposed to his work. I'm not sure how my other students responded to these books, although I imagine there were others like you who connected with them. I knew what was good, and I presented to my students. I didn't worry about whether they liked it.

Q: MLK once stated that intelligence plus character makes for great education, which is how you taught. What did you expect of your students, and what did you see?

A: Thank you. That's a very satisfying kind of praise, since I took teaching very seriously. I expected my students to make the most of their talent, which would require dedication and hard work. They had to come to class on time, prepared, and willing to listen to critical analysis of their work. Some of my students later became pretty well known poets: Rod Santos, Chris Buckley, Richard Katrovas, David Martinez, to cite a few that come to mind.

Q: You were obviously a disciplined man, a father figure perhaps. I took many classes from you, undergraduate and graduate, so much so that you labeled me a "dinosaur." Did you intend this following to be a poetry outcome?

A: I like the idea of being a father figure; that's what Levine was to me until the day he died. I don't know that I intended to create a following, but I am passionate about the work of poetry and I'm also hard-headed about my ideas about form and music. So I'm sure there was an intention of creating a specific attitude towards poetry in my students. Also, I wanted my students to have a memorable experience in my classes, akin to those I had in Levine's workshops.

Q: *August Fires* came out in 1978, again with Harry Duncan after he had moved to the University of Nebraska. It's a beautiful handmade edition in hard cover. This probably my favorite book of yours in content and design. A number of poems are printed in facing columns on the same page and it uses Romulus Italic type. How do you see the type and design fitting with the poems and subjects?

Leather Jacket

I put my jacket on a boulder
and went back down the path
picked   straw daisies   tied blue
washed rocks   in a hanky.
when I returned   my jacket
was full of air. the black creases
of the elbow   were sailing
down the cliff. skull
and crossbones painted
on someone else's back.
when I looked inside
I saw   white stretch marks
a few clumsy stitches. the neck
gradually darkened with sweat
and became smooth.
from the first day
I wore it like armor
neat's-foot oil rubbed in
deckles of light.
I was a deer   or a lion

a leopard in his fiery spots
heart   beneath the cross hairs
opening   like a shot wineskin.
when the seams pull apart
I open all at once
words pouring through my
fingers
every part of me   a target.
I move quickly to the
edge of the cliff and watch
my jacket dangle   far below
from a bush   as if the bush
were a man with habits.
I could imagine the sudden step
into air and the mind
crying no!   I could almost see
the white blades of the shoulders
driven through the skin.
I climb down these rocks
like a man rescuing a friend.

A: At first I was disappointed in *August Fires* when it came out. I had expected something more like *Bandaging Bread*. But I love it now. I love Harry's work and I feel bad that I didn't at first recognize how lovely this book is. And of course the design of the book reflects Harry's conception of what the poems are. Most are looser formally with gaps in the lines to achieve a sense of time lapse and because of this the poems' rhythms. The type is not so formal; it seems to go well with the looser forms like isochrony used in "August Fires." The fiery orange color of the cover evokes central images of heat and combustion, as does Lawrence Bradshaw's beautiful woodcut frontispiece. The ragged edged soft maidstone paper gives the book the feel of a timeless artifact of artistic witness, which I meant it to be.

Q: "Leather Jacket" is one of my favorite poems in the book. I love how the imagination enters into such a concrete object and everyday event, how it elevates it. There is, as I remember, a story behind that jacket. In the early days at Fresno State, a leather jacket was a marker or emblem of the poets there, at least for those who could afford one. Tell us about that and about how the poem came to you.

A: This poem is, in part, about a deerskin jacket I bargained for and bought in Tijuana. I attached many of its physical qualities to personal significance, like its being a kind of armor, its making me like an animal, etc. So it meant a lot to me. Then one day I wore it to Peterson gym and locked it in a locker when I went to work out. When I came back an hour or so later, the lock had been cut through with a bolt cutter and my beloved jacket was gone.

Q: The other very moving poem in the book is "Sanctuary." It reads as if it comes out of personal experience. Can you talk a bit about the basis for the poem and how you manage to transform the narrative and imagery beyond the experience?

A: This was one of the most painful experiences of my life. My mother drove up to the orphanage in a cab. She wouldn't get out of the cab but had the driver go to the door and ask the nuns to summon us. It seemed as though she wasn't eating; her skull looked like someone in a concentration camp. We sat in the cab with her for a while. It was very scary. Then the nuns came and comforted us. Enfolded into this one poem are other instances of her coming to get us for a visit at the orphanage. After that, my aunt came down to have her committed to a mental hospital. I'm not sure I do transform the narrative too much beyond the experience. Except that I organize the content into blank verse, perhaps a way of taking control of my experience with my mother. Maybe readers are moved by this poem because our relationship with our mothers is fundamental, and when it is broken pain is inevitable.

Q: In the poem "Helios," you have an affinity for natural terrain. What was your connection to this landscape—the mountains east of San Diego? Was your writing an homage to the cycles of nature planned, or was it an act of art, and how strong a theme of human exploitation do you see in this poem? How does the Greek God Helios fit in?

A: I lived in this landscape, in the mountains east of the city. It was undeveloped and beautiful. I intended to write an homage to the coming of summer, to life, to light and warmth. For me, planning to write an homage and it being an act of art are the same thing, except maybe the art is revealed slowly as I wrote it and images like "the mad red hair of the poppy" unfolded. I predict the human exploitation in this poem, but at the time of the poem I do not see much of it—I know it is coming. The Greek god Helios is a pagan god, and to my mind much closer and immediate to nature than the Christian God. And of course Helios is the god of the sun, a personification of some latent physical force.

Q: How did the solitude of living in the foothills east of San Diego cause you to realize the importance of heart, and its connection to nature as you made that drive in the "August Fires" poem?

A: The quietness of the landscape gave me a kind of meditative connection to the land, which led to an emotional connection to it—a love for nature, an intense deep feeling for it. And especially what was being done to it by man.

Q: "August Fires" celebrates nature purifying itself, and is a wake-up call to California's lack of ability to do so. What is your reflection now, some 40 years later, considering the current events happening in California and other western states?
A: It's almost like I could see what was going to happen. I wanted a purification and could imagine it, but all these years later it's like not enough people in power heard the wakeup call in "August Fires." I'm still hoping for purification, but it's even larger than that now—climate change and the refusal to acknowledge our impact on nature. It doesn't look like we are going to even try to solve this problem, so I don't know why I keep hoping.

Q: Your third book *Legend* was published by Wesleyan, one of the venerable publishers of contemporary poetry; how did that come about?
A: I was at San Diego State but I knew that I would like to have my work published by Wesleyan. Levine encouraged me, even told me to send my manuscript there. He and David St. John wrote supporting letters, which I'm sure were helpful.

Q: Your books reveal spiritual, mythical, and Biblical elements. In "August Fires" you find three seeds in a handful of earth. Is this a conscious act in your writing, or an artistic blessing? And how does this focus in *August Fires* then carry over to *Legend*?
A: Probably a little bit of both—I imagined three seeds and then said Wow, that fits. My Catholic background was powerful to me, and I'd been studying the comparison of Western religious thought to Eastern, especially Chinese religious thought with Allan Anderson at San Diego State. In *Legend* there are both mythical and spiritual themes. Like "The Wedding Feast" and poems based on the Arthurian legends—and certainly that sequence is spiritual in its essence.

Q: Talk a bit about writing in traditional forms as it is something you practice and value, and it seems to fit with the mythic quality of many poems in the book?
A: I think you connect with some universal form of the beautiful when the content is expressed in formal poetry, not always but sometimes. The deep music you perceive in good formal poetry connects powerfully to the reader/listener, maybe somewhat in the same way a myth or legend connects to the heart. Another thing is, the formal has an intense relationship to memory, and when we draw on these myths we also draw on memories from these myths that our forbears thought were important. Finally, legends and myths have formal structures and specific narrative arcs, so maybe formal, structured poetry is a good vehicle.

Q: I generally prefer your work in free verse, but it is clear that the disciplines of inherited forms influence your free verse poems and give them a tighter structure and rhythm, almost out of force of habit? Do you see it that way?
A: Yes, sure. But also a lot of times the free verse lines exhibit ghost meter, just naturally because of the nature of the language, English In my case. So words connect, and you have iambic feet. To really write formal poetry well, you have to train your ear. So this training might result in tighter rhythm in my free verse.

Q: One of my favorite poems in *Legend* is "My Brother." Can you talk about this poem's composition and achievement in light of the former question re traditional forms and free verse?

A: "My Brother" is in free verse, obviously. At times it comes close to being iambic trimeter or actually is—"and saw your tiny fist/wave above you like a bud." Structure is action, and the demands of internal action guide the structure of the poem.

Q: Turning to "Your Father's Hands," the poem for Larry Levis…this poem is written in blank verse, right? How did that discipline help move the specifics of the narrative along? What was your connection to Larry?

A: Yes, this poem is in blank verse. Blank verse is a great narrative vehicle; it's flexible and rhythmic. It demands great craftsmanship,and working with it causes details to come into the poem that I might well not have gotten otherwise. I didn't know Larry Levis that well, but I met him at some poetry functions in San Diego, maybe through Bruce Boston. I heard about him through Levine, and I read and appreciated some of his poems. When this poem took place, Levis was well known if not as famous as he would later be. He told me about his son because I had my own son Michael with me, and his sadness moved me. We weren't around each other much because of geographical distance.

Q: There are two impressive longer sequences toward the end of the book: "Ursa Major" and "The Owl." I want to talk about "The Owl" that was printed in a letterpress folded broadside at Gary Young's Greenhouse Review Press in Santa Cruz. It was a long process and I remember a crew of us up there working on the last runs through the press and the collating and binding: Gary, Jon Veinberg, Tim Sheehan I think, and Gary Soto was down from Berkeley. Can you talk about the mix of imagination and narrative—the design, structure, your keen eye and observations are iconic, and I would say you are an Owl. Is there also some larger suggestion there at the end?

Owl 5

II

My bathrobe opens in a sudden gust.
Its gray silk puffs around the shoulders—black
lines run down the sleeves, white down at my chest.
I'm at the window, fingers in the crack
where cold air issues as I hunch my back
to lift and see thorn branches whip the air;
wind ruffling the light plumage of my hair.

Wind wearing at the skin of temple and jar
of the owl who dives into my moonlit yard
and the wings splash on the mouse stuck with straw.
When he rises I think I see eyes starred
like cut glass and I try to disregard
these heavy bones; move like the owl, the shark
of night, and pick whatever is, from the dark.

A: We had this barn in the Santa Cruz mountains at my aunt's house, and there were owls. They frightened us, for sure me. The narrative of "The Owl" was based partially on experience, not only of Santa Cruz, but also on mythic elements of the owl as in Macbeth, where the owl says, "Come sealing night, come scarf up the tender eye of pitiful day," etc. The owl is partially a symbol of death and also of mysterious forces. And there are sections in which the owl in fact kills. I see myself as like an owl, a predator if also wise like Athena. Every section of the poem has a metrical organization: the first is ottava rima, Sections 2 and 4 are iambic trimeter, 3 is iambic pentameter, and 5 is rhyme royale. First of all, this was a task I set for myself. As I met the demands of form, it enhanced inspiration. I believe the last section is one of the best formal poems I've ever written.

As for the end, "like the Owl, the shark/ of night and pick whatever is from the dark." It's the power of the predator, the same instinct human beings have and take delight in. There's also something philosopher about picking whatever is from the dark—because "whatever is" is that which has essence, which is important. Which is essentially good in philosophical terms. It's also the absolute determination to find that which has essence and being.

Q: Also, the owl is also exemplified in your sage-like traveling through "The Fun House" *(Bandaging Bread)* **and "August Fires"** *(August Fires)***. I wonder what your take would be on such a comment from a former student?**
A: Maybe the three seeds in "August Fires" is an example of picking whatever is from the dark. I'm also impressed by your linking of these two poems to the Owl poem.

Q: About half of the poems in *Separate Lives* **are in blank verse/iambic pentameter. What compels you to choose this, and which poems in the book do you think are most successful using it?**
A: I often write in blank verse because it is one of the great expressive forms in our language. Blank verse does not have the pressures of rhyme, but it has the subtle rhythm and music that appeals to me. Also it gives a certain amount of resistance during composition that I find fruitful, as the demands of the form force me to be creative and disciplined. And that fifth foot of each line prevents the meter from getting too regular. And above all pentameter feels more beautiful to me. "Cloud Train" is just about perfect as blank verse, as are "The Gamekeeper" and "Tai Chi."

Q: I am most engaged by poems here that come from experience. Talk about "Children in the Arbor." This seems to me to be a poem that issued from your many trips back to Fresno, but what else is also driving the poem?
A: Yes, this poem did issue from my frequent trips from San Diego to Fresno. More significant than the mere number of trips is what I am noticing: how the children move and live, the lives of people whose experience is different from mine. I imagine the lives of people who work in the fields, poor, hard-working people of Mexican heritage. The children I see seem free of the concerns of work or time, their ignorance of the hardships of their parents and the future marked by the voices of their mothers.

Q: And "The Hemorrhage" I am pretty sure comes right out of experience also. As I remember, you had a brain hemorrhage at the end of a Karate work out. How did you develop and resolve the poem based on that?
A: This poem comes out of the experience of getting a subarachnoid hemorrhage. I was sparring at the end of a Kung Fu class and got kicked in the back of my head. I wanted to write a poem re-creating the best I could the actual details of those days when I was in

intensive care: the pain, the environment. And then the last three lines are meant to reflect my survival and my awareness of the fragility of my bodily being.

Q: "There Are Photographs" ends the book and is a very evocative elegy for the Fresno poets we lost way too early in their lives. I also recall a photo I think Franny Levine has showing you and some other poets in your early years at Iowa. The imagery here qualifies a big portion of all of our lives, of those we have lost. Talk a bit about the Fresno Poets and your other poet colleagues over the years in terms of this poem.

A: The Fresno Poets had a common vision of excellence and because of this there was a camaraderie that we shared. We all had the same teacher (Phil) and the same experience of place that informed our work. In all my years in San Diego, I never became part of a similar community—competitiveness and different goals and a smaller circle of poets seemed to prevent that. Since the time of that poem, others from the Fresno round table have gone on: Peter Everwine, Jon Veinberg, and the most devastating loss for me personally: Philip Levine.

Q: In the title poem "Spring Drive", you write "So metrical accents beating like a heart/may replicate in someone else's breast". What might be your response be to a reader, such as myself, that has parallel thoughts regarding some poems in *Spring Drive?* For example, in your poem "A Navy Pilot's Wife" I find a reminder of Galway Kinnell's *Body Rags,* or in your poem "Burial Dream," an echo of William Stafford's "Traveling Through the Dark"?

A: That's really the purpose of the metrical line, to make a poem reverberate in someone else's consciousness. Although I love Galway Kinnell, I don't feel the connection with "Body Rags," (even though I admire the poem). "Traveling Through the Dark" is a favorite poem; in fact, at one time I had it memorized. So it may have exerted some influence on "Burial Dream." Especially the experience with a deer that triggers something deeper, in my poem a wounded personal relationship.

Q: *Spring Drive* is largely a book of elegies—for friends of your youth, mates from the Navy, a letter to your brother, even for your first car. Can you speak to the formation of the collection and focus on elegy?

A: I had reached an age where the losses had begun to accumulate and I was facing more losses—of youth, loved ones, and time itself. Elegies, being lyrical songs of mourning, fit the subject matter I wanted to express.

Q: Some poems reach further back, "My Pagan Name" for instance and "Summer Dream"—David St. John in his introduction to this book says, "Glover Davis has placed the question mark of mortality, inverted like a hook, hanging before our eyes." How does the distant past still inform your theme and vision here?

A: The pain of those experiences has indelibly impressed itself on my memory. So in a way, memory is a way of compromising mortality. Memory makes the distant past part of the present.

Q: "Burial Dream" is the final poem in the book. As often is the case, you work from a particular experience and have the concrete details reach emblematically upward to your theme. How does this poem especially resolve and conclude this book?

A: Emblematically, the last three lines of "Burial Dream" cover the whole book. Those are images of finality and life being eclipsed by natural forces, but the poet still maintains agency: "I would cover the old grievances…" So in the end the poet manages to make something living out of loss and death.

Q: In the title poem of *My Cap of Darkness*, there is a keen personal realization of the inner self, and of man's general demise that travels onto images of resurrection that are ongoing in your poetry. How do you maintain this theme in your writings?
A: It's an intrinsic part of my personality. There's a part of me that, in spite of everything, remains optimistic. And I've been lucky. After great loss, I have found great happiness.

Q: Clearly, a large part of the "Darkness" in this book is contained in the poems for your wife Sandy, whom you lost to cancer many years back now. How were you able to write these poems and handle such deep loss and emotion?
A: The way I've written all my poems—I've remembered, imagined, and exerted some control out of chaos through form. And by the time I wrote these poems about Sandy, at least the published versions, some time had passed since her death, which was not sudden. I've had a lot of loss in my life, beginning with my mother as a small child, and I've been able to develop strength in dealing with deep loss—a kind of stoicism that doesn't erase pain but that gives a sense of one's ability to survive it.

Q: You have a poem for the character Pollard, which I recall from your early poems and even days at Iowa. How is it that he comes back here all this time later?
A: Pollard is my version of Weldon Keys' Robinson, whom I imagine to be something like my father. I knew a guy named Pollard who was nothing like the guy I write about but whose name I liked. I invented him at the prompting of an assignment at Iowa by Donald Justice. Pollard reappears here all this time later as a symbol of the enduring presence of my father in my memory.

Q: A number of poems toward the end of the book—"Beneath the Mission Walls," "Fresno's Underground Gardens," "Earthquake, Mission San Miguel," and more issue from landscape. How are these working for you at this point in the book?
A: I'm coming back to places and landscapes very important to me as a Californian, part of the essence of who I am as a man in place and time.

Q: In the poem "Boulder Creek 1955," you give hope and success for mother-earth to "assert" herself to rectify man's plundering. 1955 was a fair time ago; tell us how this early awareness of such plight developed, and how you began to alert readers with this theme in your poems? What might we find next?
A: Boulder Creek is on the San Lorenzo River, and it used to be clear and beautiful still in 1955. I went back there a number of years later and saw what had been done to it. My experience with beloved landscapes over time saddened me always—and in my work culminated in *August Fires*. In my newest manuscript *Academy of Dreams: New and Selected Poems*, the most recent vivid expression of my concern with ecology is the poem "My Auto de Fe," which was recently published in *The Southern Review*. This poem encapsulates my anger at the ongoing crimes against nature.

Dennis Saleh

Dennis Saleh's books of poetry are *Palmway, 100 Chameleons, Z,* and *This is Not Surrealism* which won the first chapbook competition from Williamette River Books. He was co-editor of the poetry anthology, *Just What the Country Needs Another Poetry Anthology.* His poetry, prose and art work appear widely in such magazines as *ArtLife, Happy, In the Grove, Pacific Coast Journal, Pearl, Prairie Schooner, Psychological Perspectives,* and *Social Anarchism.*

from *Down At the Santa Fe Depot,* 1970—Dennis Saleh

I suppose I am something like an Anglo-Egyptian; my father's parents came to Fresno from Egypt, one Elia and one Saleh, and my mother's maiden name was McKoy. My father was born in Fresno, left for some years, and returned to go into business as a painting contractor in 1948. I was born in Chicago in 1942 and raised in Fresno from 1948 on.

I attended Fresno State College, the University of Arizona, and the University of California, Irvine, where I received a Master of Fine Arts Degree in Creative Writing. I taught one year at U.C. Riverside and am teaching now at U.C. Santa Cruz. The most interesting job I ever had was working for Mid-Tower Publishers in Fresno, when their *Sex Life of a Cop* was in flower, and when Fresno was called by at least one Crusader "the smut capital of the world."

One of the few things I have to say about poetry is to acknowledge the great debt I owe to Philip Levine. He helped me not take my writing seriously when that was important, and when the time came, was the first to suggest I ought to take it seriously.

from *How Much Earth,* 2001—Dennis Saleh

To remember one's childhood from the remove of fifty and more years, is as much imagination as memory. Let alone the effort of recollection, usually, what is most real is what is gone. I have essentially no memory of Chicago, where I was born, and the traces of arriving in Fresno at the age of six are wisps, a best. And that's what Fresno was, my childhood.

Cloud masses in brilliant sun, piling impossibly ever higher. Fresh-cut lawn steeping wet, seven-thirty in the morning. Fall afternoons dimming with burning leaves. January scraped near-bare of color. Then school, friends, romances—precious details now, that are fragile, like antiques. One takes care with the past, lest it go away entirely.

Like the stars, most gone of all. Lying on my back, nights were so thick with stars, they tinted the sky like blue, glowing coral. Stare up long enough and you felt you could fall up into them. Of course, they were real, but now, as the atmosphere thickens like a sadness, they seem almost imaginary, a lace. Now, the stars are more like embers.

"Fresno," Spanish for "ash tree." The kind of splendid compression possible in a single word. A kind of simultaneity, different times at once. Conciseness pronouncing a fate. Or, a phoenix of imagination rising in a bed of memories. The eyes cast up. Stop-frame. In childhood, time doesn't really exist. It's for later.

Poetry Fresno: A Precis," 2020—Dennis Saleh

I first began taking poetry writing classes with Phil Levine, in the early 1960s, at Fresno State College, in bucolic Fresno, California, where anything that grew could probably grow. My wife, Michele's, Father, C. B. Johnson, had a large crop-dusting business those days, and I would hear such talk. And—news alert—that Francis Gary Powers, famed pilot of the U2 shot down by Russia during the Cold War, had been to see C. B. about a job. Pretty heady stuff, but I was sitting in classrooms.

Gene Zumwalt, English prof and later department chairman, a good friend, was my comp prof and faculty advisor, and took me down the hall to meet Phil, who was the go-to-guy for writing then. What Phil taught was how hard to be on yourself; if you could take his roughing up, why, you might be able to take anything, even from yourself, which, of course, was the real lesson and instruction: Can you be your own best—most demanding, editor/critic.

"Fresno Poets" were inklings, sprouts, then, maybe a couple dozen people, meeting furtively with scribbled sheets of paper, talking over the latest last-man-standing session in one of Phil Levine's classes. We were all writing juvenilia, things we would rather forget than remember, with journeyman's practice.

One particular time, Phil broke down his discussion of a student poem, concluding, what he liked best about the piece, was the word, "the," and he pointed out in which line. But because he was usually very funny about usually anything, it was difficult to misunderstand his good will. and thoroughgoing warmth. No matter what he might say, there was never any mistaking his correct intention.

Those days, Fresno State did not have a literary magazine, unlike many of the CSUs and UCs. I knew this, because a close friend, Jim Merzon, had been corresponding with student editors and writers around the state. What? In Fresno's loamy soil nothing sprung eternal? How could it be? Determinedly, Jim fired off salvo after salvo of inspired entreaties about a literary magazine for Fresno State.

Letters rounding up support, endorsements, all manner of schemes and connivings, presentations to the college administration, pitches for funds. He sent inquiries re costs, and found a printer in Ireland who sent sample copies of his presswork, very early copies of Robert Bly's seminal poetry magazine, *The Fifties*. . . .

A new prof, Peter Everwine, had come to Fresno State, accomplished musician, folk singer, and guitarist, and good friend of Phil Levine's. A member of the English Department, he volunteered a concert. with admission fee, to raise money for the magazine, soon monikered, *Backwash*. One bright sunny noon, Scotty Wilson, Dean of Students, was seen at a student events booth angrily tearing down a large banner for the event: *Great Big Folking Song Concert*.

Student newspaper stories and articles, more posters, mimeos, word of mouth frothing. The first editor of *Backwash* was Ollie Simpson, a poet, and Phil Levine's occasional baby sitter, in time married to Robert Mezey, also hired by Fresno State to join the English Department. The second editor was Jim Merzon; I beat the drum of publicity for *Backwash*. Sandy Avakian, a high school classmate of ours who worked in the English Department, provided the cover artwork for the first two issues of *Backwash*, and with time, married Glover Davis.

A bit before noon on the debut day for *Backwash*, on the second floor of the Business Building, home of the English Department, a toothsome young co-ed in a bikini bathing suit, Jeannie Allard, climbed out a window onto a ledge walkway, screaming and running, pursued by an enormous gorilla, to a second window she disappeared into, followed by the gorilla.

All manner of nuisance ensued. Glover Davis and I rode our motorcycles through classroom hallways. The gorilla and the girl came and went, now and again, unpredictably. And at the student activities booth, several other locations, and the English Department, stacks of *Backwash* stood ready for purchase.

Backwash continued for decades. Nationally known poets and writers contributed to its pages: W. S. Merwin, John Haines, Charles Simic, Galway Kinnell. 1970: publication of the first "Fresno" poetry volume: *Down at the Santa Fe Depot* (David Kherdian, James Baloian, eds. Giligia Press). Twenty poets, many deceased. Over the years, many subsequent Fresno books and collections have appeared.

Phil's students began to be known as "Levine's Legions" as the number of them increased, traveling far and wide as graduate students in writing programs, and into eventual teaching positions in colleges and universities. Many became editors of journals and magazines themselves. Numbers of books of poetry by students of Philip Levine are always increasing, and multiplying.

My own peripatetic path was an eventual parallel. I left Fresno State with a BA Degree in Psychology, and entered a PhD program at the University of Arizona, on a Clinical Traineeship from the National Institute of Mental Health. In Tucson, though, came the light. I heard of a new writing program starting at UC Irvine, and returned to California newly invigorated.

At Irvine I did well, receiving an MFA Degree in Creative Writing. A prof there, Jim McMichael, invited me to co-edit with him an anthology of contemporary American poetry: *Just What the Country Needs, Another Poetry Anthology* (Wadsworth, 1970), my first book publication. My second Fall at Irvine, in The Writing Center were more of Levine's Legions: Jimmy Baloian, Bob Jones, Syd Bowie, and DeWayne Rail.

With my new degree, I began teaching as a university lecturer. Over a decade, I had positions at two UCs, Riverside and Santa Cruz, and two CSUs, San Diego and Fresno; at both UCs, I also ran poetry reading series. I published several books of poetry, and at length, my wife, Michele, and I began our own press, Comma Books.

I've done two books in co-imprint arrangements: *Rock Art: The Golden Age of Record Album Covers* (Comma Books/Ballantine, 1977), and *Science Fiction Gold: Film Classics of the 50s* (Comma Books/McGraw Hill, 1979). I've also written a novel, unpublished to date, *Pomegranate,* about Oscar Wilde's 1882 lecture tour of America.

Through UC Extension, I offered the first two classes on "The Fresno Poets," featuring evenings with a half-dozen or more writers, reading and discussing their work. Tape recordings I made of the series might perhaps some day be thought historic. The first evening setting up, I had a phone call.

William Saroyan was on the line. He knew about the class, and wanted to wish all every success. We had a wonderful conversation. Whether he recalled or not, he pretended to understand what I meant by the two brothers in one of his early short stories, my Father, Bill, and Uncle Eddie, who'd grown up on the same downtown Fresno playgrounds as Saroyan.

Remembering this was the 60s, the story slides sideways into a kaleidoscope, a fish-eye photo-lens, swirls, a mosaic, names tumbling turn into scores of them, stacks of books sway higher, decades dance, people even begin dying, ultimately. Poetry contests and prizes named for the departed. Ghastly unendingness. But the shards, the anecdotes, divine.

Larry Levis does a crack-up imitation of Mick Jagger singing "Time Is on My Side," into a bottle-opener microphone. This is the night before a party of us see The Rolling Stones, in Radcliffe Stadium! at 11:30 in the morning; there may have been white crosstops involved. Walking down the block from Bruce Boston's house to the liquor store, he in his Sgt Pepper's finery, a long, orange-and-purple velvet overcoat made by his seamstress wife, Marsha.

At countless gatherings and parties, how many times in a row could we stand to hear The Rolling Stones' "Connection." Marsha's historical Thanksgiving dinners, featuring her turkey of just repute. Galway Kinnell, called a king of one-night-stands, is talking to Marsha about going off to Bob Mezey's place up in the hills; Bruce, standing there, asks, "Can I come, too? I'm her husband."

In Laguna Beach, where many of The Writing Center students live, a large party is underway, feting the success of the evening's program, a reading by litree lion, Robert Bly. Bly is still wearing his ceremonial serape. standing near a fireplace hearth, vamping a coed, arm extended with a glass, when the drink slips from his fingers dropping to the brick floor shattering. Bly stands startled, his arm still out in the air, staring to the floor at the co-ed's feet.

In the decades from 1960 to 2020, such tales and episodes abound, more than could be recounted in a library of volumes. Some stories become legendary, others only whispers, that may not be repeated by any means, neither written down on paper, nor threaded into electricity, to protect the innocent. Only the future will remember, and it is mute, choked with details, unraveling.

A signed-slipcase limited-edition volume of poetry by William Carlos Williams, enscribed by Bob Mezey to Michele and me for our wedding, with a note, "for an ounce of the finest come harvest time." Glover and friend, Milton Savage, traveling up from San Diego for the event. Phil's wife, Franny, gives me a special hair "do" for the ceremony, a "razorcut."

Santana Blues Band travels down from San Francisco to play a free concert on behalf of Bob Mezey, ensnarled in controversy over his pro-marijuana, anti-Viet Nam War views. Allen Ginsburg also comes to Fresno and gives a poetry reading, in support of Bob. Ron Turner's Last Gasp Comics releases a "Fresno" boardgame.

Following a grand *soiree* at Gary Young's in Bonny Doon, outside Santa Cruz, Jon Vineburg and I are at a Jack in the Box. I'm driving and insist Jon check for french fries, which he thinks funny, then hilarious, when he finds there aren't any.

Late in the evening, I'm sitting with Chuck Hanzlicek, and his wife, Diane, in their home in Fresno. I'm pursuing nuances of rock and roll music, and ask Chuck how good a guitar player is Waylon Jennings. Chuck replies, measuredly, "Well, Waylon Jennings doesn't play guitar. He strums it." *Touche.*

Roberta Spear and her husband, Jeff Shelby, live across the street from us a couple of years; Jeff likes to visit. and after two or three calls, Michele is able to confirm Jeff is drinking our kids' cough syrup. The bad lad became a fine, upstanding MD, though, to be sure.

One early summer evening, Omar Salinas and Gary Soto appear at our door unannounced, to sit in the backyard for a standard, rich-and-pointless Fresno poetry sunset conversation. When they go, the light in the dimming sky is mauve, almost like a sigh. But after all, what is not like a sigh. After a while, at some point, it is all simultaneity, and Fresno's massive, piling, climbing, white cloudheads.

DeWayne Rail

DeWayne Rail was born in 1944, in Round Prairie, Oklahoma, but he entered the world of poetry at Fresno State College in the late 60s in classes taught by Peter Everwine and Phillip Levine, two men who seem larger than life to him even now. DeWayne's work has appeared in a number of magazines and journals, among them *Antioch Review, Western Humanities Review, Poetry Now, Poetry Northwest, Cortland Review,* and in several anthologies. His two longer chapbooks are *Going Home Again, published* by Walter Hamady's Perishable Press in 1971, and *The Water Witch,* published by Blue Moon Press, 1988, in their Valley Chapbook Series. He now lives in Austin, Texas, with his wife, Tori, and has lately come back to poetry, after some time away. He has recently published another chapbook, *The Book of Days,* Panther Creek Press, 2019. He is currently working on revising old poems, writing new poems, and preparing another small chapbook.

"Interview with DeWayne Rail," *Cortland Review,* **March 1999, by Muffy Bolding**

Muffy Bolding: What is the first thing you notice about a poem when you read it? And, are you of the mind that poems need to be heard as well as seen?
DeWayne Rail: Actually, the first thing I notice is the way it looks on the page. Some poems are ugly on the page, and I have a hard time even reading them. But, yeah, I have to hear a poem read aloud before I can really understand it. I really need to hear myself read it, if that doesn't sound too weird. Perhaps that's why I read so many poems aloud to my students. I like to run my voice over the syllables, you know, and hear myself say the lines a few different ways before I can grasp what's in there.

MB: When did you first start writing poetry, and why? Was it the whole "to impress chicks" thing, as Charles Simic so unashamedly and refreshingly admits was his primary motivation—or was your reasoning purer and more vestal than that? (although I find myself quite hard-pressed to find a reason purer than THAT...)
DR: I started writing stuff at a very young age. My father and grandfather were both great story-tellers, and I think I began writing poems as a way of fitting myself into that tradition, of being like them. In high school I wrote poems to amuse my friends, but even there I was aware of my debt to the stories I had heard at home. None of the stuff was very good, but the impulse was there. It doesn't seem as if there was a definite time at which I started to write poems.

MB: While an undergrad at Cal State, Fresno in the late 1960's, you studied under the poetic instruction of Philip Levine . . . as well as alongside several classmates who would eventually go on to carve out extraordinarily successful careers as poets, including Larry Levis. I adore the story you tell about how Levine—when finally fed up with a class that was not enthusiastically participating in the day's discussion—would saunter to his desk, take an apple out of the drawer, and in

retaliation, proceed to sit and loudly and purposefully crunch on it to fill the resounding silence. Besides "The Phil Levine/Granny Smith Showdown," what was he like as a teacher, and did his writing and teaching methods in any way influence your own?

DR: Actually, Levine produced the apples from somewhere deep in the pockets of his jacket. Suddenly he would just reach in his pocket and pull out an apple and then eat it. It was the most marvelous act. He ate it with such aplomb and self-possession, with such elaborate relish. The most accurate thing I can say about Levine is that he was more of an electrical phenomenon than anything else. When he came in the room, it was as if someone had turned on a powerful current, and the air would just about hum. He was very directive in his teaching. He said what he meant and he pulled no punches. What more could you ask? Some people couldn't take it, I guess, but those of us who could loved it. I can remember going to the coffee shop with Bob Jones, Chuck Moulton, Jimmy Baloian, and Larry Levis after class. We would sit there and repeat the things Levine had said, you know, trying to imitate him, and laughing ourselves sick over the incredible wit of the man.

I could never sleep after one of his classes. I would lie in bed, and my arms and legs would literally just twitch as the electricity ebbed away. His writing and teaching both influenced me a lot. I loved his poems, but I didn't want to sound like him at all. It was a different voice, you know, Detroit, not me at all. But in teaching, I did want to be like him. After a few years, though, I realized I just couldn't pull it off. You can't be a Levine imitator with an Oklahoma accent. The vowels are just too slow. What I did keep from him was the refusal to lie. And I think I learned a wonderful eclecticism from him. He was very good about appreciating different voices and different approaches to poetry, within the limits of good sense, of course.

MB: Who are your favorite poets to read? To teach? Who are your influences?
DR: My favorite poets to read right now are Ted Kooser, Billy Collins, and Stephen Dobyns, and those are the poets I like to teach. My influences—the early ones, the ones that matter—were Frost and Roethke. And maybe almost equally Stafford and Larkin, if that isn't too strange a brew.

MB: Has the "perfect" poem been written yet?
DR: Yes. Evidently, several have been written. I say this because a few years ago I was told that I had written a perfect poem by the editor of a very prestigious journal, but he said the last line of the poem needed to be changed. I changed it, and he said it was even more perfect, but he was tired of publishing single perfect poems in his journal. He said he liked to publish a group of at least 4 or 5 perfect ones by any given writer, and that I should study his publication to see what he meant. So, hell yes, perfect poems are pretty common, or at least they were at one time.

MB: Many of your poems are earthy and rural, and frequently invoke your father and the world of the Oklahoma Dustbowl that he inhabited . . . in what ways did he and that world influence your work and your poetic (and perhaps life) outlook?
DR: Well, I don't think we ever get away from the images and symbols of the first few years of our lives. Gaston Bachelard has that wonderful book, "The Poetics of Space," where he writes about houses as a kind of matrix out of which your imagination develops. I think this is especially true of people who are sensitive and artistic. For example, I've

lived in California so many years now, but I still consider the weather, first of all, in terms of what it might do to or for the crops in Oklahoma. There's a limitation in this, sure, but there's strength in it, too. It centers you. You know who you are. So that world, and my father, are present in every moment of my life. Sometimes I just laugh out loud when I hear my father's rhythms and phrasing in my own voice. Lately—it may be a function of aging—I find myself using the vocabulary and dialect I grew up with. This is comical to my wife and children, and we all laugh over it, but, truth to tell, I think it has been a strength in my poems.

MB: You have been teaching poetry for nearly 30 years. Given that hindsight and experience, in what ways have poetry students changed in that span, and is their approach to the study and writing of poetry different than when you began? If so, how have you had to adjust the methods you use to teach them?
DR: I don't think the good students have changed much. It's odd, though. The enrollment at the community college where I teach has doubled, at least, in the 29 years I have been here, but the number of students who respond and catch fire has pretty much remained the same. The average student has changed tremendously in that time period. They dislike reading more, are less willing to be interested in things outside the entertainment culture. And they have been encouraged in their insularity by the popular culture itself, so much so that they take pride in it. So, I haven't changed my methods all that much. I've become kinder, I think.

MB: What do you think of the value of the poetry workshop setting . . . in regards to both the beginning and the advanced writer?
DR: I think poetry workshops are wonderful and necessary for the development of poets. Where else are they going to learn? There is so much artificial wisdom around, you know, poets who have had the advantage of years of workshops suddenly deciding that the poet must learn directly from life. Well, life goes on all the time, even if you are also taking a poetry workshop. And, of course, bad workshops and bad teachers are everywhere, but you have to have the sense to get away from those and find good ones.

MB: Do you have a favorite poetic form to read? To write? To teach?
DR: I don't have a favorite poetic form to read, but I have had tremendous luck teaching the sestina. It's a mystery to me why it works, but it does. Every semester the students complain like hell, and then they turn in some wonderful stuff. Most of us have only one good sestina in us, however. I have never written one.

MB: If you weren't a poet and a teacher of poetry, what instead would you choose to do with your life?
DR: Lord, there are so many attractive possibilities. I love visual art so much I would probably choose to be an art dealer. I can't draw or paint, so that's out. You name it, I've wanted to be it at one time or another.

MB: You tell of a poet, of some time ago, who used to perpetually maintain a bowl of over-ripened apples; the poet would then set these on his desk before him as he sat down to write . . . for it was solely that specific aroma—sweet and funereal— which somehow inspired him to compose his best work. Do you have any rituals that you employ when sitting down to write a poem?

DR: I think that was Schiller. As I remember it, he would leave an apple in his desk, so that it would rot and give off that sweet odor when he sat down to write. I've always loved that story. Yes, I'm as ritualistic as they come. For one thing, I have to write poems by hand and in a bold, dark ink. Flair pens are wonderful, but they can't have a fine point. I have to have a certain kind of notebook, or the poems just don't look right. I really need coffee nearby, and in a nice cup. You can't write beautiful poems while drinking from an ugly cup. I used to smoke, and damn, I hated giving that up. Well, this could get boring, but rituals should be taught in workshops.

MB: In your class, you also tell a marvelous story about a former student being inspired to write a most extraordinary poem after noticing a small freckle on his hand one day—pondering its creation and its impact on the future. What is the most seemingly insignificant thing that has ever compelled you to write a poem?
DR: Years ago, I was driving home from work one day when I saw a crow in the middle of the road. He seemed to be guarding a small puddle of water. Since he wouldn't move, I stopped. He squawked at me and wouldn't budge. I watched him awhile, and we had what amounted to a conversation, though neither of us spoke the other's language. Then I backed up the car and went around him and drove on home. Right after that I wrote a poem called *The Field of Crows*, and, as a matter of fact, crows find their way into my poems pretty regularly.

MB: To whom do you show your work before sending it out, if anyone?
DR: Right now I don't show poems to anyone while they are in draft. When the poet Don Jones lived in Fresno, we used to meet and show each other our poems once a week. He was a very good critic. He moved, and for a time I met with Ernesto Trejo very regularly to trade poems. He was so enthusiastic and encouraging that it gave me a real boost.

MB: Many of your more recent poems make mention of aging, and the passage of time. What, poetically speaking, do your eyes see different now that they did not, say, 30 years ago?
DR: The passage of time, yes. I'm acutely aware of that now. I'm more aware of the comedy of it all, I think, and of the terror of the situation, to borrow a phrase from Gurdjieff. Poetically speaking, I see the paired opposites of most situations very quickly, so that I am always aware of having a kind of double-vision. For example, I see the beauty and the absurdity of a human trying to maintain some kind of dignity in a difficult situation. Seeing things this way makes me laugh a lot, sometimes in situations where it doesn't seem appropriate, but it is really only a manifestation of my appreciation. I have that same double-vision about this interview, for example. Why should anyone care? And yet . . .

MB: How do you view the onset and emergence of online publishing in poetry?
DR: I'm excited by the possibilities of online publishing. I just love the radical egalitarianism of it all. Can you imagine what a boost online publishing would have been for the poets of the past? Shakespeare? The French Surrealists? John Keats? And why not for us? Doesn't that make the poles of your psyche wobble, just to think about it?

MB: In what direction do you see poetry moving in the future?
DR: I have no idea, no clue. I think it is as unpredictable as the stock market, or, more

likely, as unpredictable as genius. Search the prophecies of Nostradamus or the Book of Revelations. I think that even as we speak the Great Poet is among us, ready to lead us in a direction that seems wrong to us in our blindness.

MB: What are your thoughts on the criticism that conventional poetry has lost its "edge," and has degenerated into either a refuge for frozen, rote, threatened academics . . . or a venue pandering mainly to literary self-interest groups (i.e. feminism, culturalism, victimism, etc.)? What "isms" can you suggest that might give American poetry a good, swift, much-needed kick in the ass?
DR: Well, things are always degenerating, and, at the same time, something new is arriving. The "isms" are pretty boring whether you encounter them in ersatz poetry, in politics, or in conversation. But there is so much good stuff being published right now. Or am I being misled by the three or four books I am reading? What scares me is not the state of our poetry, of our art, but the state of our popular culture.

MB: If you could have a dinner and salon with any five poets or writers—from now or in the past—who would you choose, and what would you eat?
DR: This is difficult, but: Kit Marlowe, Rabelais, Baudelaire, James Joyce, and John Keats. Wouldn't the words and images just fly? I just wouldn't say anything at all, and John Keats would probably be pretty shy. But think of Joyce and Rabelais, their enormous heads filled to capacity, and witty Marlowe, who would at last get credit for having written the Shakespeare plays, and the acid tongue of Baudelaire. They would probably wind up killing each other eventually, but until they did it would be grand. And home cooking—they would love the food.

MB: Who and what are you reading right now?
DR: I am reading *Questions About Angels*, by Billy Collins, a book about London in the time of Chaucer, a book about the savings and loan rip-off of a few years ago, an historical mystery novel by Iain Pears, and *The Conspiracy Reader*, by the editors of *Paranoia Magazine*. All good stuff. I read several books at the same time, and I read a lot at night, so the books I am reading change rather rapidly. I'm having a storage problem. I can't stand to get rid of books.

MB: Besides the possibly portentous word "exile," do you have any other favorites in the English language?
DR: I'm a cheap drunk with words. I remember getting high on the word "the" when I was about three. I would say the word over and over to myself, and suddenly I would sort of disassociate, you know. My head would feel enormous, and I would get dizzy. In one of his letters, Dylan Thomas asks a friend if he doesn't think "aerodrome" is the most beautiful word in the English language. Not a bad choice. Lately I've become enamored of "tolling." Isn't that just a beauty?

MB: Your son, Evan, is quite successfully making his own name as a poet. Do you think your life and your work have influenced him at all—in much the same way, perhaps, that your own father influenced you?
DR: Well, I certainly hope I have influenced him. Not to (after raising him) would be odd, to say the least. Yeah, I can see the influence in his language, and, in fact, in the language of all four of my children. My two girls will call me up from, say, New York or

Los Angeles, or my youngest boy will be talking, and sometimes they will say something in that metaphorical backwoods way. It's comical, really, because they are both aware of what they are doing and unable to say it any other way. It's a good thing. I think Evan sees it as a positive thing in his own poems. The kids influence me, too. They are always passing on things to read, for example. They discover the good writers for me now, and the girls, especially, are always trying to make me less backwards, more couth.

MB: To make mention of the use of poetry as a way to liberate and exalt our own humanity (and strictly as a display of brazen pretentiousness), I shall now proceed to invoke Kafka, who once said, "Art should serve as the axe for the frozen sea within us." Do you agree with this statement?
DR: Well, now I want to ask Kafka to come to dinner. That's a wonderful, stunning statement. It spoils the pithiness of it, but I want to add "and the frozen sea around us." I do think art leads us to better places and to better versions of our unfinished selves. I have always said that my discovery of poetry in college saved my life. People always misunderstand and think that I was depressive and on the verge of suicide. I was never depressive, and suicide was never attractive to me. But I was lost in our culture, you know. The commercial gaudiness of it, the religious fanaticism, the self-righteous arrogance of people, the stunning self-centeredness of everyone—it was all killing me. It's corny to say, maybe, but poetry changed my life.

"Tuesday Nights, 7-10 pm"—DeWayne Rail

Like many students, I kind of wandered into the poetry world. After moving back and forth between Oklahoma and California a number of times, my family stayed in Fresno, where I graduated from high school and started at Fresno State, as it was called then. I majored in almost everything, changing from one to another like changing shoes, vaguely unhappy with every one, but finally I just admitted all I really wanted to do was be an English major. All those years of reading just shouldn't go to waste, I thought.

And I had a sneaking desire to write. So when a friend told me about a fantastic poetry writing course he was a taking I was captivated. I asked around about that fabulous teacher he was always talking about, but when I went to sign up for beginning poetry writing, he was on sabbatical, and his classes were being taught by Dr. Peter Everwine, about whom I knew nothing. Turned out he was wonderful. He had been through the poetry writing program at Iowa, the same as Philip Levine, and they were friends it seemed.

Pete Everwine's classes were a great introduction to the world of poetry for me. He was calm and laid-back and always seemed to me to be constantly amused about something. He was pretty non-directive and would let us all talk and make declarations, before he eventually stepped in and made a few calm suggestions about whatever poem we were discussing. This was good for me, a good grounding and preparation for future classes. Pete would gently name certain poets he thought were interesting. It was he who suggested I read Ted Kooser and William Stafford, two poets who are among my very favorites to this day.

The following year—1966 or 1967, I think—Philip Levine returned from a sabbatical year, and I began to take classes from him. He was very different in his approach to teaching. He was anything but calm and gave the impression of being charged with some sort of latent energy that might burst forth at any time. He was electrical. He was brilliant—there is no other word for it—and incredibly well read. In fact, I don't think I have ever met anyone else who had read as much poetry as he had.

I loved his classes. In our first class, he talked at length about his approach to poetry and to teaching poetry writing. My takeaway was that he had made a deal with himself long ago not to lie to students about what he thought, not to soft-pedal his criticism. He said we had to accept that and that if we couldn't take it, we probably ought to drop. He was incredibly funny, as many people have noted. I thought at the time that he had missed an opportunity to be a great stand-up comedian. He asked us to turn in a poem for the next class meeting a week away. I did, holding my breath with dread and anticipation.

The second week he brought dittoed copies of all the poems turned in, as well as the poems themselves, commented on and marked up. The classroom fell deathly quiet when he walked in, as it continued to do every meeting. He had a large manila envelope containing all our poems. He opened the envelope, peered inside, then brought it up to his nose to sniff. He made a face and turned away, as he dumped them out on the table, claiming that he thought something, or maybe several things, had died in there. All of us grinned and chuckled a bit self-consciously, knowing that it was probably our own poem giving off the foul odor.

Class consisted of Phil reading from the copied poems and inviting our thoughts. The poems were copied without our names on them, so that in our discussion we wouldn't be pandering to anyone. After we had talked for a while, Phil would give his take, which always took longer than we did, with our sometimes tentative comments. He was eclectic, capable of appreciating all manner of approaches to poetry. He seemd to try to enter into the poem completely. He would comment, make suggestions, name poets we should be reading, and so on. He gave each poem his full attention, whether he liked it or not. I don't think I ever disagreed with his analysis of a poem.

Honestly, I don't know how I would have reacted if he had not liked and praised the very first poem I turned in. But he did like it, and I knew I would stay. Levine had the uncanny knack of reading our poems and guessing who we had been reading that week. After he read my poem that week, he seemed to think for a minute. Then he said, "Oh, I see you've been reading Karl Shapiro. Good!" I still don't know how he knew that. I had been reading Shapiro! It was his ear for language, I think. He was like a musician with perfect pitch. He could hear echoes and influences in a way that seemed like magic. He did that several times that year, always right on the money. He didn't like every poem I turned in, of course, but after that first night I decided I could take whatever criticism he threw my way.

He could be rough, but even if he was being rough on one of my poems I always thought he was right. In addition, he was just terribly funny, and I would have stayed just to listen to him riff. He once said about a poem that the poet had used the words "and" and "the" beautifully and appropriately, but that the rest of the poem lacked something. He suggested that a new poem be written, saving those words and building on them. This poem had great comma placement he would say, before telling us what he thought was wrong with it. Another poem had a great title, followed by a terrible poem. He suggested the poet scrap the poem, save the title, and write a new poem the title deserved. One poem had a line so sentimental he defended it, saying he was quite sure no one in our class could write a line that bad and that the poet's mother had suggested the line to her darling little boy, saying she was sure Levine would like it. He sat back and studied each of us in turn. "But Levine doesn't like it," he said, and turned to the next poem.

It's true that after that first class about half the students dropped, but the six or seven students remaining became disciples. We were committed. We thought Levine was great and could hardly wait until the next Tuesday evening when, if we were lucky, he might praise one of our poems. Actually, he didn't have to like the whole poem. Praise for one line, one phrase, or one image was enough to get us high and energized for a whole week.

Part of the luck of being in Levine's poetry writing classes was meeting the other students. I had really good luck. I was in the class with Robert Jones, Larry Levis, Jimmy Baloian, Chuck Moulton, and Bonnie Ritchie (Hill). These were wonderful poets and people. As often as not, we would go to the coffee shop on campus when the class ended. Levine was never one to end a class early, so that meant we went at about ten o'clock. We were always as high as kites, going over the comments, laughing uproariously at the least thing, until we all settled down enough to go home and sleep. I usually couldn't sleep at all after class I was so charged with a strange energy that didn't seem to wear off for two or three days.

Later I met and made friends with some of the great students who had gone before me and came after me. Bill Childress, Herb Scott, Dennis Saleh, and Glover Davis come to mind of those who had gone on to the Iowa poetry program. The later ones included Bruce Boston, Sam Periera, Ernesto Trejo, Roberta Spear, and Jon Veinberg. Years later my own good students went into the program from my classes at Fresno City College. I remember Dixie Salazar and Robert Vasquez especially. (There are others in each group, but my memory isn't what it used to be.) Some became friends, many were friendly acquaintances, but all of them inspired me.

I went on to the writing program at University of California at Irvine. I had many fine teachers there as well, including Charles Wright and Galway Kinnell. I returned to Fresno to teach at Fresno City College, where I started and developed a really extensive writing program in both poetry and fiction. Those were good years too.

Today I live in Austin, Texas, that blue city in a red state, with my wife, Tori. We try our best to stay sane in this insane world. Poetry helps. I'm getting back into it, after a time away. I'm remembering how poetry once seemed to bring everything into focus. I hope it can do that again.

Philip Levine and Sam Pereira in Levine's front yard in 1990.

Sam Pereira

Sam Pereira attended California State University, where he received his B.A. in 1971. He continued through the following year, earning his Standard Teaching Credential in Secondary Education. From there, he was accepted into the well-known and respected University of Iowa Writers' Workshop, where he was granted his M.F.A degree in 1975. Mr. Pereira has published six books of poetry, thus far, which include: *The Marriage of the Portuguese* (L'Epervier Press, 1978), *Brittle Water* (Penumbra Press/ Abattoir Editions, University of Nebraska at Omaha, 1987), *A Café in Boca* (Tebot Bach, 2007), *Dusting on Sunday* (Tebot Bach, 2012), *The Marriage of the Portuguese—Expanded Edition* (Tagus Press, University of Massachusetts, 2012), and *Bad Angels* (Nine Mile Press, 2015). He recently retired from teaching, and currently lives in the San Joaquin Valley of California, along with his wife, Susan.

"A Fantastic American Swagger: Interview with Sam Pereira"—Millicent Bórges Accardi, *Poetsquarterly.com*, 2015

Darkness remains mysterious. Light is wonderful, but you only get there through darkness first. It is the very nature of why I write.

Unassuming and often under the radar, the poetry of Sam Pereira has been hailed as "part John Berryman and part Richard Hugo, part Hemingway and part film director David Lynch," but Pereira has yet to achieve the accolades his talent warrants. At the famous Iowa Writers' Workshop, Pereira's classmates included Larry Levis, Marcia Southwick, Angela Ball, and David St John, who praises Pereira's work as having "a fantastic American swagger."

Pereira's first poetry book, *The Marriage of the Portuguese*, was republished three decades later and is still as topical as it was in the 1970's, an ode to life's uncertainties, "This is the work of someone fully experiencing what it means to be human in a society that continually threatens that humanity" yet true to his Portuguese heritage.

Today, Pereira lives with his wife and fellow writer Susan R. G. Pereira, in a rural community in the San Joaquin Valley of California, where he works as an English teacher in the public school system. His books of poetry include *The Marriage of the Portuguese, Brittle Water, A Cafe in Boca* and his latest *Bad Angels*. Individual poems have appeared in several anthologies: *Piecework: 19 Fresno Poets, The Body Electric*, and *How Much Earth: The Fresno Poets* as well as in *Alaska Quarterly Review, The American Poetry Review, Antioch Review*, and *Poetry* (magazine). He is married to fellow writer Susan R. G. Pereira.

Pereira received a Bachelor of Arts degree from California State University, Fresno (CSUF) and a Master of Fine Arts degree from the University of Iowa, where he was part of the legendary Iowa Writers' Workshop. Literary influences include poets Philip Levine, Richard Hugo, Mark Strand, and Norman Dubie.

Millicent Borges Accardi: How does your latest collection _Bad Angels_ differ from previous books?
Sam Pereira: In _Bad Angels_, there is a prevailing need to focus on a particular period—both chronologically, as well as emotionally. The period is one of expectations, some met, others only imagined. It is also a re-invention of my days as a graduate student in Iowa.

More importantly, though, it deals with a return to a time I played badly in most cases, a time that today, due to a late-blooming maturity I suppose, I can relatively skate through unscathed.

MBA: What is the significance of the title?
SP: I was raised Catholic, and grew up in a largely Catholic community of Portuguese and Italian families. While that has changed somewhat over the years, it encompasses the foundation of things for me, a foundation that I have worked very hard to sculpt more to my needs as I have grown older.

Bad Angels refers to, in my mind, the segment of the mythology that has always drawn people like myself toward its doorway. Darkness remains mysterious. Light is wonderful, but you only get there through darkness first. It is the very nature of why I write.

MBA: If you had to select one poem to share with our readers from _Bad Angels_, which one would it be?
SP: Absolutely, and thank you for asking. "A Modern Romance" I think distributes many of the things I have been working with over the years, and continue to hold dear even now. It is a poem that taps into human needs and desires, but also includes that need for genealogy we all seem to desire, either publically or privately. While it is not one of those chronological pieces I mentioned earlier, it is a marker, I suspect, on whatever this road I've attached myself to takes me.

A Modern Romance

Sometimes, there is just sadness
Everywhere a person looks.
This morning, it was
The drum of the washing machine,
Gyrating in some kind of dance
Designed to end with her bra, tied
Around the leg of a pair of pants.
Ultimately, sadness, even though
The percussion said otherwise.
This morning, that old briar
Allows him to think about being
Related to an otherwise forgettable
Portuguese man and wife,
Who managed together, in simplicity,
The joining of earth to sea.
Truly, the perfect sadness;
That absolute kiss of soil and cod.
They looked past each other, and
Marveled at the magic of their darkness.

It had become expected,
In the years since Pessoa roamed
The exact same streets, talking
To himself; talking to darkness, which
Was only in its childhood back then.

MBA: How has being Portuguese shaped you as a writer?

SP: Funny thing, that. For a number of years I tried to detach myself from a particular lineage, and yet I found it presenting itself here and there along the way. It obviously wanted to be included. So I stopped fighting it. Much of the basic grounding in whatever Sam Pereira has become is due largely to certain classic old world beliefs. Being Portuguese, like being a part of essentially any nurturing culture, provided me with a certain system of laws on how to be a man, how to live a life. Sometimes I broke those laws, which often led to poetry.

MBA: What poets do you teach in your classes?

SP: Because I teach middle school, and am somewhat expected to abide by the educational practices du jour, I am forced to find places in the school year to teach poetry.

What the suits feel poetry plays in life and what I feel are worlds apart, but I have managed to do so, I think. Not an easy trick, but along with Robert Frost and Edna St. Vincent Millay, I have used poets like the incomparable Philip Levine, a friend and teacher, who died in 2015; Robert Bly, who remains a powerful voice, in spite of taking something of a back seat in popularity of late; Jane Hirshfield, a truly unique voice in contemporary poetry; and, yes, even the troubled and exquisite work of John Berryman.

How can someone share these brilliant minds with students who would rather be listening to the latest hip-hop artist? Carefully, I guess, carefully, and with love.

MBA: Your wife is a writer too, have you collaborated?

SP: Actually, Susan and I did that very thing early on in our relationship. We are currently working on re-submitting it for possible publication, once we do a few nip-and-tucks along the way. It is a collaborative novel, actually, which involves the use of poetry and prose as a device. It works. At some point, we are hoping the public agrees.

MBA: How do you write your poems? What is your process? (Dreams? Does a line come to you? Or the whole poem?)

SP: It varies, but one thing I have done now for the past few years is to set aside the early hours of the day to do nothing more than write, and by early I mean 5 A.M. or so. It is so quiet then, so peaceful, that I am usually able to focus simply and clearly on an idea and take it to its conclusion.

I have no set "process" other than that, and it seems to work. This past year, starting on January 1, I have written at least one poem a day, and we are now in the middle of summer as I write this. A lot of it is hopelessly bad, but some of it will appear in future books. Being the son of a man who loved working in the garden, I like to think weeding is among my skills.

MBA: Is there a "thread" or through-line, a central theme running through the poems in this book?

SP: Maybe. I'm not sure that it is all that different from some of my earlier work, but I think it is more cohesive in Bad Angels, than it was in other collections I have done. I like to think

I am somewhere in between the worst romance writer in the universe and Samuel Beckett. It gives me a rather large game board to work with.

MBA: Do you have an editor, writing group or proof-reader of your poetry? Before you finalize it?
SP: When I married Susan, I not only married the woman I had been in search of for several decades; I also married a grand editor. Everything I write generally goes through Susan's brilliant eyes before I show it to anyone else.

Also, I like to run poems I am particularly happy with by my long-time friends, the poets David St. John and Norman Dubie. Their insights and doubts are always welcome, as are Susan's.

MBA: Who did the cover? Can you talk about how the art was selected?
SP: I decided, along with the publisher of *Nine Mile Press*, Bob Herz, to use a photo of a monument located in Oakland Cemetery in Iowa City, Iowa, which is, coincidentally, where both Bob and I attended the Iowa Writers' Workshop back in the 1970s. The Black Angel, as it is referred to, has a long and disturbing history to it, and that alone drew me to using it as the cover. There is one very memorable evening when Norman Dubie, and I ended up walking out to the cemetery and the monument, in particular. I think Norman wanted to make sure I had first-hand knowledge and vision of the place, and I am forever grateful for that gift.

Bad Angels

He rests on her inner thigh, a bad angel,
In a room fit perfectly for its darkness.
Whatever this is, it's not because he thinks
He is a great lover. That is simply laughable.
He believes the most important time
Is a sigh at its middle; the purest wetness,
Those captivating tears. She tells him
About the white light; how it's nothing
To fear. . .

MBA: Are there any poems in the book which represent your Portuguese background?
SP: In "One for the Contractor, Frank Beans" I am addressing the owner of a construction company that my father worked for in his early years.

My dad was a carpenter in those days, and built the house I grew up in, pretty much as a one-man show, when he wasn't building homes for others. Frank Beans—a nickname, obviously—his real name was Frank Pereira (no relation), was someone my father respected greatly, and I think of him and my father having something of the type of relationship I have had, learning from poets and writers who are/were slightly older than I am. I am 66 now, so there are fewer and fewer of those folks around these days.

MBA: The poems in *Bad Angels* seem biographical driven by an objective force rather than a subjective force, with some more subtle than others—Did you use a biographical or historical information?
SP: You pick up something in your question that is, I believe, at the center of how these particular poems came to be.

They are "subjective" in the sense that they have a certain sense of direction that can only be derived from the writer's perspective. They are "objective" in large part due to their insistence and need for foundational stability. From that platform of objectivity, I am allowed, or gifted with, the joy that comes from creating something new and, hopefully, memorable.

MBA: You graduated the Iowa Writers Workshop in its legacy years. Who were your classmates?

SP: The interesting thing with a question like that is the fear of leaving people out. The place was, and is, crawling with talent, both poets and fiction writers.

The ones that I felt particularly close to during my time there included, of course, my amigos from Fresno—David St. John and the late Larry Levis. Also, a guy named John Bowie, who had been a student of Larry's from L.A. State, I believe, and who had followed the call to Iowa, as so many of us lucky enough to have been chosen did. John was a dear friend during much of that time in Iowa City and, strangely enough, shows up in my work on occasion. For example, the poem "Losing Myself in the Snow," which appears in *Bad Angels*, is dedicated to John, who died of a massive heart attack a couple of years later, in 1977.

There were people like Adam LeFevre, who is a fine poet and playwright, but also a well-known character actor today. He has gone on to be in several motion pictures, most recently *The Lucky One*, I believe. There were also many brilliant women in the Writers' Workshop when I was there, among them Marcia Southwick, Pamela Jody Stewart, Angela Ball, and I could go on, but you get the idea…a veritable Land of Oz for writers in their early creative years.

MBA: Your teachers?

SP: I lucked out again in that regard—nothing but the best—not just my opinion, but pretty much the world's. The list includes the two teachers who were permanent fixtures at Iowa during that time, Donald Justice and Marvin Bell. Norman Dubie, who I mentioned earlier, was also teaching in the workshop then.

Along with those three, nationally and internationally known poets and writers would spend a year on staff, and that list was incredible as well. During my two years, I had a chance to take classes and spend enormously valuable time with people like Mark Strand, Sandra McPherson, and Charles Wright just to name a few. I hate using the term "blessed," but I was blessed, dammit!

MBA: In Iowa City, did you have a favorite place to write? To hang out? I was there for a conference a couple of years ago and went to the famous Hamburg Inn #2 (a key stop for Presidential hopefuls)

SP: Yes! There is a poem in the new book that exists because of the Hamburg Inn.

I wrote largely in whatever one-room place I happened to be living at the time. The first was an efficiency apartment in the basement of a house. The second year, I managed to go up-scale to the ground floor of a two-story house, divided into rooms for rent. I felt gloriously free. During that period, Iowa City was undergoing urban renewal and many of the businesses were set up in what amounted to trailers, while the downtown was reconstructed into what it is now.

One of those buildings, a bar called the Deadwood, which exists today in a far slicker format I am told, was where many of us spent far too much time with the romance of thinking we were writers—a necessary step, I suspect, toward reaching the actuality of that dream.

MBA: The title poem "Bad Angels" seems to be about giving in to one's urges and also the contrast between life and death (that in darkness–as you said– there is also light, the shining light that people–who have had near-death experiences–see. There is a campy playfulness in the poem, a shared secret lucky couples have. It could be a sex scene or contemplation in a graveyard. Can you describe the setting you imagined while writing this?

SP: Or, if you will humor me here, a sex scene in a graveyard? But, seriously, your insightful question does a lot to answer itself, I think. The poem encompasses all of those aspects, I believe, but with the overriding quality of privacy, selectively shared with the reader. It's a kind of cat and mouse thematic that I and, I would bet money, a good many other writers find attractive. It is, finally, a poem that matters to me in ways I trust come through by the end of the entire collection, *Bad Angels*.

MBA: In *Bad Angels*, is the statue of the Black Angel significant?

SP: Let me say here: It is an image that anyone passing through [Iowa City] must, at some point, be aware of. Use it. Don't use it. The mystery continues to be written in stone.

"Sam Pereira Interview," connotationpress.com, 2017—Al Maginnes

Al Maginnes: In a time when many poets, especially younger ones, are shying away from narrative, you embrace it. By the same token, your poems tend to be accessible in language and content. Are these things related and are they important to you?

Sam Pereira: Actually, I have always considered myself a narrative poet with lyric tendencies. The idea of telling a story in metaphor and with brevity is, I think, creating the nectar all good poets want to drink from. As to accessibility, isn't that kind of the point? Striving to be incomprehensible seems like such a waste of time. I know any number of ways to waste time, and have proven it for what amounts to about a third of my life thus far, but at 68 years old now, I just don't have any extra hours or minutes to waste on not being understood in my work. It's not fair to the reader and it's not fair to me.

AM: You are associated with the Fresno poets such as Philip Levine, Peter Everwine, David St. John, and Larry Levis. Are there any associations or memories of this group or of poets associated with this group that you'd like to share?

SP: These people are some of the reasons anyone has ever taken Sam Pereira seriously in the first place. When I came to Fresno as a kid who'd read a little Shakespeare and knew that Dostoyevsky was Russian, I needed to be shaken a bit; told that my ideas were, for the most part, crap. If I was truly interested in writing well, then I'd best listen. I did. Phil was the one everyone feared, mostly because of his brutal honesty. He was also the guy who, once he believed you were the real deal, would go out of his way to support and help in any way he could. He was a friend for more than 40 years. Sometimes, if I look real hard, I can still see him nudging me to go on.

Peter was there before Phil as one of my teachers, and before Pete, Chuck Hanzlicek. Both of these generous men eased my work along, Pete with gentle, dignified coaxing, along with an undercurrent of firm beliefs about what a poem could and should be. Chuck—because he was a bit younger than the other two and was my introduction to poetry at the college level--was able to get my complete attention and devotion to the art by introducing his classes to great poets like James Wright and Robert Bly, and, yes, the one and only George Oppen, who deserves a shelf all his own. I hate the word "blessed" most of the time, but dammit, I was blessed! David and Larry were there with me, both at Fresno, and later at the Writers' Workshop in Iowa City. I still rely heavily on David's responses to my work, along with the thoughts of my teacher and friend, Norman Dubie. These two poets are essential to me in ways I can't even begin toexpress clearly.

Larry Levis was and is an enigma to me. I go back and read his poems on occasion, usually at difficult times, and every time I do, much as I did years ago with the poetry of John Berryman, I find myself so wrapped up in the sounds and ideas, that I begin to write like *them*, and not myself. At least, it feels that way to me. So I have to put their work aside for a while and grab my own voice back before it goes away forever, looking for trouble.

By the way, this year, the fine poet, Michele Poulos, who is also a wonderful film maker, directed and introduced to the world a documentary about Larry's life called *A Late Style of Fire: Larry Levis, American Poet*. I was honored to have been included in the film, even though it is a brief moment. Our dog, Sonny, also makes an appearance in the film. He walks around the house now as though he's Whitman reincarnated.

AM: You write a lot about music. So what is on your turntable, CD player, ipod as we speak?
SP: Honestly, this question made me think of an old Jerry Jeff Walker song that came out sometime in the late 1980s. It's called "I Feel like Hank Williams Tonight," and it goes through all the possible background music of a man's life, be it classical, or rock, or jazz, or country. A marvelously mellow and honest song!

As for me, I listen to a lot of jazz vocalists. Sinatra, of course. Julie London. June Christy. Nat Cole. Ella Fitzgerald. No surprises. I still believe in the power of rock 'n roll, but only as God intended: dark & joyful, with just a hint of ennui coming from a Fender bass. Country when it's the pure stuff—Merle, George Jones, Hank (the old man, to be clear). Classical? You bet. Bach, Vivaldi. Not Strauss, and for the most part, not the Russians.

AM: Finally, here is a question that was posed to me when I was interviewed by Connotation Press. What superpower do you wish you possessed?
SP: The ability to cure pain. Not doctor magic. Shaman magic, where you take a person's soul and rip it to shreds, then painstakingly put it back together again in some new, more useful configuration. On a good day, I like to think poetry cures pain.

"Breathing In and Out 101," 2019—Sam Pereira

Everything seemed hinged to that year. 1967. I had just graduated from Los Banos High School, and like many of my classmates at the time, we were either going off to college, or heading out to the Southeast Asian campus of life. I was one of those who would be heading down Highway 99 in the direction of Fresno. For the next five years, this tough, yet open, city would shape the rest of my life in ways I hadn't expected.

My plans had been decided before going: a degree in English, with a minor in History, the required nonsense called Education courses; then, Presto! High school

English teacher/pillar of the community in place. A funny thing happened to that idea almost immediately, however.

At about the second or third semester into my well-laid plans, the Introduction to English courses whetted my appetite for more satisfying revelations. I had been writing my own pathetic schoolboy stuff since about the age of 15 or so, and figured I'd try a little creative writing to hone my skills. I was instantly humbled and provided the knowledge that this valley of grapes, almonds, figs, tomatoes, cantaloupes, and—well, you get the idea—was also producing a hearty crop of poets, as well. I was merely one small part of the magnificent whole.

My first writing teacher was Charles Hanzlicek, who had recently graduated from college himself. He had a wonderful self-assurance about him, while sitting behind his desk in the San Ramon Building. Maybe it was the pipe he was almost always smoking. Maybe it was simply that he *was*, in fact, self-assured. Whatever it was, I learned a great deal from Chuck every time I'd stop to have him look at my latest fired-up piece of young man's BS. He never gave me any negatives designed to shut me down. In fact, as I recall, he always had something instructive to say that would send me back to the drawing board. Exactly what a young writer needed to encounter in order to grow.

A little after that, I branched out into other writing courses; other sage wisdom from the likes of Peter Everwine, who had a PhD, but never flaunted it, or threw it in one's face like some of the professors at Fresno did. Peter, too, was kind about student work. I remember writing a poem once and dedicating it to him. He was probably about 40 at the time, and had the beginnings of what would later become a full head of gray hair. The poem touched on this fact: how he was old and wise. He smiled and thanked me sincerely. Years later, while listening to a recorded reading that Pete had given at the University of Arizona in Tucson in the 70s, I realized that he had been somewhat taken aback by my seeing him as this ancient, almost biblical, creature in my poem. He didn't mention me by name during the reading, but I knew he was talking about me and that particular poem. I don't think he ever really forgave me for my ignorance.

When Peter passed away a couple of years ago, I wrote another poem for him, this time with my own gray hairs in place. It was, I suppose, a way of letting the dead know that I finally got it. In the poem, I mention that Pete, during the one or two times he was asked to introduce me at Fresno readings, would always include something about driving in the direction of my hometown to go duck hunting. Another surprising fact: this gentleman and scholar hunted ducks once upon a time. In his introduction, he would say how he always knew when he was getting close to his destination, because the smells of cattle and various crops on and in the ground would always alert him. Then he'd say, "It is also a place where a terrific poet lives." What a grand and giving soul he was.

Philip Levine, even back then, was legendary. This was long before he took to wearing sport coats/suits to his readings. I had worked my way by now to the point I felt comfortable taking a writing class from him; felt I could handle whatever he would dish out about my less than stellar work at the time. The stories were endless about how Phil would cut a person down to size in class if they needed it. To say that I wasn't just a bit terrified would be a lie. To my surprise, I never experienced any of that. There were times he didn't care for something I had written, but would always stop just short of telling the class it was shit. And there were times, in hindsight, it was! There was also the time, just before one of Phil's writing classes was to begin, he looked over at me and said he had just come back from Arizona, where he'd given a reading. This was about the time that the magazine *Ironwood*, edited by Michael Cuddihy, had just hit the streets with its first printing. I was in it, and hadn't said anything about it. Phil looked over at me, and in front of the entire class said, "Your publisher says 'Hi.'" In one brief statement, he was having a bit of fun with me, but also acknowledging my accomplishment. I will never forget that moment.

I recall, as well, a non-writing class that Phil was teaching, something like "20th Century American Poetry," a survey course designed to be four relatively easy units, or so we thought. Phil was very serious in his attempts to enlighten us, and would share his vast knowledge with any of us willing to take the class as seriously as he did. On one occasion, I recall there was a nun taking the class, who came to it dressed in her habit, which was the norm in those days if you were a nun. There was also a guy in the class, who was in the English program because he was looking for what he saw as an easy ride, so he could spend time at his true love, gambling. Several of us would take advantage of this fact and go play the horses with him when the Fresno Fair came to town. We'd engage his skills for profit, and it usually paid off, but in Phil's classroom—at that particular moment in time—this guy made a huge mistake! He mumbled a comment about the nun that everyone could hear. She valiantly ignored it, but Phil—who had heard the comment, too—raged at the guy; told him to get out of his classroom NOW! If I hadn't figured it out before, I did at that moment. Philip Levine would always be the defender of the underdog, in this case a mild and unassuming woman in a habit, trying to learn a little bit about poetry.

Over the years, and through many dark times in my own life, I counted on being able to come to Phil and Franny Levine's home, unannounced, or with an hour or two of notice. I was always welcome there to sit, talk, watch a boxing match, whatever. I will be forever grateful for this grand gesture on their part.

Years later, I learned that Phil had been diagnosed with pancreatic cancer and was near death. David St. John had emailed me telling me the sad news, and letting me know that I should contact Phil and Franny while there was still time. I called immediately, not realizing just how close the time actually was. Franny was strong, telling me over the phone how Phil was comfortable with all of it and ready for the inevitable. I cried. I was a blubbering fool as I recall. Franny was consoling and she, of all people, should not have had to be. I like to think Phil would have slapped me and reminded me it was all part of the plan and to shape up! I like to think he would have been gentle in doing so, but probably not.

Soon after talking with Franny, I wrote a poem and dedicated it to Phil. It was supposed to be an attempt at acknowledging what he'd meant to me for nearly five decades; what he'd meant to the world for a much longer time than that. I never got to show the poem to Phil. Several days later, on February 14, 2015, Philip Levine stopped writing his powerful poems forever. I miss that power, as well as missing the man himself. I haven't had a drink in nearly twenty-five years, but if I did, it would be to raise a glass to Phil.

One final thing, that I have left for the end deliberately for reasons I can't quite put my finger on. Perhaps, it's because mixed in with all this talk about teachers being the driving inspiration, there was also the quite powerful brotherhood/sisterhood of my fellow students. Among my closest friends, while at Fresno—and later in Iowa City at the Writer's Workshop—were David St. John, Larry Levis, and Ernesto Trejo. Those who I knew only from Fresno were fine writers and great people, including Lance Patigian, Grep Pape, Mike Cole, Roberta Spear, and Michele Hester. All of us were affected in various ways by Fresno. Some of us have now left the planet, while the rest of us remain caught between our memories and how we will turn what's just around the corner into a poetry that those angels still hovering over this San Joaquin Valley of ours might recognize and shiver at just a little.

Larry Levis—1946-1996

Larry Levis was born in Fresno, CA, September 1946, and grew up on his parents ranch in nearby Selma. He attended Fresno State and earned a B.A. in English. There he met Philip Levine who became his lifelong mentor and friend. In 1970 he received his M.A. from Syracuse University where he worked with Donald Justice. Larry then taught for two years at Cal State L.A. after which he moved to Iowa where he received a Ph.D. in Modern Letters. *Wrecking Crew*, his first book of poetry, won the United States Award from the International Poetry Forum in 1971 and was published by the Univ. of Pittsburgh Press in 1972. *The Afterlife* was the 1976 Lamont Poetry Selection of the Academy of American Poets and was published in 1977. His third book, *The Dollmaker's Ghost*, was chosen by Stanley Kunitz as a winner of the open competition for the National Poetry Series and published by E.P. Dutton in 1981. His fifth book, *Winter Stars*, appeared from Pittsburgh in 1985 and was followed by *The Widening Spell of the Leaves* in 1991. A collection of fiction, *Black Freckles*, was published in 1992, and *The Gazer Within*, a collection of his prose on poetry, was published posthumously in 2,000. *Elegy*, a posthumous collection of poetry edited by Philip Levine, was published in 1997; *The Selected Levis* appeared in 2000, edited by David St. John who also edited *The Darkening Trapeze: Last Poems*, published by Graywolf Press in 2016.

Levis was awarded the YM-YWHA Discovery Award, three fellowships from the National Endowment for the Arts, a Fulbright Fellowship, and a fellowship from the John Simon Guggenheim Foundation. He taught at the University of Missouri from 1974-1980, at the University of Utah from 1980-1994, and was teaching at Virginia Commonwealth University at the time of his death from a heart attack in May 1996.

"Philip Levine" from *A Condition of the Spirit*, 2004—Larry Levis

One night I wrote a poem. I think I actually composed it while listening to music, to some sticky orchestrated sound track from a movie. The poem was awful of course; even I knew that. It was awful except for one thing. It had one good line in it. I was sixteen then, almost seventeen, almost a senior, and about important things I did not deceive myself. One good line at the age of sixteen was lot. I decided then that I would go to sleep, and if the line was still good in the morning, then I would become a poet. I remember thinking that I might qualify the decision by saying that I would try to become a poet. The word "try" seemed dead of exhaustion. No, that was no good. I thought immediately. One either did this or did not do it.

When I got up, I looked at the line. It was still good.

Everything crucial in my life had been decided in less than thirty seconds, and in complete silence.

My great good fortune came a few months later disguised as a grade of D in my photography class. That dark mark meant I could not go to Berkeley or to any University of California campus. I tried to persuade my teacher, Mr. Ferguson, that most students thought the course was a kind of joke. This turned out to be the wrong argument. And in fact I deserved the grade for I had hardly attended the class. The D meant I would have to go to Fresno to attend college. Yes, Fresno, Dust and Wind State.

How lucky I was though my little destiny was completely disguised as failure, for at Fresno State I would spend the next four years in Levine's poetry workshops, although I could not have know that then. No one knew anything then. It was 1964.

"Larry Levis" from *A Condition of the Spirit*, 2004—Peter Everwine

I have a photograph of Phil Levine, Larry, and me probably taken in the mid-1960s, when Larry would have been an undergraduate at Fresno State. We're standing in a hallway of the old Administrative Building: Larry in his familiar slouch, holding an armload of books, the three of us smiling as if we've just come from a lecture on happiness. But the camera has caught Larry at a moment when he's closed his eyes and turned his face slightly away, so that he looks boyish and shy, as if he smiled at something inward and too intimate to be surrendered to the viewer. Seen from this side of Larry's death, the photograph has an air of innocence that is painful.

In the years after Larry's graduation I mostly saw him on those occasions when he returned to the valley to visit family and friends. We'd meet over dinner with Phil and Franny, evenings there were generous with laughter and high spirits. One of the pleasures of being with Larry was in listening to him tell, in his easy, valley-inflected voice, the marvelous, often odd and funny stories he brought with him from wherever he'd been. It was one of the ways he had of "joining one thing to another, / Myself to whoever it is. . . ." In more serious light, this is also a description of the task Larry has set for himself as a poet. "It magnifies & I can't explain it."

One can hear this gift for narrative in his mature work, especially in the poems of *Elegy*, with their wondrous, expansive sense of freedom and improvisations, their capacity for inclusion, like some crowded cabinet of wonders. "You have to tell a story," Lester Young once said about playing jazz. I think he meant that it wasn't simply a matter of knowing the lyrics to a tune; you had to get as much of the world as you could into your horn—what you knew of its joy or grief or anger. I think this was certainly Larry's sense of story; he came to know a great deal about the world, and he's made of that wisdom a passionate and elegiac art.

In one of his last poems, Larry wrote, "Poverty is what happens at the end of any story, including this one. . . ." It is, perhaps, one of his saddest lines. Time darkens us.

"After the Obsession with some Beloved Figure: An Interview with Larry Levis"— Leslie Kelen

First appeared in The Antioch Review, *and* A Condition of the Spirit, *2004. This interview with Larry Levis was conducted at his home on the north side of Salt Lake City. Levis has published four volumes of poetry:* Wrecking Crew *(University of Pittsburgh Press, 1972),* The Afterlife *(University of Iowa Press, 1977),* The Dollmaker's Ghost *(E.P. Dutton, 1981), and* Winter Stars *(University of Pittsburgh Press, 1985).*

Leslie Kelen: Would you start by describing how you began to write poetry?
Larry Levis: I was in high school. I was sixteen, and I lived on a ranch. We call them

ranches in California, but they're actually large farms, vineyards, and orchards. My sister brought back books from college, Shakespeare and so forth, but also books as recent as Thom Gunn's *My Sad Captains* and *Fighting Terms*. So I was reading them, but I didn't like them much. The first poet I really loved was T. S. Eliot, and I still do. I was reading Eliot, primarily, and Frost, and a little Pound, a little Rimbaud; I decided I wanted to become a poet one night, so I tried to write a poem.

LK: You decided to become a poet overnight?

LL: Oh, it was a longer process, but I actually remember wondering whether I should make that decision, then going ahead and deciding, actually deciding that that was all that was really obsessing me. My high school English teacher had seen one of these poems I was doing. They were just so awful. She was so kind and she said, "If you want to do this, you should really go and study it somewhere." I said, "Where?" She said, "San Francisco State has a writing program. You might think of that." I told her I wanted to go to Berkeley, but I couldn't get in because I got a D in photography. And you couldn't go to the university if you got a D at all in high school. Then she said, "You might think of Fresno because Philip Levine is there." So that was a curiously lucky series of circumstances. I met Philip Levine when I was seventeen, I think. I was still seventeen when I entered college.

LK: How did your family respond to your writing?

LL: When my first book came out—I was twenty-five, I guess—my father was talking to my grandfather-in-law (the book was around and my father was looking at it) and he said, "Well, I don't understand it. It's kind of like nuclear physics." I mean, there wasn't even a recognition of poetry. My mother, on the other hand, had had two years of college just before the depression hit, and she had actually studied Shakespeare in those years. She would quote it to us around the house. She would use Shakespeare to tell us to do things. If I was lying around, she would look at me and say, "'Filths savor but themselves.' " If my sisters were looking bored and lazy and doing nothing— "Adolescents?" she would say. "Look at them. 'Lilies that fester smell far worse than weeds.' " She'd actually committed a lot of it to memory. So we would hear this weird Shakespeare in this place where most of the people spoke Spanish. I mean the people who worked there. My father, you see, farmed. My mother was a housewife. And we were well off. We weren't rich, but we were always very comfortable. Middle class. I worked on the farm as did my brother and my sisters.

LK: In those years when you felt yourself drawn to poetry, do you remember what in the poetry you were reading attracted you? What qualities did the poems have? Can you identify them?

LL: I'm not sure I can except that it gave voice to a kind of adolescent loneliness or alienation I felt. And it made sense of things. It was also incredibly beautiful. I mean, the language moving into that state of being where it was a condition, or is a condition, of the spirit. It seemed utterly convincing.

It's difficult to say what else I was looking for, but even then, when I was very young, what was very clear, from a social standpoint, was that I had the luxury to make that decision. You see, I worked with people who worked on that farm and on other farms, and for them it was for keeps. That was life. Life wasn't going to get much better. What you were always reminded of, working alongside of them, was that you were lucky, because it could just as easily be for keeps for you. So there was that. I thought, well, you ought to do something with your life that you really want to. Otherwise, what's the point?

Then, in 1963, there was a profound event, a large public event—the assassination of Kennedy. I remember driving the tractor in an almond orchard the day after it happened, and it seemed as if the world changed. The world was no longer quite as settled or as free from chance, from random fate. It shook everybody. And, in a curious way, it opened a lot of things. The country began to change. In a good way and also for the worse. Vietnam was going on and you knew you might have to go there and nobody wanted to.

I joined the California Air National Guard when I was nineteen, because I knew they would never go to Vietnam. It was a kind of country club and they flew jets around the Sierras. . . . I lasted four days. I got a medical discharge because they thought I had a tumor and I should get exploratory surgery. Actually, it was an old operation and my hometown doctor had sewn the membrane in such a way that it looked like a tumor. So it was a fantastic bit of luck. They didn't want me and instead of sending me into the regular army, they just discharged me. I got a I-Y deferment and I called Fresno State College and said, "Can I come back in?" They said, "Yes. Just come out and register late." So I did and they put me in classes with people like Philip Levine and Peter Everwine, studying things, not going to war. . . .

LK: What was the impact of people like Philip Levine and Peter Everwine on you?
LL: Enormous, wonderful, and conclusive. They represented a way in which people could live, do as they wanted to do, and be poets. And they were also fabulously interesting in themselves. They seemed to have mastered some very basic but enormously difficult things in life, such as the belief that other people in the world are, in fact, real. They're not just categorizable ciphers. They had a kind of humanity they brought with them daily. They were also incredibly sophisticated. Phil was at that time beginning to write the poems which would go into books like *Not This Pig* and *They Feed They Lion*. Pete was coming back from a long absence from writing poetry and beginning to write the poems that went into *Collecting the Animals*.

There was this incredible energy there because of the presence of these people and because people were thinking about their lives a little differently. There was also a kind of anti-establishment mood afoot. One wanted to be hip, not in a cynical sense, but hip to the fact that you were alive and had certain alternatives. Vietnam made all of that urgent.

People, everywhere, were changing. They were growing their hair longer and taking less shit. Quite frankly, it was a great deal of fun. And part of the fun was that it was taboo to do certain things, and everybody was saying, "Well, screw that, let's go and do it anyway. Let's try to live up to this freedom." Actually, no real taboos were transgressed, but there was a countercultural move against the present system. It made you invent more and think of doing things differently, because your whole being was called into question.

LK: Did the writing of poetry create a way for you to respond to what was happening around you?
LL: Yes, I think so. Not that poetry necessarily had to be political, but the poetry answered some of the demands of the energy of the times. Poetry still seems like something one does. Poetry is something. It is not necessarily about something.

LK: If you went back and reentered the process of writing the poems that went into your first book, *Wrecking Crew*, how would you describe the imagination or the point of view of those poems?
LL: A lot of the poems came out of being involved with the poetry around me. Poets as different, say, as Creeley and Charles Simic. Poetry comes out of poetry, often enough. I

don't mean to make it sound as if everything is utterly literary, but poetry is like a huge living body in which a poet doesn't have his meaning all alone or in isolation. Creeley doesn't happen without an Olson; Olson doesn't happen without a Pound; Pound doesn't happen without a Cavalcanti or a Fenellosa. So a lot of the things around us went into the poems we were writing.

I tried to write as tersely and concisely as possible, to build a great deal of energy into a very small system. It seemed to me that what was important was to get it as tersely there as you could, so that everything essential was there and, at the same time, it wasn't diffuse or discursive.

LK: Unlike your later poems, which rely heavily on the usage of narrative, the poems in *Wrecking Crew* seem devoid of it. There's an almost anti-narrative feeling to the book. How would you explain that?

LL: I think what I was doing, and what a few other people were doing, was so tied to using the image to encompass or embody experience, that it insisted on terseness. In other words, the one thing I didn't want to do was editorialize or in any way seem to be didactic or reasonable. We were against reason, I think, reason via Dulles and Malaysian oil rights and other things, against whatever made it possible for our friends to go off and get killed in Vietnam. Eddie Zamora, a friend from high school, came home in a box. Thirty years of foreign policy—and that's the product! So reason no longer seemed an adequate vehicle.

LK: How did the "Magician Poems" sequence in *Wrecking Crew* come about?

LL: The magician was a figure of contemporary rock and counter-culture. In a minor mode, our generation went through something similar to what the French did in World War I. Do you know about the Dada exhibit where they gave you a hammer when you came in and if you didn't like something you smashed it? It came out of a reflex toward World War I. I mean, they thought what the hell good does it do to have a classical French education if it means your friend comes back with a head injury like Apollinaire? We thought—if this is what all of our technology, all of our rational American traditions lead to, all that Calvinism, then to hell with it. So there was an insistence on other modes. Irrational things: the magician, the sorcerer, the shaman, the magical properties of things. Trying to get back to that intuitive irrational sensibility. Jules Michelet would probably say that when God goes too far in his righteousness, the Devil comes to help. Which is to say, hey, I raise an objection to all this goodness, because this goodness is resulting in death. Why don't we try a little evil here to protect some lives?

LK: The poems in *Wrecking Crew* begin and end in odd, unexpected ways. It is as if they know they're coming out of nowhere and you as a poet are coming out of nowhere. Is that a fair reading?

LL: I think it is. It's one I haven't paid enough attention to, but I think it's quite right and quite fair that the poems seem to be self-generating in this way. They do that because they occur in the image. I wonder if they don't always do that. I mean, no matter how much more deliberate and formally organized my later poems are, I think, to some extent, they are always self-originating. Certainly other poems have more reason for being. I mean, they have elegiac reasons for being. They have reasons that have to do with trying to assess what's happened in, say, a life, a personal life, or another's life. But when you're young and really don't have a life or nothing much has happened in it, then they come even more from nowhere, supposedly. And there's nothing wrong with that....

The thing about the book, though, is that the times in which the book was written, while it made everything more urgent and inventive, also made me adopt a poseur, a mask in which the me in that book seems tougher than I ever was. I don't know if that makes sense.... But it all seemed part of the poetry.

LK: When were the poems in your second book, *The Afterlife,* begun?

LL: I didn't do anything for a year after *Wrecking Crew* came out. I was twenty-four when it was accepted. Like anybody with a first book, I thought, oh, boy, I'll be famous, totally unaware that there are about 40,000 books published every year in this country. That's a lot of books.

So I didn't write a thing. I just waited to become famous. And nothing happened. It was great. It's a wonderful education, the way the world works, its utter indifference to your heartfelt thoughts. [Laughs] But the book was noticed by people whom I wanted to notice it. Other young poets would write to me. So I was in the world in that way. Then I began to be troubled by the fact I wasn't writing. When I moved to Iowa City, I realized I had to start. . . . So I wrote a couple of the early poems in *The Afterlife.*

LK: What took you to Iowa City?

LL: I had a first book coming out, but I didn't have a Ph.D. I just had an M.A. and a two-year contract at Cal State University of Los Angeles, and they wanted me to get a Ph.D., so....

LK: So you went to Iowa to get your Ph.D.?

LL: Yeah. And there were a lot of good people at Iowa. Just to think about the students who were there is startling. David St. John was there, Tess Gallagher, Laura Jensen, Denis Johnson, Michael Burkard, Michael Ryan, John Skoyles, and several others. All of them have published books and published well. It was an exciting time.

People really pushed each other to do their best work. You were being challenged and you couldn't simply repeat what you had done previously. And that's what a workshop should be. It forced you to make decisions, to take certain stances toward experience and toward literature.And what we were doing, perhaps without knowing it totally, was coming to the recognition that what had been done had been done and had been done well. It was time to move on. . . . We were, I think, discovering another mode of doing things. Actually, we were going back to an older mode, a meditative mode, quite old and Wordsworthian in some ways. It was far less insistent on the image and much more insistent on thought and the presentation of thought by various moods.

LK: The poems in the *Wrecking Crew* have a gritty, streety, spirit-of-place to them. The poems in *The Afterlife,* by comparison, seem disengaged, out of touch, uninvolved with real people. What happened to make the poems in your second book take off in such a different direction?

LL: I think it had to do with a feeling that there was a danger of becoming provincial if one kept in the same place. Moreover, I did not know what more to say about certain of those places. Secondly, my new poems seemed to require an imagined place. I mean, there's a poem in which somebody lies down like a country in South America. So, I think, that was part of it, being interested in the fabulization of place.

LK: I understand what you're saying, but that doesn't explain to me why the two books differ so greatly in terms of tone. Wrecking Crew, for example, is pugnacious and playful; *The Afterlife* is resigned and despondent. What do you think brought about that change in tone?

LL: I got married for one thing. [Laughs] I was married to a nice woman; we just should never have been married. And the marriage eventually ended. But I felt an immense sort of depression about it, because the marriage seemed to be one of those things that went on eternally but very little happened. You know, an eternity of some kind, or an afterlife. And that's exactly what it was! After the event of life came the non-event of eternity. . .

And I had wanted the marriage to work. . . So I think some of my resignation or despair had to do with my recognition that it could not.

LK: This resignation seems to have had a direct effect on the form of the poems. The shapes or the edges of the poems in the book seem soft and indistinct.
LL: Yeah. In *Wrecking Crew* it seems I was working in hard-edged acrylics. *The Afterlife* looks like oils, or water colors perhaps.... I think part of that has to do with fabulization. If you move into fabulizing, edges will be blurred, because you won't have Fulton Street, which is hard edged, but a Bolivia that is not really Bolivia.

LK: At the time of the writing of the poems did you realize you were exploring new psychological realities?
LL: Well, I think, defeat. . . . I mean, I had this marriage that was sort of hopelessly unhappy for both people. And I felt defeated about that, as well as defeated by not making it in America, being unemployed essentially, despite the fact that I had a good fellowship from Iowa. So I think there was that sense of defeat and a sense of defeat also about the purpose of the other poems. The figure I created in my first book no longer seemed present in the life I then had. So *The Afterlife* seemed to me a grievous book, a book involved in mourning.

LK: Did you feel something had ended or had died?
LL: Perhaps. There was a distinct sense I had once of something leaving me as I was driving down the California coast highway, some kind of raucous, funny person. And it was partly myself that was saying goodbye, going away. It felt like a guardian angel or something. . . . It was actively at that moment saying goodbye. And there seemed to be no way I could get it back. It had gone. I remember having this absolute impression. I don't know whether it was because I was involved in a marriage that shouldn't have been, but it certainly was a convincing moment.

LK: Was there anything you could have done to reclaim that spirit?
LL: I might have reclaimed it by changing my life at that point. But, you see, it actually felt like I'd betrayed something or cut something off. Kundera says in some statement that then you can go ahead and betray something else, but that doesn't mean you've reconciled yourself to the first thing or that it will come back. Some betrayals are final.

LK: I found it exciting to move from the writing in *The Afterlife* to the writing in *The Dollmaker's Ghost*, because the latter seemed alive with new rhythms. The poems also seemed quicker, keener, and suppler, as if you suddenly had access to a greater range of emotion.
LL: I think that has to do with a couple of factors. Part of it has to do with a kind of cadence or rhythm, a dancelike rhythm that would move from initial to terminal stress with great suppleness, more or less the way a dancer might move. Whereas, traditionally, in poetry, one might think of rhythm being linear, one could begin to think of it more architecturally, as not only a linear but a vertical figure, establishing itself in rhythms or variations, both across the line and then vertically down through the poem, picking up repetitions and motifs. And, usually, more or less, the way they are used in music.

Actually, all this begins a long time ago in America with W.C. Williams and others. Those little poems by Williams that look so flat and so bare, if you put them into prose they'd sound like Faulkner. They move with that kind of velocity. When you break them up, you get that velocity slowed down over a large point of time. All those things were coming into play there; I was reading Faulkner as well. A lot of the rhythms in *The Dollmaker's Ghost* have something to do with Faulkner.

LK: What aspect of Faulkner's style affected you?
LL: A long sentence capable of moving in various ways, describing certain things and leaving others out, and coming back. I admired the prose rhythms in Faulkner. When I think of *The Dollmaker's Ghost*, it seems to me that every line break in the book is absolutely scrupulous and careful and deliberate. Although, sometimes now when I go back, I wonder, why, what exactly was I thinking?

LK: It is interesting that the poems in *The Dollmaker's Ghost* are much more accessible than the poems in your first two books.
LL: I wasn't consciously trying to make anything accessible, nor was I trying, on the other hand, to be obscure or priestly, as the Modernists tried to be. I have nothing against being accessible. I think there's a certain pleasure in that—the poems being vulnerable to being understood. A lot of young poets don't want to be understood, because they feel that when they're understood, they're dead. But I think that fear only comes from criticism—the vast inhibition they get from reading critics who, because they can understand something, simply decide not to deal with it. I think it's very difficult to deal with a fantastically complete, utterly accessible lyric by Thomas Hardy, which already says everything it intends to say. It defies criticism. It says to Harold Bloom or Helen Vendler, sure, come ahead, say what you have to say; I'll make you look hopeless.

Donald Justice comes to mind in this way. He wanted to write a poem so completely that the only thing he could say about it that would be accurate would be its recitation. Larkin thought that, too. You'll find very little high-powered criticism about Larkin. You can't do it. His poetry is too shrewd, too cunning, too mean. Scrupulously mean, as Joyce said. Now I like that . . . as a method in art. Not because I have anything against criticism, which is unavoidable and necessary and as natural as breathing. . . . But to make a poem that absolutely declares everything, one that has no hidden resources or anything—I mean, that's another idea, you see.

Sometimes we assume that in order to write well one has to be formidably armed with all sorts of ideas and theories, but when you go back to Yeats you find things. He says: men own nothing but their own, blind, stupefied hearts. . . .

I was teaching Yeats once and he appeared to me in a dream. He'd come to Salt Lake City because due to the effects of the moon and certain other things, papers he had left in London had . . . stayed in the same place, but the world had moved. So the papers now happened to be in my apartment in Salt Lake City. And Yeats simply walked into my little studio apartment down on Third East; he saw all my notes scattered around and this new annotated text of his poems that had just come out. He looked at me and said, "What are you doing this for? Passion is all that matters in poetry. As a matter of fact, it's all that matters in life, too."

I believe what Yeats said. Passion is what matters in poetry; and sustaining one's art sometimes depends on really not giving a shit about anything else but just doing it. It also has to do with a certain nonchalance and ease and arrogance by which one goes about it, as if you don't have any debts or obligations to pay. The people who are telling you that you do have obligations, moral ones . . . to their morals, are essentially just bullshit. You don't have to pay attention to that. At any rate, you've already paid that debt and you paid it yesterday. What they want to do is keep you in line and make you behave.

LK: Let's discuss your most recent book, *Winter Stars*. By way of introducing the book's heavy reliance on narrative, would you trace how the narrative element has developed in your previous books?

LL: You can discern the elements of it all the way to *Wrecking Crew* in a poem like "Fish." There actually is a story, or half of a story, in that poem about an arrest. I think the narrative mode drops out of my poetry after that, except for a muted narrational quality in the long poem "Linnets," in *The Afterlife*.

Then it comes back far more strongly in *The Dollmaker's Ghost*. The trouble with narrative is that sometimes when a poet writes for narrative, the narrative overwhelms every other consideration. When I go back to *The Dollmaker's Ghost*, if I see any deficiencies, it's that the poem is racing so much to be a narrative that other considerations, such as the integrity of a line, or rhythm, sometimes disappear. In *Winter Stars* the subjects themselves have the narrative so implicitly about them in elegies that all one needs to do is allude to it, repeat a certain thing (like a motif), and the narrative moves into that image or that line.

In *Winter Stars*, too, I was consciously writing a rather traditional five-beat line against some of the free verse in the book. But I wanted it to remain unnoticeable; I wanted the rhythm to work unconsciously. What intrigued me was coming back to a very traditional poetic source, while at the same time using or involving myself in narrative. So there was this tension between the two. The narrative was always wishing to break into prose, which is our narrative tradition. And the older line, which once contained any kind of narrative you would possibly want to write in, was coming back in the position of poetry and saying, well, there are certain things we won't do.

LK: I'm glad you contrasted *The Dollmaker's Ghost* and *Winter Stars*, because I found the narrative styles of the two books very different. The poems in T*he Dollmaker's Ghost* are generally high- pitched, almost like arias, while the poems in *Winter Stars* are, in comparison, quiet and self-possessed.

LL: A particular friend of mine, an editor in New York, said, after reading the manuscript for *The Dollmaker's Ghost*, that he found it to be full of mountains and cliffs, without what he thought were necessary valleys or lowlands.

LK: In what circumstances did you write the poems that went into *Winter Stars?*

LL: I think I began writing the book in Iowa City. I was asked to come there and teach as a visiting poet for a year and it turned into a two-year job . . . I'd been reading Robert Hass and other people and I was considering saying things in an abstract manner and using autobiographical material. I was interested in asking things like: Does this statement match experience? What is interesting about it? What may be interesting is the discrepancy between the abstract statement, which you think you believe, and your own experience, which in fact disproves the statement. Structurally, that came into play in the writing. But, basically, I simply sat down and was thinking about certain things in my life. . .

My father, at that time, was dying of Parkinson's disease, and the title poem had something to do with what he was like during the years he was deteriorating. His death, you see, had not occurred, but it was inevitable in many ways. And it caused me to think elegiacally long before he died. His death actually took about four years, during which time he slowly deteriorated, his mind being deprived of its attention of everything. . . He could remember things that happened thirty years ago quite clearly but would forget what had just happened or would think I was seventeen and would ask me if I'd brought a certain tractor home from a particular other ranch we had.

LK: Photographs play an important role in _Winter Stars._ They seem to help you focus and explore, penetrate a certain subject. Would you discuss that?

LL: I've always been interested in photographs. My first wife was a photographer and she'd bring home books of prints by people from Kertesz to Gary Winograd. One of the things that interested me was that a photograph is an image. A poem is often trying to create images. And they're both involved, insofar as they create images, in one of the larger projects of art, which is stopping time.

In a poem like "Easter 1916," Yeats stops history. So that the Ireland you thought you had is not the Ireland you have after he writes the poem. A poem like that, written by a great poet at a time of great political turmoil and stress, affects a nation and affects nations around it. What goes on in Ireland can no longer be ignored, you see. In order to make it unignorable Yeats had to, in those little three-stress accentual lines, stop time, make it impervious to its interruption by subsequent history. That's what great art can do.

And because the poem is so consummately written, it seems to me that it becomes a cultural artifact, one that no one in the British government could, after a certain amount of time elapsed, any longer ignore. If you can't ignore the poem, then you can't ignore the political reality it comes out of either.

LK: In poems like "The Cry" and "My Story in a Late Style of Fire," the narrative's reliance on a repeating motif has broadened, deepened. I'm wondering if you could address this.

LL: I can talk about it in individual cases. In "The Cry," for example, I was using a particular metaphor I'd seen in a poem by Joseph Brodsky, his "Elegy for John Donne," in which all of England goes to sleep, then all the world goes to sleep because John Donne is dead. It's a wonderful idea. I mean, once John Donne dies all the attention of John Donne dies. And so, therefore, all the things that were given energy or life by his attention fall asleep. Anvils die, compasses die, ships die. The birds that sail after them die. They don't die, actually, they sleep. So I took that from Brodsky: it was a stylistic choice and I acknowledge the theft at the end of the book. . . . But I thought if he can make all of England sleep, maybe I can make the three or four square miles of the east side of San Joaquin Valley fall asleep.

"My Story in a Late Style of Fire" was written quickly in Iowa City, and I thought, at the time of writing it, I would never show it to anybody. Because at the time it had to do with a love affair. But my marriage ended and the love affair ended, too. So then it seemed all right for the poem to be published. But I was uneasy with the style, because the lines were so long. The sentences were long and it seemed to move passionately toward the state of a kind of prose, almost a prose poem. So at the end of the poem I defended it by saying this "late, florid style," or something. A style that I could see myself having at some point in the future but did not feel, at that point, altogether comfortable with.

The poem talks about New York and going to see a particular woman there, and breaking up with her. Breaking up sounds so grand and pure, like adolescents break up. Grownups get in a taxicab and go to Penn Station and grab a train south. . . . But there's a lot of energy in the poem, the energy of something being released finally, something no longer being kept secret.

LK: I want to say that I was delighted and startled by the love poems in this book. They were candid, revealing, and introduced a subject that was ignored in your first three books.

LL: A friend of mine, a woman poet, was looking at these poems, particularly the love poems in *Winter Stars*. Not a close or a good friend. And she said, "Well, I really like it. I'm amazed by these poems because the kind of pain or melancholy they feel is exactly what a woman feels when something like this happens." And she said, "Usually, you don't find men writing this frankly about these feelings and you suspect they don't have such feelings." I said, "You mean as a species?" She said, "Well, not really." But she said, "There's too much macho self-defense that goes on."

LK: Did you have the sense that you were exploring a new part of yourself?

LL: A new part of the self? Yeah, I suppose. I couldn't exactly state what it is or where it occurred. I think it's a matter of getting rid of an adolescent preoccupation with the fact that you're going to die. And the fact that you're going to die makes you very sad for yourself. So you go around grieving for yourself. At some point you realize, you're not alone in this and it's not an endlessly fascinating subject. There are all sorts of other things that are quite important and if you're preoccupied with that obsession, you won't pay enough attention to the world, which is terrible and ugly, but also fantastic and exciting and sexy. So the particular melancholy and sadness in *The Afterlife* seems to be a young man not enough preoccupied by Eros and too preoccupied by the other instinct, Thanatos.

LK: It's interesting to note that the poems in *Winter Stars*, even when they're grieving, seem more solid, more positive, as if they have a new-found ability to cope with death.

LL: I think in periods in your life when certain large calamitous things happen to you such as divorce and leaving (at that point, my wife and my son), you realize the amount of daily good you can do is suddenly and enormously limited. In other words, you're no longer there. But the world itself, what you see in it, becomes far more real to you. The real world comes rushing back after the absence of the obsession with some beloved figure. And that's one thing that happens throughout the whole of *Winter Stars*, I think. In the end, there's this sense in which the speaker, me, can do little personal good in his own life, but he becomes a better witness to the world in a larger sense.

LK: As I was reading *Winter Stars*, I first felt that the preoccupation with the past was a preoccupation with memory, with the events of the past. Later, it struck me that the poems were actually fascinated by revealing fate itself the fate of individual lives and the fate of communities.

LL: When you mention fate, I'm reminded of the way in which fate overrides, often enough, individual will. You may think of yourself as having one kind of life or being one kind of person only to discover with new experiences that you're not that particular person, or that something seems to have chosen you to be otherwise to change; I think that's an aspect of the book. There is a kind of progress in the book from one kind of person in the first part to a far more singular person, the one who exists because of a particular fate he has to live out.

LK: And the destiny of this person irresistibly involves him in the destiny of other communities and other kinds of social processes?

LL: Yeah. "The Assimilation of the Gypsies" has to do with the policy of the Soviet officials in Slovakia who wished to break down the roving bands of gypsies and to assimilate them within the larger socialist structures of Czechoslovakia, Hungary, and other countries throughout Eastern Europe.

But how do you assimilate a people into another group? Well, one of the things you can do is have people within that particular gypsy tribe kill members of their own tribe, perform executions. In so doing, you have prima facie evidence of their repudiation of it. Therefore, afterward, a particular vulnerability to assimilation by other social forces develops. It's disgusting, but that's one element in the poem. You assimilate a people by making it commit a kind of self-murder. And that seems a particularly modern fate.

So, yeah, I'm interested in community processes like that. *Winter Stars* begins out of singularity, elegies and love poems, and then, I hope, widens into an increasing singularity. I'm alone in the end of the book, but thinking about larger communities, larger groups, what I mean by history.

LK: The tone of *Winter Stars* is different from the tone of any of your previous books. The writing feels quieter, more balanced, more assured of its effects. Would you say *Winter Stars* are the stars that appear at the end of *The Afterlife?*

LL: I think so. There's a kind of leveling that goes on in *Winter Stars*. In other words, you come down to talk to people who run barges down a river. I talked to my friends when I was writing the book, and a good many of my friends were bartenders and musicians. People who worked late at night at various jobs. They weren't intellectuals. They weren't dumb, but they weren't sitting up late reading Jacques Lacan. There are a number of people in the book who seem to me people with lives of such work, and the book tries to approach them, make a kind of bridge to them. And this leveling is important to me, a leveling by which I am really like other people. I am a poet. Right. But that doesn't mean I'm necessarily superior or that I put myself in a kind of pristine privileged position in which I am the seer or something. That's one of the older ideas about Romanticism that we forget; Wordsworth really did go out and speak to the leech gatherer and was terrified about the prospect of the loss of his poetic powers in that poem. He's quieted by this man whose life is more hopeless than his. That's part of the leveling, I guess. It's an old tradition of poetry, but an important one, I think, for me and for what I want to do.

LK: As a final question, I'd like to ask you to sketch, in a summary fashion, how you perceive your movement and/or development throughout these four books.

LL: I think my poems began with all the possibilities of dream and neo-surrealism. And there was a particular luxury they had at the point of being able to make myths and fables. . . . In *Winter Stars* it seems to me I had to confront certain things that happened in my own life. My father died. I was divorced for the second time and separated from my son. All of this happened in the space of two years and I really think I was using poetry as a necessary way of facing that and changing it into something else, changing it into the next state of understanding. You see, you stop being obsessed with death when finally somebody does it for you. Once your father dies, it's no longer all that fascinating. He's prepared a way for you by going before you and doing it. And it no longer looks as impossible as it does when you're eighteen. It now looks like another thing one has to do in life. So there were all these personal things happening. And they seemed large and immense. I think writing about them at the time, or slightly after, might seem rude or selfish to some people. But I wasn't trying to get poems out of it. I was just trying to confront my life, and it seemed necessary to try to write about it in order to survive it.

from "An Interview by David Wojahn," 1982—David Wojahn

David Wojahn: How do you respond to California when you go back now?
Larry Levis: The landscape I grew up in still looks as beautiful and as hopeless as it did then. I mean it always looks exactly like that: beautiful and hopeless. I grew up in what Joan Didion calls "the real California," where things are more resistant to change. Even if Fresno is now a huge sprawling town, it's essentially unchanging.

DW: I ask these questions because your poems are often very focused on a particular landscape or locale, yet the speakers and personas of your poems always seemed exiled from the places that are important to them. I'm thinking of some of the poems in The Dollmaker's Ghost such as "Picking Grapes in an Abandoned Vineyard" and "The Ownership of the Night."
LL: Well, I guess I feel that way, or that my life has taken that particular path of flight away from that location, from that place; or else I feel exiled from it in some way. You go along and what happens to you happens to you. You wind up in strange locations and towns and even apartments for all sorts of reasons that you can't figure out. I grew up in a house which my family has owned since the Gold Rush, and I only left our farm when I was eighteen and went to college in Fresno, which I thought was a really big city. That sort of upbringing has a lot do with how I think of myself. If you moved around from place to place when you were a child you no doubt have a more sophisticated perspective about home. For example, I went to a little schoolhouse where there were only three people in the first grade: there was Ronnie Barker, a girl named Margery Elm, of all names, and myself. It was a three-room schoolhouse, so they had the first and second grade in the same room; they had a real bell on a rope that the teachers would ring. My grandmother once taught there in the 1890s. So there was a sedimentary layer of a family that had been in that place for a long time, at least by California standards. I saw *few faces*. The school was so tiny—there were only about thirty-five people in it—that when neighboring schools would come in to compete in athletic contests, I was always struck by the variety of faces that could exist. I didn't think that there could be such an incredible array of eyes, faces, and bodies: I remember, actually, thinking just that as a child. It was wonderful that there were so many certain faces; but how could they exist? They were so out of place, shocking, strange. So obviously I was an incredibly sheltered child. I would just stand there marveling, watching people get off the bus. The naif of all naifs. I'm not proud of this sort of upbringing. I would never argue for it. To the Mexican Americans or to the Armenians or to the Japanese or the Filipinos, I must have been, as an adolescent, just another dumb Anglo.

DW: Do you think there's anything cathartic or therapeutic about your obsession with ghosts, especially in the last book ? I mean both the ghosts from your own personal past and the imaginary pasts of others. Sometimes I feel that the difference between, say, your persona poems and those of someone like Norman Dubie is that somehow you seem to write about your characters because to do so is the only way to free yourself from them.
LL: That's probably true. For me, the ghosts are also ways to talk about parts of myself that I wouldn't feel decent talking about from the first-person point of view. I don't feel brave enough to talk about them in the first person, or I felt too modest at a certain point in my life to talk about them as if those parts were, in fact, me-even if in fact they may have been me.

There is something different, of course, about the method of Norman's poems. His are personae poems, and are often based on real historical figures. My figures are often imagined or else they're anonymous and private. His use of persona is more definite or precise. The voice doesn't change or become, too overtly, Norman's. It isn't as *violated* as mine.

DW: I guess that leads me to my next question, which is how does this personal, autobiographical self, which is portrayed in your poems, and the imagined selves—all of your characters and persona—how do they interact? I think of poems like "The Blue Hatband," and your poems about Hernandez and Herbert- it's almost like we see this speaker's self-conscious and private voice give way to a more selfless voice that seems almost beyond the self of Larry Levis, more like a medium or an adopted mask.

LL: Well, the Herbert poem came from Herbert himself, who was a friend of mine for two years when he taught at the same place I did, California State University, Los Angeles. The Hernandez poem I wrote because I admire a number of his poems and I've always sympathized with him: he was just a shepherd kid from Orijuela who went to Madrid, which was eventually the scene of his great triumph. His life was particularly moving: his first book was ignored, he fought in the Civil War, and when he was imprisoned by Franco after the war he grew sick and died. I'm attracted to his openness to both ecstasy and misery. To me that was exceptional, and very touching. One poem I've always wanted to translate was one in *El Ultima Rincon,* "The Last Loner." In it he's both tired of living and overwhelmed with loving. It's actually a very Keatsian poem, in which he implies that he is *too* happy, *too* fulfilled. And it ends with some breathtaking lines, "Despues del amor, la tierra. / Despues de la tierra, nadie," which means "After love, the earth. / After the earth, nothing, no one." So I was thinking about those lines and I tried to write a poem for him. The Akhmatova poem came into being after I read D. M. Thomas's introduction to his translation of her poems, in which he tried to contextualize her writing in terms of her son getting locked up and the political events she lived through. Writers such as Herbert and Akhmatova lived in a world that is much harder than the world is for most American poets right now, though it could get harder at any moment.

DW: Do you consider yourself to be principally an elegiac poet?

LL: I often feel that that's' what I *am* as a *human.* I would like to explore other areas; I would like to write a really funny poem, a poem of wit. But I really don't know how to do that yet. Also, it seems to me, or has seemed to me for a long time, that the elegiac poem, the poem that is meditative and narrative, simply touched me more deeply. Yet I agree with Roethke when he said that a poet should try to show as many sides of himself or herself as he or she, in all decency, can.

DW: One thing about a lot of the Ghost poems that is striking to me is that as you've said, you've given a voice to people who wouldn't have had a voice otherwise. Sometimes I think, too, that many of your poems since *Dollmaker' s Ghost,* which focus very heavily on memory, are similarly elegiac. They 're trying to capture a past that's always elusive, always decisively lost.

LL: Well, some of them are overt elegies, for example four poems for my father, who died about a year ago—died hard, of Parkinson's disease. I guess one's own parents' deaths are difficult to think about. I can tell you I *did* when my father died, but I can't explain. I think you go a little crazy. At one point I was totally crazy. My father was cremated, and my sister and I had to drive into Fresno, going in to get this box of "ashes"—that's what they're euphemistically called. I knew it would be heavier than simple ashes, but I think my sister imagined they would be light and wafer-like, and that her father had been transformed into a dandelion. Actually, the box was quite heavy, and I remember driving and making sure I didn't tip the box over, which *was* heavy, so as not to disturb her any more than she was already disturbed. I remember coming out into this hot Fresno street, and you know it's a Western city with all that awful Soviet Realism architecture—it looks as bad as Phoenix. And I'm walking out with this box of, you know, bits of bone, grease for the wheels of heaven, and ashes, and part of me is thinking about poetry. I hate to say this because it will seem cruel, but the secret of poetry *is* cruelty. Part of me is always a poet, still observing, still trying to put things together and unify—and I was blasphemously thinking: "This moment is probably going to be important, what you notice is going to be important." What I noticed was an overweight woman in a T-shirt walking her springer spaniel on the street and her T-shirt read, "Kl 09 Rocks Out in Chicago!" and I couldn't get the incongruity of it out of my head. It wasn't incongruous, really. It was just my life, not a poem. I almost hasten to quote James Wright here: "I don't say it was a good life. I say it was a life." So some of the new poems are elegies; some of them are love poems. Sometimes you have to address things that are happening in your life that you really don't clearly understand and that's difficult. All the new poems I write are *me;* no personae.

DW: I guess all these questions are circling around a question. And that is, why do you write?

LL: I write, first, for myself. I was talking to my wife last week, from whom I'm separated for now, and she was saying, "Why? Why this, why that?" She would say in letters, "You're still writing. You write all the time. Just keep writing," and I would reply, "I'm afraid if I stop I won't do it anymore." And she said, "Well, why? What are you afraid of?" And I said, "Well, writing keeps me feeling good about myself, keeps me feeling alive, keeps me . . . ," and then I said, "It's the only thing that keeps me interested." And she said, "Yeah. You said it—I didn't." Suddenly everything comes back and it's at once crystal clear and also meaningless: that tree disguised in shadow in summer, sunlight on a doorstep that transforms it into a threshold of desire and then of loss, just the pure phenomenon. Sex has an *x* in it because the lover's cross just *there* and forever, and that letter, that character, has, in itself, no meaning, and no sympathy or mercy. And we're stilled, bewildered by those people who are truly happy *all the time,* who have a cash box for a heart or have a little wizened raisin far too small to contain one. Almost everyone else has an enlarging kernel of doubt.

DW: Do you find the process of writing to be painful, or is it pleasurable? Sometimes the very starkness of the subject matter is so chilling to me that I can't help but feel that your releasing that poem must have been sort of an agonizing process. Yet in that essay of yours, "Notes on the Gazer Within," you talk about how the times when you sit down to write a poem are those rare times when you 're at peace.

LL: I am at peace, at least during the moment of composition. The thinking has to get done, it seems to me, before I sit down to write. Yet writing, obviously, is about discovering something in the *act* of writing, as Robert Creeley said. But if you were just flat out weeping or crazy or ecstatically laughing, it would be difficult to make the pen move. I want to give you a very high-toned, intellectual answer. But it is also like *Garp* where the kid shows the story to the woman he's about to marry and she's in tears and she says, "That's the saddest story I ever read." And *he's* leaping up and down with joy!

Yes, there's emotion involved there, but it seems to me it's emotion that has been distilled, made palatable, pungent with its loss and with history, a myth. In readings I always end up including poems that I know might be frightening or depressing to people, but I never feel like changing or altering them. I've always thought the truth was hard.

DW: How do you sit down to begin a poem?
LL: Well, I begin by listening to music. I make a pot of coffee, I might have a drink, and I put on something, usually jazz, but sometimes rock 'n' roll, sometimes classical. It is important to listen to the best performers—Perlman, Gould, Stern, et cetera. And I listen for a while and I doodle for a while; sometimes I draw pictures. Usually everything begins with a letter, with a syllable: often it's the "k" sound, I don't know why. Must be infantile. Donald Hall says sounds in poetry satisfy infantile pleasures; *I'm* probably saying "caca" all the time. But I'll leave that diagnosis to Erikson or Piaget. Just a sound, a little phrase, that you might want to translate over into something else, to take from that into words, into .a musical phrase. And that's harder to get into English, since we have an inflected language. It's a language that seems to me less musical than Spanish, for example . . . I begin to get a few lines and then the whole thing begins to form. Then I'll cross out things that seem coarse, bad, overly conceptual, convoluted; but I do try to get a first draft at one sitting. Then I spend a week or two tracking down the alternatives. That's what's really fun, of course: just going and seeing where it goes.

DW: How long does the process of revision take?
LL: Oh, a few weeks. Sometimes less: sometimes only a week, it depends on how many problems, formal difficulties, a poem presents. I don't essentially measure a meter unless I'm openly working in one. Grammar is music. Everything is in the sound, the syntax, the grammar. When I revise I listen to the music of the thing. That's what I do—I listen. I listen very closely.

DW: Does the recent interest in a kind of narrative poetry have anything to do with a renewed interest in writing poems in traditional form, traditional meter? One reads a lot of, say, sestinas, in magazines today, and that's a form that seems to invite meditative and narrative concerns if it's going to work—and I know some of your more recent work is in blank verse or in syllabics.
LL: Yeah. I've written syllabics and blank verse and, well, the other day I wrote a poem in five-beat quatrains. I wanted to make sure I could still do it. When I began writing I wrote for two years in traditional meters—pentameter and blank verse, tetrameter, trimeter, syllabics. By casting something a blank verse line, you can make uninteresting language suddenly a lot more interesting—if only because of that slight pickup in rhythm. I don't think meters need to be used in that way, but I am saying that the ear deserves some respect. Yet I also think we ought to define form in a much broader way. I think Williams has been important, and Creeley and Olson, too, as people who broadened our ideas about form. I can't see any reason to rush back to a formal measure with rhyme unless one really feels that one can do something in a renewed capacity in the way that, say, Hart Crane did it in his poems. Or as Hugo did, or Philip Levine. The best recent formal verse I've seen comes from Gjertrud Schnackenberg—who employs form very strictly. But I guess I'm more interested in the people who are idiosyncratic masters of form—like James Wright, or more classical masters at it like Donald Justice and Richard Wilbur. I think Justice always used the form and did not let the form use him. That's a

real difference. I can't see using formal verse and saying, "Here's the answer." A lot of the formal poems I've seen—the bad ones—remind me of bad formal verse in the late fifties. I see no reason for that era to be revived.

DW: I'd like to ask you about your use of the line. The other night you were talking about Jarrell's capacity to push a ragged line to its limits, and I sometimes feel that you deliberately roughen up your lines through varying line lengths and unexpected enjambments. Few of your lines seem predictable, yet they generally seem right. What's the purpose of that technique and how do you go about working on that strategy?

LL: I think in the case of *Dollmaker's Ghost*, I had an idea that I wanted a kind of linear energy—something that went *across* a line. But I also wanted a kind of vertical energy to move down through the poem, thanks to the way in which the stanzas were shaped. One of the things that helped me to do this was a particular kind of enjambment, a violent runover of the line. But they're not enjambments so violent that the reader can't sense my pause at the end of the line. I want the individual lines to always keep a certain integrity. To capitalize the letter of each line also helps to draw attention to that fact, helps to say that it's still a line and not something arbitrary. A line is what *time* says to you, in the intimacy of terror; it's something in your ear when you think you're just driving home. At a certain point in writing *The Dollmaker's Ghost* I was very aware of the shape of the poem, the way it looked on the page; aware in some sort of silly little way of how important that shape was to me. So much happens in the heat of composition, at least in free verse; and it happens so quickly that I often feel that lines may be broken in the heat of that moment. But at the same time I feel that the line establishes itself as a distinct unit—it becomes almost like a dance step.

DW: How do you know when a poem falls into a stanzaic pattern?

LL: I think it announces itself pretty clearly and pretty early for me. I find it difficult to go back and place a poem into stanza form after I have done a rough first draft. It always seems to announce itself in the first draft. You need to stay out of the poem's way and be smart enough to get rid of your preconceived ideas about what you want to have happen. The poem you're writing, your own luck, and your subconscious may know more than you do.

DW: One very distinctive aspect of your work is a quirky use of punctuation. Dave Jauss calls it a "preponderance of punctuation." There are a lot of internal caesuras in the line that are the result of commas that aren't grammatically necessary, a lot of dashes, that sort of thing: What is the purpose of these techniques?

LL: A lot of times I think the caesura is done for dramatic effect. I'm not disparaging that as a term—you know, I think dramatic effect is important in art. When you see ballet dancers move across a floor, you are aware of sudden stops, caesuras or pauses in the body that don't seem quite natural and yet on second thought they seem to be very artful. That line of them going across a floor becomes something more sensuous than it was before by virtue of stopping, of moving very quickly and then suddenly slowing things down as if there's as much pleasure and sensuousness in slowing down, in stopping and then going on, as there would be in simply moving very rapidly. I think that's something I had in mind-conceiving the line as a kind of body moving through time and space on the page. I was not thinking of that consciously, just feeling it, feeling that capacity to hurl forward and then, suddenly, quickly and briefly stop. So much has to do with music, you know. The particular music you're hearing.

DW: How about shifts in diction, shifts in tone? I frequently see your work alternating between a kind of colloquial language and a more abstract kind of diction, also between a kind of high seriousness and a kind of black humor. Those extremes often operate within a single poem. Ashbery does that a lot, Marvin Bell does that. For example, a section of the—new long poem you read last night, "A Letter," contains a long erotic passage followed by another passage that is densely metaphysical, but bridged by the statement, "To fuck is to know." This seems to be a good example of what I mean.

LL: In that poem I wanted to try and talk about sex and, well . . . it seems to me that one could not know what one knows in this century and make a charmed case for sex being the answer to all the riddles of life. Lawrence and cummings tried that and did as well as anyone to try to make one recognize that; and you *do* recognize it to some extent, in culture and history and also in one's own life. But sex seems to be so many different things: it can be awful, it can be ecstatic, it can be boring. There's a cynicism in that poem, but it's essentially a poem of praise for the erotic. .I wanted to get all that down and I thought that one way to write that poem was to get everything to conform almost monochromatically to a certain level of diction. A poem like that inspires our trust because we feel it's by a poet with a steady life doing one thing well. I was thinking about that. The influence of Ashbery on my diction in that poem is also impossible to neglect or ignore—as is that of Levine in his most imaginative book, *One for the Rose*. . . It seemed to me one can move easily from certain levels of diction or even themes or considerations about all this just by simply fusing things together. It might look disquieting in terms of the shifts things make, but that's all right, too: one could have art that would make someone slightly anxious or could put them off as well as comfort them. An earlier draft of the section you're speaking of was spoken by a dead ancestor of mine, a woman who became more and more interesting as she began speaking—but who in fact could not have said the things that are said in that section, such as "To fuck is to know." So I thought, well, that's really what *I'm* saying: I took the poem away from her, partly because I didn't want to embarrass her.

DW: The final poem in *The Afterlife,* "Linnets," and "A Letter," the poem you read last night, are both long sequences. How do the longer poems differ from some of your shorter efforts. How does that earlier poem, "Linnets," differ from your newer one?

LL: Well, "Linnets" is much more imagistic and much more concerned with the natural world; it's a parable poem in which my brother shoots a linnet and there's a strange retribution for doing all this. It is, I guess, like shooting an albatross, though on a much smaller scale, I'm sure. So, anyway, the poem's all tied up in a kind of little myth. I think it differs from "A Letter" in that way, in that it has a mythical or hermetic method behind it, although you can say that about "A Letter" too, since the quoted thing from Ovid is spoken by Orpheus when he's petitioning the gods to descend to the underworld. He wants to go down to find Eurydice and bring her back, and there are little clues there about never looking back at each other as they *descend from* cliff dwellings. So those things are used, but in another sense "A Letter" is simply a love poem; it isn't playing elaborate games. Those games are interesting, but I just wasn't thinking of such things. I wasn't in that particular frame of mind.

DW: One thing that seems to distinguish *The Afterlife* poems from *The Dollmaker's Ghost* and some of the more recent poems is that there's a kind of mythic stance,

mythic concern or manipulation of the archetypes in the earlier book that you don't see in the later one.

LL: Maybe one has to choose between history and myth. A lot of the poems in *Dollmaker's Ghost* are concerned with people who actually lived, such as Hernandez or Zbigniew Herbert or Akhmatova; and I think you would feel—at least with those people or even with Kees or those two men, Tea and Angel, two men who picked grapes and did a lot of other things out in Fresno—I would feel that a mythic texture brought in or imposed upon them would simply violate any dignity they ever had. What a figure like Akhmatova asks you to do is simply not to falsify her life, nor to falsify history itself. If you tried to make her into a myth, it would look literary in a bad sense. Of course, myth is so ancient and so large that anybody who is a real mythologist could see it everywhere; I have friends who in fact do that. Of course, they're often Greek and they often teach comparative literature and they've read everything under the sun. The daily is mythic to them.

DW: How do you go about structuring a collection? I know that both *The Dollmaker's Ghost* and *The Afterlife* seem to follow an arrangement that makes each book grow more assured in its vision as it comes to its final sections. Few individual collections I can think of seem to be constructed as carefully.

LL: *Afterlife* fell pretty casually into place. I wanted to have a. strong beginning section and then a kind of interlude or meadow in the middle with shorter poems and more quietly lyrical movements. And I knew I wanted the long poem to come at the end. *The Dollmaker's Ghost* was a real problem, as I remember: a problem not only in arrangement but in poems, of knowing what to include. I sent the book to a friend, Daniel Halpern, to see what ideas he had about arranging it; I had some short poems that I kept out of that book, and Dan said something like, "Well . . . it's fine, but you have one peak after another here. No reader can take that for long. No reader should want to take it." And he was absolutely right, I thought, so I put the shorter poems back in, poems like "Truman, Da Vinci, Nebraska," "A Story," and a number of others; and I put them back in at points where they would lessen the action. I mean, even though we know people don't pick up poems and read them page 1 through page 72 or something, it's still important to have a strong continuity in the book. So I put the short poems back in, and other things, too. There's a little Weldon Kees poem that fit in with other things I was working on, though it is essentially different in style. The final thing that happened was when I met with my editor at E. P. Dutton, Jack MacRae, whose only suggestion was to move the poem "Picking Grapes in an Abandoned Vineyard" to the beginning of the book because he thought it a strong poem, and that the book needed a powerful opening.

DW: Who, excluding contemporary writers, has influenced you?

LL: Well, Eliot, when I was a kid, when I was fifteen or sixteen, and I still like him. I memorized a lot of him, so I don't even read him now. Yeats. Stevens. Rimbaud. Keats, especially in the odes and the letters. Coleridge, partly. Blake, Shakespeare. I mean, it goes on and on.

DW: Hart Crane?

LL: Hart Crane, certainly. Definitely Hart Crane. And George Oppen, to give you a counterbalance to Crane. Both of them were around at the same time; Oppen is amazing. Totally different from Crane, and we haven't even gone outside the language, I guess, except for Rimbaud. Pavese, Lorca—the list goes on and on once I start mentioning names. Reverdy, whom I translated at one point but whom I finally gave up on. Borges. Vallejo. Neruda. It's impossible: this thing of influence, it changes, you see, day by day. There was a day last winter when I realized how strongly I'd been influenced by Milan Kundera, who I think is wonderful at what he does. I read fiction, too, because good fiction is so vastly sophisticated about language. I like Barth and Hass but I also like Gardner, and his rebuke of the metafictionalists—it's all interesting. Ashbery, of course. So I'm omnivorous, heterodox. I might like to have some sort of clean lineage, but I don't. And it would be silly, anyway, to exclude contradictory influences.

DW: What was Levine like as a teacher?

LL: Fantastic. Unbelievably sweet and funny and harder than anybody else I've ever seen. But his great talent in teaching was to make you laugh at your own mistakes so that you could overcome them almost cathartically within a few days. Going to a class taught by Philip Levine was like going to no other class on earth. It was going to a class taught by a man who was, for one thing, a master comedian—and also one who had great passion, and who could change the emotion of the class immediately and you could suddenly participate in some dark meditation by Hardy or Yeats on death. He'd read the poem aloud and then would bring it all the way back home to the level of emotion and humor. It wasn't so much going to a class; it wasn't anything *like* a class. It was like going to hear life and poetry and the unbelievable coincidence of the two. It's nothing I've seen anybody else do, and it was particularly important to me when I was between the ages of eighteen and twenty-two, when I studied with Philip. Peter Everwine was also a wonderful poet and a wonderful teacher. Then I went to graduate school and studied with Donald Justice. Justice, unlike Levine, didn't care what you said but cared deeply about the phrasing and your care with saying something. And it was an incredible refinement: you learned so much about *words* studying with Justice; not only words, but also their nuances and their music. You could write *anything* you wanted in his classes: you were unbelievably liberated from any preconception, even those you had about your own work and what *you* wanted to do. He has the most unique mind I've ever met and one of the richest and kindest.

DW: You've taught creative writing at several universities and you've edited *Missouri Review*. A number of poets one talks to feel that teaching and editing sap some of the same energy that one would usually devote to one's own writing, that ultimately this damages one's potential as a writer. How do you feel about that?

LL: Oh, God, I feel you can only write poetry for about three hours a day—five at the most when you're really there doing it—and you've got to do something else with the rest of your time. I *like* teaching. I never liked editing, but I do it because *Missouri Review* is there, where I teach. I don't enjoy editing and I'm one of the wariest of editors. Teaching doesn't sap me. I used to work jobs where I'd work in a warehouse or a cannery or drive a truck ten hours a day: *that* saps you. If you work for ten hours a day or eight hours in a physical job or even an office job, I'll tell you one thing: you may have a lot to say, but you won't have any energy to say it. If you don't go to sleep and stay up writing a poem, which is the way I write poems—far into the night—and suddenly it's sunrise and I'm there and maybe I've got a first draft of a poem, and its time to go to sleep for a few hours, that's one life—and not an easy one. But if you have to get up at 5:30 to drive a truck, you won't do that. No one has the stamina to keep doing both things.

DW: Your new manuscript is tentatively titled *Trouble*. How do its concerns and method differ from *Dollmaker's Ghost*?

LL: Well, for one thing, there are no personas being used: there's no ghost network going on. An odd thing happened to me one day in New York. Marcia and I were staying with an old friend of ours and we'd all gone out the night before. Stephen Dunn had had dinner with us and come over briefly for a drink. It was great to see him—he's an old, old friend—we'd talked and drunk a lot of scotch during the night. The next day I got up; and it was a beautiful day in New York; I went around the corner to get bagels to bring back for breakfast, and I had this sudden idea of myself being able to say something that was terribly frank and honest and uncompromising and which might, in fact, be poetry. I was thinking that it was *poetry* and that it was what I really wanted to do, to say something terribly unequivocal. Not a literal or pedestrian honesty but an honesty of the imagination. And I've thought a lot about that moment—it disappeared, it evaporated almost immediately after coming back in and having coffee and bagels and cream cheese and all that and talking about nothing, talking about the *New York Times,* talking about this and that, listening to whoever was on the radio. But I'll never forget that moment: it was an avenue into something, and it made me understand what I really wished to do in my poetry. In my life. I understood the kind of power I've always wanted to have in poetry. It is a sort of energy, the way Yeats has it in, say, "Easter 1916," when his energy isolates a moment in time and makes it stay there forever and live in that present. It's what Eliot means when he talks about that Chinese vase, with its pattern always moving, and yet always still. And I think I felt that I could have that quality by talking very *directly* in a poem. That's what I'm doing now—just talking very directly from a first-person viewpoint during a rocky time in my own life. My father died about a year ago; my wife and I separated in August; we have a son. . . . All these things coalesced at one point. I used to think that one could only write about such things long after they had happened. But it seemed to me that there was no other choice but to try to write about them *as* they happened. Now maybe this is wrong. But there seemed to be nothing else to say, to talk about. . . Anyway, that's what the book seems to be about. I didn't plan it that way. I didn't imagine that I even could write directly about things that had just happened; but I finally discovered that if I tried to stay off subjects like that, I felt foolish. I don't want to be a "professional" and just write competent poems. I'd rather go into the whole sorrow of the beast, or whatever the phrase is, and try to talk about it. I may fail but that's all right.

DW: You're thirty-six, and Stevens, Yeats, Williams, a number of the major poets of this century really didn't start writing in what I guess you'd say is a "grand manner" until they were in their sixties. What would you like your achievement to be like thirty years from now?

LL: I don't know. I can't really say. I would like to write my poems and leave it at that. I used to envy other poets. I'd read Bidart and say, "I wish I had his way of not being 'poetic' at all and yet being incredibly talented." I love his work. Or I envied the eroticism of David St. John's poems, which is ingrained so deeply in his language—there's a desire his *words* have for each other. But now I just want to write my own poems. I would like to be one of those people who was, in poetry, a rule breaker; someone who mattered. Poetry sometimes seems totally enclosed or secluded world, a very tiny one: everybody knows what everybody else is going through by virtue of this incredible grapevine, so much so that the other worlds are closed off to us. I think poetry ought to challenge these other worlds in the way that fiction can challenge science or that art can challenge technology. I don't know how to do that in an exciting way in poetry, and I don't want her to disappear into a mist of jargon in the process. I wouldn't want to put her in conditions where she couldn't even breathe. Poetry's such an ancient art—we still have a belief in the muse. Can you imagine any other art or any other way of thinking that still has something like *that? You* know, it's so old, and the intimacy you feel with other poets is so revealing and right—it's like no other thing that anyone else on earth has. I respect poetry, because it's very old and yet it's also new and renewing. When I think of myself thirty years from now, I have this trepidation about saying *anything*. I don't *know* what will happen; I don't know who will be around to read me, or whether I'm a shriek in the void. But it is obvious that some works might last—I do feel that.

DW: One of the things Wallace Stevens said: "No one understands that one writes poetry because one must."

LL: Yeah, must. Also, it's just better than living any other way. I mean, *I* think it's better. I still think poetry is healthy; it also has greater purity than anything else, if only because you can use the mind all the way up. You can exist in the liberated adulthood of poetry, totally uncompromised.

from "An Interview with Larry Levis" from *AWP Writers Chronicle*, 2003, & from *A Condition of the Spirit*, 2004—Michael White

This interview was compiled during the winter of 1989-1990. Levis had recently returned from a Fulbright year in Eastern Europe.

Michael White: Could we begin by summarizing the unusual developments in your work over the past few years? I'm wondering specifically what influence your travels abroad have had on your poetry.

Larry Levis: I'm not sure that I can summarize them, nor am I sure that such changes are all that unusual. For one thing, they were far more gradual and internalized than the work itself might suggest. Obviously, if you placed the new prose beside *Winter Stars*, and had no idea that the two were written four years apart, you might wonder about it, or about me. But in so many ways the new poems in *The Widening Spell of the Leaves* are similar to the poems in *Winter Stars*. The line itself is far longer in the new work, especially in the longish, narrative sequence (The Perfection of Solitude) that begins the collection. The poem has a way of circling back on itself in a sort of larger musical pattern, denying any more direct, linear narrative. Of course, I wonder: is there such a thing as a direct, linear narrative? Sounds a little boring, and it seems to me that fiction dispensed with it centuries ago, as did poetry, i.e., Homer.

And there's nothing very new in a musical pattern or in the obsession with destroying or confusing or annoying Time in a poem. We're still sitting in the glacial shadow of Modernism, a period in which Eliot and Faulkner pummeled Time into whirling dust specks. And it's hard to escape the Time in which one is born, and the ideas that occur inevitably because of that. When Mandelstam cries out, "My Age, my Beast!" doesn't he mean that he can do little but cling to the fur of it as it passes through his world, that he has no alternative? But who does?

MW: I know what you mean. But don't most of us, at times, struggle to avoid resenting the labor the art costs us?

LL: In art or in life, revision should be a pleasure. And one way of revising life is to travel. In 1983, I had a Guggenheim Fellowship, so I went to Europe and later, when I returned home, I didn't quite want to be back here yet, and I still had some time and money, so I went to Oaxaca, Mexico. Both places occur in the new poems, and Europe figures heavily in the prose.

I traveled through Europe without any plan and without much organization. I wasn't studying it. I rarely carried a guidebook or a camera, things that I thought created a shield between me and the places I was in. In the station in Rome one day, I decided to take the next train, wherever it went. I traveled alone, and walked miles and miles, and got lost dozens of times, and discovered the pleasure of losing my way on the Via Serpentia—following it to the Coliseum, which loomed up suddenly at the end of it. In Vienna I drank with strangers and simply nodded as they went on raving in German. Off the Damrak in Amsterdam, on impulse, I bought a gray sport coat with narrow lapels and didn't realize that it made me look like a polyester sleaze ball until a year and a half later.

One night I tried to find the red light district, and asked two Dutch guys how to get there, asked them in French. One of them listened closely, then looked at me in my sport coat and replied, "Why don't you just use English? It's a perfectly good language." Then he pointed across a canal. I felt so abashed I just walked back to my hotel, an ill-lit place I never liked much but never took the trouble to move from, either. It was run by Indians and had a chronic odor of curry floating through it. I saw a large De Kooning exhibit near Constantin Huygenstratt and wept in the middle of the museum and have never know why. I mean, I never cry. The paintings were beautiful. My father had died about a year before. If it was him who wished that I weep at a De Kooning exhibit, I didn't mind. One morning I saw a rat climb along the counter of a cafe that looked empty, clean and gleaming before it opened for business; a muted glow of brass lining the bar seemed old and trustworthy; the rat wasn't hurrying.

You see? All I did there had this random quality about it that you can see in the above. In Europe I began to experience things, and still remember them, in terms of prose, in terms of a journal or notebook that recorded anything I happened to notice. This is why I believe that being in Europe made prose possible for me . . .

MW: Why?

LL: I don't know, exactly, but that's the lie I tell myself. Of course, composing prose is 'the shaping of sentences, paragraphs; it is not at all random, and, for me, it remains a larger and more impersonal system than poetry. For in poetry I do not fly out of myself and into another configuration, into the otherness of a character who is X or Me plus x or Me minus Y. In prose this is almost a requirement of some kind, I think, if you want to be interesting, even to yourself. This doesn't mean that poetry doesn't spiral into larger circles; it does. Yet the conventions of lyric poetry have their reasons for being somewhat incontestable, and they are good ones. In a lyric one has the sense, or the illusion, that he is hearing, getting, the poet in all his frankness; you hear, then, the real Keats, the real Donne, beneath the conventions of another time and culture. The truth is, I really don't know. I had no intention of writing any prose in Europe, or of ever writing prose.

MW: Did you continue to write poems during this period?

LL: I wrote one poem, "Those Graves in Rome," while I was staying in Paris, and I finished the final revisions for *Winter Stars* while in Bucharest. But I did write any number of notes, impressions, things in a journal which I kept, and which began to result in poems and prose.

I did see some of the things that one is supposed to see in Europe, I guess, but I missed many others. I saw the Caravaggios in Santa Maria del Popolo and in the Borghese, and this, seeing them, resulted, some time later, in a poem called "Caravaggio: Swirl & Vortex." But that poem is far more about Vietnam and a friend who died there than it is about the painting or about one of the more fascinating bad boys of Italian art, though that life is there too, in the poem. Just now I doubt that the world is in any desperate need of another poem about a painting, and mine, I am glad to say, isn't one. Still, that is no reason at all not to go and write a poem about a painting if you need to, or even desire to. The painting by Caravaggio was not my real subject. I was standing before it with my friends Phil and Franny Levine, admiring it, and this is where things get a little eerie, for in Caravaggio's rendering of the beheaded Goliath, a self-portrait in fact, there is just a little too much there that is a likeness of a friend from high school who went off to Vietnam and never came back; in Rome he appeared before me in the moment of death, his eyes half closed, or half open, depending on how you look at it.

But I didn't go searching for anything like this. It happened that way; that's all. I did nothing very deliberately in Europe. I let it all ambush me however it wished to, and it had a serene and complete way of doing this.

MW: Do you think your writing is political in any sense?

LL: No. I mean, I'm not really for anybody or any party. And I don't write tracts or manifestos. But life is political. I buy this, or that, and whether I remind myself of it or not, I'm involved in capitalism. And I have desires: I don't want to see the earth turn into a dumpsite, or the sky fill with our waste, or witness the sea full of oil. I don't want our government sending troops into Nicaragua or any place else in Central America. I wish our leaders would stop lying and using propaganda, too, but such a wish is no doubt futile. Still, how can it make war on drugs when the CIA has been trafficking in heroin and cocaine for decades? If they were serious, they'd outlaw cigarettes. After all, part of experience is necessarily and inescapably involved with a political dimension. If you keep everything touching upon this dimension out of your work completely, despite the very real and censoring difficulties of that, such an absence would be seen, I imagine, as enormously deliberate, and would seem itself a kind of political act.

But could anyone do this? Where does the political end? Recent theory has widened its meaning rather than restricted it: gender is political; metaphor is political; the existential decision to read is political given the nature of film, video and tv now. And in terms of American culture, this interview and my consenting to do it is political.

MW: Actually, I was curious whether your experience of the politics of Eastern Europe might have been transformative in some metaphorical or metaphysical way.

LL: Sorry. I guess I simply don't know what you mean. I really don't. My poetry's political effect will have all the force of a grassblade. Still, traveling and working in Eastern Europe was important to everything I wrote later, and I feel that going over there, going east of the Danube, changed me in some mysterious way.

Let me explain, or try to. In 1983 I had a Guggenheim, but I also had a more official purpose for traveling, for I had been invited, by the Romanian Ministry of Culture and the U.S. Embassy in Bucharest, to read and lecture in Bucharest, Cluj, and Sibiu. People warned me that it must be a kind of USIA tour, and I therefore could expect a lot of banquets and bullshit, but that didn't happen thanks to Ioanna Deligiorgis and her friends, and I was able to see Bucharest without being herded along by an aparachik. Romania is perhaps the only country in the world where young women come up to you after you have read your poems, poems which some of them haven't understood a word of, to hand you flowers, bouquets of flowers. As a custom, it seemed very sweet, and if some poets consider it insincere and false, because you're even more incomprehensible over there than you are here, I think their reaction is shabby and selfish. What the Romanians respect is poetry, any poetry: whether they've understood it or not, they think it civilized to hand you a bouquet out of respect for the art. There's no such respect in this country: here, you are more often thought of as some kind of con-artist guru, or as a clown who isn't terribly funny, or as someone pretentious, someone who doesn't understand that he lives in a democracy, where we are all equal, and therefore all equal in talent and brains. And always, in such a country as ours, the poet, who publishes his work in the naive expectation of being thanked for this gift, is often judged not on the merits of the work, but for his or her life, his or her behavior, judged for his or her morals. For finally, you see, there's no money in poetry, so why is this man or woman doing it? There must be something wrong with him, with her. This is capitalism in concert with that detestable vestigial Calvinism that grows everywhere here. It's depressing. How many people attended Poe's funeral? Whitman was one of the few.

Their offerings of flowers grew immense when I read with Nikita Stanescu, who died recently and was probably ill then; his audience was aware of this. He was, and is, something of a national hero in Romania, and deserves to be.

MW: How do you compare the life of, say, a Romanian poet with your own experience of life in America?

LL: In our country, few poets become heroes, and when they do it must feel suspect. Fame? Oh, but look at the fate of Pound with his insanity trial and his eleven-year stay at St. Elizabeth's; look at the reviewers (some of them once his friends!) of Hart Crane. Frost played his role quite well, but it's interesting that his last question was: "Was I any good?" Was Frost so corrupted by his public that he could no longer know whether he was? Most poets in this country can expect little but to be neglected and unread, and they are lucky if they can turn this to their advantage, most of them are too much like the culture that has produced them; they cannot stand to be ignored. All poets are spoiled, but if you can't stand neglect you are spoiled in the wrong way. In that case you'll learn nothing from reading Keats' letters; and that seems a wonderful reason for buying a guitar and learning how to play rock n' roll, which I think is a fine and respectable thing to do. It's also a lot of hard work. But the audience might, and it often does, love you. Besides, the Talking Heads are light years more imaginative and intelligent than most of what I see published in, say, literary journals.

Be spoiled in the right ways. If your work feels mediocre, if it demeans your spirit, burn it. Burn it even if the workshop you're in likes it. After all, you didn't begin doing this in order to be a competent or even an accomplished poet. That's like being a moderately good neurosurgeon; they don't exist. No one alive is going to be as good as Keats, but that doesn't mean you have to settle for crap. In fact, it means the opposite of that.

MW: Practically speaking, what was it like abroad?

LL: The problems faced by the average Romanian are so different from the ones above it's shocking. Flowers may have been easy to get in Bucharest, but bread, meat, milk, cheese, clothes were nearly impossible. A carton of Kents was a treasure on the black market. When I was there, coffee seemed to have become extinct, and in its place was a watery barley concoction. For the first time since the age of seven, when my mother gave me a first cup before school, I was decaffeinated. Things were scarce there. I first noticed this crossing the frontier from Hungary. The train from Vienna to Bucharest is the Orient Express, but after it crosses the Danube it becomes communist, and so is bare of even necessities: no dining car, no lounge car, not even water to drink. It's not the Orient Express of the movies; in fact it's an uncrowded, oddly silent train. I was hungry and thirsty when we crossed into Romania at three a.m. There, a woman about thirty-five or forty came on board with two men in civilian clothes. She was wearing, I remember, high heels and a red dress that might have been appropriate for a prom in say, 1962. I was prepared for more stern young guards with shiny, new submachine guns, the kind of military inspectors who had got on at the checkpoint in Budapest, and who barked at me: "Visa forma, please!" Someone later told me I didn't have to worry about their machine guns; they need at least three signatures before they can fire them at anyone.

But the woman at the Romanian frontier was different. First, she apologized in English for having to wake me up in the middle of the night, then said they would have to search my luggage as well. Then after a second or two, she apologized for having to do that. Then she sighed and sat down across from me and looked at my cigarettes on the windowsill until I offered her one. She did want one, she said, but her employment forbade her taking one. After another sigh, she confessed she didn't like her job that much, that the place was too remote for her, that she missed Bucharest, but then, she shrugged, you had to go where you were sent. Then she and the two men began to go through my bags, inspecting them, until she found one of my books, *The Dollmaker's Ghost*, with my picture on the back. Holding it up, she said, "But this is you! You are the author of this book!" I admitted I was. In Romanian, she told the other two, who halted what they were doing. The three of them just stood around the book in silence for a moment, then they zipped up my bags without a further glance into them, wished me the best of everything, and went on down the corridor of the train. But a second later one of the men came back, gesturing urgently by lifting two fingers to his mouth. Finally, I understood what he meant, and gave him a pack of Marlboros from the carton I'd brought.

MW: Let's change the subject a little. An interesting comparison might be made between your poem "Picking Grapes in an Abandoned Vineyard" and Frost's "Directive." Each poem involves an imaginative return to origins, to a creative source. Frost's poem directs us to move "back out of all this now too much for us"; your poem takes the speaker "back to the house/where I was born." But the journey, in your poem, is peopled with the immigrant farmhands of a mythologized childhood, while Frost's poem is remarkable for its eerie, ascetic absence.

LL: Such a comparison is interesting only if restricted to the ideas you mention. "Directive" is one of my favorite poems. My own poem is like Frost's, I'd say, even where you imply it differs, for mine is peopled by the absence of those workers, just as Frost's is inhabited by the absence, or imagined presence only, of those who once lived and worked in that New England town and countryside which they have subsequently and mysteriously abandoned. And the house at the end of my poem, which is the house I grew up in, is silent anyway, empty of what it once was, with only the past meaning of its solemnity intact, something there but inarticulate.

But I wasn't thinking of Frost's poem when I wrote mine. If his influenced me, that influence was by then so internalized as to be unconscious, I suppose. It may seem strange but I believe that poems are written because the poet engages in a special form of forgetting and therefore is enabled to concentrate upon the composing of a poem; that is, the poet deliberately, skillfully, insouciantly, cunningly, faithfully, unforgivably forgets. It is the only kind of forgetting which is also a form of remembering, yet it does no good to reflect upon the greatness of Wordsworth in such moments, and, from a certain perspective at least, the poet in those moments simply doesn't give a shit. I'm sorry, but this is the way I see it.

MW: I'm reminded here of the striking appearances Whitman makes in *Winter Stars.*
LL: I'd have to guess that Whitman appears in my work because, first of all, I'm an American. In a way Whitman is like a language or a weed, ineradicable. Like the Civil War which gave this nation its most profound history, and of which he is irrecoverably a part and a witness, he is part of American thought whether one reads him or not. At its best, this manifests itself as part of our large, generous, open-minded health and democratic grit and idealism. But in a strictly material sense, that thought becomes a blight on the land: freeways, tract homes, replications mindlessly proliferating in the form of business loops, suburbs with those thin, just-planted trees lining the streets and what they suggest: the impossibility of any history ever taking root there. But the uglification of the world is not Whitman's fault, just as Stalin's pogroms and his extinction of the kulaks is not the fault of Karl Marx.

MW: Who do you see as your precursors? I'm thinking of Harold Bloom's sense of the word.
LL: I don't know if you're asking who my precursors are or who, specifically, influenced me. But if it's the latter, then it's easier. When I was sixteen, I read all of T.S. Eliot I could, read him constantly, and after him went on to Stevens, Frost, and Auden, and after that came back to Eliot. By then I was seventeen, I think. But I should say that if it hadn't been for Philip Levine's workshops, shortly after that, I'm unsure what I would have become. A shoe salesman who has no meaning at all? A drug addict who has his meaning entirely to himself? Both? Well, I include this fact, because facts are important now in an art presently infatuated by (and sometimes nourished by) the psychoanalytic theories of Bloom. But it wasn't Milton and Wordsworth who changed my life back there at Dust and Wind State College; it was Levine, his poetry, his teaching, the purity and fire of his genius that did that, and this further effected a change that my reading of Eliot had already begun.

MW: And perhaps, with such an intensely personal view of poetic growth, you might also have intensely personal sense of a poetic?
LL: Somewhere my poetic must have begun to internalize itself just as radically as my influences did. But, all right, I try to write clearly, not because there may not be something in not writing clearly; there might be, you see, but it just wouldn't feel like me or wouldn't feel enough like me, and would seem bogus, a posturing, false. And I know that wanting my poems to have a kind of authenticity has nothing to do with that particular cultural vanity, which is a fear of change itself. For my work has changed.

So, yes, I suppose I do have a personal sense of a poetic, but having a sense of it does not mean that I can articulate that poetic. And I wonder if I would want to, even if I could.

MW: But surely you must have an idea of the larger theoretical effects of this poetic? Its "political" effects?
LL: No, what I do as a poet is different. In literary theory, in philosophy and history, we're accustomed to extending the use of the word "political" to an enormous range of preoccupations, and we're comfortable in speaking of the "political" nature of gender, sexuality, metaphor, patriarchal language, a Freudian history. In revising a past, the extension of such a term is meant to give way to a possible future. I'm less comfortable than others

with speaking in this way, if only because Theory itself, and its usual codification and institutionalization in universities, allows its visionary energy to travel in the closed circuitry of an authorship and readership who are content with their isolation from the world of political action; by their abstention from such a world, they in effect reinforce, however temporarily, a kind of status quo. Of course, I'm glad that Foucault and Lacan and Kristeva are there, that they can be read, contemplated, and after all, it would be ridiculous to expect justice in a world where everyone seems glued to the set while Nature, as we've known it, is ending because, as Bill McKibbern argues, we've tampered with its independence.

In the world, of course, politics still means power, and there's a significant difference between Theory and Power. I mean, I haven't any political power in that sense; few of us do, and this is the case whether one works in a library or a meatpacking plant. But I would suspect that everyone's poetics, even Mallarme's, is political in at least one sense: it is vulnerable, no matter how scrupulously aesthetic it may be, to history, to time, to an ethical and therefore a political formulation or interpretation within a culture, a formulation which often makes the actual work seem distant by classifying it. In this way, the Symbolist becomes not the revolutionary, but the spokesperson for Art, and therefore for the status quo, not for those who might wish to overthrow it. Similarly, the revolutionary poetics of Pound or Eliot are complicated by a discernible and naive fascism which characterizes some of their opinions, just as it does the opinions of Hemingway and Lawrence. On the other hand, at times an actual choice, such as Eluard's dismal embrace of socialism after the war, resulted only in those empty, crooning lyrics he made during that period as he turned into a kind of Marxist cheerleader. Others, great ones like Vallejo or Mandelstam, retained an independence only at a great cost, and one might say that Mandlestam died because of it, because he challenged Stalin. It is rare to have the luck of a poet like Brecht, who was characteristically cunning when he was subpoenaed by McCarthy. When asked at the hearings if he knew any communists, he answered that he did. When asked to name them, he did that too, the German names lifting off his tongue in a long roll call of the absent. The senators witch-hunters went on furiously checking their lists and finding none of those names on them, so Brecht was then asked if he knew where any of those communists he had mentioned were living. He answered, surprised, "Why no, I don't. They're all dead now. The Nazis killed them all."

Actual politics often seems like an adolescent who insists upon Either/Or, upon answer, classification, completion. It is all Keats did not mean by negative capability. Poetry is an ancient art that insists upon Both/Neither. Politics can't understand this. When Robert Lowell followed Bobby Kennedy around the house in Hyannisport reading aloud to him from *The Education of Henry Adams*, Kennedy finally went into a bathroom and closed the door. Lowell opened it. "Do you mind?" said the young candidate, and shut it and locked it.

Of course when Lowell published his refusal of Johnson's White House dinner invitation—a refusal that indicted the president for his escalation of the Vietnam conflict—on the front page of *The New York_Times* at about the same moment Johnson received the actual letter Lowell had sent, that was understood, of course. A White House aide recalled that "the roar could be heard all the way from the Oval Office." But Lowell had no such luck teaching the doomed young brother of the slain president anything more complex, and literature is always more complex. But publishing such a refusal is an incident of Lowell exercising the maximum amount of his political power. His attempt to teach Kennedy something is politics in this other, larger sense of the term, and is interesting because of its ineffectuality and failure.

MW: What makes that interesting?

LL: It reveals a world that doesn't care much about poems or poets. I, my whole generation, we were all violated by a little bit of history, by the Vietnam era. I won't go on with any prolonged analysis of it, and don't want to bore you. But to see friends from high school go off to fight needlessly in it, to see other friends wind up in jail for protesting it, affects you. And finally, to see a friend go off and never come back from it has a much larger and more lasting effect on you. He dies, you go on living, and it seems at first unfair, then odd to do so, then strange to be able to do so with such ease. But you don't forget it, and you can't forget it. This is the way history enters you.

MW: That seems like a somewhat passive view of things.

LL: No. History enters you belatedly and far more effectively after it has happened around you. It strikes me that the opposite is true. Forgetting, ignoring is passive. To ignore the history that has in a sense created what you have become is passive. But remembering it is active, an acknowledgement not only of time but also of one's acceptance of it. And such remembering is akin to poetry, as is that line in a letter by Emily Dickinson where she condemns the Civil War by saying of it: "The boys who whistled are extinct." Such remembering is why some bodies find no graves except in poems. For politics, power, at times is unwilling even to condescend to bury those whom it has used and forsaken.

Poetry takes up such a task unquestioningly, has always done so, and does it not because it is naive, but because it is worldly. From this point of view, politicians, leaders, seem a clique of rich, indifferent boys who, because they have never seen anyone die, do not believe in death itself, and who, therefore, do not really believe in the lives of others, in the very existence, the doggedly unadorned daily existence of anyone else at all.

I know this is a large, gross oversimplification, but this was the impression I got of them at that time, and still get of them when I see them lying on tv, something they do badly but often. That history makes me, and maybe my generation, anomalous.

MW: How?

LL: After the horrors of WW2, Zbigniew Herbert once wrote, in a little ode: "One might still offer, even to the betrayed world, a rose." That trite rose is deliberate and complex there, for it is offered not out of mere innocence, but out of a radical, recovered innocence, and out of the pain of that innocence, and so the offering of it, the poetry of it, reminds its recipient, painfully, at once of what is lost and of what is not lost, and therefore of what is still possible. For the appearance of a rose in the ruins of Warsaw, in bombed-out Dresden or Belgrade, is no longer trite. All the reality of it comes rushing back into its scent, the same one that has clung to it so tenaciously all through those years.

MW: Do you find any irony in the fact that you—who might in some circles be considered the loner, rebel poet—are now directing one of the more established creative writing programs in the country?

LL: No. As a title it doesn't mean much, and in fact is a departmental assignment that rotates from one to another of us on the staff here. If someone were to take it seriously as a title that meant something, like County Sheriff, well, that would be ridiculous. The only danger of such an office is identifying yourself with it. That's never been a problem with me, and, when things go wrong, I don't even take the failure personally. I just try to fix it.

"An Afterword" from *The Darkening Trapeze,* 2016—David St. John

After Larry Levis' death in May 1996, his sister, Sheila Brady, asked Larry's oldest friend, former teacher, and lifelong mentor, Philip Levine, if he would be willing to edit a posthumous collection of Levis' poems. Levine agreed, and he asked me if I would help him look through what he'd been told was a significant amount of unpublished work. This posthumous collection became, of course, the book published as *Elegy.*

I had known Larry Levis since I was eighteen years old (when he first introduced me to Philip Levine), and he had become my closest friend in and out of poetry. Except for Levine, who knew Larry's work more intimately than anyone, I felt that I had an unusual perspective on these unpublished poems, as Levis was in the habit of sending copies of his poems to me, Phil Levine, and other friends for comment long before they would appear in journals or in books. He would also send his friends a typescript copy of each new book as he was assembling it. I had agreed to help Phil in whatever way he needed and, not long after, we both received identical boxes filled with copies and drafts of Larry's poems. For the most part, this work had been pulled from Levis' computers (in his office at Virginia Commonwealth University) or found among his papers in his home office. Mary Flinn and Greg Donovan—founders of the superb online journal, *Blackbird,* and Larry's close friends and colleagues—as well his former student and friend Amy Tudor, all worked to find every unpublished poem available. What we found, as Levine mentions in his introduction to the book *Elegy,* were multiple drafts of many of the poems, some of which were clearly unfinished; yet others seemed remarkably finished. Larry's friends at VCU had been, in my view, heroic in assembling the most complete and final versions they we able to find or construct from his many drafts; at times, they had even tried to include the revisions they'd found scrawled on scattered post-its and other notes left on his desk.

I recognized a few of the poems in the box as having come from the period when Larry lived in Utah, and they'd clearly been pulled off the computer he'd brought with him from Salt Lake City to Richmond. A few other poems were originally part of a manuscript he'd sent me called *Adolescence,* but were later dropped as that manuscript became the book *Winter Stars.* Yet, to me, the most astonishing thing about looking at these poems gathered in their huge cardboard box was that the great majority—nearly 200 pages—had been written since *The Widening Spell of the Leaves.* This was almost entirely new work.

The process of working on *Elegy* was difficult for Levine and for me; it felt emotionally charged and—to me, at least—psychologically daunting. I believe that Larry Levis was the poet Levine admired most of all other contemporary poets, yet he was also as much a son to Phil as he was a protégé, as much an irreplaceable friend as an admired poet. For the first few months, every time Phil and I tried phoning one another to talk about the poems we'd been reading, well, we simply couldn't do it; we couldn't talk about this impossible task. In order to talk about some selection of Larry's poems, we first had to admit that Larry was dead. It took almost five months before we could actually have our first conversation about the work itself. Finally, over that next nine months, *Elegy* began to take shape.

Levine had a clear idea of how he wanted to present Levis' work, and that was to include a group of the shorter, more lyrical pieces we had found and to set them alongside the sequence of longer "elegy" poems, which were somewhat similar in style to Larry's late work in *The Widening Spell of the Leaves.* Yet, as we looked through the poems, it was clear that there were also many longer poems that were distinct from the "elegy" poems, and which stood apart from that sequence. Since it was impossible (for reasons of space) to include those poems also, we set them aside and, with two exceptions, included only those nine poems that were clearly meant to be part of the "elegy" sequence. Almost all of those longer, operatic, and at times wildly ambitious poems necessarily held back from *Elegy* are collected here for the first time.

Included also in this collection is a poem with a fascinating history, "Poem Ending with a Hotel on Fire," which I have always believed was meant to be the tenth of Larry Levis' "elegy" poems (some of the "elegy" poems had been titled, in their early incarnations, "Poem with..." instead of, "Elegy with..."). I believe that this poem was meant to complete the cycle of ten elegies Levis had been working toward in order to create his own *Duino Elegies*, his own *The Book of Nightmares*. Sadly, the final page of "Poem Ending with a Hotel on Fire" had been dramatically X-ed out by Levis, with an indecipherable revision scrawled down the margin alongside the X-ed out typescript. None of us—all of whom had read Larry's cursive for twenty years or more—could read the revised version. Levine, with regret, decided we couldn't publish the poem, as we had no way of knowing what Larry had intended for the final draft. Remarkably, only a month or two after the publication of the book *Elegy*, a video tape of Levis reading "Poem Ending with a Hotel on Fire" just two weeks before his death was made available to Mary Flinn (this reading is posted on *Blackbird*, which also holds a wealth of essays and commentaries about Larry Levis' poetry, including an excellent piece by Christopher Buckley on Levis' uncollected prose poems). The version that Levis read was the final, revised version we had been looking for. If this final draft had been available at the time, I might have argued to publish two separate books of Larry's poems—one volume of the ten elegies, and a second volume containing the shorter poems (as they appeared in *Elegy*), along with a dozen or so of the longer poems now collected in *The Darkening Trapeze*.

For me, one of the most fascinating aspects of editing *The Darkening Trapeze* was to be reminded again in Levis's poetry what I'd already learned from a lifetime of conversations with Larry—that he was profoundly influenced by twentieth-century painting and photography and by world cinema as well. Fellini's influence permeates the poem "La Strada," and the haunted presences of Surrealist painters and writers echo throughout Levis' wry poem, "Carte de l'Assassin a M. André Breton." Yet these are only two examples. In his earlier poetry, Levis celebrates and engages in some of his finest early work the paintings of Caravaggio and Edward Hopper, as well as the remarkable photographs of Joseph Koudelka. Still, in the poems of The Darkening Trapeze it is the influence of the English painter Francis Bacon that feels to me most constantly present and most powerfully resonant.

In the spring of 1973, Larry and I were both living in Iowa City and saw each other nearly every day. After the release of Bernardo Bertolucci's *Last Tango in Paris*—and its accompanying artistic and cultural shock waves—Larry and I would often return to one of our favorite conversations about the film: the ways in which the film's opening credits (with its voluptuous, smoky score by Gato Barbieri) had so remarkably used two of Francis Bacon's paintings, *Double Portrait of Lucian Freud and Frank Auerbach* and *Study for a Portrait*, not only to establish the visual palette for the film but also to set the stage emotionally, and to foreshadow the drama of the story to follow. For Larry, this seemed to provide poetic instruction as well offering the beginnings of a much broader range of narrative possibilities that he would later employ; it was then, I believe, that Larry began to look for more highly charged emotional valence in his poems. In my view, he continued this same reinvention of narrative strategies throughout the course of his poetry, honing it in the final poems we see in the book Elegy and, now, in The Darkening Trapeze. Many years later, Larry send me a clipping about Bacon's influence on Last Tango in Paris from an interview with Bernardo Bertolucci: it was a piece that seemed to Levis a confirmation of our talks, and it struck me that Bertolucci's reflections could easily stand as an *ars poetica* for Larry's last poems:

When I decided to make the movie, I took Vitorio Storaro (Bertolucci's
    cinematographer)
to see a Francis Bacon exhibition. I showed him the paintings,
    explaining that this was the
kind of thing I wanted to use as my inspiration. The orange hues in
    the film are directly
influenced by Bacon. . . . I then took Marlon Brando to see the same
    exhibition, and I showed
him the paintings that you see at the start of the film, Portrait of
    Lucian Freud, and Study for
Portrait of Isabel Rawsthorne. I said to Marlon, "you see that painting?
    Well, I want you to
Recreate that same intense pain." That was virtually the only direction
    I gave him on the film.

Individually, in the spring of 1975, Larry and I both went to New York to see the astonishing Francis Bacon show at the Metropolitan Museum of Art, afterwards exchanging now lost postcards from the show. What I have returned to often while reading the poems of *The Darkening Trapeze* is the recognition that, even as his stylistic virtuosity reached its most dazzling peaks, the hues of Levis's final poems repeatedly first flame than darken, often as if his speakers have been afire—a common trope in his late work—and are then slowly quenched by their pain.

After I had completed editing this collection, I decided to ask Mary Flinn, Greg Donovan, and Amy Tudor if they might offer some recollections about their original work gathering Larry's poems for that initial box of poems, especially as this took place so soon after Levis's death. Amy Tudor's response led to a realization that there was a final poem—most likely the single last poem Larry ever completed in its entirety, a poem that had not been included in the original group of poems in that box—a poem that I had never seen. Amy recounted this story:

Mary explained the system they'd started and then we worked together for a bit, talking here and there. Our goal was to try to decide which had been the most recent draft of a poem, either because the piece was dated in some way or because it showed a progression of some sort that seemed a newer version of the piece. I recall thinking that what we were going to be trying to do was attempt to parse and reconstruct Larry's *thinking* process, his creative process, and how sometimes following a conversation with him could get a bit mysterious, so this seemed a hopeless task. But that's what death gives you, I've come to think . . .

I started on the stack of drafts of the poem that would eventually become "Elegy with an Angel at its Gate." I laid the drafts out on the table like cards or puzzle pieces and read, and read, and *read*. I looked for dates first, then for significant editions ("longer equals later" seemed a good rule of thumb, at least to start), then any word changes. If there was a line that matched a previous draft but which Larry had done free-hand work on (crossing things out, rewriting), you could safely assume (if any of the assuming is safe) that the handwritten changes were likely a later draft. It was part logic, part instinct, part familiarity with Larry's voice in his notes to himself. Sometimes he would have random comments in the margins or on slips of paper. Some were incredibly funny. It was strangely like spending time with him while simultaneously making me miss him more.

I did the best I could on the poem. I did the best I could on all of it. Then I read a poem he wrote about Nick—I think it was called "God is Always Seventeen" – sitting by itself in a single draft. It was clearly recent because it had it in the *darkness* I'd seen in him all winter, something that was sort of gray-coated and not at all like the vaguely amused and wry face he presented most of the time. He wrote heavy poems, but he did not despair. This poem had an edge of that to it, and it was lonely and full of grief and honestly, it made me too sad to go on with the work for that day. I ended up sitting and talking to Mary on the couch for a while instead and then going home.

I immediately wrote to Mary Flinn, but she had no memory of seeing the poem. At last, Amy Tudor found a copy of it on files from an old computer, where she'd happened to save a copy for herself. Out of the blue, we had the concluding poem for *The Darkening Trapeze*. In my view, it is without question the final piece Larry Levis finished, the poem he'd clearly intended to use as the last poem of his next collection.

A few years after *Elegy* was published, Sheila Brady asked Phil Levine if he would also edit Larry's *Selected Poems*, but the editing of *Elegy* had come at a profound emotional expense for Levine, and he suggested to Shelia that she ask me to edit the *Selected Poems*, which I did. In the fall of 2010, a conference, *Larry Levis: American Poet*, was held at Virginia Commonwealth University to celebrate of the acquisition of a superb and varied collection of Larry's Levis' papers by the Special Collections and Archives division of James Branch Cabell Library. It was at this conference that Sheila Brady asked if I would consider editing a collection of Larry's uncollected poems, as she knew I felt strongly that there was an enormous body of astonishing work by Levis still left to be published—work that only a few people had ever seen. At first, however, I said no, admitting that I felt it would be too wrenching a project. I suggested several poets who might take on the editing of the uncollected poems, but Sheila said that she would simply prefer to wait until I was ready, as she knew that, at some point, I would be. Of course, she was right. I've titled this collection *The Darkening Trapeze: Last Poems*, and it pleases me that these last poems of Larry Levis' are no longer lost.

I continue to believe that poetry remains one of our most vital reservoirs of reflection, solace, and outrage within a world replete with horrors. Levis's poems help to remind us of our daily and necessary struggle. I see in the poetry of the poets of my own generation—as well as in the poems of the poets of the next—the lasting influence of Levis's extraordinary work. I feel the remarkable poems in this collection will now add to the conviction of many of us that Larry Levis was one of the truly major American poets of his time.

"Larry Levis" from *A Condition of the Spirit,* 2004—Philip Levine

Hearing of the death of Larry Levis, Jane Cooper, one of my oldest and surely my dearest friend in poetry, wrote me a consoling letter, one that touched me deeply and helped as much as such letters can. I think this must almost be like losing a son for you, she wrote. Perhaps once, thirty years ago when I first met Larry and got to know and love him, I might have thought of him as a son, but it was not long before we became simply friends and brothers in the impossible art of poetry. What many who knew us well failed to realize was that I took from Larry, from his advice and from the poems he wrote, more than I ever gave to him. It was easy to take from Larry, for his whole vision of why we are here on this earth had to do with giving. One sees it clearly in a little essay he wrote about teachers who mattered and didn't matter to him: "to try to conserve one's energy for some later use, to try to teach as if one isn't quite there and has more important things to do, is a way, quite simply, of betraying oneself."

In this same letter Jane goes on to describe the year spent at Iowa teaching along with Larry. "There was a gentle mysteriousness about him then which was very attractive but which at the time I respected as a kind of boundary." Amazingly, without believing she knew him well, Jane put her finger precisely on a quality of his presence I could not have articulated, for from the moment I met him Larry struck me as that rare person who knows exactly who he is and finds the mere fact of his particular existence both just and cosmically funny. That a ranch boy from Selma, California, the raisin capital of the universe, "a kind of teenage failure, an unathletic, acne-riddled virgin who owned the slowest car in town, a 1959 Plymouth sedan that had fins like irrelevant twin sharks rising above the taillights," should at age sixteen decide to become a poet always struck him as both outrageous and perfectly right. He tells us in a brilliant and hilarious autobiographical essay the decision was made on the basis of one line in a single poem all the other lines of which were awful. As a junior at Selma High he had been reading Eliot, Stevens, and Frost on his own and decided he would try to write a poem. He did this one night in his bedroom, turned out the light, and told himself that if in the morning he found one good line he would try to become a poet. And then he took back "try." "You will either be a poet," he told himself, "and become a better and better one, or you will not be a poet." The next morning he found in the awful poem the one good line. "All the important decisions were made in that moment."

From the moment I met Larry I was aware of that gentle mysteriousness that Jane wrote of. In mid-September of 1964 this tall, slender, loose-limbed, country boy entered my office at Fresno State and asked if we might discuss the possibility of his taking my beginning poetry writing class even though he was only an entering freshman and lacked all the prerequisites. I asked him to take a seat, and he did so, sprawling in a chair before me, and then he asked permission to smoke, which-being a smoker myself, I granted. I described the course to him, the fact I required the students to write poems in specific forms before they were released to the chaos of free verse, which by then they might discover was not so free after all. He smiled and nodded his approval. I wondered had he read any modern poetry, for the experience might be a richer one for him if he had. Oh, yes, he said, he'd been reading Eliot, Frost, and Stevens for two years now. He still had trouble with some of Stevens. At the moment he was struggling with Hart Crane and Rimbaud. He wondered if I might help him understand some of Rimbaud. Not knowing French, I couldn't, but perhaps I could help him with Crane.

He collected himself and rose and began to walk slowly around my small office, his mouth fixed, nodding his head up and down. A minute passed or perhaps what seemed like a minute during which he was seriously thinking, and then he leaned back against an empty desk across from mine with his arms fully extended, a stance I would become familiar with as the years passed. He looked me full in the face, his gray eyes under long lashes staring into mine, and I was for the first time struck by his physical beauty of which he seemed totally unaware. "Might I enroll in your class?" he said. "I believe it is exactly what I want. "At that moment I knew without the least doubt that the coming semester would be a triumph. And a triumph it was. It was probably the best I was ever privileged to be a part of, for week after week Larry presented us with poems. They were not perfect poems, sometimes they were not even good poems, but they were always poems. Imagine getting this description of a small town pharmacy from an eighteen-year-old beginner six weeks into his first college semester:

> In the town of 20 pool cues
> of noses broken over the

feel of pussy, among the
bottles of grease and
candy lining the shelves,
the men laughed,
they stole cars and left them in
ditches, smoldering. Their wives,
spitting at irons, never looked up.
They grew older.

from "The Town"

He may have hated Selma. ("You could die in a town like that without lifting a finger.")
But he was already Selma's one poet. The true miracle of that semester was not, astonishingly
enough, the poems Larry handed in, it was what happened to five other students, for they
too sensed someone rare and remarkable was in their midst. These five caught fire from
Larry and from his poems and began to write utterly surprising things that struggled
with the agony and humor of coming of age in the little valley towns that gave birth to
them. This was my seventh year of teaching creative writing, but it was the first time I
discovered how much one genius can give to those around him or her when that genius has
an unquenchable need to give.

I received a sabbatical that semester, and my wife and I decided to try Spain for the
following year. In late August, the night before we left there was a quiet knock on the door,
and when I answered it Larry stood shyly there in the ferocious heat with a six-pack in hand
and asked if it was OK for him to come in and say goodbye. I welcomed him into the heat
of our un-airconditioned house. The kids were in bed, and all the living room furniture—
save for one kitchen chair—had been stowed in a back bedroom so that the family renting
our house could enjoy their own possessions. The place looked like a venue for a ping-pong
tournament. I offered Larry the one chair, and he sat upright before my wife and me who
sat crosslegged before him. After some minutes of stilted conversation, the three of us
finally exploded with laughter at the stupidity of this arrangement, and for half an hour we
swapped places as Larry entertained us with a series of wonderful riffs on the theme of the
one chair. When in full flight he was the funniest man I have ever known, for his humor was
totally spontaneous and always took off from the elements at hand the way a jazz musician
might walk out into a series of variations on a musical theme.

By this time Larry had written many of the poems that appear in his first book,
Wrecking Crew, which won the 1971 U.S. Award of the International Poetry Forum and was
published by Pitt the next year. Those poems, written in his late teens and early twenties,
give only a hint of the power to come. His second book, The *Afterlife,* which won the
1976 Lamont Award, shows the expanding range of his fascinations and his style. In the
stunning long poem "Linnets"—written when he was twenty-eight—one hears for the
first time the voice that is distinctively Levis.

ONE morning with a 12 gauge my brother shot
what he said was a linnet. He did this at close range
where it sang on a flowering almond branch. Any
one could have done the same and shrugged it off,
but my brother joked about it for days, describing
how nothing remained of it, how he watched for
feathers and counted only two gold ones which he

slipped behind his ear. He grew uneasy and care-
less; nothing remained. He wore loud ties and two
tone shoes. He sold shoes. He sold soap. Nothing
remained. He drove on the roads with a little hole
in the air behind him.

By this time he'd earned an MA from Syracuse, where he worked with Donald Justice, and a Ph.D. from Iowa, where with the help of his friend the Mexican poet Ernesto Trejo he explored the great twentieth century poetry in Spanish. By this time he certainly was no longer a son to me. Indeed he had come into himself. Or perhaps I should say he had created himself, the self of which he would later write: "driving a tractor, furrowing out a vineyard of muscats for my father one day, I was for some reason immediately impressed by how lucky I was to have been born at all, especially to be born as a human being rather than, as I wrote later in a poem, "a horse, or a gnat." This was the Larry Levis to whom I mailed my new work each month—if there was work to send. He would return my poems with praise when they merited it and something else when they didn't, and I tried my best to do the same for him with an equal measure or tact and honesty.

Looking back now I can see that it was during my first year in Spain that my relationship with Larry began to change, for that was the first year of what became the crucial correspondence in my life. I was the only American poet I knew within driving distance, and so when Larry first sent me a poem for my approval or criticism I answered with one of my own. I had learned even during that first year as his teacher how sensitively and shrewdly he could read poetry, but it was only in the letters I discovered what a resourceful and brilliantly practical critic he was, and as the years passed I grew more and more need him in more ways than I can describe. I heard of Larry's death in Athens, Ohio, where I was scheduled to give a poetry reading within a few hours. My hosts, knowing of my loss, were extraordinarily considerate. The meaning of Larry's death had not begun to dawn on me, and by putting it on hold—simply by refusing to believe it—I was able to read. At a certain point in the reading I faltered, for I realized that the very lines I was reading were lines Larry had either given me or urged me to write in order to rescue a poem. The first time this happened I was able to pass over it with only a word to myself, but when a few minutes later I entered the conclusion of a poem I had 8 years before struggled with I realized these final lines I was reading were lines designed by Larry. I had to stop and tell the audience what I had to tell myself, that my brother in poetry, my dear friend, had died, and that I owed the lines I had just read to Larry Levis. I did not tell them that for thirty years his fierce devotion to his art had served as my inspiration and model. I did not tell them that I found in his poetry an originality and daring that urged me to risk more in my own writing. I did not tell them that when I am weary of the mediocrity and smallness of so much that passes for poetry I go to Larry's work and revive my belief in the value of the art we shared.

No, I never told Larry that either, nor did I tell him that I thought he had become the finest poet of his generation as well as a better poet than his old teacher. I wouldn't have dared—though I truly believe it—for he would have shambled about the room, bobbing his head up and down, and then gone off on a series of wonderful riffs on a theme such as "the most embarrassing things ever said in Fresno" or "why it is important not to drink after dark" or "how vitamin deficiency turned Levine into Edgar Guest." *The Dollmaker's Ghost, Winter Stars,* and The *Widening Spell of the Leaves,* his last three books, are collections of poetry that will last as long as our language survives, and it's likely that my greatest contribution to literature is the small part I played in shaping them.

David St. John

David St. John has been honored, over the course of his career, with many prizes, including both The Rome Fellowship and The Award in Literature from The American Academy of Arts and Letters; the O. B. Hardison Prize (a career award for teaching and poetic achievement) from The Folger Shakespeare Library; and the George Drury Smith Lifetime Achievement Award. He is the author of twelve collections of poetry (including *Study for the World's Body*, nominated for The National Book Award in Poetry), most recently, *The Last Troubadour: New and Selected Poems;* as well as a volume of essays, interviews and reviews entitled *Where the Angels Come Toward Us*. David St. John

has written two libretti: for the opera based on his book, *The Face*, by Donald Crockett, and the choral symphony, *The Shore*, by Frank Ticheli. He is also the co-editor of *American Hybrid: A Norton Anthology of New Poetry*. A chancellor of the Academy of American Poets and a member of the American Academy of Arts and Science, David St. John is University Professor and chair of English at The University of Southern California. He lives in Venice Beach.

from *How Much Earth,* 2001—David St. John

I grew up being able to look toward the eastern edge of the valley, where the Sierras stood rimmed with snow. Of course, in those days one could actually see the Sierras. Almost all of the fig and apricot orchards are long since gone; many of the old vineyards too were lost to the arrival of new houses, the ever-expanding city. Still, for me, Fresno remains the landscape of my childhood imagination, the landscape of my adolescent ideals and aspirations. It is a landscape of permission, a landscape of humor and community. It's also true that the friendships I made there have remained the essential friendships of my adult life, and the life I've made for myself as a writer owes everything to the generosity of the teachers and the many enormously gifted young poets I knew there, many of whom are included in this anthology. We are indeed a lucky band of fellow travelers.

"Philip Levine and the Hands of Time" from *Coming Close,* 2013—David St. John

Among those poets who have been Philip Levine's students at some point in their lives—and I am assuming that includes almost all of the poets in this collection—there is a clear consensus that there simply was not and is not any more passionate, wise, hilarious, useful, fearsome, brilliant, loyal, or inspiring teacher of poetry, as literature and craft, than Philip Levine.

As I've told many times, I was eighteen-years-old and a Freshman at Fresno State College when Larry Levis introduced me to Philip Levine. Over the semester break between Fall and Spring, Larry— who'd seen a few of my early inept poems -- came up to me at a rock concert we both happened to be at and told me that Phil was teaching a beginning poetry writing class that next semester. It was something he didn't always do, and Larry said that I had to take Levine's class. Larry was rarely insistent about anything, so I immediately said, Of course. Larry later made sure that I met Phil, and with both Larry and Phil as my models, my life in poetry had begun.

It would be impossible to overstate Levine's charisma at that moment in the spring of 1968. Phil looked like a cross between Woody Guthrie and Paul Newman in *Hud*— lean, muscular, intense. For someone of such an urban background, Levine seemed incredibly connected to the earth, the land. Phil had —and still has—an extraordinary sense of humor, and I've always loved watching some recognition of an absurdity crackle in his eyes just before the delivery of the exact, withering comment it would deserve. He was capable of being fall-down-funny and vulgar as well as capable of talking with exquisite complexity about Donne (or Herrick or Larkin or Dickinson) in a way that was at once practical and devotional.

Phil taught from an anthology that was historical, called *Poetry In English*, and his class was my real education in the tradition of poetry. We might be talking about one of the student poems in our beginning workshop, and Phil would find a phrase he admired (or pretended to admire) and he would say to us, "This reminds me of that moment in Emily Dickinson when . . ." or, "You know, in Whitman, when he . . ." and then he would read us these great passages as instruction and example.

This did something else as well. His method connected us (and our own pitiful poems) to the larger tradition of poetry. It made us believe that what we were writing was actually in conversation with the poems and poets who had come before us. It allowed us to understand that poems don't come out of a vacuum and to recognize the necessity of knowing the poetry of one's own language and poetic tradition. I think this may be one of the most important things I have ever learned.

Yet Levine's knowledge of poetry in translation, especially poetry from Spanish and Polish, also completely transformed my understanding of what poetry could do and be. In my later years as Phil's student at Fresno State, I began to understand that poetry existed not only in the context and conversation of the poetry of—and in—my own language, but in the context and traditions of poems from all around the world. This too felt like a stunning thing to discover, and the world of poetry opened up for me again.

Just a few years ago, for a profile she was writing on me for Ploughshares, the poet Susan Terris asked me to talk about first meeting Phil during those early years in Fresno. This is what I said:

> *Levine was the most charismatic adult I'd ever met--brilliant, wittier than anyone on the planet except Oscar Wilde, and just as vicious when he wanted to be, and a poet who was about to explode onto the landscape of American poetry. He introduced me to a Who's Who of American poetry: Adrienne Rich, Galway Kinnell, W. S. Merwin, Mark Strand, Charles Wright, Donald Justice--all poets who would become friends in later years, and Justice, of course, was my teacher at Iowa. Fresno was a quiet town then, and poets came to read and see Levine, so it was great fun. It was also the sixties, and nuts in its own special way, of course.*

One of the things all of Phil's students treasured was the extraordinarily detailed comments he would write on our poems. Always written in fountain pen, his precise line edits and more general comments in the margins served to focus our poems and to allow us to see our poems—and their possible revisions—in a completely new light. I have saved every one of those drafts with Phil's comments on them from the very first, knowing their importance to me. Even when he was living abroad, in Spain (during the time when I was an undergraduate), and trying to escape his students, he would read and make line edits on the poems that I sent him with a care that was remarkable. He did this, of course, at the expense to his own time and writing, something that took me far too long to recognize and understand. Of course, Phil's own poems are models of poetic instruction in both their vision and their craft.

Perhaps now is the place to say that Phil was also a model to us all, a living model, of how to be a writer in the world—an example of how to be an engaged and consistently humane presence in a culture that undervalued both poetry and, it has often seemed, its own citizens as well. His presence was fiercely political in the most human way; that is, he reminded us that poetry creates empathy for those marginalized by their societies, and that to live responsibly and to write with conscience were crucial elements of being a poet. Phil taught us that skepticism and a sense of humor were essential to any life, but especially to a poet's life.

He also taught us that poetry is often about time—about how the use of memory in poetry helps us to recuperate the past, those events and individuals we have lost to time. Poetry is able to help us to recover and bring back into the present of the poem what otherwise might seem gone from a life forever. For Levine, the acts of memory and reflection were, in his poetry, constant threads in an ongoing poetic reckoning with his own experiences and the details of his own past, including his sketches of those men and women who helped to make up that past, and who were themselves now gone. But one of Levine's lessons about time was, for me, of a more profoundly immediate nature. There was nothing abstract about this lesson whatsoever and it came from fiction, not from poetry at all.

One spring, I was taking a class from Phil on contemporary fiction that was being held in one of the auxiliary classroom buildings—like a series of trailers really—called San Ramon. They were adequate classrooms, if not terrifically substantial, and they were no worse than any other classroom. They were both new and temporary. We sat in the usual half-desks that torture students everywhere, and Phil sat at a small table at the front of the room, facing the students. Above him on the front wall was the typical round black-rimmed/white-faced industrial clock typical of most classrooms.

Our class was held just after lunch, and on this particular day I remember that I was late and so was hurrying across campus. I tried to come in quietly so as not to disturb the discussion, then I noticed that Phil himself hadn't yet arrived, which was unusual. I slid into a desk and waited along with the rest of the class.

That day we were discussing one of Phil's favorite recent books, one I had already read at his suggestion, Frank Conroy's remarkable memoir, *Stop-Time*. We were all looking forward to the discussion, having discovered during the semester that Levine was as brilliant talking about fiction as he was discussing poetry. Another few minutes passed after I sat down and Phil came in. He walked to the front of the room, and then sat at the small table. He looked at us in way that seemed both bemused and puzzled, as if he were thinking, Where did *they* all come from?

We all had our copies of the book on our desks in front of us, alongside our notebooks, ready to be responsible students of creative writing. Then Phil began to lecture. He hadn't taken out his own copy of *Stop-Time* and put it on the table in front of him, as he usually might. In fact, he clearly hadn't brought his own copy of the book with him at all. Still, he began to lecture about time, about the nature of time and memory, about how Conroy played with these elements throughout the course of his memoir, and how he so brilliantly manipulated us, his readers, in those manipulations of narrative time.

While speaking, Phil had gotten up from the table and had begun to walk back and forth behind the table as he talked; then he'd walk over to one of those gray metal media carts (they seemed to be in every classroom awaiting some mysterious use) that stood at the front and side of the room. He'd put his hand on the cart somewhat thoughtfully as he lectured, then he would walk back behind the table, still talking about time. Phil had now begun to talk about what time does to us, how time wants often to destroy us and take us with it. Basically, he said, time (Time) has only one message for us: It continues and we do not.

I had come to know Phil well enough during these years to realize that he was, well, not drunk exactly, but eloquently soused. He'd clearly had a great wine with his lunch. He was so calm and composed, however, that I don't think anyone else in the room had a clue about this. That is, until he pulled the chair away from the small table and moved it directly beneath the clock on the wall above him, the clock students stared at day in and day out in their academic imprisonment in that San Ramon classroom.

Phil stepped up on the chair, reached above him and took the huge round clock in both of his hands. He gripped it so that his fingers slid slightly behind the black rim of the clock, then in one incredibly authoritative gesture, he pulled that clock right out of the wall and ripped it off of its wires. He stepped down off the chair and walked over to the gray steel media cart and deposited the clock on its top shelf, where the stopped clock stared up like an open eye at the classroom ceiling.

He never stopped speaking once. He continued to lecture fluidly and fluently throughout this whole spectacular event—he was lecturing about time, even as he defiantly stopped time in our ridiculous and completely artificial classroom. What I remember vividly was looking up to see that the hole in the wall in front of me—the place where the clock had been—was not, as I had expected it to be, round like the clock itself but, instead, square as to match and hold the square metal box of clock works on the back of the clock. I have always considered this to be the day's second revelation.

For the entire remainder of that semester the torn naked red and black wires that had once been attached to the clock dangled down from the empty square in the wall up above Phil's table. The clock itself also sat for the remainder of that semester on the top of the steel gray media cart. No one came to repair the clock. No one came to start time again in Phil's classroom. Either no one cared, or no one dared. After all, if the man who taught in that classroom could stop time, then who knew what else he might be able to do.

"An Interview with David St. John" from *Seneca Review*, 1984—David Wojahn

David Wojahn: I frequently see a tension in operation in your poems, particularly between the goal of richly and sensually rendering the physical world and the goal of identifying a kind of ideal metaphysical realm. A realm of experience continually torn between an allegiance to one of those opposites.
David St. John: I think that's absolutely accurate. I think it's exactly that tension that would be called in some works a "fallen" state, and, for me, the project of the poems of *No Heaven* was to discover for myself what my own idea of one's recuperation in these circumstances might be, what reconciliation of those tensions was possible, what forms it all might take. A friend said that what he thought was both fascinating and dangerous about the book, in terms of a response to the poems, was that what was in fact a critique of a kind of decadence would be misunderstood as an embrace of decadence.

DW: The sense of opposition that we're talking about seems to manifest itself repeatedly in everything about the poems—the landscapes and the details, the narrative, and sometimes even the diction of the poems. You return again and again in all of your books to bridges, harbors, shores, to elements of the landscape that seem to signify for you that opposition. At the end of the title poem of *The Shore* you write, "In that dream we share, there is/one shore, where we look upon nothing/and the sea our whole lives;/until turning from those waves we find/one shore where we look upon nothing/and the earth our whole lives."

DSJ: Exactly. For me, that's the fascinating territory, those (seeming) lines of division and demarcation which, in fact, are illusory; every shore is in a sense a false shore. There is the constant interplay of land and water—its own yin and yang—but nothing is fixed and everything is twinned, doubled, in its own way. The regard of the outer, the regard of the inner, the regard of the one shore that's beyond the world, the regard of the one shore that is of the world—those energies are always twinned and entwined; that seems to me just a fairly descriptive way of presenting the tensions of a daily life. Those tensions are articulated in more and less extravagant ways, depending on one's temperament Say, in the temperament of the speaker in *The Shore*, certain of those tensions find their articulation and embodiment in the form of a relationship. The characters of *No Heaven* are finding those conflicts almost everywhere they step into the world and in a variety of landscapes.

DW: But it does seem that this element of opposition in your work is underscored dramatically in your poems about love relationships. So many of those poems, in *The Shore* particularly, seem to be about a gentle collapse of the relationship between the speaker and the beloved "Hotel Sierra," "The Avenues"—they seem to focus on couples who must resign themselves to never achieving that pure lasting intimacy that they so long for. In "Hotel Sierra," the speaker comes to the realization that he and the beloved have to be like those photos that she takes of the coastline, "only a few gestures/placed out of time."

DSJ: I think one of the things that I now find less appealing about the poems in *The Shore* is, in fact, that sense of resignation, and it's one of the reasons why I think the new poems are poems of greater violence. They seem to me more accurate. Certainly the poems of *The Shore* are poems of a quiet disintegration and poems of repeated attempted reckonings, and those reckonings are always asking and seeking a particular equilibrium that will allow the speaker to continue. I find now that sense of resignation, even acquiescence, disquieting. It's not that I don't find the poems emotionally accurate. I'm sounding harsher about those poems than I mean to be. "Hotel Sierra" is a poem I still like a lot, as is "Until the Sea is Dead," in which I found a violent episode to echo more dramatically and, I think, satisfyingly, the rupture between the characters. So the restraint of the poems of *The Shore* appeals to me in that I like what's happening in the writing, but I don't particularly like what it allows the figures in the poems to become to each other. That's looking back after five years, so it's easy to second-guess myself now. At the time I didn't have that problem at all or I wouldn't have written the poems in that way. I think it's also a part of the attempt of the sixth section of "Of the Remembered," to somehow put those other poems in a different kind of focus.

DW: In an earlier interview, published in *Telescope* in '83, you discuss at length that whole issue of the I and You as a principal axis around which your poems revolve. Yet you say your speakers use this "I versus you" dichotomy in an almost philosophical sense; the pronoun you is meant to be specific and intimate but it is not meant to

represent actual persons, be it a lover or a son. Instead, the "you" is meant to be a composite of sorts, an amalgamation, to some extent, of many real lovers and friends. What prompted you to adopt that strategy? Is the blurring of the "you," the you's identity, simply a device that allows you to transcend the merely personal and confessional when you sit down to write or does it stem from a more metaphysical notion, that the "you," the other, can never be fully understood?

DSJ: I would say some of each. In practical terms, it's an address that's always appealed to me because it's implicitly accusational. It's also a demanding address; it's saying *you* and *you listen*. And so, in a very underhanded way, I wanted to grab the reader and say, "Listen, you're in this poem, you're my lover, watch out, let's see what happens here." And I wanted to be able to be confrontational in that way; I wanted to be as demanding of the reader as I felt I had a right to be. I also wanted to be, then, gentle and sympathetic to the reader. I wanted to invite the reader into a more intimate conversation, and there are some poems, like "Gin," for example, where it's more clearly a self-address. The place in my own work where I find the technique working most successfully is in "Slow Dance," where the "you" weaves its way in and out of identification. It, I think, most successfully absorbs the reader into the fabric of the identity of the you. In *The Shore* there's no question that the "you" is more clearly identified as another person, a lover, and a definite other. In the poems of *Hush*, it's something I found attractive in Ashbery's work. The thing to remember is that in 1972 and '73 there weren't that many people yelling about Ashbery; outside of New York he was a fairly well-kept secret. I happened to have a number of friends who, like myself, admired him tremendously and felt that what he was writing was some of the most exciting poetry we'd ever seen. The poems in *Hush* are highly influenced by Ashbery. Obviously, there are a lot of other poets whose work has influenced my poems, both before and since. I think, in terms of admiring what Ashbery was able to get away with in using the second person address, I wanted to be able to pull it off myself, in a less abstracted way.

DW: In a poem like "Gin" the "you" obviously becomes a substitute for the speaker and it's not meant to be a separate character the speaker addresses. The "you" is used that way by a number of post-war American poets, Hugo comes to mind, Jon Anderson comes to mind. In writers like Ashbery and Michael Burkard, that issue becomes even more complicated because the pronoun often shifts without warning from "I" to "you," sometimes even to the third person, until we're uncertain if the speaker's using the "you" to refer to himself or to represent a person or reader being addressed. Why do you think our poetry has adopted that sort of pronoun blur in the last twenty years or so?

DSJ: I think I would explain this shift in the usage of the "you," this usage of free-floating pronouns, not as a reflection of lack of identity or a sense of insecurity of identity on the part of the poets but, in fact, just the reverse. It's an attempt to expand the identity, to be more inclusive, to find a way of taking the traditional "I" beyond an opposition of self and other, a way of absorbing this opposition, of saying it's an illusory opposition and that human consciousness is capable of becoming the other, of *being* the other. It seems to me that that act of imaginative sympathy is what's always the most important aspect of art. One of the things that makes art a mitigating factor in society is that it demands and initiates a sympathetic imagination in order for an audience to enter into a relationship with it—whether it's painting, sculpture, music, or literature. There seems to me a false argument in recent years about the over-abundance of the "I," of first person poetry, of post-confessional first person poetry. Phil Levine tells a wonderfully funny story about his first book, *On The Edge,* having to be held up in the middle of printing because the printer, Kim Merker, had run out of capital I's. What I'm trying to say is that, since the Romantics, the problem of a strong first person in a poem has been constant for the poet at work. Solutions to that problem are as various as poets, but one of the most interesting and complicated solutions is the way in which a second person address has been used. At this point, what's disturbing is to see how quickly it's become a cliché, and to see the poems in which it's so misused as to be foolish, as to sound foolish.

DW: You grew up in the San Joaquin Valley of California, and yet I don't think that landscape figures as prominently in your poems as it does in the work of a number of other poets of your generation who grew up in the same area. I'm thinking of Larry Levis and Gary Soto, for example, and of some of Frank Bidart's early work. I'm also intrigued by the fact that all four of you are to a large degree poets of recollection , poets of memory, and yet their work harks back quite specifically to their youths in California, while your poems seem little concerned with any sort of Wordsworthian evocation of childhood. Can you talk a little bit about that and your upbringing?

DSJ: For me, except in "Of the Remembered," the landscape of the San Joaquin Valley has never been as important to me as the landscape of the northern California coastline. It was there that I found the real embodiment, in the landscape, of what seemed to me dilemmas related to my life. Let me try to explain. Poems have real subjects, there's no question about it, and they have real figures, even if those figures are invented; yet, for me, poems aren't *about* their content, they're about the ways in which the perceiver-the writer, the figure, whether or not the figure is the same as the writer-comes into relation with whatever experience is at stake. It's that process of observation, reflection, and imagination that seems to me the sub stance of the poem. Even in "Of the Remembered," which is an attempt to write a more Wordsworthian kind of poem, there's always something else working against that; there's always section six or there's the last section with its little collation of the Tibetian Book of the Dead and the Egyptian Book of the Dead; there's always a tension fighting the simply remembered landscape.

DW: One of the things that seems clear about the way recollection is viewed in your poems is that your speakers never seem to come to terms with the process of memory beyond acknowledging its obsessive hold on them. As in Cavafy's poems, the speaker reconstructs events from his past with the conscious knowledge that this reconstruction might bring him solace but might also cause him to relive events which are painful to him. It's this receptivity towards the past that seems to give the poems their character and gravity.

DSJ: I would like to think so, yes. It's what I wanted to try to achieve; it's what remains important to me when I go back and look at "Of the Remembered." One of the poem's possibilities is solace, and yet it's not necessarily going to be solace. Again, it is that tension between the pain of the memory and its *potential* for solace-one can't enter into a state of recuperation or recovery without bringing these jagged bits of experience back up into consciousness, and it seems that the form of a poem can allow pieces of jagged, painful memory to be enfolded and absorbed, to be reckoned with.

DW: One of the things that I frequently notice in reading the manuscript of *No Heaven* is that while many of the poems such as "Woman and Leopard,"

and "The Swan at Sheffield Park," or even "The Man in the Yellow Gloves" are relatively straightforward and maintain traditional narrative structures or traditional monologues, others such as "The Lemons" and "The Day of the Sentry" seem much more telescoped and compressed in their narrative strategies; again and again they seem to shift in person with relative impunity; characters appear without much introduction, curious "he's," "she's," and they's."

DSJ: Well, it's those poems that matter most to me because they're enacting a kind of grammar of narration that I find most interesting. I think that many readers will find it troubling that the poems are so vulgarly presesential, and what I hope is that readers will begin to see that the "he's," the "she's," and the "I's" all share something in common, and that they are all sisters and brothers, in some very troubling way, all part of a"family" that is coming apart at the seams. The kind of narration that's employed in the poems of *No Heaven* allowed me, I think, much more latitude in establishing some logical climates in the poems; that's what I wanted to try to effect. I wanted the tensions to carry over from poem to poem, and I hope the little echoes will be there as the reader reads through. One of the things that is a little worrisome to me is that the poems will be seen as the poems of the decay of elegance, when in fact it's a more universal dilemma of history. It's crucial to me that the importance and impulses of history be recognized in those poems, because I think they're poems of social and cultural dilemma; I don't think they're poems of fancy.

DW: I suppose one of the reasons people might have that interpretation is that many of the poems in *No Heaven* refer to European landscapes and that few of the poems in the collection, or in any of these collections, seem to use locale and place as anything but a backdrop to the events that take place. I sometimes feel that your work, say, unlike the work of many of the poets of the generation before yours—like Wright, Levine and Hugo or even people in your own generation like Plumly and Levis and Matthews—refuses to admit that there is a nurturing sense of place; in your poems I see no abiding locale that functions like Plumly's Ohio or Levine's Detroit, no place we can come back to in order to confront again our first experiences with transcendence and loss. Instead of embracing a locale, your poems, particularly in *No Heaven* seem to embrace the act of travel itself.

DSJ: I think that's not only accurate but an important factor in the poems of *No Heaven*— that sense of there being some final and true homelessness. The characters in *No Heaven* aren't wanderers by choice, they're wanderers in search of their own homelands, and one of the symptoms of the malaise is that rootlessness, that sense of traveling over the surface of things, even the surface of the land, in a very literal way. A poem like "The Boathouse" tries to talk about that in a different way, that quality of looking for some rootedness, looking for a place that has the capacity to give rootedness, and being to a large extent disappointed. Now, this is very much, I think-to shift into a more autobiographical mode-absolutely related to the fact of growing up in California where the history of the land was pretty much the history of the latest mall. Even though Fresno is an agricultural area with vineyards, orchards—and they're beautiful—I really felt, especially in my adolescence, the poverty of any roots, any long standing historical or cultural associations. It's one of the reasons why I'm much more comfortable living in the East, and it's one of the reasons why I'm fond of New England. I think that it's a problem of my own, a problem in my own history, that I find necessary to address. Obviously, friends like Larry Levis don't feel this way. Also, I happen to like to travel; I find travel easy and comforting. I mean, traveling is hard work, as everyone knows, but I find it for my own temperament a very realistic way to live. I don't know quite how to explain it, but I find movement and travel suits my nervous system in some ways.

DW: One of the reasons why the act of travel seems so important in *No Heaven*, and in a lot of the other poems too, is that again and again your work presents a speaker whose responses are essentially passive, who works to not see the world aggressively. I sometimes feel that your poems strive to see the world with the same sort of wry curiosity in which one views the landscape from a train window; it's not like, say, Levine or the poems of James Wright in his *Two Citizens* period, that relate to the experience of travel in a way that is very aggressive and very fatalistic; your poems instead seek a kind of receptivity that defies somehow any aggressiveness, any of that sort of fatalism.

DSJ: I think the poems of *No Heaven* are trying to be representative of states of concern-psychological states of concern and emotional states as well-and yet not be passive and resigned in the way that the poems and sensibilities of the speakers in *The Shore* were, and yet be responsible to the figures of the poems. It's interesting; I find it convenient to speak of the speakers, the figures, in the poems of *No Heaven* as characters because in fact they're all drawn on real characters and figures, and yet they're functional for me as fictions in that they're enacting states that are states of concern for me, and they're states that I want to see considered in a poem, in a particular way, from a particular perspective; in that way all of the poems seem to me latent with implied decisions, implied actions that will postdate the poem. So there's a certain tension that's being created by that that I hope begins to be resolved by the poem, "Leap of Faith ." At the same time, I think there's much more humor in these poems-though whether many readers will find what I find humorous to be so is a question, especially since there is a certain amount of black humor at work. But I think humor is a necessary and useful tool in trying to consider these complicated states of emotional and psychological distress.

DW: How would you respond to the charge which some readers and reviewers have made that in terms of their language, in terms of their forms, your poems move toward the mannered despite the incredible violence that sometimes occurs in them. For example, in "The Man in the Yellow Gloves," the speaker seems very adamant towards the end of the poem of defending himself against the accusation that by wearing the gloves he may be a fop or a dandy.

DSJ: Well, that poem's both a good and a bad example, It's a good example in that what's under discussion in the poem is, of course, the way in which tragedy is masked by beauty, the way in which the violent is gloved by the elegant. And so, the speaker's defense is in some ways my own defense, that I have no particular desire myself to rip off those gloves. On the other hand, I think I could be damned much more completely by picking a poem that wasn't a persona poem. I think you could pick a poem like "Meridian" as being a poem of its own particular manners. And it's one of my favorite poems in the book, one of the key, central poems. I really in all honesty have no response to that question. If people find the poems mannered and elegant, fine. I have no complaints with people preferring to read other kinds of poems; they're just not the kinds of poems that I'm interested in writing. I'm interested in writing the poems that are in the book.

DW: More generally, how do you decide on a poem's form? Your work ranges from all sorts of vanguard pyrotechnics, unpunctuated poems that sort of follow Olson's

composition-by-field esthetic, to a poem in traditional meter, form. Several of the poems in *The Orange Piano* are sonnets.

DSJ: It's always pissed me off that it seems to be taken for granted that most young poets know nothing of traditional prosody. Here at Hopkins, I teach a course in traditional poetic forms every year. Both Phil Levine and Donald Justice were teachers of mine who emphasized traditional prosody in their teaching and it's always been important to me. Also, I found that any number of poets who are my contemporaries, or have been my students, find poems in traditional meters, poems with rhymes, to have a central place in their consideration of what poetry is. Just because they don't write sonnets doesn't mean they don't know the craft. It seems to me not only unfair but clearly untrue that young poets don't care and don't know about traditional prosody. As a way of keeping my ear tuned, I've always written poems in forms. Often I will do formal assignments for myself when I give assignments to my classes. But imposed forms do interest me less than a poem that discovers its interior form. That's what I find exciting. The activity of poetry has everything to do with finding a form for consciousness, for perception, and it's in that sinuous entity— of form-that I find the attraction, the appeal, of writing in the first place. In regards to craft, I find writing formal poems tremendously satisfying; yet what I see as the ambition for my own poems doesn't find its articulation in the formal poems that I write. The two sonnets in *The Orange Piano* I like a lot, and I'm very happy with them, but they seem to me to have ambitions that the poems in *No Heaven* don't share. The poems in *No Heaven* have their own ambitions and their own forms of suspension and satisfaction. In the poems in *No Heaven,* especially in, say, a poem like "The Swan at Sheffield Park," there are a lot of jarring enjambments, a lot of purposely roughening line breaks. In spite of the elegance of the poems, there are any number of moments that I think the readers will identify as jarring and disturbing; that's what I was after. I want to keep the reader alert, to occasionally disorient the reader so that I can exploit other moods later on. I do feel though that young poets have been unfairly accused of being "metrically illiterate." I think there's no question that most of the poetry that's being written is unmusical, but I wouldn't exempt formal poetry, highly metrical poetry, from that. Metrics and music are clearly different issues.

DW: You followed *Hush* with *The Shore* in 1980, and one of the things that seems so remarkable about *The Shore*, and what happens in *No Heaven* compared to *The Shore,* is how much it strives to depart from the concerns and methods of your earlier poems. The staccato, fugue-like movement of poems in *Hush* like "Gin" and "Slow Dance" appears less frequently. The poems of *The Shore* follow more linear narrative patterns and make use of a flatter diction. How did you seek to change your style after the publication of *Hush?* What kind of process did you go through?

DSJ: After *Hush* I really wanted a style that was seemingly more available, that had a more available surface for a reader. I wanted to try to enact the same kinds of movements, shifts, and departures that existed in the poems of *Hush,* but more underneath the surface of the poems in *The Shore.* I wanted to create the illusion of a calm, fluid surface while, in fact, being equally manipulative of the reader. Yet there's no question that the style itself was a definite shift. I was reading a lot of Elizabeth Bishop, whom I love, and her poems had tremendous influence on that book. After *The Shore* I wanted to do something very different and I wasn't sure what. I became more and more dissatisfied with the poems I was writing, which seemed adequate and interesting, yet not distinctive enough. I felt that, in the poems I was writing, I wasn't pushing what I sensed as my own limitations. I also felt that the poetry I saw around me, both in books and in magazines, was so complacent and so dull that I felt in revolt against that. I wanted to try to push the language in some other way. That's really what spurred my need to try to find the new manner, new voice, the new aspect for the poems of *No Heave n*.

DW: If there were a time period, and a place you would choose to live in, when and where would it be?
DSJ: Well, I like living in this time; I'm very comfortable in this time. I think it's a politically infuriating time, but it's hard to imagine a time that hasn't been politically infuriating. I like being an American; I have no desire to be anything other than American, but that doesn't mean I don't enjoy living and traveling in other parts of the world. In many ways I'm perfectly content to be living in this time and place, this world. For the most part, it makes me happy, and I love being able to write poems. It's the only thing I've ever really wanted from my life, and maybe this will seem to be a small expectation, but I'd like to write half a dozen really beautiful poems. If can do that I'll be pleased, really pleased. That seems like a worthwhile endeavor for a lifetime.

"An Interview by Michael Juliani, David St. John's *The Last Troubadour: New and Selected Poems*"—Michael Juliani

I. Troubadour Days

Michael Juliani: In other interviews with you, there's often a discussion about how you approach your work book by book. It's clear that each book presents something unique for you. This being your second volume of selected poems, what does that mean for you? How did you look over your previous work and decide what to use?
David St. John: It had been more than twenty years since my first new and selected poems, *Study for the World's Body*. With *The Last Troubadour*, I made the decision that, from over forty years of poems, I would select no more than fifty poems. I thought selecting 1.25 poems per year was a good ratio for any poet; if I could find 1.25 poems a year over the previous forty years, that would make me happy. Even though, as you say, with each individual book, I've always wanted to construct a book that was its own entity, I saw that in choosing poems from *all* those books I found a consistency of voice that I hadn't anticipated. Those fifty "selected" poems, for me, began to tell a story of my own life in poetry, stylistically, that I was happy to tell.

MJ: How do you characterize some of your stylistic impulses, relating both to your life's work and the new poems included in *The Last Troubadour*?
DSJ: When I wrote the book *Prism*, I found that I liked a kind of breathless quality that removing punctuation had allowed me. But I wanted to do something formally that allowed me both to race and to slow down, move quickly and then pause, and so I began working with the couplet stanza with the second line indented. I thought of it as a trellis that I could run certain rhythms and lines along. I liked being able to push a line the way C.K. Williams and Charles Wright would push a line. Charles Wright would often push toward a hexameter line, an Alexandrian line, and then come back with a shorter line, and that was something that had always appealed to me. What I liked about Charlie Williams' work was how his lines propelled the narrative. I think of the new poems in this book as highly charged cinematic vignettes; even though many of the poems are in first person, I hope it's clear that all the

speakers are not necessarily me. So, I created these more elliptical vignettes that work as mirrors all the way through.

MJ: In this process, did you gain a new sense of how your relationship to some of your primary influences has changed over the last forty years?

DSJ: I could talk forever about the poets who influenced me, writers like Eugenio Montale, Alexandr Blok, and Paul Eluard. Those poets share a kind of respect for the world's luminosity. One of the things that writing poetry at this moment necessitates for me is simply a harder, sharper edge to the sensibility. I hope the poems of the new section, "The Way It Is," have more of a sense of a whip snapping in them as the reader moves through the poems. I wanted there to be opportunity to create disjunction, both narratively and syntactically. It's a commonplace, but poetry really is about time and the experience of time in language, so I wanted the lines to be able to shift ground, to have little trapdoors within the stanza breaks that might shift the temporality, so that ideas of memory and the present become interleafed in some way.

MJ: I noticed while reading the selected poems, as you suggested, that it gave clues to me as to how you may have arrived at the forms of the new poems. Previously when I may have thought there was more of a difference between your books, I actually saw the story all the way through.

DSJ: I think that's true. One of the things I learned in reading through this new group of selected poems was that there was a continuity between all the forty years. Not simply an obsessiveness, but a stylistic impulse that kept finding other iterations, and the work is basically tonally intact from the beginning, which surprised me. I thought it would be more various. One could say, "Well, it's a unified body from forty years of work," or one could say, "He didn't do one goddamn new thing for forty years," depending on your perspective.

MJ: This reminds me of something thematic that I noticed, in relation to what you said about the poems being cinematic. There's something about how the speakers and relationships presented in these poems relate to each other, this sense that the poems elaborate on intimacies, and with that elaboration between people, there are revelations of things that may displace lovers, friends, and family from each other, and then there may be elaborations that bond them completely. There is this sense, not only in the language that displaces the reader, pleasurably, throughout the poem, but also in the narrative content.

DSJ: Absolutely. One of the things that I've often talked about in interviews or essays for many years is the sense that, for me, a poem is an enactment, in language, of a writer's sensibility. My own sensibility revolves around the notion that experience is fluid and, like the fiction of the movement of film, continuous. We know that that is not so. We know that the world is full of fracture and disjunction. You could argue that the history of 20th Century poetry is the history of fragmentation, beginning, let's say, with "The Waste Land." Disjunction and fragmentation are what any artistic consciousness has necessarily looked to confront in our own time. Much of the poetry I love is a poetry that acts as a model of consciousness and a model of the *fluidity* of consciousness, in that it's able to absorb (we hope) the jagged and fragmented pieces of experience that are thrown at us by our own lives, our own cultures, everything around us.

What art can do, I believe, when it's working well, is allow us to experience the fragmentation and the disjunction, and at the same time provide us with the fluidity of experience that allows us to absorb those disjunctions as a reader, or in looking at a painting, or at a performance of a piece of music or dance. Every art grows within and every art reflects the conditions of its own time. For this past century, and more, we have seen how much wreckage needs to be considered a part of what we consider to be inevitable, even beautiful.

MJ: How does this relate to your own poems?

DSJ: From the very first, the poems I've written have employed an I-thou kind of dialectic. What's important to me in this notion of the dialectic is that it is reciprocal. The voice may issue from one of the two poles of the conversation, but in fact, unless the poem also contains the latent *other* within it, then it's not doing what I hope it can do. For me, even though the poems continue the fiction of a single speaker, which of course we all know is a fiction in any case, that speaker is not only constructed of the fragments of him or herself, but also the fragments of that other person. The new poems, especially, are more aggressive in trying to make those little movies leaner and more exacting in the kinds of refracted images that arise.

II. The West

MJ: With the recent death of Sam Shepard, I was thinking about how he tried to live in Europe and then sort of came running back from Europe. Many of the poets you name as primary influences are European, and it's certainly no secret that you've written a lot about Rome, that that is part of your sensibility for sure. However, there is, with that sharpening of the newer poems, something more American or going-back-home about them.

DSJ: That's so true. Shepard is the perfect person to invoke here. Although the poems of my first and second books, *Hush* and *The Shore*, are filled with California landscapes, what I began to recognize (I think this was something I recognized first when I was editing Larry Levis' *The Darkening Trapeze*) was that, in one of my later book, *The Auroras,* I had returned again to California. One of the things I recognized in myself was that I was returning in my own work to a very elemental home place. I was looking back to the San Joaquin Valley, Fresno, the foothills of the Sierras, and again to the Pacific coast. I realized that I wanted to keep those landscapes alive in my new poems also.

Stylistically, I began also to move from the enactment of the cinematic to a more representational sense of the imagistic, which is why photography and the image (as well as the homage to a photographer like Weston, or the secret poem about Stieglitz and Georgia O'Keefe) appear in the new poems. I wanted the sense of a harder, more clarified edge to the images.

It's striking to me how performative these new poems are as well. In some ways, they're far more theatrical. My idea of the perfect film script is "Paris, Texas." When I went to live in Rome at the American Academy, I had a room that was basically as big as a double closet, but it was a gorgeous room that looked out on the cortile of the American Academy. I'd brought one cassette with me, and it was the soundtrack of "Paris, Texas." This is by way of saying how important Sam Shepard's work has always been to me. That language of those plays and the sense of, not just what Williams would call the American Grain, but the grain of the West. You could argue that, in some ways, Shepard went east to find what was true west. Certainly, I think one could say that about me. One could say that in some ways I've come full circle. My friend Howard Norman, the remarkable fiction writer and memoirist, who was a longtime friend of Sam Shepard's, is, other than you, the only person to recognize the huge presence of Shepard in my work. I find that incredibly gratifying that you both can see that.

MJ: I was thinking of the epigraph to Shepard's *Motel Chronicles,* from Cesar Vallejo: "never did far away charge so close." I think that sums it up. I also think of some of your poems, like "In the High Country," in relation to Shepard's stuff. A lot of people discard Shepard's poetry from *Motel Chronicles* or *Hawk Moon,* some of those rougher books of his, but I think he actually has a great ear for it.

DSJ: He has one of the greatest ears for the American language and actual speech of any poet, playwright, or fiction writer. He also understands how a voice is enacted first in language and then in physical space.

III. On and Off the Court

MJ: I thought that maybe I'd ask you what it was like to publish your first book since Philip Levine died, but that led me to thinking about how you were a tennis player when you were young, and when I was growing up, my uncle was a tennis player. He told me that in order to get better, you should play against people who are better than you, ones who are as good as you are, as well as ones who you're better than. It struck me that, in a basic way, my uncle's advice resembled how your career, and your life, really, has been defined by your friendships, by your mentors, and by your many students.

DSJ: I've been incredibly fortunate in the mentors I've had, both those who were officially teachers of classes and those who weren't. Peter Everwine, Donald Justice, Marvin Bell, and my longtime friend Norman Dubie. Most people know that meeting Philip Levine and Larry Levis at Fresno State was a defining moment for me. Levine was the most eclectic of teachers. His method of teaching was to make sure that one read great canonical poetry and poetry that he believed was, however new it was, extraordinary. From the day I first met him, at 18, our conversations were always about, "Wow, have you read this? Have you read what so-and-so just did? Have you seen this translation of so-and-so?" It's something that I think both Larry and I internalized and used later as we became teachers. I was also lucky in meeting Levine because, before I left Fresno, he introduced me to many people I ended up spending time with later, like Galway Kinnell, W.S. Merwin, and Mark Strand. A poet who was so central to me—and only a few people understand this—was Adrienne Rich. I met Adrienne when I was 19 or 20. She came to Fresno and I met her at a very difficult time in her own life. We became friends and corresponded. When I taught at Oberlin, she came to do a reading and a visit. Before she arrived for her visit, the poets there, David Young and Stuart Friebert, asked her what she wanted to do when she visited and she said, "I don't care, just make sure that David's there at dinner," and they were like, "What the fuck?" It was a friendship that continued through the years. I would see her odd places, like Key West—we were there at the same time a couple of times. Then I started to see Adrienne regularly after I moved to Los Angeles because one of her sons, Jacob, had moved to Los Angeles. She would come to see Jacob and her grandson very frequently. It was great because it gave us both a kind of built-in excuse to hang out. Also, of course, I had her come read at USC three or four times after I came here, and at the Getty Museum as well.

My conversations over the years with Adrienne had to do with political issues and questions. The poem of mine that Adrienne cared for most was my long political poem about Pasolini. That was the poem that, when it appeared in a book, she instantly wrote to me about, because it had a resonance and a scope that I think she had been waiting to see in my poems. Because she knew me, she sensed there was a political life and a range of political concerns that had only really found amplification there, in that poem

IV. The Last Question

MJ: I'm going to conclude with an old journalism school trick. They say to always end every interview by asking, "Is there anything that no one has ever asked you that you've always wanted to talk about?"

DSJ: (pause) It would be, "Why haven't you stopped writing?" The reason that's an important question is that I ask myself some form of that question every day. I ask myself, "What the fuck?" It's not "que sera, sera." It's not "Is that all there is?" It's more about asking what is it that permits me the arrogance to continue. I do it because I love doing it, and I keep doing it to discover if I can do things that I've never been able to do in language. I have no interest in writing the poems I have already written. I have no interest in those poems. I think some of them are good poems, but I don't want to write those poems. I want to write some poems that I don't think I can write. The truth is that maybe I can't, maybe I won't be able to do that. I think the delicious prospect of never writing again is always what's there in the mirror every day. I've long ago befriended that question in the mirror. I'm someone who has gone significant periods not writing. After the first long period of not writing, when I began to write again, I never was afraid of that long period of not writing ever again. What I've done is what most writers do. I just read things I love and I look for new work to startle and console me.

If there's anything good about my habits as a writer, it's that I always read new writers; I read young poets. When I was coming up, I saw too many of my revered elders making the decision that they didn't care to read younger poets because they couldn't find their own relevance to what these new poets did. The poets I mentioned earlier were not those poets, of course. Otherwise they wouldn't have read me, for one thing. And I wasn't the only younger poet they read. Somebody like Kinnell, for example, was a famous champion of younger poets, and people don't always remember that. He championed Ai, he championed Carolyn Forché, he championed me. That's how my first book was published at Houghton Mifflin—because of Kinnell. (I've told that story elsewhere.) I see it as one of my pleasures to be able to read a lot of young poets. I believe in a plurality of voices, a diversity of voices, a poetry of every issue and every stripe. Anyone who's ever been my student or who knows me, knows that's just a given in what I feel about poetry. But the question remains: why should I continue? I know there are lots of people who, when they read me saying this, will be happy to write me and say, "Please stop. We love you but please stop." Or they'll say, "We don't love you and please stop." I'll keep doing it, however, as long as it interests me and I'm able to go somewhere I've never gone. If I feel like I can't find a new path, a new door, a new drug—then I'll stop writing.

L to R: Peter Everwine, Philip Levine, and C.G. Hanzlicek.

Greg Pape c. late 1960s.

Juan Felipe Herrera, 10th grade — selfie of Browny, with Brownie camera, 1964, San Diego, CA

L to R: Gary Young, Jon Veinberg, and Christopher Buckley in Gary Young's print shop, Santa Cruz, CA c. 1970s. Photo taken by Dixie Salazar.

Greg Pape and Larry Levis at Levis' farm outside Selma c. 1970s.

Juan Felipe Herrera, 21 years old, getting ready to head to Chiapas, Mexico.
Photo taken by Tomás Mendoza-Harrell in Century City, CA.

Kathy Fagan and Philip Levine in Ohio, September 2013.

Sam Pereira and David St. John at Ernesto and Dianne Trejo's house in Coralville, IA c. 1970s.

L to R: Mickey Hazen, Thomas Emery, Herb Scott, Glover Davis, and Harold Tinkle at University of Iowa, Kenny's Bar, c. late 1960s. Photo taken by Glenn Miller Epstein.

Suzanne Lummis, 1970s, when living in Clovis and hitchhiking to Fresno State. Photo taken by Kirk McKinlay.

L to R: Philip Levine, Peter Everwine, C.G. Hanzlicek and daughter Leah, Larry Levis
c. early 1980s.

L to R: Philip Levine, Larry Levis, and Ernesto Trejo in front of Levine's house
c. late 1980s.

L to R: Jon Veinberg, Gary Young, Roberta Spear, Gary Soto, Philip Levine.

Front L to R: Jon Veinberg and Philip Levine.
Back L to R: Gary Soto and Christopher Buckley
c. 1980.

L to R: C.G. Hanzlicek, B.H. Boston, and Robert Jones.

Group photo for Fresno bookshop reading promoting publication of *Piecework: 19 Fresno Poets*, 1987. L to R: Gene Zumwalt, Robert Vasquez, Philip Levine, Jean Janzen, Jon Veinberg, Dixie Salazar, Ernesto Trejo, Sam Pereira, Gary Soto, C.G. Hanzlicek, C.W. Moulton, and Leonard Adame.

Cover photo for *Down at the Santa Fe Depot*, 1970. Photo taken by Tom Peck.

The Poets & Scholars Tennis Tournament, Fresno, CA — Center: David St. John and son; to his right is Galway Kinnell; far right is Philip Levine. Photo taken by Linda Fry Poverman.

The Poets & Scholars Tennis Tournament, Fresno, CA — L to R: Greg Pape, David St. John and son, Lance Patigian, and Robert Mezey. Photo taken by Linda Fry Poverman.

Philip Levine and Sam Pereira in the parking lot of the English-Philosophy building, University of Iowa. Photo taken by Ernesto Trejo.

Jon Veinberg and Ernesto Trejo

L to R: Gary Young, Luis Omar Salinas, Christopher Buckley, and Jon Veinberg on the veranda of Buckley's apartment, Santa Barbara, CA, 1986. Photo taken by Peggy Young.

L to R: Jon Veinberg, Gary Soto, and Gary Young, mid-1970s.

Philip Levine in the early 1960s.

L to R: Philip Levine, Larry Levis, and David St. John in front of Levine's house. Photo taken by Frances Levine.

L to R: Peter Everwine, C.G. Hanzlicek, Jean Janzen, Sam Pereira, Corrine Clegg Hales, Philip Levine, Glover Davis, David Oliveira, Christopher Buckley, Jon Veinberg, and Tim Skeen at the Fresno Art Museum after a reading by Peter Everwine, c. 1990s.

Peter Everwine and Christopher Buckley.

L to R: Nadya Brown, Christopher Buckley, Peter Everwine, C.G. Hanzlicek, David Oliveira, Dixie Salazar, and Jon Veinberg at Veinberg and Salazar's home.

Peter Everwine at Jon Veinberg and Dixie Salazar's home.

Larry Levis, Philip Levine, and Michael Harper

John Veinberg and Dixie Salazar

Robert Mezey—1935 - 2020

Robert Mezey was born 1935 in Philadelphia. He attended Kenyon College before a stint in the US Army and ultimately earned his BA from the University of Iowa. He completed graduate studies at Stanford University. Mezey's collections of poetry include *The Lovemaker* (1961), winner of the Lamont Poetry Prize; *White Blossoms* (1965); *The Door Standing Open: New and Selected Poems, 1954–1969* (1970); *Small Song* (1979); *Evening Wind* (1987); *Natural Selection* (1995); and *Collected Poems 1952–1999*, which won the Poet's Prize. Mezey has edited numerous works, including *Thomas Hardy: Selected Poems* (1998), *The Poetry of E.A. Robinson* (1999), and, with Donald Justice, *The Collected Poems of Henri Coulette* (1990).

His translations include works by César Vallejo and, with Richard Barnes, all the poetry of Jorge Luis Borges. His awards include a Robert Frost Prize, a Bassine Citation, a PEN Prize, and fellowships from the Ingram Merrill Foundation, the Guggenheim Foundation, and the National Endowment for the Arts. He taught at Fresno State from 1967-68 and lived in Fresno for a number of following years. Mezey also taught at Case Western Reserve University; Franklin & Marshall College; and the University of Utah. From 1975 to 1999, he was at Pomona College, where he served as a professor of English and poet-in-residence.

from *How Much Earth*, 2001—Robert Mezey

A very mysterious thing, how a particular place will flower for a time, however unlikely the place or the time. Fresno in the sixties was a fine place to be. Not the most beautiful of cities perhaps, but full of beautiful places, both in town and out in the foothills. And although sometimes invisible, the mountains were very close. There were a lot of literary people in that arid agribusiness town, and a lot of friends, and some very gifted young poets among the students. And every now and then you might catch a glimpse of Bill Soroyan bicycling to the post office. It was a very provincial place, but there was a certain charm in that, and there are worse things to be than provincial. For whatever reasons, I wrote a lot (if not always well) during my years there. But forget all the good parties and the general liveliness of the scene—my happiest memories are of places outside of town. A forty-acre ranch where I lived with my wife and small children and a goat and many hawks and mice. A rocky camp high in the Sierras on the North fork of the San Joaquin where Pete Everwine and I fished for rainbow trout and were vouchsafed magical visitations from golden finches and rattlesnakes and now and then a naiad or a muse. A little country church and a graveyard out in the middle of nowhere.

"Interview with Bob Mezey," *Poetry International* intern, for *Poetry International Online,* 2012—Laura L Mays Hoopes

Laura L Mays Hoopes: Bob, would you please describe your process in writing poetry?

Robert Mezey: I'm so deeply involved in the process that I can't see it very clearly from outside. For one thing, what gives me the most intense pleasure in writing poems is that I'm not really there, I escape from myself. Even if the poem is about some intimate detail from my own life, I am so wrapped up (or perhaps I should say rapt up) in the mysteries of making and in the endless flow of perceptions and questions and difficulties that I am not aware of myself at all.

The poem may begin with a line or a phrase, sometimes even a single word, or even the sense of a certain cadence, or Frost's lump in the throat, and if I'm in luck, then I'm off on the chase. But the poem has a life of its own and often seems to be leading me to aspects and notions of which I was not at all aware. I rarely begin with an idea of what the poem is about, or what sort of structure it might have, or if I do begin with that, the poem may well blow it away and go off on its own journey.

The finished poem is often a long way from what I thought I had in mind. And the finishing may take a long time—the first part of the process may be a long session of finding my way into the heart of the poem and coming up with a draft, but then I will usually go back ten or twenty or a hundred times, changing a word here, a line there.

Once in a great while, I'll get lucky: my sonnet, "Hardy", for example, I wrote in about 20 minutes while sitting in an airplane —it was as if the poem wrote itself; but to be exact, what I got in those 20 minutes was the first 12 lines; the last two lines of that sonnet took about four months to finish to my satisfaction. And I should add that what I've been describing, although true of most poems I write, is completely uncharacteristic of poems I write by command, so to speak—like those I wrote to celebrate the retirements of certain colleagues at Pomona, or to make a birthday present for my ex-wife (I've written four birthday poems for her). With such poems, the muse is nowhere to be found; she says, you're on your own, and then she's gone. I don't quite believe it's possible to write a good poem without her help, and yet I must say that some of those "forced" poems turned out very well.

LH: What kinds of ideas or feelings attract you to the translation of others' poetry?
RM: I began translating when I was 12 years old, in Latin class in high school. That first term was easy, englishing small amounts of prose while we were learning the language, but not long after, we were made to translate 20 or 30 lines of Virgil each night, and unlike my classmates, I thought it was wrong to translate poetry into prose and so I did all my translations in verse. It was a good idea, because I learned an immense amount about writing metrical verse from those assignments—I learned my craft. Before long, I began translating on my own, other poets that we read, like Catullus and Martial. When I had learned enough French and Spanish to read poems in those languages, I began to try my hand. For the most part, it was when I came across a translation of a French or Spanish poem and felt that it wasn't very good that I decided to do it right. (I guess I had some talent for it—a friend of mine sent a little sheaf of my Catullus versions, about 6 or 8 poems, to Robert Lowell, and Lowell told him that they were the best he'd ever seen and probably ever would see.) I even did some translations from languages that I didn't know, working with a native speaker (sometimes even with the poet himself). I don't quite approve of that way of working, yet it sometimes produces very good translations, and collaborating with such expert helpers, I did translations of a fair number of poems from Hebrew and a few from Hungarian and

German. The process was for the most part catch-as-catch-can, going to work on a few poems that particularly interested me.

The translation of Borges' complete poetry with Dick Barnes was far and away the best and most important work that I've ever done, and yet that started quite by accident. A former student of Dick's who was editing a literary magazine in England had had dinner with Borges, who with typical generosity gave him permission to publish English versions of any of his poems, and that young man asked us to do a few. I had never read Borges' poetry before, and Dick only a little, but after we'd done a few poems, we both realized that these were extraordinary poems and soon came to understand that we were dealing with one of the very greatest poets of the century, and over the years those six or seven poems we'd begun with grew into a collection of some five hundred. Almost every day for a good many years, I spent several hours a day and often several a night working on them, the happiest work I'd ever done. I would claim that our versions are mostly very accurate, thanks mostly to Dick, whose Spanish was a good deal deeper and more experienced than mine, and thanks to three or four people, friends of ours and friends of Borges', who read every word of our versions; and everyone who has read our book has agreed that they are very faithful, even with all the liberties necessitated by our translating into rhyme and meter. But I have come to believe that, given lots of hard work and luck, verse translation can come to seem faithful and yet not be really all that close to the original. Frost was partly right, that poetry is what gets lost in translation, but he might have added, as he well knew, that one does sometimes find real poetry in translation—almost of all of it invented by the translator, a kind of substitute for the original poetry. As I have said on more than one occasion, translation has come to seem to me, over the years, just one more way of writing poems.

LH: Do you conjure up themes that much of your poetry relates to, or do you leave that to your critics and commentators?
RM: No, I never conjure up themes or even think in terms of themes—they usually strike me as mere labels or banalities. Most good poems are too rich and nuanced to be described by a theme. When I first embark on a poem, themes are the furthest thing from my mind; I usually don't know what the poem is really about until it tells me, and that can take a while. And after they're done, I don't think of them thematically. More as kinds of poems— elegies, comic satires, love poems, etc. The only time theme comes into play, and then only very crudely, is when I'm putting a book together and I think of grouping several elegies together, and then some love poems, and so on.

LH: Do you have a favorite poem or several favorite poems, or is each poem the favorite while it's being constructed?
RM: As for having favorite poems, well, I guess I do. I could name five or six that I think especially good. (And probably forty or fifty that I think could use some more work.) I suspect my fondness for this or that poem is considerably influenced by what my friends think of it: so many have said that "Tea Dance at the Nautilus Hotel" is one of my very best that it has become one of my favorites. I never "favor" a poem I'm in the midst of constructing—I'm always too aware of its deficiencies, always thinking how far it falls short of what I was hoping for. It may grow on me later, but while I'm working on it, it's never a favorite.

B.H. Boston—1946 - 2020

B.H. Boston received his BA in English from Fresno State College and his MFA from the University of California at Irvine. *Only the Living,* was published by Helix House Press, and *By All Lights,* was published by Tebot Bach Press in the fall of 2009 as part of the Fresno Poets Ash Tree Series. His poems appeared in *Crazyhorse, Poetry Now, Black Warrior Review, Miramar, Ploughshares, and Western Humanities Review.* Bruce served as poetry co-editor and consulting managing editor for *Poetry International* at San Diego State University and curator of the Master Authors Residency Program at La Jolla Country Day School, where he and his wife Marsha taught for many years.

from *Down at the Santa Fe Depot,* 1970—B.H. Boston

I was born in Oakland, California on June 24, 1946, and have lived in California ever since. Twelve years in Walnut Creek where I remember Elvis Presley and Cheri Esquibel, three years in Colusa where most of puberty was spent in a kayak on the Sacramento River longing for a different ancestry, one year in Sanger where I met Marsha, and seven years in Fresno where we began a family, graduated from college, and learned that "occasionally poetry . . ." means what it says. We now reside in Laguna Beach, California (not far from the University of California at Irvine) struggling to live at least one decibel above the obscene roar of weekend tourism. . . . I have left California only twice: once for Las Vegas to be married and once for Oregon with my grandparents to visit the Oregon Caves. I have always wanted to travel.

from *How Much Earth,* 2001—B.H. Boston

In September of 1964, after declining a scholarship to attend Stanford University, I began the night shift as a full time orderly at Fresno Community Hospital and enrolled with fifteen units as a bio-chemistry major at Fresno State College. After a semester in Roger Chittick's advanced composition course, I changed my major to English, explaining to him one afternoon that for me science had begun to seem too sterile an occupation. A former biochem major himself, the gleam in his eye entirely undiminished, Dr. Chittick encouraged me to trust my instincts.

The Fresno scene during the mid to late Sixties constituted nothing less than a kind of perpetual miracle. For a hungry undergraduate, the writing program at Fresno State was unparalleled anywhere in the country. Many of the gifted poets and inspired teachers and remarkable fellow students I was blessed with there became my life long friends. The extraordinary convergence of people and history and poetry in Fresno still forms the heart of my spiritual and creative life. I had the enormous good fortune to study writing then with Peter Everwine, Charles Hanzlicek, Robert Mezey, and primarily with Philip Levine, whose astonishing classes and formative influence are best described in Larry Levis's superb remembrance. . . . Levine's guidance, his generosity, his courage, his poetry, his uncanny wit, his letters and friendship have sustained me in more ways than I can count for thirty-five years.

In the summer of 1969, my family and I left Fresno for Laguna Beach and the graduate writing program at the University of California Irvine, where I received my MFA. What happened after that is miraculously still unfolding, and someplace else.

"Changed Utterly" from *First Light: A Festschrift for Philip Levine on this 85th Birthday*, 2013—B.H. Boston

Poetry happens. It opens and transforms us. It builds our blood and saves lives. At least that's my experience. I would never have had anything approaching a full life, would never have taught literature and writing or edited magazines or presumed to write poems, would probably never have survived into my 60s without Philip Levine's poetry, generosity, friendship and tutelage over the last 46 years.

I first saw Phil read at the Fresno Public Library during what must have been the end of my senior year of high school in 1964. I'd recently purchased *On the Edge* at Dodgson's bookstore, a godsend on Van Ness Avenue downtown, which—along with Stanley's Armenian Deli on the one side, Anastasia's Tobacco Shop on the other, and the Sherman Clay music store near Blackstone Avenue in the new Manchester Mall—was paramount among my favorite haunts my first two years in the Central Valley, a place distressingly indifferent to the life of the imagination. Or so it seemed to me until I met Philip Levine.

As he leaned over the lectern that afternoon, squinting his left eye at the twenty or thirty of us scattered among numerous empty chairs, he remarked that in fact he had read to a smaller audience before, "in the back of a station wagon once." He then proceeded to read with such ferocity and wit the molecules of the air began to pulse at a quickened rate.

A year earlier, while doing chin-ups from a mulberry branch in our Sanger backyard, I announced, in response to my mother's question regarding my future—my parents were fans of "Dr. Kildare" and envisioned me in white coat with stethoscope—that more than anything else I wanted to be a poet. (I'd been writing sonnets to Marsha, who would soon become my wife, for months.) Phil's performance that Sunday afternoon at the library pretty much sealed the deal.

The next year as a freshman at Fresno State, I met a funny guy named Gene Winder. An ex-Marine already well into his 30s, Gene was also an enormously talented and somewhat eccentric student poet. We soon became close friends. Along with our devotion to Samuel Beckett, William Carlos Williams and Dylan Thomas, to J. P. Donleavy, cheap beer and noontime reruns of *The Andy Griffith Show*, Winder and I shared an enthusiasm for Levine. Gene raved about Phil's poetry and teaching, often quoting him verbatim, and recommended I take one of his classes as soon as he returned from his first year abroad in Spain. As I remember it, enrollment in Phil's undergraduate creative writing seminar would be limited to twelve students, no more. Imagine that.

When September arrived with its copper haze and glare, I tentatively approached Phil's office in the Humanities Building—erected from previously existing architectural drawings intended for California State penitentiaries—to find him standing in the hallway smoking a cigarette. Dressed in a plaid button-down sport shirt, burgundy sweater vest, white tennis shoes and Levi's, Phil might have been a student himself. As if on cue, a rather patrician gentleman marched out of another office down the hall and addressed Phil as if he were a recalcitrant stable boy, informing everyone within a five-mile radius that smoking was not permitted in the hallways, commanding Phil to stub out his cigarette forthwith. After telling the guy to fuck off, Phil showed me into his second story office with its window overlooking a strip of Bermuda grass decomposing in the quad. Amazingly, Phil agreed to sign my add card.

Gene decided to accompany me to Levine's first class session that fall. I failed to dissuade him from sitting in the front row.

My poem turned up on the first batch of dittos. After Marsha and I were married, I gave my brother a kayak I'd built in the Sacramento Valley my 14th winter. John of course had absolutely no use for such a thing. The poem, which I would reproduce here to everyone's dismay if only I could locate it, contained such lines as "I find myself knee deep in the backyard of my youth." I remember drafting part of it in the Fresno State cafeteria before I punched in later that afternoon as Community Hospital's only floating swing shift orderly, at $2.25 an hour. That first evening, Phil read my poem and finished his comments by saying, "This shows real talent." Gene turned to me and smiled. I remember little more except the feeling that in some way my life had utterly changed. It had.

It may be worth noting that in 1966, while still in his thirties, Phil was not yet the soft-spoken, ingratiating belletrist he has become today. In fact, his wit was wild and eviscerating, a bracing source of shock (Awake!) to all of us, an astounding and hilarious otherworldly amazement that focused our attention sharply on the business at hand—on the power of poetry, on the surprising possibility of living true lives. We shook with laughter even as we were being skewered. We loved it. We loved Phil. I don't think any of us ever missed a class. Phil would usually begin by reading a poem aloud to us—Jon Silkin's devastating "Death of a Son" for instance—followed by a brief and illuminating discussion. Then he'd move to the week's student poems, printed anonymously on a fresh stack of dittos. We were offered the opportunity to claim authorship by reading our own poems aloud. If the author declined to hold forth, Phil would generously read the poem himself, read it carefully, as convincingly as it was ever likely to be read. Most of us kept quiet on such occasions. When Levine read our poems, we heard them truly for the first time. Imagine. At the next class meeting, he would return to us, without fail, the original typed copies of our poems with his extensive comments in red ink:

> *This word is a little too fancy, too literary. For me. It may o'erwhelm others.*
> *This is a good, quiet and very suggestive ending.*
> *I'm sick of the winter, the winter poems my students write. . . . Still*
> *this is pretty damn nice; you let it build, you under write the ending,*
> *& your language is interesting.*
> *this is dangling—it's the tree & not the display that's on its side*
> *this light, psychiatric word is awful & right*
> *Your work has improved a lot this semester: it moves better, it's about*
> *more while pretending to be about less, & it's seldom theatrical. Also,*
> *you're building your poems instead of splashing them down: this one*
> *builds very well to the bed image, where they are back to back like*
> *soldiers in a hostile land.*

Each poem would also receive an overall assessment: The best poems were marked good; the decent stuff was OK+; then came OK and OK-; and finally, the legendary argh!, which happily I saw only once, on the board that first evening as Phil explained his grading system.

In the spring of 1968, Larry Levis and I began the drive from Fresno to UC Irvine for a weekend celebration called Manuscript Day, an extraordinary confabulation of poets and students. MS Day was also a chance for the fledging UCI Writing Workshop to attract attention and prospective applicants. In 1968, the campus itself was only three years old.

There was a blur of memorable parties, dinners, and readings that weekend. Late Saturday night we wandered the beaches of Balboa Island, stopping wherever we saw a light on from a deck or an open window. When the festivities had ended and we had all somehow managed to avoid arrest, I eased the car back onto the Orange County freeways going north, with Phil as my only passenger. (Larry had taken a ride back the day before with another of the Fresno contingent.) After we'd coasted down the steep grade from Gorman and pulled over for gas outside of Bakersfield—we'd made it from Fresno to Laguna Beach and back as far as Mettler on four dollars' worth of regular— Phil climbed into the back seat. As Aretha Franklin's "Respect" crackled from the AM radio, Phil stretched out as best he could for a nap. When the song ended, Phil's head reappeared in the rear viewmirror, his hands grasping the back of the passenger seat. "How long was I out? Half an hour?" he asked. "Not quite," I answered. He shuffled through some papers and asked if I wanted to hear a new poem he'd finished the week before. "Of course! I'd love to!" As we cruised past the silos and cattle yards and swerved to avoid the dust devils crisscrossing the outskirts of Bakersfield, from the back seat of the battered VW, Phil read "They Feed They Lion" aloud for the first time. Things were changing.

Over the years, Phil's poetry and friendship have given me back my life more times than I can count. The summer I turned 26, in 1972, out of a need for steady jobs and the opportunity for both of us to teach, Marsha and I moved from Costa Mesa to Santa Catalina Island, where we began our stint at a doomed little boarding school in Toyon Bay, about a mile north by boat from Avalon Harbor.

We were blessed with a number of marvelous students there, and we gave it everything we had. But we were simply not cut out for island boarding school life. Practically marooned, besieged by insurmountable difficulty, we eventually found ourselves bereft of health and hope and any reasonable prospects for the future. We signed on for a second year.

Each day after lunch, the school's mail was distributed in front of the cafeteria on a patch of grass under a grove of ancient eucalypti at the bottom of Toyon Canyon, within view of the sloping beach line, the narrow pier, and the water. One day in March of 1974, the school's business manager handed me a manila envelope containing a signed first edition of *1933*, with this inscription:

> *For Bruce & Marsha, the poet and the painter fighting the only fight*
> *there on Mad Isle. I'm glad you have each other because there is nothing*
> *in the world that anyone could give you that would mean even an atom*
> *of that, but still it thrills me to give you this book born of people who*
> *sweated & loved & suffered as you have, & who like you kept carrying*
> *the stone up the hill because, my brother and sister, that's where our*
> *road goes. Love, Phil*

As I read this even now, everything else simply stops, and only what matters most rises into perfect focus. On the damp grass that morning almost forty years ago, I turned from the Headmaster's announcements and admonitions and opened Phil's new book to

"The Poem Circling Hamtramck, Michigan All Night in Search of You," which ends with these lines:

> If someone would enter now
> and take these lovers—for they
> are lovers—in his arms
> and rock them together
> like a mother with a child
> in each arm, this man
> with so much desire, this woman
> with none, then it would not be
> Hamtramck, it would not be
> this night. They know it
> and wait, he staring
> into the light, she into
> the empty glass. In the darkness
> of this world, men
> pull on heavy canvas gloves,
> dip into rubber coats
> and enter the fires. The rats
> frozen under the conveyors
> turn to let their eyes
> fill with dawn. A strange star
> is born one more time.

The sudden infusion of such astonishing power and tenderness had made the world habitable again. We would find our future in it. This poem, and the whole of the book as I read and reread it, imparted a new resolve and clarity. For me, "The Poem Circling Hamtramck," like so much of Phil's work, performs a kind of secular miracle, where the fallen are lifted up, where those without hope are given a voice, where something of moment becomes possible even in the face of "nothing/but love or pain." We were impelled to hold fast to what is best, to persevere, and to say our piece.

Six months later, Marsha and I were two of five sleepy passengers in a retooled Grumman WWII amphibious biplane, careening across the chopped waves of Avalon Harbor on our way toward the mainland again, lifting above the channel toward our new life, laughing madly all the way to the Port of San Pedro and what came after. As I write this, Marsha is painting beautifully and masterfully in the next room. Our daughter, now almost 50, lives in a little yellow house barely nine minutes away. And Phil is Poet Laureate of the United States, perhaps in the air on his way to Ottawa or Philly, where he might read his new poem, "How to Get There." It's a life changer.

"Gifts and Remembrances" from *A CONDITION OF THE SPIRIT*—B.H. Boston

When Robert L. Jones introduced us in the fall of 1965 on the second floor of the Humanities Building at Fresno State College, Larry Levis was dressed in a tattered navy blue crew necked sweater, paper thin khaki slacks, and penny loafers without socks, a sartorial eccentricity that would remain consistent in even the coldest San Joaquin Valley weather. He was lighting up a Camel. Larry and I were both twenty years old at the time. Bob was probably twentythree. At that first meeting, Larry's fierce dedication to poetry, his remarkable preparation and readiness, were as palpable as the tule fog that enveloped the college dorms and livestock pens, the rows of stubbed vines, the almond and orange orchards, the bowling alley parking lots and coffee shops, the apartments and old Victorian rooms we lived in then-the fog that saturated our poems and fed our longing all that winter.

Another constant was Philip Levine's astonishing weekly evening poetry workshop, where we were waking to the miraculous gift of poetry and our own lives, what Larry has called the "crucial gift which Levine gave to each of us. "At twenty, Larry had memorized more of Yeats than the rest of us had read. He had much of Eliot by heart, certainly all of "Prufrock," the Sweeney poems, "Gerontion," probably most of *The Wasteland and Other Poems,* a book he appropriated from his high school library. He'd read Crane and Stevens, whom he also got by heart. In addition to *vers libre,* he immediately began exploring various received forms, including iambic pentameter and tetrameter, syllabics, the villanelle, something like Williams's variable foot, and the sonnet, which he made his own in a chilling poem called "November Landscape,"which appeared on our workshop dittos in December of 1966. In everything he wrote, even from the beginning, there was always the unmistakable thrill of his voice.

By the third year, he was well into "The Magician Poems", many of which appear in *Wrecking Crew.* It seemed that each new poem, as would soon be true of each successive new book, evolved with huge, unpredictable, qualitative leaps. It was obvious that Larry would become one of the greatest poets of our generation. This understanding was another given, something I believe none of us ever doubted. I never doubted it. Larry's destiny was simply one of those intuitive, essential, incontestable truths of life.

By the time Larry was twenty-one, he had developed the concentration and discipline of a Capuchin monk. At potlucks or parties during this period, Larry often seemed distracted, restless, as if there were some other pressing engagement we were keeping him from. This was true, of course. We were keeping him from his muses. To drop in on him to chat or to return a book or to play the new Coltrane or Stones album required considerable audacity. To the question, "So, what are you doing?" there was usually only one answer: "Writing." Once interrupted, however, he could be enormously gracious.

One autumn afternoon in his room near Fresno's Tower District (we were in our junior year), he cordially offered me a glass of Pernod, an unopened bottle of which was displayed on a window sill looking out onto the alley. After Larry filled two spotted glasses and added tap water—there was no ice—and we watched the yellow liqueur turn opaque in the pale October light, we silently lifted our drinks and suspended our judgment. The taste of the Pernod was not really the point. Larry had been reading Baudelaire at the time and would have poured absinthe had he been able to procure it.

Whenever I think of Larry now, and I think of him often, daily, I retreat into the embrace of his immeasurable kindness, his immense generosity. The evidence is everywhere: in the bookcase housing the Norton anthology he gave me after a modern European literature course the second year of our friendship; in my first teaching job at

Cal State L.A., one of the most stimulating times of my life; in a pen drawing on note paper framed for years on our kitchen bulletin board—a lopsided circle with a squinched grimace blurred by clouds above the caption, "At night, when the moon takes over"; in the Mont Blanc he left behind during an overnight stay in our tiny apartment in Encinitas; in the Marshall Crenshaw tape Larry had autographed at a club in Missouri; in the terra cotta coffee cup and saucer from Puerto Vallarta; in the pack of ribbed condoms from a gas station somewhere between Salt Lake and San Diego; in all his letters and manuscripts; in the note card from Selma celebrating the formation of our mythical rock band (which shall remain nameless here); and most thankfully in the enduring triumph of Larry's artistic imagination and wit in the daring, darkly luminous achievement of his prose and his poems, a gift which entirely consumed him.

In the summer of 1983, Marsha and I left San Diego on a road trip to Selma, California in a caravan with Richard Katrovas, his wife Betty, Carolyn Forche and Barbara Cully. After coasting down the north slope of the Tehachapis from Gorman, we reassembled at a Marie Callendar's Restaurant off the truck route in Bakersfield. We were happy to be together, anticipating spending the night with Larry and his mother at the ranch house in Selma. We all loved Larry's previous work and were excited by the new poems which would ultimately be published as *Winter Stars*. At one point during our late lunch, in the confusion of salads and pot pies and iced teas, our curious waitress wanted to know exactly which foreign country we all were visiting California from.

That late afternoon Larry and his beautiful mother Carol welcomed us like lost relatives. We dived at dusk into their fresh water swimming pool (the spilloff from which helped irrigate an orchard) and stayed up as late as we could in the mansion's many blue rooms as Larry entertained us in a place and moment seemingly devoid of all difficulty, during what was in fact a very difficult time for him. Wanting to talk out of our own excitement and our own need, we filled the aquamarine dining room with our manic voices.

Larry talked almost without pause that night and early morning, recounting stories about the house, his life on the ranch during his childhood, his son Nick, about whatever else suggested itself to his elastic mind. At one point, Larry and Richard stood at the window in the room off the pool. During a conversational lull, after Richard had begun talking again, Larry resumed his own narrative over Richard's voice. Eventually Richard wandered off, leaving Larry alone, speaking softly into the evening shadows, gazing east over the pool and the flourishing vineyards which may as well have stretched all the way to the Sierra.

Before we left the next morning, Marsha took photographs as we all embraced and said our goodbyes. Larry would remain in Selma to continue work on *Sensationalism* (the working title for *Winter Stars)* and visit with Nick, who was expected momentarily. Well before noon, the Valley sun had already warped the air above the back county roads, and through the open windows of our van, into our hopeful faces, a hot wind ground the dust of West Side cattle yards and farms the rest of the way up 99 into Fresno.

After he graduated from Fresno State College in 1968, Larry moved to Syracuse University for his masters degree, where he studied with Don Justice, then to Pasadena to teach, then to the Iowa City Writers Workshop for his doctorate, then to a succession of teaching jobs at the University of Missouri, at the University of Utah in Salt Lake, and finally at Virginia Commonwealth University in Richmond, Virginia. Over the years, we'd meet on holidays at the ranch or at Phil and Franny Levine's home in Fresno or at the Santa Fe Depot Basque restaurant or at some reunion elsewhere in the city. Occasionally Larry would read his poems at La Jolla Country Day School or San Diego State, and we'd reconvene in San Diego.

After Larry moved to Richmond, we saw much less of him. We met for the last time in 1993 or 1994, just before Christmas, at a French bistro in the Hillcrest District in San Diego, after Bob Jones had returned from the University of Utah, where Larry had recommended him for entrance into the Ph.D. program. One of the topics of discussion that day, of no small interest to both Bob and Larry, was alimony. As I remember, we all relished the braised lamb.

Although Larry never had much patience for ontological chitchat, his love for Whitman ran as deep as being itself, and on more than one occasion we discussed Whitman's transcendentalism, as well as Malcolm Cowley's superb introduction to the reprinted 1855 edition of *Leaves of Grass*. I don't wish to speculate here on metaphysics or metempsychosis or the mysterious cosmologies of the psyche. What I do know is that Larry continues to befriend me in dream.

Shortly after his death, he appeared vividly just before dawn. He was fuming. "No one understands," he said. "This is all *Maya!*" He then defined that Sanskrit word with a sweep of his upturned hand sprung at the wrist and a few, clear phrases. I woke remembering his look and his gesture, unable to retrieve any more of his words. For anyone overwhelmed by grief, the implications of such a revelation are hard to put into practice. Such grief becomes a dimension of life , a natural force, like gravity or planetary motion. Nonetheless, Larry's dream offering was wise and helpful and at the time seemed to me worthy of the most serious consideration. It still does. Occasionally, Larry pulls up in an old Chevy or Plymouth and simply hangs out for a while. We write or read or play pool and talk, always somewhere near a vast ocean, until it's time for him to leave.

Eventually the car returns with someone else at the wheel someone I have taken to be Zamora, although we've not been introduced. After these visits, I'm left to find my own way home. Somehow, I've acquired the skill (which I attribute entirely to Larry's magnanimity) for hot wiring whatever mode of transportation inevitably presents itself. Recently, I was reminded of Larry's fondness for *The Golden Bowl*. (Somewhere I still have the dark blue Modern Library edition he gave me.) Flipping through my journal from the early days following Larry's death, I came across this quote by Henry James: "Three things in human life are important. The first is to be kind. The second is to be kind. And the third is to be kind." Larry had a genius for all three. (Many thanks to Marsha Boston for her enthusiasm and critical authority and to Richard Katrovas for his sweet remembrance.)

Whenever I think of Larry now, and I think of him often, daily, I retreat into the embrace of his immeasurable kindness, his immense generosity. The evidence is everywhere: in the bookcase housing the Norton anthology he gave me after a modern European literature course the second year of our friendship; in my first teaching job at Cal State L.A., one of the most stimulating times of my life; in a pen drawing on note paper framed for years on our kitchen bulletin board—a lopsided circle with a squinched grimace blurred by clouds above the caption, "At night, when the moon takes over"; in the Mont Blanc he left behind during an overnight stay in our tiny apartment in Encinitas; in the Marshall Crenshaw tape Larry had autographed at a club in Missouri; in the terra cotta coffee cup and saucer from Puerto Vallarta; in the pack of ribbed condoms from a gas station somewhere between Salt Lake and San Diego; in all his letters and manuscripts; in the note card from Selma celebrating the formation of our mythical rock band (which shall remain nameless here); and most thankfully in the enduring triumph of Larry's artistic imagination and wit in the daring, darkly luminous achievement of his prose and his poems, a gift which entirely consumed him.

In the summer of 1983, Marsha and I left San Diego on a road trip to Selma, California in a caravan with Richard Katrovas, his wife Betty, Carolyn Forche and Barbara Cully. After coasting down the north slope of the Tehachapis from Gorman, we reassembled at a Marie Callendar's Restaurant off the truck route in Bakersfield. We were happy to be together, anticipating spending the night with Larry and his mother at the ranch house in Selma. We all loved Larry's previous work and were excited by the new poems which would ultimately be published as *Winter Stars*. At one point during our late lunch, in the confusion of salads and pot pies and iced teas, our curious waitress wanted to know exactly which foreign country we all were visiting California from.

That late afternoon Larry and his beautiful mother Carol welcomed us like lost relatives. We dived at dusk into their fresh water swimming pool (the spilloff from which helped irrigate an orchard) and stayed up as late as we could in the mansion's many blue rooms as Larry entertained us in a place and moment seemingly devoid of all difficulty, during what was in fact a very difficult time for him. Wanting to talk out of our own excitement and our own need, we filled the aquamarine dining room with our manic voices.

Larry talked almost without pause that night and early morning, recounting stories about the house, his life on the ranch during his childhood, his son Nick, about whatever else suggested itself to his elastic mind. At one point, Larry and Richard stood at the window in the room off the pool. During a conversational lull, after Richard had begun talking again, Larry resumed his own narrative over Richard's voice. Eventually Richard wandered off, leaving Larry alone, speaking softly into the evening shadows, gazing east over the pool and the flourishing vineyards which may as well have stretched all the way to the Sierra.

Before we left the next morning, Marsha took photographs as we all embraced and said our goodbyes. Larry would remain in Selma to continue work on Sensationalism (the working title for *Winter Stars*) and visit with Nick, who was expected momentarily. Well before noon, the Valley sun had already warped the air above the back county roads, and through the open windows of our van, into our hopeful faces, a hot wind ground the dust of West Side cattle yards and farms the rest of the way up 99 into Fresno.

After he graduated from Fresno State College in 1968, Larry moved to Syracuse University for his masters degree, where he studied with Don Justice, then to Pasadena to teach, then to the Iowa City Writers Workshop for his doctorate, then to a succession of teaching jobs at the University of Missouri, at the University of Utah in Salt Lake, and finally at Virginia Commonwealth University in Richmond, Virginia. Over the years, we'd meet on holidays at the ranch or at Phil and Franny Levine's home in Fresno or at the Santa Fe Depot Basque restaurant or at some reunion elsewhere in the city. Occasionally Larry would read his poems at La Jolla Country Day School or San Diego State, and we'd reconvene in San Diego.

After Larry moved to Richmond, we saw much less of him. We met for the last time in 1993 or 1994, just before Christmas, at a French bistro in the Hillcrest District in San Diego, after Bob Jones had returned from the University of Utah, where Larry had recommended him for entrance into the Ph.D. program. One of the topics of discussion that day, of no small interest to both Bob and Larry, was alimony. As I remember, we all relished the braised lamb.

Although Larry never had much patience for ontological chitchat, his love for Whitman ran as deep as being itself, and on more than one occasion we discussed Whitman's transcendentalism, as well as Malcolm Cowley's superb introduction to the reprinted 1855 edition of Leaves of Grass. I don't wish to speculate here on metaphysics or metempsychosis or the mysterious cosmologies of the psyche. What I do know is that Larry continues to befriend me in dream.

Shortly after his death, he appeared vividly just before dawn. He was fuming. "No one understands," he said. "This is all Maya!" He then defined that Sanskrit word with a sweep of his upturned hand sprung at the wrist and a few, clear phrases. I woke remembering his look and his gesture, unable to retrieve any more of his words. For anyone overwhelmed by grief, the implications of such a revelation are hard to put into practice. Such grief becomes a dimension of life, a natural force, like gravity or planetary motion. Nonetheless, Larry's dream offering was wise and helpful and at the time seemed to me worthy of the most serious consideration. It still does. Occasionally, Larry pulls up in an old Chevy or Plymouth and simply hangs out for a while. We write or read or play pool and talk, always somewhere near a vast ocean, until it's time for him to leave.

Eventually the car returns with someone else at the wheel—someone I have taken to be Zamora, although we've not been introduced. After these visits, I'm left to find my own way home. Somehow, I've acquired the skill (which I attribute entirely to Larry's magnanimity) for hot-wiring whatever mode of transportation inevitably presents itself.

Recently, I was reminded of Larry's fondness for The Golden Bowl. (Somewhere I still have the dark blue Modern Library edition he gave me.) Flipping through my journal from the early days following Larry's death, I came across this quote by Henry James: "Three things in human life are important. The first is to be kind. The second is to be kind. And the third is to be kind." Larry had a genius for all three.

(Many thanks to Marsha Boston for her enthusiasm and critical authority and to Richard Katrovas for his sweet remembrance.)

Luis Omar Salinas—1937-2008

Since 1967, Luis Omar Salinas was an important voice in American poetry. Salinas' first book, *Crazy Gypsy*, (1970), is now a classic of Chicano poetry, reflecting the politics and self actualization of those highly charged and changing times. Given his willingness to engage social and political subjects in his poetry, a number of faculty and staff members in La Raza Studies at Fresno State College collaborated to publish his first book, *Crazy Gypsy*. About 4,000 copies of *Crazy Gypsy* sold in eight months in two editions.

In the late 1960s and early 1970s, Salinas was one of the prominent group of poets associated with major American poets Philip Levine, Peter Everwine, and C.G. Hanzlicek who were teaching at Fresno State College, as it was then known. With another professor in the English Department there, Lillian Faderman, Salinas co-edited a poetry anthology in 1973, *From The Barrio: A Chicano Anthology*. It would be ten years before Salinas published his second book, *Afternoon of the Unreal* (Abramas Publications, 1980). *Afternoon of the Unreal* reflected the influences of Salinas' reading of and interest in Spanish poetry—the generation of '27—Lorca, Jimenez, Machado, Hernandez and more—as well as South American poets Neruda and Vallejo. A deeper imagism, an element of the surreal, combined with his ability to target specific emotional states, revealed his mature voice. A sense of melancholy, a romantic longing and wildness balanced by wit and irony, would surface in Salinas' following books—*Prelude To Darkness* (Mango Publications, 1981) *and Darkness Under The Trees / Walking Behind the Spanish* (Chicano Library Press, University of California Berkeley, 1982). In 1984 he received a rare General Electric Foundation Award to support his writing, and in 1985 he was invited to read at the Library of Congress with Sandra Cisneros.

Luis Omar Salinas was born in Robstown, Texas on June 27, 1937, to Olivia and Rosendo Salinas. In 1941, Olivia Salinas grew weak with tuberculosis and died. Luis was adopted by his aunt and uncle, Oralia and Alfredo Salinas. Eventually, the family moved to Fresno where Luis attended elementary and high school. Salinas moved with his family to Bakersfield where he received an AA degree in History. In 1958, Salinas enrolled at California State University Los Angeles where he studied with the poet Henri Coulette who became a positive influence on his poetry.

Salinas began attending classes at Fresno State College in 1967, and in Philip Levine's workshop met fellow poets Larry Levis, B.H. Boston, DeWayne Rail, Greg Pape, David St. John and others of that renowned group who would emerge from Fresno in the 1960s and 1970s. There he also befriended Fresno poets Gary Soto, Ernesto Trejo, and Jon Veinberg, who would be significant in their support of his poetry.

Salinas' work has become recognized as an original and significant contribution to American poetry.

Subsequent books are: *The Sadness of Days: Selected and New Poems,* Houston: Arte Publico Press, University of Houston, 1987; *Follower of Dusk*. Chico, CA: Flume Press, 1991; *Sometime Mysteriously*. Anchorage: Salmon Run Press, 1997; *Greatest Hits 1969-1996*. Johnstown, OH: Pudding House Publications, 2002; and *Elegy For Desire,* Tucson, AZ, Univ. of Arizona Press, 2005. In 2014, as part of the Ash tree poetry Series, Tebot Back published, *Messenger to the Stars: A Luis Omar Salinas New Selected Poems & Reader*, edited by Jon Veinberg and Christopher Buckley.

"Foreword" from *MESSENGER TO THE STARS: A LUIS OMAR SALINAS NEW SELECTED POEMS & READER*, 2014—**Christopher Buckley**

In 1975 when I was a grad student at UC Irvine, Gary Soto arranged a reading on campus for Luis Omar Salinas. I knew his poems in *Down At The Santa Fe Depot*, the first great anthology of Fresno poets. I was a bit apprehensive; Omar was older, and word was he was a bit manic, on the edge. I was 25 or 26 and would never have thought then that I'd become his good friend before long. I had been reading poetry and trying to write for maybe five years then, and I did not know much. Yet little was required to recognize true and amazing talent, and I came to know and admire him immediately as Soto, my house mate Jon Veinberg and others went to a reception of sorts for Omar at—if memory serves here—Gary Johnson's sister's house somewhere near Laguna Beach. Johnson was one of the early group of Fresno poets and I think he drove Omar down for the reading. Omar was mercurial, given to inspired and impromptu rapid-fire odes, brilliance off the cuff. I particularly remember him in the kitchen that night, composing an ode to the stove, which, in seven or eight lines, was brilliant with wit and inventive imagery.

Omar was a virtuoso, a poet of intense lyric originality and inspiration, a poet of great imagination and gifts. The majority of his poems were concentrated psychological investigations of his life and reactions to the rush of experience, but with a stylistic and imagistic bravado that made his voice unique. I began working closely with Omar in 1978, the year I moved to Fresno to teach at Fresno State. Our first project was to see his second book, *Afternoon of the Unreal*, into publication. Gary Soto, Jon Veinberg, and I edited and organized the ms. which had been some eight years in the making.

Over the following two years—most often it seemed in afternoons in the fall—in my back yard or in Jon Veinberg's, we sat at old picnic tables with Soto and Ernesto Trejo, or with Gary Young and Tim Sheehan over from Santa Cruz, talking poetry over cheap beer and *chicharones* while some impoverished chicken legs and dinner franks sputtered on the hibachi. Omar would praise fellow poets, or Byron and the Romantics, the apricot tree, or Veinberg's great collie dog, Moses. We'd encourage him to jot those lines down, or one of us would transcribe them. Omar was at the inspired peek of his powers in those days and the poems he wrote and which we worked on almost every week, would constitute his next three books, *Prelude to Darkness*, then *Darkness Under the Trees/Walking Behind the Spanish*. Soto was one of Omar's earliest supporters and it was through the good efforts of Gary and his wife Carolyn that Omar's double book was published by the Chicano Studies Library Publications at the University of California Berkeley in 1982.

Omar lived very modestly; his day job all the years I knew him and worked with him was writing poetry and observing life. He would turn up at all hours at my house on Arthur Street and instead of opening a beer and just chewing the fat, I'd usher him into my study and we'd sit in front of my old office model Royal typewriter, and work on whatever notes and scraps he had in his pockets, whatever revisions I had stacked on my desk. I'd open the window to the street and turn on the box fan behind us so the smoke from his KOOLS, which he chain-smoked, blew out the window, mostly. Also Jon Veinberg was a constant reader of Omar's poems, and in Fresno for the rest of Omar's life, Jon was his immediate lifeline to the world.

Soto, Veinberg and I worked with Omar on selecting poems for *The Sadness of Days: Selected and New Poems*, 1987, and over time, I became Omar's main critic, editor, and secretarial assistant, typing up the poems, sending them out to magazines, writing and calling editors. When Omar came up with his next run of poems, I sent them off to Flume Press's annual chapbook contest in Chico, CA. The judge that year, Quinton Duval, with great enthusiasm, selected Omar's collection, *Follower of Dusk*, as the winner for 1991. Adding another twenty-some poems to that chapbook, Omar had his next to last book, *Sometimes Mysteriously*, which was published in 1997 as the winner in Salmon Run Press's national book contest; poet and Editor John Smelcer selected it from about 500 entries. It quickly sold out and today is almost impossible to find; checking abebooks.com recently, I saw one copy listed for sale at $50 plus shipping.

Then into his 60s, it seemed a good time to publish a comprehensive interview with Omar, covering his writing career over 30 years. Jon and I went for a visit to Sanger and I brought a notebook and computer printout of questions I'd prepared, and we worked all one Sunday afternoon on the patio. I followed up via mail, phone, and other visits and it appeared in *Quarterly West*, No 55 Fall/Winter 2002/2003.

Around 2000, Omar began writing poems for a project that he then called *AMORES*, essentially a collection of lyrics and love poems. He had returned to reading the English Romantics, for at heart, Omar was always a romantic, a troubadour spirit in the world. What arrived every week for the next few years, were hand written rough drafts for *AMORES*. It was my job to edit, select, type up and return them to Omar for his approval and re-writing. Omar was writing love poems at a furious rate, many too baldly emotive, lacking his imagistic inventiveness and mercurial associations that always characterized his best work. It was my job to be the demanding editor and say so. Often he would send me poems that Jon had already told him were not working—a second opinion. Often he would work it around the other way. But with rigorous editing and rewriting (how else does it ever get done?) a new manuscript began taking shape. In one envelope, Omar sent five or six short poems, none of which worked individually. But when the best passages out of each were isolated and assembled in sections with the title of one, "Elegy for Desire," we discovered a strong title poem for the collection, one with a grander vision that surpassed a collection of love poems alone. A ms. emerged in the wise, wistful, hopeful, and lyrical mode of his last book. About two years of further editing and rewriting, and I had the ms. on my computer in shape to send off to the Univ. of Arizona Press.

Once *ELEGY FOR DESIRE* appeared in 2005, I saw no more poems from Omar, and when visiting Fresno I could see that Omar was just trying to hold on to life and do the best he could to survive. He was still living in the house in Sanger which his aunt and uncle had left him. His cousins were also living there and helping to care for him. I packed up all the original manuscripts and other materials from *ELEGY FOR DESIRE* and through a book dealer, sold them to the archives of Stanford University. The money kept Omar going and he went out and bought new clothes and of course, a new hat, one of this trademarks over the years. I cannot now remember exactly when his cousins decided they could no longer give him the full-time care he had come to need and sent him off to the rest home in Fresno? I do remember his cousin, Cal, driving him down to the Univ. of California Riverside to give the Tomas Rivera *Cinco de Mayo* reading that my colleague Juan Felipe Herrera and I arranged each year, I think that was 2006, and Omar was using a walker and had a portable oxygen unit to help with breathing. He read from *ELEGY FOR DESIRE* and the poems were well received.

Omar, died in May of 2008. The last year or two of his life were spent in a rest home, suffering from emphysema and other ailments. Jon Veinberg went each week to see Omar, taking him out to breakfast or sitting outside with him in the patio of the rest home drinking diet Pepsis. Omar did not present Jon with any new poems these last years, though his custom had been to do so whenever he had a chance. He had stopped mailing hand written mss. to me each week, ending a long and brilliant career as a poet.

Jon Veinberg and I have put our heads together to present a more judicious selection of Omar's poetry than has been previously available. Indeed, of all his books, only *Elegy for Desire* is still in print. Our aim is not only to provide the very best of his output from over the years, but to also accommodate many outstanding new poems from *Sometimes Mysteriously* and *Elegy for Desire* that were published after the earlier selected poems. We offer interviews, reviews, and some of Omar's own writing on his work so there is a testament in his own words. As well, we add critical and personal appreciations that, all taken together, present an aesthetic and historical context and produce a kind of literary biography—as full a picture of the entire man and his talent as is possible in these pages. Omar was the troubadour with songs and *saludos* for all his friends. Happy, enthusiastic, often sad, he was a poet who finally found contentment in surviving and in his writing, and, as especially seen in his last two books, he was a poet who admitted the possibility of hope, of life ultimately turning out for the better.

The purpose then of this book is to not only present a new selection of the best poems but to also testify to the achievement and accomplishment and career of Omar the Poet. Equally, the aim is to remember and appreciate Omar the Man, our *compañero* in life's struggles and in poetry, a great soul who was possessed of a unique vision and a rare talent, our friend who had compassion and poetry for us all.

*Note: *Elegy for Desire* is the only one of Salinas's books still in print: Univ. of Arizona Press, 2005. For more a more detailed appraisal of Salinas's life and work see:

"Luis Omar Salinas—1937—" in *AMERICAN WRITERS*, Supplement XIII, Charles Scribner's Sons, 2003, by Christopher Buckley.

"Luis Omar Salinas—1937-2008" *The Writer's Chronicle*, Oct/Nov 2008, a publication of AWP, by Christopher Buckley.

"Looking for Omar" from *MESSENGER TO THE STARS: A LUIS OMAR SALINAS NEW SELECTED POEMS & READER*, 2014—Gary Soto

Omar arrived in my life like a rumor, or what in Spanish we call chisme. I was a transfer from City College, and a recently converted English major. I kicked around Fresno State, aware that every third person in the old Ed-Psych building was a poet, hardly an exaggeration since our instruction came from the likes of Philip Levine, Robert Mezey, and Peter Everwine. This was fall, 1972. The Vietnam war was on the wane, and the Chicano movimiento was losing its ability to bring people to its cause.

I knew Omar was somewhere on campus. In the library? In the cafeteria, lost in cigarette smoke and ancient Spanish literature? Was that him on the steps of the student union? Was he there by the fountain, one hand in the leaf-littered water and the other stroking his stubbly chin? Occasionally Chicanos marched on the administration building, in a flurry of banners and gritos for daily justice. Was Omar among them? Was he in the belly of this marching crowd? Was he the head or simply the tail?

That fall semester I took my set of English classes, and occasionally heard that Omar, that Crazy Gypsy as he was described, was walking around the campus, ghost-like, poems literally falling from his pockets. I did my homework, scribbling out indecisive essays about early American literature, employing words like "seems" or "perhaps" or "possibly." But one thing was certain. I was far more interested in what was being written then, especially by other Chicanos. I bought Omar's poetry collection, *Crazy Gypsy*, and read it as a manual of politics and instructions on writing poetry. I was twenty and wanted more than anything to become a poet, even if it meant poverty, which it did, or craziness, which it also did. I read that book until the binding cracked, and I became smart enough in English to recognize the book's grammatical glitches and the sadly ridiculous poems such as "Fresno State/stand up and/fight."—a cheerleading chant for Chicanos.

I finally met Omar in spring 1973 in front of the student union. He was with a group of friends, poets I assumed, and he was wearing a leather jacket, truly the sign that he had something to say. The group was like winter birds gathered together, stepping from one foot to the other because it was icy cold—the Fresno fog having descended to chill its citizens. I had no business to be among them, seeing that I was scrubbed-faced and they were tattered looking. But I scouted over, and didn't say anything, just listening, just turning my attention from one face to another. I don't remember the conversation, only that Omar was quiet. When he spoke, his speech was staccato-like. His warm breath went up in to the air, not unlike his poems, I assumed, the breath of poetry. We stayed out in the cold for about twenty minutes and then someone smart suggested going inside the student union. Having nothing to do, I followed them, and, in doing so, I followed this life of poetry.

That was twenty-four years ago. We Chicanos did a lot of growing up, bit into more than we could chew, but chewed nevertheless. We had to swallow this country, feast on it, become it though bone and marrow, so to speak. Omar grew too. He took smaller bites, but in his own eccentric manner ate and survived. During these three decades, he published four brilliant poetry collections. Unlike his first book, *Crazy Gypsy*, which went into print unedited, these four collections as well as the one in your hand, were tinkered with and proofed by others: Jon Veinberg, Christopher Buckley, and the late Ernesto Trejo, all steadfast friends who championed his work. Now we have a new collection and the title so aptly suggests Omar's temperament—the mysterious something of an observant man. His characteristically romantic indulgence in life is here: women, weather, madness, passing clouds, dogs, family and friends. He lifts an eyebrow for the female. His romanticism is more Mexican than Spanish, and it's the Mexican of the 1940s when the world was dressed well, not in T-shirts, sloppy jeans, and baseball caps. The waltz was popular then, and with it, the possibility of becoming dizzy with life.

For those coming to Omar's poetry for the first time, you will be struck by the turns of phrases and passages prone to a surrealistic idiosyncrasy. Granted, he had read—in the original—Spanish language poets such as Vallejo, Lorca, and Neruda. His models may be these masters, honoring the pervading rule in which a poet first studies his predecessors since no one starts off alone. In the end, though, we're just left alone to put words together, not to mention our lives. These are Omar's words, in the writing style that has been consistently his since our first meeting outside the student union. While I stood with him among those poets, all of us the color of sparrows in fog, our talk then, as now, was meant to gather warmth from each other.

"A Minute with Brother Omar" from *MESSENGER TO THE STARS: A LUIS OMAR SALINAS NEW SELECTED POEMS & READER,* 2014—Juan Felipe Herrera

Rather than move the poem with allegories, desires and macro-mythic histories of a homeland lost, of an *Aztlán* usurped, as in the key Chicano poems of the 70's or the thick archeo-lyrics of a Chicana reclamation of Aztec goddesses unchained, of *Coatlique* unbound, as in the Latina borderland Meso-American cultural critiques of the eighties, Omar Salinas, through his early poems swaggers "whimsical" and "criminal." His body, oscillates between inscape and outscape, almost as a dream-walker, in angelic rebellion "where pachuco children/hurl stones/through poetry rooms..." and "bespeckled" and "nervous," "hilarious," and "angry. This is the vantage point, it seems, where Salinas prefers to question "the modern term/man." That is to say, his poems choose to embark on spirit journeys of self, a moving, shadowy, restless, collective target "of our ways," or/ our crazy souls will not rest." This is the man I met in 1972 in Santa Clara, at the "Sol" Chicano Poetry reading organized by Dr. Francisco Jimenez. A quiet man, he seemed. Philosophical and awake, beautiful and prepared with poems beyond the early political manifestoes we all loved to write and read.

One year later, I joined him at the ground-breaking 1st Chicano *Flor y Canto* Literary Conference held at USC on November 13th and 14th. To this day, people mention this milestone where many Chicano and Chicana poets, novelists and artists appeared – raulrsalinas, Tomás Rivera, Veronica Cunningham, Ricardo Sanchez, Miguel Mendez, Lin Romero, Alurista and many more. After more than five hundred *Flor y Canto* gatherings, large and small, Omar's work still works some kind of incandescent wick that pulls me. I think of the poem, *"Late Evening Conversation with my Friend's Dog, Moses, After Watching Visconte's The Innocent."* Addressed to "Moses," the question:

> "...who is there to save us/from the crickets, those small gods/
> in armor, nagging some vague truths/transient as Visconti's light..."

Yes, impermanence, yes, the reflected and manufactured "light." And the "lost fragments of our hearts."
And finally, the last lines,

> "the heart must dance like lightning,
> burn, and save it self."

This poem, in some ways, speaks to the prophet, *el perro del barrio*, the raggedy neighborhood, self propelled and akimbo canine, holder of the teachings. Unnoticed by most yet diamond-eyed; the poem reflexive in its constructions, talks back to its maker, Omar.

Omar seemed to be everywhere and nowhere – he was there, yes; at the tiny readings in Fresno, where in the early '80s he dedicated one of his books to me, "To a caustic poet . . ." or at a deli on the edge of automobile dealer row, on Blackstone Blvd. leaning on a table, outside smoking. We traded a few words, poetry this, poetry that; he looked royal, unhurried, gazing at the big picture made out of tiny shards to be located in this odd locale. Or finally, at UC Riverside where a much deserved Tomás Rivera Lifetime Achievement Award was given to him a few years before his passing, I noticed his alluring voice, his melody, as he spoke to one of the grads. It was not his "reading" voice; it was the voice inside the "reading" voice. Similar, in its deeply personal, intimate, almost loving-music to Chogyam Trungpa's, the Tibetan Lama's tone as he would casually, off-lecture, make a request to his followers. Or was he nowhere—was he gazing beyond the first panorama, the one where we speak poetry, not the one where the poem is infinite, where you live forever. Where he is now.

Luis Omar Salinas was one of our seers. He was one of our prophets. Not a radical neon-soldier with tablets and charters and austerities for a new consciousness. Rather, a walker of life, real life, with real-heart and true-mind words. All you had to do was listen and be moved. I was moved, to this very minute.

"Interview with Cindy Veach from *Northwest Review*," 1982—Cindy Veach

Many Things of Death

Death today
smells
of apples
worms chewing
their gums

a child with mud
on his hands

today it has
the mouth of an insect
crawling through
the avenues

it has the nightmares
of fish
drunk
on rain

it has the footsteps
of a gardener
wanting to murder
a chair
it has nonsense
in its eyes
a dog barking
at a cloud

a woman opening
an awkward door

it has the stubbornness
of an owl hatching
its eggs

it has the elegance
and laughter
of clowns

many things of death
in the taciturn
protest
of ants

in the unrest of flies

(from *Northwest Review*, vol. 18, no. 3)

Cindy Veach: The Spanish term *duende* implies an intensification of the senses as if in the presence of death. Your poem seems to possess *duende*, written as if brushing past death in every line. Do you feel an urgency and intensity, such as this, when you write?

Luis Omar Salinas: I believe in poetry as mystery and would like to think of *duende* as a sort of magic captivating the poet in a kind of intoxication of the senses. It's as if someone were writing the poems for me.

I remember writing the poem, "Many Things of Death," in one sitting with little or no editing. I remember the emotion of anger. I followed my intuition like always. I didn't have to think in terms of structure or strategy. It's as if I were talking directly to death, saying, "Stay away." My first experience with death was at age four with the death of my mother, who died at 27. So in a sense, I had about forty years to prepare the poem.

CV: Could you talk a little about rapid association of images and its importance to your work? Would you consider such associations a technique or do you think it is possible for association alone to be the content of a poem?

LOS: Rapid associations are a key to my kind of poetry. In my first book, *Crazy Gypsy*, I had a lot of dazzling and striking images. In my second book, *Afternoon of the Unreal*, I made a conscious effort at toning down the imagery. I am not a poet of the Surreal, yet there are elements of Surrealism in my poetry. One can get lost in Surrealism. My best poems have a directness and a kind of urgency seen, for example, in a line like, "Poverty is the smile from a turtle." I can work with this line since I have already set the way in which the poem is to go. Yet it leaves me with a lot of freedom. Here is the poem to illustrate the way I write:

What is Poverty?

Poverty is the smile from a turtle,
it is my kin and I entering a river,
it is my nephew telling jokes, feeling
pangs of puberty. Poverty you have me
by the fingers. Mother poverty you have
things well in hand. The nite and you
are twins. When we meet to talk
over supper you never fail to appear.

> Yet your handshake is reminiscent
> of a promiscuous wench. The door
> is open please leave.

CV: In *Leaping Poetry*, Robert Bly describes the leap as a jump from the conscious to the unconscious and then back to the conscious mind. To perform these leaps, he feels, the poet must be writing with great spiritual energy. What are your thoughts on such arcs of association? When you deal with the unknown, as you do here, do you feel you have leaped into the unconscious?

LOS: In the poem, "What is Poverty," there is a leap from the first line to the second. Definitely I am going from the conscious to the unconscious. We have a lot of poetry in the unconscious. In fact, I feel, most of our poems are already prepared for us. It is a matter of assimilation.

CV: The clarity and swiftness of this poem reminds me of poets like Lorca, Vallejo and Neruda. Who and what have been the major influences on your writing?

LOS: Poets like Lorca, Vallejo and Neruda have been a definite influence on my poetry. In fact, I hold them in awe and reverence. They opened so many doors for me. My first influence was the late romantic Gustavo Adolfo Becquer. I like his sense of being haunted. I still love Becquer's poetry, though it's outdated. Lorca, Vallejo and Neruda made me see the incredible and the tragic. Of course, the great commotion and turmoil of the civil war filled Lorca and Vallejo with a kind of doom. Yet they faced the madness and wrote great poetry. I do feel the major influence in my life has been my mother's death. At age four I was sort of predestined to a tragic vision of life. Also, when madness came at age twenty I was the offspring of pain, fear, rejection. It has been one long battle with madness. These two events nailed me with no reason whatsoever. Yet poetry became like a kind of saving grace; I owe much to contemporary poets like Philip Levine and Peter Everwine.

CV: In "Many Things of Death" death seems always to be just over one's shoulder; not the sober deity of the underworld, but a child, a gardener, an owl. Would you discuss your thoughts concerning death?

LOS: Death woke me early. The only way to be somewhat victorious over death is for one to reach somewhat of a state of immortality. Sometimes I feel like Miguel Unamuno. Why should we die. If God dreamt us up. He is going to have to dream us up again after we die. Maybe we will come back like birds. I wouldn't mind being a colorful bird, and my friends as well. There is so much beauty. To spend it in a grave would be a waste. Sometimes I get the feeling I've lived before and that I will live again. Then again, if could be *finis*. But I have great religious energy. We will all meet again in a better place. We might even get a chance to meet Shakespeare, Shelly, Byron, Cervantes. Who knows where the dead go? Maybe the ghosts of great writers go to the *Corrida* on Sundays. The Catholic nuns told me it will be a fine place. Maybe I'll come back as a bullfighter. But I do see greatness in this life. And of late I feel a great lust for life. Maybe we're in heaven already and don't know it. Little miracles in my life tell me a lot. And people capable of great kindness and compassion speak a true language. I feel whatever happens will be fore the best.

"Any Good Fortune: An Interview with Luis Omar Salinas," *Quarterly West,* **Fall/ Winter 2002-03—Christopher Buckley**

In 1997 Luis Omar Salinas published *Sometimes Mysteriously,* his seventh volume of poetry, which won the national book contest from Salmon Run Press in Alaska. Most recently, Pudding House Publications has published a chapbook by Salinas in their "Greatest Hits" series, 2002. Salinas began publishing poems in the late 60s, and his first book, *Crazy Gypsy,* 1970, is now a classic, reflecting the politics and self-actualization of those highly charged and changing times. In the '60s, Salinas was part of that remarkable group of poets associated with Fresno, CA and with Philip Levine, Peter Everwine, and Robert Mezey. By the time his second book, *Afternoon of The Unreal,* was published in 1980, Salinas had been refining his style for more than ten years, developing his own unique vision in poetry.

The Sadness of Days: Selected and New Poems was published by Arte Publico Press of the University of Houston in 1987 and made Salinas' work, primarily published by small presses, available to a wider audience; it is now out of print. For his poetry he has received the Stanley Kunitz Award, the Earl Lyon Award, a General Electric Foundation Literary Award, and has read at the Library of Congress. Salinas is not only one of the most senior Chicano poets in America, but he is one of our important contemporary poets. In addition to his seven full-length collections, he has published many limited edition chapbooks and he is now at work on a new volume of poetry, *Elegy for Desire.* As well as nationally, Salinas has traveled through California and the west to give readings of his work. For the last thirty years or more, he has lived in and around Fresno, California. Presently, he lives in Sanger, CA where he writes daily.

Christopher Buckley: Let's start with a little biography—where were you born and raised and what, if any, early influences in your life made their way into your writing?

Luis Omar Salinas: The little biography I have is having attended catholic pre-grammar school at St. Anthony's in Robstown, Texas with the nuns. Early influences were the ocean where I was fascinated by seagulls, pelicans, and boats and fishermen—my relatives were good fishermen, but I was one only by observation. Also the nuns, my mother, my father, and my Aunt Bessie who taught me languages, literature, Spanish, English, and math as well as some Geography and History were obvious influences and are subjects in my poetry. I was admitted to school at the age of five and I was soon fluent and started writing poetry. I had many friends, and some became lawyers and doctors who went on to further their education. In grammar school, I studied mostly reading and writing and math, but we did perform plays in which I acted. I was a bit flamboyant at an early age. I loved the romantic Mexican movies and singing stars like Pedro Infante and Jorge Negrete. Later, I landed good paying jobs that helped me through school. I've always been writing, ever since I can remember.

CB: When and how did you discover poetry, discover that you would be a poet?

LOS: I discovered poetry the moment I was born I suppose. Possibly the books of children's rhymes which I would gloss over as a child, and aunt Bessie was teaching me English. I was no Mozart by any means, but I got a taste of the language early on. Maybe then I knew I was going to be a poet—but there are no certainties in life. Also, I'll add that on the first day of school I refused to remove my hat!

236

CB: Fresno in the late 60s, the political climate, the climate for poetry, your teachers and fellow poets there and then, what was that like?

LOS: Before Fresno, Henri Coulette had a positive influence on my poetry while I was at Cal State L.A., and he suggested that I read Sylvia Plath, Anne Sexton, W.D. Snodgrass and Donald Justice—their imagery and willingness to engage the personal had an influence on the direction of my own poetry. I remember that I wrote a series of poems that appeared in the college magazine *Statement*—something about kicking snowballs with my hollow feet, walking with a cane. Since I was moving to Fresno, Coulette suggested that I work with Levine.

Philip Levine was an amazing man. When I first met him, he suggested I take the intermediate workshop. I remember one poem I wrote for him which was called "The Train." He said something about genius—the poem was so intriguing. They couldn't decipher the last stanza. Levine was supportive but I would say more inspirational, though the authors he recommended to me I gave up on. Once I had a hassle with him, but he was right. A lot of the poets would hang out at his house—we played softball, drank, danced. In another class with Levine, Greg Pape and I sat in. They were always arguing with me, saying I repeated the "virgin" too many times. I was filled with resentment at the time, so I walked into Peter Everwine's class and almost got in a brawl with all of them. Robert Mezey I took for one semester and he was a radical, wore a beard somewhat guru-like. We sat in a circle and sipped wine, read our poems and talked about Che Guevara. I wrote the poem "Guevara" in his class. I entered it in a contest at *Kayak* magazine in Santa Cruz but did not win. The poem was included in my first book, *Crazy Gypsy*.

But poets were helpful to each other and there was a great deal of camaraderie; Fresno was a haven of sorts, not only for learning but for support and socializing. I recall Larry Levis, DeWayne Rail, Bruce Boston, James Balloian, Gary Johnson. Larry was the most sophisticated and skillful of the poets. We met in his apartment once, both sitting in rockers, a poster of D.H. Lawrence to my right and I think we were listening to the Beatles—that long ago! Later on, I met Gary Soto. Contrary to popular belief, I did not help him; I had not heard of him then, I merely met him. The irony of it is that he helped me with publishing books, he and his wife Carolyn, to whom I owe a great Thank You.

Fresno in the late '60s was a fulcrum of antipathies and antagonisms. The drama department was at odds with the English Department. The students were at odds with the teachers; the teachers were at odds with their students. A small revolution against the state and the administration took place in which many of the poet teachers there took part—Philip Levine who arrived at Fresno State in 1958, Peter Everwine who came a couple years later, Charles Hanzlicek who joined the Creative Writing program in 1966, and Eugene Zumwalt, a Shakespeare teacher whose class I took as a sophomore.

In my third semester with Levine I was working on putting together a book; he asked what the title was and I answered, *Crazy Gypsy*. This was the time of the small revolution at Fresno State, and at other colleges. A building had been bombed and a main boulevard had been blocked. Chicanos occupied Baker Hall and an evacuation took place. Under threat of damages the college president resigned. The climate for poetry was nothing short of explosive. Who lit the fuse? I really don't know. The facts are the campus was up in arms against a failing administration and poetry was a life force in those days.

CB: What about early influences—which American poets did you read early on that effected your development and your voice or vision?

LOS: It had to be William Carlos Williams whose mother was Puerto Rican, and his father, I believe, was English. I read four of his books, *Patterson*, and *Pictures from Brueghel* among them. Recently I picked up a copy of his early poems at a bookstore in Ventura. Williams' first poem in "Early Poems" devastated me, the one where he is in his house alone with the curtains slightly open, in the nude, I suppose, and he is cheerful, happy envisioning a future of great artists, and he picks up his right hand and says something like, "Who is this crazy man // in this house alone // who delivers babies and writes poetry?" The thing I admire about Williams is that he stays within his own ground and is not mannered. His style is simple and his language reaches people. He has a wonderful way of dealing with the concrete. His voice cuts through bi-cultural America without ever being pretentious or pejorative.

CB: Some of your first poems quickly became anthologized, those poems that would eventually comprise *Crazy Gypsy*. Initially, what were your concerns as a poet? Were you more concerned with craft and imagery or with the immediacy of your subjects then? This is not necessarily and either/or question, but one to ask about your thinking, about writing poetry as you began to write and publish it.

LOS: The book was unedited except for slight revisions by Luis Orozco Molina. I remember he loved Vallejo's poetry. Well, I wanted to perfect my craft and my imagery as well, but the immediacy of my subjects then was a whole world of Chicanos. I learned so much from being one of them that I endured the fracas at Fresno State in the '60s. I also wanted to write the best poetry I could; I wanted to master subtlety and wit. About my craft I ventured to think that the more I worked at it the better it would get, like a horse that was used to tilling the soil—one day, they may even unharness him and use him as a race horse!? Being a Chicano affected the poems by a sort of conviviality. In other words, live together, work together, fight together. Still, I wanted to get away from the soil and also write about the aristocracy, (or the white shirt cologne epic) and give my humor a chance to breathe the air of early summer, and in the meantime write poems, and dot the "i" on beauty and put it on the page.

CB: *Crazy Gypsy* was published in 1970; tell us a little of the history of its publication and how long you were writing and collecting the poems for the book. For instance the first section of the book is called "Early poems 1964-'67." Do you recall the critical reception to the book, invitations to read in and out of state as a result?

LOS: I worked for about a year on getting the ms. together for La Raza Studies Origenes Publication at Fresno State and it was published in 1970. The reception to the book was excellent, a standing room only crowd in a large room in Baker Hall. There was a lot of excitement that young evening; students were reading poems out loud and offering toasts to me, to my book, and to our movement. It found a niche among Chicanos. As for the critical reception, I got to travel as far as McAlester College in Minnesota where I worked for a month as a student advisor and where I sold a lot of books. About 4,000 books sold in eight months in two editions with different covers. Much has changed in my style and way of looking at things, but nothing will change that evening at Baker Hall where I entered as a novice and made an impact on Chicano poetry.

CB: *Crazy Gypsy* was one of the first really known and successful books of Chicano Poetry. Do you recall any other books at that time by say Jose Montoya or any other Chicano Poets? Didn't you co-edit an anthology of Chicano poetry shortly after your book came out?

LOS: I don't recall any other books of Chicano poetry circulating at that time. I did co-edit *From The Barrio: A Chicano Anthology* (Canfield press, 1973), with Lillian Faderman. She was a faculty member in the Fresno State English Department and she had published my poem "Crazy Gypsy" in an anthology she edited with a colleague from UCLA, Barbara Bradshaw, entitled *Speaking For Ourselves: American Ethnic Writing,* (Scott Foresman & Co.) an anthology of poetry which came out in 1969.

CB: Some of the most anthologized poems from *Crazy Gypsy,* such as "Aztec Angel" are political in a personal and social sense, in a sense of self-determination for the speaker as a Chicano. There are also more overt political poems to Che Guevara and about the Vietnam War. In your next book, *Afternoon of the Unreal,* and in your subsequent work, the political focus is absent and you are wrestling with more personal struggles. Can you talk a little about the progression of your poetry from those early political days?

LOS: The early political days seemed to have evaporated, and I was romantically involved with a young woman, pretty hot and heavy. In any form or fashion, I knew I wasn't going to make it in the political arena—I had lost faith in the Leftists for one. And so I decided to subscribe to the old adage that the pen is mightier than the sword and to be cunning as well as witty. I was no longer in my 20s and personal subjects seemed then more immediate than political ones.

CB: Everyone who has read your work knows it for its style, your ability to combine the brilliant and surreal image to a lyric vision, to make the image not only engaging aesthetically and intellectually, but to make it emotionally accessible as well. Reading Simic's essay "Caballero Solo" in his Univ. of Michigan Press' Poets On Poetry series volume, *Wonderful Words, Silent Truth,* I wondered if what he had to say about Neruda's influence on his work might not also echo some of your own feelings? Simic writes about his response to one of the first Neruda poems he ever read—"I love the wild imagery, the romantic posturings, the flowery, exaggerated rhetoric . . . Here was a freedom of the imagination that was completely absent in the American poetry I was seeing in the journals of the day." Simic goes on talking about the influence of Neruda's poetry and says, "I want to go out and live life to the fullest, eat an enormous meal, drink with friends, stay up all night long." I find this exuberance in much of your work and you seem to share an imagistic turn and romantic outlook on life with Neruda. Is this an accurate observation of the first few books?

LOS: Well for one thing, I'm a light eater, and I don't drink! Yet my romantic posturings are there and I'm all for the freedom of the imagination; the better the imagination the better the poet. I read Neruda heavily, especially in my undergraduate years. Need I say he was a strong influence, especially in my middle books? I too like his exuberance and expansiveness—his extension of metaphor into imagery. His use of metaphor, rhetoric, and the surreal combinations—I especially like his *Residencia en la Tierra.* For example, "Leaning Into The Afternoon"—"Leaning into the afternoon, I fling my sad nets/to that sea that is trashed by your oceanic eyes." Eyes and ocean become synonymous with Neruda. He has a kind of grandeur about existence and an eloquence at the same time. Ironically, I like his sadness also. I don't know if he loved the ocean or was ambivalent, the ocean being greater than man? He fishes for love. The sea is thrashed and he flings his sad nets. Image after image, the ocean becomes almost a symbol of man's search, the obsession, life's struggle, etc. And I like how Neruda deals with the elements—salt, foam, sea, night, the crust of life, pieces of love. At times, he seems to be a human fish. Neruda's images are unique in their simplicity and their mystery

CB: While Neruda may have been an early influence, what about the other South American poets and the Spanish poets of the generation of '27? Do you see now any influence on your style or voice, on your approach to the world through poetry? For instance, you have long admired César Vallejo—you have a wonderful poem for him in *Walking Behind the Spanish*—what can you tell us about the influence or inspiration of his work, and others for whom you have written odes?

LOS: Vallejo was a crucial man of letters—brilliant, taciturn, and pretty much on his own, reminding me of a doomed man with no recourse but to write and die. Vallejo had a great influence on younger poets, including me. I quote from my poem, "Letter Too Late To Vallejo"—"Your Peruvian soul grieves like a cistern in a warehouse/of love, and the toxic moody eyes of one who's seen hell/and disappeared to heaven on the arithmetic of air." Talk about a poet with compassion—he was a very compassionate man. In the final analyses, after all the labels, he was Christian. Miguel Hernandez was an influence because of his courage. Here is a bit from my "Ode To Miguel Hernandez"— ". . . On a day like this/you are walking through the countryside/with Ramon Sije, writing your betrothed/and not realizing an end/to all your prismatic dreams." Ramon Sije was his friend. Hernandez was known for his excellent metaphors and his strong emotion. Way back when, I translated "Elegy to Ramon Sije" a copy of which I no longer have. It was quite a poem that ends with the birds carrying his soul through a trestle of flowers—a great image. Hernandez died in prison at the hands of Franco and the fascists. Since I talk of most of the Spanish poets of '27 I guess they all had something to do with that book—their similes, metaphors, imagery inspired me, showed me what was possible, but I never imitated them. I'd also like to mention Rafael Alberti who survived by moving to Argentina and lived to a ripe old age. He is a romantic with wonderful metaphors and images. In his autobiography, *The Lost Grove*, he talks about all the Spanish poets.

CB: *Afternoon of The Unreal* appeared ten years after *Crazy Gypsy*—why such a long stretch between books? Was it due to difficulty in finding a publisher, or were there other struggles with the work?

LOS: True there was some difficulty finding a publisher for *Afternoon of the Unreal*. I even wrote the introduction. But there were a couple chapbooks of poems between "Gypsy" and "Afternoon"—*entrance: 4 chicano poets*, which featured Gary Soto, Ernesto Trejo and Leonard Adame as well as myself in 1975, and then a little book of 10 poems, *I Go Dreaming Serenades* from Mango Publications in 1979. But overall, I wasn't at all happy in those days. There were drinking bouts and I even took an over dose of pills. Writing "Afternoon" had been an ordeal. I'm glad it's long over and I'm on more solid ground these days.

CB: In the Fall 1982 issue of *The Berkeley Poetry Review*, Prof. Donald Wolff— then teaching at the Univ. of California Santa Barbara—reviewed *Afternoon of The Unreal* and wrote that you were a "chronicler of the dark side of the soul." Did the difficult times in the '70s find their expression in a more surreal style than your early poems?

LOS: I don't know about a conscious surreal style. I was having problems and very possibly worked them out in that kind of imagery—probably unusual phrasing and juxtaposed lines. I gave a quote for the article written on me in the 1985 volume of *Chicano Literature: A Reference Guide* which spoke about my early aims, and it said basically that then I wanted to somehow come to terms with the tragic, and through the tragic gain a vision which transcends the world." I tapped freely into my unconscious, and thus, living in a fantastic world, I conjured many visions and idiosyncrasies into a poem. "Chronicler of the dark side of the soul"—certainly the surreal events of those years left an imprint, and I would later use it in my poetry, that is, my impressions, thoughts, etc. would fuse, and fantastic imagery could, for me, convey reality.

CB: Ian Gibson, in his comprehensive biography, *Federico Garcia Lorca,* pointed out that while Lorca certainly wanted to be "modern" he did not set out to write Surreal poems, but rather wrote in the manner in which his family and people of his region of Andalusia spoke—a metaphorical phrasing to be sure, but not theoretically Surreal. Would you say that the poems of *Afternoon of the Unreal* are not an exploration of the surreal method as poetic device, but rather are the accurate coefficient for the experiences of the speaker? Can you also discuss the emotional center and the vision of *Afternoon of The Unreal?*

LOS: The emotional center is the battle between the real and the unreal, what is and what should be. The experiences I bring to the poems are the essence of "Afternoon," and the language I find translates, for me, those experiences. I am not interested in theories or schools. A Cervantian chivalry full of uncertainties speaks throughout the poems. The vision is on a grander scale—to keep sane amid the mad world, to fight for there will be many afternoons on the edge with depression to cope with. As for Lorca, of course he was a great talent, a natural, a prodigy, starting to play music at an early age and writing plays. I like his unaffected, unmannered way of presenting his material. I still have a book by Lorca in my library. His surrealism is so natural. I recall his dramas and his ode to Ignacio Sanchez. He dealt with objects and nature and music. He seemed to be everywhere at one moment. His images were not poetic device; in brilliant simplicity he tells a story, for instance about the moon, or gypsies, landscapes, the sun, trees, even lizards—"Mr. and Mrs. Lizard/in little white aprons." He tells how they lost their wedding ring. At times, Lorca acquires a feminine voice in his dialogue—"I'll start to shiver and shake like the morning star." He was definitely an original, a great poet.

CB: A last question about *Afternoon of The Unreal.* Prof. Wolff in that same review mentions the "unlooked for joy" which appears in these poems, the small or momentary recoveries that balance the dark vision. Were you consciously aiming for that, or does it simply reflect the logical struggle for meaning and happiness in life and art?

LOS: I would say it simply reflects the struggle for meaning and happiness in life and art. My friend the poet Jon Veinberg, who is a long time reader and supporter of my poetry, commented once on my resiliency, and so I think that accounts for the "unlooked for joy" in those poems. There are many things in life that I like, and though I'm melancholic with a tendency to hang in with the dark, just looking at the sun on a gloomy day is enough to inspire a poem.

CB: To move on now—between 1978 and 1980 you were writing at a breakneck pace and drafted the work that would make your next three books—*Prelude To Darkness* from Mango Press 1981 and the double book, *Darkness Under the Trees/*

Walking Behind the Spanish, 1982, from Chicano Studies Library Publications, UC Berkeley. Tell us a bit about your inspiration and writing habits during that time, and about everyday influences that effected the writing.

LOS: I was living in Lindsay in 1978 then with my family as my father had opened a business there. And I was attending the clinic in Porterville and making friends quickly. I'd go with my new friends to the coffee shop in Porterville and talk. I had a woman friend, Jane, then and she would visit and my friend and his wife and Jane and I would sometimes go to the river to swim. Jane was a source of inspiration. I would write in the mornings and early evenings then, go to the patio with a cup of coffee and write. There was a period in late 1979 I think, when I moved into Fresno and lived for a while with my friend Jon Veinberg, and then a while on my own. I spent most of the days and nights writing poems, sometimes two or three a day and one revision per day. Veinberg was a big help, and you too in those days as I worked on the picnic table under Jon's apricot tree. There was some charm to all of that because I was producing and enjoying myself. Back in Porterville, I'd drive twenty miles on a pretty road lined with trees to the clinic. I had a lot of time to think, reminisce and contemplate. My subjects came from love, my immediate environment, and from the Spanish poets of course. I was on fire for a while there.

CB: Poems in *Prelude to Darkness,* and also some in *Darkness Under the Trees,* reflect a mood resulting from a difficult or disastrous love affair and are somewhat bleak, yet these books pull out of an emotional nose-dive through humor and wit that place the experiences into greater perspective and keep them then from becoming self-indulgent. You create the character "Salinas" in such poems as "Salinas Sees Romance Coming His Way." Can you speak to the effects of irony and wit and the creation of this alter ego in your poems here?

LOS: Many times the meaning is opposite of what is said, and the outcome is contrary to expectations. I see the birds singing their sadness into beautiful songs. I love the birds taking their unselfconscious baths. I used "Salinas" in the poems to get away from the subjective, to be able to see the weaknesses and strengths, the bravado and the folly. No matter what they tell you, you cannot objectify a poem since you are writing it. However, an alter ego, the other side of a personality—love/hate, anger/happiness—can describe an event or relationship from more than one side and let in some wit, or at least the larger vision of irony. It taxed my imagination but I came through it less angry than before.

CB: Fate, God, Karma—all seem relevant notions to your work. In your 1982 book *Darkness Under the Trees* the poems speculate more directly and offer a "philosophy," engaging these abstracts in relation to experience. How do these ideas fit into your poems, particularly in poems such as "Late Evening Conversation With My Friend's Dog, Moses." "Salinas Summering At The Caspian and Thinking of Hamlet," "Salinas Wakes Early And Goes To The Park To Lecture Sparrows," or "The Odds?"

LOS: Dogs are good listeners. Of course they don't talk back. So too with God. This dog happened to be a friend's collie and he listened to you with wise and loveable eyes. Sad to say he was run over by a car a few weeks after I wrote the poem. Not that the poem had an effect on him, rather it had an effect on me. I really did talk to him. Karma, Fate, all intervened here. Hamlet has been my favorite character in literature, always figuring things out. So I took a genius with me on an exotic vacation to understand the summer there and some of the larger questions in the sky. "Lecturing Sparrows"—seems like I always wake early, and if I'm not lecturing sparrows, I'm writing. I do, in other words, listen to them lecture me—there must be a little wisdom in that? Fate, God, Karma, it's a dangerous question—hoping poetry will exact goodness. You can make your own Fate, God, or Karma hinge on what you've done—the poetry exacts forgiveness. With or without God, fate is that which is given to you in life, that which you cannot alter or change. God is whatever you pray to, or give thanks to. "The Odds"—this poem summarizes a philosophy of those that have battled the odds and survived. It doesn't take a dog to do that, but it could; this is a mere personification. I'm talking about courage in life and in death in the face of those ideas.

CB: In *Walking Behind the Spanish,* a tacit metaphysical underpinning surfaces in the poems. How much of that is due to the influence of poets such as Lorca, Vallejo, Hernandez, Neruda and Jimenez and how much to just your own vision of existence?

LOS: I read and admired them all over twenty-five years ago. They spoke my language. That is Spanish. Vallejo is mysterious and simple—Hernandez is into emotion, love and death. My own vision is a melancholic one resulting from my own experience. There is a bit of the philosopher in me. Actually, it is mostly my own vision from childhood, my own makeup. I did not imitate any of those poets, and in recent years have returned to reading the English Romantics. So I am something like a Latino English Romantic.

CB: Also in this book, we see classical themes from Cervantes and Quixote. For instance a poem like "My Quixotic Bang Up" touches on that theme while at the same time suggesting some rough psychological patches during those years. How does the Quixote theme play out in the poem/poems and how, perhaps, has poetry helped to resolve those difficulties?

LOS: I am a manic depressive, I spent some time in care. Poetry gave a voice to my illusions. You certainly can't extract any humor from being locked up. I wrote out of despair with indifference to the world. Possibly, the Quixotic vision then gave me philosophy as a safety net or defense, or self-awareness. An idealist in a world of venom you might call it. So here you are, an idealist, manic depressive, with humor and wit and irony and poetry as your way out, your code of existence, a defense. No matter how negative life might become, there is always that ray of hope, whether it be a woman, friends, family or the mysterious forces that mold us into becoming a survivor. For what could be worse than losing one's mind and having so many years at rebuilding?

CB: Something a reader cannot overlook in your poetry is your great sense of compassion for the misfortune of others—great and small—and the camaraderie you feel for friends and fellow writers. Not only are there great odes to great writers but poems of praise as well letter poems to many friends and even political figures such as Zapata. Can you talk about the importance of this aspect of your subject matter?

LOS: I write about what moves me. I think that in writing there should be a kind of closeness—poets as friends, acquaintances, writing during the same time span, sending letters or poems to those that are alive to those that should be remembered. It is not only important, but a necessity. You don't have to go to church to be compassionate. It comes from within. I have a great sense of compassion for the misfortune of others, great and small which might stem from my own suffering and sense of inner turmoil. I thought of Emiliano Zapata because he was a fighter for the *campesinos* who needed his help. For instance that lady I talk about in "Last Tango In Fresno" I actually invited to my place. She talked about her love life while I made some sandwiches. I put on some music and we danced and the afternoon whirled like a gypsy. I gave her five bucks and told her she was welcome any time. We embraced and that's the last I saw of her.

CB: As your work has progressed over the years, the instinct to praise any good fortune is more and more evident. Especially this is found in the poems that end *Walking Behind the Spanish*—**the very moving ode to your stepfather "My Father Is A Simple Man" and equally compelling in a political vein, "I Am America." The speaker in these poems has a truly honest and direct voice and lays his own life/ heart on the line, takes the risks of being involved—emotionally, politically. Can these poems be read as partial ars poeticas? Can you then talk about your overall view of the poet in his poetry in your more mature work?**

LOS: Those poems came from the heart and were deeply felt. I guess you could read them as ars poeticas. I praise any good fortune because I feel mentally and emotionally alive. I gave all out in those poems. I think it's a question of spirit.

CB: *Sometimes Mysteriously* **was published in 1997 and the vision in these new poems seems tempered, not nearly so strident as early work. Do you feel this is part of becoming older, finding contentment in just surviving? I think of a poem like "Middle Age." The view in this new book seems then to admit the possibility of hope, of life turning out for the better after darker periods—certainly the title poem supports this interpretation. How has your poetic vision turned around?**

LOS: Earlier, I wrote in rage at the uncontrollable nature of people's lives. Now I feel more whole, a reactive evolution took place. *Sometimes Mysteriously* is a more tempered book, a sort of acceptance of life and reality. I try to handle it all with irony, humor, and of course with truth. In the title poem, the theme of loneliness appears again. However here it takes a different turn. It finds a solution. Before it was madness or the edge of madness that seemed to rule over most everything I wrote. Now, I am more seriously looking for answers and being quiet; I am more concerned with an affirmation of life rather than just a negative irresponsibility. I am moving in the direction of a responsible self rather than a self betrayed, so to speak, by life.

CB: A number of poets who admire your work have commented that you are a "Religious" poet in the sense that the concept of "God" is one element that plays off others in the force-field of your work. Will you speak to the "religious" as it has a part in any of your poems, e.g. "Prayer To The Child of Prague"—God as a positive or negative force in the life of the speaker in most of your work.

LOS: Yes, you could say that—God is aloof in a way that draws me to him as something mysterious. Nature, friends, God, poetry, love, madness, are all "religious." Possibly this might be so because of my childhood rearing as a Catholic? Madness came of its own volition. For me then, poetry assumes a larger role—one of being saved, discovery of self, the responsibility it brings having thus embraced humanity in all its good and all its dirt and corruption—a kind of religion without religion. I grew up a Catholic, schooled by the good nuns. A lot of my energy comes from religion, God per se. My mother is very religious and I suppose I got the Child of Prague from her.

CB: You've just published a new chapbook in Pudding House Publications' "Greatest Hits" series. Can you discuss that project a little?

LOS: Pudding House Publications is a small press in Ohio, but they seem to put out a lot of chapbooks and poetry books. They have a series for more senior poets called "Greatest Hits" and it's a chapbook of twelve poems, you know, like the old vinyl greatest hits albums with six songs on a side. The end sheets are even that plastic black color of the old records. I think they have over fifty poets in the series so far. The book consists of twelve poems that are supposed to be the best from over the years, and also there is a narrative to begin that talks about the history of each poem. On a recent afternoon I found seventy copies in my living room, of which I now have few left. It's nice to have a little book that gives an overview over the years.

CB: Given the change in attitude in the new work, I still see your brilliant and surprising imagery and turns of phrasing, your wit, and so it seems that your style really hasn't changed that much over the years. Do you feel that is an accurate appraisal, or do you see differences?

LOS: If there are any differences, they are hard to tell. I guess I'm an old young poet and a young old poet since my writing doesn't change much in phrasing, imagery and overall style.

CB: I know you've recently had a birthday, and just turned 65, but you are writing again with energy and vigor and compiling poems toward a new book. Can you tell us about the ms. in progress, *Elegy for Desire,* and what you see or hope for the future of contemporary poetry, Chicano poetry, and specifically your own poems for the next decade?

LOS: My ms. *ELEGY FOR DESIRE* is a book of loves—impetuous, sensual, it can be called an Odyssey as well as a kind of worship. It is almost episodic with different personae and scenes. As for contemporary poetry, I hope that it continues to improve. I'd like to see honest talent rewarded—it seems to me that many good poets are overlooked. Poetry helps us endure. To say we've lived is the great accomplishment.

"AFTERWORD: The Unaffected Soul" from *MESSENGER TO THE STARS: A LUIS OMAR SALINAS NEW SELECTED POEMS & READER*, 2014— Jon Veinberg

Omar loved October. He would sit on the porch of the house we briefly shared on Brown Avenue in the early 80s and watch me rake the coppering leaves, scribbling notes in a spiral encased notebook, chain-smoking *NEWPORTS*. When I asked him if he wanted to experience the full measure of autumn by grabbing a rake, he said that his doctor forbid him to rake leaves and limited his daytime activities to poetry, food, and cigarettes. It was a mesmerizing experience raking the Magnolia and Sycamore shards off the front lawn while at the same time stealing a peek at the facial contortions Omar evoked while he wrote. It was as if I was filming a kaleidoscope of emotions, each emotion blurring into the other so quickly I expected my imaginary camera to spark into flame.

Even though I ended up having a long and trusting friendship of over thirty-five years with Omar I never revealed to him that I could predict his moods and the condition of his soul through the nuanced expression of his eyes: the fiery and vicarious romantic, the excitable child who accidentally knocks over a valuable vase, the sheepish innocent looking heavenward, the mischievous glare of a pickpocket, the quizzical tilt of a philosopher that could quickly turn into a quiet sadness locked behind the cellar door, sometimes provoking in Omar " bad patches with the unreal," and my all-time imprinted favorite, the one-browed frown that always exuded a sense of mystery. To me, there was nothing distant to those eyes. I came to believe it was the place that his personal world intersected or collided with the world at large. Whatever you call it: sensitivity, soul, intuition, myth making, wit, or simply raw talent, Omar had it. My leaf raking became a ritual, and each time I did so Omar would put on his hat, which came to symbolize that he was writing or getting ready to—almost Pavlovian—in his notebook of poems which always tagged along. I went so far, once, to consider raking leaves at midnight just to see if he was culling a secret relationship with the stars. Once he wrote three poems while I scraped wet leaves from out of the gutter after a rain, after which he asked me to look at his newly written poems. To my surprise they had nothing to do with fallen leaves, trees, autumn, me, the rake, the street, neighbors, or the rain-swept gutters. If I liked a poem, he hurriedly typed it up before I changed my mind. If I felt it needed revision he would come back the next day with a completely different version, and if I rejected the poem he would send it to our stalwart friend, Chris Buckley, who so brilliantly edited and championed his work for many years and whom Omar trusted more than Buddha, for a second opinion. Omar was consumed with poetry and no one could ever, rightfully, accuse him of a failure of imagination: " I love poetry so much, I hate / To give it up / For a little salvation."

I first met Omar at a nightclub in the Tower District in Fresno in 1972 where the music was loud and the patrons, close to closing time, were running out of steam or drugs, and dancing had turned from frenetic to musingly sad. He was a solitary figure sitting in a wobbly chair at the back wall. His hat shadowed his face and he was scrawling notes into a memo pad with a ballpoint pen that skipped. And thus a three and a half decade friendship began when I asked him what he was writing. Some of his notes went something like this: " I'm waiting for someone to unbutton the straightjacket to my heart " or " her eyes were as wistful and blue as the sea's pain at midnight." What followed was a humor driven, animated discussion on everything until we, along with the rest of the raucous and/or drowsy crowd, were herded out. Omar and I picked up some cheap beer from across the street just before the 2:00 a.m. deadline and drove to Fresno State's amphitheater where we agreed to write, memorize, and perform a collaborative Mexican-American/ Estonian play long before diversity became popular. Rhyming couplets became maudlin prose pieces. Sonnets, drawn-out dramatic soliloquies. We reasoned that we were improving Shakespeare's truth. But, as we wandered through the dark trees of the amphitheater, under the August stars, playing hide 'n seek with the night hawkish imagery, Omar kept coming up with poetic zingers off the top of his head that were as heartbreaking, lucid, and raw with vision as the tarp of stars he looked toward for approval. The images didn't stop gushing when we went for breakfast at The Eagle Café just before daybreak, and when I suggested a bicycle ride to burn off the excessive energy Omar adamantly refused, stating his acumen for bicycles was shaky and something he feared, since the last time he rode he got hit by a city bus. Consequently, while the emergency personnel were attending him, Channel 47 News got to the scene and interviewed him. He proudly declared himself a "poet of the people" and that he would be all right because he was made of "sturdy merchant stock." Omar considered this a strange phenomenon of fate because he ended up selling more books as a result of this accident and his television appearance than at any one given time in his life, even negotiating with the ambulance attendants for the ones he carried in his knapsack. He didn't want to press his luck on a bicycle anymore. "I'll make it / to heaven on a motorbike yet—/ beardless DaVinci / singing Spanish folk songs."

Most of my time with Omar was spent on porches, backyards, patios, and in breakfast joints that served gravy so thick and heavy it could crumble the boulders at Pine Flat into sand. We would pool our 2-for-1 coupons and take turns in choosing which place to feast at: Chicken Pie Shop, Cuca's, Velasco's, the Train Depot, La Elegante, Chris' Meat Market, B.J.'s, Guadalajara, all the restaurants in Omar's hometown of Sanger and countless others. My favorite time was when I went to visit him in Sanger and pick up a pound of *cabeza* or *buche* at the *taqueria*, make an emergency stop at the donut shop for Omar's weekly fix of a maple bar, then to his house where his cousin, Carmen, would cook us a monumental Mexican breakfast. From the kitchen we would adjourn with our coffee to the back patio overlooking the roses and avocado tree and lay out our poems on the table, anchor them with cups, ashtrays, and saucers, and wave off the birds so " they wouldn't steal our lines." We discussed our life's events with irony and aplomb. Our stomachs were as full as our egos until we started in on each other's poems and that's when our emotional machinations shifted into the gear of humility. It was an important event for both of us, and for me, has not been yellowed by time.

In the last few years of his life, I visited him in the rest home where he resided. Instead of cheap beer, I now carried diet sodas in my car so I could pull them out to share with Omar on my impromptu visits after wheeling him to the patio. Sometimes I would take him out to eat, wheelchair and oxygen tank stuffed into the trunk, and on our return we'd take up where we always seemed to leave off, poetry. He still wore his hat and would laugh with an outrageous burst of whimsy that it didn't match his hospital gown.

Though he couldn't see as well as in the past, he was still composing poems on scraps of paper. Instead of journeying under the eucalyptus trees we were now pulling ourselves through the dark strands of memory which to me appeared impeccably unchanged, a place where I saw the same spontaneous twinkle in his eyes that only the stars could define, childlike and painful, devouring the world. And I still hear his soul-clenching and quixotic voice, " I'm a very metaphysical cat, / someday I'll be slicing apples / in heaven."

David Oliveira

David Oliveira was born in Hanford and raised in Armona, towns about thirty-five miles south of Fresno. His Portuguese roots go back to the Azores. His maternal grandparents, Mary and Earl Sousa, were from Terceira and lived in the San Joaquin valley, where they ran a dairy. His paternal grandfather, Frank Costa Oliveira, was a native of Terceira, from where he emigrated in 1914. He married Emily Oliveira, a first generation Portuguese-American from Mattapoisett, Massachusetts. He ended up moving to the São Joaquim valley, where he owned a farm in Lemoore. David Oliveira's mother was born in 1920 in Livingston, California, and his father in Mattapoisett in 1918. The family had seven children: Beverly, Robert, Eugene, Patricia, Donald, John and David.

He is the author of *A Little Travel Story* (Harbor Mountain Press, 2008), *As Everyone Goes* (TreeHouse Press, 2017), and a chapbook, *In the Presence of Snakes* (Brandenburg Press). He is also one poet in a tripartite anthology, *A Near Country: Poems of Loss* (Solo Press, 1999) with Glenna Luschei and Jackson Wheeler. In addition, he is co-editor of the anthology, *How Much Earth: the Fresno Poets* (The Roundhouse Press, 2001) with Christopher Buckley and M.L. Williams.

Oliveira's poems have appeared in *Americas Review*, *Art/Life*, *Café Solo*, *Miramar*, *Mississippi Review*, *Poetry International*, *Prairie Schooner*, *Miramar*, and *New Virginia Review*, among others. His poems have also appeared in the anthologies, *The Geography of Home*; *California Poetry from the Gold Rush to the Present*; *Bear Flag Republic: Prose Poems & Poetics from California*, and *The Gávea-Brown Book of Portuguese American Poetry*; among others.

He was a founding editor of *Solo*, a national journal of poetry from the pages of which poems were selected for Pushcart Prizes and the Best American Poetry series. He also founded the distinguished Santa Barbara Poetry Series, now more than twenty-years-old, presenting joint readings by nationally known poets and renowned local poets. Oliveira also co-founded Mille Grazie Press in Santa Barbara, publishing a catalogue of gifted Santa Barbara and regional poets.

Among poetry honors David Oliveira has received are: an Individual Artists Award in poetry from the Santa Barbara Arts Fund; serving as the city of Santa Barbara's millennial year poet laureate; having his poem, "Why I Am Not a Vegetarian," read on the Writer's Almanac by Garrison Keillor; and being a featured reader at the Yale University conference, "Portuguese-American Literature: The First 100 years."

In 2002, David Oliveira moved to Phnom Penh, Cambodia, where he is a professor of English, teaching writing and literature.

"Poet's Statement," 2020—David Oliveira

(an earlier and shorter version of this essay appeared in *How Much Earth*)

I can tell you precisely the moment I fell in love with poetry. It was when I was a student at Fresno State (now: California State University, Fresno). I was a social science major with an emphasis in history, but I liked literature and fit in English classes when I could. I had a faculty advisor to whom I would take a proposed list of classes each term, and each term he would ask exactly one question, "Are these the classes you want?" When I answered "Yes," he signed off on the list and sent me merrily on my way. So at the beginning of my senior year, I enrolled in a weekly evening class called "Poetry Writing II" because it sounded like fun and sounded like easy units. No one seem to care that I hadn't taken "Poetry Writing I," least of all me. As I said, it was my senior year and I was coasting to the finish line. The class was taught by Philip Levine, a lecturer I had not heard of before.

I liked poetry before I got to Fresno State, had read a lot of it, memorized a few poems — Shakespeare, Robert Frost, Edna St. Vincent Millay, Ogden Nash — even wrote a little myself — snappy, ingenious profundities I kept in a personal journal. I came armed with an oeuvre from which I could draw. What could be easier?

The first night of class was fun. Levine was fun, and very funny. He had a very quick, sharp wit and joked irreverently about everything, especially college administrators and politicians. He laughed a lot and so did we. He seemed to know many of the other students already. I didn't know anyone.

We got down to work the second week of class. Most of us had turned in poems during the week to Levine's office. They had been typed up, without our names, and he passed out copies to all of us at the start of class. Levine would read aloud a poem from the copy sheets in the serious, urgent, stentorian voice I would come to recognize as the one he used for his own poems. He made each poem sound like a new-found jewel of the English canon. Then Levine would start to talk about the poem: pointing out weaknesses and strengths; sometimes admired lines or images; sometimes alluding to obscure poems or poets which this poem recalled; sometimes, many times, eliciting the trademark laughter as he went. When he got to my poem, one of the best plucked from my journal, I raised myself to a proud posture. As he read the poem, the word "bravo" poised itself on the tip of my tongue. It may have been this poem on which Levine wrote, "Frankly, I don't know why poems like this exist." Or perhaps this is the one on which he wrote, "The road to poetry does not run through these words." Though I was anonymous on the sheet, I think I gave myself away when my face turned firetruck red and I slumped in my chair halfway to the floor.

Levine's genius as a teacher was that he never mocked the poet only the poem, and he always guided the poet to a path that could make the work stronger without imposing his personality over it. Levine invited us to enter into poetry as he had done, by dedicating ourselves to the love and possibility of language. He treated students as equals and expected us to treat words with a seriousness equal to his own. His excitement was contagious and pressed us to want to make better poems.

My fellow classmates included Larry Levis, Greg Pape and Bruce Boston. Unregistered poets such as Luis Omar Salinas sat in on the class from time to time. Levine occasionally referred to former students such as Lawson Inada and Dennis Saleh, already moved to legendary status. These are the ones I recall, but I'm sure there were others. All of this happened within the confines of the English Department, but it seemed the whole school was afire with poetry then. Reading venues were full. Poets were recognized in passing. Poems were talked about. Hell, this was the middle of the Vietnam War and the whole town was on fire!

To like something, even to like it a lot, is not love. I started to tell you about the moment I fell in love with poetry. It was at the Café Midi on Maroa in the Tower District at a benefit reading for a good cause. All the causes were good in those days. I had come as a show of support for Philip Levine, my new poetry teacher. Other teachers from the English Department were there to read as well. I remember Gene Bluestein, Peter Everwine, and a young Chuck Hanzlicek, for who's multi-colored, brocaded, Nehru jacket I still lust. The Café Midi was a small place and the crowd overflowed onto the sidewalk. I managed to squeeze into a space on the floor, literally at the feet of the poets. Levine had selected work from his forthcoming book, *Not This Pig*, among the pieces, a poem titled "The Midget." As he moved through the first lines, an unexpected hush settled over the coffee house as everyone strained to hear Levine's powerful voice fill to the corners. My body stiffened. My lips parted as I held on to my breath. The hair on my arms rose as an intense heat seemed to envelope the room. The air was electric.

That's at least heavy petting if not love! But in this case, it was love—love for that poem, love for that poet, love for that poetry. I can still relive that moment clearly. It was my good luck to be there then—to be at that reading and to be in Fresno when poetry seemed to be in every breath. Levine's gift to me was an idea I couldn't express at the time, and even now must borrow his words to tell you: "Poetry is an enterprise worthy of your whole life."

"An Interview with David Oliveira—a Fresno Poet," 2019—Reinaldo Francisco Silva

Even if David Oliveira (1946-) has lived in Phnom Penh, Cambodia since 2002, where he is an English professor, he will always be remembered as a Fresno poet, a man who was shaped by the agricultural region in California where he was born, in the town of Hanford, and grew up in Armona, towns about thirty-five miles south of Fresno in the San Joaquin Valley. Living on a farm, surrounded by his grandparents and parents, a witness to the hard work in the fields, from dawn to sunset, a life with few resources and amenities, the schools he attended there and, most of all, his undergraduate days at Fresno State College and the teachers and poets who taught him the wonderful art of putting words together to create poetic beauty – this ambiance would mold him into being the poet he is today. "David Oliveira offers the reader a lyrical personal history of the San Joaquin Valley, of a childhood among roaring semis on the highway, sweet wine grapes, heat and dust," writes Carol Muske-Dukes. "Especially in the poems about life in the central valley of California," writes Christopher Buckley, "Oliveira celebrates our common struggles, cherishes the smallest particulars, and makes meaning of the past. In a singular music, he preserves these details and holds them out shining as the emblems to commemorate, and to hold on to as long as possible, our collective evanescence." Reinaldo Silva has also noted the poet's grasp of his ancestral Portuguese heritage and soul in some of his poems, the feelings of *fado* (fate) and *saudade*, an untranslatable word, the Portuguese claim, but only truly felt by a navigator, proud sea-faring people from the Age of the European Discoveries, in the sixteenth-century, fishing, shipwrecks, widowhood, poverty and emigration. A bittersweet nostalgia, bone-deep longing and an endless yearning for what one can never have again – or indeed may never have had. In these poems, we are taken by the hand into the domains of a sweet melancholy, a feeling of nostalgia for moments of being from the past.

Reinaldo Silva: At which point in your life did you sense you wanted to write and when did you actually start doing so?
David Oliveira: I came to writing, serious writing, a bit later than most, I think. Throughout most of my life, I thought of myself as a visual artist—loving to draw and paint and receiving some encouragement for that. From grade school, I turned out an occasional poem—short rhyming ditties written for birthdays and such. I liked reading poetry and would often memorize favorites as a way, I suppose, of keeping the words and feelings closer. In college, I began writing in journals—scraps of philosophy or psychology or self-indulgences to celebrate my vast intellect—these insights sometimes taking the form of a poem.

RS: So was the decision to become a poet prompted by your schooling?
DO: No, that decision came much later, long after college. In college, on a whim, I signed up for a class called "Poetry Writing II," taught by Philip Levine, not famous then. I thought that I could use those little poems already in my notebook to sail to an easy grade. Levine was a dedicated, and uncompromising teacher who didn't coddle his student's grandiose fantasies regarding their poems. I was persuaded by his firm and rather harsh critique of the first poem I turned into his class that I had no idea of how to construct a real poem, a serious poem. Levine's teaching gifts were such that his honesty didn't drive me (or other classmates) away from poetry, but made me (and them) resolve to learn as much as possible and work toward real poems. I was so stimulated I signed up to take "Poetry Writing I" with Levine the next term. I would have continued signing up for his classes if more had been offered. Those classes were the point where I realized I loved poetry and wanted to make it an important part of my life. I learned how to evaluate poems and how to appreciate the complexities of the art. But, at the same time, came to believe I didn't have what it took to write the kind of poems I admired. I had the passion, if not the gift. After college, I read poems avidly, went to poetry readings as I could, but only occasionally made a stab at writing something.

RS: Can you refer to a specific poem from your early career as a poet, which encapsulates some of these writing dilemmas, choices in your life as a writer, in particular, where your own unique voice emerged?
DO: The last poem I wrote for college was about my father and started with a riff on Whitman's "I Hear America Singing." I gave a copy to my dad and wrote the poem into a notebook, which I no longer have. It was the only poem from my college days that I felt made it as a true poem.

After college, I didn't write much. I concentrated on being an audience for poetry and working on paintings. However, there was a poem for which I had a great opening line and a great closing line but was unable to put anything acceptable in between. I worked on this poem off and on for 18 years. I kept a typed copy of those lines in a desk drawer, and from time to time I would take it out and try to write more lines only to fail. What I thought the poem was about also evolved over time, my subject becoming a bit clearer with each effort. Perusing poetry in a bookstore one day, I saw a new book by Philip Levine, *A Walk with Tom Jefferson*. His books were not always readily available then, and I would buy one as soon as I saw it. Being in this book's presence compelled me to find my unfinished lines again. This time, a few more words came. For the next three weeks or so,

I carried that poem in my back pocket wherever I went, taking it out often and trying to get the rest of the lines to come out. When I finished it, I felt I had accomplished a real poem. The story goes on a bit longer, but that poem, "Like Old Friends," released a flood of writing and opened the door through which I entered into a poetry life. I'm still fond of the poem, though it's never found its way into any of my books.

RS: Why did it take you so many decades to write the poem, "Credo," in *As Everyone Goes,* where you admit your love for writing even if you never acknowledged it before?
DO: I've written other poems about poetry. I think they are easy to write, maybe too easy. It's a topic to pull out when other ideas are being stubborn. "Credo" also addresses that poets rarely write about their other jobs, the jobs at which they make a living. It's a curiosity in my own work too, which I don't know how to explain. Most of the poets I know are or have been teachers—and many of them, especially those on the university level, teach poetry. Yet there are only a handful of poems written about teaching or students. I worked with computers for 22 years and have yet to write a poem about that. "Credo," while definitely a paean to poetry, also asks about this work/poetry disconnect.

RS: How has this background helped you to develop your own voice as a poet (the sounds, imagery, local color, etc.) and how and when did you move on to adding new elements to – if I may call it as such – your voice-in-progress? How did it evolve to take on new interests, new themes?
DO: I don't have a writing strategy. I write on whatever topic raises its head, and kiss the toes of the muse when it does. I write to explain things to myself. When you're living life, you don't always take time to figure out the importance of what's going on at the moment. When you live a long time, you gather quite a collection of memories, scraps of experiences, images that shout for more attention. Many of my poems come from trying to explain to myself why these things have stuck to my consciousness.

As for voice, I write as well as I can. If I could write better, I would. Voice comes through personality and the limitations of talent. It also develops through what a person absorbs by reading, studying, and liking what others write.

RS: Would you agree that your first two volumes of poetry, *In the Presence of Snakes and A Little Travel Story* truly reflect your California phase? Emily Dickinson in her poem, "The Robin's my Criterion for Tune – " wanted to "see – New Englandly" would you say that in some of these poems you wanted to "see – San Joaquinly"? Now that you've been living in Cambodia for about two decades, do you still "see – San Joaquinly" or is it more difficult to do so?
DO: I want my poems to "see – David Oliveiraly." I've never been able to conceive of a whole book on a single theme. I would like to try that sometime, but my poems don't come to me that way. I write them as they occur to me and I feel grateful when one shows up. All of my books have sections which reflect the variety of topics. I had already moved to Cambodia when I wrote some of the poems in *A Little Travel Story*, so I don't really think that book reflects a California phase.

Like every life, mine has moved through various stages, but it's still only one imperfect life. Whatever I planned for it was really a wish list. If a wish came true, it was more the result of chance than forethought. I have spent my life trying to figure out what my life is. My poems are part of that investigation. Spoiler alert: I still don't have any answers.

RS: Based on your poetic output in the volumes you've published so far, which would you consider the central themes which permeate your collections of poetry? Which one particular theme has stayed with you longer, that is, the one that every now and then you come back to?

DO: I think my poems touch on all the classic themes of poetry. As I mentioned, I am trying to explain my life to myself, and I have a broad spectrum of interests, both personal and societal. It's not easy for me to see separate themes in my poems clearly as I think of each poem as a facet of a whole me. I think more in terms of subjects, and some subjects recur and some reflect current experiences. Growing up in the Central Valley of California often comes to the fore, as does my family and my Portuguese ancestry. I have been an activist for social and political causes, especial gay issues, and these come into some poems. Affection for friends is another recurring topic. I have not written much about personal traumas or my relationship with my husband, Vic. I find it extremely difficult to write directly about deep personal emotions, but these do enter obliquely and continually. They are the canvas on which the paint sits. As I mentioned previously, the subjects come up as they will, but having said that, I recognize that a thread which seems to run through much of my writing is my inability to know anything for certain, a perplexing state that is only exacerbated by time.

RS: How would you compare your first books of poems, *In the Presence of Snakes* and *A Little Travel Story* to *As Everyone Goes*? Would you say that your earlier work was somehow an attempt at recording and celebrating the past whereas your more recent work seems to be more brooding?

DO: Brooding? I'll have to think on that. I think of my poems as investigations. My life is evolving through experience, as everyone's life does, and so the way I write must surely reflect the constant state of that evolution.

RS: How do you perceive yourself in relation to the cultural, social and political manifestations of American society on Otherness, conservative values, intolerance in such poems as "Piss Jesse," "President Clinton Lifts Ban on Gays in the Military," and even "Jerry Falwell Contemplates Oral Sex," among others? Has this presented any problems for you?

DO: I grew up in the Central Valley of California as a person aware of their second generation Portuguese identity in what was an ocean of "Americans," the persons who descended from a longer established Anglo-Saxon identity. We were one of many such subgroups. We thought of ourselves as American too, but there was an awareness that we were American in a way different from these other "Americans." We could feel this as children, but couldn't articulate it until becoming adults, if then.

My parents were conservative but would never have conceived of, let alone, given themselves such an identity. They thought of themselves only as patriotic Americans that happened to be gifted with an equally proud Portuguese heritage. They raised their children to be patriotic Americans with a sense that we were members of a culture believing in justice and equality in a democratic society. They also raised us to be proud Catholics. The church's teachings on charity and social justice also reinforced those American ideals.

Poets are a fairly tolerant group, or rather, being artists, they are familiar with the variety of human differences. The only time I felt censored was from an organization of philanthropists in Santa Barbara who wanted poets to read at their annual donor dinner. It was a time after Maya Angelo had read at President Clinton's first inauguration and for a while it became *de rigueur* to invite poets to events. The representative of this group stressed that they were looking for something progressive and with a political bent. I excitedly told the gentleman I had just the poem, "Piss Jesse," a poem protesting government interference in the arts. He asked to see it. I sent it and a couple more. He called to tell me I couldn't read that particular poem. I'm sorry to say that I did read at their event, but didn't read that poem. Well, the invitation came with a modest honorarium and a free wine supper which I didn't want to jeopardize. My integrity comes cheap.

RS: You have written a few elegiac poems, on the losses of friends, family members, relatives. Would you say some of your lyrical poems derive from this melancholic trait that presumably also characterizes you as the person you are, a trait which I also pointed out to you as being an echo of your Portuguese cultural heritage – that of a people shaped by fate and the sea, the Discoveries, immigration, and the fisheries? Or was it simply to honor important people in your life – or maybe both? What do you say about your poems of loss in *A Near Country?* How do they fit into this discussion about melancholy, sadness, and fate, which are quintessentially Portuguese traits? Or would you say simply universal feelings?

DO: Without question, loss has been a subject for poets since whoever wrote the first one. Poetry and its sister, song, are ways humans communicate emotions. Before you pointed out that melancholia and an embrace of fate are Portuguese cultural traits, I didn't make the connection that those tendencies in myself might be part of a cultural inheritance. I just assumed these were human characteristics which we all share to some degree. Now I can see that the philosophy my parent's imparted to me was part of this heritage. The elegiac poems, of course, honor the subject, but I also see them as being similar to funerals. They are public displays of emotion to express the deep sadness I feel at the loss. It seems important for my well-being to make these expressions public rather than to just hold them within.

RS: In your earlier writings, how much of a Catholic upbringing actually crops up in your poetry? "Stations of the Cross" is one that I admire immensely. Would you say it best captures how Catholicism and Christian values have shaped you as a person? How, then?

DO: In my mind, being Catholic and being Portuguese and being American are all one inseparable thing, the fabric of my person. I haven't been officially Catholic since I was 19, but I am aware the emotions and values of that identity that were instilled in me as a child still live in me. "Stations of the Cross," I think, successfully expresses the complicated path I followed to understand this relationship.

RS: Why did you write a poem titled, "Festa" for your collection, *As Everyone Goes?* For which purpose(s)? To retrieve your past in California?

DO: As you know, "festa" means festival or celebration. In Portugal it is always preceded by an adjective denoting which or what kind of festival is being talked about. But in California, the word is used singly to mean the Holy Ghost celebrations which are an annual feature of communities that have a significant Portuguese population. In these communities the word is usually translated into English as "Portuguese celebration." The religious aspects of the festival are minimalized, and the event becomes a grand, secular celebration of Portuguese pride. For us, festa means Portuguese.

Festas were a big part of growing up. They were our tangible connection to our ancestral culture and past. My poem, "Festa," is based on a memory of when I was in college and brought my non-Portuguese roommate to experience a festa in Hanford. The poem is a bit complicated. I wrote it to honor my family. My family was an integral part of these celebrations. I wrote it to especially honor my brother, Robert, who served in the military in Vietnam. And I wrote it to honor the Portuguese community in which I grew up. The Vietnam War was raging at that time and I was reminded that it was the Portuguese who first brought to Europe the spices from Southeast Asia that are used in the food served at festas.

RS: Feel free to respond to some additional issue, idea or aspect related to you as a Fresno poet, which the interviewer omitted, against his will, or forgot to ask you.
DO: First of all, I would like to express my deep gratitude and thanks for your very thoughtful and thought-provoking questions.

Poetry is an art. Art is human beings explaining to each other what it means to be a human being. As such, it is a complicated and emotional expression that the artists themselves do not fully understand, most of it coming from intuition rather than conscious intention. Asking an artist to explain the intricacies of their art is like asking a fish to explain the intricacies of their relationship to water. These questions have given me a lot to think about, which is a great gift. Thank you, again.

RS: As a Fresno poet, how would you like to be remembered? Which keywords or sentences would best describe your uniqueness as a member of this generation or group and that you would like to leave for posterity?
DO: Well, the opportunity to move into the realm of remembrance is surely fast approaching. After years of observation, I candidly offer that any poet who thinks they will be remembered by posterity is exhibiting a fanciful hubris that is not supported by evidence. But to honor the sincerity and spirit of the question, I will say that the last poem in the "Stations of the Cross" sequence, "XIV. David Puts Things in Their Place," is the most precise expression of my understanding of the world I've been able to make. I tried and failed to write that poem many times until one morning it suddenly arrived as a grace, the lines seeming to write themselves as I looked on. Writing can be magical. Fulfillment comes during the act of writing—the act of putting words on paper. When I am in the magic zone, the words come surprisingly as though whispered in my ear. The books, the readings, the applause, the kind words are wonderful, don't get me wrong, but none of that compares with the ecstasy when writing words that say exactly what I wanted said.

Roberta Spear—1948-2003

Roberta Spear's books are *Silks* (1980), Holt, Rinehart & Winston, published as part of the National Poetry Series; *Taking to Water* (1984), Holt, Rinehart & Winston, winner of the PEN, Los Angeles Center Poetry Award; and *The Pilgrim Among Us* (1991), Wesleyan Univ. Press. She was awarded the James D. Phelan Award and was the recipient of writing grants from the NEA, NEH, the John Simon Guggenheim Foundation, the PEN, Los Angeles Center Poetry Award, and the Ingram Merrill Foundation. Her poems appeared in *POETRY*, for which she won the magazine's Frederick Bock Prize, and in *The New Yorker, The Atlantic Monthly, Crazyhorse, The Iowa Review, American Poetry Review,* and in several anthologies including *How Much Earth: The Fresno Poets. A Sweetness Rising: New & Selected Poems*—a posthumous collection—was published in 2007 with an introduction by Philip Levine.

from *Down at the Santa Fe Depot,* 1970—Roberta Spear

Born Sept. 26, 1948 in Hanford, California. The thing I remember most vividly about childhood were my dreams (about witches). Went to school in Hanford, San Francisco, Santa Barbara, & Visalia. Spent third year at Irvine (Univ. of Calif.) where I befriended poet Galway Kinnell, an association that has probably had the most impact on my writing to date. Spent summer of '69 in Sheffield, Vermont (8 miles from nowhere) with him, his wife, and two children on their farm. While there I came to realize that things like the sprouting of the garden's first head of lettuce, the chickens laying their first eggs and the raccoon eating one of the chickens, become the most important events in daily life, and when the trees stop calling you by name, you know that you are in the right place.

Returned to California and entered Fresno State College, where I am currently studying under, and receiving immeasurable help from, poet Phil Levine. I know I'll eventually end up in the mountains again though.

I don't always fully understand my poems myself immediately after they've been written. I usually write while feeling desperate or exhilarated, and often find myself transferring those emotions into my work, especially when overwhelmed by the pure physicalness of myself, other people, or my surroundings, and when my senses and ability to express myself verbally become inadequate. Because I am a visual poet and tend to write intuitively my poems often appear to follow a dream-like sequence and defy rationalization:—momentary flashes and spurts of energy with vague transitions. I resent the common association between the woman poet and neurosis, defeminization, and kitchen sinks Because poetry should be the product of one's spirit, soul, unconscious, etc. it should not be categorized according to one's physical state, but rather that physical state should be used as a tool or an asset.

from *The Geography of Home: California's Poetry of Place,* 1999—Roberta Spear

My grandparents moved to the San Joaquin Valley not long after the turn of the century. From that time until the 1970s, the Valley consisted of small farm towns separated fro each other by vast stretches of cultivated land. When I left home in the 1960s to go away to college, I didn't expect to return. I hated the blistering heat in the summer, the fog in the winter, the lack of culture, and the absence of geography. I wanted to live in beautiful places. And, for a brief while, I did—Santa Barbara and Laguna Beach, San Francisco, New England, and, later, North Carolina. However, I eventually returned to Fresno to study poetry. I also returned to the orchards and vineyards, to the home of field workers, Portuguese dairy farmers, and my old Armenian neighbors, to the Fresno poets and the poets of Spain, to Levine and Everwine and a group of talented young writers all celebrating the place I had once mocked. Levine championed everything from the valley dust to the factory worker; Miguel Hernandez wrote of love from his infested Spanish prison cell; and William Saroyan had crafted a charming story of a bicycle ride from Fresno to Hanford, my home town. I discovered that I had a long way to go.

Over the last thirty years, I have come to learn that two essential components of this celebratory tradition in poetry are passion and careful observation. While I was never lacking in the first, the second was a task made all the more difficult by living in a place that often seemed desolate and impoverished. Difficult, but not impossible. Even now, if you drive east a few miles into the countryside or the nearby foothills, the fields of yellow grass with their outcroppings of rock and skeletal oaks are still reminiscent in their rugged beauty of parts of southern Europe. The three poems here address a landscape and people that I have taken for granted most of my life and, at times, consciously turned away from. I am very moved that my friends in this book have had the tenacity to stick it out here for more than three decades and to make, as Hernandez once did, such exquisite "lullabies for the onion."

from *How Much Earth,* 2001—Roberta Spear

I wasn't thrilled about the idea of returning to the San Joaquin valley in 1969 when I moved to Fresno to continue my studies. I had grown up in a small town nearby, and had spent the previous three years attempting to put some distance between myself and the Valley. But I had been told that the writing program in Fresno, under the direction of Philip Levine and Peter Everwine, was perhaps the best in the country—and it was true. Like the other students, I learned that writing poetry required more self-discipline and humility than most twenty-year-olds possess. But Phil and Peter were very talented, very funny, and very patient. I also learned that the return for the labor put into these workshops was that rare and wonderful occurrence—a good poem. And the camaraderie of those early classes evolved into friendships which have spanned a lifetime. Just as the poems have been shared over the years, so have the events and forces of our lives. And, as the following poems show, this exchange has been at the heart of much of my work.

Introduction: *In the Next World: The Poetry of Roberta Spear*—Philip Levine

When Roberta Spear died of leukemia in the spring of 2003, she left behind not only a grieving family, but also an almost completed fourth book of poems. Thirty years earlier, when her husband was assigned to a hospital in Fresno to do his residency, she'd returned from Winston-Salem, North Carolina, where he had studied medicine and she had taught creative writing. Thus she was back in the Central Valley where she'd grown up in the town of Hanford, some thirty miles south of Fresno. Now she was not only a poet but also the mother of a son and soon a daughter. For as long as she lived she gave herself totally to the roles of wife, mother, poet, and friend to the cluster of poets settled in and around Fresno. California's Central Valley is one of the keys to her poetry, for above all else Roberta was a poet of "person, place, and thing." The people of central California are the people of more than half her poems; the landscape and the climate of scorching summers and fog-bound winters appear and disappear in these poems. The Valley, as it's known here, is not the California of the movies, unless the movie you have in mind is *The Grapes of Wrath,* for it is exactly the place to which the Joads arrive on their trek from Oklahoma with all their hopes for a better life soon to go unfulfilled. In Hanford she would have grown up with the children of the Joads or people like them who shared that journey, as well as the children of farmers and ranchers and the Chicanos and African Americans who worked in their fields, orchards, and vineyards. And she would have watched with them as the years brought smog, chronic unemployment, and gang warfare. Once it may have been the rural idyll described by John Muir when he first crossed the Pacheco Pass and beheld it from the north. Now it is Twenty-First-Century America, the small towns bursting with the new immigrants from Southeast Asia and the American rust belt. How could a poet find so much to sing about in a place like this, for sing is what she did? From her poem "Two Trees":

> And from the kitchen table,
> I can see the shadows shift
> as the pecan breathes in the sunlight.
> I wonder if this giant,
> the grandfather of our back field,
> still has what it takes
> under these tendons of bark,
> the layers riddled by seasons of birds,
> or if the young dogwood tipped with green
> will surprise us next March.

There are two crucial words in that passage: wonder and surprise. By some amazing alchemy Spear seemed able to waken each day—or at least each day that's recorded in her poetry—with a sense of wonder in the presence of the physical world as though each dawn were a surprise, an event like none other in the history of experience. There is a kind of primal innocence in her poetry; she sees a world untainted by the brutal forces that have turned the Valley into an ongoing catastrophe. It's not that she was unaware or ignorant of what was around her; it's *simply* that the present with all its riches, with all the majesty of its being tangible, was amazing to her, a gift, each moment a moment of miraculous potential, and she saw her function as a poet to observe it, to detail it, to name it, and when all her forces as an artist were at her command, to bless it. And those forces were hers more often than nor. The answer to the question that began this paragraph—how could she sing?—is mysterious and has much to do with her sense of fulfillment as a woman as well as the glory of her individual being. She was always a creature of hope. In all the years I knew her, I never knew her to despair.

And I knew her for thirty-four years, since she was a very young woman enrolled in an advanced class in poetry writing at Fresno State, a class that someone had let swell to forty students. That first evening the class met in a cavernous, unadorned chemistry lab that appalled me, I behaved very badly on purpose, for I was determined to get it down to something manageable and to move the smaller class to a more intimate setting, and to do so I set about terrifying the students. Each week, I told them, you'll be required to hand in a new poem in whatever form I require: for example thirty lines of anapestic tetrameter without an adjective. Perhaps twenty heroic couplets in the style of Charles Churchill, a blank verse monologue in the voice of Henry Ford on the theme of the Jews. When I paused to take a breath, a fresh young blonde woman asked if I recognized free verse. I said that I did, and that I'd seen a lot of it of late. She informed me that in Galway Kinnell's class at UC Irvine, the students decided what forms they wrote in. I mused for a moment and replied that it was an interesting notion. Kinnell was certainly a marvelous poet, who—I noted—had written brilliantly in traditional forms early in his writing life. It worked: the next week only sixteen students showed up, the others had dropped. And the blonde? She was of course Roberta Spear. Kinnell had advised her to come to Fresno if she were serious about becoming a poet, and she was not about to be discouraged by my folderol. As the weeks passed I began to discover her poems and also to discover the iron-willed person who had written them.

A few years later she enrolled in a translation class I taught with the Spanish critic and scholar Jose Elgorriaga, and I believe it was there that she discovered the poetry of Rafael Alberti, Gloria Fuertes, and Pablo Neruda. She loved the sharp tongue and quick wit of Fuertes' poems, that talking back to men of prestige and power and the whole rigged system that was Franco's Spain in which an ordinary working woman might drown without anyone noticing. But for her Neruda was supreme—a poet the likes of whom she had never before encountered—for it was in his work, her friend Sandra Hoben writes, she found "the difference between most poetry and what the greats were up to." His *Odas Elementales* were especially significant, for it was in them that the great Chilean honors the things of everyday—a suit, a pinch of salt, an onion, a pair of socks, the color green—so as to create an event of cosmic significance, and he does it with wit, style, at times an almost preposterous vocabulary, and always with a smile. After Neruda her aims in poetry were never the same; she now had a standard, a far clearer notion of "the poem" she was after.

At time when so many young women poets were discovering and bathing in the river that was Plath, Spear was almost totally uninterested: she wrote that she resented "the common association between the woman poet, neurosis, and kitchen sinks." In fact she was far more interested in the poetry of Ted Hughes with its extraordinary evocations of beasts and men and the pure energy that drives his lyrics forward toward an apocalyptic moment. Not that she ever tried to imitate his raucous, grinding music nor ever accepted his vision of the eternal war among *all* creatures; the music of her poetry is far quieter and more adapted to her own vision in which the individual often merges with the *other*. In terms of the music of her poetry, D. H. Lawrence, especially in his superb Rhine Valley poems, was truly influential. Her poetry arrived, she wrote, "especially when [she was] overwhelmed by the pure physicalness of myself, other people, or my surroundings." In a singular way she envisioned herself as another aspect of her environment, the one gifted with the language to speak for all the individual creations that made up her world. That Nerudaesque urge to blend with all things and to give all things their voice you can hear swelling in many of her finest poems.

Yet a few things can be explained
by all this racket. Life must be named,
called back often before it wanders too far.
And so, a mother lifts her skin
and slowly wades into the water
after a child who would rather follow
the fish to their smoky depths.

Also, there are always those
who mean nothing when they speak,
who, like birds, love the sound of air so much
they wave their arms, their tongues
and give it away.
      (from "Cinque Terre: The Land of Five Noises")

One reviewer of her first book (Robert Peters in *The American Book Review*) wrote of her "quiet, hard-seeing way of moving at, into, and through natural objects, assimilating them into her vision." Another (Joseph Parisi in *The Chicago Tribune*) praised her gift for metaphor and imagery that suggest "the mysterious depths beneath her shining surfaces." In a prose statement in the anthology *What Will Suffice* she illuminates the source of her poem "Diving for Atlantis":

At the time I wrote "Diving for Atlantis," I was pregnant with my first child and living in the South (North Carolina). The world around me seemed unbelievably vibrant and intriguing. The children who swam around me at the local "Y" demonstrated what I had already learned as a poet—that the imagination has an infinite capacity for transforming one's identity and surroundings. . . . Just as the children dive into the water to look for the mythical city of Atlanta, the poet must penetrate the layers of the imagination until the vision is realized.

Writing of her final book, *The Pilgrim Among Us,* the poet Edward Hirsch described her as a poet who "transfigures the ordinary and pinpoints the mysteries of daily life." And Margaret Gibson, commenting on the same book, wrote that in Spear's poetry "it's the ordinary which is discovered to be the site of the extraordinary." Anyone who reads her will be struck by her ability to focus her attention on that which often seems beneath our attention, and find there the source of her own visionary poems. One of her favorite poems was "Grappa in September" by the great Italian poet Cesare Pavese, which she read both in the Italian and in the translation of William Arrowsmith. It is not a typical Pavese poem; Pavese in the poems of *Hard Labor* is most often a narrative poet, but in this poem nothing happens. The poem is merely a description of a northern Italian village at the end of summer. We discover the house at the field's edge that sells tobacco "which is blackish in color/ and tastes of sugar. . . ./ They also have grappa there, the color of water." The final stanza begins:

This is the time when every man should stand
still in the street and see how everything ripens.

If Spear saw this poem as a metaphor for her own work I do not know, but I do know that she read it over and over, and that she found in it an almost mystical sense of what the poetry she loved was capable of. I know also that she was much taken with a remark of Pavese's from his book on American literature: "The new symbolism of Whitman meant, not the allegorical structures of Dante but a . . . sort of double vision through which, from the single object of the senses vividly absorbed and possessed, there radiates a sort of halo of unexpected spirituality." It was of course that aspect of American poetry, which she found first in Whitman, Williams, and especially Stevens, and later in the contemporaries she most valued, that she worked to incorporate in her own work.

Rereading her poetry I cannot hear the least suggestion of a familiarity with my poetry or the poetry of her first poetry writing teacher, Galway Kinnell, but one teacher had a profound effect on the voice she created for herself or the voice that found her in her mature poems, and that was the voice of Peter Everwine. She had already studied Antonio Machado and Juan Ramon Jimenez and admired the crystalline quality and the precision that is the hallmark of their work. She caught echoes of something similar in those delicate love poems of Lawrence, but the first time she encountered it in an American voice was in Everwine's work. Here is that voice in a poem from his second book, *Keeping the Night*, "Perossa Canavese," written shortly after his first trip to the village of his ancestors:

> What I came for
> —all those miles—
> was to see the face of the village
> my people spoke of
> in the hour before sleep,
> and which I was given for my own like an empty locket,
> like a mirror in a locked room.

In a poem from her first book called "The Traveler," dedicated to Everwine, she answers him in that new voice that will become the voice of much of her poetry.

> At the edge of the village,
> battered stalks and then a field
> of poppies. You drop your pack
> to the ground, picking
> the few that will last
> until you find others.
>
> Among the stalks,
> an old farmer
> whose plow has died.
> Wearing these flowers
> you remind him of his son
> who let the fields
> go to seed. Not everyone
> will be quick to claim you . . .

This was written twenty-five years ago after her second trip to Italy, and it constitutes the first poem in an extended conversation with her former teacher.

Her first trip to Italy in 1967, and especially the second in '80, were of momentous importance in her development as a person and a poet. She literally fell in love with the people and the landscape, and they appear in many of the poems that were to follow. (She would return to Italy two more times, the last time in 2000 with her son and daughter.) She also fell in love with the language to which she devoted years of study so that she might read the poets whose language it was, from Dante to Ungaretti, Pavese and Sinisgalli. And occasionally translate them. Much as she admired Everwine's voice and his strategies, there was in Spear a natural volubility, a sense of luxury and abundance that was absent in Everwine's work. His line suited her perfectly and she retained it for the rest of her career, but his rigorous sense of economy; the total absence of the baroque in his writing, that urge that her earlier love and study of Neruda's odes had nurtured couldn't find room to expand and play unless she let go. This created a tension that the poems themselves exploited, for Roberta's poems had the habit of seeking a larger, more expansive format, and she had the good sense to let them. She also had a strong sense of narrative; she wanted to tell in verse the family stories she inherited, to become as it were the family mythmaker. Indeed she found stories everywhere, but like her beloved Pavese she found them mostly in the ordinary people who inhabited the various neighborhoods that had been or were to become home. And since home for the last three decades of her life was Fresno, they frequently became the stories of American immigrants, especially those from Asia and Mexico. You could say at times she saw stories where there were none or where she simply invented them, exotic stories of gypsies and pranksters, travelers and seekers, those with whom she identified. This is most obvious in what is for me her finest book, *Taking to Water*, which is truly a volume of magic, one that transforms the ordinary things of daily life into tales to conjure with, as in the conclusion of "Map for the Unborn":

> Follow the line that runs
> from the thumb to the heart
> until lines cover your face
> and your legs give in.
> Circle the mound of your smallest finger twice around the world
> until your fortune comes and goes
> and a villager opens his window
> to call you inside.
> He will take your hand
> and ask to hear your stories,
> for you have crossed the seas
> of your mother, and who can remember
> having traveled so far?

In the last years of her life she found new works to admire, poets she hadn't known, and with her usual generosity of spirit she touted them (I'm thinking especially of the late books of Larry Levis and Ruth Stone and *New Addresses* by Kenneth Koch and *Time and Money* by William Matthews) more than she pushed her own work. The discovery of a true poet that mattered was an extraordinary event for her; Zbigniew Herbert, Milosz, Syzmborska, Sabines, Nancy Willard, she came back to again and again. On several occasions I loaded her down with the books I'd received in the mail, and her joy at what treasures they might hold was lovely to behold. In truth she never pushed her own work. She decided early on she disliked giving poetry readings, and although she knew this had become one of the chief means by which a poet built a reputation and a following, she found the expenditure of nervous energy not worth the product. Furthermore they caused a disturbance in the normal flow of her life, they took her away from the primary task, which was the making of the poems. If this meant she would publish less and sell fewer copies of those books she published, so be it. This was a decision she made before she was thirty, and she never looked back.

She also made her peace with the Valley. Most of the poets who studied with her at Fresno State—Larry Levis, David St. John, Greg Pape, Gary Soto—got out as soon as they could. Italy may have been where her heart was, but Fresno was where her husband practiced medicine, her children went to school, and she wrote her best poems. For the anthology *The Geography of Home* she wrote a prose introduction to her poems that addressed exactly that.

> Over the last thirty years, I have come to learn that two essential components of this celebratory tradition in poetry are passion and careful observation. While I was never lacking in the first, the second was a task made all the more difficult by living in a place that often seemed desolate and impoverished. Difficult, but not impossible. Even now, if you drive east a few miles into the countryside or the nearby foothills, the fields of yellow grass with their outcroppings of rock and skeletal oaks are still reminiscent in their rugged beauty of parts of southern Europe.

If she couldn't live in the Italy she loved she was determined to find a way of bringing the country of her devotion to the Valley, and she did exactly that with her poetry.

In a singular poem entitled "Geraniums" from her book *The Pilgrim Among Us* she wrote,

> In the next world, I will be the one
> forever pushing open
> the warped green shutters to let
> the sunlight enter the room . . .

I wouldn't be surprised if that were true, but what I know for certain is that in this world Roberta was constantly pushing aside the shutters to let light in. The young woman I encountered over thirty years ago would never let well enough pass for wisdom. She wanted to know why: why this word and not that? Why this poem or any poem at all? My initial impulse was to urge Valium on her, but as that first semester wore on I realized I had someone rare, a truth seeker who let nothing stop her. Over the years of our friendship whenever I wanted to revive my belief in the value of writing poetry or living a moral life, I would call on Roberta, either in her poetry or in her person, and she was always there for me as she was for all her brothers and sisters in the art of poetry or the art of life. She wrote once of another being: "There are some creatures, who take/ all of history with them/ when they kneel one last time in the hard, bitten grass, / only to come back later / with their sense of life, / their nerve as crisp / as a new apple." Modest as she always was, I'm sure she had no idea she had forged the perfect emblem of her undying spirit.

Her final year was particularly difficult, what with extended bouts of chemo and a month-long stay for bone marrow transplant at the Stanford Medical Center. There had been a brief period of remission—one we measured in weeks not months—and then the resurgence of the illness. I spoke with her on the phone near the end; I'd given her a batch of what to me had been unfamiliar poems by Pavese both in the original Italian and in the new translations by Geoffrey Brock, and she called to thank me for this invaluable gift. Poetry never lost its importance for her, even with the specter of the end only days away. A year ago last spring the community of poets and poetry readers here in the Valley lost one of its guiding stars. We knew then we lost more than a poet: we lost a radiant friend for life who had enriched our years, a woman of independence and spirit whose vision will continue to sing, moving and touching readers for as long as people care about American poetry.

Philip Levine Fresno, July 2004

Greg Pape

Greg Pape was born in Eureka, CA. He received his BA and MA from Fresno State and his MFA from the University of Arizona. He was a fellow at the Fine Arts Work Center from 1974-76, received the Robert Frost Fellowship in Poetry at Breadloaf, was awarded the Discovery/The Nation prize, two NEA fellowships, the Pushcart Prize, and the Richard Hugo Memorial Poetry Award. Pape is the author of eleven books, including

Little America, (The Maguey Press) *Border Crossings, Black Branches, Storm Pattern* (University of Pittsburgh Press), *Sunflower Facing the Sun*, winner of the Edwin Ford Piper Prize (University of Iowa Press), *American Flamingo*, winner of a Crab Orchard Open Competition Award (Southern Illinois University Press) and *Four Swans*, Lynx House Press. His poems have been published widely in *The Atlantic, Iowa Review, The New Yorker, Northwest Review*, and *POETRY*. For many years he taught in the writing program at the University of Montana, and he served as Poet Laureate of Montana from 2007 to 2009.

from *PIECEWORK: 19 Fresno Poets*, 1987—Greg Pape

I discovered poetry in Fresno. I lived there, on and off, from age six to age twenty-five, when I left for Arizona with a Master's degree from Fresno State and a manuscript of poems. I went to Ft. Miller Jr. High and McLane High School. I played basketball, swam laps, dragged the main, shot pool at the Mecca. I learned things about love and violence in certain parking lots and in the orchards outside of town, and worked in the orchards and in the canneries in Kingsburg, and, as a laborer, helped pave certain roads and parking lots. Fresno was the place from which I set out on my first big adventures—to the City, the coast, the Sierras—and the place to which I returned.

from *How Much Earth*, 2001—Greg Pape

When I began attending classes at Fresno State in the mid-sixties poetry was in the air. The classes I took with Peter Everwine, Robert Mezey, C.G. Hanzlicek, and Philip Levine were to me memorable life-changing experiences, sometimes challenging but always eye-opening. I am grateful for all I learned and shared with my classmates and the other poets who were or are a part of this fabulous ongoing community of Fresno Poets.

"Finding Levine" from *FIRST LIGHT*, 2013—Greg Pape

I started classes at Fresno State in the fall of 1964. I had the vague idea that I would study law. My first class as a pre-law English major, Business Law 101, met at 8 a.m. in a large, crowded auditorium. The instructor lectured with a microphone, and the sound of his voice hissing and popping through the faulty sound system had the almost immediate effect of inducing sleep. Later in the day, after lunch and coffee, I went to my Introduction to Literature class taught by the poet Peter Everwine. Peter was a soft-spoken man with a Fu-Manchu mustache, a smile like the Buddha, and when he read a poem the words seemed to hover in the air and give off light. He must have noticed my enthusiasm for poetry and at some point recommended I take a class from Philip Levine. So I went looking for Levine. I asked around, and I heard things: "he's brilliant," "he's hilarious," "he's intimidating," "he lives and breathes poetry." Of course, I hadn't read a thing he had written, but on campus at that time his presence was in the air.

In high school I was in an English class taught by Mario Chavez, who had mentioned Levine in passing as we were reading the poetry of John Keats. Chavez had taken at least one class from Levine, and Keats's poetry, Chavez intimated, was a gift Levine had given him. And Chavez passed that gift along to me.

I continued my search for Levine. I went to his office, but he wasn't there. Browsing the bookstore, I found a fresh stack of paperbacks with his name on the front cover and his picture on the back. He looked more like an athlete than a professor, which made him seem approachable. He was standing in the sunshine at the edge of what looked like the San Francisco Bay, a smile on his face, a book in his clasped hands. I opened the book at random and read "An Abandoned Factory, Detroit." It sounded nothing like Keats, but it cast a spell. "The gates are chained, the barb-wire fencing stands,/An iron authority against the snow. . ." Standing in the aisle of the bookstore I was transported to a place where "the hum of mighty workings" was stopped, "caught/In the sure margin of eternity." And the abandoned factory was a monument to "the loss of human power ... the loss of years, the gradual decay of dignity." It was a chilling experience to read that poem. How did he do that, I wondered. How did he put me outside the chained gate and get me to imagine the lives of the men who worked there "hour by hour," year by year until they were gone? As I read, the words turned into the scene and the feelings, and I seemed to bring in details and images of my own only suggested by the poem. Levine wrote "broken windows," and I saw the jagged edges of the glass, the shards on the concrete floor. I could hear and feel the rhythm and the rhymes, but I wasn't aware of the pattern. I didn't know there was such a thing as meter. I had been making up poems and songs and stories since I was a child, but it wasn't until my junior year in high school after the Cuban Missile Crisis, and the assassination of President John F. Kennedy (the announcement came over the intercom as we were reading Keats in Mario Chavez's class) that I decided to seriously write poems. When I read Levine, I thought just maybe I could learn to make a poem that would hold together. Hold what together? I wasn't sure. Me? The world?

When I finally tracked him down, he was just leaving his office, dressed in white shorts, heading for the tennis courts. I may have introduced myself. I may have asked him if I could take his poetry class. What I clearly remember is handing him my most recent poem and standing there while he glanced over it, watching as a vaguely pained expression came over his face. He handed the poem back and said, "Come back during office hours, and bring something better than this," and he walked off. I stood there and read the poem again to myself and thought, "Yeah, I see what you mean." Levine didn't know it yet, but I had found my mentor. That night I read and reread On The Edge. High on the power of the poems, I wrote something better than what I had first handed to Levine. A couple of days later I stopped by his office. He was busy with another student, so I placed the poem on his desk and left. I would come back another day and ask him if I could take his poetry class.

Around this same time I picked up a copy of *Howl* for 75 cents. I was blown away by the fierce, incantatory power of its long looping lines. I remember reading the whole first section aloud to my friend and roommate Terry Holmes, who stared at me dumbfounded, and finally said something like, "Far out, man! You know," he said, "Ginsberg is coming to campus on Friday. We should go see him."

That Friday we sat on the grass at the amphitheater at Fresno State with hundreds of others and listened to Ginsberg chant his poems as he accompanied himself on the harmonium. Just as the performance was ending, I saw Levine walking toward us. "Hey, Pape," he said, and squatted down beside me. He had my poem in his hand. He pointed to some lines in the middle, "Here's where the poem starts. The rest is shit." I may be misremembering. He probably said something funnier; such as, "The first ten lines sound like Little Lord Fauntleroy imitating Ferlinghetti." Still, the message was the same. He was telling me what I needed to hear. And then he said, "Why don't you come sit in on my class next week." He handed me the poem with his markings on it, slapped me on the shoulder and walked off. That was my first workshop with Levine. I was deeply pleased and honored that he had read the poem, carried it around, and singled me out of that crowd to give my poem and me a clear and honest response.

Over the next few years I would take every class I could from Levine. All that I had heard was true; he was brilliant, hilarious, utterly honest, constantly challenging us to dig deeper, to write like our lives depended on it, which they did. I felt lucky to be accepted into those classes and to be a part of a community of young poets including Larry Levis, David St. John, Roberta Spear, Ernesto Trejo and others, galvanized by Levine's energy, humanity, and fierce commitment to the art of poetry.

When Levine returned from a year in Spain, he brought Spanish, Latin American, and world poetry back with him. His classes were animated with readings of Miguel Hernandez, Claudio Rodriguez, Gloria Fuertes, and many other poets very few Americans had ever heard of before. Just as he had given Mario Chavez the gift of Keats, he was giving us Lorca, Neruda, Vallejo, Milosz, Herbert, Holub, Hikmet, Montale, and Pavese. I still have many battered paperbacks and mimeographed sheets of poetry in translation from that time. But much of the work of translation was yet to be done.

One of the last classes I took from Levine was a translation workshop co-taught by Jose El Gorriaga. Half the class was made up of Spanish majors, the other half poets. Jose and Phil alternated between clowning around, weighing and debating the best way to render some Spanish phrase into an approximate equivalent in English, and giving passionate readings of poems in Spanish and English. The class was a joy and seemed to consume the semester. It was a great lesson in imagination and craft to try to inhabit those poems in another language and bring them, still living, into English. I lugged my hardbound Velasquez Spanish Dictionary everywhere I'd go, and I spent many wonderful hours going over poems with Ernesto Trejo, my Mexican classmate who was perfectly bilingual.

Levine let us know that the work of a poet was hard and worthy work, that it was the work itself and how that work spoke from an individual to a shared humanity that mattered. His gift to us as a teacher and as a poet is a lasting one. His poems are about people whose lives are tough, people who struggle to hold on to their dignity and their sanity, people who work to keep their souls alive. He writes about soldiers, prisoners, factory workers, teachers, laborers of all kinds, men and women and children who experience hardship, failure, exploitation, oppression, and, because they are alive, they also experience joy and occasionally triumph.

As a young man I loved Levine's audacity, his sense of humor, his eloquent anger, his generous spirit. I still do. I'd like to say of Levine what Levine said of Keats: "He remains a wellspring to which all of us might go to refresh our belief in the value of this art."

"The Opening Within Us: An Interview with Greg Pape"—Richard Jackson from *The Poetry Miscellany 14*, 1984

Richard Jackson: One of the things that's so difficult for student writers to learn is that there has to be something larger than yourself at stake in poems. The best poems have the most at stake in them. What's at stake may not be right there in front of the speaker, either, but only triggered, as Hugo says, by what's there. It may be a larger context, as Plumly says in "Sentimental Forms," something that's absent, lost, past. This is what gives a poem resonance. It's present in all your poems – where you go to a place where a girl was once before and a double story evolves, in the poem, "In San Antonio," for Dick Hugo.

Greg Pape: For me, I think there's always a lot at stake. In *Black Branches* I wanted to affirm the things that are important, though. I guess the danger is that the resonance would be true only for myself, and therefore would be sentimental. I try to tell my students Kinnell's version of this – saying in its own music what matters. In that poem you refer to, "In San Antonio," the landscape is really important. I guess it's because of the way I've lived my life since I was a kid. I've travelled a lot and found myself in different landscapes. I was never able to take landscape for granted in a sort of comfortable, secure way that I imagined some of my friends at school did. They had their being in their neighborhood. They had their places where they went, and I'd have to ask: "What is there?" "What am I going to find of myself in this new place?"

I think part of the sense in the San Antonio poem, dedicated to Hugo, was returning to a landscape I hadn't been in since I was a child, and talking to him there. It was a time I didn't know how sick he was. In the poem I say, "I was in love with my mother," referring to the earlier time. At that time I had only wanted to see the Alamo, like something out of the movies. And then I say, "I didn't know then what I know now." There was all that death at the Alamo, but there was also the sick and dying Dick Hugo in the later visit. I didn't know. I ended the poem, "In San Antonio the river is green and tame," and it means something else now. So I guess what's at stake in that poem is change, and the way what's at stake changes – everything "passes through us/like a river that outruns its name." It's different than Heraclitus' river; once you step into it you can never get out of it. You know it in different ways.

RJ: Well, like "Part of An Old Story" – trying to escape the sense of things fated, of unwittingly playing a part in a story you don't want to be in.

GP: Yes. That came out of a particular experience of teaching on the road in Arizona where I would go and be a stranger for a week not knowing what I was getting into. I was like a fictional character because the people had it all figured out who I was, what I would do. They had events planned. And a lot of the poems, I think, are like fiction. I've worked a lot with narrative as a way to hold the poem together, as a way to find structure beyond simply a kind of lyrical structure. But the narratives I try to write are lyrical narratives that work with a line and breaking, using the line to try to find the music in the sentence.

RJ: As you were talking I was thinking of "Sharks, Caloosahatche River." There's a fabulous quality to the poem, beginning with the magic of the sound in that name. You begin thinking of the fins of the cars, and then the image tends to generate the narrative. You get a sense of the narrative emerging out of

the details of the poem – and this happens in the other poems, too. The mind's re-thinking and re-feeling become part of the plot, too. And all this enables the poem to have its alternate ending.

GP: When you set out to write a poem you have things brewing in you; you have your whole life to work with, but you have to find connections, and that's the fun of it. When you start to find connections where things start to generate a state of mind, when that is successful, the poem is successful. You've gotten excited, found some way to say a truth, to say what's at stake, or what matters, and it's there for you in the music of the language, in the precision of the images, in the connections that are made. If they work, then it's there for the reader because you've created a new kind of thing.

That particular poem is interesting to me because I wanted to write about that period of time, but I didn't know quite how to do it. In a way, I began by just talking to myself. I was trying to get centered, to focus. I began: "It's so quiet. It is 1957," as the opening line, then because of that I thought of past car crashes, and then I began to think about the images from this piece of time. That brought the car fins, then the shark fins, the sense of violence. I worked my way through the narrative, and one of the things that was in my mind was that the character in the poem is a child who goes to the movies and first witnesses this brutality. He's living in a motel, which is a place of darkness and dissociation of landscape, and he becomes a character from the movies, does this imaginative thing to shatter his world. He steals a car, drives it into the river, stops time, stops the river. In the end he becomes a sort of hero, steps dripping from the river like a child who'll lead some children's crusade. But then I thought, come on, you can't do that. So I questioned where the romance of the poem had taken me, and it started to break down. I added the other ending and got all excited about the poem again. I thought – now I'm starting to show the kind of polarities that work through us. I was starting to get much closer to the truth. Now it ends with the "silver glinting" of the river, or the blank screen; it is still mysterious, but in another way, as an imaginative place. You have to go to your childhood if you want to write what's essential, or, as you say, find what's at stake. Garcia Marquez said about *One Hundred Years of Solitude* that the book all came from experiences he had when he was eight years old. He said by the time he was eight years old he had learned everything he needed to know.

RJ: You mentioned polarities, and certainly the title of the first book, *Border Crossings*, suggests a variation on that. One of the gestures that book makes is to try to dissolve borders. And in *Black Branches* the first poem has a sort of border, time, around the edges; there's a tension between black and white, inner and outer, that you try to break down. There's a sort of emergence from within – "He is beginning to live/in those rooms above and below/opening within him." That emphasis seems to make the shift between the two books.

GP: I use the epigram from William Carlos Williams as a sort of guide for what you are talking about: "Who shall hear of us/in the time to come?/Let him say there was/a burst of fragrance/from black branches." It's an affirmative image, and an affirmative tone, but there's also a kind of vanishing in the image, too. The burst is not from the flower – he doesn't say the flower – he leaves it out; it's a sort of absence, and while it's a definite image it is also wonderfully ambiguous. The dark, the blackness, then is important if the polarities are to be recognized. In the title poem, the elegy for W. Eugene Smith, the photographer, I try to be faithful to his vision which was full of profound loss, full of pain, yet somehow affirmative. One of his problems was that he worked for *LIFE* magazine and they always wanted to take the dark out of his photographs. That was a terrible problem for him because he wanted that dark closing down on his images with a sense of mystery and death. In one picture is a child in a woman's arms. The child has been poisoned and we only see her through a little available window light.

RJ: There's a rhythm established by this play of polarities, between the tragic and the light, the romance and the reality, light and dark. Discovering the rhythm is discovering the subject, and it seems that your rhythms have become more expansive, can scoop in more of these polarities.

GP: Yes, when you change rhythms you change the terms of everything. It puts all kinds of new things at stake, in focus, and gives them a reality, something to be. The rhythm accumulates and makes connections in that long poem about Smith, allows me to call on a certain kind of spirit unavailable in a closed, shorter lyric.

RJ: There seems to be more trust, authority in the voice.

GP: I believe you really have to trust language. There's a lot of distrust of language now in my students, and in students of literature. There are some positive things that come out of the newer critical questioning, but when you fully deny the author then you have a sort of disembodied language. I think there's a lot of choice in language, and I find I trust language because when I reach a certain imaginative intensity then there is a real give and take between me and the words, an electrical connection. It is language verifying itself. It's language that's coming true.

I think that if X is there, it is partly there because of language, because of our ability to name things, like the kind of scene that you do when you include the landscape in your poems. All of a sudden, if you can be inclusive rather than exclusive, you are revitalizing the language. I think that's one of the things that poets do, they make the language come true. They give it a kind of spiritual, physical being by living through it.

RJ: What relationship do you think this has to the need for forgetting? You open "At the Edge of the River" with – "Sometimes you must forget everything/then remember it all."

GP: The way I see the poem is – here I am, standing on the edge of whatever I'm going to think of. If you really want to know what's at stake you have to erase the blackboard of preconceptions – whatever you thought was important – and then, as Rilke says in his *Letters to a Young Poet*, try to experience what you love and lose like some first human being.

RJ: One of the interesting things that's occurring in poetry is a resurgence of rhetoric. We can think of poets like Levine, Bell, Matthews, Jim Tate, for instance. It involves an expansiveness, more inclusiveness – some of the things we've been discussing. It involves looking beyond images and to the way things, images, and abstractions get connected.

GP: I remember hearing Gary Snyder read, and in one poem he says the word "apple," and the damn apple seemed to come right out of the air. It was there. I mean he believed in that word so much he made it real for me. But there's a limitation to those rhythms and that thinking, and I wanted to include more other voices in a more discursive way of thinking so the poems could open up and have longer subjects. I think a lot of people have changed this way. The last time I talked to Bill Matthews he was saying he felt pretty good about his writing because he was writing bigger, including more stuff. You know what we may do? We may fall back in ten years to a resurgence of the deep image. I don't want to leave anything good behind. I tried to take what I could out of *Border Crossings* and bring it into *Black Branches* and make it longer. You want to take with you the things that transcend fashion.

RJ: I think one of the most attractive things about your poems, and it relates to the expansiveness and inclusiveness we've been discussing, is a sense of embrace. The poems open their arms to all sorts of experience. It's not just a technique, I mean, but a vision, a way of seeing and feeling.
GP: Part of that is an acknowledgement that we live in two worlds – the past and the information about it we receive from imagination, or the present and the past. You have to include whatever is possible. That's what the poem, "The Porpoise," is getting at. It ends – "the skin of the porpoise shines/with the light of two worlds,/this one and this one." For me, it's just ambiguous enough to be right because it's an inclusiveness. There's a difference, and I like it that I could say it with the same words, lay them side by side.

RJ: There's a real harsh world portrayed in the poems so that the embracing gesture becomes all the more authentic. Yet there are more victories.
GP: The harshness of this world is something I have to digest, make sense of. I've learned a lot from reading and from writing. I think I found myself in poems when I needed to when I was a young kid. The language – I trusted it even then – freed me and made it possible for me to deal with the experiences of my life. Maybe it is a kind of power, too. Sometimes poems don't have to just look back with an awful feeling, but can do something for you, re-see something. They have to put the world on the page and then do something with it, not just photograph it but do something with it.
"An Arched and Lighted Entrance: An Interview with Greg Pape," 2013—Drew Pomeroy from *Poetry Matters*

Friends of poetry, for this month's post, you're in for a real treat as guest-blogger Drew Pomeroy interviews poet Greg Pape about his most recent collection, Four Swans. *— Nancy Chen Long*

Drew Pomeroy: Readers of *Four Swans* (Spokane: Lynx House Press 2013) may know that some of the poems included were originally published in your chapbook *Animal Time* (Lexington: Accents Publishing 2011). To better understand the process of composing a chapbook before a complete collection, could you speak to which of these works was first in your mind: the chapbook or the book?
Greg Pape: *Four Swans* was a work-in-progress long before the idea for *Animal Time* came to me. I have always been interested in animals and the ways we human animals interact with other species, how we are connected, or disconnected, with each other, how we share or infringe on each other's habitats, what we give and take from each other. But the idea for the chapbook *Animal Time* grew out of a lecture I gave at Spalding in which I considered the ways poets have engaged imaginatively with animals. After looking at the work of Whitman and Dickinson, Elizabeth Bishop, James Wright, Gerald Stern, Philip Levine, various Chinese and Japanese poets, and others, I looked at my own work and made a gathering of poems in which animals figure prominently. Those poems developed into the chapbook *Animal Time*.

DP: That deep interest in human and animal coexistence seems to be the heartbeat of *Four Swans*. I find myself often wondering what animals might think of us or say to us if they could speak. For you, as a poet, how does this very human concern become a poetry of coexistence?

GP: I like your idea of a poetry of coexistence. *Four Swans*, the book, began with the experiences presented in the title poem. I had just spoken with my mother on the phone. She was in the hospital in California. I was worried about her, thinking I needed to get down there and see her. I drove to the National Wildlife Refuge near my home in the Bitterroot, a place I often go to walk, think, write, a place set aside for people and other creatures to coexist. There were four swans on Whistler pond close enough to observe without binoculars. Beautiful creatures, calm, dignified—I describe them and name them in the poem. They seemed to give me access to something I needed. I don't know what they thought of me, but they were aware of my presence and seemed to be untroubled by it. They were in complete possession of themselves, at home on the ice and the water, feeding, preening, stretching their big wings. I wondered what it would be like to be one of them. Then I thought in some way I am one of them. I guess that's a poetry of coexistence.

DP: Your poem "Tracks & Traces" *(Four Swans* 17-18) begins with the speaker expressing a nearly child-like curiosity when he says, "It must be fun to be an otter" (line 6). However, at the end of the poem there is a profound moment of coexistence revealed beneath an uprooted Ponderosa pine, which you describe as "a time of violence / become a place of shelter, part of the story / that houses us all" (50-52). Can you tell us more about the curious and wise speaker of this poem?

GP: The speaker of "Tracks & Traces" is a guy like me walking through the woods in winter reading the signs, the tracks left in the snow by animals, trying to discern the stories those tracks tell. It is something I do often in the winter, a form of walking meditation, a state of concentration and observation much like a hunter's, except I am after something else besides deer or ducks and geese, some other kind of sustenance. These winter walks can start off serene and peaceful then turn, as the weather turns, fierce, or you come upon the carcass of an elk with ravens feeding on it, or you step down into a hole at the base of a lovely old Ponderosa pine that's blown down in the last storm. It's hard not to think of the violence as well as the beauty that's written on the land, and in us.

DP: The presence of Nature in these poems, captured in both the vivid imagery and a beautifully-wrought diction of the land, is a powerful one. What is the importance of the human element that is thinking and living within the powerful Nature of these poems?

GP: I think it's important to describe and try to articulate all sorts of experiences. If our poems and other works of art help us live our lives, and that seems to be one of the primary purposes of art, it is by articulating, questioning, and shaping experience, sometimes making sense, providing insights or feelings that can be shared, sometimes just putting something out there we don't completely understand, adding to the conversation. If we have learned anything it's that the human element is not something apart from Nature but something within Nature.

DP: There are four separate but very carefully connected parts to the book *Four Swans*. How did each of these parts become its own?

GP: When I began organizing the poems, written over several years, into a book, I found there was a kind of narrative arc that traced the infirmity and death of my mother from the first poem, written in winter, to the last poem, written in fall, and the seasons, more or less evident in all the poems, shaped and commented in a strong way on the arc of the book.

DP: The poem "Elegy for Big Red" (*Four Swans* 38-40) is perhaps the most humorous yet equally heart-breaking poem of the collection. In it the speaker tells the tale of a rooster named Big Red, whom he describes as a "bastard hatched / in Nebraska, shipped to Montana / in a box with dozens of others" (lines 1-3). Why was it important to have this poem in Four Swans?

GP: Swans, roosters, people, the beautiful as well as the good the bad and the ugly are all part of the tapestry. "Elegy for Big Red" is both a lament and a celebration, and maybe a warning. My relationship with Big Red was complex. We seemed to bring out the worst in each other. But when I found him headless in the chicken coop one morning I realized what a beautiful creature he was, and how petty and self-indulgent I had been toward him at times, and how much I respected him and would miss him.

DP: In the poem "Big Lost River Breakdown" (*Four Swans* 57-60) you write "under the cottonwoods, the smoke / sweetening the summer air dawn to dusk / makes us recall Dreamland" (lines 35-37). Some readers may initially see this Dreamland as an imaginary place of the poet to be further explored in the next stanza, but as a former native of Alabama, my mind (and taste buds) went straight to the plate of Dreamland barbecue you later describe. Do you find yourself thinking and writing about a place, like Montana or Alabama, when you are surrounded by it, or do you tend to write about a place when you are away from it, wondering about it, longing for it?

GP: I think I was writing in my journal in Arco, Nevada sitting at a picnic table when I smelled that barbeque smoke, so I was there, fully present, and certainly hungry. But that smell took me immediately to Dreamland, which as you know is the name of a great barbeque place outside Tuscaloosa. So the answer to your question is both. By writing about one place you make associations with other places, and depending on your aims or needs, you follow your pencil. In this case to Dreamland.

DP: While nearly all of these poems occur in a natural world, Parts III and IV contain many poems about people, specifically family and friends. Can you describe the necessity of these more human poems in *Four Swans*?

GP: I think all the poems occur in the natural world. There are poems in Parts III and IV that are elegies, poems that remember the lives and mourn the deaths of friends and family, but they are mixed in with sketches of particular places and people—life and death side by side of necessity.

DP: Several poems in *Four Swans* present a speaker looking through a window, either out onto the natural world or into some other world. What do these windows reveal, or hide, from the human element of the poem?

GP: I like to write outdoors, and I do as much as I can, even sometimes in winter. But when I'm writing indoors I often keep in touch with the outdoors by gazing out the window. Emerson said, "the health of the eyes demands a horizon," and I believe that is true literally, as well as metaphorically. A window lets light in, and lets one see out. It is both an entrance and an exit. I'm never completely comfortable in those rooms without windows.

DP: There is this consistent presence of faith, hope, and patience in Four Swans. This is especially true of those poems at the end of the book. Do you see these elements as an extension of yourself in the poetry, or is it a result of the Nature, the possibility of regrowth, in which many of these poems exist?
GP: Where does one find faith, hope, and patience? More good names for swans. Certainly we need those to get through tough times. I think we discover and develop those things in all sorts of ways. We learn from each other, from literature, from religion, from rivers and swans and ponderosa pines.

DP: The final poem of the book, "White Church in Wiborg" (*Four Swans* 82-83), presents a speaker looking into the window of a church and imagining a scene taking place inside. In that scene is a captured moment of human, perhaps family, history. The speaker leaves this imagined moment and follows another down the wagon-rutted mule path all the way to Cumberland Falls, where one can "watch the Moonbow / rise above the river, like an arched and lighted entrance / through earthly air that made those who saw it lean closer" (33-35). Why did you choose to end the book with a sense of entry into another world? Should we be anticipating anything? Another book perhaps?
GP: My mother's stories of her childhood in Kentucky had always fascinated me. She was born in Wiborg in McCreary County, one of eleven children. Her father and mother were both born in the southern mountains, descendants of the first European settlers. They made their living from the land as hunters, gatherers, subsistence farmers, and later as coal miners. She had a hard life. Her stories of childhood were vivid and memorable, and sometimes scary, but not without love for her early home place. After she died I took her ashes to Kentucky and searched for, and found, the small family graveyard near where she was born, and placed her ashes and monument there. The white church in Wiborg was established by her grandfather. I was lucky to be able to visit it and make it part of the setting of the last poem (it has since burned down). The other setting of that poem, Cumberland Falls, where one can see the Moonbow, is a place of great beauty and natural wonder, and for me a place of intimate connection to my family's past, to my life before I was born. And to witness the Moonbow with others, I've felt a sense of awe and kinship, an *entrance*, not necessarily to another world, but a deeper sense of this one. If all goes well, there will definitely be another book.

Suzanne Lummis

Suzanne Lummis was a 2018/19 COLA (City of Los Angeles) fellow, an endowment to noted Los Angeles artists and writers to create a new body of work. She did--in seventy one, (mostly) 280 character stanzas, "Tweets from Hell." Suzanne received the George Drury Smith Outstanding Achievement in Poetry Award from Beyond Baroque in 2015. Poetry.la produced 13 episodes of her YouTube video series, "They Write by Night,"

in which she explores film noir and poets influenced by those black and white crime movies of the 40s and 50s. Her full-length collections are *Idiosyncrasies*, *In Danger*, *Open 24 Hours*, and the new, not-yet-published, *The Garden of So-Called Eden Again*. She has appeared in *The New Yorker* and is included in Knopf's popular "Everyman's Library Pocket Poets" anthologies, *Poems of the American West*, *Killer Verse: Poems of Murder and Mayhem*, and *Monster Verse*. She teaches for the UCLA Extension Writers' Program.

from *How Much Earth,* 2001—Suzanne Lummis

I studied with all three mainstays of the Fresno legend, Philip, Peter, and Chuck, and found that while each had his own means of approaching our poems—or those rawboned, knobby formations we hoped might evolve into poems—all endorsed qualities that pointed us toward a clear resonant language rooted in the sensations and images of the physical world. And, in ways both subtle and direct, all advocated a commitment to the emotional truth (a thing not always in lock-step with the literal truth). I believe these values still comprise the foundation of my work. From time to time, however, other elements show up, moods decidedly . . . what? Un-Fresnoesque? No, that sounds quite wrong. Non-Fresnonian. For example, the FSU sensibility gave rise to many deeply humane bodies of work, so the program can't be held accountable for the acerbic tone in certain of my poems. And if anyone should ever detect a trace of irony in some poem of mine, they must not blame Fresno."

"*Open 24 Hours*: An Interview With Suzanne Lummis" from *Poets' Quarterly,* 2014— Georgia Jones-Davis

Suzanne Lummis' collection *Open 24 Hours* won the Blue Lynx Poetry Award in Washington State and will be published in Fall 2014. Her poems have appeared in such journals as *Ploughshares*, *The Hudson Review*, *New Ohio Review*, and she has one forthcoming in *The New Yorker*.

She's included in *California Poetry from the Gold Rush to the Present*, *How Much Earth: The Fresno Poets*, and the Knopf anthologies *Poems of the American West* and *Poems of Murder and Mayhem*. Known for her irreverent humor, she was a key figure in the Los Angeles-based, Stand-up Poetry movement of the 90s—and also known for her essays defining the poem noir. In 2013, NPR's *All Things Considered* aired a segment on her, "Writing Noir Poems with L.A. as a Backdrop."

Georgia Jones-Davis: Why is it a poem if it doesn't rhyme? I have been asked, especially by older people. I reply that the piece in question is a poem because it is a "history of secrets." I said that without fully knowing why or what it means exactly, except that it some angle of poetry's mystery has been illuminated. Would you talk about what you believe brightens those shadows that make up poetry's mystery, your "history of secrets"?
Suzanne Lummis: I love your answer to that question—it's in many respects a more appealing answer than mine would've been, and a hell of a lot shorter. Before I address poetry's mystery or shadows, I'd like to back up and approximate what I've sometimes said to people who think (still, after these many decades) poetry must rhyme. I ask them who do they imagine might be the most popular U.S. poet around the world, the one translated into all major and most minor languages, who has influenced other giant figures in poetry around the world, and whose appeal never wanes –the most American of American poets. It is Walt Whitman, who rarely wrote in rhyme. It's hard to imagine anyone today suggesting that Whitman wasn't a poet. He never saw the 20th century. Non-rhyming poetry has been dominant since the 1960s, but was around long before that – it's not some fad that sprung up lately.

Ancient poetry took the form of spells, incantations, prayers, cries to the supernatural forces, a kind of beseeching, or an expression of the will to draw the visible out of the invisible. Those are the roots of poetry, that's where it all began. And those early expressions rarely rhymed. Instead it used a chant-like, trance-like repetition.

> Comes the deer to my singing,
> Comes the deer to my song,
> Comes the deer to my singing.

> He, the blackbird, he am I,
> Bird beloved of the wild deer.
> Comes the deer to my singing.

This doesn't rhyme in the Navajo language.

Rhyme came into poetry in part because in past centuries most of the population was illiterate and rhyme made the words easier to memorize. The way things are going in the schools, and judging by some of the posts I see on the Yahoo news threads, rhyme may soon have to be reintroduced to poetry for the same reason.

Regarding shadows, mystery and secrets—I like all this, to be sure. I don't think these elements exist to the same degree in poetry across the board, and in some poems not at all. We probably wouldn't describe Bukowski that way, or Frank O'Hara, or, on a totally different end of the spectrum, Edna St. Vincent Millay. Those poets say what they mean, straight up. I do think your description works especially well for poets such as Louise Gluck and David St. John (though David can be both clear and shadowy at the same time.)

It's poetry we think, we hope, if it's efficient in its brevity (brief compared to fiction, even short fiction), surprising in its movement—its progress—vital and lively in its language. If it is narrative, let us not foresee what's coming next. And if it is mad, let there be a method to the madness.

Oh, and line breaks! Unlike playwrights, novelists, short fiction writers, memoirists, screenwriters, journalists, bloggers, advertising copywriters, poets turn the line. Yes, few make a fuss over this; no one's ever been moved to tears by a line break–well, maybe three or four people—but it's something very special about poetry. And it's best when the poet knows what the heck she's doing. Not all line breaks are equal.

GJD: *In Danger,* your first book of poems, is a remarkable, novel-like sequence of "noir" poems. There are characters—unsavory lovers, the city itself, and a tough-skinned narrator whose skin gets thicker as we travel through the narrative. She tells us early on about how, "I would listen to no one/especially me" and "my own radiant/dangerous origin, choices winking/like the city at night." And then the shocker: "Let poetry dump her off here." How did you come to braid the "noir" Chandleresque narration with a poetry that creates such hard-boiled lyricism? Who were your earliest influences in writing? What voices did you hear?

SL: Oh I am so glad that you see a kind of narrative thread or progress in that book, because—unfortunately for me—I've never been able to plot out a whole book of poems in advance. Nowadays, poets get "ideas" for poetry collections the way writers get ideas for novels, and creative writing students are encouraged to think that way. That's a good, sound approach and I wholly approve of it—and I don't do it. I write poems as they come to me, which is only once in a while. I'm not prolific, in part because I reject a lot of poems that I get ideas for, or I'll write half a poem then abandon it. For the poem to make the cut I want it to stand out in some way. They don't all have to be great—they can't be, I'm not that good—but each one has to offer something distinctive, and be … not boring.

Though I wrote each poem without knowing what the next one would be, the cohesion in *In Danger,* such as it is, evolved because environment matters to me, "a place for the reader to plant her feet," as I tell my students. Often I was drawing from the environs I inhabited at that time, that building, and certain lowbrow hangouts around East Hollywood.

For those who haven't read the collection and might get the wrong idea, I should mention it's not Bukowski-like in the least because, for one, I wasn't living quite such an improvident lifestyle, and even more importantly, I'd had a rigorous workshop background. By rigorous I mean, Philip Levine—Chuck Hanzlicek and Peter Everwine too, all those guys—would let us know when our poems were no good. And at the beginning anyway, and for quite a while, they were never any good. Quite a few dropped out—I'm talking the undergraduate experience, not later—but those who remained were forced to get better.

So, I was living in these kind of urban underclass circumstances but with acquired formal skills, and native talent—I guess—so I turned out poetry that was of that world but more disciplined than what we usually get from someone in those environs, who is usually someone entirely self-taught. With a few notable exceptions, that self-taught stuff is so damn loose, so slack, and nearly always absent of imagery. Or for that matter they could be living in a summer cottage on the Rhine—same thing. It's always absent of imagery.

You mentioned Raymond Chandler, and as you know, his writing struck a chord with me. Through Chandler's classic "hardboiled" detective fiction and certain films noir I discovered not only the makings of a voice that I could change and adapt to our times and my own sensibilities, but also a point of view. I don't like sentimentality or melodrama. Other people don't like it either, but I dislike it even more. There's a way that Chandler and the best films noir strip away every last vestige of sentimentality and melodrama that interested me. They supplanted both with traces of dry humor—that's what interested me.

My earliest influence might have been Eugene Field's children's poem, "Winken, Blynken and Nod." I believe it influences me to this very day. Even as a little kid I got its power, its other-worldly spell-casting mood.

GJD: What poets are you reading now? What other kinds of writing do you turn to for inspiration or ideas or simply fun?

SL: Well, you say "now," and I want to be totally literal about it—you caught me when I'm reading Goethe, *Faust, Part One*. But I'm not usually reading Goethe. In fact, I never am, except at this moment. Every once in a while, though, I like to dip into some writing that's stood the test of time, and to read work not originally written in English.

I'm going through a Graham Greene craze. If I ever start to get a swelled head, I read him to remind myself I'm just scratching the surface. I admire the depth and breadth of his knowledge of other countries, a knowledge that embraces every aspect: the machinations of the political system, the social structure, the people themselves—culture, customs—the characters of individuals and the atmosphere, the climate, what air feels like, what scents the winds bring in.

For a time Greene worked undercover for the British foreign intelligence service. He was a practicing Catholic, a true believer, but also a kind of hedonist. Many of his novels set forth subtle, moral problems that have no easy solution. He was a genius. And spy. Having said all that—I can't see that Greene's novels have had any influence on my poetry. But it'd be nice if they did.

GJD: Your new book, *Open 24 Hours*, is just about to be published and is the winner of the Blue Lynx Poetry Prize. Please tell us about your new and much awaited new book, the inspiration or vision that lead to it.
SL: Yes, I did win the Blue Lynx Poetry Prize for *Open 24 Hours* to be published by Lynx House Press in Washington state. On Thursday, October 2, there will be a publication party and reading at Beyond Baroque in Venice, California.

How to describe this book without getting all abstract? It's not sufficient to say that it includes comedy—some fairly outrageous (I mean, for poetry)—melancholy, atmospheric poems, and certain sharp-tongued dark poems. That doesn't tell us much. Maybe it would help to describe the three sections. The first, "Substandard Housing," has poems that rose out of that four-story brick building in East Hollywood I lived in long ago. The second, "Broken and in Need of Repair," plays with the idea of ill-functioning or broken things, including rules—rules that various professor poets had advised their students never to break. In the final section, "The Fate Cookies," each poem's title is taken from an actual fortune cookie. The collection ends on Sunset Strip after dark, the last poem.

It's a strong book I think, and markedly unusual. No one who knows contemporary poetry is likely to say, "oh no, not another one of these." In any case, it's the kind of poetry I believe in.

An Interview with Suzanne Lummis, from *La Bloga*, 2014—Olga García Echeverría

It's not surprising the Suzanne Lummis' newest collection of poetry, *Open 24 Hours*, was the winner of the 2013 Blue Lynx Prize. These are poems full of texture and poetic sass; they're urban dwellers that live in gritty places, where " . . . The rubble of smashed / glass makes the sidewalk shine..." In these poems "tenants bitch" and poets get stopped on street corners and asked, "Are you saved?"

These poems, born of earthquake and the "art of disaster" ride elevators, witness car crashes, dream about red shoes that do not quite fit. They are heavy-eyed in the A.M. and wide-eyed at night. They're Open 24 hours and they're over-caffeinated. You can hear the racing heat beat in verse...

    because you've stayed up
    all night on nothing
    but blues and black

coffee and the sound
of windy traffic
outside your door
which reminds you
of death or is that
the coffee?

And although there is lost love and death and even a prisoner in a Chinese fortune cookie factory in this book of poems, there is no whimpering. Only late night Facebook posts that rage against bozos who insist that Obama is a Muslim, who call Oprah "fat," who write things like, "Let the socialists Marxist Libtards / go out and wash all the oil off the fish / and birds, ha, ha, ha." Lummis fires back with:

Maybe you just popped out this way,
an ignorant, crude baby determined
to get worse. Oh there's no hope, no hope
for you, except—this: read books, books of quality...
Read the true news or, at least, news
that's closing in on the truth, watch smart TV—
it exists! Aspire to be less stupid.

Not even the Sacred Word gets a free pass in Lummis' poetic world. Hey, if it doesn't pay the rent, crown the poet "Most Celebrated Aging Poet Princess in the Land," or birth worthwhile images, then Lummis declares:

Pack your bags. Take a hike.
Make yourself scare. Hit
the road, Jack. Blow
town. Split the spot. Buzz
off, push off, shove off. Go fish!

Packed with honesty and humor, Lummis delivers a solid collection of verses and curses in *Open 24 Hours*, and because she rocks she also joins us here today for an interview.

Olga García Echeverría: Suzanne, welcome to *La Bloga* and congratulations on your recent publication of Open 24 Hours and on receiving the 2013 Blue Lynx Prize. That must feel pretty wonderful.
Suzanne Lummis: Yes, I'd like to thank the screeners who did not pass earlier versions of this manuscript on to contest judges, because if it had won a prize and gone to press a few years earlier it wouldn't have been as good. And some people's favorite poems, fairly recent ones, wouldn't have been in it. Moreover, Lynx House Press here on the West Coast is a better publisher for me than some of those others might've been. Yes, it was the right publisher, right time, and great good fortune for me.

OGE: That is very interesting and inspiring. As writers we sometimes think that rejection (of publication, for instance) is a tragic dead-end, but as you mention, sometimes being denied entry in one place/space leads to other possibilities. Are there others you'd like to thank for rejecting your work?

SL: I'd also like to thank the two lesser literary journals that rejected "How I Didn't Get Myself to A Nunnery," because their rejection made it possible for Paul Muldoon to accept that poem for *The New Yorker*. (However, let me be clear, I would not like everyone to reject all my writings from here on out, with the idea that rejection is probably in my best interests. I think I've had enough for this lifetime, thank you very much.)

OGE: I love the cover and the title of *Open 24 Hours*. It feels like a welcome sign at a diner where the everyday and the odd-houred can enter. Is this what you meant by it or does the title mean something else entirely?
SL: I'm so glad you like the cover—yes, it makes a forceful impression, nothing wispy about it. For me the title evokes the idea of night owls, restless people awake while others sleep, maybe leaning over a Styrofoam or porcelain cup in one of those low-end hangouts that stay open all night in L.A., donut shops and chain coffee houses. I mean it to refer to a marginal, nocturnal world.

OGE: Did you have any challenges with deciding on the final title of your book?
SL: It came to me fairly early on, maybe a third of the way into the manuscript. I was feeling perplexed about what I might call this collection-in-progress. Then I glimpsed a particularly striking Open 24 Hours sign and knew that was it. I knew I wouldn't come upon anything better, and I didn't.

OGE: The first section of your book, "Substandard Housing," has a very strong sense of place. How did this section of your book evolve? Did you plan on creating a series of interconnected poems that lived in the same building or was it more of an organic process?
SL: It's odd, in a way, because I haven't lived in that building for over 15 years. I wrote many of the poems while there, but continued to write about some of the tenants and memorable incidents after I'd left. I didn't scope out a design for the manuscript ahead of time, no, in fact, it changed shape many times. At one point the middle section, now called "Broken and in Need of Repair," was called "Hopeless Desire and Other Common Complaints." It was damn hard to get these poems to lie down next to each other, because in terms of voice, and sometimes even style, they vary wildly, crazily. It's not as noticeable now, not jarring anyway, because I finally did organize them so that one leads into the other without causing the reader to yelp in alarm.

OGE: My favorite poems in this first section were "7.3" and "664-8630." The former because the poem, like any good earthquake, rattles. I love all those things you worry about in the poem as the earth's tectonic plates are rumbling beneath your feet. I think many of us Angelinos can relate. I've included an excerpt of "7.3" here for our readers to enjoy:

> But I don't have time to review this life flashing
> past my eyes like the preview of a low budget movie,
>
> there's death to work on.
> Who has copies of my unpublished works?
>
> If my cats crawl out of the wreck, how will they live?
> Does this mean I'm off the hook for those parking tickets

and credit card debts? Like a fool I follow
everyone's advice, leap for the doorframe,
   which will snap like breadsticks when the floor
caves, the ultimate letdown.

When it stops my sense of The Real won't quit
shaking. Bad

Earth. The blue-dark mother holds us and her love
turns.

Your other poem "664-8630" really spoke to me because a dear friend of mine, tatiana de la tierra, died in 2012. We used to spend a good amount of time on the phone talking and texting. It was one of the things I missed most when she was gone. After she passed, and long after her phone had been disconnected, I used to sometimes send her random texts with some crazy hope that maybe she'd reply. Your poem that ends in that ringing with no answer really struck a cord and made me feel less crazy about wanting to reach the unreachable via a phone number.

SL: Olga, thank you for this comment. Yes, it does seem this poem might apply to many lives, and many losses. The phone number was Ted Schmidt's—he produced both my plays at The Cast Theater, which flourished from the 80s through the mid 90s, and an important playwriting award is named after him here in Los Angeles. However, years later I kind of wished I'd saved that poem for the phone number of the family home in San Francisco, the number that was in use for my entire adult life. When my father died, I called it one last time and felt it ring and ring in the house that would soon be sold.

OGE: That childlike question in the poem (why do people die?) is so simple, but I am sure it resonates with anyone who has lost a loved one. Here is the poem you wrote for Ted Schmitt (1940-1990) and for so many others:

I pass this number
in my phone book, the seven everyday
digits a sequence I won't dial
anymore—

like passing a house abandoned but
filled with echoing
rooms that were lived in. Till
now.

If I called I would hear
...what? A buzzing like a station
shut down for the night,
the TV screen filled with
snow?
 Or has the phone line snapped
overhead, the late messages
heading for a long

fall?
 No good asking like a child
why do people die? I call

but in a room where a man's
things have been folded and packed
as if to follow him on the next train
after a phone rings,
rings, and there is no
answer.

In the second section of your book, "Broken and In Need of Repair," you take some writing rules given by poet professors and friends, such as "No self-pitying poems," and you purposely break them. What inspired this cool rebellion?

SL: During a UCLA lecture open to the public, the late short fiction writer Donald Barthelme mentioned a rule he advised his students never to break, and quite instantly I imagined a way I could write a poem that avoided the problem Barthelme seemed to warn against. That started me on the series. I collected these rules from poet professors, and some were serious, some given to me in a spirit of fun.

OGE: Did certain rules inspire more rebellion than others?

SL: I discovered the rule had to present a real challenge or I couldn't come up with anything good, and it had to come from a poet or reader who knew what they were talking about. Once, some random person I'd mentioned this series to said something like "I think there should be a rule no more poems about dogs and cats, because there are already so many of those." Well, that's absurd. There isn't really a super-abundance, and, anyway, most poems about animals, so long as they're written by real poets, poets of talent, tend to be quite good.

OGE: Do you have a favorite?

SL: Above all I love the poem that closes *The Selected Poems of Weldon Kees*, the one that begins "What the cats do/To amuse themselves/When we are gone/I do not know." And the reader is aware that Kees would eventually end his life by throwing himself off the Golden Gate Bridge (presumably, his body was never found). But the cats go on, "crying, dancing." It's such an innocent, almost childlike poem on the surface, but it takes on an eerie power because of what we know. Talk about structure—brilliant of Donald Justice [the editor of the collection] to place that poem at the end of the book.

OGE: Can you share a source of inspiration you keep returning to?

SL: I continue to like a poem you don't see anywhere anymore, very early W. S. Merwin, "The Sands," and one that's easy to find, "Sheep in Fog," by Plath, and one that you can't find anywhere, by someone few have heard of—and, indeed, I hadn't heard of him—"Looking for Bluefish" by Jon Swan. Oh, and one that can be found with a bit of luck, "Smudging," by Diane Wakoski. Gorgeous, the way it gathers to a force at the end. Levine's "The Story of Chalk"—yes.

And as for the unruly side of the poetic spirit, Gregory Corso's "Marriage," and the fantastically wild and outrageous "Me viene, hay dias..." by Cesar Vallejo. I don't know why that one isn't used in creative writing workshops around the country—it's so freeing.

Sandra Hoben

Sandra Hoben was born in Naugatuck, Connecticut and she received her B.A. from St. John's College. She studied writing at CSU Fresno where she received an M.A. in English, and at the University of Utah where she received a Ph.D.

Her poetry and translations have appeared in *FIELD*, *Alaska Quarterly Review*, *Antioch Review*, *Ironwood*, *Partisan Review*, *Quarterly West*, *Raleigh Review*, *Three Rivers Poetry Journal*, and *Western Humanities Review* as well as in the anthologies *Claiming the Spirit Within: A Source book of Women's Poetry*, *Tangled Veins: A collection of Mother & Daughter Poems*, *How Much Earth: The Fresno Poets; Beside the Sleeping Maiden*, *Bear Flag Republic: Prose Poems & Poetics from California*, and *Aspects of Robinson: Homage to Weldon Kees*. A letterpress chapbook, *Snow Flowers*, was published by Westigan Press, and *The Letter C* was published by Tebot Back in the Ash Tree Poetry Series.

from *How Much Earth,* 2001—Sandra Hoben

It was a day in early August 1973, my first day in Fresno, and I was looking for a place to live when I discovered that the steering wheel of my Volkswagon was too hot to touch. Even so, I found an apartment and moved in. I had a chance to study with Peter Everwine and Phil Levine, and to be part of a widening community of writers. My writing and my life would be forever changed and enriched by those years. The voices of my teachers continue to echo when I sit down to write, and lasting friendships, especially with Roberta Spear and Suzanne Lummis, have been invaluable to me as a writer. But that first six months, I wasn't writing, at least not well, and sometimes gripping my pen was as painful as touching that burning wheel. I remember thinking that perhaps I should spend my small savings on a trip to Europe rather than staying put. It was around this I wrote "Pennies," the first poem I kept that year, and a beginning, I believe, of a new lightness in my work. I had so many pennies around because I was in the habit of consulting *The I Ching* ("*The I Ching*," I can hear Phil groan, "not *The I Ching.*") But the ancient book would approve of what was going on in Fresno, and would agree with the values that Phil would articulate twenty years later in *The Bread of Time*. Along with the emphasis on rigorous and exacting craftsmanship, and on telling the truth illuminated by the imagination the heart of the program was the same as the one Phil describes in how own essay on his graduate school experience and his mentor: "We were all taking pride and joy in each other's accomplishments." That winter of '73, wondering if I should stay in Fresno or go to Italy (I can hear Phil groaning, "Fresno, you chose *Fresno?*") I threw the three coins six times and came up with hexagram 58, "The Joyous." Knowledge, it reminded me, comes only through "stimulating discussion with congenial friends," and that "in this way learning becomes many-sided and takes on a cheerful lightness, whereas there is always something ponderous and one-sided about the learning of the self-taught."

The Proof of My Patience—from *Coming Close,* 2013—Sandra Hoben

(An earlier, shorter version of this essay was published in *FIRST LIGHT*, 2013.)

"Send me some poems," he said.

It must have been 1972, the Squaw Valley Community of Writers. Phil had read for scholarships, and I received one. And of course Phil took the time to send a letter to Edith Jenkins, the teacher at Oakland's Grove Street Community College who'd written me a reference. "You must be a poet", Phil wrote to Edith, "because your students are writing so well."

I recall little about what went on in the workshops at Squaw. I don't recall Phil praising my work, or blasting it. What I do remember was the conference I had with him.

I remember the rather crappy cafe at ground level where I was waiting for Phil to show up for our conference. It was summer, but the sky opened up and lightning struck all over the mountain. David Perlman, science editor of the *San Francisco Chronicle,* stood with me, watching the bolts, the downpour. "This doesn't happen," he said, "in the Sierra in summer." Then he counted the seconds; I learned something new about the distance between lightning and thunder. And I was about to learn something else: that Philip Levine would become my teacher, my mentor, my friend.

Phil finally arrived at the cafe. Again, I don't recall that we went over any of my poems. We talked. We drank coffee that tasted like pencil shavings. "There are three students here that are writing well," he said, "and you are one of them. I'm never coming back here," he said. And he never did.

"Send me some poems," he said, and gave me his address. For a year we corresponded; we got into a groove. Each month I would mail off three poems, and he would reply with a letter on yellow legal paper, written with a good pen; and he'd mark up my poems and comment on them. It was a wonderful year. I had him to myself once a month. And of course I had taken to writing on yellow legal pads, and had obtained an expensive fountain pen, a Parker 6I, the one that inks by osmosis. I couldn't afford such a pen, but I found it at the UC Berkeley bowling alley. The pen just sat there, in a lovely wooden groove, where a writing instrument could rest. Is any of this true? Did UC Berkeley even *have* a bowling alley? What was I doing, who was I with? But I kept the Parker: it was a sign. No. Somebody left a pen behind, and I slipped it into my bag. Yellow pads and expensive pens: that was going to do the trick. Poetry turned out to be a lot more than paper and pen: the art of poetry would be work, hard work, and would take a long time, and a lot of failure.

And the letters themselves, well, that's another story.

Some time in the spring of '73, I made my decision: I would move to Fresno for an MA in English, with an emphasis in creative writing. I had a BA from St. John's College, a lot of science, math, philosophy, and some literature dressed up like philosophy. No creativity in that scene. I had moved to Berkeley and was grateful to have had Edith Jenkins and the Grove Street Community College.

When I left Berkeley, I lost my community of friends, the original Peet's coffee shop, I lost the fog and the breeze, the used book stores, and the trips to Shell Beach.

I was lonely in Fresno that first semester and couldn't write a decent poem for months. My poems were like roadkill, nothing to resuscitate. Couldn't I go back to my Berkeley house, my friends, the year of exclusive correspondence with Phil? Correspondence is one thing, a workshop with Phil and a handful of talented students—that was a whole different deal. And Phil was not easy on me. I was somewhat buoyed up when a kid confided that Phil never praised him, or made fun of that student's work. I didn't say it, but I got it: this kid had no talent, and Phil was not going to shred a young person who'd never be a poet. I understood : Phil was hard on me because he believed in me.

One of Phil's ways of dealing with bad poems was to make you laugh, but when you got home things weren't very funny: my poem stinks. Then there was the evening everybody failed and turned in bad poems: "These poems are worse than a newspaper, and poems are supposed to last forever."

Sometime in that semester I walked into Phil's office and sat down. "I can't write anything." His response: "You must change your life." What I needed and what I would slowly receive was the friendship of my peers: Roberta Spear, Paul Saupe, Ernie Benck, Suzanne Lummis, Jon Veinberg, Ernesto Trejo.

Without noticing it, I'd written a poem. A found poem. Each day I wrote in my journal and would look over the week's work—and there was "Pennies." I didn't recall writing the piece, but it was in my journal and in my handwriting. I turned in the poem to the workshop, not expecting much of a response. Phil asked what the group had to say. And they went after me; after all, I'd been writing poorly: "She's using *it* too many times," or "too many repetitions of *here.*" Then Phil had his say. He didn't say *terrific,* he didn't say *marvelous,* but he was clearly taken with the poem. He was delighted. An immature character had shown up in the last stanza, in the last lines:

I could spit
mouthfuls of pennies at him,
but I know he'd spend them on himself
and write,
saying he'd fallen in love,
saying *thank you.*

"Yes," Phil said, "he wrote to her, perhaps a postcard . . ."

The next two semesters of workshop were with Peter Everwine and Chuck Hanzlicek, during which I wrote poems, some of them good, and some had to be defenestrated. But I was writing, and both Chuck and Peter were wonderful teachers.

In the evening workshop, Phil was tough; in the afternoon's Spanish Poetry in Translation class, he had a different demeanor. Phil and Jose Elgorriaga co-taught the course. Elgorriaga, a native speaker and chair of the Foreign Language Department, helped us with our Spanish, the puns, the colloquialisms. Phil pushed the poems, turning them into American English. The word *genial* was used a lot in that class, maybe more so from Elgorriaga, but also from Phil. And the stakes weren't as high—if you make an error in a translation, no big deal; you weren't facing your own poems, just bad translations. Phil was teaching the class, but he was also working on his own writing, translating the Gloria Fuertes book. His own creativity was in play—sometimes he'd just stare out the window at the afternoon light.

Once Roberta Spear arrived late (she had finished her master's but sat in on some classes; she didn't attend workshops, she'd found her own voice). When Roberta walked in, Phil looked up and said, "Hi, sweetheart," something he wouldn't say in a workshop. Or so I think.

In translation class, the most hilarious error was made by Roberta. She'd been working on a Gloria Fuertes poem—a street scene, a tough neighborhood, and its characters. Then she spoke the phrase "and Pepe plays golf." I thought Elgorriaga might fall off his chair: "Pepe plays golf? No! Pepe is a pimp!" But Roberta was certain she'd looked up the word. Check with me first, Elgorriaga said. It was easy to laugh at errors in translations. I can still hear her laughter.

Then the discussion about which poems are untranslatable. Phil said that "The Emperor of Ice Cream" could never be translated. Not possible.

Like my experience in workshop, I was slow on the mark for Spanish Poetry in Translation. I'd chosen the early work of Pablo Neruda—oh, the despair. I dragged in another Neruda poem based on a pun. If the poem isn't any good, then the translation can't fire. Then one day I brought in a Juan Ramon Jimenez poem, "Yellow Spring." It was about yellow and about spring. There was music in the piece, but I hadn't noticed. Phil looked up at me and said one word: *talent* .

I also took an individual study on rhyme and meter with Phil. Again, a slow start. My first piece was about dolphins communicating, something from the news, I suspect. "You don't care about this," he said. But then I succeeded. I don't recall the whole poem, but it started with, "Get up, let out the cat and stare/ at children." I was writing about ordinary things in my life, and the rhymes, the off-rhymes, the meter worked well. "Where did you get this? Where is your time card?" he wanted to know.

I continued to correspond with Phil when I was at the University of Utah, and beyond. I finished the PhD but was soured by academia. Everwine warned me about going to Utah—"just get a job," the wise man said. But I didn't listen. After Utah, I just wanted a job, not a position. While I was finishing my dissertation, I worked as a paralegal in San Francisco, and I liked the action. I had personal knowledge of certain activities (a tweaked sentence, stolen from Didion). Then I had enough of that job.

Roberta Spear worked for a while as a social worker, and brought up a family; she continued to write. And Jon Veinberg had, well, just a job, while writing his poetry and other creative endeavors. There is a tradition of poets having a day job—Wallace Stevens at The Hartford, William Carlos Williams with his patients. Many of Phil's students went on to head creative writing programs and did terrific work. But some of us took other paths. Whatever the path, I had enduring friendships from the Fresno poetry community, and help with my writing, especially from Roberta Spear and Phil.

After I married and had a son, I settled in Mill Valley and taught at a college and as a poet-in-the-schools. My favorite students were first-graders, with their wonderful imaginations and their fearlessness. I returned to Fresno as often as I could; I'd meet with Roberta, Jean Janzen, and sometimes Dixie Salazar, and we'd go over our poems. Roberta was my first reader. She was an essential part of the Fresno poetry community; Phil made that statement in his letter to her, which she showed to me at the Stanford Medical Center. Her death, in 2003 was a devastating loss.

Sam Hamill, of Copper Canyon Press, suggested publishing the new and selected poems of Roberta Spear; Phil was to select the poems and write an introduction, which he did. Because Sam was no longer with Copper Canyon, we chose publisher Malcolm Margolis of Heyday Books. Phil, Peter, and I facilitated the publication of Roberta's *A Sweetness Rising: New and Selected Poems, Edited and with an Introduction by Philip Levine.* A terrific book, and again, there it is: Phil's generosity.

My friend Tilly Nylin, a visual artist, has a mantra: *go where the art is*. I'd noticed that there was a lot of activity around the 2001 Levis Symposium at the Virginia

Commonwealth University, Phil the keynote speaker. *Go where the poetry is.* The symposium was a blast, old friends and new, a wonderful gathering, a celebration of Larry Levis's life and work, and of poetry itself. When I left, I reinvented the manuscript I'd fought with for forty years.

"You, Sandra," Phil once said, "are the proof of my patience."

Philip Levine has given me so much: he's given me laughter; he's spent his own creative energy helping me with my writing; he was there to slash the weeds and let the poem bloom, when no one else could. He believed in me. When I wrote to him, he always responded, with letters that ended with—*Love, Phil*

Ernesto Trejo—1950-1991

Poetry was not the major concern of Ernesto's early life, and in 1967, he moved to Fresno to work at his aunt's restaurant and to attend CSU Fresno State. Although he took an M.A. in economics, his interest turned to poetry and he took writing classes with Philip Levine, Peter Everwine, Robert Mezey and C.G. Hanzlicek. Among many poets he worked with and befriended were Gary Soto, Luis Omar Salinas, David St. John, and Jon Veinberg. In 1973 Ernesto's poems began to appear in literary magazines such as *Kayak*, *Partisan Review*, and *Backwash*. In 1975 a selection of his work appeared in the book *Entrance: Four Chicano Poets*, along with Soto, Salinas, and Leonard Adame. He was accepted into the Iowa Writers Workshop and while there also worked in the International Translation Program.

In 1976 he published *The Rule of Three*, a book of eleven poems translated from the Spanish of Tristan Solarte. In 1977 he published a chapbook of poems in English, *The Day of Vendors*, with a small press in Fresno, Calavera Press, and a chapbook of poems in Spanish, *Instrucciones y senales*. In 1978 he published a second chapbook in Spanish, *Los nombres propios*. Writing poetry in Spanish, Ernesto was concerned with poetry free of the rhetorical style of early modern Mexican Poetry. This concern attracted Ernesto to the poems of Jaime Sabines and with Philip Levine he translated and published *TARUMBA: The Selected Poems of Jaime Sabines*, 1987.

Ernesto returned with his wife Diane and son Victor to Fresno in 1983 where he taught part-time for the Spanish and English departments at CSU Fresno. In 1984 he published his last book in Spanish, *El dia entre las hojas*. In 1985 he took a position in the English Department at Fresno City College where he taught until 1990. In 1990 Ernesto's first full-length collection of poems in English, *Entering A Life*, was published bringing together old work with new. In 1991, barely 40 years old, his life was cut short by cancer. He was survived by his wife Diane until she also died of cancer in 1998. They are survived by their son Victor and daughter Kerry. Ernesto was a much admired poet in and outside of Fresno; he was a beloved husband, father, and friend.

—CB

from *Piecework: 19 Fresno Poets*, 1987—Ernesto Trejo

I was born on March 4, 1950 in Fresnillo, a small, decaying mining town in central Mexico, not far from the birthplace of Ramon Lopez Velarde, the poet. My family soon moved to Mexico City, where times were hard. I remember learning to talk in the sing-songy manner of the natives, streetcars, and magical visits to Chapultepec Park. When I was four we moved again, this time to Mexicali, where I grew up. At the time, the mid-fifties, Mexicali was seen as a frontier town where everyone came with the hope of starting a new life. Thirty years later, they still keep coming. The most pervasive sensation of my childhood was the brutal heat, which nevertheless also explains he beautiful desert landscape and the breathtaking sunsets of such a barren city. Growing up as the fourth child in a family of five, I remember being left alone to pursue what I pleased: boxing and basketball. In school I memorized countless pages of 19th Century Mexican poetry, by and large the worst stuff, which I was good at reciting and which I've luckily forgotten. I moved to Fresno to continue my education. At Fresno State I got an MA in economics in '73. In the meantime, around '69, I became absorbed by poetry after I read Paz, and the beginnings of a friendship with Luis Omar Salinas had a decisive influence on me. Then I met Dianne Lambert, who became my wife. Together we lived in Iowa City for two years while I attended the Writers' Workshop and she managed a motel. For a few years we lived in Mexico City, two blocks away from Chapultepec Park, and traveled by car throughout the country. Then, with the birth of our two children, I learned humility and gained a measure of maturity. Another exciting thing in those years was publishing *Latitudes*, a chapbook series. Publications: three chapbooks of poems, one full length poetry collection, and three volumes of translations. I presently teach at Fresno City College.

"An Interview with Ernesto Trejo for *Arte en Palabra*"—Eleanor Lazardo
(Transcribed from a taped radio interview with Ernesto. Thanks to his daughter Kerry for finding this in his archives and to Dixie Salazar for bringing it back from Mexico.)

Eleanor Lazardo: Hello, my name is Eleanor Lazardo, and today for *Arte en Palabra* we are going to be talking with a poet who lives here in Fresno. His name is Ernesto Trejo, and he is currently teaching English at CSUF. The first thing we should talk about Ernesto is if you can give us a little background in your career as a poet?
Ernesto Trejo: Sure. I started in poetry around eighteen or twenty years old, that's when I became very interested in what language did to me and then the possibilities of language mainly through poetry. And it was the reading of Octavio Paz and Pablo Neruda and Luis Omar Salinas that had a very decisive influence on me.

EL: You are from Mexico?
ET: Yes.

EL: And so you've lived here most of your life though, yes?
ET: No, I have lived here part of my life. I lived here in my late teens and early twenties and then I lived in Mexico for seven or eight years, and I'm living here again now.

EL: So your schooling was in Mexico then? Or partly?
ET: Partly in Mexico and partly here. Yes.

EL: Did you always know that you wanted to write poetry?
ET: No. I think it would be very presumptuous to say that. I think one starts out just like everybody else. You hear very often that children are poets, and I think that's true. I think something happens later on that kills the poetry in children. You know how it is with kids, they say crazy things; they say very imaginative things. They make wild connections between things. They interpret the world in a very poetic way, but something that comes along around the age of seven perhaps, leads you to believe that somethings are rational, and somethings are crazy. That somethings make sense and somethings don't make sense, and I think that's when most people start losing that poetic quality to their thinking and to their ability to express things. So I think I regained this perhaps at a later age.

EL: Your poetry deals with issues or realities of contemporary life. What are your concerns when you write your poetry?

ET: When I'm writing a poem I'm not thinking of issues. I'm not thinking contemporary life. I'm not thinking of large abstractions. I'm thinking mostly of what I want to say about something very specific at that particular time. Whether it is the death of a relative, the passage of time, having children, common experiences that everybody has, but which I perceive to be unique in my case.

EL: Ernesto, you have several books that you have in print. Tell us a little about them whether they are done in English or Spanish.

ET: Sure. The first book that I published, actually a chapbook, a small book, is called *The Day of Vendors* and that was published here in Fresno in 1977 by Calavera Press. And later on I published another book in '77 in Mexico called *Instrucciones y señales*. Then another book in '78, *Los nombres propios*. In 1984, *El día entre las hojas*, another book in Spanish. In addition to that, I published a book of translations of the Panamanian poet Tristán Solarte called *The Rule of Three* in 1976. And in 1979 a co-translation with Philip Levine of the poetry of Jaime Sabines by the title of *Tarumba*.

EL: Would you like to recite a poem from that particular book?

ET: Sure. I think Jaime Sabines exemplifies the ideal of somebody who is very earthy, yet a very profound poet. Not the least affected in his language or his expression, and yet he has managed to create some of the great poems in the Spanish language in this century. I'm going to read something from the elegy that he wrote on the death of his father.

From *Something on the Death of the Eldest Sabines* (Part Two)

II

While the children grow and the hours talk to us,
underground you slowly go out.
Alone and buried light, wick of the darkness,
vein of horror for whoever unearths you.

It's so easy to say, "My father,"
and so hard to find you, larva
of God, seed of hope!
Sometimes I want to cry, and I don't want
to because you enter me
like a landslide, because you enter
like a tremendous wind, like a chill
under the covers,
like a slow worm along the length of my soul.
If only I could say: "Papa, onion,
dust, weariness, nothing, nothing, nothing!"
If I could swallow you with one gulp.
If I could stab you with this ache.
If in this sleeplessness of memories
—opened wound, vomit of blood—
I could hold on to your face!

I know that neither you nor I,
nor a pair of valves,
nor a copper calf, nor those wings
upholding death, nor the foam
in which the sea is wrecked,—no—nor the beaches
the sand, the stones humbled by wind and water,
nor the tree that is grandfather of its shadow,
nor our sun, stepchild of the branches,
nor ripe and incandescent fruit,
not its roots of pearls and fish scales,
nor your uncle, nor your great-grandson, nor your belch,
nor my madness, nor your shoulders,
will know of the dark time that races through us
from the lukewarm veins to the gray hairs.

(Empty time, blister of vinegar,
snail recalling the undertow.)

Here, everything comes, everything passes,
everything, everything ends.
But you? but I? but us?
why did we lift up the word?
what good was love?
which wall
held back death? where was
the black child who guarded you?

I put decapitated angels at the foot of your coffin,
and threw earth, stones, tears on you,
so that you won't leave, so that you won't leave.

EL: That's beautiful. I should mention to our audience that we are unable to have Ernesto read some of his works because we didn't talk about bringing something in English. We do have a lot of his work that he has read in Spanish in another interview. We regret that we can't have you recite any of your work.
ET: Yes, I'm very sorry. Maybe some other time maybe when I publish a next book, I can read something to your audience.

EL: That would be wonderful. We'll look forward to that. Going back to your poetry, who were your major influences while you were writing or while you are still writing?
ET: I think I've had different influences at different times like all poets. At the beginning, as I said, Pablo Neruda was tremendously important to me. The sense of despair of his book *Residence on Earth* was very moving to me. César Vallejo, T.S. Eliot for different reasons, William Carlos Williams for different reasons. Octavio Paz has been an influence all along, different portions of his work at different times. Jaime Sabines, José Gorostiza, it's been different poets at different times. I try to read a lot of poetry from various languages from various countries, so a lot of it has been in translations, French poetry, Chinese poetry.

EL: Just a lot of different poets then. It almost seems that language or art, poetry rather, transcends perhaps languages?

ET: I believe so. What really has a strong reality to it beyond the individual voice of each poet is what the times are like. We are now living in the period of modern poetry, so whether you read poetry from Greece or from France or from England or from Argentina, there is a spirit to it which is the spirit of the 20st century, the spirit of despair, the spirit of the feeling that this may be the last century that we are here and a lot of that seeps its way in through the poetry.

EL: Ernesto, why don't you talk a little bit about, say people that would like to get into poetry or perhaps that is the wrong term, but if they wish to write poetry, what should they do? If someone is out there in our audience listening and they have that urge to write.

ET: That's the most important thing, the urge to write. If you do not have that urge, you'll never become a poet. You can study, you can read, you can hear, you can take classes in literature, classes in history, classes in psychology or anthropology, whatever you think that is going to be of use to you as a poet, but if you do not have that urge to write, to say something, what use to be called inspiration or the call of the muses, then you really have nothing. If you don't have that, don't bother. Maybe do something more useful with your time. But if you do have that inclination, then stick with it. Whether you get recognition or not. Whether you publish or not. Whether other people are aware of the place that your poetry has in your life. Be faithful to your vocation, be faithful to your poetry. Poetry will give you everything that you give to it back and much more. Read, that is, gain a command of the language, that's what you have to work with, words. Nothing more, nothing less. So educate not only your taste but your sensibility.

EL: How would you do that? By reading?

ET: Well, I suppose by reading. First, it is important to read what other people your age are doing, what contemporary poets are doing, what young poets are doing in this country. Or, if you write in Spanish, you want to know what other poets are doing in Spanish. You want to read the masters, the modern masters. You want to read the old masters. So, if you're going to write in English, you have to read Yeats. You have to read Hopkins; you have to read Shakespeare. Those are not going to be your themes or your concerns but hear that language and see what it says to you, hear that music. Read E. E. Cummings, read Wallace Stevens, those are the masters. A very useful thing for poets is to educate your sensibility, which may be an elevated way of saying, really learn the most that you can about what it is you want to learn. Don't be distracted by bad poetry.

EL: What would you term bad poetry?

ET: Bad poetry is pretentious. Bad poetry is silly. It's rhetorical. If it moves you, if something moves you, I think you have a very good first indication that that is poetry.

EL: That's interesting. Ernesto, poets have often been compared to gods since they both create. How do you feel about this statement?

ET: I think that it is a little bit overblown. I think poets are actually a more humble form of life. I think they may be gods in a metaphorical way in the sense that they create worlds, they create entire theaters of the imagination where things take place, where emotions are played back and forth. Maybe in that sense you can speak of little gods, but I don't think it's in the spirit of arrogance. It isn't that at all.

EL: Ernesto, is there anything more you would like to add to this interview as we come to a close?

ET: Very little. I want to thank you Eleanor for having me here and for giving me a chance to read some of my poems in Spanish and translations and for giving me a chance to speak to your audience.

EL: Thank you so very much. We really appreciate you being here. We've been taking to Ernesto Trejo who is a poet here in Fresno. For Arte en Palabra, this has been Eleanor Lazardo, we thank you for your kind attention.

"Ernesto Trejo," *Dictionary of Literary Biography, Chicano Writers* Edition, 1992—Christopher Buckley

A spare and considered surrealism resonates throughout the poems of Ernesto Trejo. From his early work to his recent, whether in Spanish or in English, Trejo celebrates the imagination and its power to breathe a sense of expanded consciousness into the objects and events of the world. He employs inventive language and imagery, yet he is never overtaken by abstraction or the temptations of style for its own sake. His landscapes and scenarios are centered in the simple yet often unexpected situations of daily life. Trejo manages to keep a clear narrative path moving through most of his work while at the same time his phrasing emphasizes compression. This technique makes the emotions and ideas of his poems accessible to the reader even though Trejo is working at the edge of the surreal image making process. With both a powerful imagery and a great sense of compassion, his work enlivens those portions of life we often take for granted. His poems make us take a second and third look at the world around us and at ourselves

In a 1986 interview he said, "The first time that I saw Dali's barren landscapes, I recognized them immediately, for they were all around me in Mexicali. Looking back, I could say that I searched intuitively and found my sources as a poet; the truth is that I was brought up on some good, but mostly bad Modernists, the Mexican post-symbolists. I had no idea that the great Lopez Velarde—the first innovator and father figure of twentieth century Mexican poetry—was born in a town near Fresnillo. " But poetry was not the major concern of Ernesto's early fife. In 1967, drawn by the prospects of an education and a degree in engineering, Ernesto moved to Fresno, California. He worked at his aunt's restaurant and attended California State University, Fresno, where his interests switched from engineering to economics and then to poetry. He received a B.A. and an M.A. in economics while studying poetry and poetry writing under the now-famous group of Fresno poets and teachers, Philip Levine, Peter Everwine, Robert Mezey, and C. G. Hanzlicek. Trejo's peers were the last of many groups of good young poets to come out of Fresno; among poets he befriended and worked with were Gary Soto, Luis Omar Salinas, David St. John, and Jon Veinberg. Around 1973, Trejo began to publish some poems in literary magazines such as *Kayak, Partisan Review,* and *Backwash.* In 1975 Trejo's poetry appeared, in *Entrance: 4 Chicano Poets,* which also included work by Soto, Leonard Adame, and Salinas. After Fresno, he was accepted into the prestigious Writers' Workshop at the University of Iowa for the M.F.A. program in poetry, and he received his degree in 1976. While at Iowa, Trejo also worked in the International Translation Program and published *The Rule of Three* (1976), a book of eleven poems translated from the Spanish of Tristan Solarte, the contemporary Panamanian poet and novelist.

Since that time Trejo has published poems in both Spanish and English and as translated English poetry into Spanish and Spanish poetry into English. Although he moved to Mexico City in 1976 to take a position as an economist with the Jose Lopez-Portillo government, he continued to write poetry in both languages. In 1977 a small press in Fresno, Calavera Press, published his first book of English poems, a chapbook entitled *The Day of Vendors*.

In these first groupings of poems Trejo established a voice and style which remain his hallmark. Sharp turns of image and language as well as narrative characterize the poems; his work focuses on the individual imagination and how it is tied to the deeper and more concrete events in life, how the imagination can transform the ordinary and make for an illuminated sense of experience. Often he begins with a mundane occasion and then allows the imagination to take over and change and amplify it. A good example of this can be seen in the poem 'This Is What Happened," in which Trejo explores the possible meaning of an incident by letting the imagination rewrite the plot of the first section of the poem in which the speaker tells of his car crashing to avoid hitting an animal. The second section of the poem treats the incident in a more magical, sinister, and weighty manner:

> You forgot the words and made some up. You were
> confident. You knew
> I would die that night yet you were confident.
> You opened the door and swerved the car at the
> curve. There were no animals.
> There was only me on the shoulder of the road. My
> body a still river, my head on a lagoon.
> You thought you saw a swallow, a
> black swallow, and still you didn't lose
> control. The mountain to your left collapsed
> and I leaped on you, where1 have been ever since,
> lodged somewhere between your neck and your
> shoulder.

Even when Trejo creates a poem which proceeds primarily on images, he anchors those images in a very personal tone, as in the opening of 'The Day of Vendors":

> Before dawn I called for you, my poem, but you didn't come.
> I had woken up to the song of the cardinal perched
> on the fence. You weren't at my desk in all the words
> chat I wrote down and crossed.
> You weren't in my shoes nor in the letters chat had come and gone all
> month nor in the space held by a window, its fourteen trees, its seven
> stars that always lag behind.

All of Trejo's work, whether in Spanish or in English, demonstrates a fine balance between imagination and startling imagery, and the personal and poignant tone of narrative. In 1977 Trejo published *Instrucciones y senales* (Instructions and Signals), and in 1978 he published another chapbook of poems in Spanish, *Los nombres propios* (Proper Names). The poems of *Instrucciones y senales* are more in the imagistic/surreal vein, while *Los nombres propios* moves more in a narrative mode. Both books show Trejo's concern with writing poetry in Spanish that is free of the rhetorical style of early modern Mexican poetry. This concern attracted Trejo to the poems of Jaime Sabines and moved him to his major work of translation (co-translated with Philip Levine), *Tarumba* (1987), a bilingual book of the contemporary Mexican poet's work. Many of the hallmarks of Sabines's work could well be those of Trejo's; Sabines's vocabulary is colloquial, his themes are personal, and his strategies are often imagistic. In the introduction, Trejo and Levine state, "Sabines gives a human shape to his images, so that the cumulative effect is to give us a reflection of ourselves in the world, a world transformed into our spirit." The poems of Sabines filter the illogical and ungenerous details of life and offer a reality that, while not always desirable, is compassionate in its awareness.

Much the same can be said for Trejo's work to date. *El día entre las hojas* (The Day Among the Leaves, 1984), his book-length collection of poems in Spanish, Trejo is out to dissect appearance and reality and those fleeting moments made accessible only through the power of memory. The book is divided into three sections: imagistic, narrative; and a third section that combines aspects of both styles. There are "voices" in some of these poems; we hear Sabines giving conflicting answers to his conscience, Georg Trakl speaking of the "heavy song" as he listens to his sister sobbing and sees her blue tears in the moonlight, and Dante as he fights back his own arrogance and greed. The short poem "Imaginaciones" (Imaginations) echoes Ezra Pound's famous "In A Station of the Metro": the ducks in Chapultepec Park are white petals in the darkness, and black umbrellas under the rain have "black veins" trembling with every step. Do these images signify impending death? The answer, or a certain balance, may appear a few pages later in a poem dedicated to Luis Omar Salinas, "Ciscara de día" (The Day's Rind). A catalogue of everyday events—kids and dogs playing in the street, two drunk lovers making love on a creaky cot, people shopping on credit—is followed by nothing but the oncoming darkness.

Trejo's most recent publication is *Entering a Life* (1990). This is his first full-length collection of poems in English, and it brings together old work with new. Any of the new poems and the longer poems in this book show Trejo's skill with narrative and autobiographical material, for while the subject is personal and many poems often have "plot," Trejo is masterful at demonstrating the many dimensions one event might take on. The title poem is a fine example of the many takes on experience that Trejo's imagination and speculation can bring to an everyday domestic situation:

> I remember that when I was 12
> I heard about an uncle who twenty years before
> had gone away for good. But he hadn't died
> like his younger brother, whose life was taken slowly
> by TB. My uncle who disappeared simply stopped
> writing home, stopped sending money & postcards
> from exotic places: Los Angeles, Pittsburgh,
> Des Moines . . . [.]

The poem goes on to explore the family story about Uncle Felix and the rumors about his whereabouts. The speaker makes up stories that show his compassion for his uncle's life; he imagines him alone running a motel in Missouri, doing time in El Paso for smuggling workers, or prospering as the owner of a jewelry store. Finally, he brings his imagination into the service of honor—he wants an honorable memory for his uncle and by extension an honorable life for himself:

These stories went on for years, even after your parents died
& your brothers & sisters were scattered around
like bruised fruit.
Uncle, after 20 years of stories I know so little . I want
to imagine you content, honoring your name. I want you
falling in love once with a girl whose love
matched the intensity of yours. I see you boisterous &
the two of you drunk with love for a few years.
Until one day she runs off with a lover & leaves you
with two daughters whom you raise. Years pass
& you are left a little less happy & unsure
of everything & ashamed at being shortchanged.

Trejo pulls out all the possibilities to get at the uncertainty of our lives, but always he shows in his speculation great compassion, for all of the outcomes are possible and real—all are earned by the true and human emotion which enters each poem. Even in the marvelous and somewhat surreal "E." poems in which Trejo creates a character who moves through life and is moved by it, we can tell that the poet's inventiveness is firmly anchored in the real world where often it is only imagination and song that lift us above our suffering and allow us to cherish our lives.

In 1983 Trejo returned to Fresno where he taught part-time for the Spanish and English departments at California State University. Trejo was on the English faculty at Fresno City College from 1985 to 1990, and he taught creative writing, basic writing, and an introduction to literature course that emphasized Latin-American writers. From the late 1970s to the present Trejo's poetry, translations, and critical expertise have been acknowledged and valued. As early as the late 1970s small literary magazines in America were paying attention to his work. In 1978 *The Chowder Review* ran a very favorable review of his first chapbook in English, *The Day of Vendors*, and in 1979 a review of *Entrance: 4 Chicano Poets in Abraxas* also praised Trejo's early work. In the early 1980s Trejo's poems drew critical praise in Mexico. Sandro Cohen, editor of the anthology *Palabra nueva* (1981), wrote that "Ernesto Trejo is a poet of measure, of contemplation. . . . Like those of Wordsworth's, Trejo's emotions are only valid when they are safely installed in the past, and this makes his poetry tranquil, meditative, with a power that is not perceived in action but in the recuperation of an ever slippery yesterday." Reviewing Trejo's *El dia entre las hojas* for the journal *Vuelta* (5 October 1984), Cohen wrote, "There are in Trejo's poetry two aesthetic poles . . . there is the need to build elaborate metaphorical apparatuses: strange turns of language which owe their ethereal character to the fact that their metaphorical structure does not rest on specific properties of the immediate world. On the other hand . . . an opposite ethics . . . one which addresses objects directly to explore them more for what they are than for that which they could represent. 'One must sing the thing in itself,' could be the motto of his poetics."

Trejo was in demand for readings and conferences throughout the 1980s. In October 1985, along with Philip Levine, he was invited to give a reading of his own work and lecture on Sabines's at the New Latin American Poetry conference m Durango, Colorado. In 1987 he presented a paper on "Border Literature" in Mexicali sponsored by Dirrecion de Asuntos Culturales and the Institute for the Regional Studies of the Californias of San Diego State Umversity. He also gave poetry readings at the University of California, Santa Barbara, and at the University of Southern California, Los Angeles. In Fresno, Trejo often gave readings of his poetry; he read at the Metropolitan Museum m 1984 and 1989, at the Fresno Art Museum in 1990, and at the "Day of the Dead" reading in 1989 sponsored by the Art Americas Foundation.

It is important too that Trejo's work is recognized by many well-known contemporary poets in the United States. Edward Hirsch, David St. John, and Gary Soto have all volunteered comment for Trejo's *Entering a Life*. Hirsch states, "Ernesto Trejo is a poet of mysteries and incarnations, of secret unnamed presences, of the magical interior spaces of childhood and the luminous floating world that flares and throbs, that burns in time." St. John has written that "Ernesto Trejo's poetry is filled with an extraordinary exuberance and vitality. These are poems of enormous humor and wisdom. These poems are like our fondest, wildest dreams—those which suddenly speak to us with the diamond-edged voice of true experience." And Gary Soto affirms, "He writes with great invention a long-lined, ambitious poem as well as a refined lyric. In both instances, it is evident that he cares about his subjects, namely family, friends, childhood in Mexico and his adult years in the United States, the everyday life he carves for himself, and that often romantic but shadowy figure he calls "E.""

"Afterword—Ernesto Trejo and the Making of *Tarumba*" from *Tarumba: Selected Poems of Jaime Sabines*—Philip Levine

This collection of the translations of the poems of Jaime Sabines has had several starts and now it has a second ending. It began back in 1968 when Mark Strand asked me to translate the poems of Jose Emilio Pacheco, Efrain Huerta, and Jaime Sabines for a volume he and Octavio Paz were editing to be called *New Poetry of Mexico*. Mark seemed to know I would not be excited by the work of Huerta and Pacheco, and so he offered Sabines as a lure. He was, of course, shrewd, for I fell in love with Sabines' unique voice and wild imagination, as well as his use of the vernacular. I had never before read a poet writing in Spanish who came so close to sounding like me, only a me with more daring and wit, a me obsessed with sexual love and furious that the world provided no place for it to flower. I was especially drawn to his book *Tarumba* in which he creates and addresses an alter ego who is no more and no less than his own soul wandering in the wilderness of his own lost self. I was reminded of Weldon Kees' Robinson poems, of which there are only a few; whereas Sabines had created an entire collection in which the poems were by turns morose, skeptical, outrageous, and comic, Kees' poems were consistently in the same desperate, suicidal voice. Seven of my translations—I'd done nine—appeared in the Strand/Paz collection, published in 1970. And that was that for a few years.

In the spring of 1971 the Spanish scholar and critic Jose Elgorriaga—then the head of the Foreign Language Department at California State University, Fresno—approached me with a proposal that together we teach a course in translation into English of the poetry written in Spanish during the then-present century. As I was also working on the poems of Gloria Fuertes, Jorge Guillen, and Miguel de Unamuno for Hardie St. Martin's marvelous anthology *Roots and Wings*, I agreed to try it. My finest student from the previous semester, Ernesto Trejo, then pursuing a graduate degree in economics at Cal State, enrolled, and this present collection was about to get its second start. I don't really know if Ernesto discovered Sabines in that class, or if he already knew him, but when I brought to class the first draft of a new translation from the *Tarumba* poems Ernesto caught fire.

Ernesto on fire was something to behold. His brilliance and energy lit up his amazing face until I thought to myself, People this beautiful don't exist, for in truth I think Ernesto was one of the most beautiful creatures I have ever seen and by far the most beautiful person who failed to recognize his own beauty. What I did not know about Ernesto was that he was publishing poems in Spanish in his native Mexico; in truth I did not then know he was Mexican, for he had almost no accent. I should have suspected, for his English was always perfectly grammatical, a rare condition among my students educated in California's

Central Valley. I made the discovery after I'd asked him where he was from; he answered Fresnillo (little Fresno, *little ash tree* in translation); I asked where that was, believing it must be a nearby town so many of which have Spanish names—Merced, Madera, Mariposa, Malaga for example. It was in the province of Zacatecas, he told me. He had come to the States at the age of seventeen. Startled, I asked why his English was so perfect; his answer was that he'd studied it in high school. (I studied French in high school and can't ask for a glass of water.)

In Los Angeles he located a copy of *Tarumba* in Spanish and began furiously translating the poems. I took up the challenge and did likewise. So each week the class would meet, and Elgorriaga would savage my translations for their inaccuracies and Ernesto's for their proximity to street English. This produced several heated arguments, for Ernesto was committed to the notion that Mexican poetry had to abandon its rhetoric and its elitism and get down to where the people spoke and lived. Jose was, in truth, a Spaniard as well as a dues-paying member of academia, and the cultured and hermetic voice of Juan Ramon Jimenez, the formality of Guillen, and the high-flown diction of Unamuno in no way bothered him: for him, this was modern poetry in Spanish. Both men defended their positions with passion; Jose felt tradition was on his side, a tradition which Ernesto found suffocating. Their biggest quarrel came when Ernesto translated a few of my poems into Spanish: "You can't do that in Spanish," Jose shouted. Ernesto was too civil to shout back; he merely pointed out that he had already done it, and furthermore, that Mexican poetry in the future would be in the spoken language of Mexicans.

When the semester ended, Ernesto suggested we keep working on the translations of Sabines and that instead of doing them separately we might do them together. I recognized immediately that this would make it easier for me, as I had learned Spanish in Spain from Spaniards and quite often I failed to grasp the subtleties of Mexican Spanish; nor did I even hear Mexican Spanish in my head. Castillian is far more metallic and "quick" than Mexican Spanish, which to my ear is softer and more beautiful. With the exception of the final poem in the collection, all the work in the last section of the book we did together. Before the year ended, I thought we were nearing the completion of a good-sized collection, so we applied for a grant from the Columbia Translation Center and got it. Ernesto, now married, was supporting himself as a cook in his aunt's restaurant, and the grant allowed him to devote more time to the work.

I no longer remember why it took almost six years for the completed book to be published. Ernesto went off to the University of Iowa to continue his education in the writing of poetry in English; after he got his MFA he and his family moved to Mexico City, where he was employed as an economist by the administration of Lopez-Portillo. Twin Peaks Press of San Francisco published the original version of *Tarumba: The Selected Poems of Jaime Sabines* in 1977. The first draft of the introduction to that volume—which is also the introduction to this version—was written by Ernesto and revised by me. The owners of Twin Peaks Press (after also publishing a volume of the selected poems of the Dutch poet Rutger Kopland) moved to Holland with most of the copies of our Sabines; what became of those copies no one seems to know.

In 1983 Ernesto's family—which now included his son Victor and his daughter Kerry, as well as his wife Dianne—moved back to Fresno where Ernesto took a position teaching literature, composition, and creative writing at Fresno City College. He had already published chapbooks of his poems written in English and in Spanish, and in 1984 he published a large collection of poems in Mexico City, *El dia entre las hojas* (The Day Among the Leaves). In 1990 Arte Público of Houston published *Entering a Life*, a collection of forty-six of his poems written in English. The voice he creates is marvelously resourceful; in the space of a few lines he can go from utter seriousness to surreal comedy; the two constants are compassion and wit. In the background one feels the presence of Sabines, but a Sabines who has read and learned from Wallace Stevens to create a poetry like none other in English. Like Sabines he creates an alter ego, the mysterious E, though unlike Sabines he usually speaks in the voice of this imagined self:

E. CURSES THE RICH

San Teodulo, give them vinegar when they thirst.
Holy Peter, when they hunger look the other way.
St. Frigid, if they bleed have some salt on hand.
John the Baptist, drown them.
Blessed Caldron of St. Ursula, bubble in their ears . . .

For me his most moving poems are those in which he celebrates the boundless gifts of his ancestors, which he embodies, and those in which he turns inward to investigate that strange and mercurial creature we call the self. It is in the latter especially we encounter his astonishing gift for invention and his almost sculptural sense of exactly how the world appears:

You forgot the words and made some up.
You were confident. You knew
I would die that night yet you were confident.
You opened the door and swerved the car at the
curve. There were no such animals. My body a
still river, my head on a lagoon.
You thought you saw a swallow, a
black swallow, and still you didn't lose
control. The mountains to your left collapsed
and I leaped on you, where 1 have been ever since,
lodged somewhere between your neck and your
shoulder.

(from "This Is What Happened")

Less than a year after the publication of *Entering a Life*, Ernesto was diagnosed with cancer. He fought it with all his will. "I will not roll over like a dog," he said to me. So murderous was the chemotherapy he had to take a leave from teaching. That spring it so happened that for the last time I was teaching the course in translation with Jose Elgorriaga. When Ernesto discovered this he asked if he could attend, which he did every week no matter how ravaged he was by the therapy. His love for poetry in Spanish and in English was so great and so obvious that on days he felt even slightly human he brought a radiance to that shabby classroom. In the spring of 1991, one week before the end of the semester and only a few days after his forty-first birthday, he died. The poetry world of Fresno has not recovered from his loss.

In 2005, having only two copies of the original version of *Tarumba* and having been asked for copies for some years, I decided to seek its republication. I have added several translations of Sabines' poems whose existence I was unaware of in 1975.

Philip Levine
Fresno, May, 2006

Gary Soto

Gary Soto has published more than forty books for children, young adults and adults, including *Too Many Tamales, Chato's Kitchen, Baseball in April, Buried Onions* and *The Elements of San Joaquin*. He is the author of *In and Out of Shadows*, a musical about undocumented youth, the one-act comedies *Novio Boy* and *Nerdlandia*, and, most recently, *The Afterlife*, a one-act play about teen murder and teen suicide. His books have sold more than five million copies and some have been translated into French, Italian, Japanese, Korean and Spanish. His poem "Oranges" is the most anthologized in contemporary literature. He lives in Berkeley, California.

from *Piecework: 19 Fresno Poets,* 1987—Gary Soto

Born in Fresno 1952 and raised in industrial South Fresno and near Romain playground where I was known as "Blackie" from having spent years in the sun. Was no good at playground sports but enjoyed them nevertheless: kickball, four square, tether ball, "jump and die" on the swings, and softball. Went to Emerson, St. John's, Jefferson, Washington Jr. High and Roosevelt High. Went to school, as my mother put it, "to eat my lunch," because I don't remember learning a damn thing during my twelve years in school. Along with my sister Debra, though, frequented the Free Public Library, which I consider a great gift to the poor. Devoured the *Meg* book series (*Meg Goes Boating, Meg and Her Friends, Meg on Lost Island*) during my elementary school years and later, after wasting my junior high years in cadets, read Steinbeck and Bram Stoker and Jules Verne. Also read Poe but found him a bore. Went to City College with the unfounded notion of becoming a city planner. Was saved, though, when I discovered poetry: Edward Field, Kenneth Koch, Gregory Corso. Transferred to Fresno Sate where I took two classes from Philip Levine. Decided to try graduate school and went to UC Irvine where I roomed with fellow poet Jon Veinberg in Laguna Beach, which was such a boring place that by the end of two years I had written two manuscripts of poems. Graduated with and MFA in 1976, began publishing and, after a few stops here and there, have lived in the Bay Area since 1977. Have four books of poems, two essay collections, and a novel. Have been married for eleven years to the former Carolyn Oda, am the father of a daughter, Mariko, and teach at Berkeley.

from *The Geography of Home: California's Poetry of Place,* 1999—Gary Soto

I conjure up inside my head an image of our old street, one that was torn down in the name of urban renewal at the beginning of the 1960s. It was, as some might imagine, a blighted area: junkyard to the left of us, a pickle factory across the street, broom factory and warehouse of books and magazines down the alley, the almighty Sun-Maid Raisin refinery in the distance, and weedchoked vacant lots. Braly Street was an area that was almost all Mexican. This was south Fresno, where there were plans to bulldoze our barrio and make room for an industrial park. Nothing of the sort was constructed, and the good people of Fresno remember this. To this day there are empty lots, weeds and rubble, and the meandering of stray cats. This place, this emptiness, and these few totems of the past haunt me and have shaped my work and its sense of loss.

These pictures muster up memory, imagination, and the willingness to care for the smallest of objects. It's not unusual for me to close my eyes for a moment or two, to see people and things in their place, from my father, dead now, and an uncle, also dead, to our dusty-white house, the bean plants, the almond tree where I hung ridiculously by an army belt, the fishless pond, my uncle back from Korea sleeping in the sun porch. Nothing much happened. No one pushed ahead, no one got rich. Everyone leaned their sadness on fences, sat in twos and threes on porches, or, if you were younger, bobbed on car fenders. We all faced the street, that river of black asphalt, and kept our eyes busy on every car that passed. I spent my first six years running like a chicken from one dirt yard to another and I can't think of a more curious or unadorned childhood. It's these images that I take to the page, whether the subject is that street or another street and time. It's these first images, these first losses when our street was leveled to the height of yellow weeds, that perhaps made me a writer.

from *How Much Earth*, 2001—Gary Soto

For me, Fresno's streets have mattered, especially the crisscross action of Divisadero and Van Ness where I once lived with my bride, now my wife of twenty-five years. This location is where I became a poet in 1977. My first book, *The Elements of San Joaquin*, had just been published that spring, but I was still feeling around for a strategy to writing a poetry that was my own. I believe my brief tenure in the cottage apartments at Divisadero and Van Ness helped me grow. The place itself was an urban solitude as these small cottages (six of them) were holdouts of the last dwellings of what had been at one time a vital neighborhood. The houses were gone by then and were replaced by small offices, ramshackle bars, a funeral home, a bridal shop, half-way houses and the adult theater called The Venus, in whose shadows breathed the moist grunts of its patrons. It was under this influence that I began to read Pablo Neruda deeply and saw that his work was closer to my spirit than any other poet, ancient or otherwise. I read him in our little bedroom, my head on a pillow and my wife, a seamstress, in the other room cutting patterns for me on the floor.

Fresno's streets mattered and still matter. I can name them off by the dozens and none of them, however, are north of Shaw, let alone the sprawl north of Herndon. I don't know those people up north and I, suspect, they don't know me. It's the southern reaches of Fresno, the Westside, Calwa and Malaga, that know me. I appreciate my readership, both the young and the grown, the educated and those picking up books for the first time. I appreciate the other poets of Fresno, a salty bunch. Their genius shines under the sun of a place I call home."

"Where Can You Go? An Interview with Gary Soto" from *Quarterly West*, 1998-99 & *Appreciations*—Christopher Buckley

Christopher Buckley: Ralph J. Mills, the poet-critic who wrote many reviews in the late '70s and '80s, wrote of *The Elements of San Joaquin*—your first book—that "I am reminded a little of Jean Genet's imaginative, utterly personal transformation of what is vilified, outcast condemned into objects of scared awe or veneration." How do you think this description of your early work is true?

Gary Soto: First, this book came out when I was twenty-four, a tyke really, and when I first read this comment I was baffled by the thoughtfulness of phrasing and, my God, I was being compared to a French writer! Second—as I recalled then and I recall now—I was fully absorbed with the small details of my childhood. I was in awe of them, from my little pinto beans on Braly Street to a couple of dirt clods on Thomas Street.

CB: But do you think that every small detail deserves attention? Since you and I are from the same generation—poets who completed our MFA's in the mid 70s—we were encouraged to write about the everyday. Was this good advice?
GS: True, the mundane gets plenty of coverage in every beginning poetry workshop across the country. I find no fault in this. I even encourage the worldliness of the everyday. When one of my teachers gave me the go-ahead to write about the seemingly insignificant, I had enough fodder to fill a number of notebooks, I think that if you truly feel for those small moments or small "things," if you look at my essay collection *A Summer Life*, then you as a writer shouldn't feel embarrassed. *A Summer Life*, as you probably remember, is a collection of forty essays just about such ordinary objects as shovels, bikes, inner tubes, etc. I was five when, for instance, I discovered a handbrake and it was just about the most interesting contraption that I had come across.

CB: Writing in _POETRY_, Alan Williamson said, "[Soto] may be the most exciting poet of poverty in America to emerge since James Wright and Philip Levine." Does poverty play an important part of your appreciation, your veneration of the small?
GS: Perhaps my early work could be characterized as the stuff of poverty. Where I grew up in south Fresno, there wasn't a whole lot, either in the house or in the neighborhood. It was Chicano Zen there, the nothingness of nothingness, the *nada de nada*, a wiped-out planet of vacant lots and abandoned businesses. I think the emptiness of the place made me a poet. If I had lived in a typical neighborhood filled with conveniences and commercial crap I would have been another person. In fact, I'm still saddened that we had to move from the area. The City Fathers had condemned homes in the name of "urban renewal," a policy that never took hold. To this day no large factories arrived to replace chose homes that were torn down. The entire neighborhood laments our move from what people driving past could see only see as a blighted area. But that *barrio* was recently celebrated with a picnic of the oldsters from the area, this done at Kearney Park. Everyone dressed up in their '50s outfits and we tried as best we could to bring it to life.

CB: It sounds like you have a lasting tenderness toward the area. Can there possibly be any nostalgia for the trappings of poverty, now that you've moved so far beyond it?
GS: Of poverty, no. Of being able to exercise my childhood to its fullest on that emptiness, yes, I agree. That little area of Braly Street was exciting because we had the run of the place, we Mexicans and hard core Okies with nothing but dirt under our feet. It was a neighborhood, landlocked from the better parts of Fresno, separated by train tracks, hidden away by the jutting skyline of factories, and we were like our own country. To take a look at this place, I think you have to read my early prose, either *Living Up the Street* or *A Summer Life*, and my early poetry books, *The Elements* and *Where Sparrows Work Hard*. Then you'll grasp my love for it. As I said, I'm sorry that we had to move from that area and am full of awe for one friend's family that stuck it out. They lived on Van Ness all the way through her college years. At this picnic that I mentioned, she told me, "I was wondering where everyone was going." We abandoned her and in doing so we lost out.

CB: What do you mean by "lost out?"

GS: I think that if we as a family had continued to live on Braly Street a whole mess of experiences would have opened up. There would have been more veneration for debris. I would love to have awakened to weeds and vacant lots, especially on a Saturday morning. I loved those Saturdays when the machinery from the surrounding warehouses and small factories stopped.

CB: Looking back, what was the likelihood coming from your background that you were going to become a writer? How did you feel about your chances of receiving an advanced education coming out of high school?

GS: No likelihood at all. I was such a lousy student from day one. I could barely tie my shoelaces by the end of kindergarten and by the time they were graduating students in 1970, if you spelled your name correctly you got a diploma. I graduated high school with something like a 1.6. There was no way my first grade teacher, Mrs. Yamaguchi, would count on me to grace the world with poetry. I remember her dragging my skinny little ass to the front of the class and asking, "How many of you want Gary to go to the principal's office?" The hands went up like spears, even my girlfriend and my best friend, Darrell, voted me out of their lives. At least for a part of the day. And that was the beginning of my education! Then again, being Mexican, no one thought that I or others could create something other than, say, employment for cops and security guards. This was the late 1950s and every family that I knew, we all knew, were working in the fields, Sun-Maid Raisin, warehouses, in schools as janitors, in gardens as *jardineros*.

CB: Readers of your poetry and nonfiction know that you lost your father at an early age and that together with your brothers and sister you suffered an abusive stepfather. Does the atmosphere of family affect writers?

GS: Family won't go away, and the hurt you cause them and the hurt they cause you is permanent. A couple of years ago I was on "Voice of America," the radio program, and I behaved badly when the interviewer asked something like, "There must have been a lot of storytelling within your family." She suspected that Mexican Americans must have sat around the kitchen telling these wonderful and touching stories. I could have played along and said, "Oh yes," to storytelling—cuentos—in order to reinforce their impression of Chicanos. I told her that our household was a chilling zoo of drunkenness and vicious yelling. Paul Zinder's *The Effects of Gamma Rays on Man-in-the Moon Marigolds* looked simply divine compared to the years in my family household. As for the death of my father, yes, of course, that had to have had an effect on me, my brother and sister, and the effect of uncertainty was amplified when I started Catholic school. Just about every day someone dead was being rolled up into the church and then out of the church, a sort of assembly line. Until I was thirty-two and just about out of the woods from a major depression, I recall having dreams in which I was trying to rebuild the house. In these dreams, I was holding a hammer and more than once was patching the roof. What could be clearer than my desire to maintain a house, even if it was just flashes of light behind my eyes?

CB: What drew you to writing poetry?

GS: It's the same with so many other poets: I fell in love with reading poetry, especially the beat poets, who were cussing up a storm and seemingly wild in their pursuit of shocking the reader. This was 1972 and I was at Fresno City College. Plus, there was a set of experiences that suggested to me, that poetry was the right art in which to let my fingers bleed.

CB: Then you went to Fresno State and studied with Philip Levine and Peter Everwine?

GS: No, I never took a class from Everwine there, and I can't say that I "studied" with Levine. No one really studied with him. You listened to jokes and stories, most of them not entirely true but a pleasure nevertheless. When he got to actually teaching the class, you listened up. I was completely sold over to poetry by the fall 1972 and I wanted someone to tell me how to do my own. I was no-nonsense and a good listener, the best kind of student because I didn't whine or deny the criticism. I was such a poor writer at the time, so Levine mostly corrected my grammar and sorry writing. He helped me, as he helped others, by showing us, nearly line by line, how to use language. I'm grateful for his attention, which, as I think about it, amounted to not more than five hours of actual individual instruction. I got my hours and ran with them.

CB: What do you mean by "five hours?"

GS: I mean that Levine looked at six poems in fall of 1972, and he probably spent about twenty minutes on each. A year later, he looked at another six poems. If you do your math, you figure that the individual instruction was not intense or built on a palsy-walsy teacher-student relationship. But whatever he told me stuck; I didn't need a relationship with him outside those two semesters. I don't see him or ever write him. Again, I wasn't bullshitting around, and if any of my teachers tended to bullshit for their living; I moved on. I was in love with reading poetry and, in time, in love with writing.

CB: Can you talk a bit about your early narrative style, especially in *The Tale of Sunlight* and *Where Sparrows Work Hard?* These collections are consistently charged with fresh imagery and inventive phrasing. Were South American writers an influence?

GS: I believe so. I remember reading Garcia Marquez's *One Hundred Years of Solitude* in the summer of 1973, reading it in front of my girlfriend's air conditioning and thinking, "My God, what is this?" It didn't sound like Steinbeck. And it wasn't *The Great Gatsby*. It was just about the most exhilarating writing a reader could encounter. Garcia Marquez didn't give a reader time to rest. It was one marvelous image or perception or immensely universal feel on every page. His genius was unfair to potato heads like us English majors, but the beauty of his creation is lasting and for everyone. And then, of course, there was Pablo Neruda's poetry, especially the odes, which were thin as string, full of cadence, and so imagistic . . . The *Sparrow* book was a slight departure from *The Elements* or *The Tale of Sunlight*. It was an ugly world in these poems, though still imagistically driven. There is less promise of earthly rewards in these poems and the narratives are less swift and, imagewise, not so much filled with flash of me showing off. I'm convinced that my own poetic batteries are recharged by other people's work. We're not speaking of imitation but the happiness you get from reading. A half-hour of reading solves all problems, including stylistic ones.

CB: Do you have favorite poets?

GS: Too many to number, really. I do admire, however, some prose stylists immensely and wouldn't mind mentioning their names in print: God bless Thomas Berger, Harry Crews, Evan Connell, James Crumley, Pete Dexter, Carson McCullers! My favorite book is *Hunger* by Knut Hamsun. It's the story of all writers who are reduced to selling buttons off their shirts. You and I have been there, haven't we?

CB: Plenty of times. You were a pioneer in the building of Chicano literature. You were the first to appear in leading magazines, such as *Poetry* and *The New Yorker,* and the first to have a university press do your poetry. We're, of course, speaking of *The Elements of San Joaquin.* What is your connection to other Chicano writers? How are you perceived?

GS: Initially, there were some Chicano poets who wanted to tar-and-feather me because I wasn't political enough, that my bravery of *viva la raza* stance wasn't apparent. I remember one student asking, "How can you stand being Gary Soto?" And that was just the beginning! But I don't hold grudges because those tirades were justified. *El movimiento* of the late 60s and early to mid-70s was serious business, that is, the movement to improve the lives of so many in the shortest period of time. We were a hurting nation. Other poets didn't like what I was up to, namely the imagistic nature of my work, but I can't blame them. They were reacting to my seeming non-committal to *la raza*. Truth is, I was committed to *el movimiento*, then and now, but committed in my own way, which was—and still is—to get our experiences down on the page in such a way that others might see that our command of language, English or Spanish, is equally moving and taut as theirs. Poet Victor Martinez said jokingly recently, "There was a time when you either hated Gary Soto or loved him." I now think people—especially teachers and students—do understand my creative motives.

CB: You spent many years at Cal Berkeley, first as a part-time member of Chicano Studies, then as an associate professor of Chicano Studies and English, and then as a part-time faculty member in the English Department. Then you quit altogether. Can you describe your rationale?

GS: I would rather not. I'd have to swig down a whole bottle of Maalox. But since we're talking about university life, of which I am no longer part, I do have a few things to say, some of them not so kind. A lot of people are suddenly against affirmative action and I have to wonder whether they have thought it out. People are calling out "reverse discrimination," but is it really? Did it really ever occur? I think affirmative action worked best for white women, who, in turn, paired off with white men, which improved their overall financial score immensely. Affirmative action never worked for hiring practices for Chicanos in the universities in California. If I look at Chicanos in the university, I don't know any of them with good jobs in the humanities, which also carries over to the hard sciences. If you look at the UC system, meaning nine major campuses—Los Angeles, Berkeley, Davis, Riverside, etc.—and if you look at the departments of English or literature taught in English, you will add up 440 tenure-track positions. At last count Berkeley had 60 such appointments and Los Angeles 43 appointments. If we have 440 jobs with steady paychecks and all the goodies that go with them, how many are Chicano? Six. Six out of 440 in a state where there are 9 million Latinos, and two of these six are no longer in the classroom but in administration. I quit Cal Berkeley because I was thrown a bone, and I don't eat bones. I eat meat. When I quit, I was a senior lecturer, and the half-time salary was something like $28,800. This after twelve years. You would have to be an idiot to continue at such a snail's pace of advancement.

CB: Is it the same scenario across the country?

GS: Definitely. A scholar friend and I recently counted up the numbers of Chicanos teaching in English departments nationwide. Of course, we were drinking some brew, so perhaps our numbers are wrong but not horribly wrong. I think we got to twenty-nine and just stopped because there was something funnier on TV. Twenty-nine such profs out of god-knows how many thousands of tenure-track positions at four-year institutions. Even at the state college system in California there are only about seven Chicanos teaching, seven out of nearly 700 tenure-track appointments. I may be wrong, but I think the English Department at Fresno State has hired only one Chicano to its tenure track during its entire history.

CB: Let's lighten the conversation and return to your poetry. I'm particularly struck by *Home Course in Religion*, which I consider your best book to date. For me, it's at once a serious and tremendously funny look at religion, the absurd trappings in which metaphysical constructs are presented. How did you decide on this subject and this new style?

GS: To talk to God, most religiously minded people might fall to their knees and pay him homage through prayer. To talk with him, one might think that an honorable language must be employed. When I chose the theme of religion, and for me a Christian God, I discovered a deadpan kind of humor, a sensibility that was naive and quirky, perhaps even the stuff of a community college student in bonehead English. Where I got it, I'm not sure, but it was consistent. Look at something like this, as an example:

> In second grade I still had to stand faraway
> From the urinal to get my pee in.
> This made me nervous. I opened myself up
> To bacteria and dust swirling in the shafts of sunlight
> I worried more and more about disease.
> I was still looking at the medical dictionary
> And staring at the Chinese boy in
> His iron lung. We became friends.
> I would open the dictionary
> And by habit the book fell open to his face.
> I looked at him, and more than once I grew scared
> Because I thought it was my face in the iron lung picture
> And if I closed the book I might go away,

The reader might have asked, "God, is this guy ill or what?" I have another poem about air captured inside of a mayonnaise jar and my childhood fear that this foul air was the ingredient for my personal destruction if I should get a whiff. And I felt that it was true and I was scared that I lived in the same house that would be responsible for tainting and killing me, and others too. Boy, did I need help! I enjoyed writing those poems, which are thick-lined and very long, and one of the most honest efforts from me. Also, when I wrote these poems, I was singing to the page. I don't know how other poets operate, but sometimes I sing out the lines, repeat them as in, I guess, a kaddish. *Que Lastima*, it's out of print, having never really made that second printing leap from the shelf into buyers' hands. The intensity of writing the book was real, though the readers weren't. Two reviews, and it was gone.

CB: Your *New and Selected Poems* was selected as one of the five finalists for both the National Book Award and the Los Angeles Times Book Award in 1995. Yet, it also received only a one review in a literary magazine. To what do you attribute this lack of attention?

GS: First, let me say that the NBA nomination was a career highlight. I am speaking of the company that I kept the night of the ceremony, I mean, there was Kunitz, Justice, Barbara Howes, and Josephine Jacobsen. Of course, I realized that they're going to give it to Kunitz since he was senior to us all—every one of the nominees was in their 70s or 80s. I was forty-two at the time and Kunitz was something like 90. I kept thinking, "Hey, give it to Youth!" But it was right that we should have honored this man. As for the reception of my *New and Selected*, I think poetry in general is not getting attention in large newspapers or the slicker magazines. Venues are disappearing; we are seeing a proliferation of books but no vehicles to discuss or review these books, certainly no fault of poets. It would be wonderful, if not cagey, if literary magazines devoted more space to reviews. I'm not unsettled by the lack of reviews of my poetry and some of my prose. I'm just like any nearly invisible poet out there, hours and hours of writing, and nearly no response! Then again, my poetry publisher is Chronicle Books, which is known for its colorful cookbooks and travel books, plus other fashionable subjects such as cigars, cats on diets, and pens. They've been good to my four books of poems and an anthology of Chicano fiction. I have a new book in their corner. It's called *A Natural Man*.

CB: Could you talk about the new collection?
GS: *A Natural Man* is a group of poems about how sordid the world is or will soon become. No, it's not about the depletion of the ozone or polar caps sliding into the ocean. Serious problems for sure and directly attributed to us greedy humans. But this new book, which is a continuation of *junior College* in its comedy of the poorly educated, is just about the depletion of beauty and our position in a world of ugliness. We've got strip malls, the homeless, the nationalization of books and films, etc. We get winos, and we get pastoral pictures of me lying in the sun with a duck plucking the gray hairs on my chest. The world is uglier than thirty years ago and, if you're Chicano, then you describe it as *rasqitachi*, messed up.

CB: It sounds particularly depressing. It sounds hopeless.
GS: Oh, there's hope. I think you can live in squalor and utter poverty, such as the characters in this new book, and yet still behave in such a way that we witness honor and bravery. Look at the character in Hamsun's *Hunger*. The man can barely walk from his hunger, and his surroundings are not Beverly Hills. Yet, you see something noble in his actions . . . . We're going to have to get used to this, the absence of natural beauty. Yet, there will always be generous people. The best people that I have met—Cesar Chavez, Dolores Huerta, Jessie de La Cruz, Nancy Mellor—worked in the most arduous places, really ugly places in order to budge the scales of fairness. They worked among the *rasquachi*, some really "messed up" situations. One other way of understanding this word is to take a look at feng shui, the Chinese art of placement. With *rasquachismo*, it's the opposite, everything is out of whack.

CB: We look forward to that book.
GS: I do too. You can never tell when a publisher will abandon you.

CB: Over the recent years, you've been expanding your energies and writing in many fields. Talk about your new audience.
GS: My new audience is about three feet tall. I'm thinking of kindergartners! Nowadays I can't give a straight poetry reading, with some of the more steamy language and images, for fear of those little tykes holding some of the children's books I've written. Since 1990, I have written many children's books and am proud to have presented Latino youth on the page. And I'm not a cheerleader for these youth. I'm not painting rosy pictures of these chavalos. My new book of short stories, called *Petty Crimes*, is anything but Captain Kangaroo with a brown shade. It's a funny yet brutal summary of Chicano youth. What are we going to do

with kids who literally wear funeral suits in Fresno. Funeral suits, by the way, don't have backs. It's easy to dress the dead with such a fashionable cut. . . . And in writing children's literature, I've had gobs of hate letters from parents and a few students. God, with poetry, you' re lucky to get a reader, but with some of this kid's stuff, people are up in arms because some of the characters are gang members. I have had some of my books banned. In fact, I've had one person stand up and say, "A teacher friend of mine thinks you're evil? What is your comment about her feelings?" Hell; at least I'm getting a reaction from my work!

CB: Is there more poetry beyond this new collection?
GS: Yes, but first I'm completing a couple of novellas under the title of *We Ain't Asking Much*. If I were running for public office, that would be my slogan. Just a little bit, folks. The novellas are sad. Sad because they both feature men and dogs, and the dogs, I'm afraid to say, are far more noble. When your lives come to that, where can you go?

"Simple Beauty: The Honest Work of Gary Soto" from *Catamaran*, 2019—Maggie Paul

Poet, memoirist, novelist, essayist and playwright Gary Soto is nothing if not prolific. Drawing upon his upbringing in Fresno, over a career spanning 25 years, Soto has given voice to the everyday experiences and challenging forces that shape the lives of Mexican immigrants in California. But the reach of his oeuvre does not end there. As Raymund Paredes once noted in the *Rocky Mountain Review*, "Soto establishes his acute sense of ethnicity and, simultaneously, his belief that certain emotions, values, and experiences transcend ethnic boundaries and allegiances." In Soto's own words, he is a writer who " provides portraits of people in the rush of life."

Gary Soto was born in Fresno, California in 1952 to working-class parents. As a young man he worked in both the fields of San Joaquin and the factories of Fresno. Despite being a disinterested student, his early discovery of Hemingway, Steinbeck, and Frost, among others, led him toward a writing life. Even as an adolescent, Soto has said, "I was already thinking like a poet, already filling myself with literature."

A first volume of short stories for young readers, *Baseball in April, and Other Stories*, was published in 1990. These eleven stories depict Mexican-American boys and girls as they enter adolescence in Hispanic California neighborhoods. *Living up the Street* (1992) was awarded The American Book award. The popular novel *Buried Onions* (1997) and its sequel *The Afterlife* (2003) are widely taught in high school and community college classrooms.

The author's ability to reflect his own readers is a remarkable element of Gary Soto's work. In *Quartets* (1988) a collection of essays, Soto shares slices of life that draw upon experiences from his childhood, experiences many young people and particularly Mexican American youth, can see themselves in. One reader on the website *Good Reads* posted: "He talks about things that are real; I like how the author has nothing to hide from his readers. The last section of the book is about how he became a writer." Indeed, Soto is very forthcoming about the trajectory of his career; a collection of poems entitled *A Fire in My Hands* (2013) includes a candid interview with the poet and features a brief explanation of how each poem came to be, demystifying the creative process and how his personal experience provides material for his work.

Another refreshing element to Soto's unique relationship to his reader is his incorporation of Spanish into English text. One could argue that Gary Soto does not write for his reader, but to his reader; he is directly, openly speaking to them. His body of work reflects the triumph of making honest art out of difficult circumstances. His inspiration and dedication as a writer is best expressed in his own words: "I tried to remain faithful to the common things of my childhood—I wanted to give these things life and to write so well that my poems would express their simple beauty."

Maggie Paul: You're a poet who writes in genres that include poetry, nonfiction, fiction, children's literature, and plays. How—or why—did this happen?
Gary Soto: At heart I'm a poet; in behavior I'm also a poet; in appearance I'm more like a successful insurance agent—let's laugh here, people… There's no getting around that I have stepped beyond the noble boundary of poetry to have a crack at other genres. Most writers remain faithful to the genre of that first magnetic force that willed them to pick up a pencil or pen (I date myself) and put their first tottering sentences on the page. And, boy, did I totter. My first efforts were ghastly. I burned my first poems (like a mortgage-burning party) and in the process polluted the air with the smoldering.

MP: Did you know that you were going to become a poet and writer?
GS: I did. As young as ten, I imagined writing a book. I recall very clearly a rack of romance novels at Mayfair Market in Fresno and thinking, "I want to write one of those." It was a bodice-ripping cover that starched me with attention. Later, after skirmishes on the playground, after my odyssey of kicking around Fresno streets, after a couple of college composition classes, I abandoned my geography major in favor of literature. When I told my mom that I was majoring in English, she said, "Don't you already know English?" That's my family.

MP: You say that poetry is an act of attention? Explain this notion.
GS: I think that we have to give ourselves over to reading and rereading poetry. I still reread the poets of my youth, namely Neruda, Merwin, early Simic, mid-career James Wright, mid-career Adrienne Rich, and one my favorites, Edward Field, from whom I discovered that humor has a place in poetry. But by "act of attention" I refer to close readings of a text, not unlike, I suspect, how art critics assess what's before them.

MP: But you haven't mentioned the Beat Poets?
GS: True, I read them early on, but they are poets—all grand figures—I'm no longer attracted to.

MP: You have a large readership among Latino youth. How did that come about?
GS: I make a public confession. I left my first love—poetry—at the altar and drove away to write prose! What a sellout! Still, we admit that a fairly well-written novel gets lots more attention than poetry. This was certainly evident after the publication of my first middle-grade book, Baseball in April. I recall attending an educational conference in Wisconsin and attracting a crowd at my table. Of course, as a poet, I was excited; then I realized, as if for the first time, the power of words and stories and the legacy of literature—then saw beyond book sales to the readers themselves. I began to really look at my readers, many of whom were brown as me, Spanish speaking, polite, the sons and daughters of immigrants. Then I recognized my purpose.

MP: What has been the response from readers?

GS: Letters, lots of letters, from young readers and teachers—a hundred or so a week. It appears that I have touched something deep within them, and, in turn, they have touched me deeply as well. By this, I mean to say that I created stories and images that were absent in children's and young adult literature. I took my role seriously. I did my best to write at a level that was both enjoyable and meaningful, possibly artful. True, I wrote a couple of what they call chapter novels, that is, third-grade novels and poems that were sweet as candy and not by any means great. But when I wrote my more serious work—*Buried Onions*, *The Afterlife*, *Jesse*—I did so with every intention of making them strong efforts. I had to compartmentalize my work for younger readers—quick reads or sturdy durable work.

MP: You say that your work has influenced others. Do you have a specific story?

GS: Yes, I recall reading at a community college in the San Diego area when a woman—a Mexicana, I believe—told me why she loved my story collection *A Summer Life*. With very limited English skills she had read that book, dictionary at hand, over and over until she became bilingual. She expressed her appreciation. It was a moving encounter, for me, for her, for those who were listening to our conversation. I recognized how literature matters. There are so many other stories like that.

MP: Can you give me another example, please?

GS: This one involves my musical—yes, that's right, my musical, namely *In and Out of Shadows*, a play that I was commissioned to write at the insistence of Emily Klion, the producer. I went into the project like a wailing brat—I didn't want to do it! You can't make me! Secretly, I was scared that I had gone too far beyond writing poetry into a territory where *Hamilton* exists. I say I was scared because the musical is about undocumented youth, Dreamers in other words. I was given two hundred-plus pages of interviews with Dreamers and Emily said get to work. *Ay, Chihuahua*, I thought. I read those pages, came up with a structure and after about a year's work wrote the musical. It played at the Marsh Theater in San Francisco and numerous other cities. It was a small-time success but big on emotion. I recall how a dance troupe from Modesto called *Los Falcones* arrived to see the musical. They loved it. It was all about them, some of whom are the children of undocumented parents. Then Laura Malagón, the co-director of the troupe, beckoned me outside the theatre. Out on the sidewalk, the troupe danced for me—thirteen girls in full ballet folklorico ruffled regalia dancing for me, a poet. What higher honor is there?

MP: And what are you doing creatively now?

GS: Is looking for a publisher a creative act? Well, I'm trying to find a home for a manuscript titled *Sit Still! A Poet's Compulsive Behavior to See and Do Everything*. That aside, I'm working on two films based on my poem "Oranges." Go ahead and rub your eyes and ask if you have read this correctly. I repeat: I'm working on two movies--a short film called "Oranges," which will be atmospheric, plus a feature-length romantic comedy titled "A Fire in My Hands." Perhaps I have gone too far—not one film but two simultaneously? Not too much for a compulsive poet who can never just sit still! I'm also teaching myself to bake cookies and other desserts.

THE ELEMENTS OF SAN JOAQUIN by Gary Soto—88 pp. Chronicle Books—Angel Garcia

(This review first appeared in MIRAMAR, *2019)*

Over four decades after its initial publication in 1977, a reprinting of *The Elements of San Joaquin* by Gary Soto is being made available by Chronicle Books. Including eleven new poems and prefaced with an important introduction, Soto states, these poems "[are] work from the past but current for many who witness urban violence and odd moments, who live in rural areas such as the San Joaquin Valley, and who face simple yet mystifying childhoods." An important collection for its crucial role in the canon of Chicana/o poetry, this work was, as it still is, absolutely essential considering the current political climate in 2018: the pushback against immigration from the south, the surge of anti-immigrant rhetoric, and the detainment and deportation of thousands of immigrants. But for the many who "witness," there are the thousands more who do not—who have little to no understanding of how "without fieldworkers, all immigrants, there would be no crops or livestock, and finally, nothing on dinner tables or for foodies to assess on their palates." This poetic and political purpose, to write against the erasure of migrant and immigrant experience who have been "historically ignored," is the power of poetry and what, over the many years, makes this collection timeless. In an address to the reader, the speaker reminds us, "We won't forget what you failed to see, / And nothing will heal / Under the rain's broken fingers."

In the sectioned title poem, dedicated to Cesar Chavez, the speaker observes in "Field", "Already I am becoming the valley, / A soil that sprouts nothing / For any of us." And here, we are introduced to the conflict and contradiction of the field as a place that grows life, meant to nourish, and how that field also takes, aggressively so. In "Campesino," a new poem to the current collection, we hear what one must sacrifice, "I was a math teacher in Mexico, / But now I'm a number squeezed into a white van" and later, "In a year, my face will be tooled like my wallet. / Dark and creased." The hardship, just as much economical as it is physical, is also spiritual, "I pound sand from a boot like an hourglass. / Time pours forever and forever." The work is undeniably unforgiving. Nature is unforgiving; the patron, too. The laborer does what she or he must do to survive, "The farm worker possesses tools— / Scarf against wind and dust" and "Cloth gloves soft as flour." But so too, the laborer finds small graces. Moments, even if short-lived, of reprieve. There is prayer in these poems. Not invocations to God necessarily, but to the enduring spirit of how one survives. These poems summon survival. In the earth, where the dead have been buried deep in the soil, lies memory and recollection of the things, places, and people of the past.

Much like the fieldworkers who through hardship could imagine a better future and began organizing for their rights, so too these poems offer hope. From the darkness, there is also light. Where is it found? In the very field where men, women, and children toil and where the "cotton plants, / Like small hands / Wav[e] good-bye." It is found in the meat shop where "ropes of chorizo are big enough to skip through." It is in "the song of a woman" that turns into "a broom stroke," and in the inevitable light that shines through poem after poem, "I saw the sun take its first step / Above the water tower at Sun Maid Raisin / And things separate from the dark." It is also found in communion. Several of these poems longingly recall the memory of what is gone and lovingly speak to those en el otro lado. In perhaps one of the most touching poems, the speaker communicates with his father who's passed:

We know you came back father
And in the doorway
Leading to your bedroom
Wanted to fog
The family's photo
With the breath
You didn't have

It is in small gestures such as these that one realizes we are not alone, "In our house / A cupboard opened" and later, "A garage light came on / Burning silent / As your jealousy." There is a history, a memory, a spirit that shows us the way.

But it was you   father
Who sent me across
A dry orchard
Where I pointed
To a thin cloud
And thought
That beyond that cloud
You lived in Limbo
God's Limbo
And were watching
And soon   for
The first time
You would come to me
Calling   *son*   *son*

That calling, too, is found in nature. In the field, in the wind, among the stars, the sun, in the rain, fog, in the dust that eventually covers everything. What the speaker is these poems asks of us, like he asks his brother and sister is no matter how far away we move, to remember. For those readers familiar with *The Elements of San Joaquin* there will undoubtedly be new experiences and memories of the collection. For those new readers coming to this collection, those who have not witnessed the beauty of this harsh landscape, these poems will ask you to notice even the smallest of gestures of why everyone's humanity is important. They will ask you to remember.

Jon Veinberg—1947-2017

Jon was born in a German refugee camp after his family fled Estonia. Upon arriving in America he briefly lived in New York, Connecticut, and Pittsburg before his family moved to Fresno where he graduated from Roosevelt High School and Fresno State. He then received an MFA from U.C. Irvine. His work has appeared in *POETRY*, *Ploughshares*, *The Missouri Review*, *The Gettysburg Review*, *Black Warrior Review*, *Quarterly West*, *SENTENCE*, *ThreePenny Review*, *New England Review*, and *Miramar*. Veinberg spent his adult life writing and working as a mental health counselor in Fresno. He is the author of the books *Nothing About The Dead*, *An Owl's Landscape*, *Stickball 'Till Dawn*, *Oarless Boats*, *Vacant Lots*, and *The Speed Limit of Clouds*. His last full-length book, *Angels at Bus Stops*, was published by Lynx House Press in 2015 and a posthumous collection of his poetry, *Uncharted Stars: Last Poems*, was published by Brandenburg Press in 2017. Jon was a recipient of two National Endowment for the Arts Grants and won The Vern Rutsala Ward from *Hubbub* Magazine. He was married to Fresno Poet and artist Dixie Salazar, and he was a treasured member of the Fresno writing community until his death in 2017.

from *Piecework: 19 Fresno Poets*, 1987—Jon Veinberg

Jon Veinberg was christened Juhan Ernst Veinberg in the town of Geisinglenstein, Germany after his mother fled the Baltic state of Estonia, leaving behind her dead husband, Jon's father. Jon had red, wavy hair and dimples and didn't utter a clear word until he was four years old and then in a fit of temper.

After a long boat ride to America, he spent his early childhood in New York, Connecticut, and Pittsburgh, PA, places which went largely unnoticed by him. Along with his mother, his aunt, and sister Katrin, and his uncle, he packed himself into a two-toned turquoise Dodge loaded down with all their belongings and headed west, fleeing the snow. He remembers his uncle driving hell bent across the U.S. hoping to reach the west coast before the gold was all used up. He fell asleep in motel room under the watchful eye of the newly discovered color TV—a habit he still finds endearing. On the first day of his arrival in Fresno it snowed. He remembers a landscape so flat that he thought it unnatural for a human being to be able to see so far in all four directions, the orange trees tipped with frost and not a movie star in sight. Here he learned to nurture an implacable desire for sunflower seeds and Basque chicken. He graduated from Roosevelt High School where he rose to the grand height of 6'4". It took him a series of broken bones, a BA in Psychology, writing classes from Phil Levine and Peter Everwine, and an MFA from UC Irvine to stubbornly discover that he was only 5'9", and that in a good pair of shoes. Jon still lives in Fresno, continues to Write, and holds jobs that never last more than a year. His neighbors, his creditors, and the Department of Motor Vehicles all refer to him respectfully as John.

from *What Will Suffice: Contemporary American Poets on the Art of Poetry,* 1995—Jon Veinberg

On the back of my book I am rewarded with a blurb that uses the words "Drama' and "Imagination," two words that always held negative connotations while growing up. For instance, in the fifth grade, I was absorbed in devising a plan for dropping cherry bombs into our public school restroom. A perfect strategy when completed which I could share with my classmates in the simultaneous sensation of seeing and hearing shit and porcelain explode. This act was always met with failure, admonition, and the principal's recurring lecture on the parameters of drama and imagination. There are other examples:

The harpooning of goldfish with a number two lead pencil after reading *The Old Man and the Sea*, the transplanting of rattlesnake tails onto the body of a turtle in hopes of generating a better way to crawl. One could say that I now write poems because I am being rewarded for things I was once punished for. One could say but it wouldn't be true.

In "Stickball 'Till Dawn" a group of boys are playing a typical game in a forbidden place and time, a place and time of their own devising. Whether they know it or not they are sensing human drama unfold. It is not unlike the act of writing poems that these boys should return as poets to rehash this experience over a few beers, to return to a point of reference where their passion for a silly game has surpassed their fear of darkness. The journey they take is through the myriad sounds and symbols of each one's specific memory. The trouble is that the journey never ends in the same collective place, or they, as a group, would fly there to quench their imaginative thirsts without ever having to set foot on the ground. They have been lucky enough to begin at a similar place, a spot of familiar experience. The bombing of toilets in a grammar school bathroom or the playing of stickball under the meager arc of neon isn't a bad place to start dramatizing and embellishing.

from *How Much Earth*, 2001—Jon Veinberg

Over the past forty years of living in Fresno I've put a great deal of thought into why I live here and can never come up with one concrete reason. It's become a cliché that the San Joaquin Valley is the agricultural breadbasket of the world and I'm beyond embarrassment when I still rely on the expertise of my friends to point out the difference between a peach and nectarine tree. I've yet to read a Chamber of Commerce pamphlet that doesn't espouse being two hours from the mountains and three from the ocean. I'm not all that crazy about staying in a cabin in the woods for more than two days and my beachfront deck has whittled away into the mist of a dream. When I'm writing, the two most recurring thoughts that come to mind, no matter where I am, are God and Fresno's imagery and I've yet to make a connection. Today my reason for staying is that I'm doing penance for, on a sweltering pre-summer day in the sixth grade, having locked Henry Lopez in the ball shed. It was at least a couple of hours before the teachers heard screams they couldn't pinpoint and discovered him missing. When they pulled him out all he could talk about was spiders. While the school officials grilled me about a motive and kept asking if things were okay at home I saw through the window poor, dehydrated Henry waiting for me outside the school fence. Even as a twelve-year-old Henry always carried a knife. It was our shared secret though it took that day to figure out why; for people like me. When I stepped outside the gate and apologized I saw the scar that ran from the corner of his mouth to below his chin, something he never talked about, quiver as he broke into laughter and told me, "hope you didn't get into too much trouble, besides it'll toughen me up for what's ahead." The last I heard Henry was doing time and I doubt he's the same, and wonder what shed he might be trying to scratch out of now. What I find in Henry is what I find in abundance where I live, Fresno: toughness and vulnerability, secret pains, the capacity to forgive and to spit laughter into the mouth of hardship. If I were to someday run into Henry I'd want to see that same scar quiver as it once did though I don't know what I'd say to make that happen, maybe if I told him that I now write poetry he would laugh so hard that that scar would disappear. I'd have to tell him that it toughens me up for what's ahead.

from *Bear Flag Republic: Prose Poems & Poetics from California*, 2008—Jon Veinberg

I ask more of my poems than they ask of me. The first I ask of any poem, while it's still in my head, is for it to identify itself, whether by title, theme, or form. One day when it exclaimed a desire to be a prose poem I thought we would both journey down a doomed path without a hiccup of sense. It kept reminding me of how I could enhance all the elements I once espoused: a storytelling personality and temperament laced with humor, the adventure in using a myriad of themes and as many circular patterns as my subconscious could handle, exaggeration to the level of the preposterous, unlimited spokes of transition, softer language yet more venom per bite, and best of all, I would exude greater clarity of thought. I don't know if any of these expectations were fulfilled, however; in writing prose poems I always feel as though I'm committing a crime, albeit a misdemeanor akin to stealing hubcaps from the grand limos of novels and/or verse when the rest of the world is asleep. I'm addicted to my crime and my adrenaline is popping.

from "My Great Good Luck: Jon Veinberg 1947-2017"—Christopher Buckley

In a 2007-2008 interview Jon related: *I come from a family of scientists. My father was an anatomy teacher. He was well read and spoke five languages. There were a lot of doctors in my dad's family, and he too, earned a medical degree. He came to America in 1930 under a Rockefeller scholarship. Then he went back to Estonia. From this experience, he felt America was the most opportune place to go for Estonians caught under the Russian regime. My mother was pursuing being a doctor. During that time, Estonia was an egalitarian country. Women held a lot of occupation weight. She was his student. My dad died over there in 1946. After fleeing Estonia and giving birth to me, my mother wanted to catch the first boat out. We missed the first boat, but it blew up after it hit a mine. We missed the second boat because my sister broke her arm; it went to Paraguay. We caught the third boat and by happenstance or luck it was going to America. When we arrived at Ellis Island, my mother didn't speak any English.*

So in one sense, my great good luck began in Germany when Jon and family missed those first two boats out of the country and caught the third one to the U.S. More practically, it began at Fresno State which offered an office of "Evaluations" to which a student could apply to have his/her course work evaluated with regard to how they were proceeding toward graduation in a major. About 1971 or '72 Jon went to the Evaluations window and handed in his request, later to discover that he had in fact completed enough courses for his degree in Psychology but was short two elective courses. Without knowing anything about Philip Levine or poetry writing, Jon signed up for a poetry workshop, thinking, *How hard could this be?* That course with Levine was hard—Phil was a magnificent but rigorous teacher—and it changed Jon's life as he discovered his vocation in poetry. And it changed mine, giving me the great good luck to meet Jon a couple years later and have him as a friend in poetry and in life for 43 years.

Although Jon would, for most of his working life, have a career and hold down a day job in mental health with his degree in Psychology, he found poetry and became a poet— hands down one of the best, most compelling, and original of our generation, and one of the outstanding poets of The Fresno School. Our mutual friend, Gary Soto, was in that class at Fresno State, and Soto recalls that one of Jon's first poetic efforts was titled, "Green-Eyed Ants," which early on demonstrated Jon's penchant for looking outside of himself for his subjects. My good fortune really began in my first MFA workshop at UC Irvine that found me in the room with Jon and Soto, Gary Young, Tim Sheehan and Deborah Gorlin. Diane Wakoski was the visiting poet for that first quarter and Jon and I agreed she was a terrific and exact teacher as well as a generous mentor.

Jon kept a house in Fresno while he was in grad school and drove home often. It was Jon who introduced me into the circle of Fresno poets by first inviting me up to stay one weekend. He suggested we go over to Levine's house and visit, and that seemed to me impossible and presumptuous . . . you could just go over to his house? Jon called Phil and Phil said sure, come by for a drink the next afternoon, and so, apprehensive as I was, we went. I had met Phil years before at San Diego State when he was down for a reading, and we played a couple sets of tennis together, but I would then have never thought of calling up and going by to visit. Phil was very friendly and relaxed, as was Jon, who chatted easily with Phil and Franny. I can't remember saying much of anything that day.

I taught several places in southern California for a couple years and then moved to teach part-time at Fresno State. During that time, I got together with Jon every week for a talk about what poets we were reading or to exchange poems. I often nagged him about finishing up rough drafts, getting work into the mails. Jon was not writing letters or emailing editors, not at the post office promoting himself in the mails. Rather, he was working in mental health. He was a great student of the human condition, the mind, the wounds it receives in the rush of experience. And with his great compassion, helped many.

While teaching at Fresno State, I learned letterpress printing on a press in a colleague's garage. The first book I printed was a chapbook by Jon, *Nothing About the Dead*, 1980. Only recently, I found a copy of it on the internet and bought it, first one I have ever seen for sale though the colophon says I printed 250 of them? "Dog Poem" from that chapbook, though an early poem, is still one of Jon's best. Over many years of teaching beginning poets, I always advised them to avoid sentimentality and subjects like the death of a dog or cat. I would bring in Jon's poem with it's fierce and original approach and resolution to an old subject, its gravity and shaking mortality, and show them the one exception which proved the rule.

I landed a full time job at UCSB but still drove up to Fresno to stay with Jon, and he sometimes drove down to Santa Barbara, and we sent poems back and forth in the mails in those days prior to e mail. In 1986 I placed a book with Vanderbilt University Press, and soon began screening poetry mss. for them. I suggested Jon send his first ms. in to Vanderbilt, telling the director, John Poindexter, that I thought it was an amazing book but that I was a close friend of Jon's and should not review it officially. I suggested he send it to Ed Hirsch and Chase Twichell, which he did, and they both gave it enthusiastic support for publication. Vanderbilt published Jon's *An Owl's Landscape* in 1988, about which Ed Hirsch wrote: "His poems have a strong sense of conflict and drama. They try to tell the truth about ordinary people—they also grant these people their individuality and dignity."

Introducing Jon at a reading I said: "Line to line and poem to poem, few poets today can sustain language and imagery this brilliant and inventive, a subject this deeply human, a voice this true, this powerful. . . . His is a vision of the world being pieced back together, a world shining in its shattered parts. These poems celebrate the power of the spirit unadorned and yet illuminated with integrity." I was not exaggerating.

We traveled to Europe together, saw each other almost daily when I lived in Fresno, and he remained my great and wonderful friend for 43 years. I could write pages and pages about Jon—his generosity, compassion, fierce intellect, critical insight, grounded sense of democratic values, and his amazing poems and sustaining sense of humor . . . no one like him. In 1991 he married Dixie Salazar, a Fresno poet and artist and they made a mutually supportive, joyous, and creative life together for thirty years.

As I said at his memorial service, it's always seemed to me that truly great poetry is a result of great character, not simply skill with language alone. Jon was a man of great character, of great insight, imagination, and compassion, and that gave rise to his exceptional poetry. To my mind, he was largely overlooked by those who purport to be champions of poetry. Jon was a true individual. He realized early on that he wanted no part of academia with its duplicity and political agendas, and he would not network or curry favor, play poetry politics. He worked longer hours than those of us who were teaching and likely did more good in the world, especially working with teens at risk the last ten or fifteen years of his life. Yet he published five books, and, most interestingly to my mind, received two National Endowment for the Arts grants for his poetry, a competition in which the applications are judged anonymously. Each time, I imagined the celebrated judges reading his work and wondering where this great poet had been the last several years, and wasn't this someone whose work they should know?

In addition to his two NEA grants, Jon also received the Vern Rutsala Award from *HUBBUB* magazine, and had work selected for *POETRY DAILY*. Along with Ernesto Trejo, he edited the important anthology, *Piecework: 19 Fresno Poets* in 1987. More recently Jon and I edited *Messenger to the Stars: A Luis Omar Salinas New Selected Poems & Reader* for the Ash Tree Series published by Tebot Bach, 2014. Jon's poems appeared in many anthologies: *What Will Suffice: Contemporary Poets on the Art of Poetry*; *Highway 99: A Literary Journey through California's Great Central Valley*; *The Geography of Home: California's Poetry of Place*; *Many Californias: Literature from the Golden State*; *Bear Flag Republic: Prose Poems & Poetics from California*; *Aspects of Robinson: Homage to Weldon Kees*; and *One for the Money: The Sentence as a Poetic Form*.

Of Jon and his poetry Peter Everwine has written: "I have for years admired the way a Veinberg poem makes its fierce and insistent music taking up, not another lyric subject, but rather entering the lives of others and giving over his vision and passion to the dignity of the individual trying to do his or her best on earth. Jon's is a selfless poetry and engages the basic mysteries of our existence, and elbows and shoulders its way toward the light, toward some concrete meaning that we might wrestle with a little anger and compassion, with great imagination, and with hard won beauty."

Jon's passing was a crushing blow to his family and friends, a roadblock on that path of hope we all try to follow. For most of my life I knew that joy, hilarity, insight, and camaraderie were only a phone call away, a three hour drive to Fresno—that great good fortune I carried with me since the first day I met him 43 years ago. When Gary Soto called with the terrible news, I felt a lot of the luck of my life evaporate. But realistically, I have to make myself understand how fortunate I was to have Jon as a friend all that time. Jon wrote exceptional poetry that resulted from his unique and compassionate character, his incisive intelligence, his understanding of irony countered with joy in the world. He wrote in the voice of animals, in the voices of the disenfranchised, in the voices of the lost whom he reclaimed. His last book *ANGELS AT BUS STOPS* is one of the finest books by anyone of our generation. We have lost a great poet and a luminous and original soul. Here's Cicero's famous line from his funeral poem to his brother, # 110: *Atque in perpetuum frater ave atque vale/*And forever brother, hail and farewell.

"In Conversation with Jon Veinberg"—J.J. Hernandez

(As part of the Spring 2015 Reading Series presented by the Master of Fine Arts Program in Creative Writing and the Fresno Poets' Association, Jon Veinberg read Friday, Feb. 13 at Fresno State. MFA poetry student J.J. Hernandez spoke with Veinberg about exploring the intersection of art and poetry, taking on other voices when writing a poem, and seeing the pomegranate as a gateway to the spiritual.)
Regarding Fresno poet Jon Veinberg's latest collection, *Angels at Bus Stops*, fellow poet Christopher Buckley says, "his cast of characters populate the poor side of town and he is their voice, their witness—a larger conscience for us all." Veinberg holds a bachelor's degree in psychology from Fresno State and an MFA from UC Irvine. A two-time recipient of NEA grants in poetry, Veinberg's work has appeared in literary magazines including *Ploughshares, Poetry, The Antioch Review, The Missouri Review, Miramar,* and many more. His work has been included in multiple anthologies including *Highway 99: A Literary Journey through California's Great Central Valley, How Much Earth: The Fresno Poets, The Geography of Home: California's Poetry of Place,* and *Bear Flag Republic: Prose Poems & Poetics from California.* Most recently he edited, with Christopher Buckley, *Messenger to the Stars: A Luis Omar Salinas New Selected Poems & Reader,* 2014.

J.J. Hernandez: I know you have lived and written in Fresno for many years. What has that been like? Or, maybe more specifically, how has the central San Joaquin Valley shaped and influenced your writing?
Jon Veinberg: In an amazing way. I don't know how much of my work you have read, but the poems are all sort of landscape oriented. I go from what the landscape tells me, and I always find something that is integral to myself or someone else. I don't really write about myself, and if I do it is usually figuratively, like I am taking on the voice of another person or animal, like a bird. When Peter Everwine read the book, he called me a ventriloquist, which to me is one of the best things I have ever heard anyone say about my poetry. It's a compliment, as I can actually be believable and not stereotypical.

JH: Taking on another voice is probably one of my greatest difficulties as a poet. In your latest collection, *Angels at Bus Stops,* I notice how effortlessly you do it in your ekphrastic poem, "Woman at a Red Table." In the poem, you seem to take on the woman's voice, which interested me.
JV: That's interesting. That was an interesting poem for me. Léon de Smet was a great Belgian impressionist painter, and when I saw that painting, I thought, this woman has a voice. I don't know if it's correct, or what, but he's dead, he can't fault me.

JH: I felt you really captured her voice, as I looked up the painting myself and saw her in the poem.
JV: Wonderful. I'm really glad you got that out of the poem. My first teacher Philip Levine told me . . . well, let me start here. You see, when I went into poetry, at the very beginning, I

had already finished the requirements for my psychology degree. I had a semester to waste. So I took a beginning poetry class with Levine [not really knowing who he was]. I remember having the wrong impression of poetry at first. I thought it was self-inflated, and I don't really like to talk about myself, and definitely not write about myself. But Levine says to me, "You've got the right idea. Why write about yourself, when you can write about something interesting." And so I just began writing about others. I remember getting compliments doing just that, yet they didn't know they were complimenting me. I had a poem called "Stretch Mark Cafe" and people said things like, "God, I didn't know Jon was like that," which to me was a compliment, because it was not me in the poem.

JH: In what I've read, T.S. Eliot hardly ever spoke on himself either. I'm drawing on that similarity, as much of your work takes on those other voices. I really like that about your craft, yet I love how straightforward your poetry is, while Eliot bridges the obscure.

JV: You're right. Eliot was a genius, but he was also one of the most confusing poets I have ever read. I always say, I still can't understand some of my favorite poets. You know, I envy the hell out of you students. In my whole career as a student, I was only able to take one other English class, and in that class I convinced my teacher to let me write fiction instead of all of the essays. I never really cared for essays until I began writing essays for poetry.

JH: That brings up another question I'd like to ask. I notice the inclusion of prose poems in your new book. How do you define the line between writing genres?

JV: There are a lot of lines I draw on. One major one is rhythm. If I cannot exact the image and it becomes more narrative than exacting the image, then I make a prose poem out of it. I've written a lot of prose poems lately. The French poet Paul Valéry – though I don't like much of his work [Veinberg says Valéry was a much better prose writer than a poet] – once said: "Prose is walking, poetry is dancing." And with these prose poems, I feel like I am walking. Maybe I'm walking fast, but I don't have the same drive I do, as when I write in verse. I don't have the energy, but I have a story to get out.

JH: Also in your latest book, I liked your poem "When Salvador Dali Camped on My Roof." Do you choose the paintings you write about, or do they sort of choose you?

JV: I didn't choose any of the paintings for that piece. You know what I chose was the character of Salvador Dali. I just pictured a painter that would paint like Salvador Dali and wrote it. He was such an interesting character. He was all over the place and so full of himself. I really like how "beyond this planet" and surreal his imagination was. And by no means do I consider myself surreal, yet I see a lot of surrealism in this world around us day by day, and I just wanted to place him in a poem doing something weird like camping on my roof.

JH: So, how did the Léon de Smet painting find its way into your poetry? I looked up the painting and I was drawn to it as well.

JV: Léon de Smet was a wonderful painter. This came about like all poems. I start with an image, de Smet's painting, and I let the image drive me. And it usually does. It's not hard for me to start a poem it's hard for me to finish a poem. That painting also has an underground history to it. The war that my family went through [as they fled Soviet-occupied Estonia to Germany in the early 1950s], and the loss of family is similar to how "the woman" is just at this table, basically meditating on what it was like before things fell apart, before her husband was taken away, before she lost her children. Yet she still dresses up and looks good, but something is still lacking, which, to me, is the life she could have lead. More impressively though, she is still driven to remain beautiful, which is what I was trying to portray in the poem.

JH: Another poem in the collection I thought really deserves some attention is "Stealing Pomegranates." Could you give some insight into the poem?

JV: The pomegranate is so visually beautiful to me. It's like an oyster that is filled with pearls. You know how oysters are kind of crusty, but then you break them open and find the pearl. Well there are hundreds of pearls in this pomegranate, and to top it off they taste good too, which is why I was driven to steal these wonderful fruits. Also, towards the end of the poem I try to make Biblical sense of that sin of stealing, and how it is related to the first sin of Eve eating the fruit.

JH: Could it also be related to an "Original Sin" or a sexual awakening?

JV: I'm so glad you were able to see that. I was hoping the poem would be something more than just a poem about stealing. To me the pomegranate is a sexual fruit, and I was hoping the reader could draw on this.

JH: I do finally want to come to this last idea, which is religion, or God. You seem to come to this in the book, and I was wondering what your thoughts on the subject were.

JV: I do seem to use it. Particularly for this book, but I hope I use it in more of a spiritual sense. I tried to include much of the mystical language. I wanted to delve into the mysteries of the soul, yet we don't really know what happens. But I don't really think it is a religious piece.

JH: Yes, a more spiritual sense to the work, rather than a religious one. Yet I do see this God, or omnipresent being, in the work. Is that the case?

JV: You're right. Yet, it is more transcendent. I wanted it to go beyond. For instance, the title *Angels at Bus Stops*, I see angels who are supposed to be transporting the dead to another world, yet they are here at bus stops accompanying people throughout Fresno. I think it's a metaphor. Who knows? Let someone else decide if it's a good one or a bad one.

Christopher Buckley

Christopher Buckley was raised in Santa Barbara, CA. He has taught at CSU Fresno, UC Santa Barbara, and UC Riverside. He has published three books of creative nonfiction and twenty-seven books of poetry, including *STAR JOURNAL: Selected Poems* (Univ. of Pittsburgh Press 2016), *Cloud Memoir: Selected Longer Poems* (Stephen F. Austin State Univ. Press, 2018), *AGNOSTIC* (Lynx House Press, 2019), and *The Pre-Eternity of the World* (Stephen F. Austin, 2021).

He was a Guggenheim Fellow in Poetry for 2007-2008 and a recipient of NEA grants in poetry for 2001 and 1984. He received the William Stafford Poetry Prize from Rosebud in 2012, and the James Dickey Prize for 2008 from *Five Points* Magazine. He was a recipient of a Fulbright Award in Creative Writing to the former Yugoslavia, four Pushcart Prizes, two awards from the Poetry Society of America, and the John Atherton Fellowship in Poetry to the Bread Loaf Writers' Conference. He was awarded the Tampa Review Prize for Poetry from the Univ. of Tampa Press for *Rolling the Bones*, 2009, and the Vern Rutsala Poetry Prize for *The Far Republics* from Cloudbank Books, 2017.

With Gary Young, he edited *The Geography of Home: California's Poetry of Place* and with David Oliveira and M.L. Williams, *How Much Earth: The Fresno Poets*. For the Univ. of Michigan Press' *Under Discussion* series, he edited *The Poetry of Philip Levine: Stranger To Nothing*, 1999, and in 2013, *FIRST LIGHT: A Festschrift for Philip Levine on his 85th Birthday*.

He has also edited *Bear Flag Republic: Prose Poems & Poetics from California* (with Gary Young) 2008, *Homage To Vallejo* (Greenhouse Review Press, 2006), and *A CONDITION OF THE SPIRIT: THE LIFE AND WORK OF LARRY LEVIS*, (with Alexander Long), 2004. The Backwaters Press published *Aspects of Robinson: Homage to Weldon Kees*, edited with Christopher Howell in 2011, and in 2012, again with Gary Young, *One for the Money: the Sentence as a Poetic Form*. With Jon Veinberg, he edited *MESSENGER TO THE STARS: A LUIS OMAR SALINAS NEW SELECTED POEMS & READER*, and in 2020 *The Long Embrace: Contemporary Poets on the Long Poems of Philip Levine*, Lynx House Press.

"Levine y yo" from *The Los Angeles Review of Books,* 2013, and *Holy Days of Obligation,* 2014—Christopher Buckley

The first book of contemporary poetry I ever read was Philip Levine's *They Feed They Lion*, that was 1972, my first semester in graduate school at San Diego State where I was enrolled for the MA in English with the creative writing concentration. Lion had just been published by Atheneum, the biggest publisher for poetry at the time after Wesleyan University Press, which had published Levine's second book of poetry, *Not This Pig*, and who turned down *Lion*. Mistake for Wesleyan as *Lion* saw many printings.

When I met Philip Levine it was on a tennis court at San Diego State University, it was 1972 or '73, and poetry and readings then drew substantial audiences; he read the poems that would go in his next book *1933* in Montezuma Hall to 350 people as did Gary Snyder that year. I had, in the summers, continued to teach tennis in Santa Barbara and was weighing the offer of a job at a club there against the precarious prospects of becoming a worthwhile and/or successful poet—a sure thing vs. the longest of shots. I had some good idea of the odds.

In the '70s everyone was playing tennis and taking lessons—Johnny Carson, Woody Allen and Diane Keaton, businessmen, professors, students, and even administrators. Phil was an avid player and while he was in town he wanted to get in a couple sets, and Glover asked me to hit with him. I couldn't believe my luck. What I knew about poetry could be written on the back of a gum wrapper, but I knew who Phil was and he was even staying at Glover's house, and had Pablo Picasso walked out of Glover's kitchen, it would not have impressed me more. I let Phil have what we called back then a "courtesy game" or two each set, moving him side to side, feeding him an occasional forehand volley put-away. Phil returned the courtesy the next day by mercifully passing quickly over my miserable poem in the special workshop whereas others were held to more rigorous account. A few years later, Phil remembered our meeting a bit differently; he gave me a copy of On the Edge and Over and inscribed it, "For Chris, who lost 6-0, 6-0, with grace, under pressure, Phil."

Later, I was invited to a small reception at Glover's house, where I said hardly anything. Just into my 20s and struggling to finish one or two poems a semester, it didn't occur to me that I might see Levine again, much less become his friend.

From San Diego State I went to the University of California for the MFA program in poetry and began to write criticism and reviews as well. The first review I published was of 1933; no one seemed to notice that I was still a kid in my mid 20s and I placed that review and others without too much trouble. At Irvine, two of my best friends were poets Jon Veinberg and Gary Soto, both from Fresno and former students of Levine's. I started visiting them in Fresno and occasionally we would drop by Levine's for a chat or drink, though I was not entirely comfortable doing so.

After Irvine, I taught part time at several community colleges in southern California and when Proposition 13 cut the funds from the colleges and put the money in the pockets of big real estate interests, I was out of work. I moved to Fresno and eventually picked up part time teaching at Fresno State. Living and teaching there for two years, I became part of the Fresno group of poets, the best group of local talent I've ever seen in one city.

I left Fresno to take a job at UC Santa Barbara from 1980 to 1983, and from UCSB I moved to Murray State University in Kentucky, and during that time I published an essay on Phil's poem "Belief" from One for The Rose. In 1985 I escaped Murray and returned to teach at UCSB and soon published a review of Sweet Will; by then I was sending Phil the published copies of what I wrote and he was gracious in his responses. While at UCSB I invited Phil to campus for a reading in the series I had organized; he was very generous to his friends and I guess by this time I had become a friend as he let me underpay him severely for the reading. We did work it out to coincide with dates when he was coming south anyway to see his mother in L.A., and also he wanted to visit his brother Eli who had moved into an amazing house on the Riviera in Santa Barbara. He gave a great reading and Eli provided an elegant reception at his house which overlooked the harbor and lights of Santa Barbara. Eli encouraged me to bring along two of my students; they were timid and quiet but at least managed to ask Phil to sign their books. Already, things had come full circle.

In 1989 I received the John Atherton poetry fellowship from the Bread Loaf Writers' conference and asked to be assigned to Levine for 1. an assistant workshop teacher which was our duty, and 2. for a conference on my new manuscript, which was my privilege as a fellow. It was a great two weeks at Bread Loaf, working with Phil and socializing with him.

He went through the manuscript of my 5th book, *Blue Autumn*, and gave it a thorough going over, with many cuts and slashes, completely candid, no punches pulled, and it truly helped tighten and shape the book.

I had recently taken on the job of editing the critical collection on Phil for Donald Hall in the University of Michigan Press' *Under Discussion* series, and so I spent a good deal of time with Phil discussing reviews of his work, setting chronology and bibliography, obtaining general background. (*On the Poetry of Philip Levine: Stranger to Nothing* was published in the University of Michigan Press' series in 1991.) We played some professors' doubles on the clay tennis courts and ate dinner with a group, all of whom could be counted on to contribute wine to the table. Most nights it was Phil, Bill Matthews, Mark Jarman, Rick Jackson, and one or two others; we alternated contributing bottles of decent and occasionally interesting wine; at Bread Loaf, if you want wine you have to bring your own, and wine-moochers at dinner are a perennial problem. By that time I had taken a position teaching creative writing and directing the creative writing program at a small state university outside of Philadelphia where again Phil came to read for next to nothing as he was only a short train ride away. This was in 1989 and he was reading the poems that would be published in *What Work Is*, which would soon win the National Book Award. Before Phil came for a reading, I arranged a printing project with my colleague Michael Peich, publisher of Aralia Press, and he printed a limited edition letterpress chapbook of a few of Phil's new poems entitled *BLUE*.

I had long been a collector of Levine's books. One day in 1995 or so, it occurred to me that many poems and books were now out of print and that even the *New Selected Poems* left out many fine poems. I suggested to Phil that we publish a collection of those poems and worked with my long time friend and fellow poet, Gary Young, and with the additional support of Jon Veinberg, we brought out an edition of these poems. Phil titled the book *Unselected Poems*. Phil and I exchanged many letters re the actual content of this book—I always wanting more, thinking of rescuing as much as possible, thinking historically, Phil trying to take poems out, keep it down to the best of what was available. In 1997 we printed a paperback edition of 2,000 with 35 special copies in boards. They sold out and Gary Young's Greenhouse Review Press printed a second edition.

In addition to seeing Phil in Fresno informally and at readings, I would try to touch base whenever we drove up to New York City. He taught at NYU almost every Fall, and when Nadya and I would go up to visit galleries and her artist friends from her New York years, we would get together with Phil and Franny for dinner, or at a book party, or reading. The last time we all spent an evening in NYC was 1997 in April and we were having dinner with Bill Matthews and his new love, Celia. Bill had just received the Ruth Lilly Award and Phil had been one of the judges. That was the last time I saw Bill. I of course spent some time with Phil in Nov. of 1996 in Richmond, VA for the memorial service for Larry Levis—Phil's best student, his great friend and helper and critic.

Before I escaped Pennsylvania, I set up one of my former poetry students, who had also become a fine letterpress printer, with a chapbook manuscript from Phil of new poems. Tim Geiger, had just taken a position at The University of Toledo and was trying to get a book arts program going. He printed a handful of new poems in the chapbook but led off with an early poem from *Not This Pig*, "Coming Homeward from Toledo." *SMOKE* was printed in a handsome wrapper edition with 25 copies in boards just in time for Phil' s 70th birthday in January 1998.

Since returning to California and working at UC Riverside, I've had Phil to campus twice as the featured writer at the Annual Writers Week. In 2001 I chaired the AWP convention in Palm Springs and Phil was our keynote speaker. I know of no one more generous with himself and his time than Phil. As a teacher, he is unsurpassed and there must be at least 100 poets with careers and books and a life in poetry out there that owe much of it to Phil.

I have written the critical/biographical essays on Phil for Scribner's *American Writers* series and for Oxford University Press's *Encyclopedia of American Literature* in addition to several reviews, interviews and other essays. Each time I introduce Phil at a reading, I am hard pressed to improve upon the superlatives I want to attribute to his recent work as well as his career, but I try and he often congratulates me for "that very accurate introduction." Phil has one of the best senses of humor of anyone I know, and that is a fabulous complement to his poems which are some of the grittiest and most profound we have in the last fifty years, poems which consistently rescue our dignity and humanity.

Phil is a great letter-writer and over the years, I have heard from him about every month, or sometimes he phones. One of my most prized letters from him is the one he sent me from Vanderbilt—where he was visiting for a semester—the day after he received the Pulitzer Prize. It was honest and showed a humility and modesty that was at once true and hard to believe for a poet who is arguably the best poet living in America.

Whatever I have learned about writing poetry, a good deal of it is the result of reading Phil's work. As a young writer, I never studied with him. It took two of my two and a half years at San Diego State to quit trying to steal his lines, I was so much in awe of his poems as a young man. Now, somehow, I am in my 60s, and I discover that much of what it takes to be a reasonable and democratic human being, an individual who values character and our common dignity—whatever small parts of that I have managed—I learned not only from his poetry, but from the gift of just knowing the man, Philip Levine.

from "An Interview with Christopher Buckley," *Smartish Pace*, 2001—Maggie Paul

In his new book, *Star Apocrypha*, the poet Christopher Buckley reaches for a higher lyric pitch and succeeds exponentially. Buckley's poetry addresses matters of this world and of the soul, daily life and the life of the imagination with brilliant language and finesse. His poems perform an eloquent dance between memory and the here and now, turning time into the very same stuff as the clouds and stars. In the following interview, the poet discusses contemporary poetry and his latest book, *Star Apocrypha*.

Maggie Paul: Can you recall some of your earliest experiences with poetry and how they influenced your decision to become a poet?
Christopher Buckley: My earliest memory of poetry is from Mt. Carmel School in Montecito fourth grade, fifth? I wrote a poem for Mother's Day in class, the nun passing out white paper and blue construction paper to paste it on. I remember this because I found it years later in a trunk; my mother had saved it. It was in fact in quatrains rhyming abab, three or four of them with sunlight and bluebirds flying about the edges of the stanzas. I came across it her garage while working on my M.A. in grad school and was amazed at how adequate I was with forms at that age, though I must have simply been repeating platitudes and greeting card sentiment. I wrote bad poetry—truly inaccessible, encoded, meritless poems—through high school and college. I never had the benefit of contemporary poetry as a model in either place. But I was always interested for some reason, in poetry. I was a surfer all through my teenage years. One day I opened *SURF GUIDE*, one of only two surf magazines in those days, and the center spread was a huge perfectly breaking wave and

superimposed in the curl of the wave was a stanza from Algernon Charles Swinburne's "The Garden of Proserpine." What great music he had. It's one of the few pieces of poetry I still have committed to memory. But as far as making a "choice" to be a poet, I'd have to say two things moved me in that direction. The first was the regular working world. I'd taken my B.A. in English and was working in a grocery store, a liquor store, while teaching tennis part time. Heavy boredom. I had a folder of bad poetry and didn't know any better, so I headed off to graduate school. The second thing was deciding to risk failure; my first teacher at San Diego State, Glover Davis, explained that, and what re-writing and work really were. So I decided to invest the time and risk everything else to try and do this little thing that didn't seem to matter to most people.

MP: Who are your favorite contemporary poets? Who are your favorite poets of all time?

CB: My favorite contemporary poets are Philip Levine, Peter Everwine, Charles Wright, Gerald Stern, Diane Wakoski, Mary Oliver, and closer to my own age Larry Levis and Bill Matthews, whom we lost not too long ago, and Mark Jarman, Robert Wrigley, Gary Soto, as well as two poets who don't get as much notice as the more celebrated, Richard Jackson and Jon Veinberg. James Wright and Richard Hugo—both who should still be with us—are all time favorites as well as William Stafford. Philip Levine and Charles Wright and Peter Everwine have been my main influences starting back in 1972. Also great and early influences have been Nazim Hikmet, Jaroslav Seifert, and many Spanish and South American poets —Machado, Hernandez, Alberti, Lorca, and Gerardo Diego, and of course Cesar Vallejo, Carlos Drummond de Andrede, and Neruda. These days, I read a great deal of Milosz, Szymborska, Amichai and Zbignelw Herbert. Go figure—the voices that speak most deeply and directly to me, a regular Irish extraction lower middle class American, are those of older Jewish men and older eastern European men and women. It's the directness that holds me.

MP: Has teaching creative writing influenced your work in a positive way? Do you think that the proliferation of creative writing programs across the country is having a good effect on the field of poetry in general?

CB: Sure, teaching creative writing has a positive effect. The only more positive effect would be not having to work at all, having my time only for writing. But if you have to work as most of us do, to be actively engaged in your own field helps keep you vital and open to change and possibility. Moreover, I've been blessed with years of fine students, many of whom have become fine writers, have published, and now are teaching other writers. It's a cliché to be sure, but if you're paying attention, you do learn from your students.

Yes of course all the new MFA programs have a good effect on poetry. Anyone who tells you different has some ivory tower, elitist, self-important agenda. A lot more folks are interested in writing and are learning, to varying degrees, how to write and better read. This creates a larger audience, a more informed public and more support for the art(s). What could be wrong with that? Of course not everyone is going to come out a Phil Levine or Mary Oliver. But that was never the proposition. Do we hear complaints if the enrollment of English PhD or Philosophy PhD programs increases, or MBA programs? Of course not. Whenever I have read the usual articles about how bad MFA programs are or that poetry is going to the dogs, etc., there is usually a sub-text that says, "However I, (who have NOT attended a graduate writing program), know the true and better way, and finally, am a better poet than most." I have never agreed with Gioia's article in *Atlantic Monthly* years ago. He made some good points about the audience for poetry, but he painted with a broad brush and smeared many good writers/poets who are effective, dedicated, conscientious teachers. Sure some "star" poets take the easy road, don't put much effort in the classroom. But he never named who exactly he was talking about? In over 25 years of teaching creative writing, I've come to know good and hard working teachers who out number the "stars" who do not do their job by 25-1 at least.

MP: Does the public sometimes confuse you with the political satirist/novelist Christopher Buckley? How do you handle this? Has "the other" Christopher Buckley ever contacted you in this regard?
CB: YES, of course, all the time. In 1981 I had a poem in *The New Yorker*, and they forward letters if people respond. This was the first time it happened. The letter I received was surreal and crazy; I read it to my colleagues with whom I was teaching then at UC Santa Barbara and none of us had a clue. Later, Ernesto Trejo sent a magazine piece on the other CB and I got it: the woman writing me via *The New Yorker* thought I was the other CB and was picking up more or less from where she had left off talking to him when he was visiting in Detroit. So then "the lizard erased from your hand" and some notions about the use of language made sense. I've been called to be on *The Today Show* and had to say something pretty direct about what I thought of George (Daddy) Bush to get them to realize that I was not the man they wanted. The other CB is the Yale-educated son of the famous conservative William F. Buckley, and besides writing novels like *The White House Mess*, he was a speech writer for Bush, twice. Our politics are 180 degrees different. Once I was giving a reading at the museum in Philadelphia in their First Wednesday series; they had jazz and movies and food and wine downstairs, and a poetry reading far back in the cloisters of the second floor. After I read, one of the twelve people in the audience approached me with a magazine in his hand, pointed to a picture of the other CB (tall, thin, blond) and said, "You're not Christopher Buckley; he comes in to my dock every summer in Connecticut and buys gas for his yacht!" "So that's what happened to my yacht!" I wish I'd replied. No, the other CB has never contacted me, but I still receive calls from editors and magazines asking for him. I direct them to *TV Guide*, *Esquire*, and *The New Yorker* for which he has written small humorous pieces.

MP: The epigraph to *Star Apocrypha* comes from a poem by the late Larry Levis. Can you tell us what kind of an influence Levis was on you and your work?
CB: Well, I published a 20-page essay on Larry in the inaugural issue of *POETRY INTERNATIONAL* and also wrote the bio/crit essay on him for *AMERICAN WRITERS*. It would take something about that length to really answer your question. In an interview I published with Levine for *Quarterly West* a few years back, Phil said essentially, that not only was Larry the best poet of his generation, at times he was just the best poet writing in America. Larry was an absolute original and had, before the age of 50, achieved the kind of poetic wisdom, and humility, that allow a great poet to speak directly and inventively and originally. No one sounds like Larry; no one has at once the craft and the honesty, the intensity of imagination serving the human condition. Larry's poems offered an intimate sense of detachment that allowed him to examine himself as an objective character, an emblematic character in the world, and yet write of the most personal events and aspirations and ideas in an objective, factual style. He was a brilliant image-maker and consistently found new ways to approach the lyric and historical. Rhetorically, emotionally, he pointed the way for the rest of us; we learned from him. No poetry gives me more satisfaction nor better enunciates the conflict of body and soul in a music absolutely personal and convincing.

MP: Your Catholic upbringing surfaces in a number of these poems. How much do you think your Catholic school experience contributed to your imagination and interest in the world of the soul and matters of the spirit?

CB: The Catholic upbringing is largely behind it all. I attended Catholic schools through to my undergraduate degree. I stopped buying into it at about 11 years old. But it gave me a target. And once free of hypocrisy and superstition, I was left with a big question nonetheless about the soul and matters of the spirit, as you say. In my 20's and 30's, if I was close to anything, it would be Hinduism and mysticism. Anymore, I flip-flop week to week between faith and doubt. Charles Wright, who I admire immensely, has said something to the effect that his poetry is an ongoing argument with himself about the unlikelihood of salvation. Ditto. Wish I had said it. Nevertheless, it's all we have and it has always seemed to me that we have art so we might formulate some notion of the spiritual. We could well be chasing our metaphysical tails, but I hope not.

MP: Images of nature, i.e., clouds, stars, the sea, trees, etc. figure prominently in your poems, not only in the new book, *Star Apocrypha*, but in your other books as well. Can you talk a bit about how or why nature is so effective in conveying a sense of what it is to be human in a world largely mysterious to us, despite our knowledge of math and science?

CB: Well, nature as moral tutor is hardly original with me. I in fact did not think about it; I was not a Wordsworth scholar. It was just my good fortune to grow up in a fairly edenic place, Montecito, a woodsy suburb of Santa Barbara, in the 50's. One of the first afternoons in 2nd grade at Mt. Carmel School, I was sitting in back of the new classrooms with a handful of other kids I did not know well at all, but who were plenty nice to me. We just sat in the wild grass or leaned against sand stone boulders beneath the palms and acacia trees and ate our sandwiches and Fritos and drank our little cartons of milk. We were in the foothills, the sky was bluer than it would ever be again and a few great white fair weather clouds floated overhead. Among friends in the luscious breathing world I got it; that was my theme long before I ever thought to write about it. Here are a few sentences I worked up for my publisher that never came to any use, but which, I think speak to your question: "Beyond our own invention, beyond myth, beyond the transcendence of light in the trees each day, what can we be sure of? Cosmology, theology, philosophy, politics do not sustain us against the hard and fast questions of mortality. What are the claims of the past, and in their attempts to offer meaning and unpuzzle the burden and brilliance of a physical life? Don't those claims, doesn't that past, offer us a clear glimpse of transcendence, of salvation, as any new and immediate knowledge of science?" Nevertheless, I love the new ideas and data emerging from science and cosmology; I read it and write about it a great deal. For the most part, I find the information to be new and extended metaphors for the basic questions of the soul/or not?

MP: Do you see *Star Apocrypha* as being different in some way from your previous books or as part of a continuum?

CB: *Star Apocrypha* is more of a continuum. Stylistically, however, it is different for the most part; the language is more compact (for me) and tight, and the phrasing and lines lean a bit more toward the intuitive than the narrative. There are still poems such as "Last Days of the Hot Rod Kids" which are more discursive. There's the Charles Bukowski prose poem in there, too, which folks seem to like. But for the most part, the poems are trying to reach a higher lyric pitch.

MP: The third section of *Star Apocrypha* stood out as containing poems of praise, contentment, the speaker embracing the ability to derive joy from life's small pleasures. Can you comment on how you see the shape of the book, the movements, so to speak, of the three parts, and what determined the three sections?

CB: The subjects of the three sections are slightly different. Section I has poems of a biographical nature, more childhood. The poems in section II all have some other person or persons involved as important catalysts—Zeno, Bukowski, Benito Juarez, etc. Poems in section III are the most ambitious and risk more strategy and style and voice. It is a more imagistic book than the previous though it is of course lyrical. The view is skeptical while the voice reaches for further music. My hope is that by that point in the book a reader will know the voice and the focus well enough to find them accessible and worthy.

MP: In your poems you move seamlessly between the "black and white" 50's and the colorful 60's of your childhood to the present where you have reached, pardon me, middle age. These childhood memories are as vivid as if they had just happened yesterday. Is there something in the present that acts as a trigger and brings certain experiences back to a writer so clearly that it could have been yesterday?

CB: Yes of course, there is always a trigger. But it is specific to each poem. There is no secret, no "method" to employ that will bring it back, every time. A writer's business is largely memory, and individual bits and details will stimulate an entire event or emotional complex at times. I pay attention to the past and try to make sense of it, try to remember some detail that will recall much more. So I am interested in old photographs, TV shows, magazines, beer labels, anything I just try to keep my satellite dish on and ready to pick up information.

MP: How do you resolve the sense of the infinite with the day-to-day particulars of life?

CB: A sense of the infinite is a source of hope, dare I say some moderated Joy, if I'm in the right mood. What should we love, what should we cherish given the rush of experience? Isn't it possible that the metaphysical is contained or at least glimpsed in the physical? Shouldn't we praise the smallest portions of our lives, the narrative that teaches us modesty, regard for the earth and yet a desire for something more, beyond that? Might not some truth be found in the simple attention the soul pays to all that surrounds it? How tenuous is the evidence of a grand design. In the humbling face of infinity, isn't there some practical work to be done each day?

from "An Interview with Christopher Buckley," *Asheville Poetry Review,* 2016—Al Maginnes

Al Maginnes: I know that you have written and spoken about many of your friends and contemporaries in poetry such as Philip Levine and Larry Levis, Jon Veinberg and Gary Young and many others. Is there anything you'd like to say about the advantages of having comrades in poetry? And are there any drawbacks?

Christopher Buckley: I met Gary Young and Jon Veinberg—two poets whose work I admire immensely—at UC Irvine in the MFA program, oh so long ago now . . . . Before that I took a risk and got lucky. I was writing poems without knowing anything of contemporary poetry. I had no critics for feedback other than my drinking buddies and they were wise enough to ignore me when I walked into the room with a few papers in hand. I was teaching tennis and working in a liquor store at nights. A pal from 2nd grade at Our Lady of Mt. Carmel was back from Vietnam and wanted to go to San Diego State to finish his B.A. in business. I looked at the catalog and saw they offered an M.A. with a creative writing emphasis, and, realizing that I was going nowhere fast, and decided to take a chance and move there with him. My first semester tuition was $89. There I met Glover Davis, one of the early group of young poets from Fresno State studying with Levine and Everwine, and Glover's classes saved my life. Like Levine, he was absolutely rigorous in workshop. It took me 2 & ½ years to write enough poems that he thought were finished and good for a thesis, perhaps 20 poems total. It had taken me a year and half to stop stealing Levine lines to end my poems; Glover always caught me on that. After Irvine, my real blessing was Gary and Jon who have been tireless editors for over 30 years. I don't think I'd have a poem without them.

If you do not have such comrades who are absolutely rigorous with you, I think you turn out a lot of uneven and self-indulgent work. At the end of our MFA time, it was Veinberg who had the good sense to tell me to can my first book ms. that had come close in the Yale contest. He was right of course, it was lousy, even for a first book. Despite a wonderful note from Kunitz that kept my spirits up for years, I was fortunate that it was not chosen. Phil helped me with 3 or 4 poems over the years. I rarely bothered him though we were friends. He had a ton of former students sending him work for help and then all kinds of other folks who were not his students sending work and asking for things. I tried not to add to the burden. Larry Levis, for me like so many, was a teacher by virtue of his amazing work—no one like him. Any new book by Larry was an event. Larry was a big help when I was a very young poet. We were maybe only a year apart in age but he was light years ahead of me. I've written elsewhere about an afternoon at the MLA convention in L.A. in the early '80s. I had one book and no prospects so went to the convention just to see people like Larry. While everyone was up in the rooms interviewing for jobs throughout the afternoon, we sat in the Biltmore bar drinking glasses of a green white wine and talking poetry. We had the bar to ourselves and I asked lots of questions about his work. Just that he would share that time with me and talk poetry gave me a boost that lasted years. Without such comrades, I don't think there are many of us who would make it to any level in poetry. The drawback would be working solely on your own.

AM: Looking over your body of work from 1980, when your first book was published (although several of your early books are not represented in your Selected) to _Back Room at the Philosophers' Club_ what changes do you see, other than a man and a poet growing older? Have your concerns changed at all?

CB: Well yes of course. I hope they have expanded, though there is a sub-current, a fault line, that runs through most of the things I have written. Like many writers—I even think of playwrights such as Tennessee Williams as well as novelists—the early writing often concerns family and is autobiographical. I tried to understand my early life and cherish and preserve those who loved and cared for me, all who are gone now, so I am glad I made the effort. My parents, relatives in Ohio and Kentucky on each of their sides take up a lot of focus and subject matter. My first publication ever was in graduate school; Gary Soto, in a completely generous moment, started a small press, Calaveras Press, out of Fresno and published very modest chapbooks by Ernesto Trejo and myself. _6 Poems_ was about family and who knows if anyone other than friends and family ever saw it, but it meant a lot to me at the time. Soto of course also went on to publish the famous Chicano Chapbook Series that promoted more than 30 young writers. I think by my third or fourth book I began looking to my poetic heroes and writing some poems in homage to people like Philip Levine, Charles Wright, though there is a poem for Robert Lowell in the first book. I also was writing ekphrastic poems before anyone was using that term. From my first book onward, I mixed in a few poems on paintings in each book as the subjects/images presented themselves. Then there were a few years during which I was responding to Georgia O'Keeffe's work; I published a collection, *Blossoms & Bones*, with Vanderbilt Univ. Press in 1988 but I had been working on them since 1980. It quickly sold out as O'Keeffe was very popular about that time. I've joked before that you could have sold sand in a can if it was labeled Georgia O'Keeffe Sand. As more poems came to me over the years, I finally put together a book that collected all the O'Keeffe poems plus the Vanderbilt book long out of print: *Flying Backbone*, Blue Light Press, 2008.

None of the poems on painting etc. are in the Selected, and for the last several years I have no poems that work in that direction. I moved on to poems of place and a theme of "Lost Eden" forgive the cliché. I had to move from my home in California to Pennsylvania for a job (for my sins as I said in a poem somewhere) and so the contrast in environments was acute and influenced my focus. Also in the late 1980s, I began to read articles and books on cosmology, astrophysics and such. I'm light years—pun intended—from being any kind of scientific intellect, but there were many articles and books written to reach folks like me who have some interest but not the schooling, so they break it down into imagery and comparisons—perfect for me, like finding money in the street. These cosmological subjects especially offer me ideas and imagery that work around that underlying theme of faith and doubt—as I cited in the previous response quoting Charles Wright. Philosophy as well has become a catalyst over the last fifteen or twenty years. Attending a catholic college, we read a great deal of Philosophy, which at the time was no treat; it was the late 1960's and I was more interested in The Jefferson Airplane and The Rolling Stones, but somehow it all stuck somewhere in the grey cells. Much later then, some of the ideas and a lot of the irony and obfuscation come back when you think of it and reread it. It has been a fertile jumping off point for poems.

AM: Your interest in cosmology, as in the title poem of this collection, serves as metaphor and as a means of meditation about our enterprise here on earth. How was this interest born and how were you able to make what some would consider strictly the territory of science fit your poems?

CB: It all presented itself by happenstance really. I picked up a copy of *The New Yorker* in 1987 I think and there was a long article on dark matter and recent cosmological discoveries. I saw some programs on *NOVA* on PBS about the scientist who discovered dark matter. It was quite a thought. I then picked up a couple books by Timothy Ferris and Marcia Bartusiak intended update folks like myself with an 8th grade education in science on the recent theories and discoveries. These were popular science type books and to reach us, to sell the books, they had to write down to our level which meant using lots of metaphors and images and photos, keeping it simple. But that got me started and from there I read and continue to read these books for pleasure as well as keeping up on articles in Scientific American and on PBS. Just this month there was a substantial article in Scientific American on Gravity Waves, their discovery confirmed 100 years after Einstein has predicted them. I published a book, *Dark Matter*, 1992, whose poems largely dealt with recent discoveries, though they are out of date now. And those concerns and subjects have stayed with me to the present. A couple years back I published a longer sequence titled *Chaos Theory*.

The scientific evidence of our place in the universe, and indeed ideas about our universe, string theory, eleven dimensions, parallel universes etc fits right into, or up against, my usual concerns about faith vs. doubt in so far as an afterlife—that hope vs., as the basketball cliché has it, one and done! My project has been not to simply repeat or report the facts and discoveries; for that you would go to the books or articles. Rather, I hope to combine them with a lyric voice and concrete specifics to render something like a lyric/speculative poem that arm wrestles with the facts and faith. The scientific data work wonderfully as imagery to amplify this contrast with the metaphysical.

AM: In reading your work and the work of other California poets such as Larry Levis and Philip Levine, who has written about this landscape as well as anyone I'm aware of, I get a sense of spaciousness that I do not get from descriptions of the land in the south, where I've spent the majority of my life. Do you have any thoughts on the relationship between landscape and poetry?

CB: It seems obvious to say we are shaped by where we come from. One of the first things people initially ask you, is Where are you from? Place is the filter through which we see experience; it is a crucible, a forge. No matter where you come from, your responses are often related to, are seen in the light of, the imagery and particulars of your native environment. California, for the most part, is unique in space, light, geography, flora et al. But I think someone growing up in a big city can be just as attached to landmarks there and find transformation or transcendence, which is what I look for, which is what Phil and Larry found time and again in their poetry. Recently I have written a handful of poems that touch on our drought in southern California, now in its fifth year. I have not set out to write environmental poems, but living here it is something you cannot ignore, something you want to address and deal with as it touches you every day. I was very fortunate to grow up in Montecito, a suburb of Santa Barbara in the foothills, with the ocean only a mile or so away. Edenic is the exact word to describe it. Remembering that childhood, observing the loss of that unique place effects a lot of my writing in poetry and prose.

AM: One of your constant concerns seems to be time and its passage. For instance in "Sleep Walk," the protagonist of the poem is younger, and time seems to be his ally while in other poems, such as "20 Years of State Jobs and Grant Applications," there is more a sense of what is gained and what is lost in the passage of time. I'd love to hear your thoughts on this.

CB: Nostalgia and growing up in the '50s and early '60s have always been main concerns; I keep trying to rescue the time and imagery before we forget it altogether; I keep trying to cherish it and have it help make sense of our lives—where we were or began and where we have come. What are the values? And of course some of it is just great fun to remember. I just finished a new poem that will have come out in *NEW LETTERS*, titled "You Tube" in which I am looking back at *American Bandstand*, Don and Phil Everly, Martha and the Vandellas and more. Those were wonderful, if not wholly conscious times. Time is an ally only when you can put yourself back into a specific moment via its first hand detail and allow that to resonate and suggest how glorious, perhaps, that time was.

It's not all glorious of course; often we can see what idiots we were, what unfairness in class structure and race obtained then as well. Many years back, spending that afternoon in the Biltmore bar with Larry Levis while everyone else was up in the rooms doing interviews for jobs at the MLA, I asked Larry what he was trying to do in his work and he told me, "Stop time." A poem can do that if well remembered, if well realized and resolved. But the view back over time also offers a more political and candid perspective. I find I have written more poems the last several years with a socio-political edge as the injustices seem to rise out of the nostalgia, out of time passing, not to mention time present. Hence a poem like "20 Years . . ." looking at how I had to fight through the political agendas of administrators and insider trading in academia.

AM: We've mentioned Larry Levis and Philip Levine, poets who are no longer with us. Can you name some living poets whose work sustains you and explain what you like in their work?

CB: Probably at the top of that list would be Peter Everwine, Charles Wright, and Gerald Stern. Of those three, Everwine is the least celebrated and should be much more widely read and appreciated. But what is there to say about the vagaries of celebrity that has not been said? Peter's *New & Selected* and most recently, *Listening Long and Late*, are luminous books that will inspire anyone interested in poetry. He is absolutely unique in his clarity, voice, and precision, his attention to the particular detail, moment, or gesture which will reveal the glory and impossibility of our lives. His work is luminous like no other. And I am enunciating the obvious to say Charles is brilliant as an image maker, but for me he especially engages— with every bit of exotic, inventive, or hipster lingo—the large metaphysical question; he wrestles faith and doubt and does not flinch. Gerald Stern was an inspiration for me from the get-go; he encouraged me to risk putting your individual "stamp" or thumbprint on a poem and showed the way to use your life to discover your poetic project. I'll mention also Diane Wakoski whose poems were a great example for me early on. Two very different poets whose work I greatly admire are Call Dennis and Adam Zagajeski. I'll just mention too my long-time friend Luis Omar Salinas who died in 2008; he was a truly unique talent and his poems have inspired me and many of my students as well as all of his Fresno compadres. Of my own generation there are too many I admire to name them all, but some well-known names that come immediately to mind are Mark Jarman, Robert Wrigley, Gary Young, Naomi Shihab Nye, Chuck Hanzlicek, Dorianne Laux, and Fleda Brown. Gary Soto's last book, *Sudden Loss of Dignity* is a terrific book, one of his best ever. The Fresno poet Jon Veinberg should be much more well-known than he is. Jon is possessed of a voice that is incredibly powerful; it has huge classical texture and volume, but at the same time is contemporary and gritty. *Angels at Bus Stops* is his latest and an amazing read. No one I know gives himself as completely to his subject. Frank Gaspar from Long Beach has become one or our best poets, and Christopher Howell in Spokane is a spectacular poet. With all of the politics in poetry, it is very easy to be overlooked.

AM: What draws you to the European poets. I find mentions of Milosz, Pessoa and others in your work. What do these poets have to say about the human experience that American poets cannot?

CB: Well the answer to this question looks to me to be book-length, a book written by someone much more intelligent and articulate than myself. I have always read many poets in translation. In Milosz and Szymborska and Herbert it is for me a matter of Voice, the direct voice, the art that makes the artifice disappear, the most difficult task in writing poetry I think. They have the craft, the wit and logic, to speak sincerely, directly, and to be original and compelling line to line. Amichai is a poet I have read a great deal and whose honest and personal voice I found inspirational. They all do not hesitate to take on, very directly, the thorniest and deepest problems of our daily lives and hold them in some kind of relief against the metaphysical, or what we hope is the metaphysical.

And I have always been a reader and admirer of the great Spanish language poets. Neruda, Machado, Lorca, Herenandez, Alberti, Blas de Otero, Luis Cernuda, Vallejo,

Ernesto Cardenal, Julio Cortazar, Jaime Sabines and many many more They all are brilliant and inventive image makers and that will charge your batteries of course, but all of that is in service of a Voice, a personal and credible human voice that a reader can believe, that he can place at street level, a common blood running in our veins. These poets have a gravity and a larger hope for all of us especially when compared to much that is currently celebrated.

AM: You've edited a number of anthologies of poetry and prose. And recently you started up the journal *Miramar*. Can you speak about the importance of such work?
CB: Ghandi said something to the effect that, The little thing you do will not be important, but it is important that you do it. A guiding principle for me over the years. And then there is that line from *Butch Cassidy & The Sundance Kid*: "Just keep thinkin' Butch, that's what you're good at." I kept having ideas. So if I could convince a publisher that my idea was worthy, it resulted in an anthology of some kind. I began writing reviews of poetry books as early as graduate school. I thought it important to point out things I observed in the work of Levine and Charles Wright, but the *NY Review of Books* and such places were not as convinced. I mainly focused on trying to promote good work by younger poets I thought might otherwise be overlooked. I published in small magazines, but did what I could to help draw any attention to good work.

I wrote the long critical/biographical essays—ten to eleven thousand words each—on Levine, Everwine, Levis, and Salinas for Scribner's *AMERICAN WRITERS*. These were "my poets" from what has been called The Fresno School, and it was an opportunity to properly appreciate what they had accomplished, and I felt obligated to testify to their achievements. Simply put, we owe those who have gone before us and given us so much. I was a friend and great admirer of Larry Levis and wanted to put together as comprehensive a book as I could to preserve his life and work. I had a verbal contract with the University of Georgia Press for the book and was awaiting the contract in the mail when my editor there left abruptly to head another university press. Georgia then cancelled all the books she had on her desk. So it took me a while to find another publisher, and in the meantime folks at Virginia Commonwealth Univ. sold the idea to Univ. of Michigan Press and reprinted most of the prose work I had in my ms. before I could land another contract. So I had to shift gears, but in doing so organized a book, over 600 pages, that uncovered more of Larry's prose and incorporated many appreciations and memoirs about his work and life. It was something that I felt needed to be done, that his life and genius deserved, and so I did the work.

I took on the book in the Univ. of Michigan's Under Discussion Series on Levine. I knew Phil and it was work I wanted to do to be certain of a book that properly represented his unique achievement in American poetry. I have done many such books now and think I am done. But it is something I feel you owe the muse, if you will. When I retired from teaching I started up a poetry journal to cash in on the huge profits available in that field. . . . Seriously, everyone knows that this is a bad business model, but I felt I wanted to pay something back and so taught part time for two years and put that salary and money out of pocket into producing a journal of poetry, reviews and essays that would promote work of a certain clarity and humanity. *MIRAMAR* takes its focus from Machado; "Every man has two/ battles to wage:/ in dreams, he wrestles with God;/and awake, with the sea." It is a dead loss financially, and I just hope I can keep it going for a while longer. I think it is important that poets review and write about poetry. It's a small contribution but we should, I think, support each other and the work that we find worthy and have given our lives to.

AM: In a review of your book *Sky*, I mistakenly identified you as a former student of Philip Levine's. You, of course, were not a student, but you did know him for many years and you edited the wonderful anthology of essays *Stranger to Nothing* about Levine and his work. I wonder if you could talk a bit about those years of friendship and what he meant to you both as a poet and a friend.

CB: I was never a student of Phil's, officially. My friends in the MFA program at UC Irvine in middle '70s, Jon Veinberg and Gary Soto, were students of Phil's and I pretty much became part of the Fresno school of poets through them. My teacher at San Diego State was Glover Davis, one of the early group of students from Fresno State along with Larry Levis, St. John, Roberta Spear, Ernesto Trejo and many many others.

The first books of contemporary poetry I bought were *They Feed They Lion*, Red *Dust* and *Not this Pig* by Phil. I was hooked; I loved the fierceness of that early work, the grounded but fiery, visionary voice, the deep humanity of the poems. That far back I didn't know much but I could recognize Phil's exceptional gift. I met Phil at San Diego State when he came to do a reading—1973 I think—which was a big deal with 350 people or more filling Montazuma Hall to hear him.

The one time I was in a classroom with Phil was several years later when I was a fellow at Bread Loaf, assigned to help Levine with workshops and conferences. In the first workshop a contributor turned in a poem on Caravaggio, and no one seemed to know the references or allusions so Phil asked if anyone could give some background or explain. I had studied Caravaggio's work and immediately raised my hand; he was hoping for one of the contributors to offer something and kept looking around the room. When there was no one to call on he finally pointed to me saying, "Ok Buckley, but don't tell us everything you know!" We had come to know each other pretty well by that point. While at Bread Loaf, I began the interviewing and data gathering needed for the Univ. of Michigan Press book, *On the Poetry of Philip Levine: Stranger to Nothing*. In addition to collecting the reviews and historical response to the poems, I also wanted to include a section of original essays, appreciations. I asked Larry to write an essay for the collection, and the result was "Philip Levine" an essay that is the hallmark of the book, a remembrance at once hilarious in recalling Phil in the classroom in the '60s, and poignant in its tribute and testament to the value of great teachers. That essay alone is easily worth the price of the book.

I knew Phil 43 years. In all that time I think he helped me with three or four poems. Since I had never officially been a student of his I was hesitant to send him poems asking for help and direction. So many did so already, students and people who just were friends, people who weren't and who presumed. He was so generous and such a great correspondent, he always wrote back—hundreds of letters in the days before ubiquitous e mail. In those years, I don't think a month went by without a letter from Phil, even when I was living in Menorca for a year. When back in California, I saw Phil on my regular visits to Fresno. Wherever I was teaching, I could count on Phil to come and read, most always for much less than other places could pay him. I don't think I've met anyone else who was truer to himself. He turned down very lucrative readings because he did not admire the people or the place; he'd take less money to help someone out. Each time I was editing an anthology, Phil contributed and arm-wrestled his publishers to waive permission fees.

Phil gave countless interviews during his career, and in an early one he was asked about teaching, if he held a little back in the classroom so he might have some energy and inspiration left for himself and his own writing. His answer was No. He did not; to do so would be to betray yourself, the students, and poetry.

from _Star Journal_ Interview Questions, from _NEW LETTERS,_ 2016—Alexander Long

Alexander Long: You dedicate _Star Journal: Selected Poems to Philip Levine._ You never were officially a student of Levine's, but he seems to have served as a mentor for you nevertheless. Can you talk about how you came to know Levine, how your relationship with him evolved over the years, & how he has influenced your writing, especially as evidenced now in _Star Journal?_

Christopher Buckley: A long story, 43 years worth . . . Bless Phil and all he did for poets and poetry, the brilliance and inspiration of his body of work. My first teacher, Glover Davis at San Diego State, was a student of Phil's in that amazing early Fresno group that included Levis, Omar Salinas, Roberta Spear, St. John et al. I first met Phil in the early '70s then when he came to SDSU to read. Tennis was huge in those days, everyone played and Phil was avid. He did not want to miss his weekly game while on the road for the week and asked Glover if he could find someone to hit with him. Glover knew I was still working as a teaching pro, and so I met Phil on the courts. Later that day I was invited to a small reception for Phil at Glover's house. I don't think I said five words all afternoon, just kept looking around amazed to be there. A year or so later while in the MFA program at UC Irvine, I published a review of _1933_ and sent Phil a copy. From there, we exchanged letters regularly; Phil was an incredible correspondent and wrote hundreds of letters to many people, back in those honorable days before email. Proposition 13 hit mid to late '70s in California and part time jobs dried up, so I moved to Fresno where there seemed to be a little work. I was 29 when I came to teach at Fresno State. Friends had already won book awards, money prizes, had tenure track jobs, and had published in the better journals. I was feeling a bit left behind in the dust, with my three early morning classes of composition to teach. But soon—as I said at the memorial held for Phil on the campus of Fresno State in February 2016—I received the major poetry award of my life: I was assigned to share an office with Phil. He gave me advice not just about poetry but about how to keep my head on straight through all the vicissitudes present and future. His advice and care were essential in getting me through those early years—he emphasized the value of work for its own worth, patience, fortitude, modesty, dedication, and honesty, especially with regard to yourself. And there was no one who gave so much of his time, gifts, insight and experience. Over the years, Phil was incredibly generous, something I can never adequately repay, and I expect many feel this debt. There are four anthologies of poets who came through Fresno and who have lives in poetry as a result.

We became closer as the years went by. He was an incredibly loyal friend; he wrote letters for me for over 20 years when no one could have blamed him for passing on the requests, especially on the Guggenheim. Most of the poets I know who received the fellowship did so with one or two tries and so did not have to bother Phil year after year as I did for the letter. Something like 20 to 25 applications went in before I was awarded one. First thing I did was call Phil and say, "I have good news for both of us!" I was a fellow at Bread Loaf in '89 I think it was, and was assigned to Phil to help with the contributors in conferences and workshops. As part of your fellowship, you were able to present a ms. to a senior faculty member for review/critique. _Blue Autumn_ was the only ms. of mine then that Phil really saw, and he offered some significant cuts and changes. Also there we did the initial interview for the Univ. of Michigan Press's volume in the Under Discussion series I would edit, _On The Poetry of Philip: Stranger to Nothing._ Phil was a loyal supporter; whenever I came up with an idea for an anthology, I could always count on him to contribute and help arm wrestle his press re. permission fees. To say that his poems were a consistent beacon of inspiration in craft and imagination, in the essential dignity of the individual and the writing of poetry, is an understatement. But I do not really know how much specific influence Phil was on the poems in this selected, other than to try to write the best poem I could at the time. The dedication then is not to say I had some special relationship with Phil; he had so many friends and no one was more generous. It is just to acknowledge a huge debt to someone that gave me my life in poetry and hence my life.

AL: If I had to describe your poetic voice, it would involve a flurry of paradoxes, something like: desperately hopeful, or seriously comic, or cosmically grounded, or genuinely & intimately political, or all of the above. Voice is a tricky thing, as you know, for writers, & by & large it is—unlike, say, a sense of rhythm or image making—impossible to teach. Your voice has changed over the years, but it hasn't. I know when I am reading a Buckley poem before I look at the name. How would you describe your poetic voice, & was there a definitive moment, or poem, when you realized you had found your voice? Or has it been a slower process of revelation & evolution over the years?

CB: Ah well . . . a real opportunity here to be immodest, but I would have to say it has been a slow process of evolution, though I agree that I don't think my voice has changed essentially from the beginning. To me, it has just become a bit more clear as I begin a poem which aspect of my voice is presenting itself.

But I think your observations re the conflict or paradox in there are accurate, and I would vote for "all of the above" in answer to your question. The battle between hope and despair is the bedrock of a lot of the work. I realized early on that I shared an essential view with Charles Wright who said, "All my poems seem to be an ongoing argument with myself about the unlikelihood of salvation." That is what an orthodox religious upbringing will do for you, once you realize what is most likely in the cards. And if you share that view with Charles, there are not many crumbs left on the table when you get there. Nevertheless, there it is and I seem to come back to it often. My interest in science and cosmology, which started in the mid '80s, is one half of that as it opposes most metaphysical notions. But voice has always been my concern, the authenticity of its tone that comes from essential human concerns.

I sometimes see the poems moving to a higher lyrical resonance and sometimes toward a more ironic and discursive character or pitch. In 2008 I put together a book of new prose poems, *Modern History*, that has most of the latter. In the last fifteen or so years, I think I engage politics more overtly—and I think that often brings in the ironic and comic— whereas you would think it would be the province of a younger man really. But I figure there is nothing they can do to me now, so why not? As for realizing when you find your voice, it is hard to say. You think that is the case many different times in your writing life it seems to me. I remember a poem I wrote near the end of grad school, thinking I had finally hit it, and then later abandoning the poem. I think my third book, *Dust Light, Leaves*, way back in the day, marked something for me; at least I seemed to have a firmer grasp on what I wanted to say and how I was going to go about it by that point. Jerry Stern was a big help about midway; the example of his own poems of course, but some things he said about putting your own thumbprint on your poems, risking more, really helped and freed me up as far as voice is concerned. I think I hit something in *Star Apocrypha* and more recently in *Rolling the Bones*. So there, I have worked myself around to being immodest after all.

AL: Every writer has his/her idiosyncrasies that manifest themselves on the page; or at least every writer that matters does. Larry Levis' use of the ampersand, Charles

Wright's low-rider line, Dickinson's varying dashes & unconventional capitalizations, Berryman's idiomatic & grammatical manipulations, Merwin's abandonment of punctuation altogether in various books, just to name a few. I would identify some of your idiosyncrasies to include the ellipsis, your own interpretation & utilization of the low-rider line (which Wright adapted, of course, from W. C. Williams), & frequent use of epigraphs. These Buckleyian signatures run consistently throughout your publishing career; I see them serving as markers of metaphysical doubt (the ellipses), a different kind of pacing of rhythm, & therefore thought & meditation, down the page (your low-rider line), & an enlargement of the context of the poem (the epigraphs). They seem to be very conscious choices, but maybe they're not. Can you offer some insight into why you return to these devices so consistently, what you hope they bring to the experience of your poems?

CB: Well again I have to agree with your reading of the work; most of my answer is in your question really. Ellipses are part of me and regularly get me in trouble with editors; they are always something I take second and third looks at due to their frequent employment. But yes, metaphysical doubt, letting the questions hang, trail off into the aethers, if that does not sound too pretentious. And as well for pacing and rhythm, allowing thought or meditation to breathe a bit more. As for Charles's drop-line, he certainly is the most notable practitioner, but I think it first caught my attention as a style/strategy with some poems of John Logan, how he orchestrated the poem on the page, and so some subjects now present themselves that way. The three-step Williams form is a discipline as well for me, as is the long line coupled with a half line . . . all little disciplines to help me order and tighten, to let the phrase or image or idea baste a bit, something I am always conscious of needing to do. But I still write a poem in the short three beat line a la Levine mid career. A tennis analogy works here I think. When I was playing a tournament match, what I did not do was go over the correct mechanics for hitting an overhead or half-volley; instead I relied on muscle-memory, the years of practice, and concentrated on a strategy immediate and appropriate to the guy across the net. So at this point, the form pretty much presents itself to me early on the process, though I am not precious about it finally. I write so many drafts of each poem that I am open to changing the form I began with if I see the lines work better or the form better fits the voice.

As for epigraphs, well, I will take all the help I can get. I use them for the obvious reasons you enunciate above, to enlarge the context and ideas of the poem. I try for irony a lot as you do not want some spectacular lines of a great poem to completely overshadow your efforts.

AL: The selection process of what would make it into *Star Journal* & what wouldn't must have been an especially difficult one. Can you talk about what guided your thinking as you made those impossible choices?

CB: Well the practical overwhelmed the aesthetic—not a lot of choosing and hand-wringing then. Pittsburgh said an initial ms. of no more than 124 pages, and the final ms. of 95-100. I left 6 books out completely. But "selected" means just that, selected. I just went through picking what I thought were the best poems from each book—as obvious as that—the exception being, as I said, leaving out long poems. I had to start over several times as I would get to the page limit with still 4 or 5 books yet to select from. Eventually, I cut to the bone, trimmed the ms. to the page limit and sent it to Ed Ochester who went through and edited out even more poems. He is consistent in what he likes and thinks works. In a larger format, if I had my choice, I would have included a number of the higher lyric pieces, many published in *POETRY*, and a handful of the longer poems as well as more prose poems. Just not in the cards. But I think we ended up with a tight and representative book.

AL: Like me, you're a recovering Catholic, & your years in parochial school have left their psychic scars, which appear in your poems with simultaneous great comic effect, serious spiritual questioning, & metaphysical gravitas. Earlier in your career you seemed to look to the natural world to replace the fire & brimstone the nuns shoved down your psyche. Later in your career, you return repeatedly to quantum physics & philosophy, all while still remaining faithful to your California landscapes. Was this a conscious shift from, say, the earth to the mind & spirit, or one that gradually & naturally developed almost without your noticing, per se? Is there something inherently spiritual about your California?

CB: Long ago, I saw a bumper sticker that proclaimed: "I survived Catholic School!" but I don't think anyone really does. At about age 11 though, I began to doubt all the flimflam and psychic torture the nuns had put us through in parochial school. Catholic high school only pushed me further away from orthodoxy. That said, the essential groundwork of metaphysical questioning, the hope that some bit of it might obtain, was the basis for a lot of the poetry. And in St. Mary's College we read philosophy every semester—a tough time to do that and have it stick in the late '60's: Hare Krishna, tie-die, Haight-Ashbury, spare change, Jefferson Airplane, Sgt. Pepper's, Jimi Hendrix and were we experienced?— add in Vietnam. But later it comes back with inquiry, and with its irony and impossibility. I find philosophy a rich source of ideas and contradictions, but there is nothing I follow specifically as a discipline of thought. Grist for the mill.

In 1999 Gary Young and I edited the poetry anthology, *The Geography of Home: California's Poetry of Place*. Our contention, somewhat obviously, was that place was essential to poetry, and was the filter through which we understand experience. That pretty much has always been one of the two or three lines of thinking I have followed. It hit me especially hard when I moved to Pennsylvania for a job. As soon as I landed in that alien environment— snow, ice, heat and humidity—my poetry and nonfiction turned to a "loss of Eden" theme in recovering my life growing up in southern California. In "Saint Emmanuel the Good Martyr" by Miguel de Unamuno, he has his protagonist suggest that there is in fact another world, but it is shining within this one, so of course I find something spiritual in the environment here, always have, though I was not aware of that per se as a kid growing up.

AL: Right around your mid-career, I want to say 1996 or 1997, you received sabbatical & went to live in Spain for six months. Two things strike me as crucial about your time in Spain. First, when you returned, you were on hot-streak of publishing some of your best poems in rapid succession across the span of about four or five books in seven or eight years. Second, I have a photograph of you feeding a herd of street cats in Spain. When you returned to the states, you immediately got two cats. Maybe my memory is foggy on all details, so please correct me. More importantly, what happened to you as a poet that obviously was a transformative experience for you & your writing?

CB: After 20 years of teaching, I had my first sabbatical in 1994-95. I'd been burning the candle at both ends and in the middle teaching at a third rate state college in PA—a huge teaching load plus several committees and program direction, not to mention a crew of "colleagues" anyone could do without. I sold popcorn at the football games on Saturdays in the fall and Simonized the President's car once a month . . . paycheck to paycheck for many years there.

It was difficult to get the poems written. I was doing it, but I could feel the flames at my heels. After the torturous process of application for sabbatical, you could choose, if you received one, either half year off at whole pay or whole year at a bit less than half pay. We had no money but I knew I needed to get away, needed that block of time all writers need to relax the brain and remember what it was you used to be obsessed about—so I took the full year. My wife had a friend with a flat she was not using in Menorca and she gave it to us for something like $300 a month. We scraped by. Thought we would travel over to Mallorca and to Barcelona every now and then but we could not afford to get off the island. I had time to clear the grey matter and read a lot of Neruda and take care of a herd of wild cats that lived on the cliff, and repair for the time being, a wonky rhythm in my heart from stress. Took lots of walks every day, re-focused on what was important—being alive. We were there 9 months. The only thing that "happened" was that I realized that there was no longer a point in having any ambition re poetic acknowledgement. Helen Vendler was not going to anoint me; I was never going to NYC to collect a prize. That boat had sailed and was not coming back, so I let it go, gave up, quit worrying about what I was writing or who might or might not approve, read, or publish it. Just do the work. That set me straight. That is all I can think of that might have changed me or recharged the psychic batteries. A load off, as they say. So no specific event took place. Living took place. And Menorca was much like home, like Santa Barbara, all the same plants and light and sea. I finished up *Fall from Grace* and had notes and experience for *Star Apocrypha*. Menorca saved my life. It was depressing to return to PA, seriously so, but I had one more year to serve there before I got lucky and turned up a job back in California, where my wonderful cats Cecil and Lizzie were waiting for us.

AL: I'd like to talk about one poem in particular, "Father, 1952." I'm drawn to its elegiac subject & how you manipulate time. I'm particularly drawn to how you try to stop it, & ultimately realize both the enormity & smallness of both time & our attempts to defeat it: "—this is not that long ago…" Such an especially tender & devastating refrain line, which is to say, one that is hitting all the right notes. You've written many other elegies, but the immediacy, the relentless reminders of the past cast in the present in "Father, 1952" is singular. What are you trying to do to, or with, time in this poem?

CB: I am trying to do exactly the things you describe in your question—he said modestly— so thanks for a good and close reading of the poem. I think most of us learned moves re stopping time, gliding back and forth, the sustaining light of the past resonating forward to us, from Weldon Kees, the immediacy of the specific in memory—thinking here especially of "1926." It is I think, the exact and specific image—the porch light coming on again, the brown autumn light above Anacapa Street—that can summon the present tense, and so stop time. Poetry comes from Poetry the cliché has it. So for me the poem works mainly in the detail, the child's memory of being there, the indictment of the place and the light and the plain fact of how memory illuminates and replays our lives with intensity, the attached emotions, when we go there, when the meditation of time and place distill. Simple mortality and the rush of experience. The moment of realization.

AL: Your poems have been unapologetically nostalgic in as long as you've been publishing. Much of your work could serve as a guide to pop culture for 1950s American film & music. What is so alluring about your past, which by all accounts seems to have been—to borrow a phrase from William Matthews—a happy childhood?

CB: A good portion of what I find emblematic, what grounds and yet suggests the larger questions, I find in the particulars of my childhood in the '50s and '60s. To say it was a different time and that the world was a substantially different place to live, is, I think at once a true statement, and yet one that any generation, looking back can claim to be true simply due to the nature of time passing. But it was—going back to an earlier remark—more of an "Edenic" place, especially growing up in Santa Barbara and Montecito, on the relatively unpopulated and verdant edge of the Pacific. Certainly slower, kinder, gentler, but beneath all that was the institutional racial and economic inequality that has not disappeared today.

I touch the specifics there and they sing to the grey cells and remind me of what we thought might come, all the light that was ours and which we thought would keep us comfortable forever. Not so, as we found out quickly enough, but when wrestling with the possibility of a metaphysical outcome or impetus in our lives, those are the details and the moments that together, help to form the argument for the value or outcome of our lives. Growing up then, you had your immediate frisson of the times—I remember replaying my first 45 of "Walk Don't Run" by the Ventures at least ten times when I got it home—as well as the recent and lingering history of your parents. My father was a DJ and a singer and my brain was imprinted early on with all the lyrics and songs from the '40s and early '50s—"Street of Dreams," "I've got the World on a String," "Time on my Hands," "I Cover the Waterfront," and a hundred others—such amazing romanticism floating over most everything. Now of course you have to play that off against the social realities as they existed then, as they evolve in front of us on 24 hr cable TV news, but that is the paradox poems try to work through it seems to me.

AL: Your influences are wildly diverse, far-reaching. Levine, of course, & Gerald Stern & Charles Wright, but also your American contemporaries William Matthews & Larry Levis, the great Turkish poet Nazim Hikmet, the great Peruvian poet Cesar Vallejo, the great Israeli poet Yehuda Amichai, the great Portuguese poet Fernando Pessoa, the two great Polish poets Milosz & Szymborska, I even recall you saying that early on in your writing life that Swinburne served as a kind of guide . . . there are others, of course. (I'd love to be at that cocktail party!) Obviously, these are very different poets, but they all seemed to have struck resonant chords with you. What does their work provide for your work? Do you hear them hitting similar notes in myriad ways & languages, or does the wide range of the totality of their poetry appeal to you in important ways?

CB: Good surfing story . . . I was 14, no swell that day and I stopped in the Bottle Shop to check the magazine rack. Only 2 surf magazines those days, John Severson's *SURFER*, and a lesser production called *Surf Guide*. New issue of *Surf Guide* was just out, and in the very center, covering right and left pages, was a photo of a perfect 12 foot wave and in its center was a stanza from A.C. Swinburne's "Hymn to Proserpine." I was taken with the soaring sounds and sea-roar of the rhymes, the steady and compelling meter. That started me off down the path to poetry, though I wrote horribly through my teens and early 20s, and Swinburne's great musical inflation did me more harm than good. What saved me from going all the way down the rabbit hole of uninformed self-indulgence was the appearance of William Stafford on my college campus to give a reading. We'd been reading T.S. Eliot in my Lit class, so Stafford's poems were like nothing I'd ever heard, direct, subtle, accessible. It took me several more years to try and write under his clear example. The first two books of contemporary poetry I owned were *They Feed They Lion* by Phil and *Collecting the Animals* by Peter Everwine. I imitated Phil for two years in graduate school and was caught by

Glover each time I stole a line. I then switched to Everwine, trying to write as succinctly and deceptively simply as Peter and soon saw that was impossible. But good lessons nonetheless. Everyone else you mention are poets I read and love; you have most of my favorites there excepting perhaps Neruda and the Spanish poets of the generation of '27. In each instance, it is voice that compels me, the direct voice, the art that makes the artifice disappear, the most difficult task in writing poetry I think. They all have mastered the craft to speak sincerely, directly, and to be original and engaging line to line. I believe there is a thoughtful human being speaking with an honest and personal voice I find inspirational. They all do not hesitate to take on the deepest problems of our daily humanity and hold those problems up against what might be a metaphysical background.

AL: So few poets get touched by fame, & some of those who are, one has to wonder how & why? What has sustained you all these years to keep going?

CB: My wife Nadya has always said I am tenacious, I guess you could read "stubborn" there. I think I probably complained too much for too many years but I did not let myself be ultimately discouraged. Strong work ethic, I kept writing and rewriting. And I especially enjoyed teaching; I have had many talented students, so I kept going, doing my job, despite spirited opposition from administrators of all stripes. William Carlos Williams said a successful poet is one who writes a successful poem. So I have gone with that as the jobs and prizes did not come through. I have good friends, especially my group of Fresno poets; we all have hung together over the years for mutual support, and man, what a gathering of talent that is, all mentored by Levine and Everwine. Jerry Stern has been a sweet, and inspirational presence in my poetry life. One day many years ago, he called me up in Pennsylvania after talking to Levine, and just started in as if we were old pals. I owe Jerry a lot and his support really picked me up in the middle of what I am calling a career. I give a lot of credit to my friends Gary Young and Jon Veinberg who edit and respond to all my work. And to Gary Soto whose support helped keep my head above water when we were just out of grad school. Wonderful poets and selfless pals. I have no networks at the top of poetry, no one asks me to lunch in NYC. I received two NEAs very far apart in time, and just got lucky with my mss. falling into the hands of the right judges finally as judging is supposed to be anonymous. I still am not sure how I received the Guggenheim after all that time; I joke that I had so many applications in the office that they needed the space for new applicants and so finally relented. Some good soul on the Literature Committee had mercy. I always thought I had a chance there as they read the work you submitted, and beyond that I have realistically never expected anything. But you can't win the lottery if you don't buy a ticket, so I do my due diligence and fill out the forms, send the money and books off and forget about them. I go to my desk each day hoping for the next poem.

Christopher Buckley and Jon Veinberg, Menorca 1995

"FRESNO" from *Holy Days of Obligation,* 2012—Christopher Buckley

I grew up playing tennis and surfing in those days when courts and parking lots were open and free. My life was charmed; my home was the foothills and the beaches of Montecito and Santa Barbara. Movie stars and the ridiculously rich lived there but you did not have to be one to do so; my father worked as a radio DJ, my mother was a secretary for the public schools. I had never heard of Fresno.

But in my first semester of graduate school at San Diego State University I found myself again very fortunate, though I did not realize that right away. Glover Davis was my workshop teacher; he was one of the early group of poets who had gone to Fresno State and studied with Philip Levine and Peter Everwine. I'd had a very traditional English major education at St. Mary's College in northern California, and so the first books of contemporary poetry I ever read were *They Feed They Lion* and *Collecting the Animals* in that first class with Glover. I soon discovered the anthology *Down at the Santa Fe Depot* and the poetry of Larry Levis, Luis Omar Salinas and many others. These books and poets, and Glover's rigorous approach to writing, gave me my poetic life. I had no idea. At the time, the landscape of the future was pretty much a blank.

After San Diego I went to UC Irvine for the MFA and met Jon Veinberg and Gary Soto, and Gary Young, my best and oldest friends in poetry. Soto and Veinberg were both Levine students from Fresno, but our friendship did not start off all that smoothly. Problems with housing had me joining our workshop two weeks late that first fall quarter, but I hit the ground running as I had just come from 2 & ½ years of workshop with Glover Davis at San Diego State. I did not know who Gary Soto was, but he was the poet in the workshop who had published the most, in places like *The Iowa Review, POETRY,* and *The Nation,* and so had more poetic medals on this chest than the room combined. In those days I carried a large shoulder book bag that a friend had made for me from thick leather. Soto later described it as big enough to house a V8! I pulled out the worksheet and a pen and jumped into the critique. Soto had a longer poem up first and I offered that the next to last stanza could be cut and it would improve the poem. Soto clearly was not used to much criticism and looked down the line at me and said, "Maybe you just don't understand the poem?" To which I replied, "I understand it just fine; that stanza is weak and has to go." He was not pleased. But after the workshop was over Soto came up to me outside with his pal Jon Veinberg and asked me, "Hey, do you want to get a Coke?" "A What?" I said? There was a college bar across the street from campus called the Spritzgarden, and so I said, "I'll go for a beer." And Veinberg seconded that motion. It had been Jon who convinced Soto that my comments were well founded and would help the poem, and so that encouraged him to try and make friends, which we did, over a beer. Gary was known through the years as "two-can Soto" due to his inability to drink more than two beers and remain cogent, so I think we talked stretching out a single beer.

During that time, I began driving up to Fresno and spending weekends and holidays at Jon's—the first time in spring, all the almonds, crepe myrtle and plums blossoming—a wonderful place I thought. I still recall Gary and Carolyn Soto's wedding there near the end of our second year at Irvine. A large outdoor affair in late spring, a perfect almost beatific light filtering through the stands of eucalyptus, the sensational chicken mole and Spanish champagne, Veinberg in his best man's tux and gold Converse tennis shoes. Tim Sheehan, Jon, and I had driven up from Irvine to share in the celebration. At Irvine, we had complained consistently enough about the department poets recycled to teach the workshop that they hired Peter Everwine to drive down once a week while he was on leave with a

Guggenheim. He taught our last quarter there and so rescued what had been—aside from Diane Wakoski visiting and teaching our first quarter—two years of a moribund program.

I began teaching part time at several colleges around Orange County, but when Prop 13 hit the schools with budget cuts, I moved to Fresno. I had good friends there, there was an amazing community of poets, and there was part-time teaching at Fresno State. Composition classes at 8:00, 9:00, and 11:00 am, MWF, students nodding off in the first row in the 8:00 class despite my intriguing lectures on parallel construction, 75 essays to correct each weekend. Baseball got me through the papers along with a huge armchair from the Salvation Army with large flat arms on which to stack the essays—the Cubs, Giants, and Braves usually on one channel or the other as I sat there all day Saturday and Sunday. If the Dodgers won, the grades were usually a bit higher. But I had a job, was getting by, and was young and grateful. I wasn't paid much but there were bonuses. Somehow, I was assigned to share an office with Levine, and often in the afternoons as I was leaving and he was coming in, he would take time to talk with me and tell stories and give me advice, and you can't put a price on that. As I have said elsewhere, that was the major poetry prize of my life. Over the years, Phil was incredibly generous, something I could never adequately repay, and I expect many felt this debt. I also befriended Chuck Hanzlicek there. I still remember the day he was assigned to observe one of my composition classes and wrote one of the funniest, most witty and irreverent reports I've ever read which put the whole process in true perspective; it opened with comments on the student in the front of the class applying lavender lipstick while I was assiduously declaiming the pitfalls of the comma splice.

I rented an old clapboard house on Arthur Street with a backyard and a garden where our crew of young poets spent a lot of time. I had two old hibachis and sometimes picked up huge dinner franks from Hestbecks Meat Market or some packs of skinny chicken legs. When I could afford to, I picked up hard biscuits, sweet butter, and some Carignane from Piemonte's at $2.50 a bottle which was the ceiling of the wine budget then. Omar especially liked those biscuits with the butter. Often the group would gather at my house late afternoon for a beer. As the light began to fade, we'd start thinking of dinner as I did not always have provisions on hand. We'd then start peaking into our wallets to see who had money and count up our collective cash. We needed $4.95 a head plus tax and tip to hit the chicken dinner at the Santa Fe Basque Restaurant. Usually we had to count down to the change in our pockets to cover Omar and Leonard Adame. If things totaled up favorably, we headed downtown to the best dinner we knew. Half a perfectly cooked chicken, but first all the extras: bread, a plate of celery, carrots, olives and salami, then salad with shrimp and potato salad, or if it was Friday, the rice and clams, my favorite, (tongue on Thursday's, Veinberg's favorite) then soup, then the huge hunk of chicken. We ate everything brought to the table and were often full by the time the entre arrived, and so each of us left with a white plastic "doggie bag" of chicken—no money left to be waylaid by the long beautiful bar and the snifters of Fundador—looking like thieves in the night, bags in hand slipping out the front door into the night. But that only happened if Veinberg was truly full, for no one cleaned a chicken bone like Jon, not a scrap of meat, skin, or gristle remained as the bones stacked up on his plate in a kind of pyramid and glistened like porcelain.

Veinberg, Adame, Omar Salinas, and Soto would regularly come by, Ernesto Trejo often, sometimes Gary Young and Tim Sheehan over from Santa Cruz. Someone might have a new poem to pass around and we'd talk about that before adjourning to pitch bocce ball and sip beverages through the afternoon and into the warm evening. I ran a long extension cord from the house to the back yard and plugged in my 12" portable TV on top of the picnic table, adjusted the antenna, and we watched baseball or on occasion a heavyweight title fight.

One fall evening I even remember our rowdy group inside before my tiny black and white to watch a production of *Carmen* on *Live from the Met*. We were silent, captivated absolutely as Carmen and the cigarette girls sashayed across the stage to the habanera. October of 1979 I had a packed living room as I had just purchased on a payment plan, a portable color TV, the first color set any of us owned. A postage-stamp screen by today's standards, but we pulled our chairs in a semicircle five feet away from the 12" screen and enjoyed each game, most of us supporting Pittsburgh. After four games, Baltimore, with over 102 wins that season, was leading 3-1. Leonard Adame thought he saw an opportunity for an easy buck and offered to bet me $10 on a Baltimore victory. Baltimore had the pitching—Jim Palmer, Steve Stone, Scott McGregor and Mike Flanagan, easily superior to Pittsburgh and needing only one more game to close out the series. But Willie Stargell ended up hitting .400 with seven extra-base hits and the Pirates came back to win in seven. Leonard never had any money, but he felt he had a sure thing if I took the bet, which I did; I just had a hunch. I think that was one bet Leonard actually paid off, though he still owes me and others on a number of other bets.

I managed to keep the bills paid supplementing my teaching salary by working at Soto's brother's Graphic Design business. I would meet with Rick and his clients and work up ad copy for the newspaper and magazine ads he designed. It was trying work sometimes, but the extra check every now and then kept me afloat. Rick did excellent work and we tried to keep the copy fresh. Nevertheless after a few very nice ads for the Olive Advisory Board that were featured in *Cuisine* and *Bon Appetite*, they did not hire us for more, and went with some firm that trotted out the old Kraft Foods cliché, "Simply Delicious." I then took on the area coordinator's job for the Poets In The School program. I'd meet with teachers and administrators in high schools and junior highs, and pitch the advantage of classes in poetry writing as a support for language skills and the arts. It worked most of the time and I taught workshops with the MGM (advanced) students as well at the Title I. seventh graders who were reading at 3rd grade level. The seventh graders especially perked up and enjoyed writing with the Soto poems I brought in as models as they saw they could write about their own lives in pretty much their own language.

I lived month-to-month, little if anything left over at the end. But what a great two years. I shared an office with Phil; Peter Everwine and I wrote a grant and received some money to run a visiting writers series on campus; Veinberg and I traded help with poems almost every week. Ernesto Trejo often came to town as he was working for a while in Mexico City for the government as an economics advisor. I still remember Ernesto coming over to the house on Arthur with his first child, Victor, bald and bundled up in a white blanket, looking like a small Pope as he reached his hand out to bless us. Ernesto was a wonderful poet and one of the sweetest people you could ever meet. And Omar Salinas who usually lived with his aunt and uncle in Sanger, moved into town for a while and Jon and I helped him find an apartment. He stopped by at all hours, and each time I would take him in my study and put him before my large Royal office typer and we would work on new poems and rewrites as he chain smoked KOOLs. I'd open the window to the street and put a fan on behind him to flush the smoke, but we got work done writing and typing up *Afternoon of the Unreal* and *Prelude to Darkness*. Omar, moved in with Jon for a while on Brown Street and worked prefabricated construction for a couple weeks on the night shift, but it proved too much for him finally and he moved back in with his relatives. Still, he would show up on weekends usually, and we all would sit in the back of Jon's house—cheap beer and sausages on the grill—and take notes as Omar extemporaneously recited odes to the apricot tree, Jon's dog Moses, or his exploits as a *Romancero*, a buccaneer of love.

For two years at Fresno State I taught three miserable sections of composition a semester, a full-time load for which I was paid part-time, but I was happy—writing a lot, living among the fog and fruit trees, the sycamores with leaves the size of dinner plates, among so many wonderful friends. Then, a full-time position came up at UC Santa Barbara, and I took it and moved back home. It was good to be by the sea, to escape the scorching Fresno summers and the barely efficient swamp coolers, but it wasn't long before I was driving back up to Fresno, sitting out into the night under the clear stars, visiting with my compadres.

Through the late '80s and well into the '90s I was sentenced for my sins to teach in Pennsylvania at a fourth-rate state college. But every chance I had, summers and Christmas breaks stretched with unpaid and underpaid readings, I was back to California. Nadya and I would escape the snow and land in Palm Springs to stay with my mother. We'd then borrow her car and drive to Fresno. I would go along with Jon on Saturday mornings to Sanger to take Omar out to breakfast, something he did without fail until Omar's passing. When I finally managed to land a job back in southern California, I'd still drive up to Fresno every few months and sit out with Jon, drinking a lite beer and remembering the great poets we'd lost—Ernesto Trejo, Larry Levis, Chuck Moulton, and Omar among the others. We'd visit with Phil and Franny, Peter, Chuck and Dianne Hanzlicek, walk through the Tower District praising the old pines and grand houses, and stop into Piemonte's for a sandwich, for the rich nostalgic air of good times already gone.

I am always, it seems, planning a trip to Fresno, staying with my friends Jon Veinberg and Dixie Salazar. For several years, my wife Nadya and I would go thrifting with Dixie who was a regular at all the best thrift stores, and we'd return home with the car full of tables and lamps and imitation leopard collared jackets and such. Dixie is a painter as well as a poet and she has a big studio down town, Fresno now a place where artists can afford space in the old central area. Nadya, also a painter, always wanted to see Dixie's latest work and we headed down for a private showing and then crossed the street to Emerald Thrift and a couple adjacent stores. Jon usually found a chair and observed the mental processes of the shoppers. Later, there were trips to celebrate Philip Levine's appointment as US Poet laureate, and a year following, his 85th Birthday—spectacular and energy-filled occasions among friends of many years. The speeches were smart, funny, appropriate, and mercifully short. At his 85th birthday party luncheon Phil stood to say a few words in thanks after the speeches, and, looking around the room at many people he has known for forty years or more, said, "Sitting here for the last half hour I have been wondering—Do I look as terrible as all of you?" And the room roared in laughter. Most of us see each other regularly, or we might not recognize one another? Sharp, witty as ever, Phil and over sixty of us had a wonderful afternoon celebrating his generosity and genius centered for fifty years or more in Fresno.

A ritual for the last several years and one of my favorite things to do in Fresno, was a visit with Peter Everwine. Jon rounded up whoever was in town, and we all went out for a nice dinner together and visited afterwards at Jon and Dixie's for a drink. But usually on a Friday or Saturday afternoon, Jon and I would hit Piemonte's for a Piemonte's Special sandwich, then drive a few blocks over to Peter's house. I'd saved up my best bottle of Pinot for these occasions, and Peter matched it with something he had turned up and the three of us sat in his living room and relived the past, laughing and telling lies, giving each other the business as the sunlight streamed through the sycamores. So much good will and friendship, it was almost beatific, at least as close as we are likely to come. Fresno—as silly as this may sound—is something like a spiritual home to me—home of the best people, poets, and poetry I know.

"My Teachers" from *Blackbird,* 2019—Christopher Buckley

One book from a small press or a Pulitzer Prize deep into a substantial career—whatever level of celebrated accomplishment or unsung private satisfaction—almost no one gets there alone.

Along the road, you develop friends and fellow writers who, if you're lucky, are candid, rigorous with their response. But what brings you fully to face and embrace your life, to risk the real possibility of failure, the lack of rewards, and a lifetime of thrift store shopping, is a good and generous teacher. For what little the world cares about a book of poetry, the humble life most of us are fortunate enough to make in the endeavor to write it, we wouldn't have even that modest portion of it if not for dedicated and gifted teachers.

When I arrived in the MFA program at UC Irvine in my early 20s (the Punic Wars had recently come to an end and we'd just sold off our swords and shields) my great good fortune was to have Gary Soto, Jon Veinberg, and Gary Young in my workshops, all who became lifelong friends in poetry. Most of us were struggling, just beginning to find a voice, the sense of a line, but Soto had already found his style and subject and was publishing in places like *POETRY, The Iowa Review* and *The Nation*, journals the rest of us only dreamed of. Veinberg was writing distinctive and consistently engaging poems, both students of Levine and Peter Everwine at Fresno State. I was writing just well enough to be the last one into the program as the door closed—no grants, no TA. Skin of my teeth.

However, almost entirely due to Glover Davis, my teacher at San Diego State, I had the poems that got me through the gate. Glover had been an early student of Levine's at Fresno State in the '60s, and he ran a rigorous workshop. Nothing weak got by; no one was patted on the head and told they were special—no participation trophies were handed out. He'd learned that fierce and rigorous sense of craft from Levine. And like Phil, Glover was generous. He had long office hours, and back then in the early '70s there was always a line outside his office, five or six students waiting to go over rewrites of their poems. (There were large audiences for poetry in the early '70s; I remember Montezuma Hall on campus being filled with 350-400 people to hear both Philip Levine and Gary Snyder.)

My first semester in graduate school, I managed one finished poem and Glover must have seen 15 drafts of it over as many weeks. But I had at least one finished poem and was grateful for that. Did students appreciate the help? Some did. In my first semester's workshop there must have been 20 poets, most writing better than I. Up to that point I had not read contemporary poetry or worked with a poet; I was, like many, self-anointed and my "work" was likely influenced by the Moody Blues or Crosby, Stills, & Nash. But one afternoon, walking out of the building after workshop, Glover paused and actually talked to me about writing, something I did not expect. The thing that resonated, that stuck, was advice he passed on from his teacher: most beginning poets will not risk failure. You needed to be "all in" as the poker cliché now has it. That saved me. That, and the required books for the workshop: *They Feed They Lion* by Levine, *Collecting the Animals* by Peter Everwine, and the anthology *Naked Poetry* by Berg & Mezey in addition to *Down at the Santa Fe Depot*, the first anthology of the Fresno Poets. I was not writing well or with any real facility, but I was committed to doing the best I could each week, and Glover took the work seriously and suffered my tireless re-writes—no guarantees.

I spent two and a half years with Glover before heading to UC Irvine for the MFA.

My first quarter at Irvine Diane Wakoski ran the workshop with a similar focus. At the time, she was writing regular columns for *APR* that addressed overall attitudes about poetry, concepts, strategies, approaches to different poets and poetries. In workshop though, she was a very specific line-by-line editor and she was a great help to those of us who did not let our egos get in the way of solid critiquing. Wakoski could as well tie in her specific suggestions to the larger picture of the poet's intention or the culture of ideas, the overarching traditions of poetry, old and new. As well, she was very generous and supportive, especially for someone as popular and in demand as she was then. Diane regularly would take some of us to dinner at restaurants we could never have afforded, and often she invited the workshop to her house for dinner and wine. Those days, I cooked a lot of spaghetti dinners and tuna casserole surprise; they were the "gourmet" meals I shared with my mates, so Diane's kindness and generosity supported body and soul. She was there for only the first quarter of our two years at Irvine, but she remained a mentor over the years, responding to poems and corresponding in letters—a teacher who continued to take the time to support her students.

Our last quarter at Irvine, we demanded a poet of some national reputation and accomplishment, as, after Diane, the department simply recycled the faculty poets whom we had already seen a couple of times and who were deeply uninspiring. One reason you went to Irvine was the list of celebrated visiting poets that they advertized taught the workshop each year. The other reason of course was Charles Wright. Our great misfortune during our two years at Irvine was that Charles Wright was gone both years—one year on a Guggenheim and one on a visiting position to Iowa. A group of us made forays into the Chair's office to lodge our protests until, amazingly enough, he listened.

We were in luck as Peter Everwine was on leave with a Guggenheim during that time and was persuaded to drive down from Fresno for ten weeks to lead our last workshop. The reason Fresno poets had developed a substantial reputation was that Peter was teaching there as well as Levine. I was not writing well and poems I submitted for workshop would not have been much improved by specific editing. I seemed to have lost focus, something the modest talent I possessed could not then rescue. Peter spoke to me about poets I should be reading, the way I should be thinking about voice, my understanding of what a poem was, and this saved me from despair. I threw away most of the work of the last year and half. I was aided in this by my friend and fellow poet Jon Veinberg, who after my first book ms. had come close at a big contest and I was talking about the title I'd come up with for my second book, put me back on track; he said I should use that new title for my first book, that I needed to toss that first ms. I reviewed it and saw he was right. So Jon, one of my peers, was a teacher for me as well.

There are many ways to learn of course. I became friends with Charles Wright after I finished the MFA at Irvine and he was a great teacher of mine though he never saw any of my poems in drafts. I just read his books, every one of them, again and again. It was inspiring and disheartening both, as it turned out that we shared a similar approach to a mix of metaphysics and doubt—to the cosmos. I was never going to write as well as Charles. A quick and easy realization. He did not leave much meat on the bone for those of us who came to the table later with a similar take on experience. But he was a supreme example of what you might aspire to, and each of Charles' books suggested new ways to approach my subject. There was high and exceptional imagistic translation of the metaphysical quandary, inventive language that soared combined with a hip and popular lingo and an existential irony, and yet a sober glimmer of hope—an incredible mix. Then I was reading *The Southern Cross*, *The Other Side of the River*, and *China Trace*. As with Philip Levine's work, I had to keep myself from "borrowing" too obviously from Charles. At San Diego State, I had Glover Davis to do that for me in the workshops: "Buckley, you can't have that; those are Levine's lines." Imitation, the sincerest form . . . etc. But though I kept having to revise the endings that I "shared" with Levine in my poems, I learned a lot from all of the close reading and the brilliance and fierce music of his voice. The same with Charles' work.

Over the years, in addition to specific help with some poems, Phil gave freely of his time and spent a lot of it talking to me about poetry, poets in the tradition, contemporary poets, how to approach the vagaries of writing, the lack of rewards, the important work that is the writing itself. I was 29 when I came to teach at Fresno State. I had friends who had already won book awards, money prizes, who had tenure track jobs and had published in the better journals. I was feeling a bit left behind in the dust, with three early morning classes of composition to teach. Up early to stand in front of a class clamoring for more information about the dangling participle, I suffered the two or three nodding off in the front row despite my energetic declamations. And I had to be observed to be sure I knew what I was repeatedly talking about. I was fortunate here in that Chuck Hanzlicek, one of the poets on the faculty there, was assigned for the observation. He wrote a short and hilarious report about my best efforts lecturing on the comma splice while a student was applying her best shade of lavender lipstick just one row back. I learned something from Chuck about collegiality in that, as well as a good reminder about the value of the pure clear word which his poems exemplified.

I was assigned to share an office with Phil whose office mate was out on medical leave. I taught at 8:00, 9:00 and 11:00; Phil did not come in until the middle of the afternoon. For a couple years then I sat at my desk correcting piles of essays, waiting for Phil to arrive, at which time I'd ask a question about a current poem or poet or journal, and my tutorials in poetry and life would begin. He gave great advice not just about poetry but about how to keep my head on straight through all the vicissitudes, present and to come. His insight and advice helped me keep my head above water through those spare early years. I complained about a book prize awarded to yet another less than mediocre talent and Phil said, "Oh, life is not fair? Just do the work." He emphasized patience, fortitude, modesty, dedication, and honesty. Our discussions always came back to the point of doing the work and not betraying your talents. Whatever I learned, however slowly, about what it takes to be a poet, a writer, an ethical and democratic human being, I learned from the time Phil spent talking with me. There are many forms of instruction.

In the 43 years I knew Phil, I think he actually looked at/helped with four, maybe five poems. Again, I learned from reading and rereading his poems, and from talking with him about contemporary poetry. Phil was absolutely amazingly generous with his time, which is one reason I did not dun him with poems for help all the time. He had many students who, after graduating and moving on, still sent work, and there were many people who asked for help who had never been his students. The price of fame.

My favorite memory of Phil helping with a poem goes back ten years or so. I rarely asked, wanting to save up grace for times when I was really in trouble with a poem. Moreover, I had bothered Phil for letters for twenty some years, those letters you must have for grants, for academia, for fellowships. He wrote for me for at least twenty times, perhaps more, until I received, finally, the Guggenheim. When I got the news, I called him immediately to say I had good news for us both: I received the fellowship and he would not be asked to write any more letters! So, the poem "Poverty." Gary Young and Jon Veinberg had each taken some whacks at the four-page poem, had cut it down, suggested shifts, slashed and burned. I had written my usual 25-30 drafts. But I knew who would not pull any punches and bring it to heel if, that is, it could be made to do so. I sent Phil the most recent draft and took a yellow highlighter to about twenty lines near the beginning that I felt were still suspect, different in voice. Phil wrote right back saying, Yes, most of those lines should go. He tweaked another couple and then, saying the ending was not quite right, wrote in new lines to finish with. I went through the poem, re-writing, cutting, tightening up, feeling back to the original voice. I sent back the revision and Phil responded that Yes, this was more like it, but the ending still needed work! He re-wrote the ending yet again and sent it back. This one was even better. I did not let my ego get in the way, smart enough by that point in time to know a gift when I'd been given one. I sent the final version back to Phil and he approved, saying any time I had a poem this good to feel free to send it to him. No pressure there. I sent it off with a couple others to the fine journal *FIVE POINTS* for their James Dickey Prize and it won. The phone call was a real surprise however, as you try lots of contests and never hear anything. But then, when I thought about it, about the help I had received, it was not so far fetched. I owed Phil a good bottle of wine. I owed him much more than that.

An obvious testament to the excellence and importance of Philip Levine as a teacher is found in the four anthologies of his students from Fresno State and elsewhere. In addition to *Down At The Santa Fe Depot* (1970), which showcased the early group of Fresno poets, there were two other anthologies of poets who had come through Fresno. *Piecework: 19 Fresno Poets* (1987) was put together by former Levine students Gary Soto, Ernesto Trejo and Jon Veinberg, with Trejo and Veinberg doing the actual editing. *How Much Earth: The Fresno Poets* (2001) was edited by David Oliveira, M.L. Williams, and myself. *Coming Close: Forty Essays on Philip Levine*, edited by Mari L'Esperance and Tomás Q. Morín, was published by Prairie Lights Books/Univ. of Iowa Press in 2013. While the previous anthologies were a tribute to Levine mainly through the quality of the poems presented, *Coming Close* is a collection of essays acknowledging Levine as teacher and mentor from students and friends, older and younger. Just prior to *Coming Close*, I edited *FIRST LIGHT: A Festschrift for Philip Levine on his 85th Birthday*, with a largely different chorus of poets and friends testifying to Phil's generosity and accomplishment over the years. There has been no one over the last half century who has given more to students, to poets and poetry, than Phil.

This brings me to Larry Levis—Phil's most exceptional student. The voice of genius in my generation was Larry. Hands down. He was a teacher for many of us. Each time Larry had a new book out, it was an event; every poet I knew would be talking about it, would be energized and inspired with the new and imaginative moves Larry was making in poems, the risks he was taking—from "Linnets" in *The Afterlife* to "Winter Stars" to "Caravaggio Swirl & Vortex" in *The Widening Spell of the Leaves*. There were always new rhetorical strategies, inventive images, and yet the poems were always anchored in experience and accessible. And Larry helped me become a good teacher. One of my best poetry students ever, Alexander Long, found his way in poetry through Larry. After a semester or two of rigorous critique of Alex's early efforts, I put him on to Levis. From there on in, Larry became Alex's teacher and Alex found his voice and realized his vision of Sharon Hill, PA where he grew up, and became a good and true poet publishing books, winning contests. All I had to do was show him Larry's poems.

Yet despite his immense talent, even Larry did not succeed on his own; he had Phil and Peter early on at Fresno State. And later, Larry became a critic, a teacher if you will, for Phil as the years went on. Over time, Phil and Larry exchanged many poems, and Larry suggested changes and edits for Phil's poems as Phil did for Larry's. A substantial portion of the letters they sent each other regarding their poems over the years is in the Berg at the New York Public Library.

I was editing a book for the Univ. of Michigan Press's *Under Discussion* series—*On The Poetry of Philip Levine: Stranger to Nothing* (1991). These volumes on senior poets regularly collected the published response to the body of work, but I also wanted some essays commissioned just for the book that offered more substantial appreciations. Larry was the first poet I called to ask for one. The result was his essay "Philip Levine," which is one of the most poignant and entertaining essays I know about the education of the poet—a loving tribute to the value of a true and great teacher, Phil's dedication, his rigor, his humor and practical advice which helped to mitigate the critiques. It was first published in a small literary magazine, *Pacific Review*, from San Diego State where a student of mine, Chad Oness, was editing the magazine and studying with my former teacher and one of Phil's early students, Glover Davis.

Larry's essay alone is worth the price of the book. He recalls Levine's classes from the '60s at Fresno State—specifically capturing Levine's wit and amazing sense of humor. But the essay goes far beyond that. The complete essay can also be found in *A Condition of the Spirit: The Life and Work of Larry Levis* that I edited with former student, Alexander Long.

The essential value of teachers. So who was Phil's teacher? John Berryman, at the University of Iowa. Phil's now famous essay, "Mine Own John Berryman" is a wonderful and candid testament to the good that a hard working and conscientious teacher can do, and it is found in *The Bread of Time: Toward an Autobiography*. Phil also mentions Robert Lowell with whom he had a workshop at Iowa. At that time, Lowell was easily the more famous poet, and Phil notes that while Lowell was not much help in the classroom, he was kind and supportive on a personal level. But it was Berryman who gave of himself, who took the time, did the detailed preparation and work of responding and inspiring, who instilled the rigor and direction the writing life would demand. I can't recommend that essay highly enough. The core of Larry's essay is reprinted earlier in this book in the Philip Levine entry.

Peter Everwine was Phil's best friend lifelong, and Phil turned to Peter consistently over the years for edits with poems, for evaluation. Timothy Geiger, directs a fine letterpress at the University of Toledo. A few years back he printed a very handsome oversize limited edition chapbook of seven of Phil's prose poems, *The Language Problem*. Phil dedicated the book to me as I had nagged him about getting the prose poems out in the world, and he sent me one of the first copies he received. When I turned the page to the poem "Islands" I found that the middle of the poem, about 9 lines margin to margin, had been crossed out in blue ink, and I recognized the fine point nib of Phil's favorite Pelikan 800 fountain pen. At the bottom left of the page there was a hand-written note from Phil: "Revision suggested by Everwine, taken by Levine." This was no joke. When the trade Knopf book, *News of the World*, was published, that middle section was missing from the poem. We rely on our fiends, we continue learning.

And Phil was rigorous with himself, throwing away many poems that he felt did not come up to his standards, keeping many poems in the drawer that did not fit into a new book thematically, not placing everything published in magazines in his books. Over the years, Phil told a few variations of the story of the writing of the long poem, "A Walk with Tom Jefferson," but essentially patience and rigorous standards were the bottom line. He had written half of the over 600-line poem and then hit a wall. Actually he had written 600-900 lines and cut back to that first 300+ half. He put it away and many months later came back to it with an idea to complete the poem—the work of two years or more. He never let himself off easy. After the publication of *New Selected Poems*, 1991, it occurred to me that there were many fine and memorable poems left out. Together with Jon Veinberg, I talked Phil into publishing a book that collected those poems. Gary Young at Greenhouse Review Press liked the idea and together the three of us published the book. Phil came up with the title *UNSELECTED POEMS* (1997). My main idea was to make available most of the rest of his work, but during the process, Phil whittled away at the overall selection, wanting only the best of what remained. At one point he agreed to include "The Sierra Kid"—a long tour-de-force syllabic poem from his first book *On The Edge*, one of the best syllabic poems in contemporary poetry. But finally it was cut. Phil did include a small selection of new poems all of which made it into subsequent books; the poem "Ascension" was printed on the broadside handed out at his memorial tribute. Phil had a judicious sense of a "book of poetry" and saw the poems working together on a theme and variation strategy, a specific emotional strategy or vision, or so it seemed to me. So, many fine poems were left in the drawer and have yet to be collected into a book. Ed Hirsch, Phil's literary executor, is working to go through all of the poems that were unpublished to see which might contribute to a *Collected* at some point.

We have become thin on the ground, the Fresno group. We lost many way too early: Ernesto Trejo in 1991, C.W.Moulton 1995, Larry Levis in 1996, Sherley Ann Williams and Andres Montoya in 1999, Roberta Spear 2003, Luis Omar Salinas in 2008, and several others. The brilliant poet and my wonderful friend, Jon Veinberg, died of a stroke in early 2017. It was Jon who had me reading the variety of eastern European poets when we were just starting out. I learned something about craft and imagination every time I showed Jon a poem, all the way through our 60s. Arthur Smith died at the end of 2018.

And recently, the last of our first teachers. The most recent grief and loss is Peter Everwine who died at the end of October 2018. Peter saved my poetic life back at the end of grad school, and over the last twenty or so years we had become especially close; I drove to Fresno a few times each year to visit with Peter and Jon. Over the last few years I had started to rely on Peter as well to help with drafts of poems, to continue teaching me. He was so modest, and would say that he hoped we would still be friends after I saw what he had to say about the poem, as, when it came to responding, he was rigorous in cuts and edits, strategy, sections to be dropped—he saved several new poems for me.

Here I am then, retired from teaching, remembering the tribute and memorial held for Phil on the campus at Fresno State a year after his passing. Hundreds of family, friends, colleagues, and many of his former students attended and testified to his genius, generosity, and importance to their lives . . . remembering the memorial reading for Jon Veinberg in 2017 with Soto, Gary Young, Timothy Sheehan and myself—all mates in our 20s from grad school—almost too shaken to speak our eulogies. We have now done the same for Peter Everwine this last April, 2019. Mercy on us all. . . .

Somehow, I have a selected poems from the University of Pittsburgh Press . . . Larry's press as I often think of it. It's a slim volume, as the press prefers—not near what I came to know as a Selected Poems as a young man, a book a good inch and a half thick, something you could drop from a balcony and crack the sidewalk with. But I feel fortunate indeed, never sure that I would have even this much. And celebrity being what it is, there were few reviews—Oprah did not call. But it represents a life, a life in poetry I have been blessed to have—a life that, without the selfless efforts and support of great friends, great teachers—almost all from Fresno—I would never have had.

Jean Janzen

Jean Wiebe Janzen was born in 1933 in Saskatchewan, Canada, and raised in Minnesota and Kansas. After marriage to Louis Janzen she worked and studied in Chicago where her husband was a medical student. Following residency in Los Angeles, they moved to Fresno in 1961 to begin a pediatric practice. In this fertile valley they raised four children and enjoyed the majestic scenery of the mountains and ocean.

Janzen completed her BA in English at Fresno Pacific College, and in 1982 she graduated from Fresno State University with a Master of Arts in English/Creative Writing. When Jean ventured into first poems in Peter Everwine's workshop, she received the nurturing guidance which allowed her to enter a whole new world of possibilities with language. Philip Levine returned from a sabbatical to add his excellent critique as she continued to develop her craft. Professors Hanzlicek, Zumwalt, and Logan were also inspiring teachers, and in these classes she met fellow students who became lifetime friends. The lively community of poets in Fresno, most of them products of the university program, have provided important stimulation and reading opportunities, as well as sustaining friendship.

Janzen's first book of poems, *Words for the Silence,* was published in 1984. Additional collections are *Three Mennonite Poets, The Upside-Down Tree, Snake in the Parsonage, Tasting the Dust, Piano in the Vineyard, Paper House,* and *What the Body Knows.* She also has two books of essays, *Elements of Faithful Writing,* and *Entering the Wild.* Her poems have appeared in numerous anthologies and journals including *Poetry, Gettysburg Review, Prairie Schooner, Image, and Christian Century.*

A number of Janzen's poems have been set to music including a major work, *This Sturdy Vine,* by Alice Parker. Janzen has also written hymn texts, several of which, based on the writings of Hildegard of Bingen, Mechtild of Magdeburg, and Julian of Norwich, have been included in various hymnals in the United States and Canada, and also in Scotland, Germany, and China.

Among other awards, Janzen has received a National Endowment for the Arts fellowship and has been twice nominated for the Pushcart Prize. She has taught poetry writing at Fresno Pacific University and Eastern Mennonite University in Virginia.

from *What Will Suffice,* 1995—Jean Janzen

We work in the dark. The writing is a dig. Nothing new, really, except sometimes the smell of earth as discoveries are made. This poem feels true to my writing experience. The common metaphors for poets in the common act give me a sense of connectedness that enriches me. My writing has moved me to the stories of my ancestors and of others, creating a wider, more fertile field. I plant them for continuity and nurture, and out of an internal necessity. The vision is partial, even as I long for the elemental, a singularity of sight that multiplies.

from *The Geography of Home: California's Poetry of Place,* 1999—Jean Janzen

To claim California as home is to claim both immensity and looseness. The open spaces of this great valley and the fine clay dust breathe an unsettledness for me, while the grand Sierra on one side and the ocean on the other shape the wild borders. It is an awesome home, one for which I have spent years trying to find language.

But home is an imaginary construct, some say, the place where we most truly live. These poems, which investigate the deprivations as well as the plentitude of this valley, recognize that we are indeed east of Eden, and what we most desire is somewhere else. Meanwhile, the velvet summer nights and the fragrance of magnolias modulate the harsh realities of labor and loss, and the mockingbird celebrates desire, singing for us our origins and our destiny.

from *How Much Earth,* 2001—Jean Janzen

I was married in the Dust Bowl of the United States—western Kansas in1954, and after seven years in Chicago and Los Angeles, was brought to another dusty place by my husband as he began medical practice in Fresno. We arrived in the slamming heat of midsummer, and found that sweetness could rise out of the hard earth and fill our mouths and the summer nights. In this valley, surrounded by awesome landscape, we raised four children who claim Fresno as home.

An unexpected gift was the teaching I received at Fresno State University beginning in 1980 when I free to explore writing. I ventured into first poems with Peter Everwine's nuturing guidance, and found a whole new world of possibilities with language. Philip Levine returned from a sabbatical to add his astringent critiques as I continued work toward a masters degree and a collection of first poems. Their continued support and friendship is a high honor as I write, their high standards of excellence the goal for which I reach.

from *FIRST LIGHT,* 2013—Jean Janzen

When I entered Phil Levine's poetry writing class in the fall of 1981, I brought with me forty-seven years of life experience and a semester of poetry workshop with Peter Everwine. Early poems had moved me into the story of my father's immigration as an orphaned teen from Russia to Canada.

By mid-semester I gained the courage to write about the secret story of his mother's suicide. I unwrapped that sorrow and created a poem which I brought to the class for critique. From both Phil and Peter I had learned that sometimes silence is better than the poems we brought:

"Does the poem arise out of necessity, or is it art for art's sake?" I had also learned the necessity of some silence before comments were offered.

Phil's tender response to the poem allowed it to live and to become the center of my thesis with the title, "Words for the Silence." Since that day I have continued to seed the music of language for the variations of life while I have breath.

"Entering the Wild with Poetry," 2020—Jean Janzen

When my husband and I moved from Chicago to Los Angeles in 1957, we crossed the Rocky Mountains in a rainstorm. Slipping off the edge of the road without harm, we sat in gratitude for a few minutes, then drove on toward the "wild west." My husband did an internship and residency in Los Angeles where we lived in sight of mountains, then chose to practice pediatrics in Fresno. Here we raised four children, and in this agricultural setting we felt kinship to the measured acres of vines and fruit trees, even as our childhoods in the Midwest were dominated by wheat and corn fields. But here we could drive out into the foothills, and in another magical hour stand in the presence of the majesty of Yosemite and Sequoia Parks. And within three hours from home we walked the beaches at Monterey and Carmel, the sense of "the wild" entering and expanding us.

In January of 1980 I walked into Peter Everwine's advanced poetry writing class, and by the end of the semester I knew that I wanted to continue exploring the creative life. When Philip Levine returned to campus, I continued to study with both of them and with Chuck Hanzlicek who drew me into the wonder of contemporary American poetry. I have named this amazing time as "entering the wild."

Even as my life was somewhat typically "domestic" as I stayed home and raised children, the events of the 60's and 70's aroused questions about faith and tradition. We opened our apartment in our large home to Pacific College students who were active in the anti-war efforts. Our church community was a newly-founded group which was lively with discussion and activism. My husband's love of history and visual arts took us to Europe a number of times. And always there was music, singing in choirs and attending the philharmonic concerts. It was, however, my father's death that drew me into unknown territory. He had immigrated from Ukraine to Canada as an orphaned teen in 1910 after his mother committed suicide, leaving nine children. Not until the morning after his death did I learn how his mother died. When I chose to tell the story with the poem "These Words Are For You, Grandmother," I stood in a wilderness alone. I remember the silence in the classroom after I read the poem, then Levine saying, quietly, "I think it's done."

That poem and my interest in family history opened the door to publication with Mennonites, a pacifist branch of Protestantism. While few artists had emerged from this "quiet group" of people, I now was joined by others in the United States and Canada who were breaking the silence. The publishers at Good Books in Pennsylvania were willing to print my poems in collections. And here in Fresno I was blessed with friendship and support from this vibrant poetry community. The Visiting Poets Series under the direction of Chuck Hanzlicek offered an amazing exposure to the best poets actively writing and publishing. Roberta Spear and I shared our poems in progress through the 80's and 90's, and Peter Everwine offered his kind critique until his recent death.

I now live in a retirement place not far from my beloved house of fifty years. The gardens around the buildings are trim, but my view out of west windows is over a wild slough over which the sky is offering gorgeous sunsets. My villa is set on ground which once was a vineyard, a place of order and routine, like a poem with its attempt at making something out of the wild. The day opens, the day ends, a rhythm that offers renewal.

Kathy Fagan

Kathy Fagan's latest collection is *Sycamore* (Milkweed Editions, 2017), a finalist for the 2018 Kingsley Tufts Poetry Award. She is also the author of the National Poetry Series selection *The Raft* (Dutton, 1985), the Vassar Miller Prize winner *MOVING & ST RAGE* (Univ. of North Texas, 1999), *The Charm* (Zoo, 2002), and *Lip* (Carnegie Mellon UP, 2009). Her work has appeared in *The Paris Review, The Kenyon Review, Slate, FIELD, Narrative, The New Republic, The Nation,* and *POETRY,* and is widely anthologized. Fagan was named Ohio Poet of the Year for 2017, and is the recipient of awards and fellowships from the Ingram Merrill Foundation, the National Endowment for the Arts, The Frost Place, Ohioana, Greater Columbus Arts Council, and the Ohio Arts Council. The Director of Creative Writing and the MFA Program at The Ohio State University, she is currently Professor of English, Poetry Editor of OSU Press, and Advisor to *The Journal.*

from *How Much Earth,* 2001—Kathy Fagan

Every morning on the school bus to Clovis High, while the other kids dozed or crammed or fooled around, I looked at the cows. I'd come from New York City and didn't know from cows, didn't know there could be snow in the mountains in spring, didn't know raisins began as grapes. And I didn't know much about poetry until I met Ben Jameson at Clovis and later Phil Levine and Peter Everwine at Fresno State. I studied at State three years, graduating with my B.A. in 1980, a time when one heard the not-so-whispered names of former illustrious grads enough to want to be them—Levis, St. John, Spear, Inada, Soto, the list goes on. When I think now of the readings I attended in the late seventies, of Mark Strand "subbing" for Phil one rainy spring, of the opportunity I enjoyed editing what was then called *Backwash,* I wonder what undergraduate anywhere ever had it so good. It was like a Juilliard for poets, this dusty little town with its shaggy trees and flat broiling avenues. I was utterly and perfectly lonely in it, thoroughly sopped in landscape and language. I didn't know then that it was the beginning of a life, but I was wise enough to be grateful for it at least, to recognize that here were readers and writers who worked and thought and created a lively literary community in an unlikely setting. If one source of poetry is the need to say the unsayable and one goal of poetry is to discover the undiscoverable, then Fresno is the continuum, for me, on which poetry lived entire.

"Homage to Mr. Levine" from *Coming Close: Forty Essays on Philip Levine*—2013

Once a year or so, when I forget myself and say something incisively critical about a student poem in class, bluntly, sometimes humorously; when I state with conviction what's "wrong" with a poem, or missing from it, or messy with it; when I joke about a bad move a poem has made, teasing it a little bit, acknowledging failure as quickly as success; I am not so much forgetting myself as remembering how I was taught to talk about poetry when I was young. I am lapsing back into the way my college classmates and I spoke to one another—

the way Phil Levine spoke to us—as if we were, all 12 or 15 of us, little Levines, nearly every semester for three years. I realize now that it was like a private language, the kind some siblings develop. Once I entered grad school, I understood that my spoken comments—blessedly few thanks to a natural shyness—were considered hard-ass. I was instructed to preface my remarks with phrases such as: "It seems to me that," and "If this were my poem I might," and "There is so much to admire here, but I wonder just a bit about the...." Diplomacy didn't win me any new friends, but it didn't gain me new enemies either. And when I began to teach workshops of my own, as a blonde, blue-eyed, 25 year-old doctoral student, leading 18 year-old Mormons through the mine field that is Frank O'Hara, Sylvia Plath, and Langston Hughes, I was grateful to have had my poetry passion tempered. In those years and all the years since then, I have been reminded over and over that there is really only one of us who can get away with being Philip Levine, and it's not me.

In autumn 1977, I enrolled in Philip Levine's poetry workshop at Fresno State. I was beginning my sophomore year after a disastrous year as a scholarship student at a wealthy, Christian, southern California college. I felt defeated, but my idea was to use up my California state tuition money for the year and then beat it out of Fresno, where my parents were living, as soon as I was able. I'd written poems at a nearby high school and knew about the legend that was Philip Levine. He lit student poems on fire with a cigarette lighter and stomped the flames out with his motorcycle boots. He cussed in the classroom. He was a card-carrying Communist. So the stories went. After the year I'd had battling fundamentalist right-wingers and Malibu millionaires, I thought, *Bring it, Levine.*

As it happened, there was no lighter, no motorcycle boots, no brandishing of membership cards. Phil, as he asked us to call him, had recently given up smoking and wore gym shoes every day. He was going to the gym. He complained about vision problems. He complained about almost everything. He laughed about almost everything, too. Or praised it: the perfection of the pear, the charm of the mockingbird—as if fruit or bird had just that morning come into being for him. He praised his wife's sense of humor, her cooking, her gardening skills. I had never heard a married person speak so fondly of their spouse, and that alone made Phil exotic to me.

Even after he'd published over five books and won a couple of significant national literary awards, Fresno State assigned Phil the requisite faculty load of composition courses. He walked to our class from one of them, stopping to pick up his mail on the way. Phil sat at a lab table-with-sink in front of the chalkboard—poetry workshops were held in one of the Agriculture buildings—and flipped through his mail as students shuffled in, raising an eyebrow to a thin new volume of poems or wisecracking about a big poetry paycheck. He might read short passages to us from the books he was teaching in comp, Studs Terkel's *Working,* for example, before moving on to our work, chosen and mimeographed by him, two to five purple poems to a page. Often the odor of cow dung hung in the air, laced with the scent of gardenia on the best of days, pesticide on the worst. It was always either too hot or too foggy. An inversion could mean no blue sky for days, even weeks. In those days, Fresno State students were preppies in Izod, Ag kids in cowboy boots, or Bulldog fans in ball-caps, but few of these enrolled in poetry workshop. It's possible I've conflated two or three workshops in my memory, but I know I capture the spirit of most of them when I say they consisted of a handful of badly dressed white kids like me, one or two Latino kids, a couple of veterans, a girl who rode a Harley, and two or three older, non-traditional students with full-time jobs and families. The glory days of Levis and St. John, Roberta Spear, Lawson Inada, Gary Soto, Sherley Anne Williams, Sam Pereira, and other notables were long gone, and we newbies were irremediable dopes. But their legacy was palpable—perhaps because of the overt pride and pleasure Phil took in their successes—and I remember thinking of them as the older brothers and sisters who'd learned well, worked hard, and gotten the hell out of Fresno. Years later, when Larry Levis was my teacher at University of Utah, I felt we indeed shared a psychic familial shorthand. Like Phil, Larry wore his intellect lightly. Like Phil, his devotion to the craft was infectious.

In the late '70s, Phil's career was coming into full bloom. Stephen Yenser published an insightful and influential essay on his work in *Parnassus* in 1977, before Levine turned 50. It is remarkable to consider that he had already written his poems, "Belle Isle, 1949," "On the Edge," "Animals are Passing from our Lives," "Heaven," the widely anthologized "To a Child Trapped in a Barbershop," the singularly spectacular "They Feed They Lion," and the disturbing "Angel Butcher." He was head-hunted to teach elsewhere. Spring semester '78 he went east to Tufts; someone named Mark Strand took his place at Fresno State. In three years Phil would leave Fresno again to teach at Columbia, where I was a beginning MFA student. If it hadn't been for Phil, I wouldn't have been there. I remember distinctly, in 1979, looking up what the acronym MFA meant. I discussed programs with Phil, by which I mean he told me what three schools to apply to. I did as he said and got into all of them. A few months before I graduated with my BA in English, Mr. Levine, as I called him then—I was such a nitwit—Mr. Levine told me there were three things I'd need to be a poet: talent, perseverance, and luck. "You've got the talent," he said. "Only you can tell whether or not you've got the perseverance," he said. "And I'm your luck." The talent and luck parts sounded good to me. And though I thought I understood about perseverance at the time, I had no idea.

Phil often said to us in class that we had more interesting things in our pockets than in our poems. And he was right. That lint, loose tobacco, and couple of cents were infinitely more interesting than anything in our poems, and more useful. A similarly effective pedagogical method was to shake our poems above his desk—the lab table—and listen for the "real stuff," the good stuff, for *any* stuff to fall out of them. These were the best lessons in the value of concrete language and the importance of specificity, image, and detail to poetry that I've ever learned, and I use them with my own students and, secretly but without fail, on my own poems to this day. He also used baseball metaphors in class. One student was batting 200 with his poem one day, another student 300: "But you know what that means, don't you? You write one more hit and your batting average goes up to 400 and you sign a million dollar contract."

Eager to "stuff" my poems and improve my batting average, I submitted to workshop one semester a serial poem based on the immigration experiences of my Irish grandparents. After discussing two or three in the series, Phil urged me to title the poem. I said I was considering, "The Irish in America." Phil said, "Who are you, James Michener?" We laughed. Even I had heard of James Michener. "Very ambitious, very ambitious work." The poem was awful, of course, but I wrote poems off the energy of that single comment, "Ambitious," for years.

In those days it was true for the majority of Levine's Fresno State students that Poetry lived on the East Coast, if not in England, and we lived on the not-quite-West Coast. Crappy luck. Except Levine lived among us, too. He'd lived among those like us in Detroit. He continued to live in Detroit in his poems and continued to live in Fresno in real life. By choice. We were delighted when he complained about his "private school" students after returning from one of his east coast teaching gigs. I'm not making too much of this when I claim that what Levine's work in the classroom and on the page did was stir our spirits out from under the crush and devastation of the ordinary, ugly, and poor, and because of that, poetry became possible for us. Because of Levine's subject matter, his prosody, his humor, his anger, his allegiances to and alliances with the political and social underclass, his students found not only a way to speak, but were reassured of their right to. The courage and confidence we'd been in danger of losing—to observe the world, criticize it, mourn it, praise it, analyze it, create and recreate it—was restored. And it became clear that if we chose to, and worked very hard, we might just make poets of ourselves, as Philip Levine had. Literature that had once seemed largely inaccessible or irrelevant to me and to my peers suddenly seemed necessary—ours for the taking and, most astonishingly, ours to make.

One story about Phil that I've doled out to only my nearest and dearest over the years happened while I was his student at Columbia University in 1981. Phil was then the age that I am now. I honestly don't know how strange it was for him to be teaching at an Ivy League, but for me, to be living in the dormitory that my grandmother had once cleaned at one of the most prestigious universities in the world made me both wildly happy and incredibly nervous, as if I could be found out and kicked out at any moment. Phil's appearance that year provided me with a touchstone, a sort of footing, though he treated us all the same and behaved in the classroom exactly as he had in Fresno. A poem once came up for workshop with the phrase "Habla espanol?" Bizarrely, I'd managed to pick up no Spanish, either in New York where I'd been raised, or in California where I'd finished high school and gone to college. "What does that mean," I asked, "Habla espanol?" "Do you speak Spanish," Phil answered. "No," I said, "that's why I'm asking." Phil dropped his head down on the workshop table and laughed. As if I had made an absurd and deliberate joke, which I hadn't. When I realized my gaffe, I suffered a moment of panic. I had exposed my ignorance, my inexperience, and an apparent ability to flaunt both.

I was not, after all, thrown out of the hallowed halls of Columbia University. Nevertheless, the memory made me wince for a decade at least, and for years after, when I was finally willing to tell the story, I told it with some embarrassment. We are all of us breakable, but the unformed thing is especially fragile. There is a tenderness to most young people. I am gentle with my students because Mr. Levine was, in every essential way, gentle with me; I attend to their poems with seriousness because Mr. Levine attended to mine with seriousness. Writing of his teacher, John Berryman, Phil comments on Berryman's ability to "devastate the students' poems without crushing the students' spirits." Alas, there is no poet or teacher good enough to teach someone how to survive a life, much less a life of poetry. But Mr. Levine comes close. There is only one Philip Levine: just my luck.

"Interview between Maggie Smith & Kathy Fagan," published in *The Rumpus,* 2019

Maggie Smith: One of the things I admire most about you is how each book of yours feels like its own thing--not a continuation of the previous book or a preview of the next one. Could you speak to the idea of "reinvention" in your life as a poet?
Kathy Fagan: Thanks, Mags. I've heard that remark leveled as a criticism of my work as often as praise, but I don't have a whole lot of control over it. For one thing, I don't write quickly, so the books aren't finished fast. For another, they tend to appear with many years between them; until recently some of that had to do with not having a single press to rely on. I've spent decades practicing the craft of poetry, and have—surprisingly, given the odds—built a life on it, but until my fifth book was contracted, I didn't have an independent publisher with as deep a commitment to poetry as Milkweed has, along with the financial stability to back that commitment up. For 30+ years, each of my books up to *Sycamore* had

been shopped over long periods of time until published, with little to no support system in place for review opportunities or marketing. Such is the state of the art; there are more poets than not contending with such conditions.

On another, more personal note, much of the reinvention you speak of happens because I change. I'm open to try stuff, in life and poetry. Some I choose and some happens to me, but I'm changed every time. Poetry as an art is so capacious, so limitless, it's able to absorb and reflect each new music, image and influence: medieval iconography, tree diseases, historical personae and deeply autobiographical material. I've come to terms with the fact that I'm an experiential learner and writing poems helps me discover what I need to know, and even (this would have caused me all the shudders when I was young, but now—what the hell!), even how I feel, maybe especially that.

Also, I revere the line above all things in a poem. Most of the play and work of a poem for me is experimenting with how a line and the sentence it lives in work together to create rhythms and meanings adjacent to the poem's content. They create pacing too, of course, which is related to the modulations of voice one hears in a poem—reserve, sarcasm, despair, affection, resignation, ecstasy—and the intimacy of that is very appealing to me, essential really. It's an element that goes beyond craft that we don't much talk about in poetry, but which goes a long way toward explaining, I think, a lot of what's inexplicable about its power.

MS: Your most recent book, *Sycamore,* is one I've been keeping close at hand. It seems to me to be a book about loss and upheaval, about finding the spring in ourselves after a long winter. Maybe even reinvention? How do you see this book as different from or similar to your previous collections?

KF: *Sycamore* has an emotional connection to my 2nd book, *MOVING & ST RAGE*, which took 14 years to finish because I stopped writing when my best friend died. The loss behind *Sycamore* was equally gutting for me, but it generated poems rather than shutting them down. If silence was the reply I made to my friend's death, poetry was the reply I made to what I felt would be my own.

I've thought a lot about these two responses to loss—my age had something to do with each of them—but I remember feeling slammed closed when my friend died and broken open when my marriage did. What I mean is, there was light and air for me in the second loss; it didn't matter that it was winter light, and air so cold it hurt my lungs, I wrote in the kind of fever then that writers envy and fear—I know you understand this. I lived for my poetry and my trees. When the fever broke, I had a book to make, and that was about discovering how the sycamore poems and the speaker's grief were related—they are, more subtly in the book than in my life, but it took me a little time and therapy to figure out how.

I thought of the book following *MOVING & ST RAGE*, *The Charm*, as a sort of antidote to grief—it investigates the magic and terrors of childhood and casts little spells or charms to ward off loss and death. My fourth collection, *Lip*, swings widely away from personal matters; in fact, it's a collection of persona poems. I did so much research for that book, and built so many different kinds of poem vessels in it. One of them, at least, brought me back home—I still do a lot of research for my poems, but the true work is largely internal now.

It was my therapist, for instance, who recommended I read Herodotus's *The Histories*, specifically passages on the habitual sale of women and the excruciating hierarchies of such purchases; before that I'd found Aristotle's writing on animal prudence, the title of one poem in the new manuscript, which inspired further research into predation. From there, to monthly visits with my father to the VA Clinic, to research in falconry, and my obsessive tracking of AccuWeather reports (its "Real Feel" temperatures and Daily Hunting Forecasts, for example), I've learned many little lessons in language, gender, health, reproduction, and survival as commodity, painfully relevant to all of us.

MS: How do you go about arranging a book? At what point do you even know that what you're working on is a book and not a pile of disparate poems?

KF: You're so very skilled at it, Mags, but I find it hard to arrange a book of my own. I know when the poems are all there—I know that the poems for my next book are all in. But I was on a very clear trajectory with *Sycamore*, and the seasonal arc of the book supported the emotional path behind it. My job was sorting and revising—which poems were "real," finished poems, which potential poems and which best kept in a journal.

The new book, also thematically based, poses a different challenge: I have to create in its arrangement the right set of psychological, what I might call, vistas. The new poems explore multiple levels of perception and predation, perception itself a predatory act, and to make poetry, to some degree, attempts to keep fresh the wounds of the prey. That is, to make poetry, for me, engages the space between what is universally relevant and deeply personal, useful and beautiful, nameable and mysterious. In poems—indeed in all the art I love best—I hope to find a bridge to span that space, creating dialogue, tension, and possibility: the experience *inside*. I'd really love if the collection as a whole did that work as well. When I catch a break this semester, and with dad-duties, I'll get on it.

MS: Whose career—or life, as I find myself cringing at the word career—in poetry has inspired or motivated you? What specifically do you admire or respect about how that person has made their way?

KF: Oh my, but it *does* become a career, doesn't it? Once you devote a couple of decades to a thing, its making and its presentation? I remember thinking career as in careerism, and maybe it is that for some, but for me it's my vocation. As I get older I find myself in awe of women who hold down jobs and spend years care-giving while making poems. Many of them don't get the accolades they deserve. Some of them don't even have the advantages of a committed press or a writing community to support them, and yet they remain active, generous and adventurous in life and writing: teaching, editing, sharing their various experiences and expertise.

I've tried to take all of my joy—maybe it's not so much joy as fire? the bright light of attentive inquiry?—I've tried to get that from the work. I was ambitious when I was young but didn't know where my focus should be. I was first-gen college, poor. I didn't want to be a housewife or do a 9 to 5, but I had no clue what grad school demanded either. After that I had to work to support myself and help my family, with no model of what the alternatives could be for someone like me, of what an artist's life could look like, and struggled to see myself in poets I read and admired, even women poets.

There are two brief stories, though, encounters with poets' lives that have stuck with me, that I've returned to when I need a jolt of motivation. One is a story I heard first from the marvelous poet Brenda Hillman, about Russian poet and dissident Irina Ratushinskaya—when Ratushinskaya died, too young, in 2017, I was reminded of this story in her obits. While incarcerated, she was not allowed paper and pen, so she inscribed lines for poems into bars of soap with matchsticks, memorized them, washed, inscribed, memorized, and so forth, until the poems could be somehow smuggled out. The second, equally compelling and resonant inspiration came from reading Audre Lorde's *Sister*,

Outsider, specifically her discussion of being a different learner, and "feeling" her way toward poetry. There is so much in Lorde's work and biography I wish I had found when I was a queer young writer, so many perspectives she had that would have made me feel less singular had I encountered them then. Both women instruct me how to be, as a poet, one's most obsessively focused, courageous and devoted advocate.

MS: One of the things we've talked about before is "playing the long game." Could you talk a little about what that means to you?

KF: In the last two years, I lost my mother; my father, who lives with us, is in steep decline, deaf and dementing; and *Sycamore* was published. These are personal and professional details that can't help but inform both my writing and my way of being in the world. Hearing my father attempt to repeat simple words during a hearing test in a soundproof room, for example, or to be present during a neurological MOCA (Montreal Cognitive Assessment) test, allow me to approach language, fluency, memory, and so-called "executive" skills in particularly refreshing ways as a writer, and citizen. I am privileged and challenged, both, to continue to make poems about what I learn, to continue to learn what poems can say.

Beyond that, I *wish* I had a more robust professional plan, a strategy to meet the milestones, an end-goal I could articulate, finally, after all this time in the biz, but I'm not especially good at it. I try to submit poems and grant applications, and I read as much as I can. Social media helps—and hurts—that way. I read way more than I post, occasionally posting pictures of my cat, retweeting former students' poems, or announcing local readings in Columbus when I'm aware of them. Sometimes, I post a link to a poem of my own.

I'm not young, nor was I ever beautiful or a genius. The long game, for me, is to remain alive long enough to write my best poems, by which I mean open to poems conscious to the art and the life. I feel the urgency of that work. And to mentor with greater care than I was mentored, to remain as steadfast and resolute in my work ethic as humanly possible, to know when advancing or retreating is best—for me—and to behave kindly, because I wish to be treated with kindness, yes, but also because there is too little justice in the world already.

"Interview between Izzy Montoya & Kathy Fagan" in *Superstition Review,* 2016

Izzy Montoya: This book opens with a very interesting first piece, "Platanaceae Family Tree." I wanted to know what inspired you to work in this form, and how you managed to find moments for creativity within it?

Kathy Fagan: I am so grateful that Milkweed was willing to keep this—what would you call it?—"legend," as the frontispiece for the book. It's as close as I've ever come to an illustration—I never dreamed of submitting it to a literary magazine because I never thought of it as a poem. I very much wanted it to suggest, in visual and verbal ways, the magnificent stands of sycamore I'd been visiting. But of course the piece also becomes a sort of wink and nod to the construction of the cosmology of the book, I think, an homage to lineage, in this case the lineage of the tree family and genus, but also of poem-making, image by image, linguistic turn by linguistic turn. It's the mind of the poet I was as I wrote *Sycamore* that I was attempting to map.

IM: Speaking of form, readers will find a few formalistic poems in this collection, including "Kaboom Pantoum," but by and large this book is free verse. How do you balance these two techniques, and what informs your process?

KF: I've written pantoums for years—several appear in my previous book, *Lip*. I love how the pantoum allows for the refinement or refutation of observation or idea. More than anything in poetry I value the music of the line. Whether that happens in a traditionally formal line or what's called a free verse line doesn't much matter to me. My growing sense over the years is that the poem finds, in its time, its most appropriate container. I'm not suggesting that happens by magic, but I do think the more one reads and practices forms, the more likely one is to know in which vessel the sounds, the words, the lines, and the sentences live most memorably.

IM: Many of the poems in *Sycamore* give poetic voice to an actual Sycamore tree. Can you tell us a little more about what made you want to write from this perspective, and what it revealed to you?

KF: One or more sycamores, yes. Before I wrote poems for *Sycamore* I found myself taking hundreds of digital photographs of the trees—on daily walks around my Ohio neighborhood, on hikes near the river, on visits to other cities and countries. I was so drawn to them that I geeked out on sycamore tree facts, doing research, following the appearance of sycamore in myth, legend, and the arts. As some of the poems address, sycamores thrive all over the world, in wild and urban environments; they can be incredibly long-lived, and grow so large that humans have been known to live inside them. The bark, notable for its white sheen, cracks and sheds to allow for expansion. There's something about those physical details, broken and strong and womanly all at once, that touches me. When the poems emerged I called them self-portraits—one titled as such survives in the book—but I gradually understood that the poems were a series of studies, in the spirit of Monet's haystacks and cathedrals. I became interested in recording the trees in conversation with the weather, the light, and the landscape, with both natural and human history. When a long-term relationship ended abruptly, I turned to the trees—and to the poems—for shelter. And both accommodated me.

IM: Something I really enjoyed about these poems was how they incorporated nature into the artistic vision. For example, we see the theme of hibernation explored in several poems. Can you describe how you took something concrete and scientific, like hibernation, and made it into something poetic?

KF: Yes, as I mentioned, the sycamores felt to me emotionally sheltering during a very difficult time, they still do, like the best imaginable (giant) family, but the poems themselves mostly rose out of the darkest places, an underworld of sadness—my own "comas of survival," as I put it in the poem "To You for Whom I Broke." Poetry and psychotherapy plumb multiple layers of understanding. Likewise, one can't stand at the base of an old-growth sycamore looking up and not feel both terribly mortal and bound up in history all at once. The ultimate in negative capability, hibernation is the life-death state, one in which survival and death are completely interdependent—Daphne, Persephone... The resonances are endless.

IM: The poem "Cinder" is a meditation on another artist's work. In what other ways, maybe less direct, do you feel the experience of art becomes part of your own craft?

KF: Aside from Ovid's *Metamorphosis*, the poems in *Sycamore* draw specifically from arts other than the literary, like film (Fellini and Herzog are credited in the book) and video (the Gaillard demolition video you mention that "Cinder" engages), dance (ballet and Kabuki), sculpture (Bernini, of course), architecture (the destroyed and the extant;

there's a poem about California's first woman architect, Julia Morgan), and even music, which to my uneducated ear reads as almost pure abstraction and emotion. As usual for me, there's a mash-up of characters in the poems, too, aside from the individual and choral groups of trees: many, many saints, Caesar Augustus, Edgar Poe, Alice Toklas, Virginia Woolf, and Michael Jackson, to name a few. Travel has also allowed me to see sycamores and their cousins thrive along the Tiber, for instance, in Rome and the Seine, in Paris, cities I can't help but equate with the visual art found in them. I mentioned Monet's studies earlier; I like also to think of poems as constructions, like Leonardo's inventions, each created as experiments devoted to different purposes. I'd say that finally it's languages and weathers that these *Sycamore* poems have made themselves from, seasons of listening to and watching everything, including art.

IM: *Sycamore* is your fifth collection. I am curious to know what has changed for you, as a writer, since your first book. How is your process different? Do you see writing differently? How about publishing?

KF: I'm more humbled by the process of writing and publishing now. But I'm also more relaxed about both. As long as I'm scratching out some lines now and then, collecting them on paper, trying them out in my head while walking or driving, seeing—when time allows—what they look like when I put them together in different combinations, I'm alright. In other words, I feel less precious about the process. I need fewer rituals and props, I need less quiet and time, though I still yearn for both every day. I'm much more aware now of my work in conversation with the living as well as the dead, of my responsibility as a poet—we "unacknowledged legislators," to quote Shelley—to community and the planet. I guess what I'm saying is I feel less precious about myself, too. I'm shy and awkward and inward-turning, but I live here; and while I'm alive I have a responsibility to be fully human as a poet and a person. Coming up I saw some poets who believed they got a pass on that last thing; they don't.

IM: *Sycamore* is divided into three sections. In your eyes, what divides these three sections?

KF: Well, when I was finally at the stage where I was making the book, I realized that I didn't want it to be "about" trees any more than I wanted it to be "about" a bad break-up. I wanted the poems to tell a larger story together, but not a story that moved in any linear way, which feels false to me. What that left me was a much more naturally cyclical, seasonal way to organize the material. I was conscious of beginning the book in winter—and, in keeping with the mythic undertones of that, balancing mid-winter with mid-summer, the invisible with the visible, the young with the old. I hoped that the two over-arching "events" of the book (the speaker's grief and the tree studies) would weave in and out of the whole, allowing for discovery alongside recovery. One of the reasons I adore the image that Milkweed has given to the cover of *Sycamore* is its aerial perspective; the photograph is taken from above, and the objects photographed suggest the tops of trees—or barbed wire, or brain synapses. The poems spend so much time on the ground (or, as you noted earlier, under the ground!), that there had to be a vertical movement upward, too, a literal branching. The three sections of the book provided the space or air, it seemed to me, to promote multiple perspectives.

IM: The final poem of the book begins "When I was dead, one of the whiter/ sycamores who live on the river said,/ Kathy, why didn't you live in your body

more?" Can you tell us more about the ways you feel nature speaks to us, and how you incorporate that into your craft?

KF: I come from an urban, working-class, Irish-Catholic family. I'm second generation American, first generation college. Until I went to graduate school I wouldn't have been able to identify an artichoke. But there were books and there were trees, and both were revered in my family. There was a willow, for example, that my parents dug up and moved from one place to another in New York because they were entrusted with its care. Incredibly, it thrived. I think I internalized early that notion of the tree as a being, and over the years I've carried close inside me some small discoveries, like, for instance, the etymological relationship between the word beech tree and the word book, and the beech's Latin name that rhymes so closely with my own (fagus). Though I never claimed to be an environmentalist poet, writing *Sycamore* has taught me so much about the natural sciences that I'm a card-carrying Sierra Club member, support the #NoDAPL movement, and am devoted to stewardship causes in ways I was ignorantly unaware were even necessary before.

IM: You are the Creative Writing program director at Ohio State University. How does work as a teacher inform your writing? Do they feel connected, or compartmentalized?

KF: When I was a young poet-teacher I definitely compartmentalized writing and teaching. Interestingly, back then I was writing less and teaching more. Now that I'm older, I am more clearly able to integrate my creative and working lives—in fact, I see very little distinction between the two where teaching specifically is concerned; administration is another matter, of course—and I learn both with my students and because of my students' engagement with their poems and our world. In very practical terms, my relationship with students keeps me alert to how language evolves, to how the culture of art—and I mean by that the makers of art, not the sellers of art—is trending. Together we trace influences and departures and patterns. I also feel frankly honored to witness my students' progress as poets, and I know that gives me the courage to continue to grow as a poet myself.

IM: Finally, I'll end with our traditional question. What does your writing space look like?

KF: There have been so many! Always with three things in common: a window, real or remembered books, and a pen.

Corrinne Clegg Hales

Corrinne Clegg Hales is the author of three full-length poetry collections: *To Make it Right*, winner of the Autumn House Poetry Prize for 2010; *Separate Escapes*, winner of the Richard Snyder Poetry Prize from Ashland Poetry Press; and *Underground* from Ahsahta Press. She also has published two chapbooks: *Out of This Place*, March Street Press and *January Fire*, Devil's Millhopper Press. Her poems have appeared in *Hudson Review, Ploughshares, Kenyon Review, Prairie Schooner, Southern Review*, and *North American Review*. Awards include two fellowships from the National Endowment for the Arts, the Devil's Millhopper Chapbook Prize, and the River Styx Poetry Prize. She helped shepherd the transition of Fresno State's MA in Creative Writing to an MFA degree in the 1990s, served as program coordinator off and on for many years, and was named the James and Coke Hallowell Professor of Creative Writing for 2011-2014.

from *How Much Earth*, 2001—Corrinne Clegg Hales

I was born in Tooele, Utah in 1949, and lived in Utah until I left for graduate school in New York late in 1980. I earned a B.A. and M.A. at the University of Utah and a Ph.D at SUNY-Binghamton. In 1985 I moved to Fresno with my husband and children, and, with the exception of two visiting appointments at the University of Oregon, I've taught in the English Department at CSUF ever since. I've had the opportunity at CSUF to work with some of the very best writers in the country, which I consider a great privilege, and the students, coming from all over the Central Valley, are the best I've encountered anywhere. Although the Central Valley landscape and its wonderfully diverse plant and animal life have inhabited and influenced my poetry for many years, it's the changing nature of the *human* population in this valley—the undeniable clashing and mixing of culture and ethnicity and class—that has made the most difference to my writing. This is a place where profound truths (both positive and negative) about American life are working themselves out in plain sight every day. In many ways, it seems to me the truest place I've ever lived.

"An Interview with Poet Connie Hales," from *PackingHouse Review*, 2011—David Dominguez

David Dominguez: Connie, congratulations regarding the publication of your latest poetry collection: *To Make It Right*. The cover is a deep glossy black, and it has a bold spine with white lettering. The back of the book features a wonderful blurb by Juan Felipe Herrera, who says regarding your work, "I am in absolute awe." The book looks beautiful, and it is beautiful. For example, I'm blown away by the eclectic group of people who appear in the poems. Did you feel a desire to tell their stories? In other words, did people inspire them?

Connie Hales: Thanks, David. I'm excited about the book. I guess I do think in terms of personal stories and I'm interested in how people's lives affect each other—how we are connected—even across time and space. When I started writing many years ago, one of my goals was to tell the stories of the people I knew—to somehow bring those stories into the light.

DD: How do you decide which stories are worth retelling in poems? You write poems that focus on dead pigeons while others focus on your ancestors. That is a wide range of material. What advice would you give to the young poet who has many ideas swirling around in her head and can't decide which ones deserve to be put on the page?

CH: Well, it's sort of like an itch. When an image or a story or a phrase just keeps popping into my head, it becomes a problem that demands attention—a type of obsession. Of course they don't all go anywhere, but I really can't tell if something will become a good poem until I work on it for a while—so I just go ahead and try them all out on the page. Many get stalled at the draft stage, but that's my process. I tend to think things through on the page rather than in my head. I also try to see if there might be relationships between seemingly unrelated stories, memories and images, and I might bring several incidents from different times and places to the same poem. If there are several images bouncing around in your head at once (or several stories swirling) they might be strangely connected somehow, and there's often a way for them to shed light on each other.

DD: For all the teachers reading this interview, I would like to say *To Make It Right* would work wonderfully in the classroom. One reason is because you tell stories, and these stories are packed with images. The lines in "Unburied," for example, unfurl one image after another. What role do you believe images play in a poem?

CH: I tend to rely heavily on sensory images to drive the poems. Our senses obviously help us receive, engage with, and understand the world in a primal and powerful way, so I try to create a physical experience for the reader as much as I can and hope that will provoke an emotional and an intellectual experience. As a reader, there are certainly rhetorical poems and voice driven poems that I admire very much, but the poems that move me most deeply are those that invite me to consider a topic with my whole body as well as my intellect. When I write my own poems, I work hard to engage the reader on a sensory, imagistic level, and I generally trust the analytical part of the experience to develop from the sensory impression. Physical/sensory experience, after all, is the primary source for humans. It's our first way of knowing.

DD: Images often contribute to clarity, and I think clarity is important; otherwise, it's too easy for the reader to walk away and go see a movie. Is being clear one of your goals, or does it just happen?

CH: I absolutely agree with you. Clarity is extremely important to me, and the effort to move toward it is a big part of my writing process. It may be the main reason I write at all—an attempt to clarify the world to myself. The world is amazingly complicated and mysterious—and often contradictory—and it's actually extremely difficult to be clear about what we encounter. When I am unclear or obscure in a poem, it's never deliberate—it's because I failed to be clear, not because I wasn't *trying* to be clear. Or it's as close as I could get to clear communication in that particular poem. I want to add that for me, clarity is not simplicity. I don't want simple or simplistic answers—they are hardly ever true—but I don't want deliberate obscurity either. I'm not talking about avoiding honest ambiguity or ambivalence—these things are an important part of the clear and honest portrayal of human experience. I'm talking about avoiding a type of pretentious obscurity that sometimes passes for intellectual discourse in poetry, and avoiding the temptation to settle for vague but beautiful language. I'm talking about constantly working toward the (probably unattainable) ideal of precise communication with one another.

DD: Yes. Very nicely said. I especially appreciate you saying "clarity is not simplicity." Another defining quality of your work is the strength of your lines. Some are long, some are short, some are indented, and others aren't indented. What determines the shape of your lines? Is it the poem, or is it you?

CH: Well, I work hard on the line as a distinct unit of speech—separate from phrase or clause or sentence. It seems to me that the line break is the one piece of punctuation that makes poetry distinct from prose, and it offers poets a unique and powerful tool. So—I think about concerns of sound and rhythm and pacing when I decide on the shapes of the lines in a poem, but I also try to use the line to push toward complexity in meaning, sometimes by breaking at unexpected places that might allow the reader to read the line one way as a unit and another as part of the sentence that continues on through the poem. I want the line to create a type of tension inside the sentence.

DD: I've also noticed that setting plays a significant role in your work, such as in "City Cemetery Love Poem: 1975." How does a person craft a poem so that the landscape comes alive?

CH: This is related to the question about image. I'm attracted to poems that are alive in the very physical world of the imagination, and it seems to me that one way to breathe life into the poem's speaker is to stage the poem firmly in the physical world—the world outside of the speaker's head. I think it helps to ask yourself such questions as "Where is the speaker of the poem standing? What is she wearing? What can she see or hear or smell from where she is standing? What objects are near? What is in the distance? What is she holding in her hand? What is she doing while she speaks? If you watch actors in a play, you see them moving about the furniture on stage, picking up objects and generally reacting to the physical setting as they speak lines. This helps tell us how they are feeling and what they are thinking. I think we can learn a lot from stage performances—and from film—about how to use setting effectively. Setting is also extremely useful as a practical set of tools. The world around us is full of stage props that can be summoned to communicate an emotional situation or even an idea. Why not make use of them?

DD: Finally, when I read a poem, I'm always looking for a sublime moment. Longinus said a sublime moment was like lightening hitting the ground. Do you think a sublime moment just happens or does the poet have to sweat over the page to help make it happen?

CH: That's a great question. In my experience, both things are true—it seems to just happen, but usually not until you've worked very hard and opened yourself up to many possibilities. Some people call this the lyric moment, or an epiphanic moment—or a moment of light. Robert Penn Warren calls it "time out of time." It's like we jump the temporal fence for a second into the realm of astounding clarity and knowledge. Humans have always valued and searched for these powerful moments of altered consciousness, and one way we access them is through art and the power of imagination. You can't force a moment of realization or brilliance to happen—and you certainly can't make it happen when or how you plan for it in a poem. I think you have to work hard at your craft and keep yourself open to unexpected profundity—and be ready to accept it when it shows up.

"In the Company of Poets: Fresno 1980s," 2020—Corrine Clegg Hales

On a July afternoon in 2019, Chuck Hanzlicek and I sat ourselves down on the floor of the Philip Levine Reading Room in the Madden Library at Fresno State to shelve books from Peter Everwine's personal library. Peter had died the previous October, and Phil had been gone for four years.

The Levine Reading room is a large, rectangular space with a high ceiling and lots of light. One long wall is nothing but floor to ceiling windows overlooking Fresno State's Peace Garden with its beautiful landscaping, and statues of Mahatma Gandhi, Martin Luther King, and Jane Addams. The opposite wall is lined with tall glass and wood bookcases holding books from Phil's personal library—both from his home in Fresno and from the Levines' Brooklyn apartment. There are at least 2500 books, including first editions by prominent poets, signed and unsigned books by poets who were Phil's peers, his friends, his former students—and simply poets he liked to read.

Thanks to the generosity of Franny Levine and the hard work, persistence and negotiating skills of a small group of Fresno poets—and a supportive dean and provost—we were able to open the Levine Reading Room on May 5, 2017. Franny donated Phil's entire personal library to the university's College of Arts and Humanities to be housed in a space where they could be found and read by students, teachers, scholars, and community poets. A usable space. This would not be a dusty mausoleum—it would be a busy classroom, meeting room, and work space, open to students and the general public during library hours, and used regularly for creative writing workshops. Many of the books here have Phil's distinctive, angular handwriting in the margins—talking back, arguing with—in conversation with the voice on the page. A clear check mark often notes what he likes, and some books even have a letter or a separate note tucked between the pages. It's an amazing place to spend an afternoon.

When my graduate poetry workshop met there that first semester, we opened all the glass bookcase doors and the students browsed excitedly until they each came back to the table with a book. Then each young poet read a poem out loud from the book they had selected—a poet whose voice they found on Levine's shelves. Someone read Jaime Sabines in Spanish and English (from an edition translated by Ernesto Trejo and Phil Levine). Someone read Sharon Olds, and Omar Salinas, and John Keats. We heard an early Audre Lorde poem from a rare 1973 chapbook, at least one Lawson Inada poem, and a couple of Ai's harrowing persona poems, and more. In this way, the voices of all those poets began to join us around the seminar table, sitting with us as we settled into our work.

Fortunately, enough shelf space remained in the Reading Room after Phil's books had been placed, so when Peter Everwine's sons gave Chuck some truly essential books from Peter's collection, he thought it would be both fitting and practical for those books to be accessible to students, scholars, and other readers alongside Phil's books. Chuck got Franny's blessing, we got permission from our dean, and we went ahead.

I brought the keys to the bookcases and my hand truck, and Chuck met me in the parking lot with four boxes of books. We adjusted and organized until we had three shelves cleared at the bottom of one of the large cases. Chuck had carefully selected which of Peter's books to bring to this room. Mostly, he chose books that might not be easily available elsewhere—several hard to find copies of Peter's own books, for instance, including a very rare copy of his first book, *The Broken Frieze*, published in 1958. He brought signed copies of books by Luis Omar Salinas, and books signed to

Peter over the years by other Fresno poets, and many more. In addition, there are six stunningly beautiful fine art poetry books made by Brighton press—one of them Peter's own *How It Is*, (poem by Peter Everwine, woodcut by Bill Kelly), and one of them *The Mahler Poems*, (poems by C. G. Hanzlicek, etchings by Oldrich Prochaska).

Of course it took us much longer than it should have to shelve the books because we couldn't resist opening them, reading a little—and Chuck had wonderful stories and details to share about many of them. We sat there on the floor, surrounded by stacks of extraordinary books—two old poets, an occasional puzzled student wandering in and out, the Fresno sun lighting up the room, and the energy of all those voices.

It's a powerful thing to have all those voices gathered in that room together. It's an intense and eclectic chorus—poets from many cultures and from the distant past, poets who were Phil's and Peter's peers or former students—and many poets who are not at all aesthetically or philosophically aligned with the work of either Peter or Phil. There are books by many of my own favorite poets, and books by some of my own former students (Brian Turner, Blas Manuel De Luna, Sasha Pimentel among them). They all remain in constant conversation here, and anyone who walks through the door is welcome to join in.

This is how all of Fresno seemed to me when I first came here in 1985—brimming with a huge variety of poetry and poets. There truly were (still are) an astonishing number of poets here. They seemed to be everywhere—more than a few nationally known poets were on faculty at Fresno State and Fresno City College, in the larger community, and across the valley as a whole. You'd find outstanding poets teaching high school, working in offices, bookstores, grocery stores, working as teachers' aides, as social workers, interpreters, firefighters, waiters and bartenders.

Previously, I'd heard about (and was attracted to) the English Department at Fresno State because of its 1970s history of protest and righteous clashes with administration— and I understood that the poet Robert Mezey had been fired over a free speech issue. I was also aware that Philip Levine taught in the English Department—but I'd never been to Fresno before I moved here. I had no idea how deeply and widely poetry was rooted in the Central Valley.

My husband John had been hired in the English Department, and in summer of 1985, we moved to Fresno with our two almost grown children from upstate New York (where we'd both just completed graduate school). I started as an adjunct, teaching composition and humanities/classics courses. I had a PhD and a book of poems coming out, and I was determined to get a tenure track job somewhere in the area as soon as I could.

The English Department at Fresno State then consisted of 28 tenure track faculty members. Three of them, Levine, Hanzlicek, and Everwine, were very well known poets, several more were practicing and publishing poets and translators at various points in their careers, and quite a few of the adjuncts (like me) who taught classes intermittently during those years were also writing and publishing poems. Fresno State clearly didn't need another poet. Fortunately, I was qualified to teach other things, so I did that, and I applied diligently for jobs elsewhere. I also applied for a generalist position at Fresno State, thinking it would be great to avoid a commute across the valley, and understanding what an incredible opportunity it was to teach at this poetry-rich school in the same department as three of my favorite writers in the world, no matter what I was teaching. Three years later, I was hired as a generalist. It was the same year that the department hired Steve Yarbrough, committing itself to a re-vitalized fiction program alongside the poetry program, and Steve, (along with Liza Wieland, hired a few years later), began to make that happen.

Before I came to Fresno, I'd never been to a place where the literary community, poetry, in particular, was so *visible,* was such an expected (and respected) part of daily life. In those days, I'd run into Omar Salinas, or Mike Clifton, or Robert Vasquez, or Dixie Salazar, or Ernesto Trejo, or Jon Veinberg at the Upstart Crow, a bookstore/coffee shop in the Manchester Mall, or walking down Olive Avenue headed for coffee or breakfast in the Tower District, or I might spot Chuck Moulton working on a poem at one of the green vinyl booths at the Chicken Pie Shop. I remember chatting with Roberta Spear at the Farmer's Market on Blackstone Avenue, and I'd often spot Ernesto Trejo walking and talking with students at Fresno City College near where I lived with my family. Unless they were deeply involved in something else, any of them would wave or call out. They'd stop and ask how the writing was going—like other people might ask about your family or your job.

I sometimes rode city bus number 28 from our house to work at Fresno State, and I was used to people reading novels on the bus (this was before cell phones), but on this bus I would almost always see at least one person reading a book of poems. One morning, I saw a young woman, probably still in high school, reading a book of poems by Adrienne Rich, and I asked her what she thought of it. She said she loved Adrienne Rich and proceeded to explain in literary and political detail what she loved about this book. *Are you a teacher?* she asked, noticing my bag of textbooks and papers. *Yes*—I said—*and a poet*, still feeling a little bit self-conscious about saying that out loud. *Me too*, she said matter-of-factly, and went back to her reading.

It wasn't just that there were a lot of poets around, it was that everyone *talked poetry*—and everyone *read* poetry—and they took it seriously. When I went to the downtown library, I'd often find that the book I wanted was already checked out. And most of the poetry books had been checked out many times. As any poet knows, this isn't usually the case. This literary community was for real. It wasn't about po-biz or career building or posturing of any kind. As Phil often said: *This is Fresno—not New York City.* You could expect to overhear a heated discussion in a bookstore or a coffee shop—or even at a bus stop—about lyric versus narrative, or the virtues of a prose poem, but you would rarely hear a cynical discussion about fame or how to achieve it. The ongoing conversation was about the *poems*—about craft and content, about the how, what and why. There was an abundance of opinion and passion, but there was very little of the petty competitive sniping or the suspect praise I'd seen elsewhere.

During my first few years at Fresno State, I taught everything *but* poetry writing: freshman composition and classics, intro to lit courses, American literature courses, even beginning fiction and non-fiction workshops. I loved the students right away—they were curious and smart and bold, and they were eager to learn. Every class included students from all over the valley, from many different backgrounds, circumstances and ages. I found the teaching both challenging and exciting, and I was starting to feel at home in Fresno. Then, in the semester after I was hired on a permanent line, I noticed that the Beginning Poetry Writing course had been assigned to me, and I thought there had been some mistake. I went to the chair and asked why this was on my next schedule. He said Phil and Chuck (as Coordinator of Creative Writing) had asked him to assign me the course, and to switch Phil to a GE course in its place. I was happy and grateful. Neither Phil or Chuck ever said a word to me about this, but after that I was rotated into the poetry schedule as a regular part of my schedule.

The poets at Fresno State had a certain kind of subtlety—a quiet dignity. There was never a lot of fanfare, no hyperbole, no extraneous drama (though there was plenty in the English Department as a whole). One semester Phil visited one of my classes to write a faculty peer evaluation for my tenure file. When I saw him in the hallway, I caught up with him and thanked him for the generous evaluation. He stopped walking and looked me straight in the eye: *It wasn't generous*, he said raising his eyebrows as he often did when making a point. *I'm never generous.* And he went on his way. In fact, I knew him to be incredibly generous—with his time, his expertise, his hospitality. But after I thought awhile, I knew what he meant. He was telling me he didn't lie. Not in class, not in letters of recommendation, not to avoid hurting someone's feelings, not to get someone a spot in graduate school, a job, or a promotion.

In fact, I never heard Phil—or Peter or Chuck—offer gratuitous praise or avoid telling a difficult truth—to either students or colleagues. But none of them subscribed to the "brutal honesty" workshop model either. I never saw any of them be petty or cruel—or condescending—in class. In quite different ways, they each relied on clear, tactful but straightforward, communication. They were exceptional teachers partly because they treated students and their work with respect, and they were able to find ways (often using humor) to help a student or—a colleague—hear what might be difficult to hear.

My first full-length book, *Underground*, came out that first fall semester after we'd moved to Fresno, and I didn't really know what to do. I didn't know anyone well enough yet to set up a book launch reading—and I was so naïve that I didn't even know that I *should* do that. I was still a bit intimidated by the faculty poets and hadn't yet dared to even knock on office doors and introduce myself. I worried way too much about whether to give them each a copy—or whether that would be too presumptuous—so I did nothing.

After a few weeks, one afternoon when I was grading papers in the office I shared with Martin Paul, the door wide open and my chair nestled among Martin's wonderful, jumbled heaps of poetry books—Chuck Hanzlicek walked up and sort of loomed in the doorway. I was so surprised I don't remember if I even said hello. He had with him not only a copy of my new book, but also a copy of the chapbook I'd published the previous year. *These are good poems*, he said simply, and asked if I'd sign his copies. We had no online bookstore then—no Amazon, no Google. You had to make a real effort to find out that a book had been published by a small press, and you had to look up the press's address at the library, and you either had to order a book by mail or by phone–or ask a local bookstore to order it and wait weeks for it to arrive.

In spite of my own initial and ongoing awkwardness, Chuck had made it his business not only to get my books but to read them—and to come by and quietly tell me he liked the work. That meant everything. Chuck became a kind and generous (unofficial) mentor to me, actively supporting my promotions, my tenure decision and other department hurdles, but most importantly—he consistently supported my work. I'm sure he was behind more than a few anthology solicitations I've received over the years, for instance, and he was the chief instigator of my nomination for a Fresno Arts Council Horizon Award in 2010, an award that's especially important to me.

When the second printing of one of my books was horribly filled with typos and errors (the press was new to scanning and OCR technology), Chuck calmed me down and strongly advised me to simply not accept this—even though the press had already run the whole printing, sent me a box of 50 author copies, and shipped boxes of books out to the distributor. He even offered to write to my editor himself. In the end, the whole printing was re-called and re-done beautifully. Chuck helped me navigate the English Department, the university and even the town. If John and I needed a plumber, we knew we could ask Chuck for advice, when we wondered what backyard bird or native plant we were looking at—we'd call Chuck (and we still do that). He taught me many things about teaching, about poetry—and everything I know about how to run a creative writing program and a reading series.

In the 1980s and 90s, there were frequent poetry readings on Fresno State campus and at Fresno City College, and Chuck Moulton ran a legendary once-a-month Fresno Poets Association reading at the Wild Blue Yonder, a nightclub in Fresno's Tower District. Various local and out-of-town poets would read to a full house–often people would be lined up at the bar and standing at the back of the room. There was a small stage and a microphone, and many of these readings were recorded. I recall the loud dinging of the cash register and the clanking of coins and glasses, and people shuffling back and forth to the bar and the restrooms—but the audience was there for the poetry, and it was always packed.

Thanks to Jacqueline Pilar and Chuck Hanzlicek, who took over the FPA after Chuck Moulton died, many of the recordings were saved, and thanks to Jefferson Beavers (Communications Specialist for the English Department) they are now digitized (including readings at the wild Blue, at the Fresno Met, and later at the Fresno Art Museum) as part of the Fresno Poets Archive Project. Each video is being close captioned and made available on an ongoing basis on Fresno State MFA Program's YouTube Channel.

In addition to all the usual readings and events, during my first year in Fresno, Chuck and Peter offered an entire course in the English Department devoted to poetry readings. Somehow, they secured money from the university to bring a well-known poet for an evening reading every single week for the whole semester—there must have been at least a dozen different visiting poets. The readings were open to the public and the class members would stay for class discussion afterward. My friend Michael McGuire (a wonderful poet who was also an adjunct faculty member and a Fresno State alum), attended all of the readings with me, and made sure to introduce me to the poets. Guest poets included alumni who had gone on to become very well-known poets: Sherley Anne Williams, David St. John, Gary Soto—as well as other prominent poets such as Sandra McPherson, Stanley Plumly, and Nobel Prize winner Czeslaw Milosz. It was a remarkable few months. Recordings of these readings are (or will be) available on YouTube as part of the Fresno Poets Archive Project.

Various other readings took place on a regular basis, both on campus and off. Often a poet friend of Phil's or Peter's or Chuck's, such as Ed Hirsch, Gerald Stern, Sharon Olds, or Larry Levis, might be in the Bay area (or in Larry's case, nearby visiting family), and make a side trip to Fresno. The Levines frequently opened their house and their dinner table to such guests, and their abundant hospitality helped make it possible for Fresno students and residents to hear many major poets read their work in person. They'd do a reading, answer questions, and often visit a poetry class. I was always welcome to attend any of Phil's classes when a visiting poet was involved, and welcome to stop by his office to talk poetry when he was there. It seemed like he read and remembered everything. If I published a poem in a journal, he'd often have seen it by the next time I ran into him, and he would comment on it. He'd often point me toward interesting poems by others in recent journals, or suggest a poet—or a new book—that he thought I might be interested in.

Sometime in 1991, Phil came into my office and set a thick manila envelope on my desk. I'd been talking with him recently about long poems, and poems in sections, basically asking him for advice. I'd been trying to push myself to deal with larger topics in a longer form—trying to lean more outward in my work—and the poem I was currently grappling with wasn't coming together. No matter what I did, it felt disjointed and distant. *This is what you need to read,* he said. I asked what it was. *It's the book that should get the Pulitzer this year,* he answered—*but it won't. Read it, and give it back to me as soon as you can.* It was either the galleys or a copy of the manuscript (I can't recall which) for Adrienne Rich's *An Atlas of the Difficult World,* which would come out late that same year. And he was right—it was exactly what I needed to show me what could be done and why it was worth doing.

The Levines hosted many wonderful dinners at their house. They always involved great food (thanks to the truly amazing Franny Levine), lots to drink, and wide-ranging conversation. Sometimes it was gossipy talk about the larger poetry world, funny anecdotes about writers' conferences or behind the scenes stories about awards and publishing. Sometimes it was stories about Fresno State and the creative writing program's early students. These were some of the smartest, most interesting people I have ever known, and dinner discussions were often passionate—and everyone didn't always agree. I recall one dinner listening to an intense but friendly argument between Peter and Phil about the merits (or not) of Robert Bly's poetry. This was at the height of Bly's *Iron John* popularity, and he had recently visited campus. They were quoting poems and telling stories, and from time to time, Peter would just shrug and laugh and say: *I still think Bly is under-appreciated as a poet.*

At one dinner party, I asked Phil why he thought Fresno State got so many talented poets to enroll in our program. I realized as soon as I said it that, of course, the obvious answer was the three superb poets sitting here in the room with me (it seemed like I was always putting my foot in my mouth). But that wasn't where Phil went with it. He paused, leaned forward and said with all seriousness: *Where else can they go?* It was an acknowledgement of a simple fact. Many of our students had considerable family obligations and full time jobs—or simply could not afford financially or logistically to move away for a couple of years to study creative writing. UC Merced didn't exist then and there were only a few low-residency programs across the country. Even Bakersfield was a 2-hour drive. This is still the case for a large number of our students, and this valley is filled with people who are living profound lives, who have important stories to tell—stories that we need to hear.

Living and teaching in Fresno isn't especially comfortable or easy—the chorus of voices in our classrooms and our streets has always been large and disorderly. It's comprised of varied and urgent voices that might disagree on many things—they might sing opera or blues or even off key—but they all strive to sing with intention and intensity. They all believe in the power of words to somehow bring us together, to help us move in the direction of understanding, of some type of clarity, of connection. And that chorus is always growing, changing, making room for new voices. Years ago, when I was first studying Whitman, one of the critics I read complained that Whitman's legacy wasn't a great American cathedral, but amounted to "a series of antinomian chapels." *Yes!* I wrote in my journal. *That's exactly what he hoped for.* And that's sort of how I feel about Fresno poetry.

What we have here is not one elegant construction, where people follow the same leader and subscribe to the same set of assumptions. It's a large assortment of poets who are happy to learn from each other, who influence and are influenced by each other, but who do not become replicas of their influencers. Fresno poetry can't be defined by a specific style of writing, by the philosophies of any specific teacher, or even by subject matter. I think of the distinct poetries of Lawson Inada, Larry Levis, Sasha Pimentel, Brian Turner, Soul Vang, Omar Salinas, Suzanne Lummis. Ultimately, I believe Fresno poets have only two things in common: a deep connection to Fresno and the Central Valley, and a belief in the essential power of poetry—the importance of the work. They might have grown up here, been students here, or moved here for some unrelated reason, and decided to stay. Somehow, the place itself seems to give a hefty nudge those who want to speak. It gives them space, permission, and a supportive community. The vitality of Fresno poetry thrives on the curiosity, courage and perseverance of individual poets.

What was so astonishing to me when I came to Fresno, what made me understand that I could live the rest of my life here, was that there were so many passionate voices devoted to writing poetry. It gave me hope. Right here, in this conservative, scrappy, dust-covered, *un*California part of California—there were so many voices singing.

Since the 1980s, when I first came to know it, the Fresno poetry community has continued to flourish. It has grown in every way you might imagine. In 1990, Juan Felipe Herrera returned to the valley to teach Chicano Studies at Fresno State, and he and Margarita Luna Robles have been powerful poetry arts activists and leaders here ever since. Poets Ruth Schwartz and Tim Skeen joined the faculty at Fresno State about a decade later. And even after retirement, both Phil and Peter remained regular and generous participants in Fresno's poetry community, always showing up at readings, offering advice to young poets, visiting poetry classes, and reading their work (often at benefit readings) in town. Chuck has done the same since he retired. He also single-handedly managed the FPA community reading series for many years, and more recently, he was a central and persuasive part of the negotiations to establish the Philip Levine Reading Room at Fresno State.

Today, Fresno is home to many more literary events, organizations (and organizers), and poets and prose writers, than I could possibly list. An astonishing number of former Fresno State students and community members have won national awards and published excellent books of their own—and that number increases each year. I'm very proud of my part in this exceptional community—as a poet, and as a teacher. And now, as I retire from teaching, Fresno State has hired two brilliant poets, Mai Der Vang and Brynn Saito, who both happened to grow up in this poetry-rich valley. The future is in good hands.

I'm acutely aware of how lucky I've been to teach and live in Fresno for the past 35 years. It was a transitional era for the community in many ways, and it's been an extraordinary experience, beginning with the improbable opportunity to work alongside the three poet/teachers who founded Fresno State's creative writing program—and who built into it such integrity, and who made such a huge difference in so many lives. By the time I came along, they had been close friends with each other for many years, and even their friendship seemed like a lesson in living. Each, in his own way, modeled for students (and for newcomers like me) what it might be like to live your life as a writer, and to live your life in the company of poetry, and poets, that you love.

Dixie Salazar

Dixie Salazar was born in Chicago, Illinois and studied art at California State University, Fresno. Also an author, activist, and educator, she has been a working artist and writer for more than forty years. She has published six books of poetry: *HOTEL FRESNO; REINCARNATION OF THE COMMONPLACE* (national poetry award winner) by Salmon Run Press in 1999; *BLOOD MYSTERIES*, 2003, and *FLAMENCO HIPS AND RED MUD FEET*, 2009, were both published by the Univ. of Arizona Press; *ALTAR FOR ESCAPED VOICES* by Tebot Bach in 2013 in the Ash Tree Series. and *Voice of the Wind* from Brandenburg press in 2018. *LIMBO*, her novel, was published by White Pine Press in 1995. She taught for many years at CSU Fresno and has also taught extensively in the California prisons and the Fresno County jail and is currently involved in The Eco Village Project to develop housing for the homeless. Her recent projects include a photographic exhibit of a homeless encampment in Fresno and serving on the board of the Eco Village Project and the Dakota Eco Garden, which provide sustainable, green housing for the homeless in a community environment. She's also active in Fresno Filmworks. Some of Dixie's awards include a Horizon Award and Award of Excellence from the National Women's Political Caucus.

from *What Will Suffice*, 1995—Dixie Salazar

I want to read and write poetry that breathes through the music, breathes through the meaning. That means poetry taking place in and out of the world—poetry that has its feet, not just on the ground, but in the mud. Because poetry is dirt under your fingernails, and between your toes, and recognition of the beauty and terror contained in the process itself, which is really the act of living.

This is poetry that is not alienated from our inner lives, not separate and compartmentalized, like a subject to be studied for a semester; but as integrated and fully realized part of ourselves.

By entering poetry, I have learned to trust myself more, and the rightness of failed memory; to let imagination play in the minefield of memory. Learning to believe in what we can't see, touch, taste, smell or hear involves trusting in memory and imagination, trusting in a force greater than our intellect or senses, and continuing to live in a state of amazement.

from *How Much Earth*, 2001—Dixie Salazar

It's the best of places, it's the worst of places; but ultimately, the place one always returns to is the place inside. That's where the small town girl hides who flew on her second-hand Schwinn over brick streets lined with maples spinning leaves into dust, to the library to become *Becky and the Bandit, Girl Detective; Lowilla, Gypsy Girl of the Pyrenees;* or *The Lost Indian Princes of Ghost Hollow Canyon.* And for all her days cast away in stacks of dusty books, she'll be perplexed when the whole third grade bursts into laughter at the Indian name she chooses: "Princess Moonshine."

So how does she come to reside and write in Fresno? Let's be honest, when was the last time you saw a listing for gypsy-princess-detective who speaks Iroquois in the want ads? But Fresno is very much like a small town, and with a credit card and a phone, you can order any book you desire, and until you can prove your secret royal Indian heritage, you can live cheaply on figs and oranges in your back yard, with acres of space and time to explore all the uncharted territory within.

from *Bear Flag Republic: Prose Poems & Poetics from California*, 2008—Dixie Salazar

T.S. Eliot proposed that "the supposed freedoms of free verse are only negatives: (1) absence of patter, (2) absence of rhyme, (3) absence of meter." If this is true, where does that leave the prose poem? Now we are giving up the line in addition, which could lead to the question, what could possibly be gained by using the prose poem form (another contradiction)? Already backed into a corner, the only possible answer that comes to my mind is that one gives in to its oxymoronic, contradictory nature, although super-condensed. The rest of the story must be told in individual and personal terms.

These recent poems of mine also were the result of a negative. Let me explain. For about fifteen years I had been teaching visual are and creative writing in the California men's and women's prisons. The poems that resulted from those experiences took mostly a first-person narrator's point of view, an involved viewer/visitor/observer, the outsider looking in. The voice in the poems was a kind of disembodied, floating voyeur. This stance seemed limiting and at times dissatisfying to me.

The discovery of writing in other voices, those of the inmates, was quite liberating, but also challenging. Like attention-starved children, they had pored out their stories, remarkably uncensored. Occasional attempts to color reality seemed almost feebly transparent. The need to be heard and paid attention to, that most basic of human needs, is most effectively denied the incarcerated, and they clamored to be heard.

These voices became the disguise I needed, and with that intact, the need for a vehicle arose (the getaway car, let's say). The prose poem seemed a natural vehicle, with its engine the dominance of narrative. These stories that would be told made their own demands for simplicity and veracity, and the prose poem complied.

It has been a number of years since I have worked in the prisons, but as the voices continue to break out, I am amazed at their strength and the worthy urgency of their demands.

"Finding Poetry in the Fig Orchards of Fresno," 2020—Dixie Salazar

Even Fresno natives take part in Fresno bashing at times, but I, along with many other Fresnans, had to discover its attractions by leaving. It wasn't until I spent two years living in New York that I realized that unbeknown to me, a subtle and alarming osmosis had taken place and I had become a Fresnan. It was alarming because I had planned to try and move somewhere nicer after graduate school and there I was missing Fresno fog, freeways and funky thrift stores. There was much to love in New York (when I wasn't battling it) but it was as if aliens had planted a microchip in me, and now I actually preferred grape vineyards and visual impoverishment.

It's easy to love Barcelona or Berkeley, but to love Fresno takes a keener eye, to see beyond the Golden Arches and giant Long John Silver anchor hooked into the gray, conversion layered skyline. Loving Fresno is like learning to love one's nose or hips or chronic skin condition. It takes a certain maturity and almost zen-like enlightenment to embrace a landscape that boasts one of the longest stretches of fast food restaurants in the world. But it is precisely this "commonplace…that can be endowed"…as Ray Carver noted "with immense, even startling power". And it is that magical-mundane quality that has continued to draw my scrutiny and filter into my writing (I hope).

My teachers at Fresno State Philip Levine, Charles Hanzlicek, Peter Everwine, and before that Dewayne Rail at Fresno City College also reinforced and in truth demanded this deep rooted reality check of our poetry. They ruthlessly but lovingly nurtured my poetry instincts and I am forever grateful to them all. This desire for "keepin' it real" as they say in the blues world informs and sustains me still in both writing and visual art.

I did not think of myself as a poet originally. I had always been primarily a visual artist. Poetry was something I stumbled into, but from my first class with DeWayne Rail at Fresno City College, poetry switched me on. Part of the attraction was escape from an emotionally stagnant childhood and stultifying marriage. And there were all these male professors in corduroy jackets with arm patches and new, enticing ideas, encouraging me, a culturally starved housewife. I was in love with this new world of ideas and images. I would haul bushels of poems to Dewayne's class and he would hand them all back pulling out two or three, saying, "these are good…those others, don't do that again." This academic world was an elixir for my soul and the early exposure to poets like James Dickey, Elizabeth Bishop, and Richard Hugo took the top of my head off (as Emily once said). I tried them and many others all on for size and it wasn't a bad way to hone a craft.

By the time I reached Phil Levine's class, I had committed the most serious poetry felonies and was ready for his critical but discerning eye. Phil was brilliant, funny and at times biting. Almost every class someone left in tears. He did not hold back when his bullshit detector went off.

We were held in the grip of a collective cringing that was palpable when a fellow classmate was being skewered but always, it was undercut by humor. I would find myself laughing at Phil's scathing critique, thinking, thank God it's not me on the rotisserie. Later, at Columbia, I was exposed to many of the major poets of the 1980's, from Joseph Brodsky to Richard Howard to Sharon Olds, but I never encountered another teacher who could cut to the center of a poem and deconstruct it in a way that made perfect and obvious sense the way that Phil could. He was our prophet, guru, and poetic father figure. And I absorbed it all like a nerdy poetry sponge.

"Can you really hear anyone you know saying this? " he'd ask or "This line has five adjectives that describe nothing real". Always, we were cautioned against bullshit and esoteric nonsense and encouraged to explore our immediate world, the Ho Ho cafes, the vineyards of the Central Valley, the Crest Theatres, the Cherry Auctions, at the same time, dipping into the deep, rich imaginative well of poets like Neruda, Lorca and Gloria Fuertes. And the craft of poetry was not neglected. We studied Robert Frost, Sylvia Plath, Wilfred Owen, and Emily Dickenson. When Phil introduced Philip Larkin, I was intrigued and rushed to the library to look for his books, only to be told they were all checked out. When I told Phil about this at the next class, he quietly suggested I go and look again. Lo and behold, they were all there.

You had to have a thick skin to make it through Phil's classes. I sometimes wonder if it wasn't his way of weeding out the less than serious. During one class, in the process of critiquing a student's poem, Phil said, "there's only one thing that will help this poem." He proceeded to fold the poem into a paper airplane and fly it out the window. But if you were awake and engaged, you learned. The list of poets that emerged from his classes is phenomenal: Larry Levis, Gary Soto, Roberta Speer, David St John, Sherley Ann Williams, Jean Janzen, Lawson Inada, Jon Veinberg, and many more; all became published and noteworthy poets. I owe my poetic career to Phil. When I shyly suggested after class that I was thinking of applying to Columbia University MFA program, he said, "You could be a poet." It was as if he had handed me my driver's license and now I could charge forth into the world of poetry.

But I was incredibly lucky to have had other amazing teachers at Fresno State. After a divorce, I lived in a small apartment with my daughter Krista, part time teaching jobs paying for this and a beat up Datsun with no reverse gear, which made parking on campus crazy, an already nightmarish experience. Added to this, the need for babysitters made night classes almost impossible. Luckily for me, at the first class meeting, Chuck Hanzlicek suggested we meet off campus, and I readily volunteered my place. The rest of the semester the class of about fifteen met in my tiny apartment. Chuck became another trusted ear. He also ascribed to the same no BS—reality first approach to writing poetry. He perhaps had an even stronger commitment to un-fanciful language. Chuck had a great fondness for the Eastern European poets and introduced us to Transtromer, Havel, Kundera, Milosz and others. Chuck was not a harsh critic but his standards were high. I remember one student in particular who brought very obscure, almost inscrutable poems to class and every week Chuck would say, "I haven't the vaguest idea what you are saying." But each week he'd return with another batch of enigmas. I'll be eternally grateful to Chuck for making it easier on me to take a night class and always grateful for his generosity, insights and encouragement. Both Chuck and his wife, Dianne became dear and valued friends of Jon's and mine.

The unselfish, supportive spirit of these teachers was nothing short of amazing to me and still is. Jon and I also became friends with Phil and his wife Frannie. I never quite got over my awe of Phil, but he never played a superior role with his students and an incredible amount of them became his friends over the years. He was always ready and willing to look at poems or write letters of support or recommendation. When he found something to praise in a poem of mine, I would float in the glow of his words for weeks.

Peter Everwine became another trusted ear. There was a humble elegance about Peter and his poetic sensibility was flawless and finely tuned. I loved his academic poetry classes but did not have him for a workshop. Jon did though, and recounted how in one class, Peter had ripped apart someone's poem. After class, Jon overheard that student and another: "He sure tore your poem up didn't he?" "No. I think he kind of liked it," the student said. Jon attributed this to Peter's erudite criticism, and his graceful facility with words. He could cuss you out and make you think it was a compliment.

Hard to believe now, but when I was in Peter's class, smoking was allowed and in one class where I had settled in to soak up another brilliant Everwine lecture on Romantic poetry, I watched in horror as a plume of smoke rose up from his shoes. Peter had a soft but deep and sonorous voice that fairly hypnotized the listener. But I had to interrupt his passionate treatise on "Ode on a Grecian Urn" to tell him that his shoelaces were on fire.

Peter was a prince of a man, as highly principled as he was generous and I always paid attention when he talked about who he was reading and discovered many new poetry finds through him, particularly Leondardo Sinisgalli and the Dutch poet, Rutger Kopeland. Shortly before Peter passed away in 2018, I had stopped by his house for a quick visit. I asked if I could borrow the Kopeland book and assured him I would take good care of it and return it promptly. "Don't worry about it," he said, and I suspect now that he had a presentiment about his own mortality at that time.

Probably the second greatest influence on my poetry, after Phil, was the man who would become my husband, Jon Veinberg. I knew Jon and I were committed, the day we combined our poetry collections. We never had a class together, but when we began to date, we were already part of a close knit poetry tribe: Chuck and Dianne Hanzlicek, Peter Everwine, Phil Levine and Frannie, Roberta Speer, Chuck Moulton, Omar Salinas, Jean Janzen, Ernesto and Dianne Trejo, Sandra Hoben, Robert Vasquez and others. Roberta Speer was at the epicenter with her monthly poetry potlucks and Chuck Moulton with his Wild Blue Yonder poetry readings, a local nightclub owned by the Bixler brothers that served up incredible music and poetry on a regular basis.

There was never a really strong critical aspect to Jon's and my poetic communing. I probably showed him more of my poems than he did me, and he always had insightful comments, but gradually, we each maintained our own poetic space. Jon was an avid reader of both poetry and fiction and I could always count on him to find new and exciting voices. Our mutual love of poetry was a constant and I do remember nights in the backyard and discussions of various writers and aspects of poetry. I appreciated Jon's ability to take on other voices such as a stray dog, a prostitute, a pastry chef and a buzzard. Jon said that Phil had once said to him, "Why would you write about yourself when you could write about somebody really interesting?" In my book, *ALTAR FOR ESCAPED VOICES*, I risked also taking on the voices of inmates I had worked with in the prisons and homeless people I had come to know through my work in a homeless shelter. But usually our nights in the backyard came around to a couple of glasses of wine and a lot of laughter. Jon was very funny and a natural story-teller, and I think this element came through in the narrative quality of many of his poems.

I hadn't realized when I first moved in with Jon that his house was a refuge for wayward and rambling poets. Chuck Moulton had stopped by once to watch a football game and stayed for eight days. Omar and Gary Soto had to be reminded to knock now that I was living in the house. Omar at his best was probably one of the most natural and organic poets imaginable. But both Jon and Chris Buckley spent many hours editing his work and shaping his manuscripts. Omar had the soul of a mystic and the honest and pure vision of a child but he needed parameters. Jon told me once that there were words or lines in Omar's poems that he had written. But it was always Omar's vision. Before I arrived on the scene, Omar had lived with Jon for about a year, but it finally did not work out. Omar had his demons and Jon needed his space.

Ernesto Trejo was a handsome and genteel dreamer and an incredibly imaginative poet who loved life fully. He was all heart. He and Dianne bought a house on almost a half acre in Old Fig Garden with an older, rectangular cement pool from another era. Floating under the stars, shaking off the blistering heat of the day, "It's just like a Hollywood swim party" Omar said, dog paddling across the pool one balmy summer night. Ernesto and Dianne raised two creative and soulful children there, Keri Christina and Victor. Sadly, we lost Ernesto to cancer in 1990 and Dianne several years later.

It's about 1989, a balmy summer night after a blistering day of 100 plus temps. Jon and I are sitting under the arbor in the backyard on Brown, catching occasional whiffs of Wisteria floating through the leftover chorizo from the neighbor's yard. Omar appears, his clothes wrinkled, his hair tousled, his eyes wild with that crazy gypsy glint. He's lost his driver's license somewhere in the vineyards—he's not sure where and he can't remember how he got here. Jon talks him down, with a promise that he'll go straight home to his Aunt's house who had called earlier worrying about him. He'd been missing for several days. After he leaves, we are pouring ourselves two more glasses of wine when we hear the growl of a motorcycle out front. It's Chuck with his own Moulton growl, wanting to use our phone to make the hundred plus reminder phone calls he makes before every poetry reading. I tell him OK but be sure to be off the phone by nine because I need to make a call. Close to ten o'clock he steps off the back porch and seeing my less than pleased face, strokes his chin and in his gnarly voice says, "I heard everything you said. I just heard it backwards." I wasn't even sure how that fit the situation, but it was classic Moulton.

When we lost Chuck Moulton, in a somewhat freak accident where he fell from a fruit tree that he was pruning, it was the beginning of the unraveling of this remarkable and closely knit poetry family. We were still a family, but gradually, as things must, there were changes and as they added up over the years, the poetry scene shifted slightly and became a different animal. Jon felt that it became more academic, with the Fresno Poet's Association now attached to Fresno State.

One thing I am certain of is that the remarkable teachers I had in Fresno changed my life in every possible way, and I learned not just about poetry but most importantly, they taught me through the example of their own lives how to live a life of generosity and integrity.

"Interview with Dixie Salazar" from *SALT*, 2020—Christopher Buckley

Christopher Buckley: Tell me about your early days. When did you arrive in Fresno?
Dixie Salazar: We moved to Los Angeles and for me at the time it was like landing on another planet, from the small towns in Illinois where I had grown up. I moved to Fresno about 1968 and have lived here ever since. I always saw myself as an artist, a visual artist that is. That was all I ever wanted to be, other than a cowgirl. I would have made a lousy cowgirl. I haven't had good luck with horses. Photography, poetry and then writing fiction came later when I was in my thirties.

CB: How did you come to be interested in writing poetry?
DS: I was working on a BA degree in Art first at Fresno State. But I had discovered poetry earlier in a class at City College with Dewayne Rail and got hooked. I had taken a poetry class mostly at night every semester along with my other classes, and when I applied for my degree in Art, I was told that if I took two more classes, I could earn a degree in English, so I thought, why not? The catalogue that I had entered under had only X number of units required for a degree in English. I think part of the interest in writing was because of my frustration with art and not being able to get across visually what I wanted to say.

I began taking classes at Fresno State in 1979 and continued until 1983, sometimes only taking one or two classes a semester. I took poetry writing workshops with Phil Levine and Chuck Hanzlicek and academic poetry classes with Peter Everwine. They were all amazing teachers who set the bar high, and I owe my entire poetic development to them and to Dewayne Rail at City College.

CB: Who were some of the Fresno poets you met in workshop and in the community at large? Did you find support for poetry/your poetry among the other poets you came to know?
DS: There was Jean Janzen, Robert Vasquez, Kathy Fagan, in classes at Fresno State. But I also got to know many other Fresno poets, such as Roberta Speer, Omar Salinas, Chuck Moulton, Jon Veinberg, Ernesto Trejo and others, all supportive of each other and all so in love with poetry and under the spell of Phil Levine, that there was never any

competitive rivalry, at least I don't remember any. Jean and Roberta, Sandra Hoben and I met for awhile and shared our poems and gave each other feedback.

CB: There were many readings on campus and in the community those days by Fresno poets and others who came to visit campus; it seems those were still high-energy days. Are there any you specifically recall; did you find inspiration in those times?

DS: Yes, the poetry scene was very vibrant and alive with both local and visiting poets reading. Richard Hugo gave probably the most dynamic and memorable reading I ever experienced. The room was packed and he was funny and brilliant and lively. I remember everyone rolling in the aisles with laughter and not wanting it to end. Robert Bly came in an ethnic shirt and beads, with his drums and he read every poem twice. After he'd read it once, he'd say, "Did you like that? I'll read it again in case you didn't get it." And one semester, Mark Strand was the visiting poet for Phil Levine's class. He was not a good fit for Fresno at that time. He was perceived as snobbish and arrogant by the students, and he didn't work very hard to correct that notion. But I still got a lot from his class. He commuted from New York for the class, which was part of the problem.

CB: You attended Columbia for your MFA. How did the experience there compare to your experiences in Fresno? When did you first start to publish in poetry journals?

DS: I had classes from Harold Brodsky, Richard Howard, Dan Hapern, Sharon Olds, and many others. I was exposed to the widest range of poetry available at that time, and that alone was invaluable, but I realized that I had already had the best teachers I could have had at Fresno State. I had been publishing in a few journals already, but MFA programs were not a ticket to publication in poetry, unlike fiction. The fiction students were often courted by agents before they even graduated. I was also hired by Herb Leibowitz as an associate editor for *Parnassus: Poetry in Review* and that was another invaluable experience.

CB: Your first poetry publication was *HOTEL FRESNO*, 1988. How did that come about?

DS: *Hotel Fresno* was a small potatoes type chapbook, published by Blue Moon Press, a very small local operation. They contacted me, and I was thrilled of course at the time to get a book of any sort. I had published in some rather decent journals but was hungry for a book of my own. I remember it cost $4.00 and I am still happy with most of those poems. Most of them went into my thesis that I had to complete for my MFA in poetry at Columbia.

I returned to Fresno in1986 and I couldn't find a job to save my life for quite awhile. I remember almost begging people I knew for jobs. I was overqualified and underemployed. Surprise—an MFA degree in Creative Writing even from Columbia University is not a ticket to prosperity or even entry level employment it seemed. I took a variety of part time jobs teaching art at Juvenile Hall, parenting at the County Jail, writing and art in the prisons as an outside contractor, and even a courtroom artist until a fluke job came along and I got to work as an art therapist in a mental hospital for several years.

CB: You published a novel *LIMBO*, in 1995. How much of the novel drew on your own experience in moving to Fresno, or was it simply imagination and character driven? Have you written other novels?

DS: The novel flashed back and forth in time and place from Fresno to Illinois, and Los Angeles, all places I have lived. The three main characters were three generations of women and by flashing back and forth in time, I was trying to juxtapose events in their lives to show the parallels. So the places were from my experience, but the characters were imagined. I also published a young adult fantasy novel, *CARMEN AND CHIA MIX MAGIC*, the story of a Hmong and Mexican girl who put the magic from their separate cultures together to get Carmen's brother back who has been kidnapped by the ICE who are deporting him, trying to steal the family's property. They travel to and have adventures on Otro Mundo.

CB: When did you start teaching at Fresno State, and were you ever given poetry workshops to teach?
DS: I started teaching there about 1992 and I was given poetry workshops to teach at first, but things changed . . . no need to go into that . . . and I ended up teaching mostly composition and literature classes. I wish I had gotten the opportunity to teach more poetry classes, which I enjoyed.

CB: You were married to Jon Veinberg for many years. How did your writing lives mesh—did you help each other with poems and re writes, share interests in poets, in books, or just give each other space to do your work?
DS: Jon and I had known each other as part of the poetry community for many years, but it wasn't until about 1995 when I was home for the summer between semesters at Columbia University that we began to date. Our artistic sensibilities were amazingly alike, one of many mutual attractions. We didn't share much though in the way of editing, re-writing, that sort of thing. But we shared books and writers and artists and movies and all things creative. I trusted his poetic and aesthetic view implicitly. We were always on the same page, so to speak. I would occasionally show him a poem and he would do the same, but these were not everyday occurrences. We honored each other's need for space and autonomy.

CB: Your next book, *Reincarnation of the Commonplace*, won Salmon Run Press's national book contest and was published in 1999. Roberta Spear commented, "The crass, the bizarre, and the commonplace all receive their blessing from the extraordinarily rich imagination that governs these poems." I have always admired your image-making—a natural talent it seems—but combined with that the grit and realism you find in your subjects. The star poem in this book for me is "For a Blow Up Doll Found in a Canal." How did you choose this subject? And doesn't this subject work toward/resolve into a larger and almost feminist theme?
DS: I was jogging by a canal and saw legs sticking up from the water. I was big into found objects then (and still am) so when I realized what it was, my mind went immediately to thoughts of how this could be used artistically. I did a number of photographs and then the poem came. I think the poignancy of this symbol of perverted love being thrown away spoke to me metaphorically. I had been using dolls in both visual art pieces and writing, and this was another kind of doll, but from the adult world that carried huge symbolic significance. I carried it in the trunk of my car for a while, until one day my ten-year-old daughter saw it there and I found myself struggling for explanations.

CB: *Blood Mysteries* was published by the Univ. of Arizona Press in 2003 and the brilliance of your imagination is evident from the opening. The book starts off with subjects largely drawn from every day life in Fresno, "Nowhere Girl" and poems about a character Angel on Brown Street where you lived; but you soon move to poems of a more speculative and imagistic nature such as "Valley of Shadows," "Why I'm not Someone Else," and "Meteor Showers, Yosemite." Do you find it difficult to move from a more narrative voice to a poem that relies more on imagery?

DS: It just depends on where my head has been at the time, who and what I've been reading, and what type of tone or mood I'm wanting to evoke in the poem. I think the poem itself often dictates this.

CB: The last sections of *Blood Mysteries* contains many elegies; elegies for Fresno poets who died far too early such as Ernesto Trejo and Chuck Moulton. Can you talk these poets/about writing those poems?

DS: An elegy is one of the most difficult poems to write, for me, anyway. You want to do justice to the person who has died, to honor them and still create a poem that is made of truth and based on reality. And love comes into this equation also. The elegy becomes a way to express your feelings for this person but demands avoiding sentimentality and over-idealization. I loved and admired both Ernesto and Chuck and hope that my poems did justice to their memory in some way.

CB: Also in those last sections there are several elegies or poems of witness for the women incarcerated at Central California Women's Facility at Chowchilla where you worked teaching writing. Can you talk a bit about that work and its influence on your own poetry?

DS: I have many wonderful memories of working with the women in the prison. I learned a lot from them about humility and perseverance in the face of adversity. Their honesty was almost raw and if they trusted you, they would pour out their hearts. They were so grateful for anything you brought to them from the outside world of the arts, and they were like children at times in how they responded with such excitement to the new ideas and books and writers you brought in. Once when I had done a lesson on negative space, the next week when I came to class, a women who rarely talked and kept to herself mostly, came to me and said, "I see everything differently now." She was an amazing artist who did very complicated pastel pencil drawings on cardboard where she scratched deeply into the surface over and over in layers. I tried to buy one of her art pieces, but prison red tape made it too difficult and one day she was gone from my class before I could make it happen.

CB: This might be a good point to ask about the cross-influences of your painting and your poetry. *Blood Mysteries, Flamenco Hips and Red Mud Feet, Altar for Escaped Voices* and *Voice of the Wind* all have covers from your own art work (as did your novel *LIMBO*). How does this work for you—does one ever suggest the other?

DS: The editors are usually quite happy to use one of my art works for the cover, since that relieves them of finding something to everyone's liking and sometimes they even have to pay for the images. Usually, I don't get paid. I find there is a lot of crossover between the visual work and the imagery in my poetry, not surprising to me; after all, they all come from my over active imagination. I have gradually become aware of the duality of the different mediums, although it has had to be pointed out to me in the past. When you are working with ideas and problems to be explored, it only seems natural to me that the results could take many forms. I just happen to have these tools in my toolbox to use.

CB: *Flamenco Hips and Red Mud Feet*, 2010 Univ. of AZ Press, has poems largely centered on family members/ancestors that contribute to an examination of your dual cultural heritage. Was this a project you set out to investigate, or did the subjects just present themselves to you? There is also a lovely elegy for Luis Omar Salinas, "Yard Sale in the Fog."

DS: Thank you for the comment on Omar's poem. I had a great fondness for Omar and he was such an unusual character. I tried to capture the mystery of his illness and the intersection of that with his amazing poetry.

Identity was always an issue for me. Yes, I was trying to delve into the topic of my dual heritage. Coming from two such disparate cultures, it was hard for me to know who I was. My father's changing our name and all the moving didn't help with this. I still grapple with this issue to some degree, although not as much.

CB: *Altar for Escaped Voices* was published in the Fresno Poets Ash Tree Poetry Series in 2013. Series editor, David St. John, said, "These poems celebrate the ghosts of our pasts, the struggles of our present, and the uncertain hopes we recklessly claim for our future." I recall that there was an exhibit—was it at Artes Americas?—with many artists building altars to other artists and poets, and I guess just altars in general; I think you contributed to that? How much of this book then was a response to actual altars/art works and how much was more a conceptual, emotional, or spiritually imagined altar as the opening poems in the book demonstrate? Can you talk about your process here and the combination in poems of both kinds of responses?

DS: I was very taken with the idea of altars and found a book titled: *BEAUTIFUL NECESSITY: The art and meaning of women's altars*, by Kay Turner. I found myself underlining half the book because it spoke so directly to me. "The age old task of religious art has been to bridge the division between the sacred and mundane, the spiritual and the material, the Self and the Other." This line opens the book and exemplifies much of what I am most interested in exploring in my own writing and visual work. I think my book responds to altars as both actual/art works and also in emotional/spiritual ways. I did also create an actual altar for Ernesto Trejo at Artes Americas.

CB: You have always been active in the Fresno community, working in the prisons nearby, working for the homeless in Fresno. You had a photographic exhibit of a homeless encampment in Fresno and served on the board of the Eco Village project and the Dakota Eco Garden. You were for many years an organizer of Fresno Filmworks. Talk a bit about these community projects and you commitment to social justice in the community.

DS: I have always been involved in local activism because I hate to see injustice and working with the disenfranchised gives me a sense of purpose that is for me very meaningful. I had been attending meeting after meeting for years with endless discussions re the homeless situation, which has now reached crisis proportions in Fresno as well as all of California, and I was discouraged to see so little accomplished. When a friend bought a house and opened a homeless transitional living center, I jumped on board right away. It was a chance to be involved in something hands on that could make a tangible difference in people's lives and it's proven to do just that. We have no state or federal funding and are supported by local donors, operate on a shoestring, depending on volunteers. It's very rewarding to see people get off the street and turn their life around. The poems and artwork that resulted from this work were a bonus. We have a website for the Dakota Eco Garden which you can access under The Eco Village Project online.

CB: Your most recent book of poetry is *Voice of the Wind*, Brandenburg Press 2018. You were married to poet Jon Veinberg, who died suddenly in early 2017. He was not only one of the great poetic talents in the Fresno group, he was a generous and glorious soul, friend to all. This was/still is a crushing loss. The poems in this book are all poems to Jon. They are very personal, experiential, and still have your original imagistic and narrative qualities. I remember that you said something about the poems just "coming" to you. Can you talk a bit about that process, the vision or spiritual vision, how your received these poems and wrote the book? I believe you had not been writing poems for a good while?
DS: Yes, I had had a long dry spell poetry writing-wise. I wrote one poem for the memorial service and after that, surprising to me, more poems came. I think it was a huge outpouring from the emotional place I was in at the time, a purging of sorrow and grief and way of paying homage to Jon and maybe even posthumously thanking him for all he had given me. I have always used art as an escape so it was a natural therapeutic tool for me to use to try and deal with all the strong emotions that flooded me day and night.

CB: Finally a question about what you are working on now . . . *SALT* features two new poems by you; are you working on another book of poetry, a novel, just more paintings for a show?
DS: I have a full-length poetry collection that I am sending around titled *CROSSHAIRS OF THE ORDINARY WORLD* and I just put up a one-person show at The Fig Tree Gallery in Fresno of about twenty painted collages. One large triptych involves a collaboration with Roger Perry a local quite talented guitar player and Jeff Hallock, who plays incredible harmonica and helped with QR codes to place beside the three pieces in the show that have compositions, inspired by the art. I also have a long-term project: creating a video documentary to recognize and document the Fresno blues scene from the 1960s to the 1970's. I am a huge blues fan and know most of the blues musicians in this area, and I want to preserve this bit of Fresno musical history.

M.L. Williams

M L Williams, a Fresno native, is the author of *Other Medicines* and coeditor of *How Much Earth: The Fresno Poets*. His poetry and prose has appeared in many journals and anthologies, including *Miramar*, *Western Humanities Review*, *The Journal of Florida Studies*, *The Cortland Review*, and *Stone, River, Sky*. He has taught at the University of Utah, where he was editor of *Quarterly West*, as well as the University of California, Santa Barbara. He co-emcees the Poetry Corner for the *Los Angeles Times* Festival of Books and currently teaches creative writing and contemporary literature at Valdosta State University in Georgia. *GAMES* is forthcoming from What Books Press in L.A. in fall 2021.

"Patchwork Elegy," 2020—M.L. Williams
(Parts of this essay appeared previously in *Geography of Home*, *How Much Earth*, *Bear Flag Republic*, *First Light*, *New Virginia Review*, and *Mead*.)

Hardpan on the edge of a small city. Tule fog erasing chain link and every headlight and breath dissolving into the missing sky. Thompson seedless and fig orchards. Not a sea. Train tracks. Ice house. Dust. Hoboes. Dark pulsing canals and Lanfranco's farm fed by ditches, filled with frogs and tadpoles and tiny carp and glass shards—first biology class, first conscious crime. Dirt clod fights and hide and seek. Vandenberg's twisted cold war rainbows across a child's night sky. Dead air-raid sirens. Bees and flies and Dad's pushbutton Dodge Dart at the curb, trickle of dirty water in the gutter. Summer lightning. Bees on clover flower. Mom worrying. Mountains, white teeth in the distance every spring. My sharecropper grandmother rolling out biscuits. Skins and shirts at Quigley Park, March wind, family dominoes, all the chatter and movement. Rhythms sifting the white noise of machinery, the haze of dust, July heat baking shade at 110 degrees while hot engines tick over oil and asphalt and white lines that can't keep anything straight. Everything falls apart openly: old harvesters rust into primordial lace; beams twist over the settling ground, exposing all the failing infrastructures of pig iron and fir stud. Easton Market sags visibly over aisles of shiny cans and bags and the squeaky wheels of grocery carts and no, a mother says, not today, it's too much.

This was the Fresno I grew up in in the early 1960s, the Fresno after streetcars vanished and opulent hotels for rich travelers closed, Fresno before sprawl and mall swallowed it and spread itself over the farmland like mayonnaise on Rainbow bread. This is not nostalgia. It's just the Okie Fresno I was raised in, and it's good that some of it has gone by the wayside, become more diverse. But I can't not carry it around. I can't not see that sprinkler I wanted to run through or a long piece of grass I wanted to pull out and suck the nectar out of while I leaned back and watched the sky frail blue into a white haze. I just can't be from anywhere else. Wilson, Cooper Jr. High, Fresno High, Cal, back to Fresno to teach high school and finally get an education from Phil, Pete, Chuck, and Connie, then off to Utah to study with Larry, to Santa Barbara to raise my two kids and teach and write and work on *How Much Earth* with Chris Buckley and David Oliveira, and finally teaching poetry here at Valdosta State University in a small flat hot city surrounded by farmland on a freeway between two big cities, a lot like Fresno then except for all the trees.

Though we never spoke, William Saroyan with his magnificent moustache waved as we crossed paths on bicycles when I was a teen. We both frequented the Gillis Branch of the library; he'd sit and read or chat with librarians or friends, and I would scan the shelves on the other side of the library for new science fiction titles to keep me occupied summers between classes at Fresno High. I grew up a couple of blocks from his two houses on Griffith Ave, just down from Cooper Junior High, and I suppose he recognized me as a fellow reader and bicycle rider, that neighbor kid on his Free Spirit with a book in hand. I knew he was famous, but as a shy high school kid, I lacked the courage to approach him in the library. But that smile and wave remains my earliest connection to Fresno's living literature.

In a workshop at Berkeley during my junior year, Thom Gunn pulled out a gem of a Peter Everwine poem, "Desire," as an example of outstanding poetry, which meant to find Fresno poetry I'd had to leave. In 1983 or '84, when I was taking classes toward a teaching credential and helping edit *Common Wages*, I mustered the courage to show Peter a poem I'd written, the first since Berkeley. He encouraged me to get into the M.A. program. I still hear his low, instructive chuckle. I'd read his first two books, *Collecting the Animals* and *Keeping the Night*, and loved his work. I told him so and asked when his next book would come out. He said he it wouldn't, that he wasn't writing. He kind of shrugged, "I don't want to kill all those trees."

I would continue to pester Peter about his writing over the next few years. After I formally enrolled in the program in 1988 after taking a couple of graduate classes, I asked Phil once why Peter didn't write. He concentrated and said very deliberately, "I can't say. He's a terrific poet." Then Phil half-whispered solemnly, "I think he's more talented than I am."

Before I left for Utah in 1991, I stopped by Peter's house to bug him again. He asked me to wait a minute, stepped into another room, and the keys of a manual typewriter clacketed for a couple of minutes. He handed me a green piece of paper with a remarkable new poem: "Speaking of Accidents." He said, "I don't know. I think it's kind of talky." I told him I didn't think so, that the poem was wonderful, but since he was asking for comments, I told him I wasn't sure about the rhyme at the end. He thanked me for my praise and my comment. The following year it came out in the *New Yorker* exactly as he had typed it out for me.

Years later, after *From the Meadow* came out, I took a bottle of good California zin to his house as I often did and we talked poetry and sipped wine in his living room. I had taught the book that year and I brought the poem up again and confessed that I had been absolutely wrong about that rhyme. He just smiled and laughed, "I know."

While I was in the MA program, I'd drop by Phil's office impromptu now and then to talk about a poem from workshop or thesis forms or a good wine buy in town. But March 2, 1989 was different. I couldn't stop looking out the window. Sleet covered the ground, turning the dead lawn ice blue and the sidewalks glittery white. A grey-green funnel cloud tickled the beautiful imploded sky suddenly gone Oklahoma and I gawked. One actually touched ground and destroyed a shed—a tornado in Fresno! Phil looked, too, but he just smiled at this junior varsity version of what would have been common in his Midwest. For once, I suspect, Fresno looked a little more like home to him.

I'm feeling good about my poem. We walk in, talk fast, excited. Same time, same place, but this isn't the usual workshop. Phil arrives with important young poets we've all been reading and admiring, Dorianne Laux up from Mills College with her guest, Ron Silliman, Li-Young Lee, and our own Ernesto Trejo. Fluorescent lights buzz and chairs scrape the scuffed linoleum tiles and we make an awkward circle in the classroom.

Poems circulate, they're read. Students receive comments and advice from our guests, from other students, tougher words from Phil. He has a reputation. But the atmosphere is good-natured. Phil smiles too between serious points he makes about poetry. He's funny.

I'm feeling good about my poem. Pass it out. Read it out loud. Silence.

I remember Phil in the gym before I started taking his classes. He's in good shape, wiry and confident and quick, still that boxer's body, compact, no-nonsense, knows precisely how far his reach is, the right point of impact. You can tell.

I'm feeling good about my poem, but the silence is long. Finally the first comments, halting, uncomfortable—Loren says to cut the first part, to start on the bus, maybe. Li-Young Lee suggests taking a couple lines, using them to make a radical revision, tossing the rest. Silence. Adam points out a phrase he thinks is ok in the first part, but agrees with Loren. Silence. Dorianne looks down, wants a smoke maybe, or just out. Another student starts to go on about what's wrong with the opening.

Phil interrupts.

"Hold it," he commands. Everyone looks at Phil, whose open palm hovers over the piece of paper he holds at arm's length in his other hand. "Hold it right there. We're not going to spend another minute on this. This, this is a fucking disaster," he says. "This is just a fucking disaster. It's not worth another minute of our time."

Shock blossoms on the faces in our awkward circle. Phil has a reputation. He pulls no punches. Everybody knows it. I know it.

"Phil, Phil," I say. "Please don't hold back just because we have guests."

Everyone laughs and Phil laughs and we move on to real poems. One punch. Knockdown.

"Can we talk about that poem?" I ask Phil later that week, in his office.

"Sure," he says. He has a reputation. He smiles, listens patiently.

"It's exactly the way it happened," I explain, recounting a narrative that was only remarkable for a single banal coincidence. "It's in the poem just the way it happened. Where did the poem go so wrong?"

Phil says genially, "That's the problem. You only wrote what happened. You're not a reporter." I nod. "To be a poet, you have to be true to the poem, not to the facts. If you're just being true to the facts, you're not writing poetry. A poem makes its own truth."

Right on the point of the chin—knockout—the kind every novice poet needs.

I tell this story to my own students, pass along Phil's passion, his hopes for poetry, every workshop I teach.

I taught high school for a number of years, one of those years at De Wolfe Continuation High School in Fresno, California, the '85/'86 school year, in fact. Even though the continuation high school is where they send all the serial truants and rule offenders, the students on probation, those whose graffiti graced alley fences all over town and secret corners of my classroom, those who smoked weed and got caught by cops who kept it, the sweet girl there for poking another girl's eye out in a fight over a boy, glue sniffers and PCP paranoids, one future mass murderer, and many of Fresno Unified's pregnant girls, we huddled together around TVs on a weirdly warm January 28th and watched the Challenger explode together. It hit us teachers, and it even hit most of the students indulging our desire to watch a teacher fly, but when the flight blew up, it stopped being just a break from math and reading. Even tough kids want to believe someone can triumph, even if some had already given up on themselves, and most knew we hadn't given up on them, and that, we hoped, meant something.

One of my students that year, a young pregnant girl, never said anything. If pressed, I could get a one-word answer from her. I was a young father, and hoped to make some sort of connection. But I didn't push it. She worked a little, kept mostly to herself. I remember being delighted to have said some stupid enough thing to make her laugh out loud once. Later that year, summer vacation, I learned from a small article in the *Fresno Bee* that she had been murdered, her body thrown in Avocado Lake, no suspects. I would find out later from one of her friends that she was a victim of some kind of gang retaliation that had to do with her brother. I remembered her laugh, that she had a baby.

A couple of years later, I started graduate studies at night, and issues of cultural authenticity were prominent in academic discourse, especially after Danny "Santiago's" *Famous All Over Town* was published in 1983 to great acclaim, won some prizes and was nominated for a Pulitzer the next year. Many critics lauded the book for its authenticity, so when it was discovered that Santiago's real last name was James, that he was white and privileged, that he had fabricated his name to help sell the story, there was understandable outrage. A few Latino critics defended the novel on its merits, but most critics focused on the lie of using an ethnic pseudonym to cash in.

That was in the air when I set out to write a poem from the point of view of Lydia, my young student, the quiet, laughing mother. I showed my draft to Phil, worried to even workshop it given all the talk about cultural appropriation. He read it, demurred. "It's not hopeless," he said. The draft had two voices in it, Lydia's and a cypher for me, a teacher figure. I wanted it to be right, to honor Lydia. The teacher figure, I felt, insulated me from possible accusations that I had appropriated her voice, and I thought making it a dialog was a clever solution. Phil looked at me and said, "If you're serious, you have to get rid of that guy. He's in the way. He's not doing anything but satisfying your ego."

I was surprised. Ego was the last thing on my mind. I explained my reasoning. He got it, smiled, and told me not to worry about all that stuff. "Look, she has to speak for herself," he said, "And your job as a poet is to let her. You can't be afraid to let her have her say because you're worried about what some dipshit critic might think of you."

He pointed out that if I didn't write the poem, no one else would speak for her, and that the teacher was in the way of what she had to say, and writing in response to critics could only lead to a lack of authenticity, a lack of the kind of honesty that makes poetry meaningful as an act of witnessing. I rewrote the poem without me in it. It's not perfect, but he was right. And if Lydia speaks at all in the poem, it's because Phil convinced me to kill the ghost of the living author to let Lydia have her final say.

In Phil and Jose Elgorriaga's translation class during my last semester at Fresno State, Ernesto Trejo worked to get his Jaime Sabines translations perfect, spirit and generosity brightening his eyes even as his body betrayed him. Everyone knew his prognosis, but it didn't faze him. He smiled frequently, offered astute comments on all our translations, truly a third teacher, young, so full of life in that room of aspiring writers from both English and Chicano Studies programs.

The following year in Salt Lake, Larry Levis gave a reading from *Black Freckles* and read Ernesto's name into his story. The surprise of his name shattered me. Instead of asking Larry to sign the title page, I asked him to correct my copy so that it read exactly as he had read it that day.

Larry remarked on a poem I submitted to his last workshop in Utah, spilling out one of Frank Bidart's at length from memory. Larry scared us because we could hear him feel the poetry, while we still hadn't figured out how to touch or trust our own.

He had taped this note—*We're sorry, but Larry's not in at the moment. Thank you for your patience. —His Imagination*—scrawled across an old torn photo of the Faces looking glamorously dissipated, to his office door when he was away, but it served as no epitaph. He wrote elegies and elegies are about living, about what we lose. Only elegies for Larry, given he'd lost, all he'd lived.

While he was packing to move to Virginia, his face hovered above everything: the boxes filled with what he'd take, what he'd leave behind, books mostly either way. Signed books, unsigned books. One had the word *Notice* in the title. When I picked it out of the pile, he laughed, "Guess I didn't," with the kind of casualness that comes from too often culling anything from a life, leaving so much behind.

He was referring to the finitude of cars, how far they go, how fast, how much each car bears. Like life and words and the horrible evidence history builds against each one. Like turning the tape over to hear Ian Curtis sing "Love will tear us apart," even beyond his own death, over and over, and I still see Larry's face hovering over the plastic glint of that Joy Division cassette box, its anomalous messages.

The light in his emptying space revealed his culminating absence the way flame bears away anything. There's a light on the secretary desk he gave my daughter because it wouldn't fit in his car. I turn it on and the old grain shines, and the brass. I can only listen now to the creak of wood, to the small song of a hinge closing.

He had delivered the desk in my absence. I didn't believe he'd have time to deliver it to my house, to look for my house among all the other brick houses built to lodge the onslaught of soldiers coming home from World War II. When they built it, he was just a kid discovering the pleasure of dirt clods exploding on brick or the ringing corrugations of a shed in the heat in the San Joaquin Valley. His father owned a farm there where he learned how to work, learned to respect those who owned far less.

He wrote on a poem that I'd submitted to class, "Follow this guy without an arm. That's fascinating." In class he divided fancy from imagination, pared away outlandish ways to dress up simple thoughts or tired conceits. And he was so at ease in this, mild, as though the self-evidence of what he said was apparent, important. And he raised his voice only when he quoted poems, spoke them from memory and at great length, and they lived in his saying them aloud—Bidart, St. John, Levine, or Baudelaire—speaking them so we would have to try to be that good, that honest.

When he left, I gave him a good bottle of 12-year-old brandy for the trip or for his arrival in Virginia. I could see him already, red tail lights fading east into the flat distance past Laramie, carrying a history of truck stops, raisins, tule fog, a few loose tapes on his seat, this summer night with a window rolled down to hear the whisper of his arm in the wind.

His house was already empty. He pulled a bottle of half-full gin and told me to take it. "In Utah, you can't carry anything open in your car," you explained. "I won't take this anyway." So I took it. "When you get to the border, the Wyoming border, you can drive with it open forever, 90 miles an hour and nobody will do anything. Nothing. When you get to the border, anything goes."

After Larry died at 49 in 1996, rumors swirled about causes. Salt Lake friends had partied with him and I was hearing about some of it. People were making assumptions, speculating, talking. I called Phil to offer condolences and to find out what he knew. He was vehement in his anger at the very question of death by overdose, the only time I had ever experienced his rage. He told me to stop spreading salacious rumors. When I assured him that I wasn't, that I called him because I was hearing those rumors, and that I called in part to find out what I should say when people brought it up, he calmed down, understanding that, as *Quarterly West*'s editor, I might be contacted for comment. He said, "Say he had a heart attack. That's what happened." We talked for some time after about this huge loss both for poetry and for him and Franny personally. He was bereft.

We now know, of course, how the tox screen turned out, but Phil was right to be protective of Larry's legacy, to allow his poems to be what they were undiminished by unsavory gossip. The author was dead, but his astonishing poems remained, and that's all that mattered. Phil rightfully wanted them to bear witness, to have their own life, and they have in Larry's two astonishing posthumous collections, *Elegy*, edited by Phil and David St. John, and *The Darkening Trapeze*, edited by David.

I took a wonderful literature class from Charles Hanzlicek, who read poems from John Berryman's *Dream Songs* out deeply so we could feel the music; now I can't read Berryman without hearing his ponderous basso, and after hearing Berryman's recorded nasally fake British accent, that's been a blessing. When he came to South Georgia, we smoked cigars in my back yard. He enjoyed his; I mangled mine. After his reading here, students gushed over the complexity he achieved with such simple, beautiful language.

When I was in the program, I'd drop by Connie and John Hales' house to hang out occasionally, have a beer, complain about politics, relax, talk poetry, Utah, Everett Ruess, our kids. She and John were neighbors and her brilliant son, Jason, attended Fresno High when I taught there. She taught a laid-back workshop, nurturing but serious, and she became a model for my own workshops. Her poems are fierce and unflinchingly honest, and when she came to South Georgia, she connected. Many of my students in South Georgia grew up in poverty and found in her work stories they could identify with and hope in the humanizing voice of her language. She encouraged me to be more daring in my own work, to try things outside of my comfort zone.

Jon Veinberg and Dixie Salazar were neighbors, too, and I'd often run into Jon when I went for a walk. We touched base on poetry events, but also on students that we both worked with, and we worried together about Jeremy ("He's a brilliant kid") and Sunshine and other struggling teens. He counseled youth for many years, and he sincerely cared about the young people he worked with, sometimes too much, because he suffered when he couldn't help a kid, and he couldn't say much as he perhaps needed to, because of his profession. When I asked about Sunshine, a tall, striking young woman with a smile that gave her her nickname who had suddenly vanished from my class, all he could do was shake his head and say, "I haven't heard from her. All I can say is that she was in a really tough situation. I hope she's alright." His deeply humane insights about people show up in his fine poems, and so does his extraordinary sense of humor. I remember with great fondness the day maybe fifteen years later when David Oliveira and I showed up unannounced at their doorstep and Jon welcomed us with his inimitable smile and an offer of wine, then Dixie came home and joined us and I was home again.

Called Chuck Moulton from Salt Lake in 1995 after he had fallen off a ladder helping his friend, Jacqueline Pilar; I had to talk to a nurse, who then put the phone to his ear. I said what I could to cheer him, urge him out of a deep coma with talk of future get-togethers at the Olive-Tower Café, where he read my stars once, insulting me, I thought, by saying I would be great in politics. I smiled, but protested. "No," he said. "You'd rally the masses. You'd be an honest leader. Not a politician. You've got charisma!" his voice so full of gravel and enthusiasm I almost had to consider his outlandish proposition for one long second, his gapped smile fractured and beaming, his hands on a page marked with stars and lines I couldn't fathom. He was beloved because he was kind to friend or stranger, to the poor kids he helped as a teacher's aide, or to anyone with love for the living words that he promoted in his Fresno Poets Association reading series and on public radio. His passion frayed into sweet anarchies, and he bore himself like some poetry pirate, hair sprouting whichaway as he navigated Fresno on a 100 cc bike he refused to register, crate full of books and rubber-band bound papers bungied to the rack. The nurse thanked me for calling, said it mattered. It did to me. He never woke up.

Coffee with Stephen Jamison and his Big Sur or Marty Paul at the Crow after teaching terrific kids like Morgan and Angelle and Mark at Fresno High. The student parking lot after night workshops with Loren Palsgaard and Andy Miller and Adam Hill, talking about poetry or life or memory or the weather, never trivial in Fresno. At the Wild Blue Yonder nightclub for Fresno Poets Association readings, Loretta Collins Klobah, now in Puerto Rico, reading her terrific poems and blowing a little sax for fun, where I first saw Phil read, and later Chris Buckley and his poems combining science and philosophy in gorgeous alchemy, and even dancing there a little after a Peter Everwine reading. David St. John at Fresno City College, and Larry and Gerald Stern and Sherley Anne Williams and Donald Justice and Gwendolyn Brooks and Gary Soto and Maxine Hong Kingston and C.K. Williams at Fresno State, all passing through or coming home—a poetry epicenter.

I come from a family of Paso Robles farmers and zinfandel pioneers, so wine was part of my life and also how I connected with many poets, especially Phil and Pete Everwine in Fresno, and later, Kurt Brown and Laure-Anne Bosselaar in Boston, Mark Strand in Utah and Wyn Cooper in Vermont. Phil and I would trade information on great wine buys around town frequently, so when he came to Valdosta in 2013, Alice and I opened the last bottle I'd carted cross country in my beater Plymouth Acclaim from a stash I'd stored for years in the crawl space under my parents' ranch style house in Fresno—a bottle of 1983 Chateau Margaux. Unlike the gumbo with slightly burnt roux that I prepared for the post-reading gathering, the wine was in perfect condition. "This is magnificent," Phil said, and so was the evening. When the Margaux was gone, I pulled out an expensive Santa Barbara pinot, and I asked what he thought. "That cheap pinot we had at lunch was better," he frowned. I swirled it in my glass and reluctantly had to agree, despite the wound to my wallet and pride, but it was a pleasure to be in the presence of Phil's wonderful candor once again.

Kurt Brown once asked me if I had any wine stories for an interview for his online *Mead* magazine. I answered that wine stories aren't nearly as interesting as the stories we tell while we share wine. I remember with so much fondness wine tastings and meals over the years with friends like Kurt and Wyn Cooper and Scott Cairns and Kate Coles at AWP meetings around the country, George Yatchisin, David Oliveira, Chryss Yost, Barry Spacks, and Chris Buckley from my years in Santa Barbara, Phil and Pete in Fresno, wine with poets visiting us now in South Georgia, Terry Hummer or Elena Byrne or Bob Wrigley or Barbara Hamby or Dorianne Laux and Rick Campbell, wine accompanying a quiet meal with a lover at home or in an exotic country. Wine goes perfectly with poetry. Both are ancient, and, because of their longevity, the linguistic and ritualistic crust of culture has naturally accreted and hardened around them, and I think some are more interested in the accumulated crust on the vessel than the living wine or the living lines inside. The crusty stuff matters, but certainly not more than direct experience.

But most wine and poetry nights are more about poetry than wine. Working on *How Much Earth* with Chris Buckley and David Oliveira in Santa Barbara, we chose wines that would go with Me n' Ed's pizza, our working meal and a rare connection to Fresno cuisine in Santa Barbara's increasingly rarefied food scene. We complemented David's favorite everything pizza with good but cheap Spanish Vega Sindoa or a nice cab that Chris found on close-out special someplace in Lompoc and we worked through poems, permissions, and all the complicated logistics of anthologies, pausing from time to time to read the poems to each other, to hear them again.

We refuse to lose anything, the names of those present, the names of those lost, those who remain among us in words and in all these moments woven together because of or in spite of geography and time. Poetry comes from silence, by the way it gives up to speech and the music always behind it—traffic and power mower, strident crickets, screen-door hinge and slam—silence and the road out to anywhere, sigh of tires, whistle of wind through a window wing. Every trip is long, bothered by signs opposite the oleander, train tracks and cotton greening the distance. The stone-blue August sky gives up to cumulous erupting its blood of light over all of this. Rows of vines still make a visual iambic I can't stop watching through the backseat window of an old Dodge Dart, my breath timing the light against the chugging warp of a low tire trying to keep up. Poetry's gift is its ambitious failure, its giving in to so many voices against the quietude it wants to explain. This is what growing up in Fresno taught me.

Juan Felipe Herrera

Juan Felipe Herrera was born in Fowler, California in 1948. The son of migrant farmers, Herrera moved often, living in trailers or tents along the roads of the San Joaquin Valley and in Southern California. Herrera received a BA in Social Anthropology from UCLA, a masters in Social Anthropology from Stanford in 1980, and earned an MFA from the University of Iowa Writers' Workshop in 1990.

Herrera is the author of many collections of poetry, including *Notes on the Assemblage* (City Lights, 2015); *Senegal Taxi* (University of Arizona Press, 2013); *Half of the World in Light: New and Selected Poems* (University of Arizona Press, 2008), a recipient of the PEN/Beyond Margins Award and a National Book Critics Circle Award; and *187 Reasons Mexicanos Can't Cross The Border: Undocuments 1971–2007* (City Lights, 2007). He has received fellowships and grants from the Breadloaf Writers' Conference, the California Arts Council, the National Endowment for the Arts, the Stanford Chicano Fellows Program, and the University of California at Berkeley. In 2015, he received the L.A. Times Book Prize's Robert Kirsch Award for lifetime achievement. In 2012, he was appointed California Poet Laureate by Gov. Jerry Brown. In 2011, Herrera was elected a Chancellor of the *Academy of American Poets*. In 2015, Herrera was named Poet Laureate of the United States.

from *How Much Earth*, 2001—Juan Felipe Herrera

Fresno has always been a fulcrum for the Chicano experience during the last fifty years, the other, I would say is El Paso or maybe Matamoros, all crossing points, migration stream loci. In a way, the lands, the vines, the little establishments—even though they are washed up, boarded over and in shambles in many cases—still remember the travels, trials, and stories of the people who passed through their doors and leafy veredas: from Murrieta to Chavez, from the Tulare Indians to Dolores Huerta and Felipe Veracruz, from Jose Montoya at Fowler High, home of the Red Wildcats to Pedro Infante in the fifties stepping in Fresno's Chinatown to give a show as Ernie Palomino constructed the first Chicano installation with a car and an 8mm film to Luis Miguel Valdez in the early sixties making the first teatro Chicano. We wouldn't think this is so, at first. We'd want to say Los Angeles, San Diego, Corpus, Cameron County, Texas. Each place has its own bowl, it casuelitas where our ancestors poured frijoles, manifestoes and remembrances. Fresno is such a cuento-soul-bowl, a cultural and geo-political nexus of language, culture and self-in-transition. It is also a mirage. We think we are standing still as we peer at Yosemite range. We look South and we see haze, neon and wild lights. West drifts off through the casitas and barrios, parks and barbeques. Here, we find a center that is not there, yet it provides us with a rich position to speak, write and invent a new wind, a sigh, a saludo of *How Much Earth* exists under el cielo bravo.

from *Bear Flag Republic: Prose Poems & Poetics from California*, 2008—Juan Felipe Herrera

It provides an ideal canvas to paint, that is, to mix colors, images, designs, depths and perspective into a tremulous fragmented whole. A story can be entered with more clarity. The prose poem is the most direct guide to the stuff of the poem itself. It is a bit more rebellious, more elusive, more precise. Contradiction, synthesis and ordeal find a unique conductivity in the prosarama, that is, the expansive yet collapsible structures of the form.

from *FIRST LIGHT: A Festschrift for Philip Levine on his 85th Birthday*, 2013—Juan Felipe Herrera

In the late summer of 1990 after hauling our funky furniture from living in Iowa City to a new life in Fresno and after finding a pad for our family I finally made it to the Chicano and Latin American Studies Program office which had just hired me to teach. And guess who was standing there near the cramped copy machine, smiling, and staring at me as if we had planned it all along? Phil Levine. He was the first one to welcome me to campus, to Fresno, to the Valley—since the early fifties when on occasion my father would drive my mother and me back to the fields near Fowler where I was born. It was Phil. No one else. We really had not talked before our Chicano Studies get-together. Maybe it was Gerald Stern, my prof, who called him from the Writer's Workshop in Iowa or maybe it was just Levine being there as he always is—there. Sometimes all it takes is a solid and soulful welcome from a solid and soulful human being to make everything all right for a guy rolling into a new episode in his life.

"Interview with Juan Felipe Herrera"—Michael Torres & Christopher Buckley— from *The New School*, 2020

New School: You have spoken about growing up in the small agricultural towns of the San Joaquin Valley; I think Fowler was your hometown? Which places do you especially remember and how have they contributed to your vision and voice in poetry? How much does place figure in your work?
Juan Felipe Herrera: Yes, I have mentioned Fowler quite a bit. Part of it has to do with early days in elementary school. Students were called to mention their birth place on occasion and I knew no one (I imagined) would know about Fowler, where it was or what it was. Later, I made it a point to put it on the map, at least through my picture books. At another level, the San Joaquín Valley is a highly significant arena—its social movements, its global agricultural core, its people most of all, that is, its migrant generations and immigrants. Not to mention its writers, artists and social and educational pioneering since the 70's. It is good to acknowledge people who do not ask for applause, yet who merit our full and lasting embraces. Place is always in poetry, be it local, regional, national, global— or, as Levertov said in her essays in *Light up the Cave*, "Inscape and outscape."

NS: I think your parents were farm laborers. How much of an oral tradition did they pass on to you, stories, songs etc. as a child? Looking back, does that seem a likely background for the development of a poet? Those must have been difficult times for the family?

JFH: Yes, it is true. Even though we traveled from one day to the other or from one street to the next, rambling across the San Joaquín, Lake Walefer, Ramona, Escondido, Vista, San Diego, Milpitas and San Francisco, for starters, every day was a story-telling day. And a singing day, a poetry day, riddles and sayings and word-play, a word-ad infinitum day. I lived in a world where language turned as fast as the wheels and horizons gained momentum. Only now do I realize it. I had a Mark Twain Chicano brain early on. Homespun stories, sayings, songs and remembrances were the foundations that little by little, word by word, became my literary life.

NS: So how did you come to poetry, develop as a poet? When did you first begin writing? Who were your models, who were you first reading then? And of course, how did you end up at the Iowa Writers Workshop?
JFH: Little by little. Every impromptu story my mother performed in the tiny kitchen or "living room" was a lesson, a literary track. My migrant oral lit anthology, so to speak, was The Pancho Villa Story, The Leaving Mexico City to the USA a Few Years After the Mexican Revolution Story, the Family Women Stories (they were brutal), the Young Woman in Juarez Stories, and many more. Each of these had the passion of poetry, longing, dreams, fervent remembrance—and different ways of speaking. Of course, the poems my mother happened to learn in her few years of schooling in El Paso, Texas or when she was put in Mexico City's Venustiano Carranza Orphanage in the early 1900's (my grandmother was penniless after my grandfather suddenly died at the age of 40).

Iowa? Well, everything that happens to me is by chance. Karmic choices, causes and effects. By the mid 80's, after graduating from Stanford and working for Poets in The Schools in the Bay Area, I was invited to teach, part-time at De Anza Community College. Bang! After a year or so, George Barlow, who taught English there, said, " Hey, Juan, I am leaving to Iowa City, maybe you want to apply to the Iowa Writer's Workshop?" "What is that?" I said. You go, you write, you sit in a circle and talk about it." "I can do that!" I said. Not long after that, all of us, Margarita, my wife and kids were on Highway 80 (and my brothers-in-law, along with Barlow and his family), all the way to South Johnson Street. What a magnificent experience. It was the second half of my poetry life, in a sense—the first was one of story-telling, bilingual spoken word, Chicano Movimiento empowerment and community roots. The second word-life was made of caesura, enjambment, stanza work and power hitters like József, Gombrowicz, Richard Hugo, Wordsworth, Stieglitz, Bishop, O'Keeffe and on. My professors were magnificent—Marvin Bell, Gerald Stern and Jorie Graham (whom I had seen on the cover of the American Review). Ain't that Superb?

NS: I seem to remember a phone conversation we had a few years after you were out of Iowa, early to mid '80s . . . I was at Murray State University in Kentucky and I think you were teaching somewhere in Illinois? I think you had a creative writing position—hard to come by then as now—but you said you needed to get away from there. Was it the lack of support for creative writing in the department as often is the case, or was it generally the problem of surviving culturally in an environment not the least simpatico?
JFH: I am thankful to the good people of Southern Illinois University, the English Department, specifically. We lived next to the Shawnee Forest, open country, snow, local fish fries and neighborhood Mulligan Stew—you can't beat that, even softball games with the faculty! The students were solid, super creative and open to my West Coast

experimental dadaisms. I learned much from them and their lives in Indiana, Kentucky, Tennessee, and Illinois. The difficulty was from the extreme right wing vibes that were beginning to show up in the children's banter. This was not good for our son, Robert, who was in elementary school. This marked the end of our stay. Blessings to all.

NS: When then did you come to Fresno? You contributed a lovely tribute to *First Light,* the festschrift published for Philip Levine's 85th birthday in which you recalled your first day on campus at Fresno State and Phil being there to welcome you. Talk a bit about that.

JFH: As you know, I was born in Fowler, 10 miles south, inches from the famous I - 99. Of course, just for 29 days, as my mother would tell me. Just enough time for her to almost heal-up from the caesarian surgery and head on to the next crops to be harvested. As a child, on occasion, we would return to visit the Villescas family in Fresno. Little did I know that they were from Mesquite, New Mexico, a small town about 10 minutes south of Las Cruces. After a while, I discovered that most, if not all, first-gen Mexican families are in a state of continuous migration. In 2010, I met two of my sisters (another story to tell), one in her eighties, Sarah Chavez and one in her mid-nineties, Concha Contreras. Concha told me, as she recounted my father's story, that she had lived and worked in the fields of Fowler. I was bowled over. A bold discovery—Fowler-Fresno comprised an migrant ellipse for my family since the forties. Fresno rotated back to me in 1990, the year I received my MFA from the Iowa Writers Workshop—in the form of a letter inviting me to apply for a tenure track Assistant Prof. position in the Chicano and Latin American Studies Program. Beautiful. At the Workshop, Gerald Stern often spoke about his friendship with Phil, their jaunts in Paris and on, Gerry, at that time was so magnetic and visceral that, as Phil recounted one day, that if you stared at him, he would stare back and "peel the skin off of your face." To my surprise, the first time I checked into the Chicano Studies office, guess what? Phil was there, his casual self, to receive me. No words, to express this, why would he be there—for me? As we all know, Phil was genuine, caring, warm and also, could knock you out with the plain ol' truth, in one way or another. From that point on, I cared for him, his work and most of all, his humanity. The tiny, good-hearted readings the poetry students organized in the barrio, in Chinatown, for example, Phil would join in and blast out his solid Pulitzer prize winning poems. That was Phil. This welcoming encounter with Phil made poetry and being a poet more human for me, it was not a "job" or "career," it was not just "craft," "meaning," "voice" and all that raz-ma-taz, it was, as Buber would say, "I and thou."

NS: To what extent were Levine and Peter Everwine resources for you while you were in Fresno? Were they important to you as a poet those years?

JFH: Both were deeply significant for me. I knew we lived together, in a sense, on campus, in Fresno, next door. Believe it or not, being linked in this manner, gives you (and gave me) a foundation of and for a poet's community, small or large. We wrote, we read out loud, we peeked at each other's work. We sat in the library, we hauled books and funny fountain pens, we thought about stuff—maybe we didn't care about many other things. But we cared. We were an akimbo family.

NS: How about the other poets in Fresno during that time? Were Ernesto Trejo, Gary Soto, Jon Veinberg still in town, in the workshops? And what about Luis Omar Salinas—had you known him before you came to Fresno? Did you know

his books and which ones were the most inspiring for you? And what about the work of Roberta Spear, Greg Pape, and Larry Levis; did you know their poems. So in general how did you find the community of poets then, the support and energy and inspiration?

JFH: I know these beautiful poets, except for Pape and Levis, the way poet's know each other—on that long road of poetry. Coffee bars, readings, classrooms, state-wide poetry festivals, and on one-on-one occasions. Some I knew for quite a while, others for just a click of time, and other's in-between those crazy, social sparks.

1990, maybe 1991 or '92 I ran into Trejo at Fresno State, at a reading with Li-Young Lee, both serious readers, meticulous, humble and intense. Ernesto read his "Larynx" poem, short and lethal. Li-Young, as always, leaned into the podium and scalded the mic and our mind, with work from his *Rose,* perhaps, I don't remember. Margarita, my wife, after the reading, took time with Li-Young and I with Ernesto. We chatted about Mexico City where he lived (and where my mother was born) and produced his elegant hand-sized chapbook series. Later, I would run into him on those wide streets of the capitol and also, I would bump into Li-Young several momentous times. It hurts when you lose someone close like poets can be, years later, like Ernesto. Those two magnificent writers and thinkers will be torches lighting the way.

NS: In a 2008 interview you said some of your favorite poets were the Post War Polish poets—Szymborska, Herbert, Celan, and Radnoti. What influences, moves, approaches etc. did those poets suggest for your own work? In which of your books specifically? In other interviews you listed Ginsberg and Lorca as major influences. They seem two very different responses to experience, and two very different voices and energies when compared to the Post War Polish poets, especially Szymborska's sly use of logic and directness. How have Ginsberg and Lorca then helped you with any of your earlier work, how did they influence or guide, and in which particular poems/books?

JFH: The Post War Polish poetry world as well as Celan and Rodnoti, all these earth-shaking voices start with my dear friend, the late Victor Martinez. As you know, he was a student of Phil Levine at Fresno State and a Wallace Stegner fellow at Stanford where we began our friendship. I noticed that he was deeply immersed in global poetry, in particular poetry that was written with simplicity and a hacksaw and most of all, tangled in the cables of turmoil, resistance and revolution. This was Victor—a deep thinker, reader of literature, philosophy and the Chinese classics. We happened to live a few rooms from each other at the Bell apartments building on 24th and Capp Street in San Francisco. When I looked up the authors he mentioned, I was hit by lightning. I loved Celan's tight, short-line, abstract work, his poem "Radix" is an example. A stiletto opens your mind and you must decide whether to yank it out or caress it. I caressed it. "Resistance" Polish poet and playwright, Rozevicz, became my favorite. He was displeased with "ornamental" writing, that is, poetry that floats and dances with devices and does not arise or carry the naked suffering of the people, the Jews face to face with the holocaust, an irrefutable example. The last three lines of his poem, "The Survivor," presents his case: " at twenty-four / led to slaughter / we survived." Rodnoti suffered and died at the hands of the Nazis. Yet, his scribbled notes were buried with him survived and later found. For some reason, I was magnetized by these writers, their experience and their existential choice to write this thing called poetry. Szymborska's use of symbols without deviating from the horrors of the times attracted me. Her work was akin to my sense of how to say things. It even was surprisingly knitted to my beginnings with Lorca and Ginsberg, mostly Lorca. In the late sixties, ambling on the main line of the Mission District, I discovered the only Latinx book store available at that time, Librería National. And guess what, I stumbled into that textured burgandy leatherish cover of his Lorca's *Obras Completas*, all he had written. A few years earlier, in '66 or so, at the San Diego Public library on "E" Street, I had picked up his *Gypsy Ballads*. With Lorca, it was his "green-moon" pallet, his dream-brush, his shifting registers and feverish styles, his drawings, his varied genres, his subjects and his relationships to Dalí, Buñuel and the various artists of Spain and—his formal manner. If you lived in the Bay Area in the 60's, you would eventually read Alan Ginsberg, hear him read or feel his grooves in the voices of the new wild writers. In my case, all three possibilities were true. His daring, his dedicated freedom, his deep agonies, his intelligence, his "plain-talk" poems, Beatnik pioneering, Buddhist boldness and why not, his titles and phrasing, thick imagistic concatenations, his knowledge of Jewish history, literature and thought and notions of breath, mind and line. All this and much more took me into what poetry and poetry life can contain. Being gay without fear, being a human being without apologies, contesting tidal waves of power day in, day out—my kinda dude. In terms of my books, many of them have busted chromosomes and fragments of their minds' DNA. Ginsberg and Post War Polish Poetry strands—in particular, the Sutras, in Chile Verde Smuggler and the manifestos here and there. Simplicity and writing power are key for a poem on the verge of being read and remembered by the people. And there are new ways too. Lorca and Ginsberg seem different, yet, they are true cousins of Fury and Love.

NS: In 2015 the Univ. of Arizona Press published *Half the World in Light: New & Selected Poems,* a substantial and impressive collection. The poems that stuck with me the most, made the largest impression were the "New" poems, many about your parents, poems dealing directly with "la vida," poems I think much closer in voice and vision to someone like Szymborska or Herbert than some of your other poems that you have described as being "open" or "sculpted." A poem such as "19 Pokrovskaya Street" is a poem that is a good example. The deep humanity of those poems makes them weigh more heavily with me. How do you decide then on subject, form, strategy? Is Voice dependent on vision for you? How important is memory?

JFH: Splish, splash, I go unto the page, without knowing what I am going to write and on and on until the poem is finished. Usually, two drafts. I used to ask myself "what's the first thing that drives into a poem?" The title, yes, the first line, yes — but, what is under and above and through the entire moment? The feeling. It sounds a bit old-schoolish, and romantic. Think about it. If we overthink the poem, it will wilt. If we prepare a stimulating hybrid plan, maybe. Without the mind viscera at play, we might as well forget it. Let the inspiration-feeling-blood-beat lead you as you jump out of bed and dash to the nearest scrap of paper and write whatever it wants to be.

NS: Also re. *Half the World in Light,* I remember the first time flipping through and landing on, or perhaps being drawn to poems from *Notebooks of a Chile Verde Smuggler*. There's something I find particularly fascinating about the epistolary poems in that section. Maybe it's the fact that the form can be one part welcoming (I assign students to write Letters-to poems) and another part gut-wrenching. Those poems demand a lot of vulnerability of the speaker. I'm rereading the

"Undelivered Letters to Victor" series, wondering why the epistolary form for what you had to say here?

JFH: Letters, what else is there? They flow. They are personal. They give you room to lay on the wide floor of thought, syntax, idiom, and ideas, discussion, secrets, whispers, and shouts, dreams and raps. In this case, with Victor, who was always open to digging deep into whatever occurred to me, would "listen"—I wanted his "listening," I needed it. Yes, you do have to be vulnerable, or it is not a letter. But you don't think about that while you are writing, you just write a "letter." How did I get to the letter form, you ask? Having had many a discussion with Victor and Francisco X. Alarcón who was mad about Julio Cortazar, sooner or later you would end up writing an epistolary poem. With Cortazar's novel, Hop-Scotch (Rayuela), the universe cracks open for the poet and the novelist. Mexico, Latin America and the Caribbean, will mess you up and turn you into a writhing new kind of poet—we forget we live in an "American" writing culture, it is good to notice hemispheric and world writers, what they say and how they say it.

NS: Lately, I've been thinking about the capaciousness of a poem. I ask my poems: "What can you hold for me," which is another way of admitting I cannot hold everything myself. The facts of the sacrifices my family made for me. The things that happen in a life, that we try to concretize in poems. I'm wondering if you thought/think about why poetry? I found myself agreeing with poems like "The Glue Under." I see the speaker struggling with what a poem can hold: "This is not a *lyric* as they say in the Nomenclature./ This is not a *manifesto,* as they said in Rodchenko's Moscow, it is/ not even a dream or a poem anymore . . . " In "Enter the Void" it's the lines "I had written this somewhere, in a workshop, I think,/ yes, it was an afternoon of dark poets with leaves, coffee . . . " Your speaker seems to step out of the moment without stepping out of the poem to call the reader's attention. I keep wondering if you think about a poem's capacity, and if so, what is a poem's capacity?

JFH: As much as the poem wants to hold is the answer—as long as you do not break the "consciousness" of the poem. Artificiality in the poem's own terms will not work. This is one of many ways to consider the poem. "Too much is possible," think about Ginsberg's' "Kaddish," or Antin's "conversation" poems or Artaud's ritual, seizer poetry. And it can also be deadly when your poem turns into page talk. So many cool ways to loose yourself and fail and that is what poetry is also made of—inside that most "accomplished" poem, there are beautiful trash-basket shreds.

NS: I am thinking now of two conversations we had on two separate occasions when I was an undergrad at UCR. 1. When I decided to move away from CA for grad school in Minnesota, you said, "It's okay, we're everywhere." I was nervous to leave home/family/the neighborhood for a part of the country I knew so little about. And "We're everywhere" meant Mexicans and Mexican-Americans, meaning to reassure my decision to move. 2. Another thing you told me was: "A poem isn't an image, it's a piñata exploding." Both these instances parallel each other, at least to me, in how they exemplify a type of reaching. I was reaching for familiarity in this strange situation of moving to another state. The bursting piñata AKA the poem is another type of reaching, of trying to communicate something to the reader.

Your poem "I Forget the Date" in The Five Elements makes me think of a kind of reaching. The speaker begins, listing: " . . . soda on a tray//Women at the counter, mexicanas . . ." then moves across lands "Hidalgo// Texas// Sonora// Zacatecas// Chihuaha . . . " before happening upon (or reaching) memory: "I think of my father, for a moment—/ I see him again, robust, alone, walks to the park..." From there the poem expands and contracts, settling finally on song the speaker hears "in the distance," the end of which brings us to the poem's final lines: "why am I the only one/singin' this desolation song?" These lines seem to be reaching if not for home then a yearning that home-ness might solve. Could you talk about writing about family and home?

JFH: Wish I could do that—most of what I write is inside my head, in some trapezoid of acrylic societies and simulacrums in loaded velocities. Sometimes I talk about my family, in short poems, or painterly prose and in children's picture books—one of my favorite places to write. With "family" and "home" poems, there's nothing to hold on to—more than subtlety or poetic plain talk, or both, it will involve meditation, sincerity, respect and love. I look forward to it. As a matter of fact, this morning I thought about writing a short album of poems, the 50's-90's, the jaunts of my uncles and aunts in California after their grueling journeys from Mexico City and from the Juárez, Chihuahua / El Paso, Texas borders.

NS: Talk a little about your subjects—do they find you, or are you focused especially on social and community issues? Do you still write poems about "writing"? And do you see a shift generally in subject for your poems between your early work and your more mature work?

JFH: My subjects always find me. It is more about *how* they find me. With a line, a few words, a set of images or what comes right after a moment of empty-seeing. That is, if you scour the debris in your mind and let your clear consciousness go out there into the ethers, like an upwards fish line, it will catch you, for a millisecond. That is when you have to be micro-alert and take the insight to the table. For example, Buber's notion of "sources" of knowledge. Recently, I found that to be an incredible finding, in terms of a people's way of having a metaphysical, philosophical and historical foundation for being, for who they are, a deep core of self. Now, for the poet in these times, for the various social groups in this nation and globally, we need to ask, what are our "sources"? Or have we been suctioned by the "absurd," as Milosz has written in *The Captive Mind*, that is, by materialism and militarism, by a rootless artifice, a dimensionless nationalism? So we float in this oppressive flatness. Buber and Milosz hit a chord for me.

NS: In a 2017 interview with Donald Munro for *The Fresno Bee*, you recalled: "I remember in 1955 playing in the fountains in downtown Fresno. My father and mother and me, just passing through, and splashing around in the fountains. It was extremely hot. My parents working here in this area as farm workers, and my mother picking peaches—early cycles of my life. This is a big cycle, coming back, as I'm finishing up my laureate, I'm finishing the big journey of the story of my family and the story of many families."

And I remember that you have kept a house in Fresno for many years now, even when living or working elsewhere. For instance while we were colleagues at UC Riverside you still had a home in Fresno, and since you have retired you have lived there. How important then is Fresno to your writing, how much of a source is it, how much inspiration and seat of voice and vision?

JFH: Fresno has opened for me like a Lotus flower. I say thank you to this city. Thank you, to its students, Fresno State and all the colleges and schools, teachers and children.

I bow before its peoples. I say gracias to the land, lakes and mountains, to its plants, animals and trees—to all its workers, immigrants and migrants, its generations across many borders, how hard they have worked and continue to labor for all of us. My parents, brothers and sisters were among them, since the 40's. It takes time to realize who you are and what you are made of—I am beginning to see this now. All this finds it place in one way or another in my writing. It will be endless. It is life. My life and all of our lives. Thanks Chris and Michael, for your work, how you take time to put us all onto the page. And gracias for this digging-deep interview.

Lee Herrick

Lee Herrick is the author of three books of poems: *Scar and Flower*, finalist for the Northern California Book Award, *Gardening Secrets of the Dead*, and *This Many Miles from Desire*. He is co-editor of *The World I Leave You: Asian American Poets on Faith and Spirit* (Orison Books, 2020). His poems appear widely in literary magazines, textbooks, and anthologies including *Highway 99: A Literary Journal Through California's Great Central Valley*, 2nd edition; *One for the Money: The Sentence as a Poetic Form*; *Indivisible: Poems of Social Justice*; *Dear America: Letters of Hope, Habitat, Defiance, and Democracy*; and *Here: Poems for the Planet*, with a foreword by the Dalai Lama.

Born in Daejeon, Korea, and adopted to the United States, he served as Fresno Poet Laureate (2015-2017). He teaches at Fresno City College and the MFA Program at Sierra Nevada University.

"Fresno taught me to write, dream" from *Zocalo Public Square*, reprinted in *The Fresno Bee*, August 27, 2015—Lee Herrick

Every once in a while, I remember that I was born on the other side of the world, and it makes sense that I love looking up at the stars. Fresno, California is 9,000 miles from my birthplace: Daejeon, South Korea. I was found on the steps of a church. I was ten months old I was adopted by American couple who lived in San Francisco. When I was 26, I accepted a tenure track teaching position in the English Department at Fresno City College. This year, I was named Poet Laureate of Fresno.

More than 90 languages are spoken in Fresno County, where the heat reaches 110 degrees in the summer, the fog in winter softly blankets Highway 99, and we farm 250-some kinds of crops. When I moved here in 1997, I learned about the pillars of Fresno poetry. I felt like I was part of something, and I was. It is a tough city full of grit, but amid the heat and dust, hardworking poets blossom. Here is where I learned to write.

The late Andrés Montoya was my first influence, and the largest. I met him through our mutual friend, author Daniel Chacón. Andrés died at age 31 before his first book, *the iceworker sings and other poems*, was published. He believed that poetry fueled personal, societal and cultural liberation. He wrote about the downtrodden, the poor, the factory workers and the drug-addicted. He beautified what some deemed ugly and taught me that poetry is for all the people around you. I saw what language could do. We talked for hours about poetry, politics and race. I had found my first brother in poetry.

In Fresno, there are farmers markets every day of the week, and in Fresno, you can find poets laureate, and not just local laureates like me. Once I saw Philip Levine at a grocery store and introduced him to my daughter. In a career that saw him named U.S. poet laureate in 2011, Levine became known as a voice for the working-class, but he was more than that. My favorite of his books, *The Simple Truth*, taught me there is something extraordinary about ordinary people. I loved his ability to cut to the truth of a good poem or right through the pretension of a bad one, both as a legendary professor who spared no one the truth in his critiques, or in memorable lines of poetry, when he writes, "Some things you know all your life. They are so simple and true, they must be said without elegance." Before his death, in an interview with Bill Moyers, Levine stated that what angered him most was American racism and American capitalism. These were great models for me. I did not know him well, but when we spoke he was always kind to me. His poems and his life are true inspirations.

Juan Felipe Herrera, the current U.S. poet laureate and formerly California's laureate, lives here, too. Once, years ago, I saw him in Fresno's Tower District when his collection *Notebooks of a Chile Verde Smuggler* had just come out, and I had my copy in the car. I asked him to sign it right there on the street, which he did. Herrera's playful musicality, his political fierceness, his humility and his compassionate embrace of all people around the world are examples bar none. Juan Felipe has always been good to me, supportive of my work, and a friend in poetry. We are not close friends, but his poems are close to my heart. I count him as a friend and an important role model. I admire his tireless devotion to social justice through poetry. Much of my poetry and teaching life has been devoted to this, and I have Juan Felipe Herrera to thank for his example.

Two more Fresno poets and good friends shaped me early, and still do. First, Brian Turner served as an infantry team leader in the Iraq, and I met him when he returned home after the war. He was looking for a poetry community, and we found each other. We are good friends, and he always inspires me, with his poems, his kindness and his humility. His books are about war, the many effects on people here and abroad, and the resilience of the human spirit. I value his calm in the midst of a storm, and Brian's poems exude this, as well as a great fire of the spirit. He was raised here, and although he now lives in Florida, he is a Fresno poet to the core. I count Brian and the second poet, Tim Z. Hernandez, as dear friends.

I met Tim almost 20 years ago in Fresno. Tim is known for his gritty and beautiful novels, including his historical novel about Bea Franco, the "Mexican Girl" from Jack Kerouac's *On the Road*, but I knew him first from his early poems about manhood and Latino culture that would become *Skin Tax*. Tim is about hard work, community, and writing killer poems and novels. He shines a light on the small beauty in life to a world often afflicted with disinterest. He now lives in El Paso, Texas, and teaches at UTEP, but he too is a Fresno poet through and through. Some poets leave after receiving tenure-track teaching jobs elsewhere, but I believe that poets who once lived here and leave always keeps a part of Fresno in their heart and in their poems.

It is an honor to serve as poet laureate of Fresno. I have mentioned poets who shaped my work most, but there are so many others – those who have advocated for young poets, poets produced by Fresno, students I have taught over the years. I wish I could name them all here.

Poetry is where fires begin and smolder. So it's no wonder that poets here write killer poems in our unapologetic heat, the exhaust of the traffic, or the dream-inducing tule fog. It's no wonder that I was born in South Korea, adopted to the U.S., and wound up in Fresno amid factory workers, war veterans and farm laborers. It's no wonder that I learned to write and dream here. It's no wonder that I love looking up at the stars.

"A *Normal School* Interview with Lee Herrick," 2018—by Rebecca Evans

Rebecca Evans: I read that the anthology, *Here: Poems for the Planet* (March 2019, Copper Canyon Press) (Elizabeth J. Coleman), which includes your work, has a foreword written by the Dalai Lama, tell me about that!

Lee Herrick: My poem "A Thousand Saxophones: A Poem for the Living and the Dead," is part of the anthology. I wrote this piece following Hurricane Katrina in 2005.

The disaster moved me, and I felt inspired to work those images into words: impoverished neighborhoods, people on their roofs, bodies floating. Copper Canyon Press saw this poem, and here we are. I am thrilled to be a contributor to this new work. What I first thought, regarding the Dalai Lama's foreword, is how surreal this is. My work placed among an amazing man who has changed the world. I've had the privilege of my poems published alongside Abraham Lincoln or Walt Whitman, and it's extremely humbling. Then I ground myself. I do not allow these experiences to impact me too much so that I can stay pure to my writing.

RE: You teach English and Poetry at Fresno City College, along with Poetry at Sierra Nevada College's MFA program. How do you balance your personal creative space with the demands of instruction?

LH: Even before "balancing" creative space, I'm most mindful regarding family. Family first. This is my value system. Time with my daughter is paramount, being present for her. I try to be present when I teach as well, as my students are important to me. Balancing my writing is about remembering my writing practice – remembering what works for me. When I feel a poem or that little agitation, there is very little that will prevent me from writing it. I now know my rhythms well enough to recognize when something speaks to me. I honor that, move in that direction.

Another aspect to balance is saying no. I'm able to decline because I know my limits and I know my needs. I need to stay somewhat healthy. That matters as it impacts not just my writing, but my life. In addition to teaching, I edit and publish. I write letters of recommendations and blurbs. I'm grateful that I have a writing life.

RE: You moved to Fresno over 20 years ago and I've heard you talk about this place, how you pull inspiration from the richness of its uniqueness and the blend of culture and ideas. Can you tell me more about how place plays a role in your work, especially this one place you've chosen to live, grow, and give back?

LH: Fresno is a medium-size city with a mix between urban and rural. There is a "downtown," but it is largely agricultural, largely immigrant. We have one of the highest Hmong American populations in the US. It's around 40% Latinx. Fresno is working-class and gritty, rich with texture.

I've traveled to almost 25 countries and I've found Fresno as diverse as any place I've visited. Yet it is a city of extremes, a city of wealth encrusted in poverty. To me, the culture here feels much like a kaleidoscope and that range of humanity excites me. Summers reach over 110 degrees, and the people here push through heat, push past discomfort. They know what it means to work. I've absorbed this work ethic, which I first learned from my father. You put your head down and plow through it. I don't separate the arts from labor. Labor. Beauty. Discovery.

RE: Your birthplace, your culture, your identity is woven throughout your work and I wondered if you could talk about how your experience, adopted as an infant by an American couple, found its way into your art? Or did you find art as a way to explore your experiences?

LH: Well, if I'm mystic about this, I want to say that art or the imagination is already a part of every person before they enter the world. I was adopted at ten months by a white couple, and for many years, I didn't think of my adoption much. Very common amongst adoptees. America has a way of wanting to assimilate everyone down to one idea. One root.

Now, I'm more integrated as a whole person, inclusive of my adopted Korean self. It is always there and if the poem calls that out, I feel comfortable allowing it into my work. It is available, at "the ready," and I find it has a way of sprinkling itself in.

One of the great surprises of poetry is when a poem takes on a life of its own. This is the best feeling. The poem takes over the poet. My identity is simply a part of that.

Adoption has offered me a heightened sense of race and difference and nuance. And being raised in a white family, I'm able to see people and the questions I grew up with about myself and the world. This gives me a true interest in individual experiences. This definitely relates to *Scar and Flower*, which deals with gun violence, trauma, and how we manage it. In fact, the first half of the book is about mass shootings, like Orlando. One of my main preoccupations as a poet is trauma and how people survive it, the way they navigate life after it, sometimes, incredibly, with grace.

RE: Can you speak to the different processes that each of your three books has taken? Is there a similar thread to the way you've pulled a book together or has each one been an individual method? Has the third book become something that has grown from earlier roots in your earlier work?
LH: Honestly, each book has been different. Think of a band who has recorded three or four albums, each one a completely unique experience because, over time, everything changes: studio, producer, sound.

My first book was written mostly in South America, Central America, and Asia. I had spent eight to nine years out of the country for two to three months every summer. So the concept and theme of travel was common throughout my first book. *This Many Miles from Desire* was about discovery, and about moving away from physical desire, the idea of simplicity in life. I was sorting through my cultural identity and had only returned to Korea briefly.

Gardening Secrets of the Dead feels different because I sensed I needed to do something different. *Gardening* was published in late 2012, and, by then, I had been through a significant relationship shift. I had also become a father, which offered a wonderful and meaningful impact on me with regards to certainty. It is a much darker book because of this. It is much more certain of itself, and I'm more comfortable with that darkness.

This third book, *Scar and Flower*, feels different yet again. This is my first overtly political book. I've always been involved with politics, economy, military, and history. My passion and long-standing interests in social justice merged with the events in the world. I found myself writing about guns and mass shootings, along with poems about my daughter, and walks along the beach. At some point, I realized, this is about balance. It was also about trauma, how people regulate the impact of life-altering events. How they navigate through and, eventually, reach the other side.

RE: Did you find turning points, the arc in your own writing life, from the start of your first book to the completion of your third?
LH: A huge event that impacted my life and my writing was returning to Korea and searching for my birth family. Of course, becoming a father has completely shaped me. This is my greatest joy, but it has also forced me to think about audience and the longevity of a poem, to ask questions. If my daughter read this in twenty years, what effect would it have on her?

Travel became another pivotal point. I feel that people and places around the world have stayed with me, they enter my poems: a woman in a market in Guatemala, or playing soccer with the young kids on the banks of a river in Laos.

Not finding my birth parents nudged me into making peace within myself, sort of a forgiveness of Korea, of the adoption. Adoption is traumatic. 2008, when I did an extensive birth family search, was one of the most difficult years of my life, but through this fire emerged the most liberating and most important years of my life.

RE: I once asked you, which of your books would you recommend for me, a writer working on memoir, and you suggested *Gardening Secrets of the Dead,* snapshots of history fused together. Can you tell me your thoughts of nonfiction writers studying, not just this book, but poetry?

LH: I think any writer in any genre will benefit on and off the page from reading other genres, just like a bass player will benefit experimenting with other instruments. It is critical to read across genre, read widely, not just recent published pieces, but those works that have stood the test of time. Read and study across religions, cultures, and belief systems. I can't imagine a serious writer not wanting to read other genres. Great musicians will readily name the musicians out of their genre that they love. I read fiction and nonfiction, though poetry is my main reading. Reading across genre study provides surprise, keeping us fresh and allowing us to change up our own norms, experiment.

I recommended *Gardening Secrets of the Dead* for you because of its movement and its questions for the dead. The main question pursued is, if the dead could speak to us, what would they say? And also, if we could hear them, how would we respond? A memoirist is often concerned with this, the dead, or perhaps their past.

RE: How do you use research in your writing? Formal? Your personal interior? Interviews?

LH: I'm a big researcher, but not in a formal way. And my research typically won't make its way into a poem. There's a poem in *Gardening Secrets* that includes some research about Leo Tolstoy's death and others involved research about Korean border politics. Where I'm rabid on research is through interviews. I'm insane about this. I've listened to thousands of hours of interviews of actors, musicians, writers, comedians. I simply love interview as an art form, such as James Lipton or literary interviews. I'm not sure if that makes its way into my poems, but I love reading about creative lives. Every night, I listen to some type of interview, the methods people use to process their lives. I'm a huge sports fan as well, and my curiosity is drawn to people working through things, tough things. Overcoming obstacles.

RE: Can you share your writing process?

LH: I have so many ways to answer this. I'm very auditory. Many of my poems begin with sound. A wave. A bird. Something someone says. An echo. A vibration. I write either on a legal pad or on my laptop. I write into the direction of that moment or that idea or that sound. I'm big into revision and allow my poems to simmer for a while. My wife, Lisa, is my first and best reader. She has great instincts, and she cares about me, about my poem. My first book, I wrote a lot outdoors because I was traveling. I wrote in a notebook. Less pragmatically, I'm a bit of a dreamer, and so my imagination still has a place in poetry. Basically, I'll write anywhere on anything.

RE: Your work is not limited to the writing-poetry-academic circuit; you heavily participate in human rights, a voice for adoptees, and more. Can you speak to how these events, maybe even world events, influence your art? Do you feel a responsibility, as an artist, to help bring truth to the surface through your work?

LH: I care and am moved as a person. I don't feel like I have to write towards some global or some political event. It is more that I am saddened or angered by an event. Alice Walker once said, "Poetry is a place for leftover love and leftover anger."

The world is joyful and beautiful but hideous at times, too. I recently wrote a poem about a Korean adoptee, Phillip Clay, who was raised in America and never became a citizen. He was deported back to Korea over a misdemeanor. I wrote a poem for his memorial service after he committed suicide.

One of the great blessings of my writing life is to have connected with other Korean adoptees around the world. I've met people who read my work, tell me what my writing has meant to them. This surpasses all accolades and prizes. I've written about and supported a number of social justice efforts over the years, and I'm also working to establish a Social Justice Center at Fresno City College.

RE: Can you share a few insights into who has influenced your writing the most?
LH: Li-Young Lee, Juan Felipe Herrera, Alice Walker, Brian Turner, Sun Yung Shin, Larry Levis, and my mom who was an artist, to name a few.

RE: Can you talk about where, for you, a poem begins, that small ignited fire you've spoke of in workshops?
LH: I have this belief that writers, those who write seriously, have some experience in their life that altered their course, often under the age of ten, often traumatic or very difficult. I call that the writer's fire. It is always there. Given that, then almost anything can spark from it. Fires can jump. It can be sparked by another little spark. For the writer who is in-tune with this, knows what this fire is, their potential for writing is almost always there because it sparks from anything. It fuels their writing. My adoption is my large fire, and my smaller sparks circle around race, death, mother figures, trauma.

RE: Did any of your work surprise you?
LH: When I'm lucky, and the poems are good, they should surprise me. The good ones. The fun ones. Sometimes, you're surprised over a number of years. Hopefully there's enough rigor and a little magic and a little lyric. One poem, "Fire," does something different for me every time I read it. It surprises me every time.

I try not to think of a poem as "done" once published. We can listen to our favorite songs countless times, but we always discover something new each time. Great art should do that.

RE: What advice do you have for a student of the narrative or literary arts?
LH: Read voraciously. One must read across genre, across time, and read multiple works by an author if available. Humility and development. Cultivate thick skin and the ability to be humble. Learn. Love revision. Don't take things personally. Make room for criticism.

Take care of your lives and yourselves. Self-care is critical. Take care of your families.

Honor whatever strange, weird direction writing might take you. Don't over-censor.

Travel. Explore. Get messy. Get lost. Have some faith. Or find some faith. Find your tribe, by gender, experience, aesthetic. I'm a part of several tribes. This is helpful. I don't mean to sound remorse, but remember death — whatever that means to you —and let it fuel you.

"On Fresno Poetry Influences," 2018—Lee Herrick

We need the artful moment. In the face of racism, misogyny, capitalism, illiteracy, apathy, poverty, and violence, we need poetry. We need it as much as music, film, or any other kind of art or grace. In Fresno, there is beauty. There are many truths here: simple truths and complex truths, but we aren't blessed with instantly recognizable beauty—no Pacific coastline, no snow-capped mountains—but we are blessed with another kind of beauty: the poets. The pillars who began it and the new pillars who expand it. Sometimes at night, the summer heat cooling into a manageable temperature, I think of my own beginnings: abandoned as an infant in South Korea, adopted to the United States, in Fresno now for over twenty years, and I take a deep breath and know I am home. I'm at home among poets who know what trauma is and respect other's traumas and others' suffering. Their honor their own in stellar poem after stellar poem. I'm home in a city that speaks 90 languages, a city full of heat and grit and work and desire, a city that knows what work is, a city gathering in a flourishing way, a city of poetry and poets, working to make it right. There are four Fresno poets whose poetry and world-views shaped me: Andrés Montoya, Connie Hales, Juan Felipe Herrera, and Philip Levine. There are poets whose poems are always with me: Peter Everwine, Jon Veinberg, Dixie Salazar, Larry Levis, and my contemporaries and friends Tim Z. Hernandez, Brian Turner, and Marisol Baca. But it was Andrés, Connie, Juan Felipe, and Phil, whose poetry and humanity influenced me, shaped me into the poet I am, and served as an example of what a poet looks like in the world.

The late great Andres Montoya was the first and most impactful early influence on my writing. In his work, I saw how darkness and light rotated in the same poem, how tenderness could function amidst violence, and how love could ought to figure prominently in a poem. I also admired his ability to call out racism and his conviction for poetry and politics. We spent countless hours talking about Fresno poetry, its lure and its lore. I introduced him to his fiancé, Eleanor. We ate tacos. We talked about Czesław Miłosz, Claribel Alegria, and Roque Dalton. He lived and breathed poetry, much like I was beginning to, and it was through this lens that I cut my teeth on the Fresno poets. His premature death in 1999 left me stunned but forever inspired. To this day, anywhere I read, any time I am writing, thinking, or teaching poetry, Andrés's voice rings in my head.

Connie Hales has shaped me in ways she probably doesn't know. I was never a student of Connie's, Juan Felipe's, or Phil's, but her poems taught me something new every time I read them. *To Make It Right*, the book and the poem, is always with me. The quiet violence. The struggle with family history. Her poems are full of grace but also gravity and fire. I remember driving home from work once, listening to public radio. She was being interviewed, and she read a poem that was so stunning, I had to pull the car to the side of the road. I sat there and listened, almost moved to tears. I spoke to her poetry class once, and every time I organized an event—for tsunami victims, for Writers Resist, or any type of fundraiser, she was the first person I thought of and always the first person to sign on. She is as giving as any poet I've ever met. She is as important a poetry teacher in Fresno as anyone, I would argue.

I asked her to Skype into my poetry class once, and the students loved her, of course. She invited me to speak to her students, who were so fortunate to learn from her. Along with Tim Z Hernandez, a dear friend and another important writer from Fresno, I was on the thesis committee with Connie for the wonderful, late poet Mia Barraza Martinez, who was a student of mine at Fresno City College and who blossomed at Fresno State. She was only 29 when she died. Connie's care with Mia's manuscript and her compassion and humanity with Mia's family is something I'll never forget. Some poets teach you about writing poetry. Some poets, like Connie, show you what compassion looks like in the world. Most recently, Connie and I were part of the organizing committee for the Andrés Montoya Literary Symposium at Fresno State, which brought scholars and writers from around the country. As always, she was pure grace, pure work, pure humanity, and pure community. This is how I try to live as a poet. I don't always succeed. In fact, I am sure that I often fail. But I do my best, and I think of Connie often in times of difficulty. It has been my good fortune to have her as a poet-guide.

When I moved to Fresno in 1997, I'd only begun to seriously read poetry, and I was only familiar with one or two of Juan Felipe Herrera's poems, including the iconic, "Let Us Gather in a Flourishing Way," but he already felt like an icon. I had seen him once or twice at an event, but the first time I saw him read is forever etched in my mind. It was an event for Andrés while he was sick in the hospital, receiving treatment for leukemia. He broke out a guitar and led the crowd in a chant while he orchestrated a call and response, which I know now as one of his signatures. I'd never seen a reading like it— so spirited, so free, so joyful. I call his readings "the Juan Felipe Herrera Experience." They're like revivals.

Once, I happened to have my copy of *Notebooks of a Chile Verde Smuggler* in my car when I saw Juan Felipe at an ATM machine in the Tower District. I grabbed a pen and excitedly walked up to him when he was done. He was probably startled to see a young Korean American with a copy of his book asking him to sign his copy, but that's just what he did, inscribing it to "Brother Lee."

After the Orlando shooting at a gay nightclub Pulse, I organized a reading to raise money and to remember the 49 people who were killed. There were about ten readers, with Juan Felipe listed as the final reader. He was driving back from teaching at Squaw Valley, exhausted from the teaching and the long drive, but he drove five hours straight and made it to the reading in time, and delivered a powerful tribute to the dead. When I co-founded the Fresno literary festival LitHop with my wife in 2016, he was our first keynote reader. The auditorium at Fresno City College was packed. We had seven or eight kids, including my daughter, surprise him before his reading, each of them reading one of his poems. He was so moved, I like to think, and gave an unforgettable talk and reading, during which he proclaimed, "Fresno is the poetry capital of the world." The crowd roared. I tried to contain my pride. I took a deep breath and once again felt what it meant to be a Fresno poet. Most recently, I was asked by my former colleague, activist Venancio Gaona, to help in the effort of get the newest elementary school in Fresno named for Juan Felipe. It was an uphill battle, with local philanthropists giving large sums of money and throwing their support behind their chosen person. There were around 100 people who were nominated. I wrote a letter explaining why it should be named for Juan Felipe—his work with young people, his national and world-wide acclaim, his many accolades, and his community work. Over 100 local writers and educators signed the letter in support, and to our delight, the board voted to name the newest elementary school in Fresno: Juan Felipe Herrera Elementary School. We had lunch in celebration and talked about his ideas for the school. The mascot will be the Giant Sequoias—fitting and named for the local trees, fitting for children who will learn at a school named for another type of giant. I still carry his books with me, and if I am lucky, my poems embody even an iota of his poetics and spirit. From Juan Felipe, I learned what poetry community can be, and in his poems, I discovered why joy matters even in the face of political strife or social injustice. I learned how poetry and politics go hand in hand. How rhythm, pace, and music can drive a poem.

Soon after I moved to Fresno in the late 1990s, I attended a reading at the Tower Theater, a 760 seat art-deco mainstay of Fresno's creative arts neighborhood. It was a fundraiser for a prisoner rights benefit featuring Philip Levine and Adrienne Rich. Phil opened for Adrienne. He walked to the podium in his signature white tennis shoes and his swagger. It was one of the most commanding readings I have ever seen. I was never a student of Phil's, and I did not know him well. But his readings and his poems shaped me immensely. He mesmerized the overflow audience that night, and I was sold. Phil was everything that everyone said he was.

He was always kind to me. Once, I was at Trader Joe's with my daughter when she was eight or nine years old, and I introduced her to him as one of the country's finest poets. He probably wanted none of the flattery, but it was true, of course. We chatted for a few minutes right there near the pita bread, my daughter replying when we left, "He was really nice." And he was.

In a 2013 television interview with Bill Moyers, he spoke of his great poem "They Feed They Lion." He told a story of eating at a little restaurant that made marvelous hot fudge sundaes that he knew from his childhood. He was the only white person there. He said "the atmosphere in the place was not friendly. I got this realization. When they look at me, they regard me as exactly what I am—white and middle class, which by this time I was —-I was a university teacher. And they see me in many ways for what I am—a portion of their problem. And they had every right to view me this way because what am I doing? I'm middle age—I'm middle everything. You're either part of the problem or part of the solution, and I was part of the problem. And this poem partially comes out of that." He went on to tell Moyer about the inspiration behind his great poem "What Work Is." He was born in Detroit in 1928, and by the early 80's, the American auto industry began to struggle, given the preponderance of Hondas and Toyotas, which in part fueled a rise in racism toward Asian Americans. He told Moyer, "'What Work Is' grew out of a terrible moment. Once I was watching 60 minutes and the story was a terrible story, the story of a father and son who beat a man to death with a baseball bats, who they identified as Japanese, but he was actually Chinese. They felt Detroit collapsing around them and they felt this imposition from Japan and somehow they took it out on his guy and killed him. They were white. And I just couldn't believe it. I was shocked. And I sat down and started writing and I said something that I can't repeat on television about Detroit." He was talking about Vincent Chin, who was killed in 1992 at age 27 by Ronald Ebens and his stepson Michael Nitz. Ebens was a Chrysler plan supervisor and Nitz was a laid-off auto worker. Neither one went to jail. They were merely fined $3,000. It's abhorrent and sickening. It's a defining moment in Asian American activism history. And here's the thing about Phil, as I saw it. He did not say people overreacted. Or that a lot of people have been killed. Or that we all need to get along. He was disgusted by it. He was repulsed in the way that I felt repulsed. Moyer asked Phil what angers him most, and he said, plainly, "American capitalism and American racism. You never get over it." This is how I see the world. It felt like a shared disturbance about the human condition, the kind of agitation and anger and love that has fueled many of my poems.

I was born in Daejeon, South Korea, and as the story goes, I was found on the doorsteps of a church. I was adopted into a white family when I was ten months old and raised in the East Bay and later, Modesto, California. Somehow, I wound up in Fresno. Or Fresno wound up in me. I don't know how Fresno became an epicenter of such great poetry any more than, as Phil used to say, the boxer Jack Johnson could explain how to knock out an opponent or Rafael Nadal could explain how to win a tennis match. If I had to guess, I'd say it has something to do with the heat, the grit, the grind, and the struggle. It definitely has everything to do with its great early poets. Fresno is home. I'm a transnational Korean adoptee at home, in need of the artful moment. I have music, poems, and stories in my head. I have a fire inside of me that was lit as an infant in Daejeon. I have Fresno and poetry to thank for giving the fire oxygen. Korea made me human. Fresno made me a poet.

Acknowledgments

All work © and used by permission of the authors/editors. Additional thanks and permissions are as follows:

Introduction by Philip Levine to *A Sweetness Rising: New & Selected Poems* by Roberta Spear, used by permission of the Estate of Philip Levine, Edward Hirsch Literary Executor.

Thanks to Sarabande Books for permission to reprint "Afterword" by Philip Levine from *TARUMBA: the Selected Poems of Jaime Sabines* translated by Ernesto Trejo and Philip Levine.

Thanks to Nicholas Levis for permission to use "An Interview by David Wojahn."

Excerpt from "Sherley Williams–from Fresno to La Jolla: Raised not to Hope too Hard," *San Diego Reader*, April 13, 2000— By Jangchup Phelgyal, used by permission of Jim Holman, owner/editor.

Christopher Buckley, "Ernesto Trejo," *Dictionary of Literary Biography, Chicano Writers Edition*, Vol. II, 1992.

"Interview with Bob Mezey" by Laura L Mays Hoopes, *Poetry International* intern for *Poetry International on Line*, June 8, 2012. Used by permission of the author and *Poetry International*.

Special thanks to C.G. Hanzlicek for help and guidance with this project, and to David St. John for assistance and advice in rounding up our poets. Additional deep thanks to Dianne Hanzlicek, Frances Levine, Chuck Hanzlicek, David St. John, Dixie Salazar, Gary Soto, and Peggy Young for help with the photographs of the poets.

Works Cited

Down at the Santa Fe Depot, 1970, the Giligia Press: edited by David Kherdian & James Baloian.

PIECEWORK: 19 Fresno Poets, 1987, Silver Skates Publishing: edited by Jon Veinberg & Ernesto Trejo.

What Will Suffice: Contemporary Poets on the art of Poetry, 1995, Gibbs-Smith Publisher: edited by Christopher Buckley & Christopher Merrill.

The Geography of Home: California's Poetry of Place, 1999, Hey Day Books: edited by Gary Young & Christopher Buckley.

How Much Earth, The Round House Press, 2001: edited by Christopher Buckley, David Oliveira, & M.L. Williams.

A Condition of the Spirit: The Life & Work of Larry Levis, 2004, Eastern Washington University press: edited by Alexander Long & Christopher Buckley.

Bear Flag Republic: Prose Poems & Poetics from California, 2008, Greenhouse Review Press/ Alcatraz editions: edited by Gary Young & Christopher Buckley.

Aspects of Robinson: Homage to Weldon Kees, 2011, The Backwaters Press: edited by Christopher Howell & Christopher Buckley.

First Light: A Festschrift for Philip Levine on His 85th Birthday, 2013, Greenhouse Review Press & The Press at California State University, Fresno: edited by Christopher Buckley.

Coming Close: Forty Essays on Philip Levine, 2013, Prairie Lights Books: edited by Mari L'Esperance & Tomas Q. Morin.

MESSENGER TO THE STARS: A LUIS OMAR SALINAS NEW SELECTED POEMS & READER, 2014: edited by Jon Veinberg & Christopher Buckley.

CPSIA information can be obtained
at www.ICGtesting.com
Printed in the USA
JSHW012127080621
15706JS00001B/1

9 781622 889044